The Religious Traditions of Japan, 500–1600

The Religious Traditions of Japan, 500–1600, describes in outline the development of Japanese religious thought and practice from the introduction of writing to the point at which medieval attitudes gave way to a distinctive pre-modern culture, a change that brought an end to the dominance of religious institutions. A wide range of approaches using the resources of art history, social and intellectual history, as well as doctrine, is brought to bear on the subject. It attempts to give as full a picture as possible of the richness of the Japanese tradition as it succeeded in holding together on the one hand Buddhism, with its sophisticated intellectual structures, and on the other hand the disparate local cults that eventually achieved a kind of unity under the rubric of Shintō. Much of this book is concerned with the way in which Buddhism used the local cults to consolidate its position of hegemony while at the same time offering an example against which Shintō could slowly invent itself. An understanding of this process of constant and at times difficult interaction is essential to a deeper appreciation of Japan's history and its cultural achievements.

RICHARD BOWRING is Professor of Japanese Studies at the University of Cambridge and Master of Selwyn College, Cambridge. His interest in Japanese culture is wide-ranging and he has written extensively on such topics as Murasaki Shikibu from the eleventh century and Mori Ōgai from the nineteenth, as well as co-authoring the *Cambridge Encylopedia of Japan* (Cambridge University Press, 1993) and a number of Japanese language textbooks.

The Religious Traditions of Japan, 500–1600

Richard Bowring

CAMBRIDGE
UNIVERSITY PRESS

CAMBRIDGE UNIVERSITY PRESS
Cambridge, New York, Melbourne, Madrid, Cape Town, Singapore,
São Paulo, Delhi, Dubai, Tokyo, Mexico City

Cambridge University Press
The Edinburgh Building, Cambridge CB2 8RU, UK

Published in the United States of America by Cambridge University Press, New York

www.cambridge.org
Information on this title: www.cambridge.org/9780521720274

First published 2005
Paperback edition 2008

A catalogue record for this publication is available from the British Library

ISBN 978-0-521-85119-0 Hardback
ISBN 978-0-521-72027-4 Paperback

Contents

Illustrations

Maps

Preface

This book began life as something different. As my own interests shifted from Heian to medieval literature, where religious matters play a far larger role, I found myself handicapped by my ignorance of Japanese Buddhism. Faced with such a dilemma, one's first instinct is to turn to a survey in an accessible Western language. A number of works suggested themselves – *Japanese Buddhism* by Charles Eliot (1935), *Japanische Religionsgeschichte* by Wilhelm Gundert (1935), the work of Hartmut Rotermund, Kitagawa's *Religion in Japanese history* (1966), and Daigan and Alicia Matsunaga's *Foundation of Japanese Buddhism* (1974) – but all of them needed updating and none of them was quite what I had hoped for. There was clearly a need for a new history of the subject. Having now become sidetracked into matters religious, and intent, as usual, on running before I could walk, I devised a grandiose plan for a book on the history of one particular temple. The temple I chose was Daigoji. Soon after, I was awarded a two-year British Academy Readership (1995–97), which gave me the freedom to start on the necessary groundwork. I owe the Academy a great deal for allowing me to retool myself at what I fondly, but probably misguidedly, thought of as mid-career.

It did not take me long to realise four things. Firstly, that the choice of Daigoji had been a good one. Secondly, that the sources for a such a study were not in a usable state and that obtaining access to them (never mind reading them) would take years. Thirdly, that such was the state of the field that I really needed to write a history of Japanese Buddhism first, and only then try and deal with the history of a single temple. And fourthly, that it would be impossible to treat Buddhism in isolation from what we think of as the 'native tradition', namely Shintō. A good outline of this latter subject has been available in German for some time (Naumann 1988, 1994), and we now have an excellent short introduction in English (Inoue et al. 2003), but there is nothing that attempts an overall picture of Buddhism, let alone both traditions. There is certainly room for a wide-ranging history of Japanese religion as a whole, and that is what now lies before you. I trust that those who put their faith in me will not be disappointed by the results. It is not what was first proposed; it is only the first of a projected two volumes; it has taken far too long; but it does fill an important gap, of that I am quite sure.

The title, if I may borrow a phrase from Basil Hall Chamberlain, cost me much cogitation. Can there be such a thing as a history of religion, as distinct from, say, a history of politics or social movements? If it were not simply to be a history of doctrine, what would it look like? Should I dare to impose the concept of 'religion' on a culture that did not have an equivalent of that overarching term until modern times, presumably because it never felt it necessary, or indeed possible, to compartmentalise that particular area of human desire and experience, isolating it from other forms of activity (McMullin 1989b)? Would a balanced history of Japanese religion not end up as nothing more or less than a history of Japan, *tout court*? Perhaps, in the end then, it is simply a matter of emphasis: there are always choices to be made, and the choice made here is to focus on how a series of religious ideas and organisations affected the life and development of the nation. This is not, however, a history of doctrine, nor a history of institutions, for I have allowed the material available to dictate the approach. Some readers may, in their turn, think the results rather too scattergun, since they will find themselves being shuttled between art history, doctrine, institutions, and social and political history as and when it seems fitting. One of the most difficult tasks has been to try and treat Buddhism and the local cults together, because although for most of Japanese history they were inseparable, their stages of development have not always interlocked as neatly as one might hope.

An author who tries to cover such a wide span of history must, of necessity, make difficult choices. This book is not for the general reader, in the sense that it presumes a knowledge of at least the outlines of Japanese history. If this were not assumed, then the book would indeed have been a history of Japan rather than of one aspect of it, and it would have been twice as long. The reader should also be aware that much has been left out and that topics for further research lie on almost every page. On the other hand, it may be that I have attempted too much. The question of doctrine was a difficult one, because this was an area in which initially I had almost no expertise. I toyed with the idea that doctrine could be safely ignored, but was soon disabused of this notion: too much of what happened had doctrinal roots. I remain somewhat unsure of my ground in this area and would like to thank in particular Professor William M. Bodiford, who, as a very careful reader of the initial typescript, pointed out numerous areas where I had been either slipshod or mistaken. I hasten to add that the second half of the book has not had the advantage of his eagle eye.

Readers with some knowledge of the subjects being treated will undoubtedly find favourite topics treated too lightly or not at all. This is in the nature of the exercise and cannot be helped. Perhaps of rather more concern, however, will be the noticeable lack of reference to ongoing historiographical debates in Japan: terms such as *kenmitsu taisei*, Kamakura New Buddhism and *hongaku shisō* are not used. Although one cannot in all conscience ignore these debates, since they inform almost everything one reads, I have decided against referring to them overtly, primarily because I did not wish to burden the reader with matters of academic discussion that would not only need a great deal of background explanation to make sense, but that draw their lifeblood more from present-day sectarianism (both academic and religious) than from the past itself. The reader who knows Japanese may also be dismayed to find almost no Japanese references, but this has been deliberate. Since this book is intended mainly as an introduction to an audience that does not read Japanese, or may be only in the middle stages of that daunting enterprise, a Japanese inventory would have been out of place. It is in fact a tribute to the quality of research on Japan now being produced in languages other than Japanese that the bibliography looks as impressive as it does. If I have managed to present an adequate synthesis of present scholarship and so provide a reliable background against which future work can proceed, then I will have done my job. My debts to the whole community of scholars in this field will be obvious; debts I owe to the friendship and support of colleagues in both faculty and college are no less for being personal; and for one in particular: *shiru hito zo shiru.*

Selwyn College
Cambridge

Glossary of commonly used Buddhist terms

abhiṣeka   An act of anointing or consecrating, typically used in tantric rituals.

bīja   A Sanskrit syllable representing a particular buddha or bodhisattva, typical of tantric practice.

bodhicitta   The awakening of intent to seek enlightenment.

bodhisattva   An awakened being who aspires to become a buddha by dint of practising compassion for all sentient beings.

buddha   A fully awakened one, who has experienced *nirvāṇa* and will never be subject to rebirth again. Śākyamuni is the historical buddha of our age but there have been buddhas before and will be buddhas in the future. In Mahāyāna Buddhism these buddhas are seen as co-existing and eternal.

dharma   The physical and mental elements or events that constitute existence (distinguished from the following by being in lower case).

Dharma   The teachings of Śākyamuni Buddha.

Hīnayāna   The Lesser Vehicle. A pejorative term used by followers of the Mahāyāna to refer to all other Buddhist traditions, in particular those that use the Pāli canon.

jātaka   A story illustrating an event in one of Śākyamuni's previous lives.

Mahāyāna   The Greater Vehicle. The name adopted by those who considered that the achievement of *nirvāṇa* was not enough and should be seen as merely one stage on the greater path of striving for full buddhahood.

nirvāṇa   That state of liberation which comes about when one has fully extinguished the desire that leads to the cycle of birth and rebirth.

samādhi   Concentration, meditation.

saṃsāra   The cycle of birth, death and rebirth from which the Buddha's teaching seeks to liberate us.

saṅgha   The assembly of monks and nuns.

śrāvaka   One of those who actually heard Śākyamuni's teachings and reached *nirvāṇa* as a result. Mahāyāna Buddhists often looked down on them as being incapable of reaching the higher levels of bodhisattvahood.

Tathāgata   The 'Thus-come One'. Another term for a buddha.

vajra   A 'diamond-hard' sceptre used in tantric ritual, adopted from the thunderbolt weapon used by the Vedic god Indra. It symbolises the absolute state of emptiness towards which the adept is striving. In tantric Buddhism, the *vajra* often has a sexual connotation.

vinaya   The body of rules that govern the behaviour of the *saṅgha*.

A note on dates

The order of dates follows Japanese usage: year-month-day. The month and day are given according to the Japanese calendar, but the year date is Western and should therefore be regarded as a guide rather than an exact equivalent. Because the Japanese New Year usually started in what we think of as early February, for dates in the first and twelfth months one would probably have to add or subtract one year to obtain the correct figure. For more details on the Japanese calendar, see §7.3.

Abbreviations

Ch.   Chinese
Jp.   Japanese
Kr.   Korean
Sk.   Sanskrit
T.   Takakusu Junjirō and Watanabe Kaigyoku (eds.), *Taishō shinshū daizōkyō*, 100 vols. (Tōkyō: Taishō Shinshū Daizōkyō Kankōkai, 1922–33).

Introduction

Terminology

The decision to start this history in 500 (or 538 to be precise) and to end in 1582 was based largely on the fact that these two dates mark major events: the official arrival of Buddhism from Paekche, and the utter destruction of the monasteries on Hieizan by Oda Nobunaga. We do have some limited knowledge of the tradition prior to the sixth century, but the lion's share is archaeological rather than textual, and since I am no archaeologist and since ninety per cent of the information still lies shamefully untouched in the huge tomb mounds of the Yamato plain, I have decided not to speculate. After all, it is bad enough trying to deal with the sixth and seventh centuries, when one's earliest textual sources date from the early eighth century and when these sources were designed for the specific purpose of producing a series of masterly smokescreens.

Comparisons may be odious, but they can also be useful to help highlight characteristics that might otherwise be hidden from view. As luck will have it, another country on the other side of the globe experienced similar events at roughly the same time. The traditional date for the landing of St Columba on Iona is 563, and the dissolution of the monasteries, which caused far more damage than Nobunaga ever contemplated, happened between 1535 and 1540. This relative closeness of dates is, of course, entirely an accident, but both ends of the story help to throw the Japanese example into relief. At one end, compare the nature of Japanese Buddhism and the way it interacted with local cults with what happened in Britain as Christianity took hold. British paganism took some time to die, but die it did, overwhelmed by the new arrival that simply subsumed what it could not destroy. The local worship of gods and spirits in Japan, however, did survive, long enough and strong enough indeed to form the bedrock of a new state ideology in the nineteenth century. Why and how this happened in the case of Japan is a source of considerable interest. Undoubtedly, the flexible nature of Buddhism with its concept of multiple realities and the philosophical breathing space it gave

1

conventional as opposed to absolute truth had a large part to play. There is good evidence to suggest that Buddhism in fact created the ground on which Shintō later flourished. It is this subtle interplay that makes this history of Japanese religious traditions so difficult to write. And at the other end of the story? Well, let us just say that what are usually interpreted as the actions of a megalomaniac in the 1580s in Japan can be given a useful perspective if looked at through the prism of the dissolution of the monasteries in sixteenth-century Britain. Problems of church and state are universal.

Mention of the word 'church' brings us to the tricky matter of terminology. One answer would be not to attempt translation at all but simply to use the romanised form of Japanese names of institutions and titles; but this might well make the text unreadable for all but the specialist. The number of Japanese characters sprinkled throughout the text is already bad enough. On the other hand, one must also avoid using equivalents that mislead. In the field of religion the most natural English equivalents are so redolent of Christianity that one hesitates to use them. It is instructive that the Japanese themselves deal with Christian ranks and titles not simply by using Buddhist equivalents, but by inventing new words: a Catholic archbishop, for example, is Daishikyō 大司教 and an Anglican archbishop Daishukyō 大主教. When in doubt, I have followed their example, not by inventing an entirely new word, but by choosing as neutral a term as possible. For example, it would have been very useful to have been able to use the term 'Buddhist Church' to refer to Buddhist institutions as a group, but this would have produced the impression that there was such a thing, when in fact the lack of unity was precisely the distinguishing characteristic of Buddhism in Japan. In one sense, yes, everyone knew that all 'Buddhisms' were connected, but there was no Buddhist 'pope', no overall authority, no one god, no sense of unity, and different institutions haggled and fought more between themselves than ever against a common enemy. Any sense of fragmentation one might find in the Catholic Church in Europe pales in comparison. At the heart of this lack of cohesion lay one of the central tenets of Buddhism, namely the acceptance of, and sometimes the encouragement of, multiple truths, which inevitably led to a plethora of doctrinal differences. Since there could be no single path to enlightenment and/or salvation, each institution could have its own ideas as to what constituted the true path. It is this that lies behind one of the more curious (for the outsider) occupations of Buddhist scholar-monks, their obsession with categorising, classifying and ranking various teachings. In such a context, to use the word 'Church', even in inverted commas, would be to lay down expectations of an underlying unity that are never going to be fulfilled and that will inevitably lead to misunderstandings. Where necessary, I have resorted to the rather clumsy 'Buddhist institutions' or even just 'Buddhism', which is unforgivably vague but has the advantage of not being 'Church'.

The same goes, *mutatis mutandis*, for the individuals involved. The lines between lay and non-lay are at times extremely difficult to draw. It is tempting to use the term 'clergy' to distinguish the professionals from lay believers and supporters, but in the Japanese context this must include 'monks', a category which in the Western context is normally set in opposition to 'clergy'. Titles raise similar questions. Distinctions are made in Japanese that are not made in English and vice versa, so one has to come to some sort of compromise. Another title that causes difficulty is *tennō* 天皇, which is usually translated as 'emperor'. This Chinese term that originally referred to the divinity who appears as the Pole Star 北斗 was adopted as a title by Japanese rulers in the early years of the eighth century. Piggott (1997) uses the translation 'heavenly sovereign', which is a little unwieldy but better than 'emperor', which suggests to the modern ear an empire that never existed. 'King' would be better still but might give the erroneous impression of someone who ruled directly and personally, which was certainly not the case. When it occurs as a personal title, I have left it untranslated as *Tennō*. When it occurs as a generic term, I have preferred 'sovereign' or 'monarch', with 'royal' as the adjective. This may ruffle a few feathers.

A short glossary of Buddhist terms that are used in this book without further explanation will be found on page xiv.

Shintō

As will become clear in due course, part of the object of this book is to problematise the term 'Shintō' and the reader will find that it appears relatively late in the narrative. In the earlier sections I have preferred to use such circumlocutions as 'local cults' or 'native deities' (*jingi* 神祇), although even the word 'native' can be misleading here, since the question of what is or is not 'native' is open to much debate. I have used the word 'shrine' to translate the term *yashiro* 社 or *jinja* 神社, and 'priest' (*shinshoku* 神職) to refer to those people connected to shrines, the majority of whom were ritualists or assisted in rituals. The Council for Affairs of the Deities of Heaven and Earth (Jingikan 神祇官), as one of the earliest government agencies, had its own titles, but these are rarely mentioned in what follows.

During most of the period that we are dealing with, Shintō ranks refer not to a rank within a national system but to positions within individual shrines:

gūji, kannushi	宮司、神主	head priest
gon-gūji	權宮司	assistant head priest
negi	禰宜	senior priest(s)
gon-negi	權禰宜	assistant senior priest(s)
shuten	主典	priests
miko	巫女、神子	shrine maidens
jinin	神人	shrine servant

Buddhism

This is more complicated. The generic term for a Buddhist establishment is *tera* or *-ji*, both written 寺, a word that makes no distinction as to size or function. Early establishments in Japan were clearly temples in that their prime purpose was not to house celibate men dedicated to a contemplative life and cut off from normal society but to house priests whose duty it was to perform rituals for the peace and stability of the state. It took some time for what we would recognise as monasteries to emerge. The same building or compound might change its usage many times. Some *tera* were clearly monastic institutions first and temples second. In other cases the reverse might be the case, and in yet others there would be no sign of monasticism at all. Some were vast complexes, others were single, small buildings. At the risk of some slight confusion, it seems sensible to allow a degree of flexibility, although I have given preference to the term 'temple', since at least it suggests something non-Christian and has a wider remit than 'monastery'. Later reformist sects that began by challenging the whole significance of ordination used an entirely different term for their buildings, *dōjō* 道場. One occasionally finds this translated as 'chapel', but I have preferred the more neutral 'meeting house'.

So much for the buildings. But what about the people in them? The generic Japanese word is *sō* (Ch. *seng* 僧), which is usually translated as 'monk', although it comes to mean this via a rather circuitous route. The Sanskrit term is *bhikṣu* (Pāli: *bhikkhu*), which means a mendicant. The Chinese *seng* is in fact a short form of *sengqie* 僧伽, which transliterates the Sanskrit *saṅgha*, meaning the 'assembly [of ordained monks]'. The term then became used for a single 'member of the saṅgha'. Here, too, the reader must allow for a degree of flexibility, because many of these members of the saṅgha or 'monks' in the Japanese context were not what we would normally term 'monks' at all. Some were primarily scholars, others mainly administrators. Some had priestly functions, some were simply eccentrics who lived outside the system altogether, and at a later stage some could best be described as having a pastoral role, being leaders of congregations. The same man might act as a monk in one scenario and a ritualist in another, so I have used a variety of terms on the principle that to court occasional confusion is better than to cause constant misunderstanding. As far as women are concerned, the study of women and Buddhism in Japan is still in its infancy.[1] Although in the Nara period they seem to have had an equal role with men as ritualists, this situation did not last for long and one has fewer qualms in calling female members of the saṅgha 'nuns'. Even here, however, we are not without problems. The Japanese term *ama* 尼 is flexible and was often used with respect to women who had simply decided to 'retire', from either official court duties or sometimes just household life. It does not always refer to an officially ordained female.

The question of nomenclature arises again with respect to those official Buddhist titles which were given to members of the government office whose duty it was to oversee all Buddhist establishments, the Saṅgha Office (*sōgō* 僧綱). There were three main ranks: *sōjō* 僧正, *sōzu* 僧都, and *risshi* 律師. The first two are often translated as archbishop and bishop, but I have chosen the following slightly odd-sounding equivalents, for the very reason that they reveal difference rather than suggest a misplaced familiarity:

sōjō	saṅgha prefect
sōzu	saṅgha administrator
risshi	preceptor

In addition to these official ranks bestowed by the state, each monastery/temple had its own organisation. Here we run into the problem from the opposite angle. The fragmented nature of Buddhist institutions is mirrored in the nomenclature. A tree chart for one temple might be roughly equivalent to another, but the ranks would have completely different names. This reinforces the impression of a lack of uniformity, but to avoid a plethora of Japanese titles, the only answer is to use one English equivalent, hence the following titles, referring to the highest position in a monastery, will all be translated 'abbot': *zasu* 座主 at Enryakuji, Kongōbuji, Daigoji; *chōri* 長吏 at

---

[1]   This is true both in Japan and abroad, although the situation is improving rapidly. See Ruch 2002 and Horton 2004 for recent work in English.

Onjōji; *jūji* 住持 at Zen monasteries; *chōja* 長者 at Tōji; and *bettō* 別當 at Tōdaiji, Kōfukuji, etc. For the reformist sects, with their anti-monastic bias and their predominantly lay organisations, one has the choice of 'priest', 'pastor' or 'minister', depending on the exact relationship between lay members and their leader, although all these could also run into the familiarity trap. For the Jishū order one is even tempted to use the term 'friar', were that not so specific in a Western context.

Preview

It may be helpful at this point to give a synopsis of what follows. This history begins with the arrival of Buddhism. The Buddha is first interpreted as a strong foreign deity, whose magical powers are well worth appropriating. His cult is therefore introduced top-down and kept firmly in the hands of the ruling clans. Initially there is a certain amount of tension between the proponents and opponents of the new arrival, but a *modus vivendi* is soon found, Buddhism being simply added to the number of cults whose main duty it was to protect the ruler and maintain the status quo. There are signs here of an incipient state religion. Moves are made to bureaucratise the localised, disparate cults that had existed before the arrival of Buddhism into a hierarchical system and from that point on they always remained indissolubly linked to questions of sovereignty. In sharp contrast to events in Britain at roughly the same time, the survival and indeed growth of local cults is helped by Buddhism's willingness to accommodate rather than confront.

It should be borne in mind that Buddhism arrived in Japan after a very long journey from north India, through Kashmir and Afghanistan, along the Silk Route north and south of the Taklamakan Desert, and then through the whole of China and Korea. It called itself the 'Greater Vehicle' (*Mahāyāna*) and had developed doctrines and practices that were quite distinct from the southern Theravāda tradition based on the Pāli scriptures and found today in Sri Lanka, Burma and Thailand. The encounter with Chinese culture was decisive, and it is important to remember that to the Japanese the canonical language of Buddhism was classical Chinese, not Sanskrit or any of its many varieties.

From the mid-sixth century to the tenth, new schools of Buddhist thought and practice were developing in China and as contact between Japan and China increased, these new traditions found a secure haven in Japan, far more secure, as things turned out, than in China itself, where Buddhism often had to fight to hold its own. Each new tradition had its champions, who competed with each other for various forms of Japanese state support and patronage. There was no 'Buddhist Church' as such, merely a collection of traditions, each with its own political ambitions. Rivalry between institutions could be intense. Although it is often tempting to think of a Buddhist establishment as a simple power block, it was nothing of the sort. In fact, temples were more often than not the sowers of discord and they never managed to create a mechanism for mediating conflict. Buddhism remained in the hands of the elite until the twelfth century, and during that period it became more and more involved in the production of this-worldly benefits and protection via the manipulation of spells, magical images and gestures for which I have used the term 'tantric'. It was, to all intents and purposes, the preserve of the aristocracy.

Things began to change around 1100. With the advent of men like Hōnen, the exclusive right of members of the saṅgha to salvation was challenged. The possibility that salvation might be made available to everyone, no matter what their status, was now made explicit. The saṅgha did not disappear, of course, but they no longer had a monopoly. Some remained within the traditional structures of power and continued their role as priests acting on behalf of those who ruled, but we begin to see the emergence of many who preferred a pastoral, ministering role. The practice of faith was made easier partly by narrowing the choice of devotional object to a single Buddha, usually, but by no means exclusively, Amitābha, and partly by the invention of simple formulae for expressing devotion. Sermonising became common and Buddhist art expanded its reach into the didactic, into the production of illustrated scrolls for use by preachers. It should be stressed that these changes can be seen across the board, not only in the new non-monastic movements. Given that Buddhism had been introduced from the top, it is only to be expected that this kind of reformist movement would emerge; indeed it is slightly surprising that it did not take off earlier. There are obvious parallels here to the Reformation movement in Europe, with its questioning of the role of a clergy and its championing of the individual's right to have unmediated access to the deity, but the end result of such changes was to be quite different.

The 'opening out' of Buddhism that we find from 1100 manifested itself in a number of different ways. There was a growth in cults directed towards not just one Buddha but one specific image. Certain images in certain temples became the object of popular devotion, the Amitābha triad at Zenkōji 善光寺, for example, and unofficial holy men became the self-appointed guardians of these cults. There was also, of course, an economic imperative behind such developments. There emerged mendicant orders, and three devotional sects, Jōdoshū 淨土宗, Jōdo Shinshū 淨土眞宗 and Nichirenshū 日蓮宗, each of which had a charismatic founder. What distinguishes these sects was their insistence that they and only they had the correct message, an intransigence that clashed with Buddhism's more usual elasticity. It is not surprising that they were subject to considerable persecution and oppression, and in fact only gained real influence in the fifteenth and sixteenth centuries, at which point they became a magnet for those who were interested in fomenting large-scale social unrest.

There is, however, a danger in concentrating too much on these sects; and to do so is to obscure the fact that the more established, official institutions continued to dominate. Reform movements, such as a drive to revive proper observance of the monastic precepts which had fallen into disuse, also emerged from within. They were joined in the thirteenth century by the Zen monasteries, which were the last significant religious import from China until the seventeenth century.

All these developments need to be considered in relation to local cults. The attempt to impose a system in the eighth century was not sustainable and fell apart, but the cults as discrete entities survived and prospered by coming to an accommodation with Buddhism, which easily explained them as manifestations of an underlying unity and which needed them to naturalise itself fully. Tantric Buddhism, in particular, became involved in the quasi-nationalist enterprise of proving that Japan, as the land of the gods, was not at the end of a long developmental line but was in fact the original home of the buddhas. From here it is not far to insisting on the primacy of native deities. It is in essence the history of a long slow Japanese battle for self-justification, legitimation and self-respect in the face of the frightening debt that they owed to Chinese culture and Buddhist thought.

Part I

The arrival of Buddhism and its effects
(*c*.538–800)

Plate 1   Kōfukuji Buddha.
Bronze head of Yakushi, the Medicine Master, c.685. Height 1.07 m. Kōfukuji Museum. This strikingly handsome head was discovered in 1937 while repairs were being made to the Eastern Golden Hall (Higashi Kondō) of Kōfukuji. It was found under the main dais on top of a wooden box that contained a number of other parts of Buddhist images that had obviously been melted by intense heat. There are traces of gilt on the face and red on the lips. Most of the back of the head is missing. It is thought to be the central figure of a Yakushi triad originally installed in the Yamadadera in 685. It turned up at Kōfukuji in 1187. Kōfukuji was badly damaged by the forces of Taira no Shigehira in 1180 and although the Eastern Golden Hall was rebuilt by 1185, they had considerable difficulty in obtaining a suitable image. The monks eventually solved the problem by simply removing the triad from the Yamadadera. It survived one fire in 1369, but was destroyed in a lightning strike in 1411.

Chronology

Note that dates prior to the eighth century are based on eighth-century texts and are therefore largely unverifiable

538   Official introduction of Buddhism according to *Gangōji garan engi narabi ni ruki shizaichō*.
552   Official introduction of Buddhism according to *Nihon shoki*.
577   A Japanese envoy returns from Paekche with Buddhist texts and six specialists: a precept master (*risshi*), a meditation master (*zenji*), a nun, a master of spells (*jugon no hakase*), a sculptor and a temple architect.
584   Soga no Umako creates a building to house a statue of Maitreya that has arrived from Paekche. The Soga clan search for someone to perform ordinations and eventually find a former monk from Koguryŏ called Hyep'yon, who carries out the first 'ordinations' in Japan for three young women. Discord between Mononobe and Soga over the latter's adoption of Buddhism continues, coming to a head when the Mononobe opposition is destroyed in 587.
588   More craftsmen and artists arrive from Paekche, led by the monk Hyech'ong. Soga no Umako begins work on the Asukadera (Hōkōji), completed in 596. The three young women travel back with some Paekche envoys to study Buddhism and receive correct ordination.
590   The three women return and take up residence in Sakuraidera.
593   Work begins on the Shiten'ōji in Naniwa. Compound in use by 596.
595   The monk Hyeja arrives from Koguryŏ. He returns to Koguryŏ in 615.
600   Official mission sent to Sui China.
601   Work begins on Wakakusadera (later Hōryūji), which is completed in 607.
602   The Paekche scholar Kwallŭk arrives with a series of important works on astronomy and divination.
603   Twelve-grade cap rank system introduced at court.
604   The Seventeen Articles promulgated, with Buddhist sentiments expressed.
609   Paekche priests are shipwrecked in Kyūshū and decide to stay in Japan. They are housed at Asukadera.
621   Diplomatic relations begin with Silla.
622   Death of Prince Shōtoku.
623   Śākyamuni triad at Hōryūji produced.
624   First official Buddhist bureaucracy instituted by Suiko as a result of a priest having committed murder. Kwallŭk made saṅgha prefect (*sōjō*) and a Koguryŏ monk called Tŏkchŏk made saṅgha administrator (*sōzu*). Census of temples taken, revealing forty-six. Hyegwan arrives from Koguryŏ and is immediately made grand saṅgha prefect and accommodated at Asukadera.
628   Death of Suiko.
630   First mission to Tang China.

645　Soga clan destroyed. Taika Reform. Beginning of full state control over Buddhism with an edict reinforcing the establishment of a Buddhist prelacy.

651　Over a thousand priests (both men and women) invited to the palace to read a large number of sūtras.

661　Dōshō returns to Japan.

668　Silla destroys Paekche and unifies the Korean peninsula.

670　Hōryūji burns down.

671　Tenji falls ill and orders the first mass ordination of novices as a means of effecting a cure.

672　Civil war (*Jinshin no ran*). Succession of Tenmu.

677　Large assembly at Asukadera.

680　Tenmu begins work on the Yakushiji to save his consort. A hundred men signed up as priests to pray for Tenmu's recovery from illness.

694　A hundred copies of the *Sūtra of golden radiant wisdom* sent to the provinces to be read on the eighth day of the first month every year.

698　Yakushiji completed.

700　Dōshō requests cremation. Said to be the first example in Japan.

701　Taihō Codes.

710　Capital moved to Heijō-kyō (Nara).

712　*Kojiki* completed.

715　Genmei retires; replaced by Genshō.

716　Dōji returns to Japan.

720　*Nihon shoki* completed.

721　Genmei dies.

724　Genshō retires; replaced by Shōmu.

734　Demand for higher intellectual standards in temples.

735　Smallpox epidemic lasts for two years.

741　Order for temples to be constructed in each province.

748　Genshō dies.

749　Tōdaiji Vairocana Buddha completed. Shōmu retires; replaced by Kōken.

752　Official opening of Tōdaiji.

754　Jianzhen arrives in Japan.

756　Shōmu dies.

758　Kōken replaced by Junnin.

760　Kōken's mother Kōmyō dies.

763　Death of Jianzhen.

764　Junnin replaced by Kōken under her new title Shōtoku. Dōkyō in favour at court.

770　Death of Kōken/Shōtoku; replaced by Kōnin.

781　Death of Kōnin; replaced by Kanmu.

784　Move to Nagaoka-kyō.

794　Move to Heian-kyō.

Map 1   The provinces of Japan in the eighth century. Note that the boundaries were in many cases vague and never as clear as a map such as this might suggest, especially in the east of the country.

1　The introduction of Buddhism

1.1　Gifts from Paekche

The entry in the chronicle *Nihon shoki* 日本書紀 (720) for the year 552, winter, tenth month, reads as follows:

King Sŏngmyŏng 聖明 of Paekche 百濟 (also known as King Sŏng) dispatched envoys to Japan, led by Norisach'igye, a *talsol* 達率 of the Hŭi 姫 family from the Western Sector. They had with them an offering of a gold and copper statue of Śākyamuni Buddha, together with several banners and canopies, and several volumes of sūtras and treatises. In a separate declaration, the king praised the merit of propagation and worship, stating: 'This Dharma is superior to all others. It is difficult to grasp and difficult to attain. Neither the Duke of Zhou nor Confucius was able to comprehend it. It can give rise to immeasurable, limitless merit and fruits of action, leading to the attainment of supreme enlightenment. The treasure of this marvellous Dharma is such that it is as if one owned a wish-fulfilling gem that granted every desire. Every prayer is granted and nothing is wanting. Moreover, from distant India to the three kingdoms of Korea, all receive these teachings and there is none who does not revere and honour them. Accordingly, your servant Myŏng, King of Paekche, has humbly dispatched his retainer Norisach'igye to transmit it to the Imperial Land 帝國 and diffuse it through the home provinces 畿内, thereby fulfilling what the Buddha himself foretold: "my Dharma will spread to the East."'

That day the Heavenly Sovereign 天皇 [Kinmei] heard this declaration and leaped for joy, declaring to the envoys, 'Never until this moment have we heard such a fine Dharma. But we cannot decide on the matter ourselves.' Thereupon the Sovereign inquired of his assembled officials in turn: 'The Buddha presented to us by the state to our west has a face of great dignity, such as we have never known before. Should he be worshipped or not?'

Grand Minister Soga no Iname 蘇我稲目 replied: 'The many countries to the west 西蕃諸國 all worship it. Can Japan alone refuse to do so?' But Mononobe no Okoshi 物部尾興 and Nakatomi no Kamako 中臣鎌子 together addressed the Sovereign saying: 'Those who have ruled as kings over the world, over this our state, have always taken care to worship the 180 deities of heaven and earth 天地社稷百八十神 in spring, summer, autumn and winter. If we were now to change and worship a foreign deity 蕃神 we fear we may incur the wrath of the deities of our own land 國神.' The Sovereign then declared: 'It is fitting that we give it to Soga no Iname, who has expressed his desires. We shall ask him to worship it and see what results.' The Grand Minister knelt down and received the statue with great joy. He enshrined it at his home at Oharida and practised the rituals of a world renouncer with devotion. He also purified his home at Mukuhara and made it into a temple.

Later, an epidemic afflicted the land and cut short the lives of many. As time passed, matters became worse and there was no respite. Mononobe no Okoshi and Nakatomi no Kamako together addressed the ruler, saying: 'This epidemic has occurred because our counsel went unheard. Now, if you rectify matters before it is too late, joy will be the result. Throw away the statue of the Buddha at once and diligently seek future blessings.' The Sovereign responded: 'Let it be done as you advise.'

So the officials took the statue of the Buddha and threw it into the waters of the Naniwa canal. They then set fire to the temple in which it had been enshrined and burned it to the ground. At that moment, although there were no wind or clouds in the sky at the time, a fire suddenly broke out in the Great Hall (Sakamoto et al. 1967, vol. II: 101–02; Aston 1972, vol. II: 65–67).

This passage was written 168 years after the events it describes and is contained within a chronicle whose compilers had a very specific purpose in mind. It is hardly surprising, therefore, that the account has been shown to contain a whole host of problematic features. As might be expected, the language betrays an exclusively Japanese perspective and the representation of a Korean king sounding so humble is doubtful, to say the least; native Korean names such as Norisach'igye (the reading is tentative) had already been replaced by Chinese-style names in Paekche by the mid-sixth century; the order of titles is incorrect and should read: family name, rank (*talsol*) and then personal name; 'Western Sector' is an anachronism; and the key term 'Heavenly Sovereign' 天皇 was certainly not in use in sixth-century Japan. King Sŏngmyŏng's declaration also contains two passages which have been lifted from Yijing's translation of the *Sūtra of golden radiant wisdom*,[1] which was not completed until 703 and did not reach Japan until 718. Although the delicate balance maintained between the new foreign deity and the native gods was a likely outcome, it must never be forgotten that all passages from *Nihon shoki* are far more a product of 720 than of 552.

We are fortunate in having access to another account of these events in the *History of the Gangōji monastery with a list of its treasures* (*Gangōji garan engi narabi ni ruki shizaichō* 元興寺伽藍縁起並流記資材帳), a history and inventory that was drawn up in 747. This short work postdates *Nihon shoki*, of course, and is no less tendentious, stressing as it does the pivotal role of

---

[1] Sk. *Suvarṇaprabhāsottamasūtra*, Ch. *Jingguangming zuishengwang jing*, Jp. *Konkōmyō sai-shōō kyō* 金光明最勝王經, *T.* 665.

the Soga house, and in particular Suiko Tennō 推古天皇 (r. 592–628), in the struggle to secure the future of Buddhism in Japan; but it is nevertheless important because it gives us quite a different picture of what might have happened.[2] In this account, Buddhism is said to have been introduced in 538, there is no separate declaration, and the image that arrives is a statue of Śākyamuni as a prince, accompanied by vessels for an anointing ritual. It is strongly suggested that the image had been requested by the Soga rather than having simply arrived out of the blue from Paekche. It is now thought likely that the later date of 552 in *Nihon shoki* reflects not historical accuracy, but rather the tradition that placed the beginning of the decline of the Dharma (*mappō* 末法) in this year, exactly 1,500 years after the putative death of Śākyamuni in 948 BCE. Written in the early eighth century to legitimise the position of the ruling family, *Nihon shoki* succeeds in creating history and masking the past to an extraordinary degree; our major source for the whole period becomes our major problem.

It is, of course, quite possible that the Japanese had been exposed to Buddhist ideas well before this time; a large number of small Buddha figurines that may well predate the mid-sixth century have been found along the Japan Sea coast facing the Korean peninsula, and it is always tempting to question official dates in official texts. But on the other hand, we must avoid the temptation to assume that Buddhism had been long established on the peninsula itself. Admittedly, Koguryŏ to the north had adopted certain elements of Buddhism as early as the reign of King Sosurim (371–84), but the situation in Paekche and Silla, the two states closest to Japan, was quite different [map 2].

As far as Paekche was concerned, Buddhism was not in fact a major influence until the reign of King Sŏng (r. 523–54) himself, who sponsored the construction of the first large temple, the Taetongsa 大東寺, in the capital Ungjin 熊津. The case of Silla is equally instructive: cut off from direct contact with China, it was not until the reign of King Pŏphŭng 法興 (r. 514–40) and, in particular, his successor, Chinhŭng 眞興 (r. 540–76) that Buddhism became adopted as something close to a state religion, a pattern that was to be repeated in Japan two hundred years later. Once Buddhism had been accepted by the courts of both Paekche and Silla, it flowed on into Japan with hardly a break.

Map 2 shows the situation in Korea at the time of the gift in (let us say) 538; but this was to change rapidly [map 3]. In 551 Silla moved north against

---

[2] For the text see Sakurai et al. 1975: 7–23; for a translation, Stevenson 1999.

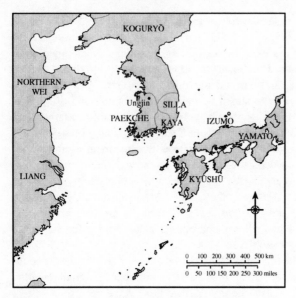

Map 2   Japan and Korea: early sixth century

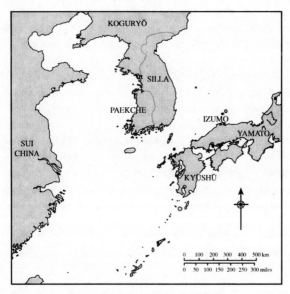

Map 3   Japan and Korea: late sixth century

Koguryŏ and occupied the whole of the Han River basin, giving itself direct access to the Yellow Sea for the first time. It continued to expand, putting constant pressure on Paekche (King Sŏng died in battle in 554) and occupying the region of small states known as Kaya in 562. If the gifts from Paekche to Japan had not been requested by the Soga, then at the very least they were part of a diplomatic offensive to ensure support from the Yamato court.

1.2   Patronage at court

Given that our earliest sources of information about this early period are dated almost two hundred years after the events themselves, the description that follows should be read as a 'traditional account'; there is little that is independently verifiable. In whatever manner Buddhism was first introduced to Japan, it is clear that the initial experiment failed in the face of opposition from both the military, in the shape of the Mononobe, and the ritualists, in the shape of the Nakatomi. But the flow of priests, artists and architects devoted to the worship of this powerful foreign god known as 'Buddha' 佛神 did not dry up. On the contrary, events on the peninsula were unstable enough to generate a constant influx. An embassy arrived from Paekche in 577 bringing gifts, texts and men skilled in temple construction. Despite further discord which surfaced in 585, the Soga pressed ahead and finally eliminated the Mononobe in a massacre in 587. In 588, three women were allowed to cross (or perhaps they were sent) to Paekche to obtain formal ordination (they duly returned in 590), and more craftsmen, led by Hyech'ong 慧聰 (fl. 595–615), arrived from the peninsula. This enabled Soga no Umako 馬子 (d. 626) to start the construction of a temple, known as Asukadera 飛鳥寺 in southeast Yamato. It was completed in 596 and furnished with a large image made by the sculptor Tori Busshi 止利佛師 in 606.[3] One must presume that most of the priests who worshipped there were from Paekche. During the long reign of Suiko, who was placed on the throne after her father's death by Umako, her maternal uncle, Buddhism gradually became entrenched under the patronage of the ruling families, despite the odd difficulty. The building of large tomb mounds came to an end around this time, to be replaced by smaller mausoleums, temples and pagodas. Recent excavations of pagodas have re-

---

[3]   Asukadera is thought to have been the first temple built in Japan. At a later date it became formally known as Hōkōji 法興寺 (perhaps in honour of the Sillan King Pŏphŭng?) and was then renamed Gangōji when it was moved to Heijō-kyō *c*.716.

vealed jewels, gold ornaments, mirrors and swords in small chambers buried beneath their central pillars – precisely the same kind of material found in the larger tombs of a few decades earlier. From the very beginnings, then, Buddhism was connected to funeral rites and commemoration of the dead.

The figure most closely associated with this whole process is Suiko's nephew Prince Shōtoku 聖德太子 (572–622), who acted as Regent. Whether they were truly 'co-rulers', as a recent study would have it, or whether Shōtoku qua male was the de facto ruler, is difficult to tell (Piggott 1997: 79–81). Unfortunately, almost nothing we know about Shōtoku can be taken at face value, because by the time *Nihon shoki* was written his persona had already taken on semi-divine attributes and he was the object of a cult; but, at the very least, he can be counted as the inspiration behind some of the most outstanding architecture of the period and he may also have been indirectly responsible for some of the earliest Japanese Buddhist scholarship (Deal 1999: 316–33). Another inventory of 747, which records the contents of Hōryūji 法隆寺, lists three commentaries (*gisho* 義疏) said to be the work of Prince Shōtoku himself.[4] This attribution has long been accepted as fact, but is probably little more than a pious fiction. There are two main problems. Firstly, given the state of Buddhist scholarship in Japan at this stage, it is simply difficult to believe that Shōtoku himself could have written them. Secondly (and perhaps more seriously), there is no reference to this extraordinary achievement in *Nihon shoki*, which in all other respects treats Shōtoku as being close to a saint. In the circumstances, it seems safer to assume that they were the work of a group centred on the Koguryŏ scholar Hyeja 慧慈, who was Shōtoku's mentor from 595 to 615. The nature of the first two of these sūtras will be described in due course, but the *Lion's roar of Queen Śrīmālā* is of particular interest here because the forceful portrayal of the bodhisattva path for both layman and member of the saṅgha that it contains is couched in terms of a discussion between a young queen and the Buddha himself. The queen emerges as a wise, compassionate ruler, responsible for spreading the Buddhist Dharma and fully knowledgeable about the tenets of Mahāyāna. Given Suiko's central role at this time, it seems a natural choice for her to sponsor and have copied.

Shōtoku is also said to have been responsible for the so-called 'Seventeen articles' of 604. Among statements of general principle, we find:

---

[4]   The sūtras were the *Lotus sūtra* (Sk. *Saddharmapuṇḍarīkasūtra*, Jp. *Hokekyō* 法華經), *T*. 262; the *Vimalakīrti sūtra* (Sk. *Vimalakīrtinirdeśasūtra*, Jp. *Yuimagyō* 維摩經), *T*. 475; and the *Lion's roar of Queen Śrīmālā* (Sk. *Śrīmālādevīsiṃhanādasūtra*, Jp. *Shōmangyō* 勝鬘經), *T*. 353.

Reverence for the Three Jewels: the Buddha, the Dharma, and the Saṅgha. These are the last resorts of humankind, pillars of faith in every realm. What world and what people fail to treasure this Dharma? The Three Jewels will not fail to win over even the most evil man, and so will the crooked be made straight.[5]

The first moves towards regulation came in 624. *Nihon shoki* reports that in that year a priest was accused of murdering his grandfather with an axe. Suiko demanded an investigation, and severe punishment would have been meted out to all priests had it not been for the intercession of a man called Kwalluk 觀勒, who had arrived from Paekche in 602. In the end it was agreed that what must have seemed at the time to be a group of immigrants rapidly growing out of control would need some form of regulation. Kwalluk was made saṅgha prefect (*sōjō* 僧正) and a Koguryŏ monk called Tŏkchŏk 德積 was made saṅgha administrator (*sōzu* 僧都). At the same time, the lay office of Dharma Master (*hōzu* 法頭) was established to oversee the financial administration of the increasing number of temples. This triumvirate was to develop later into a full-blown Saṅgha Office (*sōgō* 僧綱), which was to remain the chief instrument of state control for centuries. An opportunity was also taken at this juncture to carry out a census of Buddhist institutions. The entry in *Nihon shoki* for the ninth month of the same year reads:

There was a review of temples and priests, men and women. The reasons why temples had been built, the reasons why people had entered the Buddhist path, as well as the year, month and day, were all recorded in detail. At this time, there were 46 temples, 816 men and 569 women: 1,385 in total (Sakamoto et al. 1967, vol. II: 210–11).

Within less than a hundred years of its arrival, then, Buddhism had gained enough of a presence among the ruling elite for it to be treated as an institution in its own right. We see here the beginnings of a Buddhist establishment, and the beginnings of regulation by the secular authorities. The pattern was already a familiar one in both China and Korea. Control was made palatable because it came with patronage and no one who believed in spreading the Buddhist message could afford to turn away from such support. Of course, this ran counter to the Buddhist ideal that it was the duty of the layman to support the monk in his quest and that great merit would thereby be accrued, but at this stage in Japan there were no monks in the sense we would normally understand the term. It is clear from the entry in *Nihon shoki* with which we began that we are dealing with priests, male and female, whose duty it was to worship an image. It was to be some time before anyone

---

[5]   Piggott 1997: 92. Note that the first mention of these 'Seventeen articles' is in *Nihon shoki* and so their authenticity must remain somewhat suspect.

recognisable as a 'monk' emerged, since Buddhism was quite naturally being interpreted as just another cult at this stage.

When Suiko died in 628, the usual disputes over the succession broke out and violent confrontation continued for the next fifteen years. Finally, in 645, Nakatomi no Kamatari and Prince Naka no Ōe destroyed the Soga and forced most members of the clan to commit suicide. This ushered in what is known to history as the Taika Reforms 大化改新. There is, however, a good deal of scepticism about the reliability of the *Nihon shoki* sections that deal with these reforms and it is probable that many of the administrative changes attributed to this period were in fact instituted much later. Certainly we have to wait until the Taihō Code 大寶律令 of 701 before a new system of administration was really put into practice. But for Buddhism the impact was more immediate: patronage shifted from private (Soga) hands into those of the monarchy and the newly emerging bureaucratic state. The establishment of a fully fledged Buddhist prelacy seemed to be only a matter of time. In the same year, a long edict was proclaimed at the one state-sponsored temple to be built so far, the Great Paekche Temple (Kudara Ōdera 百濟大寺),[6] in which the principle of central control was again made explicit and ten 'learned masters' (*jisshi* 十師) were appointed to run Buddhist affairs along early Tang lines. This particular administrative system was not to last long, however, for the pattern soon reverted to that established by Suiko.

Prince Naka no Ōe was de facto ruler from 655 to 671, only ascending the throne as Tenji Tennō 天智天皇 in 668. During this period, events on the continent had considerable impact on domestic issues and it is clear that lineage ties between Paekche and Yamato were still strongly felt. In an attempt to save Paekche from being overrun by Silla, a Japanese force of some 5,000 men was sent across in 661, and a much larger fleet two years later, only to be crushed by a Tang naval force in a sea battle off the mouth of the Paekch'on River 白村江 in 663. From then until 676, when the Tang forces finally withdrew from the peninsula, Japan felt under constant fear of invasion.[7] When Tenji died, the civil war known as the Jinshin no ran 壬申の 亂 broke out, his chosen heir was killed and his younger brother eventually took power in 673 to rule as Tenmu Tennō 天武天皇. It was under Tenmu that the ruling family was finally to stake its claim to divine status.

[6]   After 677 this became known as Daikan daiji and then simply as Daianji 大安寺 after the move to Heijō-kyō.
[7]   See Batten 1986. Batten argues that major administrative changes took place in three phases: immediately after 645, from 664 to 671, and post-702.

1.3 The 'Beetle-wing' cabinet

The best, and possibly only, way to find out how the Buddhist message was understood at court at this early juncture is to look at what remains of the material culture it produced; and this means in essence Buddhist temples and images. Of course this brings with it its own problems. In the case of temples, the dating of wooden buildings is fraught with difficulties and the only thing one can be sure of today is that what one sees is not what was originally built. Not a temple exists that has escaped at least partial destruction at some stage in its life, and it is difficult to monitor change with any accuracy. Most Buddhist halls now contain a bewildering array of statues and paintings from the whole span of Japanese history, and considerable care must be taken to ensure one knows the provenance and date of each article. Some halls are little more than museums. In such light it may seem foolhardy to attempt to flesh out a history of early Buddhism in this way. Yet we have little choice. The new deities from the continent were entirely the preserve of the aristocracy and the court, who showed their interest by sponsoring the building of temples and images; in this sense, the Buddhism of this period can only speak to us through its art and architecture. We are fortunate to have one or two examples that remain to speak with eloquence.

The temple that today contains the most informative material from this period is Hōryūji 法隆寺. Originally known as Ikarugadera 斑鳩寺, it was begun by Prince Shōtoku about 607. Destroyed by fire in 670, it was rebuilt soon afterwards, but on a slightly different site. The oldest buildings in the western precinct are the main hall and the pagoda, which date from 680–90, although the murals inside the main hall are thought to date from *c.*711, as are the clay diorama and statuettes inside the pagoda.

A few precious objects were saved from the 670 fire, the most important being four wooden statues of the Four Heavenly Kings (Shiten'ō 四天王) carved from camphor; some sections of what is known as the Tenjukoku tapestry 天壽國繡帳 embroidered with scenes from a 'heavenly realm of longevity', said to have been created in memory of Shōtoku; a number of small gilt-bronze statues; two large images of the bodhisattva Avalokiteśvara, known as the Guze Kannon 救世觀音 and the Kudara Kannon 百濟觀音; the main gilt-bronze Śākyamuni triad [plate 2], which is dated 623; and the 'Beetle-wing' cabinet [plates 3–7]. An inscription on the back of the halo of the Śākyamuni figure gives a full description of its provenance.

The former Dowager Sovereign [Prince Shōtoku's mother] passed away on the twelfth month of the thirty-first year of Hōkō [621], and on the twenty-second of the

Plate 2   Gilt-bronze Śākyamuni triad, 623. Height of central figure 8.75 m. Hōryūji Kondō.

first month of the following year the Prince himself 上宮法皇 fell ill and refused to eat. His consort also took to her bed, worn out with nursing him. Together with his sons and his ministers, and in deep distress, she vowed to take refuge in the Three Jewels and to set up an image of Śākyamuni of the same stature as the Prince, hoping to turn away the illness by the power of this vow, to prolong his life and secure a peaceful sojourn in this world. But if it were already determined by his karma that he should turn his back on the world, [she prayed that] he should rise to the Pure Land and quickly gain enlightenment. On the twenty-first day of the second month she herself died and the Prince reached enlightenment on the very next day. In the third month of 623, in honour of this vow, this image of Śākyamuni with attendants and other adornments was completed.

In the end, may they take advantage of the short time allotted to them, and in the knowledge of the way, now pass from life into death in peace and tranquillity, and may they follow the Three Masters, honour the Three Jewels, and together reach the other shore. May all beings in the Six Realms, the Dharmakāya, gain knowledge, obtain liberation from the bonds of suffering, and likewise gain enlightenment. Shiba Tori 司馬止利, Head of the Saddler's Guild, Buddha Master, was ordered to make this image (Nara rokudaiji taikan kankōkai 1968–72, vol. II: 23).

Monumental bronzes of this type do not survive in China or in Korea, but the origins of the geometric hardness of the design, the long rectangular face and set jaw, together with the flared drapery, can be recognised in the stone carvings of the Northern Wei (385–535) at Yungang and Longmen, filtered through Koguryŏ and Paekche. A description is best left to an expert:

The ringlets, which were not cast with the head, are coiled in a non-conventional anticlockwise manner. Fitting them on was no small accomplishment. Some two hundred are massed on the head, all but seven missing at the back. They show no signs of gilding, so were probably painted in the blue colour specified for Buddha's hair. The back of the head is bulbous, a feature little noticed from the front . . . The *ūrṇā* 白毫 in the middle of the forehead, most likely a semiprecious stone, is missing. The exposed gilding reveals the outlines of the eyebrows. Within the 'almond-shaped' eyes are engraved balls, they too without gilding and perhaps once painted black . . . Only the outer tips of a moustache remain; the rest has flaked off. The lips are very slightly turned up at the ends to form an attractive, faint smile, and were presumably first painted red. The strong groove between nose and mouth is a Tori characteristic, as is the rather heavy jaw. In a strange way, the ears simply drop – his left ear is 1.8 cm longer than the right ear – and are unperforated (Kidder 1999: 218).

But perhaps the most informative of the artefacts that survived the fire is the 'Beetle-wing' cabinet or Tamamushi-zushi 玉虫厨子, created between 640 and 650. This cabinet is important because it tells us how far its sponsors had moved towards understanding the basic tenets of Buddhist teaching. It has been studied in depth for clues as to early architecture, gilt, lacquer and

Plate 3   The 'Beetle-wing' cabinet. *c*.650. Height with base 2.327 m. Hōryūji.

techniques of working wood, but of more interest in the present context is the subject matter of its illustrations. The cabinet without the base stands 2.18 m high and, if one were sitting level with it on the floor, one would be looking directly at the centre of the lower section [plate 3]. It has an elaborate double roof with fish-tail ends. The surviving fish-tail was stolen in 1911 and what we now see are replicas. The box section on top has double-opening doors on three sides, the back being closed with a single sheet of wood. The divider half-way down is in three sections with a single-petal lotus design known as *ukehana* carved on the underside. At the bottom are another two layers with another lotus-petal design known as *kaeribana* on top. The whole cabinet sits on a large base. The middle section has four illustrated panels.

Most of the wood used was Japanese cypress (*hinoki*) except for the lotus petals and the front steps, which are of camphorwood (*kusunoki*). The cypress is native to Japan but not to Korea, which is a strong pointer that the object itself was not imported. The wood is covered with a series of thin translucent lacquers which now give a very dark reddish tinge. The main ornament is in the form of intricate gilt-bronze carving attached to the face of the wood, but the most remarkable feature can be seen on the top section where, kept in place by metal strips, are a whole series of green iridescent wing-sheaths from a species of native beetle (*Chrysochroa fulgidissima schoenherr*). Many of these have now fallen off, but the greenish light reflected from thousands of these sheaths must have been an extraordinary sight. It has been calculated that 2,563 sheaths were used on the upper portion, so at least half that number of beetles were sacrificed to the greater glory of the Buddhist Dharma. If we include the lower section, the number rises to 4,665. Similar ornamentation has been found on a dagger and an arrow in the mid-eighth-century royal storehouse the Shōsōin 正倉院 and in Korean tombs, but examples are still extremely rare. This feature, of course, is the provenance of the name 'Beetle-wing'. The statue that is now in the top of the cabinet is not original, but there was undoubtedly a figure in this position; it may have been of Śākyamuni, but it may equally well have been the sovereign Suiko.

For reasons which will become clear later, we shall start with the panel on the right-hand side [plate 4]. The provenance of this subject is beyond doubt. It comes from Chapter 17 of the *Sūtra of golden radiant wisdom*.[8] Entitled 'Casting away the body', this is a retelling of a familiar story of how the Buddha once sacrificed himself for the sake of a tiger and her cubs.

[8]   For further discussion of this sūtra, see §3.2.

Plate 4 'Casting away the body'.

Once there was a king called Mahāratha who was a wise ruler. He had three sons, Mahāpranada, Mahādeva and Mahāsattva, the youngest. Mahāsattva was the Buddha in a former life. One day they went out into the forest and came across a tiger who had given birth to seven cubs just seven days previously. Both mother and cubs were starving. Since tigers are meat-eaters, the only food they could offer was themselves and this they were, of course, reluctant to do. Mahāsattva, however, came to an awareness of the insubstantiality of his own body and returned later to where the tiger was lying. He hung his clothes on a branch nearby and lay down by the tiger. But the tiger was too weak to move. Mahāsattva had no weapon, so went to the top of the hill overlooking the scene, drove a dried bamboo stake into his neck to produce a flow of blood and then cast himself down. The earth shook six ways, the sun lost its power, and petals and perfume rained down. The tiger ate Mahāsattva, leaving only his bones. There they were discovered by his distraught brothers. There was much grief and in the end his father and mother deposited his bones as relics in a large seven-jewelled stūpa.

The painting depicts this scene but with the minimum of violence. In the famous cave paintings at Dunhuang in Gansu Province in western China there are a number of examples of this tale, most of them depicting things in gruesome detail. By contrast, here we have the Buddha hanging his clothes on a tree, casting himself off the cliff and then lying peacefully at the bottom, giving himself to the tiger and her cubs. The essential message is here without the gore. One very curious aspect of this painting is the C-shaped rocks and caves of the cliff, depicted in slab-like sections; this continues to provide art historians with a puzzle. We find these elements on the painting on the opposite side, and they are a marked feature of the whole cabinet, but their continental source is hard to identify. Nothing at Dunhuang really serves as a reference point and so, in the absence of any better roots, it is assumed that the origin of this style must lie somewhere in Korea. The message of this panel is a fairly simple one. The first of the six perfections of the bodhisattva is that of 'giving'. Compassion for others was always seen by advocates of Mahāyāna to be what best characterised their beliefs.

What of the front panel [plate 5]? Working down from the top, we have a lotus flower in the centre supported on clouds. Wisps of smoke, perhaps perfume, rise from it. A little lower to the left and right appear two angel-like figures known as *apsāras*, who hover (descend?) holding between them another lotus. The currents that eddy around them suggest quite violent motion. In the upper middle floats an incense burner with three lines of smoke rising from it. Each of its claw-shaped feet rests on a lotus bud. Lower

Plate 5 'The worship of relics'.

still sit two monks left and right, each holding an incense burner with ladle attached. At the very bottom in the centre sits a large table with animal feet resting on a lotus base. From either side and from the top of the table rise curls of smoke which in turn support a fully opened lotus in which stands a pedestal. On the pedestal we find a round receptacle garlanded with flowers. It looks like a relic box. In the bottom left and right corners sit two Chinese lion-dogs (*shishi* 獅子) gazing up at the arrangement in the centre.

This painting is the subject of some debate. There are those who argue that it is simply a picture of an offering to the Buddha in the top section with all the usual paraphernalia of such a scene, but since the other panels are linked to texts, it would be helpful to identify some source. Perhaps Chapter 17 of the *Sūtra of golden radiant wisdom* can do dual service. Before the story of Mahāsattva and the tiger proper, the chapter has a preliminary scene in which the goddess Bodhisattvasamuccaya asks the Buddha about the occasion when in a former life he underwent countless austerities and eventually sacrificed his own body. In reply the Buddha stamps on the earth, which then shakes in six directions and disgorges a large seven-jewelled stūpa. The Buddha makes obeisance to this stūpa and when asked why, replies that herein lie his own relics.

At that time the Buddha turned to the sage Ānanda and said, 'You should open the stūpa, take out the relics that lie within and show them to the assembly. These relics indeed hold the fragrance of countless merits of the six perfections.' Then Ānanda followed the Buddha's instructions, went to where the stūpa stood, bowed in homage and gave offerings, and then opened the door of the stūpa. There he saw the relics, of marvellous colours, red and white. And he spoke to the Buddha saying, 'World-honoured One. The relics within are coloured red and white.' And the Buddha said to Ānanda, 'You should bring them here. These are the relics of the true body of the wise one (Mahāsattva).' Thereupon Ānanda lifted up the jewelled casket and returned with it to where the Buddha was and he offered it up to him. And the Buddha said to the whole assembly, 'You should now make obeisance to these relics. They are fragrant with constant practice of keeping the precepts, concentrating the mind and seeking wisdom. They are fields of merit that are extremely difficult to obtain.' Now the assembly heard these words and their hearts were filled with pleasure and happiness and they all rose from their seats, put their hands together in prayer, and gave homage to the relics of the Mahāsattva. And the World-honoured One, desirous of cutting the net of doubt for all the assembly, explained whence these relics had come (*T.* 663, vol. XVI: 354.a.6–19).

Not all the elements in the picture are explained by this quotation alone, but in the absence of any better suggestion, it would seem to be a good candidate. It is about the importance of relics.

The panel on the left illustrates yet another scene of self-sacrifice [plate 6]. The source this time is Chapter 14 of the *Nirvāṇa sūtra* entitled 'On holy actions'. Again it is a story that deals with the activities of the Buddha in a former life. Buddha recounts the story in the first person. Once, when he was a brahmin undergoing ascetic practice in the Himalayas, the gods decided to test him. Indra transformed himself into a devil and descended to where the young brahmin was practising. In a loud voice, he proclaimed the first half of a key verse that encapsulated Buddhist thinking: 'All dharmas are forever changing, this is the law of birth and death.' The astounded brahmin eventually realises that the devil, despite his appearance, has the key to enlightenment and he begs him to give him the second half of the verse. After some discussion the devil agrees, on condition that the brahmin gives himself up to be eaten, because he is starving, can find no food and can only survive on living flesh and blood. The brahmin agrees and then hears the second half of the verse: 'Once birth and death are annulled, quiet and annulment bring bliss.' Having promised to give up his life for the message, the young brahmin writes down the verses wherever he can, then climbs a tall tree and casts himself down to die. In that instant the devil changes back into Indra and the brahmin is helped gently to the ground, and praised and worshipped as the future Buddha.

The general design of this panel is very similar to the one on the right. It too moves from bottom left up and over in a circular movement accentuated by the shape of the cliff and the caves. The brahmin is also depicted three times. Standing bottom left looking at the devil, he is dressed in bark or deer-skin clothes and has the long hair of an ascetic. Half-way up we see him writing the verses on a rock, and then we find him casting himself from the top, to be saved by Indra on the right. Flowers and perfumed smoke mark his descent. The message here is twofold: self-sacrifice is a central Buddhist virtue and enlightenment is open to all, even to what appears to be a devil.

When we move to the rear of the cabinet we find another large picture corresponding to that on the front [plate 7]. It is a painting of Mt Sumeru, which was thought to lie at the centre of the Indian universe. Right down the centre we have the mountain, towering above the waves. On top of the mountain is Indra's palace, which links this panel to the last one. On both sides immortals fly on phoenixes with banners raised, and below them lie the sun and the moon. The sun contains a three-legged crow and the moon a hare. In the middle of the mountain are the four palaces of the four guardian kings and around the base winds a double-headed dragon. In the sea at the bottom stands the Palace of the Dragon King with fish-tail ends to the roof and an

Plate 6 Indra as a devil.

Plate 7 'Mt Sumeru'.

interior divided into three sections. In the middle sits the Buddha with a woman on either side. On each side of the palace in the corner sits a garuda bird, each holding a small dragon in its beak.

There are at least two sources for this panel. The first is a passage from the 'Devadatta' chapter of the *Lotus sūtra*. The crux of this chapter is the example of the Naga (Dragon) King's daughter who manages to achieve enlightenment, so giving hope to all women. This has been augmented by the painter with reference to the *Sūtra of the Dragon King of the Sea*.[9] Immediately before preaching on Vulture Peak, the Buddha causes Mt Sumeru to appear and the Dragon King comes up out of the sea to hear his message. The Dragon King then asks why it is that a decline in numbers of dragons is now being reversed with an increase. The Buddha explains that in the past many dragons heard the Dharma, became good Buddhists and were eventually reborn as humans. Now humans are becoming more and more decadent and so are being reborn as dragons. The king then allows the Buddha to preach in his palace. The women depicted are the king's wife and his daughter. The daughter hears the Buddha preaching and hears him say in particular that women too may eventually become buddhas. She then debates the matter with Kāśyapa, who believes the opposite. The Buddha informs them that there is no distinction between the genders when it comes to enlightenment and that the daughter will clearly achieve her goal. In the end the king asks the Buddha to save those dragons who are petrified with fear in case they are eaten by garuda birds. The Buddha preaches to the garudas, who also promise to uphold the Dharma.

To what use was this shrine put and why was it created? There are, of course, no definite answers but it may well have been used as a centrepiece for oral explanation. It is the correct height and holds within its panels many of the central propositions of Mahāyāna Buddhism: the possibility of enlightenment for all, compassion for others as the first of the six perfections to be practised by the aspiring bodhisattva, and the concept that the Buddha was not a man who has 'already gone before' but an eternal presence. The use of the 'Devadatta' chapter of the *Lotus sūtra* suggests that the intended audience were the women at court. Together with the statues from this early stage, it shows us that despite the fact that the Buddha was being worshipped by priests as a deity, the central tenets of the Buddhist message were beginning to be understood and honoured by the elite at court by the middle of the seventh century.

[9] Ch. *Hailongwang jing*, Jp. *Kairyūō kyō* 海龍王經, *T.* 589, vol. XV: 134–57.

2   Creating a dynasty

2.1   The problem of succession

It would be reasonable to assume that each successive monarch wanted to establish a dynasty but had not discovered how best to control the pattern of events. Certainly, the kind of upheaval that tended to surround each change at this stage was hardly conducive to stable government, and there seems to have been no law of succession. It was, of course, difficult to forestall all the problems and rivalries that might emerge after one's death, and smooth transitions were not exactly the rule from this point on, but it was Tenmu who took the first major step in this direction. By ordering the compilation of written records, and particularly of lineages, he began a process that came to fruition fifty years later in the first chronicles, whose mission it was to reveal an unbroken line of succession leading back to the beginning of time and the earliest gods. In an edict of 681, he proclaimed:

> I hear that 'imperial records' [*teiki* 帝紀] and 'accounts of origin' [*honji* 本辭] handed down by various houses have come to differ from the truth and that many falsehoods have been added. If these errors are not corrected now, the meaning of the records and accounts – the warp and woof of the Japanese state and the foundations of royal rule – will be lost before many years have passed. Therefore a study of the royal records for the purpose of selecting out and recording what is true, and an examination of 'ancient accounts' [*kyūji* 舊辭] for the purpose of rejecting errors and determining truth are ordered so that we may have true records and accounts passed on to later generations (Kurano and Takeda 1958: 45–46).

It would be difficult to find a statement more self-aware in its duplicity. He who writes the first history and manages to bury all previous and competing narratives has invented the most powerful tool of all, and we have already seen what an effective smokescreen these early chronicles create. Most of what appears in this chapter is subject to their control. Their aim was to show that the present state of affairs had always pertained, and that the tutelary deity of the ruling family had from the very beginning been at the apex of a divinely ordained hierarchy and part of the natural order of the universe.

36

When Tenmu died in 686, he left two possible heirs, Prince Ōtsu 大津 and Prince Kusakabe 草壁. The first was quickly eliminated, but the mourning for Tenmu took over two years, and before Kusakabe could be proclaimed as the next sovereign, he too died. His mother Jitō 持統 took his place, ruling from 690 to 697. In 690.1.1 an entry in *Nihon shoki* records what may be the first description of a formal investiture ceremony, and in 692.3 she made the first royal 'progress' to the shrines at Ise. This was to be the first of a number of such tours, which were clearly designed to impress the presence of the centre on the periphery, but perhaps Jitō's greatest contribution to the survival of the Japanese monarchy was to introduce the concept of abdication, a technique which made it possible for the reigning sovereign to control succession and so maintain a dynasty. Was it to avoid the elaborate rites that accompanied the death of a sovereign and to allow the shift of authority to be made swiftly and with the minimum of fuss? In 696 she announced her intention to resign, and the next year Kusakabe's son Karu became sovereign at the age of fourteen. He was to be known to posterity as Monmu Tennō 文武天皇 (r. 697–707).

When Monmu died, he was replaced by his mother Genmei 元明 (661–721; r. 707–15) who was in turn replaced by his sister Genshō 元正 (r. 715–24). The women seem to be trying to ensure that orderly succession became second nature. Although this period is often treated as little more than a trough between the high-points of Tenmu-Jitō on the one hand and Shōmu-Kōken 聖武・孝謙 (724–58) on the other, it was in fact during this time that the capital was moved to Heijō-kyō 平城京 (Nara 奈良) and *Kojiki* and *Nihon shoki* were written down and made public. In order to secure the future, the ruling family had to be able not only to control local cults and the rapidly expanding presence of Buddhist institutions; it also needed to put in place a rule of law. In 684.10.1 the old titles had been abolished and replaced by new ones which reinforced the importance of lineage: *mahito* 眞人 for members of the immediate family; the ubiquitous *asomi/ason* 朝臣 for others with blood ties to the monarch; and *sukune* 宿禰 for those close to the centre but without blood ties (Aston 1972, vol. II: 365). Penal and administrative codes based on Chinese models are thought to have been promulgated in three stages: the Kiyomihara Code 淨御原令, not extant but said to have been completed by Jitō in 689,[1] the Taihō Code of 701, and the Yōrō Code 養老律令, compiled in 718 but not fully promulgated until 757. Only the last of these survives to

---

[1] An entry in *Nihon shoki* for 689.6.29 reads 'One section of the Code in 22 volumes was distributed to all local governors'; it is thought that this refers to the completion of the Kiyomihara Code, which had been ordered by Tenmu.

any degree, but as each built on its predecessor one is justified in extrapolating backwards, if done with care. The administrative framework that emerged had the sovereign nominally in control of two main councils, the Council of State (Daijōkan 太政官) and the Council for Affairs of the Deities of Heaven and Earth (Jingikan 神祇官). The latter is usually described as being a Japanese innovation, entrusted with the delicate task of extending central control over all deities in the land, local and tutelary. That said, however, the term *jingi*, a short form of the phrase *tenjin chigi* 天神地祇, had a long pedigree in China and a number of the statutes and rituals in the Yōrō Code have precedents in those parts of the 'shrine regulations' (*ciling* 祠令) of pre-Tang and early Tang codes that are extant. We know from an entry in *Nihon shoki* for 692.9.14 that records the Jingikan presenting four 'sacred treasure books 神寶書四巻, nine keys and one wooden seal' that the institution itself was already in existence by this time.

2.2   Native beliefs

It is now time to ask ourselves a difficult question: what were the indigenous beliefs in Japan before the arrival of Buddhism? The gifts that arrived from Paekche in the middle of the sixth century could hardly, of course, have simply filled a void: so to what were the Mononobe and Nakatomi referring when they warned: 'Those who have ruled as kings over the world, over this our state, have always taken care to worship the 180 deities of heaven and earth in spring, summer, autumn and winter. If we were now to change and worship a foreign deity, we fear we shall incur the wrath of the deities of our own land'?

The question is far more difficult to answer than it appears at first sight because we immediately run into the usual historiographical impasse: there are, by definition, no native sources that predate the introduction of writing into Japan, so an early text such as *Nihon shoki* of 720 is already heavily 'contaminated' by Chinese influence and Buddhist presence. A term such as 'the 180 deities of heaven and earth' is a nice case in point: it might sound indigenous, and the magic figure 180 might possibly have roots in pre-Buddhist Japan; but the rest of the phrase has a strong Chinese flavour that clashes loudly with the nativism of its context. Things are made doubly difficult because it is precisely during the two hundred years that stretch from the early sixth century to the eighth that Buddhism was accommodated and that indigenous beliefs adapted to this powerful intruder. This fact is worth stressing, if only because attention is more usually focused in the other direction, namely on the degree to which Buddhism succeeded by being so responsive to every new environment it faced. It is true that Buddhism sometimes goes so far in this process that one is tempted to talk not of the 'Buddhist conquest of Japan' but of the 'Japanese conquest of Buddhism', but it is equally true that indigenous cults changed radically in turn. The problem is in measuring this change with little evidence other than the contents of tomb mounds, which date mainly from 300–600.[2] The largest of these were assigned to various monarchs in the Meiji period (with varying degrees of plausibility) and they have been off-limits to archaeologists ever since. By and large, the smaller ones that have been excavated have revealed large quantities of material goods of value such as bronze mirrors, swords, horse trappings, and clay replicas of human figures, horses and boats, but, as one might expect, there are no inscriptions. Any description, then, of indigenous beliefs and cults in the sixth century must remain tentative.

It would appear that from earliest times the Japanese, like most early societies, had a strong sense of sacred space and of the numinous nature of certain places and objects. The term used to describe such elements is *kami* 神, a word that can refer both to an object and to the presence represented by that object. A *kami* might be an oddly shaped rock, tree or mountain, or any other phenomenon or place that had important connotations for a particular group. These places were treated as contact points between this world and the other world from where all uncontrollable events originated. They were therefore held sacred and it was considered important that they be kept clear of this-worldly pollution; if pollution did occur, dire consequences might well result, since *kami* were a source of all that was unpredictable, of life and health but also of misfortune and disaster. Constant and regular observation of ritual was necessary in order to placate, cajole or simply demonstrate that the presence or force represented by the site was being remembered and respected for what it could do. We have here the beginnings of the shrine or *yashiro* 社.

We cannot tell at what stage temporary structures erected at sites for ritual purposes might have become fixed shrines, nor how the practice of ritual was organised, but it is probable that by the sixth century the Nakatomi family group, or *uji* 氏, had become hereditary ritualists for those shrines that had particular significance for the rulers of central Yamato, so it is reasonable to assume that others performed similar duties in other areas. This development

---

[2] See the useful chart of keyhole-shaped tombs in Piggott 1997: 32–33.

presupposes a process by which a divine presence, amorphous but specific to a locale, became the ancestral deity of an *uji*, symbolising its corporate identity. This was presumably common by the sixth century and, given the reported response of the Nakatomi in 552, one can perhaps posit a series of tutelary deities, honoured at a shrine, with a priestly family charged with ritual. This might also suggest some form of ancestor worship, but here too we have to be careful. The deification of family founders – and we know that this occurred in the eighth century with Fujiwara no Kamatari, for example – presupposes anthropomorphism and may well involve a transformation quite distinct from the process described above. There is no evidence for this kind of belief in earlier times, and its emergence may itself have been a result of the influence of imported Chinese concepts. It is also difficult to tell at what stage this kind of *kami* took on semi-human characteristics. The beginnings of such a process would lie in the impulse to name, but the nature of our sources does not allow us to state when this may have occurred. Certainly, there is no evidence of any attempt to carve images of native deities at this stage.

Developments at a later stage suggest that once the link between local deity and family had been created it was difficult to break, so that a group might well find it necessary to maintain such ties even when it moved far from its 'original' home. This could be done either by creating a legend that deity X had moved from A to B at some stage in the past for some good reason, or, as in the case of the ruling family in the eighth century with its main shrine at Ise, by making sure that one important member of the family was resident in the shrine as a representative. One important corollary of the localised nature of cults was that they were essentially unrelated to each other. Certainly, this was not a coherent system. In view of what we know of matters after 720, whatever the Mononobe and Nakatomi may have been referring to in 552, it was nothing resembling an organised 'religion'.

The most unfortunate gap in our knowledge about pre-Buddhist Japan concerns attitudes to death. Recent studies have drawn our attention to the wealth of information about burial rites for dead rulers that can be gleaned from forensic examination of *Kojiki* and *Nihon shoki*, but no scholar can escape the grip of the sources (Macé 1986 and Ebersole 1989). We know very little about attitudes in the sixth century, never mind about what underpinned the production of the tomb mounds (*kofun*) that were so conspicuous in the fourth and fifth centuries. There seems to have been a concept of a psyche (*tama* 靈 or 魂) that gave the body life but that also might wander away on occasions such as sleep, dreamtime or death; one might try and call the *tama* back with an arm-waving ritual known as *tamafuri* and it was thought that the *tama* of the deceased could well return of its own accord at certain points of the year to receive ritual recognition. But the relationship between *tama* and *kami* is unclear. What seems to have happened is that during the sixth and seventh centuries Buddhism made death its own, appropriating it so completely that it now appears to us that the native cults simply had nothing to say about death, which common sense tells us is an untenable proposition. We have been left with only half the picture. What 'native' prayers have survived are mainly concerned with agricultural rituals, and shrines seem to have had nothing to do with burial or the dead, such things being regarded as little more than a source of this-worldly pollution. The uncanny illusion is thereby created that Buddhism simply filled a void as far as the rites of death were concerned, which cannot be correct; its success in this particular arena was so complete that it obliterated what came before.

2.3 The Jingikan

To return to Tenmu Tennō and his strategies of legitimation. Given the disparate, highly localised nature of these cults and the fact that power had only just been won as the result of a vicious internecine war, hegemony could not be expected overnight, if at all. An administrative framework was needed to impose a hierarchy onto the cultic landscape. As we have already pointed out, the earliest extant statutes (*ryō* 令) that governed the operation of the Jingikan are those in the Yōrō Code of 718, but there is some justification for reading at least the outline back into the middle of the previous century. They consist of twenty short articles outlining the duties of the council, mainly concerned with certain key rites: observances for the natural agricultural cycle such as spring planting and the annual harvest rite, together with prayers for the avoidance of natural disasters and the health of the monarch. The most important of these were the Toshigoi (or Kinensai 祈年祭) and the Tsukinami no matsuri 月次祭.

1　The worship of the gods of heaven and earth should be performed by officials, in accordance with the prescribed forms. [There is no consensus on the distinction between the gods of heaven and those of earth. Tokugawa scholars have argued that the gods of heaven were directly linked to the monarchy, and those of earth not so linked, but this is only one of a number of theories.]
2　Early spring: Toshigoi no matsuri 祈年祭, for a good harvest. [Offerings were presented to all shrines in the Yamato area.]

3   Late spring: Hanashizume no matsuri 鎮花祭, for good health. [This was held at the Ōmiwa shrine. It was believed that the scattering of blossoms in the wind was linked to the spread of epidemics. Here, too, offerings were presented to the shrine.]

4   Midsummer: Kanmiso no matsuri 神衣齋, offerings of summer garments to the deities [presented to the Ise shrines]; Ōimi no matsuri 大忌祭 'the Great Taboo' [offerings presented to the Food Deities at the Hirose shrine]; Saigusa no matsuri 三枝祭, possibly to give thanks for rice wine [offerings to the Isakawa shrine, a sub-shrine of Ōmiwa]; Kazakami no matsuri 風神祭, for good weather [offerings to the Wind Deities at the Tatsuta shrine].

5   Late summer: Tsukinami no matsuri 月次祭, a 'monthly' thanksgiving [held in the Palace, but actually only on two months of the year]; Hishizume no matsuri 鎮火祭, to avoid fire; Michiae no matsuri 道饗, 'the Banquet of the Roads' [to keep the roads in the capital clear of dangers],

6   Early autumn: Ōimi no matsuri and Kazakami no matsuri.

7   Late autumn: Kanmiso no matsuri and Kanname/Kamunie no matsuri 神嘗祭 'the Divine Tasting'. [Offerings of the first fruits of the year's harvest, held at the Ise shrines.]

8   Early winter: Aimube no matsuri 相嘗祭 'the Joint Tasting' [similar to above but offerings were sent to major shrines in the Yamato area]; Tamashizume/Ōmutamafuri no matsuri 鎮魂祭 'Pacifying the Spirit' [to insure that the monarch's spirit did not leave his body; held at the Palace, this was a rite that enacted the capture of the Sun Goddess when she hid herself away in a cave]; Ōnie/Ōmube no matsuri 大嘗祭 'the Great Tasting' [the main thanksgiving festival, held in the Palace].

9   Late winter: Tsukinami no matsuri and Hishizume no matsuri and Michiae no matsuri. The offerings, rituals and dates for all these festivals are as set out in separate ordinances (*bechishiki* 別式). For the Toshigoi and Tsukinami, all officials are to gather at the Jingikan. The Nakatomi are to read the *norito*; the Inbe to present the offerings.

10 On the accession of the monarch, all deities are to be worshipped. There shall be partial abstinence for one month and complete abstinence for three days. Offerings should be prepared three months beforehand.

11 During partial abstinence all officials should carry on their work as usual; but they should not visit anyone in mourning, call upon the sick, or eat flesh. Nor shall death sentences be pronounced or criminal cases be judged. No music shall be played and no unclean or inauspicious tasks be performed. During complete abstinence, no duties may be performed except those to do with ceremonial observances. Partial abstinence is to take place before and after complete abstinence.

12 One month's abstinence is to be treated as a Grand Festival; three days as a Middle Festival; one day as a Small Festival.

13 On the day of accession the Nakatomi shall read the divine ritual (*yogoto* 壽詞), and the Inbe shall present the regalia: the mirror and the sword.

14 The [Special] Great Food Festival (Ōmube) will take place once in every reign,

presided over by the provincial officers. Other festivals shall be celebrated annually by officials from the Jingikan.

15 When a festival is to take place, the officials shall inform the government as to when the abstinence is to begin; the government shall then inform other offices.

16 All offerings of food, fruits and drink at festivals shall be examined by the chief official, who shall personally ensure they are correct and proper. No ill assorted or unclean items must be permitted.

17 When offerings are made on occasions other than the regular ceremonies, diviners of the fifth rank and upwards shall be employed for this service.

18 On the last day of the sixth and twelfth months, on the occasion of the Great Purification, the Nakatomi shall offer the purification wand (*nusa*), the masters of writing shall offer up the sword of purification and recite the liturgy. That done, the hundred officials and their families, male and female, shall assemble in the place of purification. The Nakatomi shall recite the prayers (*norito*) and the Urabe perform the cleansing.

19 When the great Purification is performed in the provinces, every province is to be provided with one sword, one animal skin, one hoe and other miscellaneous gifts. Each household is to receive one strand of flax and each provincial governor one horse.

20 The taxes levied on the servants of the shrines, whether miscellaneous or land tax, shall be devoted to the construction of shrines or to the provision of offerings to the gods. Land tax proper should be treated as rice reserve, inspected by local authorities and reported to the office (Inoue et al. 1976: 211–15).[3]

These statutes are short and perfunctory, with detail in some areas but not in others, and we have to wait another two hundred years, until the *Engishiki* of the 920s, for further information, by which time the whole system had been considerably expanded. Nothing, for example, is said about the activities of priests or about the organisation of any shrine system, possibly because no such system existed. The staff of the Jingikan was not large, with a head (*jingihaku* 神祇伯) of rather low rank, two assistant heads, two secretaries, two clerks, thirty deity households (*kanbe* 神戸), twenty diviners, thirty attendants and two servants (Naumann 2000: 47–67). Clearly, the provision of gifts and offerings from the centre was designed to create the illusion of a system, but very few shrines are mentioned by name, which suggests that the process of creating a hegemony was only just beginning. The very sparseness of the laws betrays the difficulty of the enterprise. We have to wait until well into the eighth century before we see an appreciable increase in the number of official shrines receiving such offerings; the first recorded offerings to shrines outside the immediate Yamato area, for example, is in 698.

---

[3] Trans. adapted from Sansom 1934. Note that many of the Japanese readings given here are probably later inventions.

Hidden in item 14 of this list is a reference to what is now known as the Daijōsai 大嘗祭, a special expanded thanksgiving ceremony that took place only once at the beginning of a new reign in celebration of the enthronement (Liscutin 1990). It was first held in 691 in the reign of Jitō, and again in 698.11.23 in honour of Monmu. Our earliest source for a description of this rite is the 'Rituals of the Jōgan era' (*Jōgan gishiki* 貞觀儀式) of 872, which undoubtedly represent something grander, but the main outlines were probably the same. Although the heart of the rite was private to the monarch, the whole country was expected to participate in the preparations, so it was designed to emphasise the hegemonic role of the figure at the centre. Preparations began in the spring with the choice of which two districts would be responsible for the arrangements; it was their role to provide the sacred rice, construct the buildings and send the young women who prepared the food and drink. As in normal years, the Ōmutamafuri or Chinkonsai was held just prior to the ceremony itself, to ensure that the monarch's psyche would not leave him in his weakened state near the end of the year. The ceremony itself was held in a specially built enclosure with two small lodges inside. At night, the monarch purified himself, entered each lodge in turn in the company of two maidens, where he laid out rice for the gods and shared *sake* with them; it is thought that some sacred communion occurred at the point that the monarch shared the sacred wine. A couch called a *shinza* 神座 was also present in both lodges, but there is no indication as to its use. Conflicting theories, of course, abound. There was, in addition to this, a separate enthronement ceremony (*sokui no gi* 即位儀) that was firmly based on Chinese precedent, although it was still held under the auspices of the Jingikan.

Some idea of the language involved in these various rites can be gathered from the following Toshigoi liturgy, which dates from the eighth century:

Before the mighty ancestral gods and goddesses who augustly reside in the plain of high Heaven, before the many *kami* enshrined in Heaven and Earth, we raise our words of praise. And to the mighty *kami* we humbly speak: in this second month of the year, at the beginnning of the sowing of seed, we humbly raise our words of praise even as we bring choice offerings from the divine descendant at this moment of the majestic and brilliant dawning of the morning light. Before the presence of the *kami* who govern the crops we do humbly speak, praying that they will grant a late-ripening harvest of grain. With foam on the water up to the elbows and muddy water up to the thigh as the rice is planted, may it grow into countless bundles of long-eared grain, vigorous grain. If the mighty *kami* grant that it shall ripen, we shall offer up the first-fruits of the grain, a thousand, yes, ten thousand ears.

Let offering jars be filled to the brims, let full-bellied jars be arrayed in rows. We shall offer liquid and grain with words of praise, together with things that grow in the broad meadows and moors, sweet herbs and bitter herbs. We shall offer things that live in the blue sea-plain, beings wide of fin and narrow too, seaweeds of the deep and those of the shore. And for divine raiment, we shall offer up bright cloth, shining cloth, coarse cloth, all with our words of praise (Piggott 1997: 210).

In light of the above, it is striking to find that those sections of *Nihon shoki* that cover the reigns of both Tenmu and Jitō contain surprisingly few entries devoted to cult affairs. In particular one notices the paucity of references to the shrines at Ise, which are famous for being the home of the ancestral deity of the ruling family. Exactly why the tutelary deity of the rulers should be based at Ise is not known. There is no sign that they ever had any roots there; on the contrary, the early movement into Yamato was always presented as having come from the west rather than the east. It is thought that Ise may have been adopted as late as Tenmu's reign. *Nihon shoki* tells us that he prayed to this deity for success in battle while he was in the Ise region during the Jinshin civil war, and that early in his reign preparations were made to send a princess of the blood to the shrine as a surrogate for the sovereign (*itsukinomiya* 齋王). Both chronicles record the mythical origins of this practice, but it is likely that this reference in fact records its genesis. When Jitō went on her tour to the east in 692 there is a mention of two deities at Ise, which is taken to mean that both the Outer (Gekū 外宮) and the Inner Shrine (Naikū 内宮) were in existence by this time.

And what of the deity itself? We know that they adopted a sun deity, anthropomorphised it at some stage, and placed it at Ise, but what was its name and what was its gender? Not that too many people would have known. In *Kojiki* the name is written 天照大御神, which could be read either Amateru ōmikami or Amaterasu ōmikami. In *Nihon shoki* we find both 大日孁貴, which was given the reading Ōhirumenomuchi and suggests the female gender, and 天照大神 Tenshō daijin, which is genderless. The name Amaterasu only becomes fixed with Yoshida Kanekata 吉田兼方 in the sixteenth century. The gender tended to fluctuate and for much of the medieval period the name used was Tenshō daijin with the assumption that if one had to choose then it would be male.

Having a divine ancestor is one thing. Being divine oneself is another. There is no sign in the chronicles that monarchs like Tenmu were considered to be divine in and of themselves, but the picture changes when we look at the late eighth-century poetry collection *Man'yōshū* 萬葉集, which includes much from this early period. Here we do find poems that make such a claim. It undoubtedly began as hyperbole. The poet and court eulogist Kakinomoto no Hitomaro 柿本人麻呂, when writing of Tenmu after his death, used the term *kamunagara* 惟神, 'as a very god', and in a number of longer poems the divinity of the ancestor is transferred directly to the reigning monarch. In particular the term *akitsukami* 現つ神 or 'manifest deity' occurs a number of times. It did not take long for this hyperbole to be transformed into norm, so we find that the edicts known as *senmyō* 宣命 that appear in *Shoku Nihongi* 續日本紀, a chronicle that covers the years 697–791, use this concept of *akitsukami* quite freely. The edict read out at Monmu's accession to the throne in 697 shows that the rhetoric of divine lineage was by now fully developed:

Hearken all ye assembled August Children, Princes, Nobles, Officials of the Realm-under-Heaven to the Word which he speaks even as the Word of the Sovereign that is a manifest God ruling over the Great Land of Many Islands.

He says: Hearken ye to the Word of the Sovereign who proclaims thus: We have listened with reverence to the noble, high, broad, warm Words of the charge vouchsafed to Us by the Sovereign Prince of Yamato, who is a manifest God ruling over the Great Land of Many Islands in performance of the task of this the High Throne of Heavenly Succession, in the same wise as the August Child of the God of Heaven, as it was decreed by the God which is in Heaven, that from the beginning in the High Plain of Heaven, through the reigns of our Distant Ancestors down to these days and onwards, Sovereign August Children should be born in succession for ever to succeed to the rule of the Great Land of Many Islands. And, even as a God, it is Our wish to give Peace and Order to this Realm-under-Heaven and to deign to cherish and soothe its people.

He says: Hearken ye all to the Word which the Sovereign proclaims, saying thus: And therefore all ye functionaries of every kind, even unto the officers appointed to govern the countries under our rule in the four quarters, do ye, neither mistaking nor violating the laws of the land which the Sovereign House had proclaimed and enforced, ever striving, without delay or neglect, with bright, pure and true hearts, earnestly labour and serve.

He says: Hearken ye all to the Word which the Sovereign proclaims saying thus: And all people who, hearing and understanding in this wise, shall serve Us faithfully, We will in divers ways reward, praising them and lifting them up (Aoki et al. 1989–98, vol. I: 3–5).[4]

2.4   Inventing the past

The process of inventing the past came to fruition with the completion of *Kojiki* in 712 and *Nihon shoki* in 720. We have already had occasion to touch

---

[4]   Trans. by G. B. Sansom in Snellen 1934: 169–70.

on both of these chronicles, but they demand a closer look since the stories they tell reverberated through the whole of Japanese history. From the outset it is important to note that although at various stages they were to be treated as sacred texts to be revered and studied, they were never recognised as having been 'revealed'. They were not the word of a creating deity but written by court scribes as history, the aim of which was to legitimate the pre-eminence of the ruling family by explaining its divine roots in prehistory, and to explain the status quo by illustrating how contemporary power relationships at court and within the country were a direct reflection of relationships established in the distant past between different ancestral deities. They were therefore intensely political products. This is not to say, however, that they are of no use to the historian of religion.

Kojiki covers the story of Japan down to the death of Suiko in 628, although it tails off well before that period. Written in a difficult hybrid style that retains a great deal of native Japanese beneath the cloak of a script borrowed from China, it traces the genealogy of the ruling family back to the very beginnings of the world. It does so largely in mythical style, telling its tale through vignettes and poems, mixed with the usual lists of names. Concerned mainly with domestic affairs, it hardly mentions China or Korea, organises itself not by date but by the name of sovereign and length of reign, and ignores the introduction of Buddhism completely. The suggestion that it was largely a product of the Jingikan is entirely plausible. When discussing *Kojiki*, however, one must never forget one uncomfortable fact: very soon after its compilation, perhaps within a space of ten years, to all intents and purposes it disappeared and was not read or studied again until the rise of philology in the eighteenth century. This means that although it can tell us a great deal about the ideology and intentions of the early state, when discussing the application and growth of such an ideology post-720 it must always cede precedence to *Nihon shoki*.

Nihon shoki is quite different. Written in classical Chinese, this is much more recognisably historiography, with careful dating. In the later sections it reads very much like a diplomatic history, with constant cross references to Korean sources and other variant accounts. The use of the term 'Nihon' 日本 could be seen as a willingness to objectify Japan in Chinese terms, although it could also be seen as justification for treating Japan as coeval with the origin of the sun. The historical account is brought down to the abdication of Jitō in 697 and the sections that cover the last seventy years are seen to be increasingly reliable, if just as subject to political imperatives. The earlier sections cover similar mythical material to *Kojiki* but there is a much more critical mind at work here, since many different and often contradictory versions of events are included. This has two effects: it imbues the text with a self-awareness that constantly reminds one of the slipperiness of historical 'fact'; and it also provides us with a large collection of what we might call allomyths, against which one can read the account as presented in *Kojiki*. It gives us an opportunity to study mythmaking as a dynamic process.

The use of either of these texts is fraught with difficulties at every turn. As we have seen, it remains a possibility that a written version of anything, including myth, produced in the early eighth century has been influenced by three hundred years of exposure not only to Buddhism but also to Chinese thought and institutions in general. This is clear from even a cursory glance at the preface to *Kojiki*, which is full of classical Chinese references. Nevertheless we cannot simply reject these narratives as being too difficult to use just because of the tangled web they weave. Careful analysis can give us brief glimpses of a Japanese vision of the world that predates the introduction of Buddhism. Whether it can give us a glimpse of aboriginal beliefs prior to the advent of Chinese influence is an entirely different matter. Rocher, introducing a trenchant and wide-ranging treatment of most of the early myths, writes of the problems created by this text as follows:

Two approaches stand out. Either the stories are denied coherence, broken up into a mosaic of motifs, each one attributed to a different origin as if myth can only make sense as etymology; or their systematic nature is recognised, only for it to be situated outside the realm of myth: in other words, the intelligibility of the texts becomes one of politics. Implicitly all scholars appear to assume that the mythological dimension of the chronicles belongs to a past long gone, in which case analysis is condemned to take on the guise of archaeology. One ends up repeating that *Kojiki* and *Nihon shoki* are the result of a long process of compilation; that the stories they contain were reworked, pruned, and put to the service of an imperial ideology; and that the original voice is lost to us, having passed through three stages of disenchantment: religious, ritual and ideological. In short, we are invited to believe that there is a conflict between what is political and what is mythological, as if myth could only blossom in the purest of pure spontaneity (Rocher 1997: 4).

For our purposes the most important sections of the chronicles are those that cover the 'Age of the gods' (*jindai no maki* 神代卷): Book One of *Kojiki*, and Books One and Two of *Nihon shoki*. The *Kojiki* narrative begins by recording the names of three deities (Amenominakanushi, Takamimusubi and Kamimusubi) who came into existence in the Plain of High Heaven (Takamanohara 高天原) when Heaven and Earth began 天地初發之時, but these are single deities, ungendered and originating nothing; they simply exist. Four more single deities then emerge, to be followed by deities in pairs.

Among these are the male-female pair Izanagi and Izanami. Together, as brother and sister, they create the land (of Japan) by stirring a spear in the sea, the brine dripping from the end of the spear coagulating to form an island called Onogoro. Descending to the island, they discover their sexual difference and, circumambulating a pillar, conjoin to produce offspring. The first result is a mere leech, which they cast adrift on the water. After discussion as to why the ritual has failed, they decide it was because the female spoke first. Repetition of the ritual with the male speaking first brings success. They give birth to all the islands of the Japanese archipelago, followed by thirty-five more deities, each one representing a natural phenomenon.

This apparently limitless process of procreation is brought to a sudden stop when Izanami dies giving birth to the fire deity, which burns her genitals. Enraged, Izanagi buries her and kills the offending child. Many more named deities emerge from the bloody corpse. In deep distress, Izanagi tries to follow his sister into the underworld, Yominokuni, asking her to return. In his impatience, he breaks a taboo and produces light, only to reveal her decomposing body full of maggots 'squirming and roaring'. Chased by hags, he flees using a combination of grapes and peaches as decoys. When Izanami herself comes after him, he blocks the way with a large boulder and makes his escape. They agree to part for ever, Izanami vowing to kill a number of children every day, and Izanagi vowing to replace them every day. Returning to this world, he purifies himself by washing and in the process produces a stream of further deities, among whom are the Sun Goddess Amaterasu ('she who lights the heavens'), who comes from his left eye, and two males, Tsukiyomi ('he who understands the moon'?), who comes from his right eye, and Susano-o ('the raging male'), who comes from his nose. *Nihon shoki* contains a large number of variants at this point. It uses the same metaphor of a reed-shoot emerging from a marsh, for example, but calls the first deity Kunitokotachi ('earth standing eternal') in one version and Umashiashikabi-hikoji ('male spirit of the excellent reed shoots') in another.

If, contra Rocher, one does believe that unadulterated myth can at least be approached, this is the closest we will ever get to it. One might define it as that which provides narrative explanations for the greatest conundrums of existence: why the sun and moon; why death; how does life begin; what is our place in the order of things? So what are we to read from such a narrative as this? The lack of a creator is marked and there is no attempt to identify an absolute origin. The universe begins with the spontaneous generation of solid out of liquid, and the language is full of vegetable metaphors. The impression of these opening sections is of untrammelled fecundity, of natural growth, of consumption and defecation, and finally of sexual reproduction; but rampant generation must be somehow controlled if the world is to be anything but chaos, hence the emergence of death: Izanami gives birth to something so dangerous that it kills her. Even this is not enough, because her corpse gives violent birth to a million maggots. This nightmare of uncontrolled fertility is only ended with the discovery that death must be a final parting and that the dead must be barred from re-entry into life. Within this discovery the proper cycle of birth and death is proclaimed. And is the circumambulation of the pillar a wedding rite? Naumann rejects this out of hand:

What we have here is the corrupted tale of a brother-sister pair who, either as the first pair at the beginning of the world or the only survivors from the flood, are driven to incest if life is to continue. Wandering the world – clearly discernible even in the first version with the island of Onogoro as the pillar at the centre of the earth – makes it clear to them that they are the only living beings in existence. Their meeting for a second time is a sign from heaven that their marriage is the will of heaven. Still, of course, it is necessary that the first product of such a liaison turns out badly. This motif is twisted in this slightly corrupted Japanese myth: the first failure is attributed to the fact that Izanami spoke first when they met, since it was not seemly for a woman to speak first. The deeper moral expressed here, namely the condemnation of incest, is suppressed. This was unavoidable in a land where marriage between close relatives (even half-siblings) was seen as entirely natural and was frequently practiced by the highest levels of the nobility from the monarchy down (Naumann 1988: 63–64).

Nothing like this kind of narrative has been found in sources from the continent, so it probably betrays the existence of an earlier stratum of myth, unconnected to either Chinese or Buddhism. Some have suggested that astrology might be the key to unlocking some of the more puzzling aspects. Note how, like all such texts, it manages successfully to hide from the reader the truth of its genesis: the narrative is often sustained not by logic but by a simple procession of names, names of deities that turn out to be descriptive labels of their roles and their natures. This act of naming is, of course, an intensely human activity, but what is being described is the emergence of the world prior to the emergence of man. It is important for its impact as a statement of fact and truth that this human agency be hidden from view. Here we find one of the greatest differences between *Kojiki* and *Nihon shoki*: the compilers of the latter were happy to foreground the act of composition and problematise the writing of history to a quite remarkable extent.

There is another kind of myth, but perhaps differing only in degree. It is marked by political intent; it explains things of a slightly lesser order than the first: why the status quo, for example? Not eternal truths as such, but political realities presented as eternal truths. And it is this kind of myth/history that emerges at the second stage. It is no accident that it is at this point that the main deities begin to assume quasi-human characteristics. Izanagi gives his daughter Amaterasu some jewels (the word is *tama*, which also signifies a 'psyche') and tells her she will rule Takamanohara. To Tsukiyomi he gives the night; and to Susano-o he gives the sea. The moon is never mentioned in the narrative again, but Susano-o certainly is; he becomes a central figure in what follows. Refusing to accept the fact of his mother's death, he contines to mourn her. 'He wept and howled until his beard eight hands long extended over his chest. His weeping was such that it caused the verdant mountains to wither and all the rivers and seas to dry up. At this, the cries of malevolent deities were everywhere abundant like summer flies; and all sorts of calamities arose in all things' (Philippi 1968: 72). This behaviour threatens to destroy the whole world. Banished by Izanagi, he goes to Takamanohara to take his leave of Amaterasu, but she mistrusts his intentions and thinks he has come to threaten her too. To prove his good intent, he challenges her to a duel that involves bearing children. She uses his sword and produces females; he uses her *tama* jewels and produces males. Claiming victory for no particular reason, he breaks into an orgy of destruction, ruining the paddy fields, and defecating in the sacred hall where the Harvest Festival was held. These wilful acts of pollution are followed by further violence culminating in a scene where he throws the hide of a piebald colt that has been flayed backwards into the sacred weaving hall. This leads to the death of one of the women weaving there (although the *Nihon shoki* version has his sister being injured in this act of desecration). Terrified, Amaterasu hides herself in a cave, plunging the universe into darkness. The other deities perform an elaborate ritual involving a mirror, *magatama* jewels, scapulamancy, and a lewd dance, eventually luring her forth by feigning gaity and blocking her passage back into the cave. Susano-o is subjected to purification and sent away to Izumo, where he founds a dynasty of rulers.

Interpolated at this juncture is the Izumo myth cycle, which happens to contain the majority of the most memorable vignettes and folktales. As soon as we enter the cycle, for example, we find that Susano-o has become completely transformed. Although he eventually ends up in charge of the underworld, he is fêted as the bringer of agriculture and the founder of a dynasty that ruled over Izumo. He is credited with having created the first Japanese *waka* poem, with all that meant in terms of cultural prestige, and the story of him killing a snake and finding a sword in its tale has echoes of the discovery of metallurgy.[5] The accounts in *Nihon shoki* and the gazetteer *Izumo fudoki* 出雲風土記 of 733 take this aspect much further and make it clear that he was seen as being responsible for having brought this culture across the sea from the Korean peninsula (Grayson 2002: 465–87). The cycle continues with the grand exploits of Susano-o's descendant in the sixth generation, Ōkuninushi.

We return to Takamanohara in *Kojiki*, Chapter 32. Amaterasu decides that the sovereignty of Japan should lie with one of her offspring but it turns out that the land is now in uproar and quite ungovernable; a number of her sons fail to pacify the land and it is only after much diplomacy that Ōkuninushi and his sons are prevailed upon to surrender their land to the deities of heaven, in return for which a shrine is raised in their honour. This part of the narrative, known as the *kuniyuzuri* 國讓, was to become a central element in the continuing attempts to justify the sovereign's hegemonic rule over the whole land. Amaterasu's grandson Ninigi then descends from heaven to a mountaintop in Kyūshū to claim his inheritance. Some generations later his descendants move east and conquer the central region of Yamato, where they settle. Izumo then reappears and is eventually incorporated under Yamato sovereignty after its major deity, the Great Deity of Miwa 大神大神, receives a promise that he will be duly worshipped.

This is a good example of the complexities thrown up by these chronicles. At one level we are being told about certain mythic generalities: of the necessity of controlling violence, for example, which if left unchecked may lead to the destruction of all life; an explanation for the eclipse of the sun, and the necessity for ritual to maintain good order. We also have a second tale of procreation between siblings, although it cannot be said that incest is dealt with very satisfactorily. But at another level we slip over the border into history as myth with political intent, as the late seventh-century 'present' erupts into the narrative. It starts with the mention of the Harvest Festival and the sacred weaving hall (elements that come from the time of Tenmu) and continues with the early politics of Izumo and Yamato diplomacy. So the universal theme of violence is linked with utmost economy to the story of the founding of the major 'problem' power, Izumo, and its eventual subjugation by Yamato. The narrative explains why this subjugation was inevitable. It is generally recognised that the complexity of both *Kojiki* and *Nihon shoki* is not simply temporal but geographical and that we are being presented with an

---

[5] The sword is called Kusanagi 草薙劍, identified in a variant passage in *Nihon shoki* as part of the regalia (Aston 1972, vol. I: 76).

ill-fitting coalescence of three distinct myth cycles centred on Izumo, Yamato and Kyūshū. The attempt to please all parties (while asserting heavenly ordained power to rule over all) gives the text a fragmented feel; there is little point in looking for coherence.

It is hardly surprising that with such convoluted texts various different hermeneutic approaches can be taken. Ebersole, for instance, is interested in reading the political and social realities of the time of composition back into the mythical sections, identifying certain 'charter myths' that were used to justify seventh-century practice. Considerable work has been done on the practice of double burial in the time of Tenmu-Jitō, whereby the body of a ruler was first placed in a temporary mourning hut or compound (the *mogari no miya*) for a period that could last a number of years. Ritual accession of the next ruler could only happen after the body had been given final burial. This hiatus, which may have originated in the necessity of actually seeing the fully decomposed body before mourning could cease, became a dangerous space pregnant with possibilities for intrigue over the succession, especially as the former ruler's female companions were entrusted with most of the rituals during the period of mourning. Outlining his project, Ebersole ties this into the early myth of Izanami's death:

The mythic narratives of early Japan often mirror the historical reality of the court in the wake of the death of a sovereign or crown prince. The Izanagi-Izanami myth, for instance, will be found not only to present an ideal model of the imperial funeral practices, but also to portray the 'reality' of the politics of death in the court. Similarly, the narrative detail of Susano-o's excessive mourning for the deceased Izanami and his expressed desire to visit her tomb will be found to provide the mythic charter for various forms of symbolically charged political acts in the court during the period of temporary interment. I will argue that Susano-o provided a model for imperial princes desiring to claim the throne in the wake of the death of a sovereign, while the Amaterasu–Susano-o myth links the celebration of the *niiname-sai* with the full exercise of the power and prerogatives of the sovereign (Ebersole 1989: 79).

This is a seductive argument, especially when we know that as we proceed Susano-o will become the progenitor of a rival state, which will eventually be incorporated into greater Yamato. It is difficult to deny that these chronicles, whose genesis lay in political necessity, do not offer all they might to the historian of religion and that a coherent mythical message is difficult to extract. But are all the myths we find here necessarily inventions of sixth- and seventh-century ideologues? We must take care not to reverse the whole picture and end up by reducing all such narratives to the wily strategems of those who rule.

3 Buddhism and the early state

3.1 The emergence of a religious organisation

If the Jingikan was created to try and impose by fiat a hierarchical structure on what was in essence a collection of independent localised cults with little in common between them, the relationship between the emerging institutions of Buddhism and an increasingly powerful court was very different. The status of the Jingikan was theoretically equal to that of the Council of State and it was directly responsible to the sovereign at the apex as high priest, but it is noticeable that its chief officer was not of high status, its staff small, and its remit limited. Buddhism, in contrast, certainly by the time of the Yōrō Code in the early eighth century, was involved in the work of a number of ministries. The Ministry of Central Management (*Nakatsukasa shō* 中務省) contained the Bureaus of the Library (*Zusho ryō* 圖書寮), Textiles (*Nuidono ryō* 縫殿寮), and Art and Architecture (*Gakō ryō* 畫工寮), all of which had to deal with things Buddhist as a matter of course. Personnel was the responsibility of the Bureau for Aliens (*Genba ryō* 玄蕃寮) which was part of the Ministry of Administration (*Jibu shō* 治部省). This probably came about because all early Buddhists had in fact been foreigners.

It soon became clear to the court that Buddhism was much more than just a cult of a new, powerful deity; unless it was kept under control, it might easily develop into an autonomous institution of considerable power. This was particularly so when the underlying Buddhist message became more understood: somewhere at the heart of its doctrines lay the unusually dangerous concept of liberation and a radical questioning of the status of worldly power and prestige. In this sense, it presented a far greater problem than native cults with local loyalties, carrying as it did within itself an agenda that always had the potential to subvert. There was nothing new in this, of course: Buddhism in China always had a difficult relationship with the state. It was during this period (672–724) that the Japanese rules of engagement were first established in the shape of the *Regulations for members of the saṅgha* (*sōniryō* 僧尼令). They are of quite a different order to the *Jingiryō*, being specific and restrictive. It is worth giving them in full, for they show the degree to which the court treated these members as government employees on government salaries. As is so often the case, however, we shall find that practice differed from theory.

1   Members of the saṅgha who falsely predict good fortune or disasters by heavenly omens, who speak against the state and mislead the people, who study military treatises, who commit murder, rape, or robbery, and who feign enlightenment, will be punished by the secular authorities in accordance with civil law.

2   All members of the saṅgha who practise divination and fortune-telling, or who pretend to cure illnesses by exorcism or magic, shall be returned to lay life. However, it is allowed to aid the sick through the recitation of mantras as recognized by Buddhist law.

3   If a member of the saṅgha wishes to return to lay life, the Three Deans (*sangō*) of his temple shall first record the details of his life before he became a member. These should then be notified to the Saṅgha Office if he resides in the capital, or to the provincial governor if he lives in the provinces. This shall then be reported to the Ministry, which shall strike his name [from the register]. Should the Three Deans or his master conceal this matter for more that thirty days, they shall receive fifty days' hard labour; if for sixty days or more, then 100 days' hard labour.

4   Members of the saṅgha who try to bribe officials with anything pertaining to the Three Jewels, or who gather in a group and sow disorder, or who slander the saṅgha authorities or denigrate their elders and betters, shall receive 100 days' hard labour. However, this shall not apply to meetings where matters are properly and sensibly discussed.

5   Members of the saṅgha who live outside temples, who build their own separate retreats, who gather people together to teach them; members who falsely expound good and evil, and who assault their superiors shall all be returned to lay life. Should provincial or district officials know of these crimes yet fail to report them, they too shall be punished according to law. If there is anyone who desires to beg, the Three Deans shall sign [the petition] and submit it to the district and provincial authorities. Only after they are satisfied that true ascetic practice is intended shall it be approved. In the capital, the Bureau of Aliens is to be notified. Begging shall be done before noon with a bowl, and nothing other than food is to be requested.

6   Men are allowed as servants trustworthy boys from among close relatives in their home villages, but when these boys reach the age of seventeen they must be returned to their homes. Women may also take female servants who are willing to serve them.

7   Members of the saṅgha who drink alcohol, eat meat, or use any of the five herbs will be given thirty days hard labour; although if any of these herbs is required as medicine, the Three Deans may authorize its use for a specified number of days. Men who get drunk and start brawling shall be returned to lay life.

8   Members of the saṅgha who, when faced with a problem, do not go through the proper official channels but send petitions directly to the government and pester

the authorities unnecessarily shall receive fifty days' hard labour. And if they repeat the crime, they shall receive 100 days. However, if submission is made that a decision of the officials or the Saṅgha Office was patently unfair or was unreasonably delayed, then this rule shall not apply.

9 If members of the saṅgha perform music or play games that involve gambling, they will be given 100 days' hard labour. Playing *go* and the *biwa*, however, is permitted.

10 Members of the saṅgha are permitted to wear robes of yellowish-brown, purple, blue, black, yellow, or purple-brown. If they wear colours other than these or if they wear robes of figured silk and other fine brocades, they will receive ten days' hard labour for each offence. If they wear lay clothes they shall receive 100 days.

11 If a woman stays in a man's cell or a man stays in a woman's cell for one night or more, the guilty party shall be given ten days' hard labour. The punishment for five nights or more is thirty days, and for ten days or more 100 days. Should the Three Deans knowingly permit this crime, they shall receive the same punishment.

12 Men are not usually allowed to enter a woman's cell, nor are women to enter a man's quarters, except when being interviewed by one's superior, when visiting the sick or dying, or for the purpose of religious ceremony, observance or instruction.

13 When members of the saṅgha desire to practise meditation and to pacify their minds in solitude, to shun this world and fast in the mountains, the Three Deans should sign their request. In the capital, the Saṅgha Office should contact the Bureau; in the provinces, the Three Deans should approach the relevant officials. Once the request is verified and recorded, it should go to the Council for decision. The officials in the relevant province should always know the exact location of the member's retreat, and moving to another location shall not be permitted.

14 When making an appointment to the Saṅgha Office it is essential to choose men of virtuous conduct, who have good influence over their followers, who enjoy the respect of both members and the laity, and who are good administrators. The members of the saṅgha shall make nominations and send them to the Council. Should any group of evil-doers conspire to nominate an unworthy candidate, they shall receive 100 days' hard labour. Once appointed, a member cannot be removed, unless he commits a crime or cannot perform his duties by reason of old age or sickness. He should then be replaced by higher authority.

15 Members of the saṅgha who receive a punishment of hard labour should do some meritorious task, such as keeping the Buddha Hall in order or cleaning and sweeping the temple grounds. A full day's work should be done per day of punishment. If the Three Deans are weak and fail to assign punishment, they shall be required to serve the same number of days of punishment. If there is good reason for leniency, the reasons should be investigated, the truth established, and decision made upon appeal. But if such leniency is granted for some ulterior motive and for no good reason, then the person granting such allowance shall be given the same punishment as the appellant.

16 Members of the saṅgha who by fraudulent means transfer their names to another shall be returned to lay life and punished according to civil law. The other party

shall also receive the same punishment.

17 A member of the saṅgha who appeals on some private matter and brings this appeal to the Council should do so in a temporary lay capacity. But officials above the grade of Recorder and the Three Deans who appear before the Council on matters that concern the whole community, or on other matters of merit, should arrange special audience.

18 Members of the saṅgha shall not be able to accumulate private land holdings or other forms of wealth, nor may they engage in commerce or usury.

19 When travelling, members of the saṅgha who meet persons of third rank or above should turn away. If they meet those of fifth rank or above, they should rein in their mounts, exchange salutations, and let the other pass. If they are on foot, they should turn away.

20 Details of members of the saṅgha who have died shall be reported monthly by the Three Deans to the provincial governor, and yearly by the governor to the Council via an official messenger. In the capital, the Saṅgha Office shall report deaths seasonally to the Bureau of Aliens and yearly to the Council.

21 When a member of the saṅgha commits a crime that is punishable according to civil law by one year's hard labour or more then he should be returned to lay life [and then punished], although the penalty may be reduced by one year in return for giving up his licence. If there is a further crime this should be dealt with according to civil law. If the crime deserves a punishment of 100 strokes of the stick or less, then he should be given ten days' hard labour in lieu of ten strokes. If the crime does not deserve laicisation, or if such a step is deserved but never carried out, then the member should be kept under surveillance. If the crime merits more than just hard labour but not laicisation, then the Three Deans shall decide the case according to Buddhist law and punish accordingly. Members of the saṅgha returned to lay life or otherwise punished shall not be able to lay complaint against the Three Deans or their former community, although this restriction shall not apply in case of serious matters such as rebellion or inciting the people by oracles or magic.

22 A person who sets up as a member of the saṅgha without official permission and a person who becomes a member of the saṅgha under false pretences, and those who wear Buddhist garb despite having been laicised, shall be judged and punished according to civil law. Any master, dean, or fellow member who is privy to this knowledge shall be returned to lay life. And even if that person is not a fellow member, if he condones such behaviour and harbours him for one night or more, he will receive 100 days' hard labour. And for any member who knowingly harbours a vagrant or a fugitive for one night or more, the punishment will again be 100 days' hard labour. If the crime is a grave one, then punishment shall be by civil law.

23 Any member of the saṅgha who gives a text or an image to a layman, or who teaches beyond the monastery gates, shall receive 100 days' hard labour. And the lay person shall be judged by civil law.

24 Any houseman or slave who, having become a member, is either returned to lay life for a crime or decides to return for his own reasons shall be returned to his

original master and his original status. Unlicensed members will not be permitted even though they have studied the sūtras.

25 The third time a member of the saṅgha commits a crime deserving 100 days' hard labour, he or she will be banished to a temple in the outer provinces and will not be allowed to enter the capital.

26 At religious ceremonies members of the saṅgha should not be offered slaves, cattle, horses and military weapons as alms, and if these are offered they are to be rejected.

27 Members of the saṅgha are not to immolate themselves or take their own life. Those who disobey shall be punished according to civil law (Inoue et al. 1976: 216–23).[1]

It is a matter of considerable debate as to whether these laws discriminated against members of the saṅgha or whether they in fact favoured them, for it can be argued that by giving them a code of their own, quite separate from the civil code, the state was in fact offering them privileged status. Monks and nuns were in any case meant to live under strict regulations, and many of these rules are little more than definitions of good practice copied from the rules of monastic behaviour known as the *vinaya*. The first two prohibitions, for example, deal with the perennial problem of what was and what was not false teaching and false practice, obviously very much a concern within the saṅgha. There can be no doubt, however, that as a direct consequence of the initial introduction of Buddhism into Japan by the elite, members were seen first and foremost as servants of the state, and the principle that the state should control them, correlate their ranks with court ranks, and generally assert the right to appoint to high office, became established practice.

The main organ of control was the Saṅgha Office (*sōgō* 僧綱), a group of senior monks whose duty it was to ensure that the regulations were enforced. The term itself is first used in the Taihō Code of 701. Provision was made for the members of this office to be elected from within the community of monks, but in actual practice most were simply appointed by royal fiat. In addition, by the turn of the century each institution had its own governors, who were known as the Three Deans (*sangō* 三綱), an Elder (*jōza* 上座), a Master (*jishu* 寺主) and a Supervisor (*tsuina* 都維那). The officially pre-scribed way of becoming a male member of the saṅgha was to start at a young age. A boy could renounce lay life and enter religion to serve in a temple. Later, in his teens, he might undergo initiation (*tokudo* 得度), to become a novice (*shami* 沙彌, from Sk. *śrāmaṇa*), although permission for this had to be obtained. At this point a permit was issued and the novice was

---

[1]   See also the translations in Sansom 1934: 127–34 and Piggott 1987: 267–73.

expected to observe the ten basic precepts. After some years of discipline, the novice could apply for full ordination and receive all 250 precepts, an act known as *jukai* 受戒. It should be stressed, however, that this was prescriptive and not descriptive of actual practice. Nor did it necessarily pertain to the increasing number of non-official institutions that could accept members in any number of ways.

The situation as far as women is concerned is not so clear, particularly before the setting up of state-sponsored nunneries in 741 under Shōmu Tennō, whom we shall discuss in due course. Some of the earliest 'servants of the Buddha' were women and it will be recalled that the census taken in 624 had revealed 816 men and 569 women. Women who had served at court tended to enter nunneries on retirement and there were a number of such institutions built, usually connected to a temple. At first sight, this early ratio would seem to be in sharp contrast to the situation in the Heian period when nunneries all but died out, but this is misleading since the category of 'nun' was a flexible one (see §15.1).

Details of the lives and work of the officially recognised members of the saṅgha, details that might bring them alive for us, are hard to come by for this early period. Appointments to the chief state offices are usually recorded in *Nihon shoki* and *Shoku Nihongi* and one also comes across occasional mention of one or two members being returned to lay life because their expertise was needed by the court. In general, however, it is rare to find any extended descriptions. One unusual exception is the following death notice for the venerable Dōshō 道昭 for 700.3.10.

The venerable Dōshō died. The Sovereign was greatly distressed and sent messengers to convey his condolences. Dōshō was from Tajihi in Kōchi. His family name was Fune no Muraji; his father was Esaka of twelfth rank. He maintained the precepts to the full and set great store by the virtue of endurance. Once, a student decided to put him to the test and secretly made a hole in his chamber pot so that when he used it, it leaked out and wet the bedding. But Dōshō just smiled. 'Naughty boy. Messing up my bed': that was all he said. Initially, in the 4th year of Hakuchi (653) during the reign of Kōtoku Tennō, he went to China as part of an embassy. There he happened to meet Xuanzang, who became his mentor. Xuanzang loved him dearly and had him stay in his quarters. 'In the past', he said, 'when I travelled to the Western Regions, I was starving on the road and could find no village where I might beg for food. Suddenly a monk appeared. He had in his hand a pear, which he gave me to eat. After I had eaten it, my strength returned day by day. You are another such with a pear in his hand.' And he added, 'The sūtras and treatises are deep and mysterious; they are unfathomable. Better to learn how to meditate and pass on that knowledge to the East.'

Dōshō received instruction and began to learn to meditate. He gradually became adept at achieving enlightenment and then he returned to Japan with another embassy.

At their parting Xuanzang brought him all the relics and sūtras and treatises in his possession and offered them to Dōshō saying, 'You will be able to broaden the path. Now use these works to pass on the teachings to others.' And he gave him a bowl and said, 'This bowl I brought back with me from the West. When you use it to boil up medicines, it always works miracles.' Dōshō thanked him and they parted in tears.

When they reached Dengzhou many of the party fell ill. Dōshō brought out the bowl, heated up water, cooked gruel, and gave it to all who were suffering. They were cured that very day. So they loosened the ropes and left with a fair wind. On reaching open sea, however, the ship became becalmed and did not move for seven days and seven nights. Everyone was frightened and said, 'If the wind had been favourable we would already be home, but the ship does not dare move forward; there must be some reason.' Then a diviner spoke up and said, 'The Dragon King wants the bowl.' Dōshō, hearing this, replied, 'But this bowl was a gift from the Tripiṭaka [i.e. Xuanzang]. Why does the Dragon King desire it?' But everyone else argued that unless they gave up the bowl, they would all become food for the fishes. And so he took the bowl and cast it into the sea. Immediately the ship began to move forward and they returned safely to Japan.

Dōshō built a separate meditation hall in the south-east corner of Gangōji and lived there. And all the monks in Japan who were intent on practising came and studied meditation under him. Later, he travelled the land, digging wells by the roadsides and building ferries and bridges at every river crossing. The Uji bridge in Yamashiro is his work. He travelled thus for ten years or more. Then came a decree and he returned to live in the meditation hall, meditating as before. Sometimes he would rise only once in three days; sometimes only once in seven days. Then one day an attractive scent came from his cell. His students were frightened and went to see what had happened. He was sitting there on a rope mat, not breathing. At the time he was 72 years of age. His students did as he had requested and cremated him at Awahara. This was the beginning of cremation in Japan. It is said that after the cremation his relatives and his students started arguing over who was to have the bones, when suddenly a whirlwind sprang up and blew away his bones and ashes no one knew where. And people marvelled.

Later still, when the capital was moved to Nara, his younger brothers and his students petitioned to have the meditation hall rebuilt in the new capital. This is the one now in Ukyō in Nara. It contains many sūtras and treatises. The writing is clear and there are no mistakes. They are all texts that Dōshō brought back with him (Aoki et al. 1989–98, vol. I: 23–27).[2]

Although the ideal was that the special status afforded members of the saṅgha was a direct result of strenuous ascetic practice and learning, in reality they were treated as little more than state employees doing a job of work. There were, of course, many men and women who did not fit into this mould, but these were at best tolerated by the court, regarded with suspicion, and

---

[2] It is doubtful whether this was the first cremation in Japan, although it certainly became accepted practice at about this time. Jitō was the first sovereign to be cremated, on 703.12.17.

treated as a social problem. Life must have been difficult for the more independent-minded man or woman who took self-cultivation seriously and who wished to live out the Mahāyāna bodhisattva ideal of a life spent in the service of others. A man like Gyōki 行基 (668–749), for example, perhaps the best known of these independent spirits, who simply refused to live in a community and preferred to spread the Buddhist message on foot as medicine man, ascetic and popular preacher, was seen more as a threat to public order than as an ideal to be followed (Piggott 1997: 223). He gathered around himself a large number of female followers, which must have also been frowned upon. Self-initiation (*shido* 私度) was naturally discouraged, but it too proved difficult to control and a few charismatics did manage to live outside the system and still receive recognition.

One might have supposed that it would have been in the interests of good government to have severely restricted entry into the profession via strict control over ordination. Since being a member brought with it freedom from taxes and other advantages, there was always a danger that large numbers of men and women might wish to take up the option. Ordination was certainly a matter of great concern for state and saṅgha, but sometimes things worked in the opposite direction. At times of crisis, when a ruler fell grievously ill for example, immediate recourse was had to mass initiation (if not full ordination), which was clearly seen as a form of symbolic human sacrifice: men and women were thus dragooned into religious service. It is unclear whether this was an actual expansion in numbers or merely an occasion to give self-appointed, unofficial members official recognition, but it was a natural response for a court that thought in terms of presenting 'offerings' to placate a wrathful deity. The following entries from *Nihon shoki* are instructive in this regard, since they show both profligacy and restraint in equal measure:

680.11.12. The first Consort fell ill. Having made a vow on her behalf, [the Sovereign] began the building of the Yakushiji and had 100 men renounce lay life. As a result, she regained her health.

680.11.26. The Heavenly Sovereign fell ill, so 100 men were ordered to renounce lay life. After some time, he recovered.

685.9.24. The Heavenly Sovereign fell ill and so for three days sūtras were read at Daikan Daiji, Kawaradera and Asukadera. Accordingly rice was donated to the three temples, the amounts varying.

685.10. This month there were readings of the *Diamond sūtra* in the Palace.

686.5.24. The Heavenly Sovereign had a fever, so there were readings of the *Baiṣajyagururājasūtra* at Kawaradera.

686.6.16. Prince Ise and number of officials were sent to Asukadera to command the priests: 'Of late Our body has been ill at ease. We hope that some relief may be obtained through the awesome power of the Three Jewels. Let the Prefect, Administrator, and Preceptor offer up prayers.'

686.8.1. On behalf of the Sovereign eighty men were made to renounce lay life.

686.8.2. 100 men and women were made to renounce lay life. 100 images were installed in the Palace and the 200 fascicles of the *Kanzeon kyō* read out.

694.8.17. 104 men were made to renounce lay life for the sake of Princess Asuka.

696.12.1. There was an order that ten men per year should become priests on the last day of the twelfth month to perform readings of the *Sūtra of golden radiant wisdom*. [This entry is usually thought to mark the beginnings of the *nenbun dosha* 年分度者 or 'yearly ordinand' system, which came into effective operation at a much later date.]

Scattered here and there in the chronicles are signs of a constant concern that the distinction between an officially sanctioned member of the saṅgha and a self-appointed healer of body and mind was not clear enough. In 717, for example, we find the following entry:

Item: We establish offices and entrust matters to the able so that they can teach and lead the people. We create laws and set up regulations so as to prohibit dishonest practices. Recently there are those who have ignored the regulations, who have done as they please, cut their hair and beards, and simply donned the clothing of a member of the saṅgha. They look like proper members but they harbour evil intent. This gives rise to deception and mischief.

Item: Members of the saṅgha should live quietly in temples, study the teachings and pass on their learning. The regulations state that if a man wishes to beg, the Three Deans must sign the petition. Begging is only allowed before noon; and it is not permitted to ask for anything other than food. Now there is a man called Gyōki, whose followers gather together on the streets, preach wildly of what is good and evil, who organize bands, and burn their fingers and elbows, who teach beyond the temple gates, who beg for things other than food, who fake enlightenment and who mislead the people. Morals are in chaos and the four classes neglect their work. They both mistake the Buddha's teachings and break the laws.

Item: Members of the saṅgha are permitted according to the Dharma to save people by sacred spells and to cure illness with medicines. But now we hear they go into people's homes, falsely call up dark magic, use shamanistic arts, wrongly divine good and bad fortune, strike fear into the hearts of young and old alike, and do as they wish. There is no distinction between sacred and profane and this gives rise to disaffection. Henceforth, if anyone is ill and desires to be cured, he should request the services of a man of purity, inform the saṅgha authorities, obtain the signature of the Three Deans, and ask for his services for a fixed period. This period is not to be exceeded. It is because the authorities have been lax that things have reached such a pass. Henceforth this must cease. Post this at all towns and villages and make sure that the law is upheld (Aoki et al. 1989–98, vol. II: 27–29).

In the tenth month of the next year, 718, the Daijōkan sent an order to the Saṅgha Office, which read:

All those whose intelligence is outstanding, who are promoted by their peers and who are masters of the Dharma should manifest the highest merit. And those who never tire of learning and who are always at their master's heels, those who are worthy of having students themselves, should all have their names and their experience recorded and passed on to the authorities. The learning of the five traditions 五宗 and the teachings of the three baskets are full of debates and disputation. Only a man who is fully conversant with the principles of his tradition should be made a master. Every such person in each tradition should be recorded. Next come meritorious roots, character, and whether or not they take their practice seriously. They should be encouraged to study what fits their character. Priests are not to indulge themselves in pleasurable pursuits. They should lecture on the principles of their tradition, study the teachings of other traditions, chant sūtras and practise meditation. Each one is to specialize in a subject. Intelligence and merit should be recognized and their practice and abilities recorded. Soapstone and jade, each has its own lustre. The music of Yu and Zheng do not share the same tunes. The waves of pure water created by a teacher of great merit purify the heart of the Dharma; the brightness of the lamp of a teacher of great intelligence reaches into the court. And moreover, the Buddha himself warned against members of the saṅgha who slander the Dharma and destroy the teachings. For a man to mistake the path and denigrate the laws of the Sovereign is expressly forbidden in the regulations. The Saṅgha Office should be vigilant and make correct decisions. Those men who do not live in temples, who turn away from right practice, who follow their own desires and enter the mountains, building huts or caves, sully the purity of mountains and rivers and spoil the natural beauty of the mists. In the sūtras, it is said: 'Those who beg every day and clog the markets and the towns may feel that they are pursuing enlightenment, but in fact they take it to excess.' Such types are to be discouraged (Aoki et al. 1989–98, vol. II: 47–49).

Two years later this was followed by a rather unusual incident when 320 men were confirmed as having entered religion, only for the majority to be pronounced fakes five months later; all but 15 had their permission withdrawn. The problem of legitimacy was to remain central to state–saṅgha relations for the whole of Japanese history.

And what of the temples themselves? Buddhism had begun in Japan as an elite but essentially private affair, and it took a little while before the ruling family realised that it was a resource that had to be harnessed more closely. This was done not by trying to control the spread of temples built by noble families, but rather by joining in and creating a number of state temples founded and sponsored directly by the sovereign. This did, of course, place a considerable burden on state coffers; so much so, in fact, that in 680 we already find a decree to the effect that:

Henceforth all temples, with the exception of two or three state Great Temples, will cease to be administered through the state office, although those temples that hold sustenance-fiefs will be allowed to retain them for a period of thirty years, but no longer. Asukadera should not really be administered by the state, but it was originally one of the Great Temples and has always been under state administration. It has also been of great service in the past. For these reasons, it should remain under state control (Sakamoto et al. 1967, vol. II: 440; Aston 1972, vol. II: 346).

But the evidence is contradictory. The Heian period history *Fusō ryakki* 扶桑 略記 states that during Jitō's reign some 545 temples were receiving some form of royal patronage, but in 720 there were only four officially designated state temples, known as *daiji* 大寺, where most rituals and readings for protection of the state took place – Daikan daiji 大官大寺 (home of the Saṅgha Office), Gufukuji 弘福寺 (formerly Kawaradera), Yakushiji 薬師寺 and Gangōji 元興寺 (Piggott 1997: 154).

Great effort and much funding was also put into the collection and copying of sūtras. In 673.3 scribes were put to work at Kawaradera to start a process of copying texts, and in 675.10 messengers were sent in all directions to look for material. It may have been to celebrate the completion of this effort that a large vegetarian feast was held at Asukadera in 677.8, on which occasion 'princes of the blood, other princes, and ministers were each ordered to provide one person to renounce the world, without distinction of age or sex' (Sakamoto et al. 1967, vol. II: 428; Aston 1972, vol. II: 337).

3.2   Sūtras to protect the state

One of the most important tasks that priests in the officially state-sponsored temples had to perform was the reading of certain sūtras that were known to have state-protecting powers, a ritual learned from China and Korea. Sūtras at this early stage in Japan had two main uses. Reading and studying them naturally formed a major part of the education of a monk or priest, although it is impossible to gauge how many could read enough classical Chinese to really understand them and how many simply learned the contents and teachings by word of mouth. Their main mode, however, was as ritual objects to be copied, revered and recited. Recitation in the correct ritual circumstances would ensure that the promises contained in the sūtra would come to pass. It is worth remembering that the Japanese never felt the need to translate sūtras from the Chinese; the fact that they remained in a foreign language (albeit available to an increasing number of Japanese scholars) helped the ritual process, keeping them and their contents at one remove and so enhancing their magic potential. The following entries in *Nihon shoki* are typical:

676.11.20. Messengers were sent out to all parts of the country to set up readings of the *Sūtra of golden radiant wisdom* and *Sūtra for humane kings*.

685.3.27. There was an order: 'In all provinces and in each house 諸家 a "dwelling for the Buddha" 佛舍 is to be built to accommodate an image of the Buddha and sūtras. This is for worship and offerings.' [This entry is problematic. The term 佛舍 may refer to fully fledged temples, or it may simply refer to rooms in the mansions of local magnates.]

692. (intercalary) 5.3. An order went out that the *Sūtra of golden radiant wisdom* be read in the capital and the four home provinces [to stop floods].

693.10.23. From this day the *Sūtra for humane kings* was read in all provinces. The reading lasted for four days.

694.5.11. One hundred copies of the *Sūtra of golden radiant wisdom* were distributed to the provinces to be read without fail in the moon's first quarter of the first month every year. The cost was to be borne by each provincial office.

So what was it about these sūtras that gave them such power, beyond being recognised as the word of the Buddha? It is perhaps worth investigating their contents. The sūtra most often used in this context was the *Sūtra of golden radiant wisdom* (Jp. *Konkōmyō kyō* 金光明經).[3] It is not known when it was originally composed, but it was first translated into Chinese by Dharmakṣema (385–433) sometime after his arrival in China in 414. The earliest surviving Sanskrit manuscript has been dated to the middle of the fifth century and so postdates the first Chinese version. There are also versions in a number of Central Asian languages and it was considered particularly important in the city state of Khotan on the southern fringes of the Taklamakan Desert in what is now Chinese Turkestan. The sixth-century translators Paramārtha and Jñānagupta did further work on the first version, but the results are not extant. Yijing's 義淨 (635–713) translation, with the slightly different title *Konkō-myō saishōō-kyō* 金光明最勝王經,[4] which was to become standard, was produced sometime in the early 700s and brought to Japan by Dōji 道慈 in 718, so the only version available in Japan in this early period was the first one. It opens with a passage of self-praise and, as with so many Mahāyāna sūtras, proceeds to develop not a narrative but rather a reiteration of the importance of constant performance and defence of itself, offering a litany of its own value to all who are in distress.

[This king of sūtras] has been blessed by the Buddhas in the four directions, by Akṣobhyarāja in the east, in the south by Ratnaketu, in the west by Amitābha, in the north by Dundubhisvara. I will proclaim this blessing, this excellent, auspicious confession, whose aim is the ruin of all evils, producing the destruction of all evils,

---

[3]   Sk. *Suvarṇabhāsottamasūtra*; Ch. *Jingguangming jing*, *T.* 663.

[4]   Sk. *Suvarṇaprabhāsottamasūtra*; Ch. *Jingguangming zuishengwang jing*, *T.* 665.

conferring every blessing, ruining every misfortune, the basis of omniscience, thoroughly adorned with every splendour. For those beings whose senses are defective, whose life is expended or failing, beset by misfortune, their faces averted from the gods, hated by dear, beloved people, oppressed in such places as households, or at variance with one another, tormented by the destruction of their property, both in grief and trouble, and in poverty, likewise in the plight of fear, in the affliction of planet or asterism, in the violent grip of demons, one who sees an evil dream full of grief and trouble should listen to this excellent sūtra, when he has bathed well and is pure. For those who hear this sūtra, the profound Buddha-region, with pure minds and good intentions, adorned with clean garments, and for all beings, such most severe misfortunes are forever extinguished by the splendour of this sūtra (Emmerick 1970: 1–2).

In the second chapter the scene is set with a bodhisattva called Ruciraketu asking himself why the Buddha's last life was so short. He is then visited by the whole assembly of gods, bodhisattvas and buddhas, his house and then the whole city being transformed into a pure Buddha field. The message he receives is that the life of the Tathāgatha is actually without limit, eternal. The whole assembly proclaims verses to this effect. Then a brahmin asks for a relic of the Lord. This is refused with the explanation that there can be no relics since the Buddha's life is eternal and infinite. The scene ends and the assembly disappears.

We then enter the heart of the sūtra. Ruciraketu sleeps and dreams he hears the words of a confession. He then goes to the Buddha and recites these words at length. They form a kind of prayer that all men might be saved through the power of a bodhisattva's vow, a vow that takes the form of a confession of all past evils. This confession is what releases the bodhisattva's power to help all living beings, it is the sūtra: 'I will expound this confession, the splendid, excellent Suvarṇabhāsa, by which is quickly obtained the destruction of acts and hindrances' (Emmerick 1970: 11). The implication is that whoever worships and praises the Buddhas by means of this kind of confession will succeed in achieving perfect enlightenment.

We then have a prayer, a short explanation of the concept of emptiness, or *śunyatā*, and a long succession of proclamations by various kings and gods to the effect that they will protect all those who pay homage to the sūtra. Of particular importance is the statement by the four great kings, Vaiśravaṇa, Dhṛtarāṣṭra, Virūḍhaka and Virūpākṣa in Chapter 6, where they pledge to protect all those states where this sūtra is correctly honoured. These were the four kings in whose honour Prince Shōtoku had created one of the first Japanese temples in the 590s at Naniwa, Shiten'ōji 四天王寺. The rest of the sūtra repeats its own excellence; and in Chapter 12 we read:

When a king overlooks an evil deed in his region and does not inflict appropriate punishment on the evil person, in the neglect of evil deeds lawlessness grows greatly, wicked acts and quarrels arise in great number in the realm. The chief gods are wrathful in the dwellings of the Thirty-three when a king overlooks an evil deed in his region. His region is smitten with dreadful, most terrible acts of wickedness and his realm is destroyed on the arrival of a foreign army (Emmerick 1970: 59).

The passage then goes on to warn, somewhat in the manner of Mencius, that if a king stops acting like a king, he forfeits the right be called a king and may be overthrown. Chapter 14 'On the refuge of the yakṣas' explains how those who hear this sūtra will be saved from all sorts of afflictions, and that wherever it is heard and worshipped will come under the protection of all the gods of heaven. This sūtra, then, is not a narrative or a theoretical discourse, but rather an extended proclamation of its own efficacy.

The *Sūtra for humane kings* (Jp. *Ninnō kyō* 仁王經)[5] does not exist in Sanskrit and was probably created in China in the late fifth century. There are two versions: a 'translation' attributed to Kumārajīva (*T.* 245) and a later 'revision' by the Tang tantric master Amoghavajra (*T.* 246), produced in 765–66. The first version was used in public ritual during the Sui dynasty and again in the early Tang. The first mention of its formal use in a ceremony in Japan is in the fifth month of 660 under Saimei Tennō 齊明天皇, and from then on one finds it often mentioned in the context of rituals in times of crisis. Ritual 'congregations' known as Ninnō-e 仁王會, presumably run according to the instructions given in the eighth chapter of the sūtra itself, were called for to guard against pestilence or flood. This role in state ritual stemmed directly from the text itself.

The *Sūtra for humane kings* is dedicated to the idea that the path by which the bodhisattva accomplishes enlightenment is equivalent to the path by which the king of a state achieves power, a link that was always implicit in Mahāyāna Buddhism although not always expressed so boldly. The Buddha first of all presents the bodhisattva path and then moves on to explain how a king can protect his people and his state in degenerate times. Despite the fact that this sūtra contained non-standard terminology for the stages of the path, introduced the concept of three rather than two truths (something that was borrowed and refined by the founder of Tiantai Buddhism, Zhiyi), and had an idiosyncratic dating for the onset of the Latter Days of the Dharma, in the end it was the message of the second part that led to its popularity as a staple of state ritual. The answer to the question of how the king should best protect

[5] Ch. *Renwang jing*. For a full study see Orzech 1998.

his state lay, as one might expect, with the scripture itself: the text itself, properly treated and honoured, would provide magical protection for rulers and their states in the face of all manner of calamities. Produced at a time of crisis for Buddhism in China (calamity, for example, is defined as an increase in unfilial behaviour and irreverence shown to teachers and elders), the sūtra creates a bond between king and saṅgha. By claiming to be the key to survival, it in turn ensures its own survival. Survival of the state in a time that is clearly identified as being in the 'Latter Days of the Buddhist Dharma' depended on the willingness of the ruler to support Buddhism, the most obvious sign of which would be the honouring of this particular text.

3.3   The Medicine King and the Pensive Prince

The average person at court did not, of course, read or study sūtras and left recitation to the professionals. The spiritual potential of Buddhism for most people lay in the visual impact made by images, and above all by the remarkable sculpture that was produced during this period. It was to these images that offerings were made and it was in front of them that one was made to feel the magical properties that might bring health and fortune. A sense of the sheer variety can be gained by looking at just two, very different examples. Both of them also illustrate how closely the iconography ties Japan in with the rest of Asia, in particular Central Asia, at this early stage.

It is a mark of the degree to which buddhas themselves were seen as cult images, who would repay attention offered in the form of ritual by bringing wordly benefits of good health and prosperity, that one of the earliest and oft-carved images was that of Yakushi 薬師 (Sk. Bhaiṣajyagururāja), the Medicine King. This was a fully fledged Buddha whose origins lay more in Central Asia than in India. He can be found standing but is more usually sitting cross-legged in the lotus position (*padmāsana*) with the soles of his feet facing upwards, his right hand raised in the *abhayamudrā* sign of fearlessness, and his left hand lying open above the knee with fingers pointing towards the supplicant. In the palm of this hand is a small round medicine jar, although this has often been lost.

The most spectacular example of a Yakushi image can still be found in the temple of the same name, Yakushiji 薬師寺 [plate 8]. In 680 Tenmu's consort contracted an eye ailment and the sovereign ordered the construction of a temple. What then happened is unclear, because it is some time before we find any further mention of a Yakushiji in the records; it is not referred to

Plate 8   Bhaiṣajyagururāja, the central image from Yakushiji. Early eighth century.

when Tenmu himself fell ill six years later, for example. The next reference comes in 688, when Jitō held a ceremony there. By the end of the century, however, Yakushiji had become one of the big three temples in Fujiwara-kyō, ranking in importance with the officially supported Daianji and Asukadera. This site is now known as that of the 'former', or 'Hon-Yakushiji', because in about 718 the temple was moved to its present site in the western sector of Heijō-kyō (Nara).

The Hon-Yakushiji was the first temple in Japan to have two pagodas, a feature that was carried on to the new site. Both were the equivalent of five storeys high, in this case with three main storeys separated from each other by two roofed 'porches'. Running through the centre was a core pole supporting the usual finial with nine rings topped by an intricately carved and justly famous bronze 'water-flame' (*suien* 水煙). Research into the plans of temple compounds during this early period shows a startling lack of conformity, but the outlines of a progression are clear to see. All temples had a north–south orientation. In early examples the pagoda was at the very centre surrounded by halls; then it was placed immediately inside the gate with the halls aligned behind it on a north–south axis; then the decision was made to strike a balance between pagoda and main hall, aligning them on an east–west axis, sometimes with the pagoda to the east, sometimes to west. Eventually, as in the case of the Yakushiji, we have two pagodas. The final stage was to move the pagodas entirely outside the compound, as if they were simply meant to guard the southern approaches. This gradual displacement is highly instructive, because it represents a relegation to the margins of what one would normally expect to be the central element of a temple – the pagoda qua stūpa, the repository for a relic of the historical Buddha Śākyamuni. At the Yakushiji, the Main Hall with its image of Yakushi takes centre stage and the pagodas are pulled away to the two southern corners.

There is much scholarly discussion as to how much was transported and how much built anew on this occasion, and the argument chiefly revolves around the Yakushi triad in the Main Hall. Given the quality of the casting, it is probably early eighth century. The halo behind the head of the central figure is of much later provenance, possibly seventeenth century. Yakushi sits on a rectangular pedestal over which flows a heavy cloth that falls in rich folds. Behind the cloth the pedestal [plate 9] is decorated with a series of patterns among which is a grape-vine lining the top rim, unusual for Japan, and there are exquisite renditions of the four Chinese tutelary deities of the four directions, the scarlet bird of the south, the azure dragon of the east, the white tiger of the west and the black tortoise entwined with a snake that represents the north. Each of these represents seven of the twenty-eight constellations. These are pre-Han mythological figures that can be found in stone carvings from the Northern Wei, on memorial tablets of the Tang, and inside Koguryŏ tombs. This kind of Chinese geomancy continued to exert considerable appeal in Japan for many centuries.

The figures that appear just above these signs point us even further west. In the centre is what appears to be a fat three-toed naked demon, who is holding up a column of jewels. On either side sit squat pairs of aboriginals with curly hair who seem to be listening to the message of the Buddha from within a cave. No one has yet come up with a satisfactory explanation of what these figures are meant to represent, but there are precedents in China.

Plate 9 The Yakushiji pedestal.

It has been suggested that they may represent the twelve *yakṣa* generals who pledged to protect those who accept the teaching of the sūtra, but they do not give the impression of being particularly fierce or armed.[6] The 'caves' are formed by a band in two waves that are reminiscent of the looped garlands that can be found at the base of many Gandhāran friezes and are similar to those found by Aurel Stein at Mīran on the southern fringes of the Taklamakan Desert. This pedestal is stark proof of how close we are at this point to the art of Central Asia.

A further link to this region far to the west of China proper lies in the figures of the two bodhisattvas who flank the central image, representing the sun, in the form of Nikkō 日光 (Sk. Sūryaprabha), and the moon, in the form of Gekkō 月光 (Sk. Candraprabha) [plates 10–11]. They are sanctioned by scripture, but by the same token suggest a Central Asian origin, perhaps Zoroastrian, that takes us back to Afghanistan. A glance at the Gandhāran prototype with the same elaborate jewellery on the neck and arms, and the hair swept up and back in a high cockade, immediately reveals a lineage that goes back some 400 years [plate 12]. They stand over three metres tall in a pose that suggests both gentleness and firmness. The clothes on the lower half of their bodies are a mixture of robes that cling closely to the outline of the legs with a much freer overlay of draped material that gives a feeling of lightness and accentuates hips that appear to sway.

The fact that the initial vector for the introduction of Buddhism was visual rather than textual did, of course, reduce the role of the written word. But it should not be forgotten that ultimate legitimation for the efficacy of the image lay in texts, in this case the *Bhaiṣajyagururājasūtra* (*T.* 449). The Buddhist Sanskrit version of this sūtra was only discovered in Gilgit in 1931, but it is generally considered to have been composed in the region of Kashmir in the second century BCE. The particular attributes of this Buddha – emitting strong light, accompanied by the sun and moon, and inhabiting a Pure Land that was decorated in lapis lazuli and gold – again give us reason to place his origins in what is now Afghanistan. He is mentioned in fifteen Chinese texts that range from the third to the fifth century, but worship of him in China does not seem to predate the Sui Dynasty. Like most Mahāyāna sūtras, it begins with the description of a scene with Śākyamuni Buddha surrounded by an assembly, and then moves into a question-and-answer session, the purpose of which is to persuade

---

[6]   The Ráth György Museum in Budapest has a similar demon made of grey earthernware, said to be from the Xiding Pagoda in Henan Province and dating from the early Tang.

Plate 10   Nikkō from Yakushiji.   Plate 11   Gekkō from Yakushiji.

Plate 12   Bodhisattva from Gandhāra. Second to third century CE.

Śākyamuni to proclaim on the particular merits that will be gained from the worship of Bhaiṣajyagururāja. What emerges is not a story but a description of a Pure Land, a list of the vows that Bhaiṣajyagururāja took when he was a bodhisattva, and then an exhortation to worship both Buddha and text. If one has faith, if one copies the sūtra, 'accepts' it, presents offerings in its honour, and trusts implicitly in its beneficial effects, one will experience a myriad benefits. It makes no bones about the kind of worldly benefit available if one is prepared to accept the teaching as medicine. The seventh vow, for example, is:

If there are any sentient beings who are ill and oppressed, who have nowhere to go and nothing to return to, who have neither doctor nor medicine, neither relatives nor immediate family, who are destitute and whose sufferings are acute – as soon as my name passes through their ears, they will be cured of all their diseases and they will be peaceful and joyous in body and mind. They will have plentiful families and property, and they will personally experience the supreme enlightenment (Birnbaum 1979: 153– 54).

The image of Yakushi was obviously designed to impart a sense of mysterious power over matters of life and death, illness and disease. Quite a different impression is given by the sculpture that is now known as the Pensive Prince, redolent of the inner calm that comes from meditation and detachment [plate 13]. Dated to the seventh century and made of camphorwood that was originally gilded, this image is now held in the Chūgūji 中宮寺, the nunnery that was linked to Hōryūji 法隆寺. The figure is bare to the waist and has the hairstyle of a child, tied up in two buns. A full skirt flows over the legs and down to the base of the pedestal. Some art historians argue for a fairly early date (*c.*630) largely on the basis of the folds in the skirt, which are clearly in the style of the Shaka triad in the Hōryūji [see plate 4]; others prefer to stress the quiet features and the subtlety of the hands, which, together with the fact that the image is made not from a single piece of wood but from over twenty-four interlocking pieces (a technique known as *yosegi zukuri*), suggests a much later date. It may well be, of course, that the more intimate, almost vulnerable, feel of this image has more to do with function than with date, but there is no escaping the great contrast it presents with most other sculptures from this period. It would, however, have looked different when it was first made, since there are marks that show it had a metal crown concealing the hair, necklaces and other ornaments attached. Buddhist images of this type, seated with the right leg resting on the left knee and the right arm touching the chin (the pose is known as *hanka shiyui-zō* 半跏思惟像), are rare. Most date from the seventh and eighth

Plate 13   The Chūgūji Maitreya.

centuries, and only about thirty survive, the majority being small portable gilt bronzes. It would not be unreasonable to identify this figure as that of the young Śākyamuni the moment before his enlightenment, but it could equally be said to represent the Buddha of the future, Maitreya (Jp. Miroku 彌勒). Why is this?

An explanation must be sought in Korea. Maitreya was the next Buddha in line after Śākyamuni and his cult was common throughout Central Asia and China. Some believed that one should strive to reach the Heaven of Contentment (Tuṣita), where he (and others) were known to reside; others believed that he would appear in this world at the appointed time. In Paekche, and later in Silla, this cult took a particular form. There emerged a belief that Maitreya was already present in this world as a member of a group of noble youths, known as *hwarang* 花郎. These *hwarang* later became known for their martial prowess in the service of the king but at this stage they seem to have been a religious order. There is a gilt-bronze image in the Toksu Palace Museum in Seoul which is of Maitreya in this form, although there remains some disagreement as to its provenance. It is very similar to the Chūgūji figure. Also related is another well-known statue carved from red pine and now held in Kōryūji 廣隆寺 in Kyōto. A reference dated 603 in *Nihon shoki* refers to a statue of Maitreya being sent to Prince Shōtoku as a gift from the king of Paekche. Shōtoku passed it on to Hata no Kawakatsu 秦河勝, who built the Hachiokadera 蜂岡寺 to accommodate it. An entry for 623 refers to another such gift sent from Silla in memory of Shōtoku. It is possible that the Hachiokadera was later renamed Kōryūji, but this is by no means certain. It has been argued that the Chūgūji image was probably produced and dedicated between the death of Shōtoku in 621 and the end of Tenji's reign in 673. Certainly, Shōtoku became identified with Maitreya and many of the temples associated with his name are known to have contained images of this Buddha of the future (Lancaster 1988: 135–53; Guth 1988: 191–213).

4   Monuments at Nara

4.1   Kōfukuji

It was in fact the female sovereign Genshō Tennō who oversaw the move of the capital from Asuka to Heijō-kyō (Nara) that started in 710. The scale of the enterprise was such that it took twelve years before the main palace buildings were completed. Officially sponsored state temples such as Daianji and Yakushiji were dismantled and transported north, as were a number of privately funded temples, the most important of which was the family temple (*ujidera* 氏寺) of the Fujiwara 藤原, construction of which began around 715. The Fujiwara family had been founded by Tenji Tennō, who gave Nakatomi no Kamatari 鎌足 (614–69) the separate name Fujiwara in recognition of his support. The *ujidera* had started life in 669 as a small temple in Yamashina to commemorate Kamatari's death. His son Fuhito 不比等 (659–720) moved it first to Asuka and thence to Nara, rebuilding it in grand style and giving it the name Kōfukuji 興福寺, although the name Yamashinadera 山科寺 was also used. The ground chosen for Kōfukuji, on the eastern fringes of the new capital, was already sacred to the Fujiwara house; it stands next to what later became the Kasuga shrine, their main ritual centre.[1]

Kōfukuji became one of the most important and influential of all Japanese temples, mainly because of this connection to the Fujiwara, who began to wield considerable power soon after the move to Nara. In 724, following what was rapidly becoming a tradition, at least among female sovereigns, Genshō retired in favour of her nephew, Monmu's eldest son Shōmu 聖武 (701–56; r. 724–49). Shōmu had some difficulty establishing his credentials, not least because he was the first male sovereign for some time not to have a royal mother; he was in fact the first of what was to be a long line of rulers with Fujiwara mothers and he in turn made a Fujiwara daughter his queen-consort. She is known to history as Kōmyō 光明, a devout Buddhist, who played a major part in ensuring the growth of Kōfukuji. A major step was

---

[1]   For further details on the early history of Kōfukuji see Grapard 1992a: 48–70.

taken in 734, when the monk Genbō 玄昉 (d. 746) returned to Japan after eighteen years' study in China carrying with him Buddhist images and a very large collection of sūtras, amounting to over 5,000 volumes. He was immediately appointed her personal meditation master (*zenji* 禪師) and his collection of texts was housed at Kōfukuji, transforming it overnight into an important centre for Buddhist scholarship. She also built a special temple for him called Kairyūōji 海龍王寺, a specific reference to the sūtra of that name that dealt with the enlightenment of the Naga King's daughter, which we have already discussed with reference to the 'Beetle-wing' cabinet at Hōryūji. Genbō himself was made Saṅgha Prefect in 737.[2] Work on the temple complex continued right through to 772.

Kōfukuji soon became known for its Ritual Assembly of Vimalakīrti or Yuima-e 維摩會, and for the academic discipline known as Hossō 法相.[3] The interest in the *Vimalakīrtisūtra* is usually traced back to Kamatari himself, who is said to have been cured of an illness in 656 after a woman from Paekche had urged him to chant the fifth chapter, which treats of illness and its essential unreality (Tyler 1990: 78–80). The name Kōfukuji itself is thought to have been chosen from a passage in Kumārajīva's translation. The Ritual Assembly, which we shall treat in more detail later since it became of real importance in the subsequent Heian period, started life simply as recitations of the sūtra itself, but it soon turned into a major seven-day rite during which doctrinal debates and lectures on a variety of subjects were held, partly as an attempt to encourage scholarship. The main lecturer was appointed by the sovereign and to be chosen for this position was a certain mark of future advancement.

4.2   Tōdaiji

The first twenty years of Shōmu's reign were highly unstable. There were powerful rivals, unhappy at the way Genshō had arranged the succession; there was a disastrous smallpox epidemic that raged from 735 to 737, killing, according to some estimates, almost a third of the population; and in 740 the court was faced with having to raise a force of 17,000 to deal with a serious uprising in Kyūshū. This was followed by yet further unrest when Shōmu himself caused enormous worry and expense by trying to shift the capital

[2]   For more on Genbō see Bingenheimer 2001: 107–12; Grapard 1992a: 66–67.
[3]   For a fuller discussion of Hossō see §4.7.

twice, to Kuni 恭仁 on the Kizu river in 740 and to Shigaraki 紫香楽, which was even further away from Nara, in 742. Why he vacillated in this fashion is not really known. It was only in 745 that the decision was made to remain at Heijō-kyō.

It was Shōmu who planned and oversaw construction of the monumental Tōdaiji 東大寺 with its large bronze statue of Vairocana Buddha. A project of unprecedented size and expense, it was originally planned in 743 for the site at Shigaraki but eventually built at Nara. Although, as we shall see, the native deities were still worshipped and the necessary rites continued, the reigns of Shōmu and his queen-consort Kōmyō were marked by the amount of attention paid to all things Buddhist. Buddhist ceremonies, such as the yearly confession of sins (*keka* 悔過), became prominent events at court, and members of the saṅgha must have been a more common sight within the Palace grounds. Although officially sanctioned ordinations continued to be restricted to ten per year, the number of unofficial initiations grew considerably: 900 in 737; 750 in 743; 400 in 745; 3,000 in 748; 1,000 in 749; and 800 in 757. A large number of men and women were clearly being recruited as 'offerings'. Not only did this begin to have an adverse effect on those who had a serious commitment to the religious life, it exacerbated the problem of finances, for these numbers represented a not-insubstantial diminution of the tax base.

There was also during this period a surprising shift of attitude towards those religious figures who had put themselves beyond the pale: Gyōki (668–749), for example, had been heavily criticised in 717 for maverick behaviour, and an entry in *Shoku Nihongi* for 730.9.29, which is assumed to refer to him, talks of worryingly large crowds gathering in the east of the capital to hear 'misleading' prophesies. He certainly gained a reputation as a charismatic proselytiser who was not content to remain within the precincts of a temple. But in the tenth month of 741, 550 of his followers were allowed to take proper vows and four years later in 745 he himself was raised to the rank of Grand Prefect by Shōmu. It was clearly in Shōmu's interests to harness as much support as he could for the project that became Tōdaiji.

Between 737 and 741 orders went out for the construction of more temples in the provinces and for the building of seven-storey pagodas for enshrining copies of the *Lotus sūtra*. The logical progression of this was seen in 741 with the institution of a network of provincial temples for both male and female members of the saṅgha, Kokubunji 國分寺 and Kokubunniji 國分尼寺. Ten copies each of the *Lotus sūtra* and the *Sūtra of golden radiant wisdom* were also provided for each province. In this way Shōmu tried to extend his authority far out into the provinces on the back of a nationwide temple-building project. Until Tōdaiji was completed, the central pivot for this state-wide *kokubunji* system was Daianji, which had been moved to Nara and rebuilt under the supervision of the monk Dōji. *Shoku Nihongi* notes that in 756 twenty of these provincial temples had already been completed.

It was undoubtedly Kōmyō who lay behind the addition of temples for women. We know very little about the ordination of nuns, but we do know that women carried out many of the same tasks as men at ceremonies within the Palace itself. This lasted until about 770, when Shōtoku Tennō 稱德天皇, the last female sovereign for many centuries, died. As we have already mentioned, from that point on there was a rapid decline in officially recognised female members of the saṅgha, so that by the early Heian period they receive only limited mention in the sources. The term *ama* 尼, however, which is often translated as 'nun', was also used to refer to those many women who were accepted as initiates on an unofficial basis by men like Gyōki. If anything, the number of such women increased as time went on. There were, of course, many reasons for taking such a step: bereavement, divorce and retirement. It soon developed to the point where this became a socially acceptable status for any woman who was no longer active as wife or mother.[4] It was also Kōmyō who encouraged the copying of sūtras. Partly this was for distribution to the growing provincial network, but to copy a sūtra was in any case an act of great merit and could be either done or ordered for a variety of personal reasons. Kōmyō was in charge of the sūtra scriptorium (*shakyōjo* 寫經所) that was funded by the government, which perhaps explains the production of copies on such an enormous scale during this period. The scriptorium itself and the public nature of this enterprise was not to survive the move to Heian-kyō (Kornicki 1998: 78ff).

The pièce de resistance of Shōmu's reign was undoubtedly Tōdaiji and its smaller sister, Hokkeji 法華寺. We are probably now at the stage where an institution such as Hokkeji can legitimately be called a 'nunnery' or 'convent'; the equivalent male establishment, however, was still more in the nature of a temple than a monastery. The titles reveal a good deal about their respective roles: the Hokkeji was named after the *Lotus sūtra*, the one major scripture that specifically held out the prospect of enlightenment for women. The formal name of Tōdaiji on the other hand was the Temple for the Protection of the State by the Four Divine Kings of the Golden Radiant Wisdom sūtra (Konkōmyō shiten'ō gokokuji 金光明四天王護國寺). This

---

[4]   On this as yet poorly researched subject see Groner 2002: 245–88.

suggests that what lay behind the project was yet again the *Sūtra of golden radiant wisdom* (in the second translation by Yijing), but in fact the image housed in Tōdaiji is indubitably that of Vairocana, part of a rather different tradition.

Construction of Tōdaiji was clearly intended to bolster Shōmu's position as sovereign, but the project was too large for a mere domestic audience. By presenting what might be seen as an act of gross self-aggrandisement as an act of benevolence for all, he was not just indulging in further state patronage. It was tantamount to claiming the role of ruler as *cakravartin*, or ruler on a world scale, much in the manner of Emperor Wu of the Liang Dynasty 梁武帝 (r. 502–49), who created his own ordination rituals and raised the status of the layman above that of the monk (Janousch 1999), or of Empress Wu Zetian 武則天 (r. 684–705), who also used Buddhism to great effect. And there were precedents in China for such a monumental image: there remains a ten-metre high carving of Vairocana in the cliffs at Longmen near Luoyang, commissioned by Gaozong 高宗 in 672, and we also know that Empress Wu commissioned a huge bronze image in 700. But this was something on a truly grand scale: Japan, less than two hundred years after the introduction of Buddhism, was about to produce the largest and most magnificent monument to Buddha the world had yet seen. The proclamation of 743 reads as follows:

Although of little virtue, we have humbly assumed this great rank. Desiring to succour all, we have devoted ourselves to soothing all living beings. From shore to shore this realm has been permeated with benevolence, but the Buddha's teachings have not yet penetrated everywhere. May Heaven and Earth be graced by the power of the Three Jewels, and may all living things prosper and countless generations bounteously continue their labours.

Here, on the fifteenth day of the tenth month of the fifteenth year of Tenpyō (743), we take the great vow of a bodhisattva to construct a golden image of Vairocana. The image will be cast in bronze, exhausting the copper in the realm. A great mountain will be excavated, a hall of worship erected, and the whole universe shall join us in this endeavour. Thus shall the whole universe gain benefit and reach enlightenment.

It is we who possess the wealth under Heaven, we who possess its power; and we shall use this wealth and power to erect the sacred image. But while it is easy to conceive of such a task, it will be difficult to fulfil our desires. We fear the people may be worked so hard that they will fail to sense the sanctity of the task, and, on the contrary, may feel resentment and commit crimes. Therefore, let all those who are committed to this great enterprise be assured of merit in absolute sincerity, and worship Vairocana Buddha three times a day. So will the image take shape. And if there are those who desire to bring but a blade of grass or a handful of earth to help create this image, then they shall be permitted to do so. Governors and district chiefs are on no account to importune or threaten the people, nor demand extra taxes from them. Let my command be proclaimed far and near, that all may know my will (Aoki et al. 1989–98, vol. II: 431–33).[5]

Preparations for the huge figure to be cast in Nara began in 745. The project involved levelling off a large area of land at the foot of the sacred Mt Mikasa just to the northwest of Kōfukuji and creating a compound that covered 6.6 km^2 (4 sq. miles). The layout was the same as that of the new Yakushiji, with the main hall in the centre facing south dominating a compound flanked by two pagodas, each over 100 m in height, arranged on an east–west axis.[6] This main hall now measures 57 m long, 50.5 m deep north to south and 49.1 m high, but we know that the building we see today is quite different from the original, which at 86.1 m (eleven bays) was longer by another third, giving far better proportions than the present squat construction that dates from the late seventeenth century. Inside this huge hall sat the statue, almost 16 m high. The original base remains, but the head and most of the rest of the torso dates from the seventeenth century and is unfortunately somewhat ungainly.

After some false starts the casting began in 747 and was completed two years later. This was by no means the end of the process, since the statue had yet to be properly prepared, gilded and covered, but Shōmu visited the site in the first month of the year to review progress. Some idea of the difficulties involved in this kind of work can be obtained from the following description:

The monumental statue was cast in eight stages, working upward from the base to the head. After the bronze for each level had been poured, the molds for the next level were positioned and earth was piled up around them, both to hold them in place and to provide a surface for the bronze foundries. Thus by the time the casting was complete the entire statue was covered with a mound of earth. As each level of molds was removed, imperfections in the casting had to be repaired: the flashing that would have occurred along the seams of the mold would have required chasing, and the hollows caused by gassing would have required recasting. This time-consuming process lasted from 750 until 755; moreover, the 966 snail-shaped curls had to be cast one by one and set onto the head. At the time of the dedication ceremony in 752 the image was only partially completed (Morse 1986: 51–52).

A few months after his visit, Shōmu retired and forced through the succession of his daughter by Kōmyō, Princess Abe, known as Kōken 孝謙. Shōmu was ailing and wanted to spend his remaining time overseeing the grand project and making sure that Kōken's rule was secure. The official opening ceremony was held three years later in 752 and was presided over by

[5] Trans. adapted from Piggott 1997: 104–05.
[6] See the useful plan in Coaldrake 1986: 34, which shows both original and existing structures.

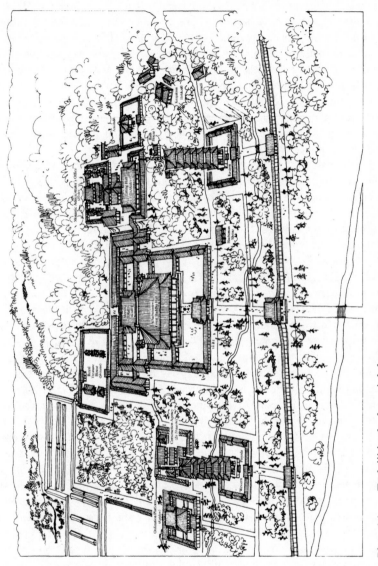

Plate 14   Tōdaiji in the late eighth century.

the monk Bodhisena 菩提遷那 (704–60), who had arrived in Japan in 734, the only Indian known to have done so in pre-modern times. Shōmu himself died in 756. In the end, the image took 444 metric tons of refined copper, 7 metric tons of unrefined tin, and 391 kg of gold leaf (which had been discovered in the north of Japan at just the right moment). The project was so vast that a special agency called the Zō Tōdaijishi 造東大寺司 was created to oversee the operation. This eventually grew to be the largest agency in the government and once the temple was completed it was transformed into a general agency responsible for all further palace and temple construction until the end of the century.[7]

Once created and in operation, Tōdaiji became the centre of all Buddhist activity that had relevance to the state. Perhaps for this reason, the curriculum was eclectic from the beginning. For academic purposes the community was divided into six groups, each responsible for studying the texts and practices of a particular academic tradition (see §4.7). Each subject had its own building, its own specialist library and its own administration. The first head of the community was Rōben 良辨 (689–773), who had originally been trained at Kōfukuji. He founded a strong tradition of Buddhist scholarship at Tōdaiji, as befitted a temple complex of such magnitude, and there was soon a full programme of festivals, readings and congregations throughout the year, designed to celebrate a wide variety of sūtras, most of them – as one might expect – of the 'state-protecting' variety (Piggott 1987: 166–87).

How was it that the central figure of Tōdaiji turned out to be the cosmic buddha Vairocana and not the historical buddha Śākyamuni? It is generally assumed that the decision to build in honour of Vairocana was in response to the recent arrival in Japan of the sūtra in which he is a major figure, the *Flower garland sūtra* (Ch. *Huayan jing*, Jp. *Kegon kyō* 華嚴經, *T.* 278). This vast work was probably compiled in Khotan sometime in the third century CE, but the Huayan doctrinal tradition to which it gave birth (and from which it should be distinguished) was a product of late Sui and early Tang China. Its founder was the scholar-monk Zhiyan 智儼 (602–68), but it reached its apogee with Fazang 法藏 (643–712), who won the patronage of Empress Wu. The empress was so interested in this sūtra that she personally invited the Khotanese monk Śikṣānanda to work on a new translation.[8] On a far grander scale than previous 'state-protecting' sūtras, offering the protection not just of guardian kings but of the cosmic Buddha himself, it was adopted as the

---

[7]   For further details of the construction and financing of Tōdaiji, see Piggott 1987.
[8]   For details of Empress Wu as a patron of Buddhism see Weinstein 1987: 37–47.

basis of a new and more grandiloquent state religion. The idea that the physical world was one and the same as the spiritual suggested that temporal power could be identified with spiritual power and so made the identification of ruler and Buddha that much easier. The sūtra was in turn adopted on the same basis in newly unified Silla, where it was represented by Wŏnhyo 元曉 (614–86) and Ŭisang 義湘 (625–712), who founded the first Hwaŏm 華嚴 temple in Korea, Pusoksa 浮石寺, in 676.

The first sign that the sūtra was in Japan comes in 722, when Genshō Tennō had it copied in memory of Genmei. Both Genbō and Daoxuán 道璿 (702–60) brought copies with them in 734 and it is usually Daoxuán who is credited with its introduction. But Daoxuán was in fact better known for his knowledge not of Huayan but the *vinaya*, and it was a monk called Simsang 審祥 (Jp. Shinjō) from Silla who first explained the sūtra to Shōmu in 740. He began by expounding the text in his capacity as lecturer (*kōji* 講師) to be followed by a series of 'repeaters', or *fukushi* 復師, who paraphrased what he had said so that it could be absorbed a second time. In this fashion he managed to cover twenty books a year, in a format that was continued throughout the Nara period (Girard 1990: 224). There can be no doubt that these monks, coming from China in the mid-730s, brought with them news of the high esteem in which this sūtra had been held by Empress Wu and its major role at the court of the Silla kings. The central figure of this vast text is Vairocana, who was the outcome of a movement to unify all buddhas under a single entity; as the ultimate transcendent buddha of Mahāyāna, representing all matter and mind, nirvāṇa and samsāra, he was a natural symbol for a ruler to adopt. One may doubt whether Shōmu knew much about the complex doctrines of Huayan/Kegon, but he was clearly interested in appropriating to himself the most powerful, all-encompassing Buddha of them all.

It is thought likely that the iconography actually came from the description of Vairocana in the *Sūtra of Brahmā's net* (Jp. *Bonmō kyō* 梵網經),[9] which had been compiled in China during the fifth century and also brought to Japan by Daoxuán. It was often treated as a closing chapter to the *Flower garland*. It is here that we read of Vairocana preaching on a throne of one thousand lotus petals, each petal containing a historical buddha, each one master of a universe containing a trillion worlds – a symbol of the Pure World that is the cosmos. This was an image of authority on not just a national but a world scale.[10]

---

[9]   Ch. *Fanwang jing*, T. 1484.
[10]   For a translation and study of the *Sūtra of Brahmā's net* see de Groot 1967.

4.3   The question of ordination

We have already drawn attention to the contradictions that arose from the clash between a desire to control the spread of people opting out of normal civil life on the one hand and the willingness to 'offer up' large numbers of men and women for initiation in times of crisis on the other. The latter habit was bound to lead to a lack of commitment and it is hardly surprising that the behaviour of priests within the temples became a matter of concern to the Saṅgha Office. Those men who had experience of life in Chinese institutions were often shocked at the laxity of standards in Japan. In 734.11.21 the following order came from the Council of State:

The survival of Buddhism depends on [the quality of] members of the saṅgha. The ability and training of ordinands is the responsibility of the relevant bureaus. Recently such training has been lax and petitions for ordination made by individuals have increased: this is against the spirit of the law. From henceforth, no matter whether it be a novice or a lay person, an ordinand must have memorised the *Lotus sūtra* and the *Sūtra of golden radiant wisdom* and in addition have prayed and practised for a minimum of three years. If this happens, then scholarship will improve and private petitions will naturally cease (Aoki et al. 1989–98, vol. II: 283).

One area of particular concern was the ordination process itself, which had always been crucial to membership of the community. Full ordination (*jukai* 受戒) was a ritual whereby the precepts of the saṅgha were conferred on an ordinand, giving him or her the right to accept alms. In return, the ordinand vowed to uphold the precepts and live according to the rules of the order. There were a number of different versions of the *vinaya* belonging to different traditions, but the one in common use in China was known as the *Regulations in four parts* (Ch. *sifenlu*, Jp. *shibunritsu* 四分律), stemming from the Dharmaguptaka tradition in India. This contained 250 precepts for men and 348 for women. It is indicative of the haphazard way Buddhism had been introduced into Japan that the *vinaya* seems to have arrived in piecemeal fashion and at this stage the stipulations were probably honoured more in the breach. Strictly speaking, indeed, no one in Japan had ever been ordained correctly because the regulations clearly stated that for an ordination to be valid ten fully ordained members had to be present, a preceptor, a master of ceremonies, a teacher and seven witnesses. In theory, therefore, one could argue that the whole Buddhist enterprise in Japan was illegitimate.

It was for this reason that moves were made to try and persuade a proper *vinaya* master to come from China and overhaul the system. On the occasion of the ninth mission to the Tang court in 733 two men from Kōfukuji, Yōei 榮叡 and Fushō 普照, were sent with the specific task of finding the necessary ten men. Daoxuán met them, agreed to help and left immediately, travelling with the returning mission and arriving in Japan in 734. He was soon setting up seminars devoted to the study of the *vinaya*. Yōei and Fushō stayed on in China as students for the next nine years. Eventually they met the master Jianzhen 鑑眞 (Jp. Ganjin, 688–763), who was lecturing on the subject at the Damingsi 大明寺 in Yangzhou 揚州. They persuaded him that his presence was needed in Japan, but it was to be over ten years before he finally arrived. On the first occasion he tried to leave without official permission and was betrayed by a student. The second and third attempts were thwarted by bad weather and when he tried a fourth time, he was arrested by the Tang authorities. On his fifth attempt the ship was blown to Taiwan and he returned to mainland China with great difficulty. It was only on the sixth occasion that Japanese envoys finally managed to transport him to Japan. He was already a blind old man of 68. Even then the Tang emperor requested that he be accompanied by a Daoist priest. The Japanese refused and were reduced to smuggling his party on board. He arrived in Japan in 754 with a party of twenty-four men and women, many of them fully ordained members of the saṅgha.[11]

On his arrival, Jianzhen was installed at Tōdaiji without delay and given the job of instituting the correct ordination procedures for Japanese monks. He set up the required platform (*kaidan* 戒壇) in the fourth month of that year and at the initial ceremony administered a number of different rites. To Shōmu Tennō and his immediate family he conferred the 'bodhisattva precepts' (*bosatsukai* 菩薩戒). This was a set of ten major and forty-eight minor precepts listed in the *Sūtra of Brahmā's net*. This sūtra, which is presented in the form of a direct sermon by Vairocana himself in response to a request from Śākyamuni, is in two sections: the first contains an exposition of the ten stages of the bodhisattva path; the second section is a list of simpler precepts, which were commonly used in China for 'confirming' laymen and laywomen as devotees of the Three Jewels, as supporters of the saṅgha.[12] He also re-ordained some eighty priests connected to the palace with the full,

---

[11] See Takakusu 1928–29, a translation of *Tō Daiosho tōseiden* 東大和尚東征傳, composed in 779 by the monk Genkai 元開.

[12] These were: not to kill, not to steal, not to be unchaste, not to lie, not to sell liquor, not to tell others of errors made by members of the saṅgha or lay supporters, not to praise oneself and defame others, not to begrudge others either property or the Dharma, not to become angry, and not to slander the Three Jewels. See Groner 1984: 119.

correct 250 precepts (*gusokukai* 具足戒). Not all this activity went down as well as it might: there was naturally some resistance from those who were unhappy to be told that their earlier ordinations had been invalid. A debate was held at the Yuimadō at Kōfukuji at which monks tried to argue the case for 'self-ordination', using as support quotations from a Chinese text entitled the *Divination sūtra* (Jp. *Senzatsu kyō* 占察經).[13] In the end, however, the majority agreed to be re-ordained.

Jianzhen's arrival therefore led to considerable changes. The first was this establishment of an official and permanent ordination platform at Tōdaiji. Two more platforms were set up in 761 to serve east and west Japan: at Yakushiji in Shimōsa, and Kanzeonji in Daizaifu, Kyūshū. Ordinations are recorded at Daikan Daiji in 703, Asukadera in 708, Yakushiji in 721–22 and 726–27, and Kōfukuji in 743, but there had been no fixed location for the ceremony prior to this point. The second change was in the way ordination certificates were granted. Before Jianzhen, both permission to become a novice and permission to proceed to the next stage had required certificates signed by the Ministry of Administration; Jianzhen managed to alter this procedure so that the second stage was left to the Sangha Office to handle themselves. Was this a major concession to self-rule? Since the issuing of novice certificates (*dochō* 度牒) remained the business of the ministry, the answer is probably 'no'. In 756.5 Jianzhen was honoured with the headship of a newly constituted Sangha Office, but it was not to last. He resigned this position in 758, persuading the court to build him his own temple, Tōshōdaiji 東招提寺, with its own ordination platform. This marks the beginning of what later became known as the Ritsu 律 tradition. All monks were initially urged to study there at some stage during their training, in line with the temple's name (招提 representing a transliteration into Chinese of the Sk. *cāturdiśa*, meaning '[all] four directions'), but the actual status of the platform itself is not entirely clear. Although the temple continued to grow and prosper into the Heian period, Tōdaiji remained the main ground for ordinations.

4.4   Explaining anomalies

Our account of the progress of Buddhism so far has concentrated on political and institutional matters, but what of personal beliefs? How much do we know, for example, about attitudes to death and the afterlife two hundred

---

[13] Ch. *Zhancha jing*, *T*. 839.

years after the arrival of gifts from Paekche? Sources are, of course, scarce but we do have the collection of tales entitled *A record of strange happenings in Japan* (Jp. *Nihon ryōiki* 日本靈異記), compiled around 820 by Kyōkai 景戒, from Yakushiji.[14] Although, strictly speaking, this is a Heian text, the majority of stories deal with the Nara period. Written by a man who was more interested in proselytising than in doctrine, this work is thought to have been prepared as a source for sermons and preaching, giving us a glimpse of what an 'ordinary' Buddhist message might look like. It is full of admonitions and dire warnings.

Good and evil deeds cause karmic retribution as a figure causes its shadow, and suffering and pleasure follow such deeds as an echo follows a sound in the valley. Those who witness such experiences marvel at them and forget they are real happenings in the world. The penitent withdraws to hide himself, for he burns with shame at once. Were the fact of karmic retribution not known, how could we rectify wickedness and establish righteousness? And how would it be possible to make men mend their wicked minds and practice the path of virtue without demonstrating the law of karmic causation?

In China the *Mingbaoji* 冥報記 was compiled, and during the great Tang the *Banyao yanji* 般若驗記 was written. Since we respect the documents of foreign lands, should we not also believe and stand in awe of the miraculous events of our own land? Having witnessed these events myself, I cannot remain idle. After long meditation on this, I now break my silence. I have recorded for future generations the limited information that has come to me in these three volumes called the *Nihonkoku genpō zen'aku ryōiki* (Nakamura 1973: 101, adapted).

The full title of this collection is *A record of strange happenings in Japan [explained in terms of] immediate karmic response to both good and evil* (Jp. *Nihonkoku genpō zen'aku ryōiki* 日本國現報善悪靈異記) and its main aim is to illustrate the workings of *karma*, the idea that actions are never random but always have causes and unavoidable consequences (*inga* 因果); and, as the term *genpō* ('retribution here and now') suggests, those consequences may be just round the corner rather than postponed to a future existence. There is another message in the title, for it stresses the fact that these strange events have happened in Japan, as well as elsewhere. There is more than a suggestion of rivalry and pride: Japan is now fully incorporated within the Buddhist sphere and its marvellous power can be experienced here and now.

Introducing the concept of karma in this way has two benefits: firstly, it has great interpretative power, providing a rational, satisfying explanation for everything from strange, untoward events to why things simply are as they

---

[14] The translation of the title takes a clue from LaFleur 1983: 26–59.

are; secondly, it turns out to be a very useful threat to encourage people to behave properly, to do good deeds, uphold the principle of filial piety, and avoid actions destructive of public order. We encounter here Buddhism as a mechanism of social control, masquerading as the bringer of salvation. It is a world of cautionary tales: 'On a man's rebirth as an ox for labour and showing an extraordinary sign because of stealing from his son'; 'On the death penalty for constantly boiling and eating bird's eggs'; and a world of poetic justice: a man who kills horses by working them too hard loses his sight when both of his eyes fall into a kettle full of boiling water. Faith brings its rewards: 'On a deaf man whose hearing was restored immediately owing to his faith in a Mahāyāna scripture'; and there are dire consequences for those who dare to ridicule the Dharma: 'On ridiculing a reciter of the *Lotus sūtra* and getting a twisted mouth as an immediate penalty'.

Karma works against the background of transmigration through the cycle of birth and death, traversing the six courses (*rokudō* 六道); these were commonly divided into the three pleasant ones – gods (*tenbu* 天部), humans (*ningen* 人間) and demi-gods (*ashura* 阿修羅) – and three less pleasant ones – animals (*chikushō* 畜生), hungry ghosts (*gaki* 餓鬼) and creatures of hell (*jigoku* 地獄). The hierarchy may be fixed, but they all coexist in this realm of ours and the boundaries are pervious; bodhisattvas, for example, may take human form (*keshin* 化身) as part of their vow of compassion; this is how one explains the existence of such shamanistic figures as Gyōki and the legendary founder of the tradition of mountain ascetics, En no gyōja 役行者. Kyōkai argues in favour of accepting self-ordination, for instance, because the person involved may just be an incarnation of a higher being; one never knows. Note that the gods in this system are still within the cycle, and gods themselves must eventually be reborn as humans if they are to achieve enlightenment, since this can only ever be achieved from the human state. Being human is therefore already a state of merit, although no one in the six courses can escape decay of the body. The anonymous poet who produced what are known as the 'Buddha's footprint poems' carved into a stone at Yakushiji in 753, perhaps some thirty years before Kyōkai's birth, put it as follows:

> The human body / is a hard thing to attain:
> It has become / a refuge for the Dharma;
> Strive onward, all! / Press forward, all!
>
> Where the Four Serpents / and the five Demons
> All accumulate – This vile body –
> We must loathe and cast away / Must free ourselves and cast away.

> (Cranston 1993: 774–75, adapted)

From the number of references that Kyōkai makes to passages in various different sūtras one might gain the impression that he was unusually widely read for a man who had little interest in doctrinal matters, but that would be misleading. In fact he made excellent use of a Chinese compendium entitled *Zhujing yaoji* (諸經用集)[15] compiled by Daoshi 道世 in 659, which consists of important illustrative passages from the sūtras listed according to theme. The Chinese flavour emerges in other ways too. In addition to karma and the *rokudō*, there are signs that the quintessentially Chinese idea of purgatory was known and understood. At death one goes into a kind of liminal state, which can last for anything up to three years. Every seven days for the first forty-nine days one goes through a critical stage, which is thought of in terms of court proceedings with the judge of the underworld Yama (a pre-Buddhist Indian figure) presiding. Rites and gifts from the dead person's family are therefore needed to help him or her on the way, but the eventual destination is still thought of in terms of karma (Teiser 1994: 1–15).

4.5   Hachiman

The Buddhist acceptance of multiple truths, the concept of rebirth, the ability of gods to reveal themselves, the Kegon concept of the interpenetration of all phenomena, and the fluidity inherent in the idea of the six courses, all pointed in the direction of a possible accommodation between buddhas, bodhisattvas and native deities. It might seem that under Shōmu, the court was allowing enthusiasm for all things Buddhist to eclipse the interests of these deities, but the sovereign, as high priest, would ignore the latter at his peril. Shōmu knew very well that on the domestic stage the legitimacy of his rule still depended on their goodwill and on the efficacy of the myths now enshrined in the early books of *Kojiki* and *Nihon shoki*. Perhaps the best way of showing how this balance was maintained is to look at two edicts proclaimed in 749 when Shōmu and Kōmyō visited the site where the image of Vairocana was taking shape. The first edict, spoken by Tachibana no Moroe 橘諸兄, used extremely humble language towards the image of Buddha:

These are the words of the Sovereign, the servant of the Three Jewels, that he most humbly offers up (奏賜) before the image of Vairocana. Although gold has been offered to us by people from other lands, it was thought not to exist in this land of Yamato since the beginning of heaven and earth. But in the east of this land over

---

[15] Jp. *Shokyō yōshū*, *T.* 2123. See Nakamura 1973: 36, n. 155 for a list of themes covered.

which we rule, the Governor of Michinoku, Kudaranoō Kyōfuku, of Junior Fifth Rank, has reported that gold has been found in his territory at Oda. Hearing this, we are astonished and rejoice, and feel that this is a gift bestowed on us by the compassion and good fortune of Vairocana. We accept it with reverence and humility and now lead all our officials in worship. Reverently we proclaim this in the awful presence of the Three Jewels (Aoki et al. 1989–98, vol. III: 65).

The second edict, which comes immediately afterwards, is quite different in tone and shows a desire to treat the 'gods of heaven and earth' on the same footing.

Hearken all ye assembled, princes of the blood, princes, nobles, officials and people of the realm-under-heaven, to the word which he speaks even as the word of the Sovereign Prince of Yamato who is a manifest deity; hearken ye all to the words which he speaks as a manifest deity in performance of the task of ruling over this land, to sit on the high throne of heavenly succession through generations and generations, to control and cherish, from the first reign of sovereigns who came from the High Plain of Heaven through the reigns of his ancestors down until this day, saying: a report has been made to us that in the east of this land, which we rule thus in benevolence through heavenly succession down to the present reign in honour and awe of the will of heaven and earth, gold has been found. We consider that of the various laws, the word of the Buddha is the most excellent for protecting the state. Thus in this realm over which we rule we ordered that the *Sūtra of Golden Radiant Wisdom* be honoured, that an image of Vairocana be fashioned, and that prayers be offered to the gods of heaven and earth. In our desire to pay due honour to the reigns of our ancestors for whom we have such awe and to lead and guide our subjects, we tried to ensure that misfortunes are corrected and dangers pacified; but even so our subjects worried lest the project be uncompleted and we ourselves were concerned that the gold was insufficient. But now we have been granted this sign of the supremely auspicious word that is the Three Jewels and the gods of heaven and earth together deem it good.

A good example of this process by which the native deities and buddhas came to support each other occurred during the construction of Tōdaiji itself. The work at Nara began in the eighth month of 745. When Shōmu suddenly fell ill the following year, help was requested from the deity Hachiman 八幡 who was resident in Usa 宇佐 in northern Kyūshū. The origins of Hachiman are obscure, but he was connected to families that specialised in metalwork, who may well have had access to the latest continental casting techniques. This may explain why he was one of the first deities to attract a Buddhist title – Daibosatsu 大菩薩, the earliest example of which is dated 798 – since casting was so central to the production of Buddhist images. It is highly likely that the first buildings at Usa were Buddhist, for we have a record of a temple called Mirokuji 彌勒寺 being built there as early as 725. Hachiman was also believed to have helped the court defeat the rebels in Kyūshū in 740, which could explain his later identification as the god of war. On that occasion, the court presented Usa with copies of two sūtras and ten Buddhist priests and ordered that a pagoda be built; he was already a composite deity for whom Buddhist gifts were not considered out of place.[16]

Exactly why this deity and this region should suddenly reach national prominence at this juncture is not known, but the catalyst was certainly Tōdaiji. Shōmu made a quick recovery and Hachiman was promoted to Third Rank. In 747, when the casting of the image was to begin, Shōmu turned to both Usa and Ise for help. Ise did not respond, but Hachiman issued his famous oracle, vowing to ensure the completion of the image by making the molten copper flow like water. A month after the statue of Vairocana was completed in the tenth month of 749 came news that another oracle had been pronounced by Hachiman announcing that he wished to move to Nara to lead all native deities in defending the grand project. As a result, a ritual icon (*shintai* 神體) representing him was brought to Tōdaiji with due ceremony. He was installed as protector of the temple and given the unprecedented honour of First Rank. In this fashion he became the prototype of all subsequent *gohō zenjin* 護法善神, deities whose primary function was to protect Buddhism. The Usa shrine was given the status of a *daijingū* 大神宮 in 756, putting it on the same level as Ise. It need come as no particular surprise that Buddhism eventually found it quite easy to accommodate Hachiman in this way. There were already a large number of deities that had been picked up en route and it is this habit of accretion that helps to explain the presence in Japanese Buddhism of Indian deities such as Brahmā (Jp. Bonten 梵天) and Śakra (Jp. Taishakuten 帝釋天), who not only acted as protectors of the Dharma but were in fact seen to rule over the gods of heaven and earth.

From the above description it should be clear that Hachiman was seen as having special status. As Buddhism continued to spread to other areas and small temples began to proliferate, we find one of two things happening: either existing local deities found themselves co-opted, or, as elsewhere in the Buddhist world, priests set about inventing local deities as being one of the easiest ways of attracting local devotees. A deity would be identified, and then named, and then worshipped in a temple. Priests often used the idea that these spirits were as much in need of salvation as anyone else. The earliest

---

[16] The well-known link between Hachiman and the legendary fourth-century ruler Ōjin is probably a later invention, given that it is not mentioned in any eighth-century source and first appears in 844. See Bender 1979 and Grapard 2003.

reference we have to this tactic occurs in the *Muchimaro den* 武智麻呂傳, a biography of Fujiwara no Muchimaro (680–737), written in 760.

In the first year of the Reiki era [715] Muchimaro dreamed that he met a 'strange person' who had a most unusual appearance. This strange man said to Muchimaro, 'That you are a person who is devoted to the Buddhist Dharma is well known to both men and deities alike. Therefore I request that you build a temple for me to help me fulfil my vow. Because of my past actions (*shukugō*), I became a deity long ago. I now want to take refuge in the Way of the Buddha and undertake meritorious works, but have not yet found an [appropriate] link [to the Buddha]. I have come to tell you this [in the hope that you will assist me].'

Muchimaro suspected that this [strange person] was Kehi-no-kami. Although Muchimaro wanted to reply, he was unable to do so and awoke from his dream. He thereupon [directed the following words to Kehi-no-kami] in a prayer: 'The ways of deities and men are separate: one is hidden, the other visible. I do not know the identity of the strange man who appeared in my dream last night. If I can get a sign [that it was you who spoke to me in my dream], then I shall without fail build a temple for you.'

At this point the *kami* seized hold of the layman Kume Katsutari and deposited him in the branches of a tall tree, thus providing the sign that Muchimaro sought. Muchimaro now understood [that this encounter with Kehi-no-kami] was real and so built a temple for him. The *jingūji* that is now in Echizen Province is this [temple] (Weinstein 1999, paper 3: 12–13).

The term *jingūji* 神宮寺 refers to a Buddhist temple that was built either in the precincts of a shrine or close by, at which daily services – usually the chanting of sūtras – were often performed for the local deity by a 'shrine priest' (*shasō* 社僧 or *gūsō* 宮僧). We meet this interesting title for the first time in the account of the founding of Mirokuji at Usa; it too suggests that Buddhist priests were taking the initiative in the worship of local deities. We do not know for certain, of course, but it may be that *jingūji* actually predate shrine buildings themselves. An entry in *Shoku Nihongi* for 766 tells us of the dispatch of an emissary to arrange for the construction of a sixteen-foot image of the Buddha at the Ise Daijingū, meaning that a *jingūji* had been established in the heart of the ruling family's cult centre.

4.6   Twice a sovereign

The period from the death of Shōmu in 756 to 784, when the decision was made to move the capital away from Nara, was one of constant upheaval. In an unprecedented move, Shōmu had named his daughter as his successor, and on his retirement in 749 she became sovereign as Kōken Tennō 孝謙天皇. As long as her father was alive, she was under no apparent threat, but after Shōmu's death in 756 discontent became openly expressed and she came under pressure from her mother, Kōmyō, who was allied to her nephew, the chief minister, Fujiwara no Nakamaro. She was forced to abdicate in 758 and become a nun, ceding her role to Crown Prince Ōi, who became Junnin Tennō 淳仁天皇. After the death of her mother, however, she reasserted herself and eventually, in 764, seized control again. In this highly unusual second reign (764–70) she took the name Shōtoku Tennō 稱德天皇. One of her first acts was to order the construction of another temple to be called Saidaiji 西大寺, clearly designed to rival her father's monument. Not much is known about this project, except that it made little progress.

It was at this juncture that there occurred one of the more remarkable episodes in Japanese history. In 766, Shōtoku began appointing monks from the Sangha Office to the Council of State and in the process went so far as to promote her personal priest and confidant, a Hossō monk called Dōkyō 道鏡, to the highest post of First Minister and Master of Meditation (Daijō Daijin Zenji 太政大臣禪師), eventually granting him the title of 'Dharma King' (Hōō 法王). The usual interpretation of this relationship is that Dōkyō was planning to take over the succession and create a Buddhist theocracy, and it is true that he was promoted well beyond the dreams of most priests; but whether we should see this as Shōtoku gaining absolute control over the sangha, or as Dōkyō gaining control over the government, is difficult to judge. There are strong echoes here of Empress Wu Zetian, who had also tried to use the wealth and power of Buddhist institutions for her own benefit.

Dōkyō's downfall came when in 769 it became known that an oracle at Usa had proclaimed he should become the next reigning sovereign. Shōtoku was forced to have the matter investigated and Wake no Kiyomaro (733–99) was sent to Usa to investigate. He received a second oracle which claimed that the first one had been a fraud:

Since the establishment of our state the distinction between lord and subject has been fixed. Never has there been an occasion when a subject was made lord. The throne of heavenly sun succession shall be given to one of the royal lineage; wicked persons should immediately be swept away (Bender 1979: 142).

Dōkyō naturally came under suspicion for having engineered the first oracle himself, but he survived a little while longer until Shōtoku's death in 770. Having then lost his patron, he was immediately banished. We shall, of course, never know the truth as to his motives or whether he was the victim of a plot rather than the perpetrator of a plot that went wrong. But why were appeals made to Hachiman in the first place? Why not Ise, for example? Was it because whoever instigated these appeals felt instinctively that Shōtoku and the court would only listen to an authority that had both Buddhist and native credentials and not just the latter? If so, this would suggest that the role played by Ise in the legitimation of monarchy had, at least temporarily, become less significant. Shōtoku was, after all, a serious Buddhist, who had even allowed monks to be present during her Daijōsai rituals (Inoue et al. 2003: 55–56). This view is strengthened when we look at one of her edicts dated 765.11.23.

Today is the day for the Toyonoakari festival as part of the Great Thanksgiving. On this occasion we are faced with an unusual situation, because we have already received the bodhisattva precepts as a student of the Buddha. Therefore first we serve the Three Jewels, next we pay homage to the deities of heaven and earth, and lastly we have returned to rule once more, intent on exercising pity and compassion on imperial princes, our ministers and other servants, and all common people in the realm-under-heaven . . .
There are those who believe that the deities should be kept separate from and be untouched by the Three Jewels; but if one reads the sūtras one discovers that it is the deities who protect and pay homage to the Buddhist Dharma. Surely therefore there should be nothing to stop either those who have become ordained or those who have taken lay orders becoming involved in the worship of such deities. What was originally thought taboo is not taboo and so we hereby order that the Great Thanksgiving Festival be held [as normal] (Aoki et al. 1989–98, vol. IV: 103–05).

This statement could perhaps be seen as a healthy sign that native rites and Buddhist rites were being considered as essentially one and the same thing, but in fact it reads more like a piece of sophistry, with Shōtoku riding roughshod over complaints and assigning priority to Buddhism; the deities were, after all, seen to be 'paying homage' to the Buddhist Dharma. In the end, we do not have enough information to decide whether Japan was in danger of becoming a state run by the Sangha Office or not at this point, but this edict suggests that, at the very least, the deities were being given a secondary role.

There is one other event in Shōtoku's reign about which we do not know as much as we might like. *Shoku Nihongi* has the following entry for 770.4.26:

After the uprising of the eighth year [of Tenpyō-hōji, i.e. 764] had been put down, the sovereign took a vow and ordered the construction of one million small three-storeyed pagodas, each 4 *sun* 5 *bu* [*c*.13.5 cm] in height and 3 *sun* 5 *bu* [*c*.10.5 cm] in diameter, each containing one of the following dhāraṇī: Konpon, Jishin, Sōrin and Rokudo in the base. Once this had all been done, they were distributed among the various temples. The officials and artisans, one hundred and fifty-seven in all, were rewarded according to station (Aoki et al. 1989–98, vol. IV: 281).

This somewhat laconic statement refers to a project that, if it had been completed, would have been another monumental achievement. As it is, some 40,000 of these small pagodas survive today. Shōtoku was trying to go well beyond Shōmu in the attempt to prove herself as bodhisattva-queen. What the entry hides is the momentous fact that these dhāraṇī spells were not written (how could they be if such numbers were planned?) but actually printed on small pieces of paper. This makes those that survive among the oldest printed items in existence. Was this simply an inability to realise the significance of the arrival of a new technique that was to change the world? Or do we put this silence down to Shōtoku's enemies, perhaps unwilling to give her the credit for such an enterprise?

With Shōtoku out of the way in 770 there was an immediate reaction against any further intrusion of Buddhism into the life and rituals of the monarch, by far the strongest reaction we have seen since the initial rejection of Buddhism in the mid-sixth century. Just before she died, Shōtoku was forced to name as her successor a distant cousin, the 62-year-old Kōnin 光仁 (r. 770–81), at which point the succession switched back to descendants not of Tenmu but of Tenji. Under Kōnin and in the early years of the reign of his son Kanmu 桓武 (r. 781–806), affairs were more or less run by Ōnakatomi no Kiyomaro 大中臣清麻呂 (702–88), who was both head of the Jingikan and Minister of the Right. He sacked the administrative head of the Ise shrines, replacing him with his own nephew, and he gave himself the new post of *saishu* 祭主, to ensure that rituals at Ise were kept under strict control. Orders were given to remove the Ise *jingūji* that had been built by Dōkyō in 766 and the whole area was cleansed of Buddhist presence. It is at this time that taboos against Buddhist vocabulary were established at Ise and Kamo, and during certain court rituals that involved the monarch, in what is now recognised as the first example of an official attempt by one particular group to produce clear water between Buddhism and *jingi* worship. One might even be tempted to talk here of the birth of the kind of self-conscious native tradition that now goes by the name Shintō 神道, were it not for the fact that the measures were confined to the monarch and to Ise. Elsewhere interaction continued apace, and even at Ise it was not long before Buddhism came to make its presence felt once again.

It was, of course, Kanmu who decided to move the capital away from Nara, first to Nagaoka 長岡 and then to Heian-kyō 平安京. Unrest continued throughout the period and Kanmu, in particular, had some difficult years at the beginning of his reign with constant fighting in the northeast of the country. It is sometimes claimed that he was at loggerheads with the Buddhist establishment and that this was why he decided to move the capital north to escape their influence, but this is most unlikely. The move, when it came, had more to do with Kanmu (being a descendant of Tenji) wishing to finally distance the monarchy from the Tenmu line, which was so clearly identified with Nara and had its home and its sacred spaces in Yamato (Toby 1985). Kanmu was not particularly anti-Buddhist, but he did feel the need to revive the kind of strict controls that we find in the *Regulations for members of the sangha*. In 783–84 the gifting of land to temples was banned, and the prohibition on simply 'initiating' people in the provinces without recourse to the Sangha Office was reinforced. A large number of these 'monks' were forcibly returned to lay life, particularly if they were found to have families of their own, and emphasis was placed on the meditational duties of priests in order to try and depoliticise their activities. In 798 an age restriction of thirty-five was imposed and candidates were required to sit a test and pass five out of ten topics set. In 801 a distinction between Sanron and Hossō monks was made and in 803 both traditions were allotted five monks each. Here we have the real beginning of the *nenbun dosha* quota system, fixing the number of ordinands initially at ten per year.

4.7   Buddhist scholarship

The constant refrain one finds in official documents bewailing low standards among members of the sangha was based on a general concern that priests were simply lazy and wasting their time, and on a more specific worry that an inability to read sūtras would interfer with their prime function: recitation for the protection of the state. As it happens, it is not difficult to learn how to recite in rote fashion from a text one does not really understand, and there is a quantum leap from this to being able to read Buddhist scholarly treatises and explain doctrine. Leaving aside the commentaries ascribed to Prince Shōtoku for a moment, it is only in the latter half of the eighth century that we begin to encounter this level of learning. Perhaps we can also now begin to talk of monks living in monastic institutions. Up to this point we have used the term 'priests' because it is likely that their primary role was of worship and ritual, but there now developed what had been there from the beginning in India: groups of men and women living in celibate communities apart from the rest of society, devoted to meditation and the study of texts, and occupying what we might legitimately think of as a monastery rather than a temple.

One commonly encounters the term 'Nara rokushū' 奈良六宗, first used in 760. It is sometimes translated as 'the six Nara schools' or even 'the six Nara sects', but this is misleading: in some contexts the word 'seminar' is more appropriate; in others 'tradition'. Certainly, in the beginning, the term *shū* was written not with the character 宗, which can have a sectarian flavour, but with 衆, which simply meant '(study) group'. By and large, the title of a seminar referred to the name of the sūtra or treatise studied. It was natural for certain monks to specialise in certain texts, and it should therefore come as no surprise to find that some temples became known for the study of one particular tradition rather than another; but there was nothing particularly exclusive about the arrangements. Tōdaiji, for example, as the hub of the whole system, was home to all six seminars. Here we shall introduce all six in outline. The object is not to discuss Buddhist philosophy in detail (which is beyond the scope of this history) but merely to illustrate the kind of concepts that were occupying the minds of scholar-monks. All except one of these traditions were of Indian origin.

Ritsu 律 was the study of the *vinaya*. This became a recognised tradition of scholarship with the arrival of Jianzhen and the building of Tōshōdaiji. As a seperate tradition, however, it did not survive past the end of the Nara period and had to be revived in a rather different guise in the twelfth century.

Kusha 俱舍 was the study of Vasubandhu's important work *Abhidharma-kośa* (Jp. *Abidatsuma kusharon* 阿毘達磨俱舍論),[17] an epistemological analysis of being, which formed the bedrock for an understanding of how Buddhists viewed the world. It covered such fundamental topics as the distinction between absolute and conventional truth, and the Four Noble Truths. These were, firstly, that existence is defined as suffering; secondly, that the cause of suffering is our insatiable thirst for life, which inevitably leads to rebirth; thirdly, that in order to eradicate suffering one must eradicate the thirst and aim to reach that state of perfect liberation from desire known as nirvāṇa; and fourthly, that the way to achieve this is to follow what is known as the Eightfold Noble Path: right views (seeing the world as it really is) and right intention, both of which have to do with wisdom (Sk. *prajñā*); right speech, right action and right livelihood, which have to do with conduct

[17] *T.* 1558–59. This was first translated into Chinese by Paramārtha in the mid-sixth century, although the Japanese used Xuanzang's seventh-century version.

(Sk. *śīla*); right effort, right mindfulness and right concentration, which have to do with meditation (Sk. *samādhi*).

Then there is the doctrine of non-self (Sk. *anātman*, Jp. *muga* 無我). There is no such thing as a permanent self and it is precisely because we cling to the idea of such an unchanging core that we experience suffering. Body and mind are analysed into five aggregates (Sk. *pañca-skandha*, Jp. *goun* 五蘊): form (Sk. *rūpa*, Jp. *shikiun* 色蘊), sensation (Sk. *vedanā*, Jp. *juun* 受蘊), perception (Sk. *saṃjñā*, Jp. *sōun* 想蘊), mental formations (Sk. *saṃskāra*, Jp. *gyōun* 行蘊) and consciousness (Sk. *vijñāna*, Jp. *shikiun* 識蘊). The self that we think we experience is nothing but a cluster of these aggregates, a grouping of mental and physical elements known as dharmas (Jp. *hō* 法), all of which are in constant flux. The categories of 'form' and 'mental formations' are in their turn subdivided into yet further dharmas. A person has no core entity, being nothing more than a set of events and elements that are causally connected over time. I am not as I was a moment ago, but neither am I a random cluster. Death is simply another event in this continuing flux. As with the person, so with the world: all objects are also made up of conditioned, transitory dharmas. Nothing is permanent. Only three dharmas exist that were considered unconditioned and hence permanent: space, the state of nirvāṇa achieved through 'analytical cessation', and the same state achieved via 'non-analytical cessation'. The fact that a dharma is conditioned does not make it any the less real. Dharmas come into existence through the law of dependent origination (Sk. *pratītyasamutpāda*, Jp. *engi* 緣起), which is analysed as a chain with twelve links. Everything is mutually conditioned, everything dependent on a cause and itself the cause of something else. So every dharma has its own set of connections, both temporal and spatial, that form its dharma-realm (Sk. *dharmadhātu*, Jp. *hokkai* 法界), although since dharmas come and go on the instant this means that everything is interconnected with everything else in unimaginable complexity.

Jōjitsu 成實 was the study of Harivarman's *Establishing the truth* (Sk. *Satyasiddhi śāstra*, Jp. *Jōjitsuron* 成實論, *T.* 1646). This was critical of the *Abhidharmakośa*, precisely because although it explained the emptiness of the self, it did not extend this to dharmas themselves, seeing them as real. The study of this text did not survive as an independent tradition past the end of the eighth century, at which point it was subsumed in what follows.

Sanron 三論 was so called because it was based on three works: the *Root verses on the middle* (Sk. *Mūlamadhyamakakārikā*, Jp. *Chūron*, 中論, *T.* 1564); the *Treatise in one hundred verses* (Jp. *Hyakuron*, 百論, *T.* 1569); and the *Twelve approaches* (Jp. *Jūnimonron*, 十二門論, *T.* 1568). This was essentially Indian Madhyamaka thought, which denied that anything, including dharmas, could have inherent existence. They were constantly changing in response to conditions and so must also in the ultimate analysis be characterised by emptiness. Emptiness is not, however, nothingness; it simply means that a dharma lacks a permanent, unchanging core; it is but the temporary sum of all that has brought it into being. And since emptiness is also a characteristic of nirvāṇa, it follows that according to absolute rather than conventional truth, conditioned existence, saṃsāra, must be the same as nirvāṇa. Sanron as a separate seminar did not survive the Nara period, but the study of these works was essential for anyone interested in Mahāyāna doctrine and it continued to form part of the training of all serious scholars.

Hossō 法相 (the name means 'characteristics of dharmas') developed out of the Indian Yogācāra tradition. It took matters a stage further and made explicit what Sanron had implied, namely that if all dharmas are empty then they can only be the product of mind. It accepted that all dharmas are characterised by emptiness and without innate existence, but it was more interested in the question of why we see things as we do. How does our consciousness work to produce the illusions it does? Such an analysis would presumably bring us closer to understanding how enlightenment could be achieved. Hossō based itself on the assumption that the objective external world is nothing but a fabrication of our own consciousness, which, because we are ignorant of the truth, produces representations of externality and gives rise to the illusion that both self and other exist. Objects do not have independent existence apart from the perceiving mind, but because of the way human consciousness works, perception continually causes us to posit real objects and (the illusion) of a perceiving self. Since existing as a human involves us in a continual flow of ever-changing perceptions, we are continually inventing for ourselves objects of desire, which, of course, lead to attachment and suffering.

Hossō starts its analysis by categorising the countless dharmas of existence into a hundred types, beginning, as we might expect, with the dharmas of mind. Eight forms of consciousness are distinguished: hearing, smell, taste, feeling, mental cognition, the defiled mind (*kliṣṭa-manas*), in which the consciousness of ego resides, and lastly the *ālaya vijñāna* or Store Consciousness (Jp. *arayashiki* 阿頼耶識), where the illusions are generated.

The mind in its active capacity, for example as intention, instigates the performance of intentional deeds (Sk. *karma*). These deeds, once performed, leave traces or consequences which are said to redound to the mind, now in its sustaining capacity as mental continuum or store-consciousness of each sentient being. Specifically, the traces of acts enter the *ālaya* by way of 'impregnation' or 'suffusion' (Sk. *vāsanā*, Jp. *kunjū* 薫習) and are thus regarded as the implanted 'seeds' (Sk. *bīja*, Jp. *shuji* 種子) of future conscious acts. The 'seeds' planted from without by the active mind mingle with the 'innate seeds' (this is a matter of some sectarian dispute) and all proceed to influence each other according to their respective moral species as pure, impure, or neutral. Eventually this process of mutual influence (again *vāsanā*) brings about the fructification or maturation (Sk. *vipāka*, Jp. *kahō* 果報) of the seeds in the form of new mental phenomena. This 'biogenetic' model of the mind serves, among other purposes, that of explaining dependent origination by showing how there can be retribution for acts when there is no personal agent or self to whom those acts might be charged (Gimello 1976: 234).

In this sense, the Store Consciousness constitutes our whole experience and ensures that the illusion of a dichotomy between self and other will continue. If this were all, of course, then there would be no way out and enlightenment would be impossible. But the Store Consciousness, which accounts for a person's continuity through the cycle of birth, death and rebirth, does contain pure 'seeds', some of them innate, which can be germinated through the practice of meditation, right thought, and a determination to see beyond the idea of self and other; the nurture of these seeds involves many acts of compassion and will take aeons to bring to completion. Hossō also posits a hierarchy of three aspects of human perception and understanding: the imagined, the dependent and the perfected.

A favourite analogy of Yogācāra thinkers is that of the mirage. The water that appears before the eyes of the parched desert traveller, for example, does not really exist; it is only *imagined*. Nevertheless the appearance or visual idea of water does exist; it exists *in dependence upon* the traveller's imperfect faculties of perception and his wishful, projective thoughts. When the traveller has realized that in the vision of water there is actually no water, then he has 'emptied' the mirage of own-being and seen the fact or truth of the matter to *perfection* (Gimello 1976: 248).

Once all the seeds in the store are pure, a fundamental transformation (*āśraya-parāvṛtti*) occurs within the defiled mind, the Store Consciousness stops generating illusions, and the opposition of self and other disappears. This is the onset of enlightenment.

The emergence and survival of Hossō as an independent tradition in Japan was the result of historical accident and is an interesting example of the vagaries of transmission. Its parent, known in Chinese as Faxiang 法相, was based not on earlier translations of Yogācāra treatises by Paramārtha (Zhendi 眞諦, 499–569), but on those produced a little later by Xuanzang 玄奘 (*c*.596–664). Xuanzang is, of course, famous for the journey he made to India and back and for the sheer number of translations he produced. The reason for preference being shown to Xuanzang's interpretations owed more to imperial patronage for the man himself than to anything else. In China the Faxiang tradition itself was not to survive the Anlushan rebellion of 755–57, but survive it did in Japan, partly because of Fujiwara patronage and partly, no doubt, because of the sophistication of its doctrines. Hossō texts were initially brought to Japan by Dōshō, who settled at Gangōji, but Genbō had also studied in this tradition and such was the influence of the Fujiwara that Kōfukuji eventually won pre-eminence for this area of scholarship.

One unorthodox element that seems to have been transmitted to Japan as part of Hossō doctrine was the idea that there was a particular class of beings (Jp. *shushō* 種姓), known as *icchantika* (Jp. *issendai* 一闡提) or incorrigibles, who, because of the type of innate seeds lying in their store consciousness, would never be able to achieve enlightenment no matter how hard they strived. This ran counter to the more inclusive Mahāyāna universalism and caused considerable controversy. It is not clear whether this theory came from Xuanzang's experience in India or from some other source, but the fact that it remained a central tenet of Japanese Hossō was perhaps not unrelated to the aristocratic nature of its Fujiwara patrons. Although there must have been a number of monks who felt rather uncomfortable with the ramifications of such overt discrimination, the term *shushō* has strong overtones of status being defined by one's birth.

The *Kegon* (Ch. Huayan 華嚴) tradition is the only one to take its name from a sūtra, the vast *Flower garland sūtra*. There were two full translations into Chinese: the first in sixty volumes by Buddhabhadra, and the second in eighty volumes by Śikṣānanda. The sūtra itself is a collection of texts from different traditions and different periods, some of which, such as the *Daśabhumika* (Jp. *Jūjikyō* 十地經) and the *Gaṇḍavyūha* (Jp. *Nyūhokkaibon* 入法界品) existed as works in their own right, in both India and China. These texts were grouped together under the general theme of man's quest for enlightenment. Perhaps best thought of as a presentation of the universe through the eyes of someone already enlightened, a bodhisattva, the sūtra consists of a series of long sermons. There are eight grand assemblies (會), two on earth, four in the realm of desire, and the last two back on earth. Vairocana is present throughout but does not speak, only emitting light occasionally from different parts of his body at various stages. The long progress of the candidate for buddhahood towards final enlightenment passes through five stages (位).

The philosophy that emerges is a complex one, treated by many as the crowning glory of Chinese thought. The central figures are, therefore, all Chinese: Dushun 杜順 (557–640), Zhiyan 智儼 (602–68), Fazang 法藏 (643–712) and, later, Zongmi 宗密 (780–841). It marks the maturation of a process by which the Chinese made Buddhism their own, often analysed as a Chinese response to Madhyamaka and Yogācāra thought. It is not a commentary on the sūtra so much as a complex analysis of the process towards, and experience of, enlightenment that takes the journey and the vision illustrated in the sūtra as its starting point.

This sinification of Buddhism began with Dushun, who started with the traditional terms 'emptiness' (Sk. *śūnyatā*, Jp. *kū* 空) and 'form' (Sk. *rūpa*, Jp. *shiki* 色), but shifted to 'principle' (Jp. *ri* 理) and 'phenomenon' (Jp. *ji* 事). He proposed three 'discernments' 觀 or meditational stances that would eventually lead to enlightenment: firstly, the 'discernment of true emptiness' 眞空觀, which was the straightforward Mahāyāna view that there is no such thing as an unconditioned dharma; secondly, the 'discernment of the mutual non-obstruction of principle and phenomena' 理事無礙觀, which marks the change in terminology; and lastly, the 'discernment of the total pervasion and inclusion' 周遍含容觀, which reinvests phenomenal reality with significance. This is seen as a necessary procedure if the paradox of the bodhisattva, enlightened yet still present in this world, is to be explained.

The replacement of 'emptiness' by 'principle' signals an important step in the direction of evolving a more affirmative discourse . . . The second discernment elucidates various ways in which phenomena and principle interrelate. Because they instantiate principle, all phenomena are thereby validated. This positive valuation of the phenomenal world culminates in the third discernment, that of total pervasion and inclusion. With this final discernment principle itself is ultimately transcended, and one enters the world of total interpenetration for which the Huayan tradition is justly famous. Each and every phenomenon is not only seen to contain each and every other phenomenon, but all phenomena are also seen to contain the totality of the unobstructed interpenetration of all phenomena' (Gregory 1991: 7).

The cosmos that is discerned in this third phase is the Dharma Realm, the ultimate absolute nature of the universe, identified with the Dharma Body (Sk. *dharmakāya*, Jp. *hosshin* 法身), the body and mind of the Buddha Vairocana.

Dushun's initial analysis was later recast in terms of four approaches, rather than three, the fourth view being particular to Huayan/Kegon. It described the terms in which a Buddha saw the universe.

1 The universe as phenomena (*jihokkai* 事法界): waves on the ocean appear
   to exist in and of themselves.
2 The universe as principle (*rihokkai* 理法界): the ocean appears as water and
   one does not see the waves.
3 The universe as the unimpeded interpenetration of principle and
   phenomena (*riji muge hokkai* 理事無礙法界): one sees the waves and the
   water as at once distinct from each other and as one, dependent on each
   other.
4 The universe as the unimpeded interpenetration of phenomena and
   phenomena (*jiji muge hokkai* 事事無礙法界): this is Indra's net, covered in
   jewels at each knot, each jewel reflecting all the others. All things that exist
   are interdependent, all in one and one in all, the part dependent on the
   whole as the whole is dependent on the part. Everything has in common the
   fact that everything is emptiness, and it is this emptiness that links
   everything in a mutual relationship: the Dharma Realm can be therefore
   defined as pure relationship. The distinction between nirvāṇa and samsāra
   collapses.

Another central element investigated by Huayan/Kegon doctrine was the idea
of Buddha Nature (*busshō* 佛性). We all have within us the potentiality for
buddhahood, that element of pure principle without which we would never
have any aspiration towards becoming enlightened in the first place. This was
also known as the 'Womb of the Buddha' (Sk. *tathāgatagarbha*, Jp. *nyoraizō*
如來藏). Enlightenment can be seen as the fusion of this individual element
with the Dharma Realm.

Part II

From Saichō to the destruction of Tōdaiji
(800–1180)

Plate 15   Shinra Myōjin

This remarkable statue of Shinra Myōjin 新羅明神 from Onjōji 園城寺 is the oldest surviving example of an image of a *gohōjin* 護法神, or protector deity of the Buddhist Dharma. Many of these were native to Japan but a number had continental origins. As his name suggests, this particular deity was from the Korean state of Silla. Onjōji tradition had it that he appeared to the founder and first abbot Enchin 圓珍 (814–91) as he was about to return from China via the northern route along the west coast of the Korean peninsula in 858. On both voyages Enchin used a Sillan vessel. Nothing definite is known of Shinra Myōjin's origins but he may well have been a protector of seafarers. His role expanded at Onjōji as a result of the bitter rivalry with Enryakuji that eventually led to the schism that produced the Sanmon-Jimon groups in the late tenth century (see §7.1). Ennin at Enryakuji had adopted as his protector the Chinese deity Sekizan Myōjin 赤山明神, tutelary deity of Mt Chi in Shandong Province, and when the split occurred Onjōji created its own deity. The first written evidence of Shinran Myōjin is a record of the court granting him senior Fourth Rank upper grade in 971.

Scholarly consensus is that this statue, which as a National Treasure is now kept in the Shinra Zenshindō 善神堂 in the Onjōji compound, was produced about 1052. It was presumably created either on the basis of an iconographical drawing or from memory but no other example of this striking figure survives (Guth 1999).

Chronology

794   Kanmu moves the capital to Heian-kyō.
796   Tōji, Saiji and Kuramadera established.
797   Kūkai composes *Sangō Shiiki*. *Shoku Nihongi* finished.
798   Kiyomizudera founded.
800   Mt Fuji erupts.
804   Saichō and Kūkai travel to Tang China.
805   Saichō returns.
806   Kūkai returns. Kanmu dies and Heizei becomes new sovereign.
809   Heizei deposed and Saga becomes sovereign.
822   The Shingon'in is set up at Tōdaiji. Saichō dies.
835   Kūkai dies.
838   Ennin travels to China.
847   Ennin returns.
858   Enchin returns.
860   Iwashimizu Hachiman miyadera established.
901   Sugawara no Michizane banished to Daizaifu.
907   Tang Dynasty collapses.
914   Miyoshi Kiyoyuki composes *Iken jūnikajō*.
924   First rites held for Shinra Myōjin on Hieizan.
927   *Engishiki* presented to the throne.
938   Kōya starts his activities in the capital. Taira no Masakado rebels.
948   Kitano shrine established in honour of Michizane.
966   Ryōgen made Tendai abbot.
974   *Kagerō nikki* written about this time.
983   Chōnen travels to Song China.
985   Ryōgen dies. Genshin's *Ōjō yōshū* completed.
1003   Jakushō travels to China.
1007   Michinaga makes a pilgrimage to Kinpusen.
1010   *Genji monogatari* started about this time.
1017   Genshin dies.
1023   Michinaga makes a pilgrimage to Kōyasan.
1027   Michinaga dies.
1052   Byōdōin established at Uji by Yorimichi. Traditionally, beginning of *mappō*.
1072   Jōjin travels to Song China.
1081   Dispute breaks out between Enryakuji and Onjōji.
1086   Shirakawa abdicates and Insei period begins.
1090   Shirakawa's first pilgrimage to Kumano.
1095   Monks from Enryakuji bring the Hie palanquin to the capital.
1102   Tōdaiji and Kōfukuji in conflict.
1113   Monks from Enryakuji and Kōfukuji in conflict.

1126 Golden Hall dedicated at Chūsonji.
1131 Kakuban requests permission to establish the Daidenpōin.
1140 Monks from Enryakuji burn down sections of Onjōji. Saigyō becomes a monk. Kakuban moves to Negoro.
1143 Kakuban dies.
1156 Hōgen Disturbance.
1158 Go-Shirakawa begins his rule as retired sovereign.
1159 Heiji Disturbance.
1160 Disturbances on Hieizan. Enryakuji monks invade the capital. Minamoto no Yoritomo (aged fourteen) escapes to the Kantō.
1163 Monks from Enryakuji burn sections of Onjōji.
1164 The *Heike nōkyō* produced.
1165 Continued disturbances.
1168 Eisai travels to Song China and returns with Chōgen.
1173 Monks from Kōfukuji burn Tōnomine.
1175 Hōnen leaves Hieizan and begins his proselytising.
1178 Taira no Kiyomori defends scholar-monks in Enryakuji against worker-monks.
1180 Tōdaiji and Kōfukuji destroyed.

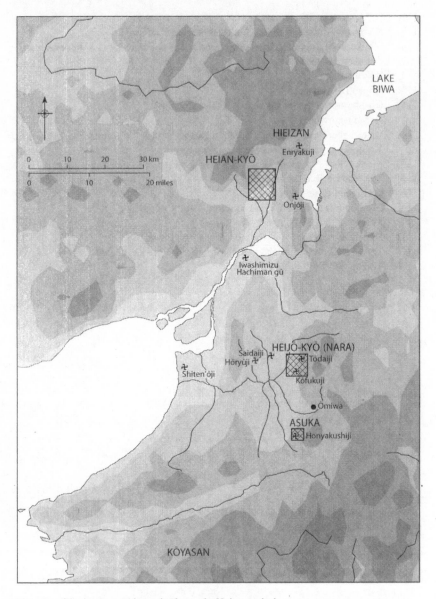

Map 4   The home provinces in the early Heian period

5   The beginnings of a 'Japanese' Buddhism: Tendai

5.1   The situation in 800

The writing of a historical narrative such as this is, of course, governed by the nature and quantity of available sources, many of which are narratives in their own right with their own agendas. Such accounts can in their turn become causes for subsequent developments, immutable parts of history with their own dynamic, so that even though one might wish to rewrite them, they cannot be ignored. Given the importance of lineage in the transmission of Buddhist teachings, Buddhist histories tend to be a series of hagiographies of charismatic monks (*kōsōden* 高僧傳). No matter how firm one's resolve might be to escape the idea that 'great individuals make history', it is difficult to avoid in such a context, since the narratives themselves and their influence form a large part of the object of study. It is with this caveat in mind that we shall approach the early Heian period through two remarkable individuals: Saichō 最澄 and Kūkai 空海. Between them, these men set the parameters that have governed the development of Japanese Buddhism ever since.

Up to this point, the process had been one of slow absorption over a period of some two centuries. There were, of course, local peculiarities, but by and large the pattern differed little from that prefigured in Korea: the introduction of a powerful new deity, or set of deities, duly appropriated by the ruling class for its own purposes. Initially the vector was visual, an impressive array of sculpture, painting and architecture, only gradually augmented by the written word; and the doctrines of personal liberation and salvation that were contained in these writings were, for the most part, hidden from all but the literate few. In contrast to China, where Buddhism encountered a number of sophisticated conceptual systems from the outset, local Japanese cults were of a very different order and could offer little philosophical resistance. Of course, the understanding of Buddhism in Asuka and Nara was governed by native concerns and interests, and in this sense Buddhism in Japan was always going to be different from anywhere else, but it was essentially an instinctive rather than an intellectual response to an external stimulus. With the emergence of Saichō and Kūkai, however, we enter a very different phase: the beginnings of what can truly be called a 'Japanese' Buddhism. This new development had much to do with the situation as it was developing on the continent.

In 676 Silla 新羅 succeeded in unifying the southern part of the Korean peninsula and was to hold this unified state together until about 889. To the northwest lay the large state of Parhae 渤海 (Jp. Bokkai), which had been founded by defeated remnants of Koguryŏ in 698 and continued to control a large swathe of Manchuria until falling to the Khitan invasions of 926. Parhae sent regular missions to the Japanese court in the early Heian period, but it is doubtful whether anything significant in terms of Buddhist influence travelled this route. Silla, on the other hand, became a major centre for Buddhism during the late seventh and eighth centuries, producing such men as Wŏnhyo 元曉 (617–86), Chajang 慈藏 (fl. 636–45), Ŭisang 義湘 (625–702) and Wŏnchŭk 圓測 (613–96). Even so, the country that the Japanese were most interested in was China, and it was to the various Buddhist centres there that Japanese monks preferred to go and study. The irony is that Buddhism was never entirely safe in China. Although it flourished in the reigns of Empress Wu (r. 684–705) and Emperor Xuánzong 玄宗 (r. 712–56), Buddhist scholarship was dealt a heavy blow in the Anlushan 安祿山 rebellion of 755–57.

The inevitable destruction of monasteries that resulted from seven years of warfare in the area meant not only the loss of buildings, which in better times could have been replaced, but also a disruption in scholarly traditions, which had far-reaching implications for the subsequent development of Buddhism in China. Many of the most significant Buddhist commentaries and treatises produced in the first half of the T'ang disappeared after An Lu-shan – although it should be noted that they were often preserved in Korea and Japan. Even such a doctrinally important school as the Fa-hsiang with its voluminous literature vanished with hardly a trace after the An Lu-shan rebellion, only to survive in Japan with its elaborate doctrinal system intact (Weinstein 1987: 61–62).

Under Daizong 代宗 (r. 762–79) there was vast expenditure on rebuilding monasteries and a concomitant concern about taxes and rampant abuse of the habit of selling ordination certificates. This led to less enthusiasm for Buddhist institutions on the part of his successor, Dezong 德宗 (r. 779–805), although he gained a reputation as a devout Buddhist near the end of his reign and authorised the establishment of the Institute for the Translation of

Buddhist Scriptures (Yijingyuan 譯經院) in 788. Xianzong 憲宗 (r. 805–20) was also a strong promoter of Buddhism, despite continued worries about its undue wealth and the deleterious effect of allowing unofficial ordinations, and it was indeed his activities that led to the famous complaint of 819 written by the Confucian scholar Hanyu 韓愈 against the emperor's reverence for a finger-bone relic of the Buddha. Buddhism finally came under sustained attack, however, in 835 when Emperor Wenzong 文宗 (r. 827–40) started a major purge of the whole institution, calling for severe discipline to be reintroduced. The *coup de grâce* came during the reign of Wuzong 武宗 (r. 840–46) in what became known as the Huichang suppression 會昌法難, which included wholesale destruction of temples and libraries, the forced laicisation of tens of thousands of monks, and reported massacres. We know a good deal about the events of these years from the diary of the Japanese monk Ennin 圓仁 (793–864), who travelled in China from 838 to 847 and witnessed much of the distress of those years (Reischauer 1955a and b). Buddhism would, of course, survive in China, but the effect on Japanese monks of this single-minded repression must have been profound. Although it would be going too far to say that China lost its role as the fount of Buddhist knowledge and practice at this point, Japanese Buddhists certainly began to feel a stronger sense of their own worth and their own abilities.

5.2 Saichō

Saichō was born in 767 and died in 822. At the age of twelve he was sent to the *kokubunji* at Ōmi to study with the monk Gyōhyō 行表 (722–97) who had himself studied under Daoxuán. At the age of fourteen he became a novice and at nineteen he went to Nara to study for ordination at Tōdaiji. It is known that during these years Gyōhyō introduced him to a wide range of Buddhist doctrines, including Kegon and Hossō texts. Having completed the required study of the 250 rules, Saichō left Nara and went north to the mountain known as Hieizan, which overlooked Lake Biwa to the east. This was a rather unusual step to take. Whether there was already a temple there is not known, but the living conditions must have been very harsh, and it suggests that he took his training extremely seriously, preferring the rigours of mountain asceticism to any advancement within the Buddhist hierarchy. Certainly, anyone who wanted to make their mark politically would have remained in Nara. Life on the mountain seems to have been divided between long stretches of meditation practice and further study, and it was during this time that he first encountered reference to the Tiantai doctrinal tradition. He then managed to obtain from Nara copies of the major works of the founder of this tradition, Zhiyi 智顗 (538–97): the *Profound meaning of the Lotus sūtra* (Jp. *Hokke gengi* 法華玄義); the *Words and phrases in the Lotus sūtra* (Jp. *Hokke mongu* 法華文句), a phrase-by-phrase explanation of the text; and *Mahāyāna calming and contemplation* (Jp. *Maka shikan* 摩訶止觀), a treatise on the meditational techniques considered necessary to achieve enlightenment.[1] These texts had in fact been brought to Japan only thirty years previously by Jianzhen but had remained largely unstudied until Saichō came across them. What really triggered his interest is not known. By 788 Saichō had managed to have a small hall dedicated to Yakushi built on the mountain, and in 793 this was renamed the One-Vehicle Calming and Contemplation Hall (Ichijō shikan'in 一乗止観院), a direct reference to Tiantai doctrine.

In choosing Hieizan Saichō was either prescient or extremely lucky, because when the new capital was established at Heian-kyō, Hieizan found itself guarding the northeast approaches, a direction that was considered to be particularly prone to evil influences. It is likely that it was Saichō's continued presence on the mountain that drew him to the attention of the court and Kanmu Tennō. In 797 he was appointed *naigubu* (内供奉), the title given to those monks who served in the palace itself.[2] By 801 Saichō was becoming known for his learning and his views on the pre-eminence of the *Lotus sūtra*, for in that year he persuaded ten monks to come from Nara to participate in a series of lectures that he had initiated in 798. The next year, 802, he was invited to participate in some seminars on Zhiyi's works held at Takaosanji 高尾山寺 to the northwest of the new capital. Partly as a result of his performances on these occasions, he was granted permission to accompany a mission that was on the point of leaving for China; he was to study Tiantai further and bring back more accurate texts. He was also allowed to take with him the novice Gishin 義眞 (781–833), who is said to have studied some colloquial Chinese at Tōdaiji.

Missions such as these were few and far between, being both costly and extremely dangerous, and over twenty years had passed since the return of the last expedition. Preparations began in 801, but the four ships involved were not ready until 803 and they ran into bad weather even before they had left the Inland Sea: three were heavily damaged and the fourth one (carrying Saichō) limped on to Kyūshū to await instructions (Borgen 1982). Eventually

---

[1]   Ch. *Fahua xuanyi, T.* 1716; Ch. *Fahua wenju, T.* 1718; Ch. *Mohe zhiguan, T.* 1911.
[2]   Originally ten such priests were appointed and so they were also known as the ten meditation masters (*jūzenji* 十禪師). See Groner 1984: 31.

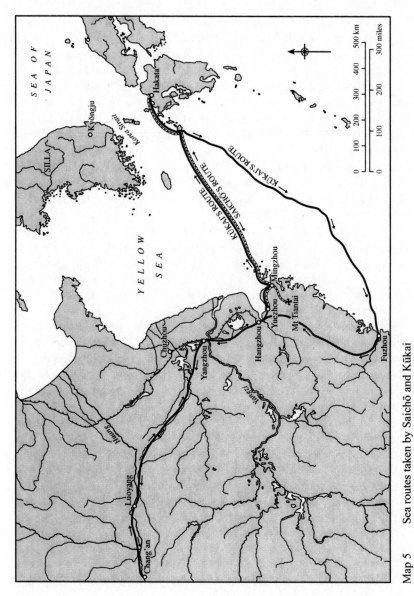

Map 5   Sea routes taken by Saichō and Kūkai

all four ships left from Tanoura 田浦 in the seventh month of 804. Unfortunately this was the worst time to sail: not only was it the typhoon season but Japanese ships lacked the keels that would have helped them run against the prevailing westerlies. Two of the four ships were forced to turn back. Saichō's ship managed to reach Mingzhou 明州 on the first day of the ninth month [map 5]. The official mission left immediately for the capital at Chang'an 長安, but Saichō headed southwest to Mt Tiantai 天臺山, where he arrived on 804.9.26. He was treated well, met the governor and obtained an introduction to Daosui 道邃, who had studied under Zhanran 湛然 (711–82), the second most important master of the tradition; it is from Daosui that Saichō claimed to have received personal instruction and certification. On 804.10.13 he is said to have received a transmission of the Ox Head tradition of Chan at the Chanlinsi 禪林寺[3] and an esoteric initiation known as the Rite of the Buddha's Pate (Jp. Dai Butchō hō 大佛頂法) at the Guoqingsi 國清寺. 'Transmission' in this context probably meant little more than learning a technique or ritual from a master, but to be able to claim such an experience was crucial to all who went to China. The legitimacy thus obtained was priceless and well worth the dangers of travel, especially if some sort of certification could be produced.

Saichō spent his time on Mt Tiantai studying and arranging for a large number of works to be copied (he returned with about 230), including the *Tantra of wondrous attainments* (Jp. *Soshitchikara kyō* 蘇悉地羯羅經),[4] a tantric text that would later be of considerable importance. In 805.3.2 he and his companion Gishin were formally acknowledged as monks of the Tiantai tradition. Both men then returned to Mingzhou, where they found that the mission was not scheduled to leave for another month and a half. Saichō took the opportunity to visit two temples in nearby Yuezhou 越州, where both he and Gishin received further esoteric transmissions.[5] Saichō then returned with the main mission in the fifth month of 805 and was back in Japan within two months. His stay had been less than nine months in total.

It is clear from Saichō's experience that a wide variety of doctrines and practices were available both on Mt Tiantai itself and at temples in the

---

[3]   See more on this tradition in §13.1. Having the patronage of Kanmu, Saichō had been given plenty of expenses for his journey. Part of the allowance was spent on a building in the Chanlinsi intended to serve as quarters for the Japanese students who would follow. It was destroyed in the Huichang suppression of 845 but rebuilt by Enchin at the Guoqingsi with funds supplied by Fujiwara no Yoshisuke 藤原良相. Groner 1984: 64.

[4]   Sk. *Susiddhikaratantra*, Ch. *Suxidi jieluo jing*, *T.* 893.

[5]   On the vexed question of precisely which transmissions were received, see Groner 1984: 52–63, and on the question of the authenticity of certain key certificates, see Chen 1998.

vicinity, and that he made full use of this eclectic mixture. Although Chang'an was the main centre for tantric Buddhism, such practice had spread widely in China by this time and, given the interest of early Japanese Buddhism in spells, rites and their effects, it is only natural that Saichō should pay it particular attention. The point here is that what we shall later describe as the tantricisation of Japanese Tendai in the tenth century was merely an extension of earlier concerns and not something out of character. Saichō was initiated into a number of different rituals and maṇḍalas. Their exact nature was to become a matter of great controversy later when Kūkai's followers tried to stigmatise Saichō's experience as inferior and muddled compared with Kūkai's inheritance of the 'true' tradition. And, as we shall see, the matter is made even more complicated since Saichō himself received instruction from Kūkai after the latter's return to Japan.

5.3   The Tiantai tradition

What is meant by the term 'Tiantai tradition' 天臺宗 and what did it signify at this juncture? The name is that of the mountain southeast of the city of Hangzhou 杭州 in Zhejiang Province, where a monastic centre had been established by Zhiyi in 575. The teachings became associated with this mountain complex and with the Guoqingsi 國清寺 that was built in memory of the master in 601. But this link should not blind us to the fact that the tradition was widespread and taught at many other centres, perhaps the most important being the Yuquansi 玉泉寺 near Qingzhou 清州 (Hubei Province), founded by Zhiyi in 593, which became known for its eclecticism and in particular for its interest in tantric ritual. It is here, for example, that the tantric master Yixing 一行 (683–727) is said to have studied Tiantai, and the kind of rituals that Saichō found at Mt Tiantai may well have had their beginnings at Yuquansi (Groner 1984: 51; Penkower 1993: 191–93).

Tiantai was the earliest of the three great traditions to emerge in the sixth and seventh centuries (Faxiang and Huayan being the other two), and it wrought a fundamental change in Chinese Buddhism, marking a shift away from the kind of translation and exegesis that had been driven mainly by a desire to understand correctly the writings of the Indian masters towards a Buddhism more in tune with Chinese attitudes, thought and habits. Numerous sūtras were studied and interpreted in ways that went far beyond a literal appreciation of their content; as we have already seen in the case of the *Flower garland sūtra*, they were used as springboards for philosophical speculation. To a large extent this can be put down to the nature of the sūtras themselves, which tended to be illustrative and discursive rather than theoretical or argumentative, open texts that invited the kind of commentary that lay claim to a discovery of an underlying meaning. In the course of the Tang, these three traditions influenced each other greatly, but they had very different functions and interests. One might describe Faxiang 法相 as a highly specialised scholarly tradition that analysed the mechanisms of human consciousness; and it was so closely tied to the fortunes of the translator Xuanzang that it failed to survive the Huichang suppression. Huayan 華嚴 was a highly speculative philosophical inquiry into the nature of enlightenment and the path of the bodhisattva. Tiantai was something rather wider in scope, a movement which tried to be as inclusive as possible, bringing some semblance of order to the Buddha's teachings, interesting itself in intensely practical matters such as how to meditate, and, above all, breaking down the barriers between monk and layman by stressing the possibility of enlightenment for all.

Tiantai teachings were not actively supported by the early Tang rulers, who may well have found it difficult to give support to a community that had been closely involved with a ruling family they had just overthrown (Weinstein 1973). When they were not actively putting Buddhism under pressure and supporting Daoism, they showed more interest in supporting Xuanzang and the Faxiang tradition that grew out of his work as a translator. The accession of Empress Wu brought a further shift in patronage as she supported Huayan scholarship and showered honours on its first systematiser, Fazang. The emphasis changed yet again under Emperor Xuánzong, who became interested in what the newly arrived tantric masters from India had to offer, a development that we shall investigate in due course. This continued low profile of Tiantai teachings throughout the period may help to explain why it took so long for them to be recognised in Japan, why both Faxiang and Huayan became the object of interest well before the Heian period, and why we have to wait until the almost accidental discovery of Tiantai texts by Saichō before they begin to make an impact.

It has in fact proved quite difficult to identify what Zhiyi's teachings actually were in the sixth century. Most of his work has come down to us in the form of lecture notes taken by his student Guanding 灌頂 (561–632) and by Saichō's time these were commonly read through the prism of commentaries composed by Zhanran, much of whose work was devoted to responding to doctrinal developments in traditions of which Zhiyi himself could not have been aware, including the growing impact of Chan. It seems to have been Zhanran, for example, who produced the indissoluble link between Tiantai doctrine and the *Lotus sūtra*, arguing that Zhiyi's genius lay in his discovery of the profound meaning hidden in this sūtra, which he had then revealed in his two major commentaries. Even so, the variety of influences that Saichō encountered in 804–05 make it plain that Tiantai was not as monolithic at this stage as later sectarian historians have tried to make out. The situation was, in fact, extremely complicated, and it is unwise to try and illustrate what Tiantai may have meant to Saichō by presenting a description of Tiantai that has been filtered through later Song polemics. Perhaps it might be safer to use a text such as Gishin's *Tendai hokkeshū gishū* 天臺法華宗義集, which was presented to the Japanese court in 830, but, although this text is readily available, it does not give an adequate explanation of the doctrines to the uninitiated (Robert 1990; Swanson 1995).

Tiantai doctrine is complex and difficult to present without lengthy excursions into paradoxical arguments. The best we can do here is offer some general pointers. Fundamental to Tiantai is the concept of 'three truths' (Ch. *san ti* 三諦). The Indian tradition had a tried and trusted concept of two truths: 'conventional truth' (Sk. *saṃvṛti-satya*), which was how the unenlightened saw reality, as saṃsāra, all conditioned things being governed by the law of dependent origination; and 'supreme truth' (Sk. *paramārtha-satya*), which was how the enlightened saw reality, as nirvāṇa, all conditioned things being characterised by emptiness. Out of this Zhiyi developed a third truth, producing a triad of the 'empty' (Jp. *kū* 空), 'provisional' (Jp. *ke* 假) and 'mean' (Jp. *chū* 中). There are in fact four layers: firstly, the state of ignorance, which assumes a complete lack of truth; secondly, the understanding that all is emptiness; thirdly, the return to the conventional, but now armed with certain knowledge of the provisional nature of reality; and fourthly, the 'mean', which affirms the second and third layers, seeing them as two sides of the same coin, the one inevitably entailing the other. Emptiness is just as real and non-real as provisionality, which can be defined as assuming something exists 'for the sake of argument', a heuristic technique (Sk. *upāya*, Jp. *hōben* 方便) to lead people to enlightenment. The ultimate form of truth therefore lies in understanding that each pole presupposes its opposite, is only definable in terms of its opposite, and is in this sense indivisible from its opposite. But this kind of truth is not exclusive and does not negate the duality; it must be seen as having equal importance to the other two, because it too is relative and reliant on difference. By saying that saṃsāra is nirvāṇa, one is not denying their difference; one is merely saying that although both are at root characterised by emptiness and could thereby be treated as identical, nothing can exist without its opposite, since everything is relative, so their difference can never be fully negated. In Zhiyi's own words, 'the threefold truth is perfectly integrated; one-in-three and three-in-one' 三諦圓融一三三一.[6] It is when one understands this truth and sees things as they really are that one is in a state of being enlightened.

The Tiantai solution to the problem of suffering lies in thinking through to the end a tendency foreshadowed in much Mahāyāna thought. The overcoming of suffering is seen as ultimately a question of coming to understand that the apparent dichotomy between suffering and liberation (enlightenment, bliss) is false, rather than the elimination of a real entity called suffering. The torment of finitude lies, in this view, in the mistaken notion that torment and bliss (as well as finitude and infinity) are mutually exclusive, in the erroneous view that to attain bliss it is necessary to eradicate torment rather than to experience that bliss within, or perhaps even as, the (first-order) torment itself . . . This identity [of good and evil] is also supposed to preserve the difference and even the conflict between the two, such that identity and difference are seen to be mutually entailing and mutually inclusive. This understanding of identity is mediated by the notion that each of the two opposite 'parts' that constitute the situation . . . is, itself alone, the whole. Hence suffering is both suffering-and-bliss, and bliss is also suffering-and-bliss. In this sense they are identical to one another, even as they maintain their difference from one another rather than being dissolved in some neutral tertium quid (Ziporyn 2000: 113).

The process by which one reaches first an intellectual and then an intuitive understanding of the 'mean', and hence enlightenment, involved three modes of calming (Ch. *sanshi* 三止) and three of contemplation (*sanguan* 三觀).

By contemplating the dharmas of mundane existence as dependently originated, devoid of self-existence, and hence utterly inapprehensible, one 'enters emptiness from provisionality' 從假入空. The delusions of view and cultivation that bind one to saṃsāra are severed, and one achieves the liberation of nirvāṇa. By applying the same critique to the truth of emptiness itself, one severs biased attachment to emptiness (i.e., the delusion that eclipses the infinite sandlike features of existence) and reaffirms its fundamental identity with provisional existence. In effect, one fearlessly 'reenters' or 'comes forth into' provisional existence from emptiness 從空入假 but this time as the self-sovereign master of saṃsāric existence rather than its naïve victim. From this point on both extremes of existence and emptiness are 'simultaneously illumined and simultaneously eradicated' 雙照雙亡. When all vestiges of dualism (i.e., root nescience) vanish, the transcendent and unalloyed middle – the third and absolute truth – is revealed (Donner and Stevenson 1993: 12).

---

[6]   Swanson 1995: 7. This three-way distinction may have been developed from a 'creative misreading' of a crucial verse in Nāgārjuna's *Mūlamadhyamakakārikā*.

Reaching enlightenment is one thing. But how can it be that we also have the possibility of reaching buddhahood, which is quite another? This can be explained by using the concept of the ten realms (*jikkai* 十界). Each consciousness has available to it ten ways of perceiving the world. Known as the ten realms, these were (in ascending order) hell, hungry ghosts, animals, demi-gods, men, gods, śrāvakas (Jp. *shōmon* 聲聞), pratyekabuddhas (Jp. *dokugaku* 獨覺), bodhisattvas (Jp. *bosatsu* 菩薩) and buddhas. Śrāvakas were those 'auditors' who had heard Śākyamuni himself preach and so achieved instant enlightenment, becoming what was known as arhats; they were not teachers and so were not in a position to produce merit through compassion; pratyekabuddhas were those who had achieved enlightenment but simply happened to have no one they could teach, so they were not in a position become bodhisattvas either; bodhisattvas have the desire and the techniques to help others achieve nirvānā and so are ranked higher than the other two. It will be noticed that these ten realms include six that have the same names as the 'six courses' mentioned earlier, but in Tiantai doctrine these are not courses into which one may be reborn but realms of consciousness, all of which entail each other (Jp. *jikkai gogu* 十界互具). And since they do entail each other and are coeval, then human consciousness can experience all of them. All things therefore have the potential to experience all realms, including that of buddhahood.

Zhiyi shared with his contemporaries a concern to bring some semblance of order to the jumble of texts that had accumulated in China over more than four hundred years of translation. Each sūtra claimed to be the final word of the Buddha but the ideas presented were often contradictory, so scholars felt the need to classify scriptures into a hierarchy with their own particular truth at the apex. Zhiyi was also interested in this kind of classification, which was known as 'discriminating between teachings' (Ch. *panjiao* 判教 – in Japanese this term was reversed as *kyōhan* 教判). But his intention was to try and synthesise rather than divide, the general effect of the exercise being to relativise the content of the various teachings and so reduce the potential for conflict. The end result of his systematisation was a division into four broad categories of teaching: tripiṭaka, shared, distinct and perfect (or integrated).

The tripiṭaka teaching (*zangjiao* 藏教), the Hīnayāna teaching of the śrāvaka, is designed for beings of dull capacity who are deeply entrenched in mundane existence. By characterizing existence as suffering, they are induced to renounce saṃsāra, remove the delusions of view and cultivation, and attain the nirvāṇa of the arhat. This goal is achieved through an analytic reduction of existence to its dharmic components (*fenxikong* 分析空) and, ultimately, the featureless quiescence of emptiness. Although the tripiṭaka teaching affords liberation from saṃsāra, it remains caught up in the duality of existence and emptiness and so falls short of the middle way. Hence it remains a biased and merely provisional doctrine – one that must wait for the more profound teaching of the Mahāyāna to be completed.

The shared teaching (*tongjiao* 通教) receives its particular name for two reasons: first, because it advocates an immediate or intuitive understanding of emptiness (*tikong* 體空) that is foundational to all Buddhist teachings, Hīnayāna as well as Mahāyāna; and second, because it incorporates the alternative soteriological ends of all three vehicles (i.e., śrāvaka, pratyekabuddha, and bodhisattva) within its scheme of the path. Both features – its emphasis on emptiness and its salvific ambiguity – make the shared teaching a purely transitional and therefore incomplete doctrine.

The separate teaching (*biejiao* 別教) is the exclusive domain of the bodhisattva: its principles, its language, its practices, its professed goals are purely Mahāyāna, unshared by any of the lesser two vehicles or teachings. For the first time the middle truth of Buddhahood is openly established as the supreme goal, and the two truths of emptiness and provisionality demoted to the status of expediency. Nevertheless, spiritual progress in the separate teaching is decidedly gradualistic (*jianci* 漸次) in character. Over a course of fifty-two levels . . . the bodhisattva proceeds in dialectical sequence (*cidi* 次第) through the three truths, passing first from mundane or provisional existence to emptiness, back to provisionality (with simultaneous discernment of emptiness), and finally to the middle. Only with the last twelve levels of the fifty-two – the ten bhūmi or bodhisattva stages, plus penultimate enlightenment (*dengjue* 等覺) and wondrous enlightenment (*miaojue* 妙覺) – are the two biased views of emptiness and provisionality shed, root nescience penetrated, and the middle truth of Buddhahood revealed. In this respect, even though the separate teaching ultimately reaches the middle, its approach is roundabout and crude, for it lends excessive concreteness to the dualism of existence and emptiness and its attendant delusions and requires a string of biased expedients to redress these imbalances and achieve its final goal.

The perfect teaching (*yuanjiao* 圓教), as its name suggests, is the only teaching among the four that conforms directly to the nature of ultimate reality. Hence it is equivalent to the genuine (*shi* 實) one Buddha vehicle mentioned in the *Lotus sūtra*. Here the perfect (*yuan* 圓) vision of the inconceivable middle truth is presented 'all at once' (*dun* 頓), without the mediation of the provisional and gradualistic expedients that characterize the tripiṭaka, shared, and separate doctrines. Being the most marvelous and profound of paths, it is intended only for bodhisattvas of keenest ability (*ligen* 利根) (Donner and Stevenson 1993: 14–16).

These teachings had been pronounced by the Buddha at five periods in his lifetime, each time with increasing insight and wisdom, the last period being that of the *Lotus sūtra*, which illustrated the One Vehicle, holding out the promise of ultimate buddhahood, as opposed to the Three Vehicles, which stop short at the stage of the bodhisattva. The One Vehicle in fact makes the assumption not only that salvation is universally attainable but that we all have the potential to become a buddha ourselves, in this very life and in this very body. From an Indian, pre-tantric, perspective this is a quite extra-ordinary claim, but it was typical of the more optimistic approach taken by Chinese Buddhists. This shift was to affect all subsequent forms of Buddhism in China, particularly the development of Chan.

The process by which one was supposed to reach this goal was described in the meditation manual *Mahāyāna calming and contemplation*, where Zhiyi went into considerable detail about how one put the three truths into practice in terms of the fourth, perfect teaching. It began with the arousal of *bodhicitta*, the determination to achieve enlightenment and beyond, and then led the practitioner through a series of stages towards the ultimate goal, stressing the need to 'seek upward for enlightenment while transforming sentient beings below' (Jp. *jōgu bodai geke shujō* 上求菩提下化衆生). The dictum that encapsulated the complexity of what one was seeking was 'three thousand [worlds] in a single thought' (Jp. *ichinen sanzen* 一念三千). *Mahāyāna calming and contemplation* is perhaps best known for its pre-sentation of four methods of religious discipline (*samādhi*), which were linked to visualisations and to which we shall have occasion to refer later: 'constantly sitting' (Jp. *jōza sanmai* 常座三昧), associated with Mañjuśrī; 'constantly walking' (Jp. *jōgyō sanmai* 常行三昧), associated with Amitābha; 'part walking/part sitting' (Jp. *hangyō hanza sanmai* 半行半座三昧), associated with Samantabhadra; and 'neither sitting nor walking' (Jp. *higyō hiza sanmai* 非行非座三昧), also known as 'following one's own thoughts as they arise' (Jp. *zuiji'i* 髄自意), linked to Avalokiteśvara. The inclusion of cult elements into meditational practice in this way was to be a matter of continuing controversy in the interpretation of *Mahāyāna calming and contemplation* in China, and in Japan it was to develop in interesting ways, especially as regards Amitābha.

5.4   The *Lotus sūtra*

And what of the *Lotus sūtra* (Jp. *Hokekyō* 法華經),[7] which had such influence in East Asia and gave rise to such intricate philosophical discourse? The first Chinese translation was produced by Dharmarakṣa in 286 CE, which predates the earliest Sanskrit MS (found in Gilgit, Kashmir in 1931) by many centuries. For reasons that are not entirely clear, the *Lotus* was never central to the Indian tradition, and the Tibetan canon contains not one single com-

---

[7]   Sk. *Saddharmapuṇḍarīkasūtra*; Ch. *Fahua jing*, *T.* 262.

mentary, but the situation in Central Asia and China was entirely different: in the guise of Kumārajīva's Chinese version of 406, it became the most influential sūtra of them all.

The sūtra opens in Rājagṛha where the Buddha has just entered meditation after having preached the 'Great Vehicle'. His listeners see a vision and Mañjuśrī tells Maitreya that this happened once in the distant past, just before a buddha preached the 'Wonderful Law' and finally revealed the true nature of all things. Emerging from his concentration (Chapter 2), the Buddha then explains to his disciple Śariputra how difficult true wisdom is to comprehend: it is beyond language, and only a buddha can grasp its full import. Śariputra has to beg him three times before he agrees at least to try an explanation. At this point 5,000 listeners get up and leave, secure in the belief that they already know all there is to know. As language is inadequate to the task, we are given not a discourse or a sermon, but rather a series of vignettes and images, some of which become full-blown parables, all designed to make the message accessible. Not for nothing did the *Lotus* eventually become the most illustrated sūtra of them all. The Buddha explains that although prior to this point he had indeed taught that there were Three Vehicles that would bring one to enlightenment, there is in fact only one. The three had been presented as heuristic devices, provisional truths to fit audiences of lesser capabilities. Now the final truth is to be revealed.

The Three Vehicles were those of the śrāvakas, pratyekabuddhas and bodhisattvas. The first two were stigmatised as followers of Hīnayāna, the Lesser Vehicle. What made them lesser examples to follow was not so much their lack of compassion as their lack of any means by which they could teach. It was the bodhisattvas, who had both compassion and the means to express that compassion, who were the true followers of the Mahāyāna or Greater Vehicle.

But what was this new, single vehicle? The *Lotus* identifies it simply as the 'Way of the Buddha'. At the end of Chapter 2, the Buddha prophesies that Śariputra will eventually become a buddha himself, and one finds such prophecies repeated throughout the sūtra from time to time. This is far more radical than may appear at first sight, since we must remember that Śāriputra was a disciple, a śrāvaka, hence supposedly one of those who followed the Lesser Vehicle. The message is the astounding one that everyone has the potential not just to achieve enlightenment and enter nirvāṇa, but to become a buddha in his or her own right. It is for this reason that Mahāyāna is seen to be a message of universal liberation with compassion at its heart. The *Lotus sūtra* represents Mahāyāna at its most militant. Unlike most other Mahāyāna texts, which dwell at length on the concept of *śunyatā*, the nature of emptiness, the *Lotus* is more accessible, tells memorable stories, and openly challenges every other path, claiming supremacy for its own message.

Now that the central message has been delivered, there should be no more to say, but the sūtra continues to expand, dealing in more detail with the question of intelligibility: how can a truth beyond language be expressed? Chapter 3 discusses the kind of heuristic techniques one may use. By using an analogy, the Buddha explains why, despite knowing the ultimate truth, he had previously preached a lesser truth. The analogy concerns children in a burning house, who can only be saved by an act of deception on the part of the father. These analogies are a marked characteristic of the sūtra as a whole. He then prophesies buddhahood for others of his followers and Mahākāśyapa expresses his delight with a further parable (Chapter 4) about a son leaving home, becoming a beggar, and later being given a menial job in a large household, not recognising that the head of the household is his father until the truth is revealed to him after many years. The menial job is a metaphor for the Lesser Vehicle, the revelation is that of Mahāyāna. Yes, says the Buddha (Chapter 5), take the example of the rain, which falls equally on the whole of nature; different plants and trees react in different ways and only a very few have the potential to end up as the largest trees. He then prophesies buddhahood for even more of his disciples (Chapter 6). They in turn explain their situation in terms of someone who has lived most of his life in extremely poor circumstances while remaining unaware that a friend had long ago sewn a rich jewel into the lining of his garment. Salvation has always been within easy reach; they have simply been ignorant and unable to see it (Chapter 8). Chapter 10 is devoted to the proposition that the sūtra itself is even more valuable than the relics of Śākyamuni and should be honoured above all things. At this juncture an immense stūpa suddenly rises out of the earth containing the body of a previous buddha called Prabhūtaratna, 'Many Jewels', who had apparently vowed to appear in the future whenever the *Lotus* was expounded. The stūpa opens up and Śākyamuni takes his place beside Prabhūtaratna. As a result, the buddha field of Śākyamuni, this world of ours, is suddenly transformed into a Pure Land and all other buddhas from all other worlds gather to honour the pair.

The message of this image is equally as astounding as the prophecies of buddhahood for all. Early Buddhism believed that although there had been buddhas in past aeons and there would be buddhas in the future, time was linear and only one buddha could exist at any one time. We were fortunate to have been born at a time when the message of the 'historical Buddha'

Śākyamuni could still be heard and practised, but Śākyamuni himself was now 'the thus-gone one' (Sk. Tathāgata). What is now being shown in the *Lotus* is that more than one buddha can exist in the same world at the same time. Śākyamuni was in fact a temporal manifestation of an eternal and infinite buddha, who is always present: we have not been left behind to fend for ourselves.

There follows the crucial 'Devadatta' chapter (Chapter 12), which was in Dharmarakṣa's version but not apparently in the text used by Kumārajīva; nevertheless, it was seen as intrinsic to the text by the time of Zhiyi. In it, Śākyamuni prophesies that even Devadatta, his cousin, who was reputed to have tried to kill him a number of times, would eventually reach ultimate buddhahood; he goes on to show how the power of the *Lotus sūtra* even allowed a young female, the daughter of the Dragon King, to achieve this ultimate goal. She admittedly achieves this by undergoing instantaneous transformation into a male, but this was good enough for the large number of women who sought refuge in Buddhism, despite its tendency to misogyny. It was largely a result of the existence of this chapter that the *Lotus* became a central text for women at court to copy and honour in various ways. The main theme of this first section, which Tiantai doctrine identified as the 'Entrance of traces' (Jp. *shakumon* 迹門), was therefore the revelation of the One Vehicle, holding out the possibility of buddhahood for all.

The second half of the sūtra is taken up with questions about the span of a buddha's life and further proof of the fact that the single life of Śākyamuni was in a sense an illusion: his life is in fact limitless and eternal. It is known as the 'Entrance of origin' (Jp. *honmon* 本門). We then have further vows and explanations of the merits that will accrue to those who propagate the message. There is constant self-referential praise whereby all manner of merits and blessings are prophesied to flow from the act of homage to the text itself, the sūtra prefiguring its own transformation into a cult object.

This, then, is the text that Zhiyi used as the main source for his philosophical inquiry. One suspects that he chose the *Lotus* over all others not only because it presented the two most important messages of the Mahāyāna in unambiguous fashion but because, as a text that proclaims rather than explains, it lays itself open to the exegete, who can then proceed to fill the gap with his own discourse. The first ten or so chapters of the sūtra are clearly coherent, but this cannot be said of the rest, which must have been the result of much accretion. This was a well-recognised fact in China and there is a long history of debate and disagreement over different recensions and added chapters. But once a scholar such as Zhiyi had decided on which text to trust, what might appear as accretion is treated by the believer as the word of the Buddha, so a perceived lack of coherence must only be apparent, something to be overcome; it becomes the duty of the scholar to discover coherence and reveal the message within the text. This is what men like Zhiyi and Zhanran felt they were doing, so what sometimes appears to us as philosophical inquiry grafted onto the sūtra was to them a revelation of the secrets within.

The *Lotus* is the most influential of all sūtras in Japanese history and we shall have occasion to refer to it often in what follows. It was always read in conjunction with two other much shorter works, *Innumerable meanings* (Jp. *Muryōgi kyō* 無量義經) at the beginning, and the *Contemplation of Samantabhadra* (Jp. *Kanfugen kyō* 觀普賢經) at the end. The descriptions in the latter sūtra became the basis for a number of meditative techniques and, perhaps more importantly, rites of repentance that included acts of spiritual purification.

5.5   The creation of Tendai

Saichō returned with the mission in the fifth month of 805 and was back in central Japan within two months, presenting a list of what he had brought with him. Copies of the main texts were ordered for the major temples in Nara, although this was a laborious process, which was not to be finished for ten years. Unfortunately, Kanmu Tennō's health was failing, so what attracted the immediate interest of the court was not so much doctrine as the possibility that Saichō had returned with new and more efficacious rituals and spells. Within a month he had been asked to perform a tantric consecration rite at Takaosanji known as a *kanjō* 灌頂 ceremony, involving the sprinkling of sacred water over the initiate. Eight monks were involved, two of them standing in for Kanmu himself, who may have been too ill to participate. It is sometimes claimed that this was the first time that a maṇḍala had been used in Japan as part of such a ceremony, but the details are sketchy. What it does show is that soon after his return Saichō was being fêted as a major asset by the court.

By this time it had already become a habit to use terms that initially identified certain doctrinal positions, such as Hossō or Sanron, as convenient administrative labels under which the continually growing Buddhist establishment could be classified and controlled more effectively. This bureaucratic use of the term 'tradition' (Jp. *shū* 宗) was, of course, influenced by the habit of doctrinal disputation between these different groups or seminars, but, as we have seen, monks studied a wide range of subjects and disputation often took the form of a ritual performance. Institutionally it was clearly important to Saichō that he achieve recognition for his 'subject' as soon as possible.

The most obvious manifestation of this categorisation was the system of 'yearly ordinands' (*nenbun dosha* 年分度者), granted as a favour from the court. Since such ordinands could have accounted for only a fraction of the men (and women) actually leaving lay life in any one year, it was more of a symbolic gesture than anything else, but, somewhat like the institution of a chair for a subject at a university, the symbolism was important. In 803 the granting of these had been specifically linked to the 'shū', and restricted to Hossō and Sanron. Saichō lost no time in suggesting a revision to this procedure: instead of the existing 5/5 Hossō–Sanron split, he proposed three for Hossō, three for Sanron, and two each for Kegon, Ritsu and his own group, to which he gave the name 'Tendai', representing, of course, the Japanisation of 'Tiantai'. These suggestions were quickly accepted by the court, giving Saichō at least some of the recognition he needed. In the case of Tendai there was a stipulation that each new ordinand would enter one of two courses of study: the tantric course, the Shanagō 遮那業, which took its name from the *Mahāvairocanatantra* (Jp. *Daibirushana-kyō* 大毘盧遮那經),[8] or the meditation course, Shikangō 止觀業, which took its name from Zhiyi's *Mahāyāna calming and concentration* (Jp. *Maka shikan*). These two categories were in use until at least 890. Kanmu died soon afterwards and the actual granting of ordinands to Tendai was held over to 809, at which point Saichō received an allowance of eight students to cover the intervening years. So 809 saw Hieizan finally begin to expand; but it also brought the return of Kūkai, who had been studying esoteric ritual in the Tang capital of Chang'an.

We shall deal with Kūkai's achievements and his difficult relationship with Saichō in the next chapter; suffice it to say here that, although it was to be some time before Kūkai received recognition, Saichō quickly realised the importance of Kūkai's experience of ritual at Chang'an. He immediately requested copies of the works Kūkai had carried back and is thought to have helped him become established at Takaosanji. In 812, he asked Kūkai to initiate him properly into the two major rituals for two maṇḍalas that Kūkai had studied in depth and that Saichō himself had not experienced. He also

---

[8]   It is important to note that this was *not* in fact one of the texts that Saichō brought back but a version that he had studied before going to China. There is no sign that he himself had ever taken instruction in these rites.

decided that students doing the Shanagō course should study with Kūkai. It must have taken considerable strength of character to admit Kūkai's superior knowledge in this manner. By 814, however, relations had soured, as Kūkai moved to establish his own tradition. Saichō's last years, from 814 until his death in 822, were spent devoted to two causes: a defence of Tendai doctrine against an attack from Hossō; and a battle for the principle that the Tendai tradition should be allowed to ordain its own monks rather than having to rely on the ordination platform at Tōdaiji.

A defence of Tendai necessitated an attack on other doctrines that did not take the *Lotus* as the final truth and that imposed a different system of classification on the teachings. Perhaps the best-known disagreement was with the Hossō scholar Tokuitsu 德一 (780?–842?), who was living in a temple in Aizu, in northeastern Japan and whom Saichō may well have met when he travelled to the Eastern Provinces in 817.[9] We do not know for certain, but the debate may have started when Tokuitsu read Saichō's *Doctrines of Tendai on which others rely* (*Ehyō Tendaigishū* 依憑天臺義集) of 813–16, where he had first proclaimed that in his view all Japanese were already advanced enough to be able to understand the Perfect Teachings. Certainly, Tokuitsu was well informed about Tendai, as is clear from his first tract *On Buddha Nature* (*Busshōshō* 佛性抄), in which he attacked the supposed pre-eminence of the *Lotus*. The debate that followed was in the form of a series of such tracts exchanged between them. There is some puzzlement at how Tokuitsu managed to learn so much about Tendai, stuck as he was in the wilds of northern Japan, but he may well have previously studied the *Fahua xuanzan* 法華玄贊, an anti-Tiantai commentary on the *Lotus* written by Cien 慈恩 (632–82) (Groner 1984: 93–106; Tamura 1985: 48–81).

It is not surprising that a Hossō scholar should have had problems accepting Tendai doctrine, since the traditions disagreed so fundamentally on the question of innate Buddha Nature (*busshō*). Tendai's wholehearted acceptance of Mahāyāna universalism as expressed in the *Lotus* assumed that every sentient being had the potential to become a buddha. Hossō, as we have seen in §4.7, took from its parent, the Faxiang tradition, the assumption that there were five different types of sentient being, a theory known in Japanese as the *goshō kakubetsu setsu* 五性各別説. There were those predestined to become arhats; those predestined to become pratyekabuddhas; those pre-

---

[9] Tokuitsu is credited with seventeen works. Only two of these survive: a series of questions about Kūkai's teachings entitled *Shingonshū miketsumon* 眞言宗未決文, *T.* 2458 and *Shikanron* 止觀論. Many others are quoted extensively in Saichō's writings. Groner 1984: 92.

destined to become buddhas; those with some 'untainted seeds' who might attain any of these goals; and lastly those unfortunates who lacked any such seeds and were therefore fated to a repeated cycle of birth and death for ever. These were the 'incorrigibles'. This disagreement then spilled over into further argument about the interpretation of certain key passages from the *Lotus*, about Tendai's concept of the 'four teachings', and about the nature of the sūtra itself. Hossō insisted that the idea of Three Vehicles was the ultimate truth and the One Vehicle was itself simply a skilful device invented to encourage the fainthearted.

The significance of this disagreement lay in the standard of debate. Tokuitsu had a fairly strong tradition of Faxiang criticism of Tiantai doctrine on which to rely, but even so his use of quotations was correct and judicious. Saichō had somewhat less to rely on, since Tiantai had not had to deal with Faxiang doctrine in such a direct manner before; he was thrown back on his own resources and showed the depth of his scholarship by using against Tokuitsu the awkward fact that the Yogācāra doctrines stemming from Paramārtha's earlier versions did not argue for the existence of an 'incorrigible' group and differed significantly from those views held by the Faxiang school as it emerged from Xuanzang's work. Japanese Buddhism was clearly ready to strike out on its own.

The second controversy that involved Saichō until his death was, in the beginning, political rather than doctrinal in nature, although perhaps such a distinction is invidious. It involved his attempt to obtain permission to ordain monks of the Tendai tradition on Hieizan rather than on the ordination platform at Tōdaiji, but it led in the end to a radical break with established ordination practices, drawing a sharp line between Tendai monks and all others. Saichō's desire to win independence from Nara was understandable in the context of his desire to establish the one true doctrine as pre-eminent in Japan, but then so was the tremendous opposition that such a proposal aroused in the Saṅgha Office, whose head at the time was a Hossō monk called Gomyō 護命. In essence, Saichō wished to have Tendai monks simply excluded from the monastic register held by the Office. This may possibly have been a sign of unhappiness at the degree of control the state had over the saṅgha, but it is far more likely to have been driven by rivalry with Hossō. The dispute ran from about 817 to his death in 822. After a number of false starts, Saichō gradually became convinced that to achieve such a goal in the teeth of powerful conservative forces, he would have to shift the argument to a debate on doctrinal grounds: this eventually led him to take an extreme position, arguing that the traditional 250 rules had been designed for men of lesser ability, for followers of the Lesser Vehicle. They were therefore quite unsuitable for followers of the Mahāyāna, especially those who were practitioners of the 'perfect teachings' exemplified in the *Lotus*. For this argument to succeed, Saichō first had to split the term that covered precepts and rules, namely *kairitsu* 戒律, into its component parts. This gave *kai*, which meant 'moral precepts' (Sk. *śīla*), and *ritsu*, which meant 'rules' (Sk. *vinaya*). The morality he identified with the Mahāyāna and so retained; the discipline he identified with the Hīnayāna and so felt free to reject.

It is worth noting that this was an unprecedented procedure both in China and in Japan, where all members of the saṅgha, no matter what persuasion, were ordained with both because they were considered indivisible. For his own Tendai monks Saichō proposed a new set of 'Mahāyāna precepts' that he termed the 'perfect precepts' (*enkai* 圓戒), which were in essence the ten major and forty-eight minor precepts listed in the *Sūtra of Brahmā's net*, the set that we have already seen being used to initiate lay Buddhist supporters (Groner 1984: 169–263). This apparent statement of equality between saṅgha member and lay supporter did not mean, however, that life was going to be easy for his students. The requests that Saichō sent to court to support his case for separate recognition make it clear that the regime he intended to impose on his students was rigorous in the extreme; Tendai students were to be sequestered on the mountain for twelve years of hard study and meditation.

Faced with a major disagreement in the monastic establishment, Saga Tennō 嵯峨天皇 refused to make a decision and sent the last of Saichō's petitions to the Saṅgha Office for further review. Saichō himself died in the fourth month of 822, his wishes unfulfilled. Such was his prestige, however, that the petition was granted seven days after his death. Perhaps the state wished to avoid the calamities of an angry spirit on the loose. Whatever the reasons, the ramifications of this agreement were to be far-reaching: Japanese were moving rapidly from the purely receptive stage to making their own contributions to the doctrinal development of Buddhism.

There is one other matter that is the subject of some controversy: the degree to which Saichō may have believed in the possibility of achieving not just enlightenment but buddhahood in this life, an essentially tantric concept that usually goes by the name *sokushin jōbutsu* 即身成佛. As a result of the disagreements between Saichō and Kūkai, their successors made great play of who should have the honour of having introduced this idea into Japan first. There can be no doubt that Saichō did discuss the subject in his later writings and he certainly used the term *sokushin jōbutsu*, as well as *jikidō* 直道 'direct path' and *tonkyō* 頓教 'sudden teachings', which meant something very similar. This was to provide a precedent for Tendai to develop a strong interest in tantrism after his death. The basis for this belief in *sokushin jōbutsu*, however, was quite different from that used by Kūkai. It came from the passage in the 'Devadatta' chapter of the *Lotus* where the daughter of the Dragon King achieves buddhahood.

The dragon king's daughter who converted others [to the ultimate teaching] had not undergone a long period of religious austerities; nor had the sentient beings who were converted undergone a long period of austerities. Through the wondrous power of the sūtra, they all realized buddhahood with their bodies just as they are (*sokushin jōbutsu*). Those with the highest grade of superior faculties realize buddhahood in one lifetime; those with the medium grade of superior faculties require two lifetimes to realize buddhahood. And those with the lowest grade of superior faculties will realize buddhahood within three lifetimes. They will meet the bodhisattva Samantabhadra, enter the ranks of the bodhisattvas, and acquire the dhāraṇī which will enable them to master nonsubstantiality (*Hokke shūku*, Groner 1989: 62).

6   The beginnings of a 'Japanese' Buddhism: Shingon

6.1   Kūkai to China

Born in 774, Kūkai (空海, or Kōbō Daishi 弘法大師 as he was to be known) entered the Daigakuryō college as a scholar in 791. This was an institution dedicated to training scholars along Confucian lines, with the aim of providing for the growing bureaucracy. It was here, for example, that the rites in honour of Confucius (*sekiten* 釋奠) were held (McMullen 1996). Kūkai concentrated on classical literature but soon found his interest waning and he left after some years to become a self-ordained mendicant. The justification for such a move can be found in his first work, *Goals of the three teachings* (*Sangō shiiki* 三教指歸) of 797, an erudite discussion of the merits of Buddhism, Daoism and Confucianism. In the introduction, he wrote that his eyes had been opened by an encounter with the Buddhist tantric ritual known as 'Ākāśagarbha's technique for seeking, hearing and retaining' (Jp. *Kokūzō gumonji hō* 虛空藏求聞持法), which promised a perfect memory:

There was a monk [at the college]. He showed me Ākāśagarbha's *Monjihō*. It says in the text that a person who recites these True Words one million times according to the specific rite will be able to memorize the meaning of all the sūtras. I put my faith in this testimony of the Buddha, watching for flames to fly from the sparks of struck flint. I scaled the peak of Mount Tairyō in Awa, I persevered in meditation as far as Muroto Cape in Tosa. The valleys did not fail to resound, the brilliant star [of Ākāśagarbha, i.e. Venus] shone down in grace. In the end, I came to shun all thought of worldly glory, day and night I thirsted for the smoke and mist of mountain crags and mired wilderness. To see fine raiment, plump steeds, and a stream of fleet conveyances instantly awakened in me grief at the phantom lightning flash [which is this life]; to see deformity and pauper's rags gave me no rest from the sad awareness of cause and consequence. Through my eyes I was compelled [to take the tonsure], for who can snare the wind? (Hare 1990: 254)

We know very little about his other activities during this period except that he must have spent considerable time studying in one of the temples at Nara, if the learning that is apparent in *Sangō shiiki* is anything to go by. His formal initiation as a monk took place in 804, only days before he was due to leave for China. He tells us that his initial plan was to stay and study in China for twenty years. In particular, he was intent on finding out at first hand about the rituals that were described in texts such as the *Mahāvairocanatantra* (Jp. *Dainichikyō* 大日經, *T*. 848), which had been translated into Chinese in the 720s and brought to Japan by Genbō in 735. Tantras were in large part ritual manuals, extremely difficult to grasp without prior experience of the ritual itself or without the guidance of a master, so it is hardly surprising that Kūkai found the text impenetrable: 'As soon as I opened its scroll to read its lines', he wrote, 'my mind grew dark. It was then that I vowed to travel to China to study it' (Abe 1999: 109).

At this point fortune smiled on Kūkai. As we have seen, the mission of 801–06 that carried Saichō ran into considerable difficulties, and a second attempt only received authorisation in the third month of 804. Kūkai's request to travel with this mission must have come at the last minute, for he was hurriedly ordained as a monk at Tōdaiji in the next month and was on board within a few weeks. His obvious facility with classical Chinese may well have been the deciding factor in allowing him to go. As it happened, he travelled on a different ship from Saichō. Kūkai was blown far to the south [map 5] and arrived on the coast near Fuzhou 福州 after a full thirty-four days. It took some time before permission to land was granted, since the authorities in Fuzhou were not used to receiving such missions. Permission to travel to the capital took even longer, and in the end only twenty-three members were allowed to proceed; the rest had to travel north to Mingzhou to prepare for the return journey. Kūkai was extremely fortunate to be allowed to go with the main mission, and even more fortunate to be allowed to stay and study. They left Fuzhou on 804.11.3 and took forty days to reach Chang'an, where they met up with some members from the second ship, which had managed a much faster crossing. The requisite imperial audience was obtained, but Emperor Dezong was already ill and died in the first month of 805. The main mission left Chang'an soon afterwards, reaching the coast in the fifth month and arriving in Japan a month later. At this juncture, the two ships that had been driven back to Kyūshū left for China, hoping perhaps to obtain audience with the new emperor, Shunzong 順宗. Unfortunately, only one of them survived the journey and Shunzong had already died by the time they reached the capital.

In the second month of 805, Kūkai was given permission to reside at the Ximingsi 西明寺, a major centre for scholarship and translation in Chang'an, and it was here that he came into contact with monks capable of reading Buddhist Sanskrit. He lost no time in learning as much as he could. Although Kūkai was probably not, as legend has it, the inventor of *kana*, there can be no doubt that the knowledge of the Sanskrit syllabary that he and others gained in China played a major part in the development of a Japanese script during the course of the century. Some four months later, he came under the tutelage of Huiguo 惠果 (746–805). Huiguo had studied under Amoghavajra (Bukong 不空 705–74), who, as we shall see, had been a central figure in the spread of tantric Buddhist ritual at the Tang court. Within the space of three months, Kūkai claims, he had learned enough to be counted a master in his own right. Huiguo died in the middle of the twelfth month of 805. It was at this point that, contrary to his initial intention, Kūkai decided to return to Japan with the second party. He was back in Kyūshū by the end of the year. Twenty years had been squeezed into just thirty months. He was thirty-three.

The only information we have about Kūkai's time spent in China comes from either his own account or later hagiographies, and there is little open to independent verification. He was certainly lucky to have reached the capital; not only was it to give him the kind of 'imperial' cachet denied Saichō, but he happened to be there at a time when tantrism was in vogue and under imperial patronage. Even had he not, as he tells us, come to China for this express purpose, he might well have become involved in any case.

Kūkai's account of his meeting with Huiguo at the Qinglongsi 青龍寺 and his subsequent induction into tantric secrets leaves us in no doubt that he was claiming a special form of transmission for himself:

I called on the abbot in the company of five or six monks from the Ximing Temple. As soon as he saw me, he smiled with pleasure and joyfully said, 'I knew that you would come! I have waited for such a long time. What pleasure it gives me to look upon you today at last! My life is drawing to an end, and until you came there was no one to whom I could transmit the teachings. Go without delay to the altar of *abhiṣeka* with incense and a flower.' I returned to the temple where I had been staying and got the things that were necessary for the ceremony. It was early in the sixth month when I entered the altar of *abhiṣeka* for primary initiation. I stood before the Womb World maṇḍala and cast my flower in the prescribed manner. By chance it fell on the Body of Mahāvairocana Tathāgata in the centre. The master exclaimed in delight, 'How amazing! How perfectly amazing!' He repeated this three or four times in joy and wonder. I was then given the fivefold *abhiṣeka* and received instruction in the grace (*kaji*) of the Three Mysteries. Next I was taught the Sanskrit formulas and rituals manuals for the Womb World and learned the yogic practices which use various sacred objects of concentration to gain transcendental insight (de Bary et al. 2001: 163).

The term *abhiṣeka* here refers to a consecration that involves sprinkling sacred water over the head (Jp. *kanjō* 灌頂), the ceremony that Saichō had performed on his return. There were usually three levels: an initiation ceremony called 'binding the relationship' (Jp. *kechien kanjō* 結緣灌頂), which involved the casting of a flower or sprig on to the maṇḍala to identify one's deity; 'studying the Dharma' (Jp. *gakuhō kanjō* 學法灌頂), which involved much learning of mantra and mudrā, and practising visualisation techniques; and 'transmission of the teachings' (Jp. *dengyō kanjō* 傳教灌頂), when one became qualified as a master. At this advanced stage the maṇḍala might simply be imagined by both master and student (Abe 1999: 124).

We are also told that Huiguo urged Kūkai to carry his knowledge back to Japan, and that Kūkai himself was chosen above all other students to write his master's epitaph. It was on this basis that Kūkai's followers were to construct a lineage and eventually claim him as the 'Eighth Patriarch of Shingon'. According to later Japanese tradition there was a series of patriarchs leading down to Amoghavajra, then directly to Huiguo and Kūkai. The implication of this is that there was a 'school' of tantric practice which came to an end in China in 805, which was then transmitted to Japan in the body of Kūkai and in the form of Shingon.

There are, of course, a number of problems with so sectarian a view. We know, for example, that tantric practice did not simply die out in China. We also know that, although Huiguo was certainly listed as one of six prominent students in Amoghavajra's will, when the master died in 774, Huiguo was only twenty-nine and it was in fact Huilang 惠朗 who was officially recognised as his successor.[1] Huilang died four years later in 778 and what then transpired is unclear, but Huiguo left no writings and would probably have remained an obscure figure had it not been for Kūkai's subsequent activities. But the main problem lies with the idea of a patriarchial tradition itself. Although transmission of tantric teachings did, of necessity, involve a student learning direct from a master instead of simply via texts, there is little sign that the tantric masters in Tang China ever saw themselves as creating a 'school', and it is of interest that neither the catalogue of the Chinese Buddhist canon produced in 730, nor that of 800, had a special section devoted specifically to 'tantric texts'. Tantrism was more a matter of individual enterprise.

A more detailed discussion of the nature and principles of tantrism will be found in the next section; suffice it to say here that it involved a special use

---

[1]   See Chou 1945: 306; Matsunaga 1973: 227–42; Orzech 1989: 91.

of language and images, elevated ritual above philosophy, and believed there to be a shortcut to enlightenment and buddhahood. But tantric masters were also highly political animals and saw themselves as full participants in the business of governing the state. This should not surprise us. It was a good reflection of how tantrism saw itself in India:

It appears that the central and defining metaphor for mature esoteric Buddhism [in India] is that of an individual assuming kingship and exercising dominion. Thus the understanding of such terms as tantra in Buddhist India would invoke, first and foremost, the idea of hierarchical power acquired and exercised through a combination of ritual and metaphysical means. Based on this power, the varieties of understanding and of personal relationships become subsumed to the purposes of the person metaphorically becoming the overlord (*rājādhirāja*) or the universal ruler (*cakravartin*) . . . It is astonishing to realize that so many significant terms found in the standard esoteric manuals and the Buddhist tantras have political and military significance as well as religious, and the bivalence or paronomasia of these terms in aggregate is extraordinary (Davidson 2002: 121).

So what did Kūkai encounter at Chang'an? Although Buddhist ritual texts had been brought to China in piecemeal fashion over the centuries, the beginning of tantrism proper is usually linked to the arrival in Chang'an of the scholar Śubhakarasiṃha (Shanwuwei 善無畏, 637–735) in 716. It was he who, with the help of Yixing 一行 (687–727), translated the *Mahāvairocana-tantra*, the text that was to puzzle the young Kūkai. He was closely followed by Vajrabodhi (Jin'gangzhi 金剛智, 671–741) and his student Amoghavajra (Bukong 不空, 705–74). From the start, these men were treated as state employees, accommodated in monasteries, put to work translating the new texts they had brought with them, and, once they had proved themselves, performing rituals for the court and the emperor. Vajrabodhi, in particular, was known for his unusual powers as a thaumaturge and was constantly on call to perform rites for clement weather or to cure an illness. He was also responsible for the first translation of the other major text of Chinese tantrism, the *Assembled reality of all the tathāgatas*, which was also known as the *Diamond tip* (Jp. *Kongōchō* 金剛頂).[2] The legend that surrounded this particular text is an interesting example of how narratives of origin could be used to create a sense of authority and power. Partial translations of this text were produced by both Vajrabodhi (*T.* 866) and Amoghavajra (*T.* 865), but it was made plain that these had been made from a much truncated version that Vajrabodhi had managed to bring from India. The far larger version, 'broad

---

[2]   Sk. *Sarvatathāgatatattvasaṃgraha*, also known as the *Vajraśekhara*, Ch. *Jin'gangding*, *T.* 865.

and long like a bed, and four or five feet thick', which had been copied from an even vaster text held inside an iron stūpa, had been thrown overboard to save the ship. The complete teaching therefore could only come from he who had seen and studied the original text, or from someone who had been taught by such a one. Of such material is religious authority often concocted (Orzech 1995).

Soon after Vajrabodhi's death in 741, Amoghavajra was allowed to travel to India, returning in 746 with yet more Sanskrit texts. It was at this point that he was allowed to create an altar in the palace so that Emperor Xuánzong could receive an *abhiṣeka* initiation. This intrusion of Buddhism into the inner sanctum was an unprecedented development of tremendous symbolic significance; hardly surprising that Kūkai was to work so hard to achieve a similar feat on his return to Japan. Amoghavajra himself survived the Anlushan rebellion of 755 and achieved even greater prestige and authority under Emperor Daizong, promoting the idea of emperor as universal monarch and developing the theoretical and ritual underpinnings for a highly politicised form of tantrism with the twin goals of sudden enlightenment for the individual and protection of the state. The small temple within the palace became a fixture and Amoghavajra became renowned as a miracle worker, with power to control the elements and call up divinities to defeat the emperor's enemies. In such an environment, it was more a question of individual presence and authority than any emphasis on doctrinal superiority of a 'school'. It was above all Amoghavajra's relationship with his emperor that Kūkai wished to emulate. It is striking that one of the texts he brought back with him was an important collection of letters that had been exchanged between Amoghavajra and Emperor Xuánzong (*T*. 2120). Compiled by Yuanzhao 圓照 (d. 800), probably in the 780s, this collection was designed to persuade the new emperor Dezong, who had reduced patronage and stopped rites being held in the palace, of the importance of tantric masters; it represented biographical documentation of an ideal relationship between master and ruler. The message was not lost on Dezong, and certainly not on Kūkai.

It is probable that most of what Kūkai took back with him to Japan had emanated from Amoghavajra and so was only forty years old at most. Although it is true that Kūkai studied Sanskrit, most of the new texts that he obtained, the rituals that he learned and the maṇḍala that he carried with him were heavily influenced by Chinese practice. The new version of the *Sūtra for humane kings* by Amoghavajra, for example, kept its original concern with the link between sūtra and state, but added a number of important tantric elements, including the Four Wisdom Kings (明王) and a long dhāraṇī near the end. Ritual handbooks produced by Amoghavajra himself make it clear that the dhāraṇī was to be seen not simply as an addition but as a condensation, the essence of the sūtra: the relationship between text and spell had been radically altered (Orzech 1998).

6.2 Fundamental characteristics of tantric Buddhism

At the risk of losing sight of Kūkai for a while, it is important to be clear what 'tantric Buddhism' means. Tantras were texts that explained and described ritual practice. There was always a strong interest in ritual in Mahāyāna, but tantrism takes this one step further and places the practice of ritual and invocation at the core. From one angle this might be seen as little more than sympathetic magic performed for worldly benefit (Jp. *genze riyaku* 現世利益). We have a tendency to look upon such practices as debased, but in tantrism the principle of non-dualism was so thoroughgoing that the mundane was never divorced from the more 'exalted' realms; it was precisely success in attainment (*siddhi*) in the latter that brought success in the former. It is this attitude that explains the willingness of tantric masters to use their powers in the service of rulers and the state. Far from being a prostitution of talent, it was a sign of their prowess.

There was, of course, what we might term a much deeper level, where the practice of ritual was explicitly linked to the search for enlightenment, liberation and buddhahood. The core beliefs of tantrism are, firstly, buddhahood is possible in the here and now, and secondly, the ultimate mystery is in some form communicable. Now for many Buddhists these are anathema, since they fly in the face of so much that was said about the long, heroic path to be trodden, and even the most optimistic doctrines of Mahāyāna universalism had always argued that the experience of enlightenment itself was beyond the capability of language to express, hence beyond normal cognition. It is useful to see tantrism as an attempt to provide an answer to the problem of language and the limitations it places on the human mind. The position was justified as follows.

It was universally accepted that the Buddha had taught various doctrines at different times to different audiences and had cut his cloth accordingly. Just as Mahāyāna saw the path of the auditor (śrāvaka) as being an inferior vehicle (Hīnayāna) compared with that of the bodhisattva, so now tantrism claimed that there was a different way, via the practice of ritual. This new tantric path was recognised to be an extremely risky one, but the rewards were correspondingly greater. It employed special methods which only those of very strong faculties should dare use, but the prize held out was buddhahood in this very life. By using incantation, ritual gestures, visualisation and other techniques, one could link oneself to beings and deities in other spheres of existence, either dominate or identify with them, and thus rise into higher spheres of being, eventually coming face to face with and identifying oneself with the cosmic Buddha, Mahāvairocana.

The rituals involved speech, body and mind, the so-called practice of the 'three mysteries' (Jp. *sanmitsu* 三密): speech, in the form of mantra or invocations; the body, in the form of mudrā or signs made by the hands; and sight, through contemplation and imagination. Language is the way human beings make sense of the universe, the tool we use to differentiate and hence generate meaning. But this process gives rise to the illusion that everything differentiated has self-presence, precisely that illusion that Buddhism is dedicated to destroying. Language must therefore be used against itself; it cannot be disposed of entirely, but it cannot be allowed to fulfil its normal function, namely to carry everyday meaning, for this would distract. The only way this can be done without succumbing to pure nonsense is if language is treated as pure sound, but sound that is known to hold within itself profound significance, a significance, however, that can only be grasped by the owner of a secret key. So it was that Chinese tantrism chose to retain the 'original' Sanskrit sounds (or what passed for those sounds). Mantra or dhāraṇī (the two were often not distinguished clearly before Kūkai) were seen to contain the concentrated essence of the teachings; far from being nonsense syllables, they were the sound of the universe. As Kūkai himself put it in 'An interpretation of the *Lotus sūtra*' (*Hokekyō shaku* 法華經釋):

> The 'revealed' consumes many words to carry one meaning. The 'tantric' unleashes countless meanings from within each letter of a word. This is the secret function of dhāraṇī. Because of this, dhāraṇī is translated as *sōji* 総持, the container of all. However, this meaning of dhāraṇī has been kept secret by the Dharma transmitters of the past. This is what I have now introduced as the mantra scriptures (*shingonzō* 眞言藏) (Abe 1999: 264, adapted).

In Japan the situation was to go one step further, from sound to shape. The written forms of the Sanskrit syllables known as *siddhaṃ* (Jp. *shittan* 悉曇) became a sacred script, and the written sign took on the same power as the sound it represented. It became the object of visualisation.

Mudrā likewise were symbolic of states of mind, the body being used to perform various gestures pregnant with signification. Visualisation was helped by the use of maṇḍala, symbolic representations of the universe. Acts of imagination were especially important since they showed that the dichotomy between form and emptiness was false. We have here an attempt to deal with the problem of language by cutting it away and replacing it with the whole human body in its every aspect, with pure form. Enlightenment is then no longer beyond language but speaks through the world in all its materiality. It was in this sense that tantrism could claim that enlightenment was communicable; the communication was to be achieved through performance.

And what was the cosmic Buddha? It had long been recognised that Buddha existed in a number of forms. Śākyamuni, as the historical Buddha, was of this earth, a manifestation of limited duration whose teachings must to some extent have been conditioned. This form was called the Response Body (Sk. *nirmāṇakāya*, Jp. *ōjin* 應身), because it appears as an object to our senses and responds to our needs. The body of a buddha such as Amitābha, who was present but not historical in the same sense, was called the Reward Body (Sk. *saṃbhogakāya*, Jp. *hōshin* 報身), which he had received as a reward for his constant practice and perfect merit. But there was a third, even higher form: the tantric teachings dealt with the Dharma Body (Sk. *dharmakāya*, Jp. *hosshin* 法身), the absolute, eternal, cosmic Buddha. *Dharmakāya* originally meant something like 'the body of the teachings [of the Buddha]' but this was subject to a process of semi-reification as 'dharma-body'. The representation of the *dharmakāya* in the figure of Mahāvairocana ran a danger of losing its metaphorical status. There was an ever-present danger of personification, of course, but philosophically the term was understood to mean absolute unity, an all-embracing 'body' that enfolded all types and forms of consciousness and was above any duality. Differences and distinctions were collapsed and both nirvāṇa and saṃsāra were subsumed within it. In the ultimate analysis, then, nirvāṇa and saṃsāra were one and the same thing, indivisible to the enlightened mind. All things partook of enlightened mind and enlightened mind expressed itself in all forms.

The consequences of such teaching were far-reaching. The material world, be it body or object, was reinstated as an integral part of truth and reality. The reification in a word like *hosshin* was not therefore accidental. The absolute speaks through the material world and we respond to it through our bodies. The impasse of language was thus avoided and we could then reach directly into the heart of the absolute. But perhaps the most striking result of this emphasis on the material, and the affirmation of all things, is that human desires are seen in a different light. They become not the root cause of

Plate 16   Mahāvairocana (Dainichi), in the form of a bodhisattva, showing the characteristic mudrā known as the 'wisdom fist', the sexual connotations of which are quite clear.

illusion and suffering but rather something innately pure, the outward expression of our Buddha Nature. The objective then becomes not to negate them but harness their energy and direct them into the quest for enlightenment. Desire is a sign of activity and without such activity enlightenment will never be attained; it is this kind of thinking that lies behind such phrases as 'passions and enlightenment are identical' (Jp. *bonnō soku bodai* 煩惱即 菩提), and behind the tendency to treat basic human instincts as a manifestation of pure energy. Sexual desire becomes a subject of serious interest, particularly since it results in physical union and a paradoxical momentary dissolution of self. Such a doctrine is open to abuse, of course, and this is why the word 'risky' always comes to mind.[3]

Since the absolute expresses itself in myriad forms, there is nothing that the mind may not use in its search for enlightenment; hence tantrism is also marked by a multiplicity of shapes and images. The normal habit of Buddhism of appropriating to itself the powers of local deities as it spread is here magnified to an astounding degree; perhaps nowhere is this more obvious than in the maṇḍala, that staple of tantric ritual. There is one extant illustration of Amida's Pure Land that has been dated to 763, a woven tapestry that survives in fragmentary form in the Taimadera 當麻寺 in Nara prefecture, but the more abstract, geometrically patterned maṇḍala are mainly connected to the tantric rituals that Kūkai encountered in 805. As representations of the universe, they are very powerful statements of mind over matter, and of a fear of undisciplined space. Maṇḍala may also be three-dimensional arrangements of statues, of which there are any number of examples in Japan, or two-dimensional paintings, which could be either spread out horizontally or hung vertically. They may be dedicated to individual deities (Jp. *besson-mandara* 別尊曼荼羅) or contain a vast number of deities surrounding a main central figure, but in all cases the maṇḍala is seen as sacred space into which a deity may be invited and, as the result of certain ritual actions and mental effort, personally encountered by the initiate. They are designed to be entered.[4] Although the examples that were brought back to Japan by Kūkai and others in the ninth century contained much that was Chinese in origin, their Indian roots are by no means erased; they retain, for example, a large number of deities that are not specifically Buddhist in origin. The rationale for their presence, which was as important in Nara and

---

[3] In this context see Astley-Kristensen 1991, which treats in detail a short sūtra well known for its argument that passion, including sexual desire, is at root pure and to be harnessed in the interests of the search for enlightenment.

[4] See Appendices for further treatment.

pre-Nara Buddhism as in tantrism, is that they have all been converted at some point to become themselves 'Protectors of the Dharma'. Appearing in a maṇḍala meant that they too were now emanations of the Buddha and so they took on even greater powers. A number of these deities therefore arrived in Japan with their own cults intact and they coexisted with more orthodox Shingon practice while remaining distinct.

6.3   Kūkai returns

Unlike Saichō, whom we have seen being fêted on his return and immediately encouraged to perform new rituals for the benefit of ruler and court, Kūkai came back as an unknown monk with few connections. He brought with him 142 sūtras, 42 Sanskrit texts, 32 commentaries, 5 maṇḍala, and a large number of paintings and ritual implements, all of which he gave to the head of the mission to take to the capital, together with an 'Inventory of imported items' (*Shōrai mokuroku* 請來目錄), but Kūkai himself stayed in Kyūshū. For some reason that is still unclear, he waited until the accession of Saga Tennō in 809 to return to Heiankyō. The exact role played by Saichō at this juncture is also uncertain, but both men certainly worked closely together for a few years. The well-known break in relations occurred later, in 815.[5]

Saichō was understandably anxious to borrow and copy everything Kūkai had brought with him. He recognised the importance of both the texts themselves and the experience that Kūkai had gained in Chang'an. Both men needed each other at this stage: Kūkai needed Saichō to help him become established, and Saichō needed Kūkai for his knowledge. It was because of Saichō, for example, that Kūkai was settled at Takaosanji to the northwest of the capital, a mountain retreat that became his home for the next nine years and where he flourished under the patronage of Saga. It was there too that in 812 he was allowed to conduct a *kechien kanjō* for Saichō, his students Kōjō 光定 (779–858), Enchō 圓澄 (771–837) and Taihan 泰範 (778–?), and more than two hundred others. The co-operation and friendship did not last much longer, however. The real reasons for the split are not known, but by 815 or 816 relations had soured. This is sometimes put down to the fact that Taihan, sent by Saichō to study with Kūkai, eventually refused to return to Hieizan, but at heart there was a fundamental doctrinal difference between the two men: to Saichō, who was, after all, convinced that the *Lotus sūtra* held the

[5]   For a refreshingly non-sectarian treatment of this relationship see Gardiner 1994: 194–224.

final truth, tantric ritual was simply one of a number of legitimate practices; for Kūkai, it represented the ultimate. Perhaps his role as master of ceremonies at the initiations of 812 convinced Kūkai that he might be able to stand on his own. Perhaps he came to realise that to succeed in becoming tantric master to the monarch he had to distance himself from Saichō, and that in the context of Japan at the time, he had to create a 'tradition' of his own. Certainly, from about this time, we start to see Kūkai composing a series of polemical texts that were to form the doctrinal foundation for Shingonshū 眞言宗, a designation first used in 834.

In 816 Saga granted him title to build a major religious centre at Kōyasan 高野山 in the mountains southwest of Nara. The first buildings of what was to be the complex known as Kongōbuji 金剛峰寺, or the Temple of the Vajra Peak, were consecrated in 819. Kūkai's intention was to design the whole complex in the form of two maṇḍala with a large stūpa at the centre of each sacred area, although it so happens that today only one large stūpa remains (Gardiner 1996: 256–58). The rest of his life was spent trying to raise funds for more building on the mountain, although he was always under considerable pressure to spend more time at court, and could never be absent for long. He could hardly complain, of course, given that the role he wished to play was of tantric master to a Buddhist ruler, a role that certainly clashed with the ideal that the saṅgha, although supporting the state, would remain independent of it. It presupposed that the Buddhist establishment would in fact become one with the state, with the ruler initiated and ordained as chief priest. In founding Kōyasan, Kūkai was again trying to emulate Amoghavajra, who had created a large complex at Wutaishan, but he lacked the necessary resources, and raising funds for this enterprise remained a constant headache for the rest of his life. He also took great care to keep in close contact with the temples at Nara, and the creation of a separate Shingon initiation hall at Tōdaiji in 822, at which it is thought he performed a *kanjō* initiation for deposed sovereign Heizei, can be seen as a major development, bringing tantric practice into the very heart of the Buddhist establishment (Grapard 2000b). This was followed a year later by an agreement whereby Saga allowed him exclusive use of Tōji 東寺, one of only two temples that had been created within the bounds of the new capital. In 824 he joined the Saṅgha Office. In 827 he himself advanced further in the Buddhist hierarchy and was made Grand Prefect. In 832 he fell ill and retired to Kōyasan, where he died two years later. Three months before his death, however, he was still intent on emulating the success of Amoghavajra, requesting permission to construct a Shingon hall in the grounds of the palace itself:

I have heard that there are two kinds of preaching of the Buddha. One is shallow and incomplete while the other is tantric. The shallow teaching comprises the scriptures with long passages and verses, whereas the tantric teaching is the dhāraṇī found in the scriptures. The shallow teaching is, as one text says, like the diagnoses of an illness and the prescription of a medicine. The tantric method of dhāraṇī is like prescribing appropriate medicine, ingesting it and curing the ailment. If a person is ill, opening a medical text and reciting its content will be of no avail in treating the illness. It is necessary to ingest it in accordance with proper methods. Only then will the illness be eliminated and life preserved.

However, the present custom of chanting the *Sūtra of golden radiant wisdom* at the palace is simply the reading of sentences and the empty recital of doctrine. There is no drawing of Buddha images in accordance with proper technique nor the practice of setting up an altar for offerings and for the ceremonies of empowerment. Although the reading of the sūtra may appear to be an opportunity to listen to the preaching of the nectar-like teachings of the Buddha, in actuality it lacks the precious taste of the finest essence [ghee] of Buddhist truth.

I humbly request that from this year on, fourteen monks skilled in tantric ritual and fourteen novices be selected, who, while properly reading the sūtra will for seven days arrange the sacred images, perform the requisite offerings and recite mantra in a specially adorned room. If this is done, both the revealed and tantric teachings, which express the Buddha's true intent, will cause great happiness in the world and thereby fulfill the compassionate vows of the holy ones (Gardiner 1996: 264–65, adapted).

The reference here is to the Misaie 御齋會, which involved recitation and lectures on the *Sūtra of golden radiant wisdom*; it was held over a period of seven days between the eighth and the fourteenth of the first month. Given that the new version by Amoghavajra was now in use, Kūkai was concerned to incorporate the proper tantric rituals. This was eventually done (but a year after his death) and the ritual, the Go shichinichi mishiho 後七日御修法, became one of the most important in the court calendar from this time on, dedicated both to requesting blessings for the coming year and to anointing the ruler (Abe 1999: 347–55).

6.4   The creation of Shingon

Driven partly by force of circumstance and partly by the very nature of what we have seen to be the tantric enterprise, Kūkai probably started the process of creating his Mantrayāna tradition (Shingon 眞言) in about the year 815. The main problem he faced was how to establish the uniqueness of his teaching when, as we have seen, tantric elements had been central to Buddhism from its inception in Japan, and Kūkai had clearly been exposed to them before he left for China. About a quarter of what are now recognised as tantric texts were already available in Japan during the course of the Nara period: Dōji had studied with Śubhākarasiṃha and brought back both the *Assembled reality of all the tathāgatas* and Yijing's new translation of the *Sūtra of golden radiant wisdom*; Genbō had returned with the *Mahā-vairocanatantra*. The use of spells against bad weather and illness, especially involving the worship of Yakushi, was commonplace, and there were plenty of tantric deities already in place. So how was Kūkai to distinguish between these pre-existing tantric elements and the tradition he wished to establish? And how was he to do this without alienating the Buddhist establishment?

There were, of course, some extreme novelties in what Kūkai brought back, in particular the use of maṇḍala and the attendant *kanjō* rite, which had such resonance with the act of coronation. There was also the central role played by the mantra that gave their name to the whole tradition, and the siddhaṃ letters that looked strange to a Japanese eye, and sounded even stranger still. In his 'Inventory of imported items' Kūkai made it clear that he saw himself as being in the possession of a new 'vehicle', which he called Vajrayāna (*Kongōjō* 金剛乘), and he was already marking a major distinction between these new 'secret teachings' (*mikkyō* 密教) and the 'revealed teachings' (*kengyō* 顯教) of Mahāyāna. But he took some care to show how these new discoveries were not really at odds with present practice; they simply operated at a much deeper level. Dhāraṇī in Japan prior to his return, he argued, had been, if not misused, then misunderstood. In their new guise as mantra or shingon they were not simply secret spells and incantations to avoid calamity or bring good health; they were the key to achieving buddhahood, which, as he explained in *On the meaning of 'becoming a buddha in this body'* (*Sokushin jōbutsu gi* 即身成佛義), could be attained in the here and now.

Japanese before him such as Dōji had certainly studied in Chang'an and worked with Sanskrit masters, but much had happened between 718 and 805. Amoghavajra had developed his links to imperial power and Kūkai had been close to the realities of mature tantric Buddhism in action. He also had the luck to return to a Japan on the cusp of a further period of sinification with the enthusiastic encouragement of Saga. In his later works, such as *On the ten stages of mind according to the secret maṇḍala* (*Himitsu mandara jūjūshinron* 秘密曼荼羅十住心論), written at the behest of Junna Tennō 淳和天皇 in 830, he developed his own version of *kyōhan* or the ranking of teachings. Here too, mindful that he should not antagonise his fellow priests, he took care not to denigrate existing traditions of scholarship but argued

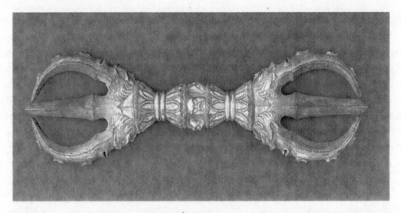

Plate 17   A six-pronged, double-ended *vajra*, the characteristic implement of Japanese tantric ritual. The chosen weapon of the Vedic god Indra, it was often identified as either a thunderbolt or an adamantine sceptre, used to symbolise the diamond-hard nature of perfect wisdom. *Vajra* can come in different shapes. The three prongs at each end are said to symbolise the three mysteries of body, speech and mind.

instead that tantric practice was simply on a different level; the very secrecy of the enterprise seems to have acted more as a draw than as an annoyance, because tantrism was to succeed eventually in permeating all aspects of intellectual life in Japan.

The first datable text by Kūkai after the 'Inventory' was his 'Written appeal to those who have an interest' (*Kan'ensho* 勸緣疏) of 815, which takes the form of an open letter requesting help in copying thirty-five scrolls of tantric scriptures. It was sent to at least ten monks in different parts of Japan, Tokuitsu among them. Indeed it was in response to this letter that Tokuitsu produced his *Shingonshū miketsumon*, which queried a number of Kūkai's assertions. On the face of it, *Kan'ensho* seems a curious way to obtain copies of something, and the ulterior motive may have been simply to bring these new texts to a wider audience, spreading the new teaching by indirect means, since it also contains a description of the tradition and details of the Shingon lineage that Kūkai was beginning to construct. One important difference between Mahāyāna sūtras and Mantrayāna tantras was that the latter were seen to have been passed down not from Śākyamuni, but from Mahāvairocana. It was this provenance that gave them their special status; it gave them the right to lay claim to exclusive truth. Both Kūkai's *Kan'ensho* and his treatise 'On discriminating between revealed and secret teachings'

(*Ben kenmitsu nikyō ron* 辨顯密二教論), written at about the same time, are known for this theory that Mahāvairocana, as the *dharmakāya*, 'preaches' (*hosshin seppō* 法身説法).

This doctrine proved to be extremely controversial. It was all very well using it as a polemical tool in the attempt to show that one's teachings were qualitatively different from anything that had come before, but such rhetoric brought with it the obvious dangers of personification. As always with tantrism, the problem starts when metaphorical language is taken literally. To say that the *dharmakāya* 'preaches' is on a par with saying that the absolute 'speaks' through the sum of its manifestations in the universe. The language through which the experience of enlightenment was communicated was that of ritual, the 'three mysteries'. But normally the absolute was seen to be entirely static, since any activity, even that of pure mind, would presuppose the existence of some form of dualism. Kūkai got round this problem by arguing that the *dharmakāya* had two aspects, that of Principle 理身 and that of Wisdom 智身; ultimate reality contained within itself the wisdom that could recognise itself, expressed in the term 'principle and wisdom are one' (*richi fu'ni* 理智不二). This dual aspect of the universe was reflected in the dual use of the Womb World and the Diamond World maṇḍala. Even so, the idea that a supposedly abstract, static *dharmakāya* could teach was disconcerting and led to a serious sectarian split in the mid- to late Heian period as to whether or not it preached regardless of whether anyone was listening. The 'old' view, represented by Kūkai, was that the *dharmakāya* preached 'independently of any union with the practitioner, directly from the fundamental source of reality (*honjishin* 本地身)', whereas the 'new' view, as represented by Kakuban 覺鑁 (1095–1143), argued that it only preached 'in the form manifested to practitioners in meditative absorption (*kajishin* 加持身)' (Gardiner 1994: 56).

6.5 The Shingon tradition after the death of Kūkai

Kūkai's followers, under the guidance of Shinnen 眞然 (804–91), devoted themselves to building temples on Kōyasan. Meanwhile, the centre at Tōji gained prestige and eventually the two major institutions clashed. In 876 Shinnen 'borrowed' certain important documents in Kūkai's hand from Tōji, took them to Kōyasan and then refused to return them. This was to lead to a bitter conflict between the two, which continued until 919, when the court decided to combine the abbotships of both institutions, so avoiding the kind of damaging split that occurred on Hieizan. As far as further trips to China were concerned, both Shinnen and Shinzei 眞濟 (800–60) tried to reach China in 836 but failed. Four Shingon priests did in fact study in China and return with a large number of texts: Jōgyō 常曉 and Engyō 圓行 in 838–39 with the last official mission; Eun 惠運 in 842–47, and Shūei 宗叡 in 862–65. Dharma Prince Shinnyo 眞如法親王, the son of Heizei who had been passed over in favour of his uncle Saga in 809, also left in 862 and managed to reach Chang'an two years later. Remarkably he succeeded in obtaining permission to travel on to India via south China, but died somewhere en route, possibly in Malaysia. The main reason for the relative decline in the fortunes of Shingon in the fifty or so years after the death of Kūkai, however, was the degree to which Tendai adopted tantric practice and robbed Shingon of its exclusivity. As we shall see, Ennin 圓仁 (794–864) returned in 847 after ten years in China and Enchin 圓珍 (814–91) returned in 858 after five years, both of them having studied in Chang'an. In a sense, then, Kūkai's mission proved extremely successful; it was simply that his own followers were not the main ones to benefit.

Despite considerable difficulties, Kūkai's tradition did flourish in another form; successive sovereigns made sure that they had their own temples, which became centres of tantric practice in their own right. Uda Tennō 宇多 (r. 887–97, d. 931), for example, who during part of his retirement lived in the Ninnaji 仁和寺 that he had founded in 888, oversaw its development into a major tantric centre; and it was also during this period that Daigo Tennō patronised Daigoji 醍醐寺, situated in Yamashina to the east of the capital. Both of these temples were to wield considerable power because of their connections to the monarchy. But problems continued to arise between the two main centres of Tōji and Kōyasan, not only over borrowed manuscripts but also over the number of yearly ordinands each was allowed. When all authority reverted to Tōji in 919 under Kangen 觀賢 (853–925), Kōyasan fell into disrepair. From time to time a major figure such as Fujiwara no Michinaga 藤原道長 would make a pilgrimage (in 1016 and 1023), but we have to wait until the twelfth-century revival under Kakuban.

7   Buddhism and the state in Heian Japan

7.1   Tendai politics

In 812 Saichō, thinking he was about to die, granted the 'seal of transmission of the Dharma' (*fuhō inshō* 付法印承) to Enchō 圓澄 (771–836?), but in the event he recovered and lived for another ten years. In 822 he changed his mind and designated Gishin 義眞 (781–833) as his successor (McMullin 1984a). The next year the Ichijō shikan'in, which had up to this point simply been known as 'the temple on Hieizan' or Hieizanji 比叡山寺, was given the new official designation of Enryakuji 延曆寺. This finally marked it as somewhere a monk could 'belong', an important development, since until that time all monks on Hieizan had been forced to register with other institutions. It was also agreed that a number of Saichō's administrative proposals be put into effect, namely that Tendai monks were to be allowed to carry out their own ordinations on their own platform, lay administrators (*zoku bettō* 俗別當) were to be appointed to test new ordinands, and the results were to be reported not to the Saṅgha Office but directly to the Council of State. Three officials (*sangō* 三綱) were appointed and Gishin was made head of the establishment in 824. He is therefore known as the first abbot (*zasu* 座主) of Enryakuji, although the first person to actually receive the title was to be Ennin. The post of lay administrator became increasingly important and contributed to the growing cross-influence between Tendai monks and the nobility, so much so that it was soon adopted by a number of other major temples. The first full ordination of fourteen monks with the Mahāyāna precepts was also seen in 823. Here again, Tendai gained considerable privilege by being allowed to have the certificates (*kaichō* 戒牒) issued by the Council of State, by-passing the more normal Saṅgha Office route to which the Nara schools were tied. It also meant that the monks concerned did not have to travel to Nara for interview and confirmation, but could stay on Hieizan and start their training immediately. An ordination platform was built in 825. As one might expect, these developments met with considerable opposition from Nara, and Tendai monks found themselves constantly blocked for appointment as lecturers to the three major ceremonial assemblies, the Vimalakīrti Assembly (Yuima-e 維摩會) that was held at Kōfukuji in the tenth month, and the two recitations of the *Sūtra of golden radiant wisdom*, the Misai-e (御斎會), held in the first month at the Palace, and the Saishō-e (最勝會), held in the third month at Yakushiji.

When Gishin died on 833.4.7 he designated Enshu 圓修 as his successor, but because Enchō was still alive this decision was challenged. The resulting conflict simmered on for some months until in the tenth month of 833 another of Saichō's students, Kōjō 光定, appealed to the court, which eventually ruled in favour of Enchō; Enshu and his supporters were forced to leave the mountain, finding refuge at Murōji 室生寺, southeast of Nara. Enshu and his student Kenne 堅慧 went to China in 842 and returned two years later with a document testifying that they had received instruction from the Tiantai master Guangxiu 廣修 (772–844?), but this was not enough to overturn the court ruling (Groner 2002: 21). Enchō died in either 836 or 837, and for the next eighteen years no one was officially appointed to the post of abbot, although it is assumed that Kōjō was in charge.

In 847, Ennin (793–864) returned home after a stay of nine and a half years in China. Ennin is perhaps best known for the diary that records his experiences in China. Entitled *Nittō guhō junrei gyōki* 入唐求法巡禮行記, it is particularly valuable for its detailed description of the activities of Buddhist monks and priests and for the picture it gives of China before and during the Huichang suppression under Emperor Wuzong that had such a devastating effect. Ennin left Japan with what was to be the last embassy in the sixth month of 838 and, after the usual difficult voyage, landed (or rather was wrecked on the coast) just north of the mouth of the Yangzi [map 6]. While the main party eventually moved on to Chang'an, Ennin found himself confined to the city of Yangzhou and in the end never received official permission to achieve his main aim and go south to Mt Tiantai. The next year he left with the returning embassy, but the ship was blown back onto the southern coast of the Shandong peninsula 山東半島, at which point Ennin managed to arrange matters so that he was left behind when they sailed. He was looked after by Korean monks at the Fahuayuan 法華院, a monastery on Mt Chi (斥山, but also written 赤山) at the eastern tip of the peninsula. Forced to abandon any idea of reaching Tiantai, he decided instead to make a pilgrimage to Wutaishan 五臺山, where, after considerable bureaucratic difficulties, he eventually arrived in the fourth month of 840. There were Tiantai monks here too of course, but Wutaishan was chiefly known as the centre of a major cult to Mañjuśrī. From there Ennin went on to Chang'an,

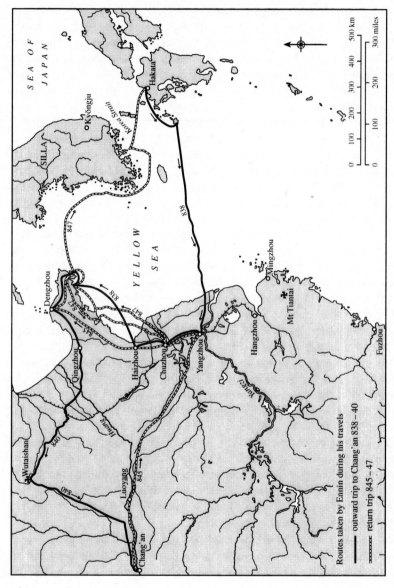

Map 6   Route taken by Ennin during his travels

where he was allowed to stay, studying under a number of masters, including the well-known Faquan 法全, who espoused a somewhat different tantric tradition from that of Huiguo. Two years later, the pressures on Buddhism started to increase and he was eventually forced to leave, travelling incognito to the coast in 845, but not finding a convenient ship until 847. He returned to Japan with 584 volumes (221 of them tantric in nature), 59 different maṇḍala, a range of painting and ritual artefacts, and a good knowledge of tantric ritual. This, above all, was to be a priceless gift for the Tendai tradition, which was becoming increasingly uncomfortable with its perceived lack of tantric expertise. He was given a rapturous welcome on his return to Hieizan and eventually appointed abbot of Enryakuji in 854. He brought back new forms of Tendai meditational practice that he had experienced at Wutaishan, but, more importantly, his return ensured that tantric practice would take proper root among Tendai practitioners. Among the new rituals he brought back were the 'Eight-syllable rite for Mañjuśrī' (Monju hachiji hō 文殊八字法), first used in Japan when Ninmyō Tennō fell ill in 850, and the 'Ritual of abundant light' (Shijōkō hō 熾盛光法), which was designed to challenge the status of Kūkai's Go shichinichi mishihō and became the central Tendai rite for protection of the ruler and the state. He also carried with him the first image of Mañjuśrī riding on a lion, and established a cult in honour of the deity Sekizan myōjin 赤山明神, to whom he attributed his own good fortune in making a safe return journey.

One monk in the party was in fact allowed to go to Mt Tiantai, the young Ensai 圓載 (?–877). It was rumoured that he stayed in China because he succumbed to the charms of a nun, and when Ennin tried to contact him in 846, he failed. But Ensai had been entrusted by Ennin with a letter containing fifty questions from the scholars on Enryakuji to Guangxiu on Mt Tiantai; these questions were duly answered and the answers sent back to Japan, so Ensai must have at least remained in contact with someone.[1] At a later stage, he moved to Chang'an, where Emperor Xuānzong 宣宗 allowed him to live in the Ximingsi and from where he helped a number of subsequent Japanese arrivals. In the end he stayed in China for almost forty years, only to die in a shipwreck on his way back to Japan in 877.

During this period the Saichō–Ennin lineage established a strong base in what became known as the Eastern Pagoda (Tōdō 東塔) of Hieizan, with its esoteric materials stored in a building called the Dhāraṇī Hall (Sōjiin 惣持院),

[1]   This exchange of letters, known as 'Decisions from China' ('Tōketsu' 唐決), is extant and available in the series *Dai Nihon bukkyō zensho*.

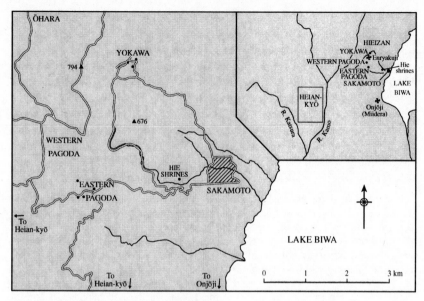

Map 7   Hieizan and the surrounding area

begun in 853 and finished ten years later. Ennin also started to open up another area to the north called Yokawa 横川 [map 7]. When he died in 864 he was succeeded by Anne 安慧, but Anne himself died four years later in 868 to be replaced by Enchin (814–91), who became the fifth abbot. Enchin had been ordained in 833, underwent the full twelve-year retreat on Hieizan, and was appointed Head of Tantric Studies (Shingon gakutō 眞言學頭) in 846, but his position was made extremely awkward by the return of Ennin the next year; so awkward in fact that he eventually decided that he must follow in Ennin's footsteps and go to China himself. He too managed to study with Faquan in Chang'an and returned in 858 with another large collection of texts and artefacts. It is thought, for example, that it was Enchin who brought back the first maṇḍala devoted to Aizen myōō 愛染明王, the King of Lust, who was to figure so prominently in subsequent tantric rituals in Japan. On his return he based himself not in Tōdō or Yokawa but at Onjōji 園城寺, near Ōtsu 大津 at the southeastern foot of the mountain, where he created his own rival esoteric centre and established a cult to his own guardian deity Shinra myōjin 新羅明神.[2]

---

[2]   See plate 15, p. 109.

This decision was to have unfortunate consequences, magnifying a personal antipathy by giving it clear physical expression. For the next century tension grew between the Saichō–Ennin lineage, based at Tōdō and Yokawa, and the Gishin–Enchin lineage, based mainly at Onjōji. Disputes constantly bubbled up as to who had the right to succeed to the post of abbot of Enryakuji, the most prestigious position in Tendai. From the monks' point of view matters of lineage were of high seriousness, but seen from the vantage point of the bureaucrat, this kind of behaviour was injurious to peace and stability. The scholar Miyoshi no Kiyoyuki 三好清行 (847–918), for example, in a strongly worded Confucian statement of 914 entitled 'Twelve opinions' (*Iken jūnikajō* 意見十二箇條) took a very dim view indeed:

The number of people initiated as yearly ordinands or in special ceremonies permitted by the court has risen to two or three hundred per year. Of these more than half are evil and wild sorts of people. In addition, many people among the farmers [without government permission] shave off their hair and wantonly wear monastic robes in order to escape their tax and corvée labour obligations. As the years have passed, their numbers have increased until two-thirds of the population have shaven heads. They all keep a wife and children in their houses. Although they resemble monks outwardly, they eat meat and fish; their minds are like those of butchers. It is even worse when they assemble and behave like a band of robbers and secretly mint their own money. They do not fear punishments from heaven or concern themselves with the Buddhist precepts. If provincial governors try and make them behave according to the law, they assemble and become violent. In previous years, when Fujiwara no Tokiyoshi, the governor of Aki, was surrounded and when Tachibana no Kimiyasu was threatened and robbed, it was precisely this type of evil monk who did so . . . If the edict from the Chancellor's Office had been late, or the court's messenger had been delayed, Tokiyoshi and Kimiyasu might have died terrible deaths. If they are not prohibited, then I fear that they may rebel [against the government]. Therefore I ask that when monks behave in such evil ways, they be arrested and forced to return their certificates of initiation and ordination. They shall then be required to [again] wear lay clothing and return to their former occupation. In addition, if privately-initiated novices join together in evil groups, then they should be put in restraints (*kentai*) and forced to do hard labour (Groner 2002: 8–9).

The court certainly had reason to be worried. Factional strife finally boiled to the surface during the tenure of Ryōgen 良源 (912–85) of the Ennin line. Exasperated by continual complaints from the rival faction, he stopped inviting them to major ritual gatherings altogether and excluded them from the process of decision making, using the Yokawa sector as his personal base. In 982 there arose a dispute over who was to become abbot of Hosshōji 法性寺, a dispute in which armed conflict was only just avoided. Matters went from bad to worse in 989, when the abbot of Onjōji was appointed abbot of Enryakuji by the court. Incensed at this proposal to give the post to someone from the opposing faction, the monks at Tōdō and the third centre on the mountain, the Western Pagoda (Saitō 西塔), dug in their heels, eventually forcing the court to back down. Four years later, the dispute between the two finally broke into armed conflict, which in turn led to much destruction of property; bad blood between the two became the norm.

Despite this failure to achieve unity, Ryōgen is seen as the man who succeeded in giving Hieizan the kind of the financial and political base that was to secure for it an unassailable position as the major Japanese Buddhist centre for the next five hundred years (McMullin 1989a; Groner 2002). He himself seems to have lacked a powerful sponsor in his early years, making his name instead through sheer brilliance in debate. Lectures, recitations and formal debates were major events in the Buddhist calendar and it was through participation in such assemblies that one secured advancement. The most important of these was the Vimalakīrti Assembly held at Kōfukuji. It had started as a private memorial service in memory of Fujiwara no Kamatari, the founder of the clan, but had since burgeoned into an assembly that tested the knowledge and scholarship of monks from a wide range of traditions. Ryōgen first became known outside Hieizan when at the young age of twenty-five he was allowed to attend this event in 937. Only about two years later he came to the attention of Fujiwara no Tadahira 忠平 (880–949), who asked him to become his personal priest. It was largely thanks to the patronage of Tadahira and his son Morosuke 師輔 (908–60) that Ryōgen found himself able to establish a power base of his own on Hieizan at Yokawa. It was a symbiotic relationship, whereby in return for acting as a ritualist for the family at crucial points, his building plans were funded. He became the first monk to perform at court the 'Ritual with five altars' (Godanhō 五壇法) to the five Wise Kings (Go daimyōō 五大明王), with which Murasaki Shikibu would begin her record of a prince's birth fifty years later, and in 977 he performed the 'Ritual of abundant light' for Fujiwara no Kanemichi 兼通, the first time a rite that was normally devoted to helping the sovereign at times of celestial disturbances (it had been introduced by Ennin and first used in 850) had been carried out for someone other than the monarch. Tantric knowledge, which had previously been the exclusive property of the ruling house, was slipping more and more into private hands.

In 950 Ryōgen was appointed religious guardian to the future ruler Reizei 冷泉; in 954 he became the official ritualist for Morosuke; in 958 he ordained Morosuke's son Jinzen 尋禪; and in 966 he became abbot of Enryakuji. He had particular need for financial support. Three disastrous fires on the mountain, in 935, 941, and in 966 when thirty-one buildings were reduced to ashes, meant that much had to be rebuilt from scratch, and his success in achieving this was an extraordinary achievement. Through his patron, he ensured that Tendai landholdings grew and that each new building came with its own support grant in the form of land. When he died in 985, he was succeeded by Jinzen (943–90), the first member of the nobility to become abbot. So began the aristocratisation of the high offices in the Enryakuji community and elsewhere. All abbots of this establishment after Myōku 明求 (1019) were either sons of the ruling family or from the senior branches of the Fujiwara.

Ryōgen's rise to the top position in Tendai was not only a result of patronage, however; it was also achieved as a result of the Ōwa Debates 應和 宗論 of 963, which were held not at a temple but in the sovereign's own apartments within the Palace compound. These debates were started because of dissatisfaction with the dominant position Kōfukuji held as the main venue for this kind of scholarly assembly. Twenty monks were invited to participate; eight Hossō, one Kegon, one Sanron and ten Tendai; one of them gave a lecture which was then subjected to cross-examination by an opponent. As usual, the main protagonists were Hossō and Tendai and the main topic of debate was the Hossō insistence on the existence of 'incorrigibles' (Groner 2002: 94–117). Although it is not known who actually won the debates, they brought Ryōgen fame as a scholar of rare debating skills. Thanks to his patrons, he became both abbot and a member of the Sangha Office. From this time on, Tendai monks, who had previously been largely excluded, gradually started to dominate this institution.

Another area where Ryōgen made substantial changes was in the education of Tendai monks. In non-ritual aspects, namely in logic, disputation and doctrine, standards had been much lower than in the Nara temples, and Ryōgen was particularly interested in improving lecturing and debating skills. He took his cue from the Vimalakīrti Assembly. We have already mentioned this yearly event, by this time funded by the state, in the context of the early history of Kōfukuji. Lectures on the *Vimalakīrtinirdeśasūtra* were followed by an examination of monks on various difficult points of doctrine. Although the event became increasingly formalised in the late tenth century as more sons of the aristocracy became involved, at this stage it was taken extremely seriously. Candidates (*ryūgisha* 立義者) prepared for this gruelling test months in advance and were marked as having passed (*toku* 得), failed (*ryaku* 略) or performed indifferently (*mihan* 未判) (Groner 2002: 132). Any monk who wished to progress into the higher levels of the Buddhist hierarchy had to have lectured at this assembly at least once. It was in Ryōgen's interests to try and create an institution to rival it, not only to counteract the endemic factionalism within Tendai but to free Tendai monks from the obligation to perform at Kōfukuji. He therefore instituted a twice-yearly examination system for which one (or possibly two) candidates would prepare for many months. There were a large number of possible topics, some limited to Tendai doctrine (called *shūyō* 宗要) and others relating to the teachings of other traditions (*gika* 義科). A selection of ten topics would be made by the chief examiner (*tandai* 探題), and the candidate had to pick them out of a box and discourse on them in turn, facing away from the examiners and towards an image of the Buddha. Seven satisfactory answers were needed for the monk to pass. Ryōgen used this institution most successfully to challenge Hossō claims to scholarly pre-eminence (Groner 2002: 150–65).

As this suggests, once Enryakuji managed to create its own tantric tradition, its main rival was not in fact Shingon centres such as Tōji or even Ninnaji, but rather Kōfukuji, which had dominated the Saṅgha Office for much of the ninth century. Kōfukuji's position was largely a result of the prestige and wealth of the Northern Branch of the Fujiwara, under whose patronage it continued to grow until it eventually became the largest landowner in the central provinces. Patronage of this kind was a double-edged sword, of course. Both Enryakuji and Kōfukuji became large landowners, benefiting from gifts of tax-free land by patrons eager to support a particular ritual, or to give thanks for a successful outcome, or indeed to provide for a son who was entering the priesthood. This kind of expansion led inexorably to the growth of large bureaucratic structures to administer large and widely spread estates, which in turn had to be supported by an expanding base of scribes, artisans and 'workers' (*dōshū* 堂衆). It also involved them in disputes over such matters as landholdings that were not always of their own making. Much like the monasteries in England, they became inextricably linked to the structures of power which gave them extensive networks of their own throughout the land but which, by the same token, trapped them in an increasingly complex web of politics and personal agendas.

By the time of Ryōgen's death in 985, it was clear that any attempt to exert state control over Buddhist institutions was doomed to failure. An inability of the state (or perhaps unwillingness would be a better term) to stop the proliferation of private temples in the ninth century meant that by the tenth century there was a large pool of small, largely independent temples available for integration into one or other of the larger religious complexes.

In and around the capital were some temples, known as *goganji* 御願寺 or 'prayer-offering temples' that had been founded by members of the ruling house for their own purposes; these were not strictly state institutions and some of them remained independent. But there was also a fairly large group of *jōgakuji* 定額寺, temples that had been given official recognition in the form of a plaque and funds for the performance of state-protecting rituals but which were essentially in private hands. Temples like these were gradually absorbed into the growing fiefdoms operated from Enryakuji and Kōfukuji. Belonging to a powerful institution helped in disputes over land rights and brought benefits for which independence was a small sacrifice. Buddhist institutions were developing into a series of major political forces in their own right.

7.2   Tantrism triumphant

Saichō had been convinced that the teachings of Tendai and the contents of the *Lotus* were the final, perfect teaching, and, on the principle that teachings were designed to fit the audience, it followed that the Japanese must, by definition, be ready for these teachings. 'In Japan,' he wrote, 'the perfect faculties (*enki* 圓機) of the people have already matured. The perfect teaching has finally arisen' (Groner 1984: 181). From here, it was not a large step to the idea that all Japanese were already in one sense bodhisattvas and so might well be in a position to attain buddhahood sooner rather than later. We have already seen (§5.5) how Saichō thought much about the 'Devadatta' chapter of the *Lotus* where the daughter of the Dragon King achieves almost instantaneous buddhahood, linking it to the concept of the 'direct path' (*jikidō* 直道). He also used the term *sokushin jōbutsu* 即身成佛, which had made its first appearance in Zhanran's *Notes on [Zhiyi's]* 'Words and phrases in the *Lotus sūtra*' (Ch. *Fahua wenju ji* 法華文句記).[3] But Saichō's use of this term should not be misunderstood. He was not suggesting that study of and belief in the *Lotus* guaranteed immediate buddhahood, merely that it was the most direct path and that those who trod that path might well reach it within the relatively short space of three lifetimes. Nowhere did he suggest that anyone was advanced enough to achieve it here and now.

It will be clear that this idea comes close to the tantric agenda espoused by Kūkai, but both the canonical texts from which these ideas stem and the

---

[3]   The main discussion of *sokushin jōbutsu* occurs in Saichō's *Hokke shūku*. Groner 1989.

method of reaching the ideal state of buddhahood are quite different. And while we know that Saichō encountered tantric teachings in China and included a course in tantric ritual in his curriculum, he still saw the 'perfect teaching' of the *Lotus* as supreme. It was left to his successors to try and work out a proper response to the challenge posed by Kūkai. The history of Tendai during the ninth and tenth centuries is one of the growth of the importance of such ideas and of ritual in general. This was not simply a matter of expediency, but was also doctrinal in intent. Both Ennin and Enchin returned from China with the crucial experience of having studied directly under tantric masters in Chang'an and their certificates of initiation gave them the status to act as ritualists as the equals of Shingon priests. The very similarity of their aspirations exacerbated their rivalry. Differences of detail stemmed from the fact that Faquan had developed his own set of secrets and, in particular, had introduced the use of a third set of rites based on the *Tantra of wondrous attainments*, which he extolled as representing the unification of the Diamond World and Womb World teachings. Although it is clear from the tantra itself that a maṇḍala was involved, neither Ennin nor Enchin brought back an example, and the rituals as developed in Japan concentrated on the use of mantra. The core mantra was so secret that it never seems to have been revealed in writing and naturally gave rise to much discussion and disagreement; there were three other mantras, linked to the three bodies of the Buddha, that were also unstable, existing in a number of variations and giving rise, as one might expect, to differing traditions. The position of prominence afforded to the *Tantra of wondrous attainments* and the rites associated with it were peculiar to Tendai tantrism as opposed to its Shingon rival.

It is at this juncture that we begin to see the development of doctrines grown on Japanese soil, and one does not have to go far to find the reason. There had always been tension in Tiantai Buddhism between the merits of meditation and the practice of ritual. One might argue that ritual, even when practised as a communal rather than a private activity, was an outward expression of the concept of non-self; and yet there is no denying that meditation and ritual can be very different activities. But this tension was nothing compared with the radical nature of the shift in direction that we find in Japanese Tendai with its turn towards a kind of tantric ritual that had emerged from a very different background. Considerable effort would be expended on trying to produce if not a synthesis then at least a marriage. The *Lotus sūtra*, for example, was reclassified as a tantric work and then interpreted as such.

The central figure in this attempt was the scholar Annen 安然, who is credited with having laid the doctrinal foundations for much that followed. Born in 841 (Groner 1987; Sueki 1994), he studied at Enryakuji under Ennin for a few years before the latter's death in 864, long enough to receive certain preliminary initiations. He also seems to have studied under two rather unusual, colourful figures: Tankei 湛契 (817–80) and Henjō 遍昭 (816–90). Tankei was forced to return to lay life by Fujiwara no Yoshifusa when he was caught having an affair with the wet nurse of the Crown Prince (the future sovereign Seiwa). Nevertheless, he remained an important presence at court, known for his knowledge of and expertise in esoteric ritual and siddhaṃ. Henjō, being himself the grandson of Kanmu Tennō, was another frequenter of the court, famous as a *waka* poet; but much of his time from 876 onwards was devoted to the establishment of the Gangyō-ji 元慶寺 near the capital. Neither of them was a very monkish monk. In 877 Annen made plans to travel to China and as part of his preparations received a series of initiations with the intention of verifying them in China. There is, however, no evidence that he ever made the voyage. Instead he returned to Hieizan and turned to writing and scholarship. He was never made abbot, but wrote some influential Tendai doctrinal works, dealing both with the status of tantrism and with the question of precepts, where he was in favour of relaxing the rules to a degree that even Saichō would have found difficult to accept.

Annen's writings cover a wide variety of subjects. As far as the important matter of *kyōhan*, the categorisation of the teachings, was concerned, he was faced with having to adapt the traditional Tiantai system inherited from Saichō in light of Tendai's now vigorous espousal of tantrism. So far had this process advanced indeed that Annen began to appropriate the term 'Shingon' and apply it to his own form of Tendai doctrine. The word 'Shingon' in the work entitled *The meaning of 'teachings' and 'periods' in the Shingon tradition* (*Shingonshū kyōji gi* 眞言宗教時義), for example, actually refers to Tendai. The traditional classification called for 'four teachings'. Instead of simply inventing a fifth to include this 'Shingon', Annen turned the whole system on its head by denying the concept of different times and different places as being itself merely a heuristic device. He argued that as all buddhas were merely manifestations of Mahāvairocana, everything was reducible to one: one Buddha, one time, one place and one teaching. This was known as the theory of the 'four ones' 四一教判. By stressing ultimate unity, Annen collapsed all distinctions. And if all teachings are in the end one teaching, then all must be affirmed. The problem with such an approach, of course, is that criticism becomes impossible: one ends up attacking not the content of a teaching but simply the myopic beliefs of its proponents.

One of the key terms in tantric Buddhism is 'thusness' (Sk. *tathatā*, Jp. *shinnyo* 眞如), how things 'really are'. In later Mahāyāna the word is used almost synonymously with *dharmakāya*, forming a central tenet in the *Awakening of faith in Mahāyāna* (*Daijō kishin ron* 大乘起心論). There are two aspects of thusness: the unchangeable aspect 不 變 眞 如 and the conditioned one 隨緣眞如. The unchangeable aspect was what underlay the mind of all sentient beings, but it tended to become impregnated with ignorance, in which case it was transformed into the conditioned aspect, which eventually gave rise to the phenomenal world, the world of saṃsāra. How ignorance arose, however, was not normally explained. For Annen, ignorance was subsumed under thusness, since nothing could be external to an all-embracing principle. The logic of this stance was that thusness transformed *itself* into ignorance and so gave rise to saṃsāra. This is a sensible way to deal with the problem of the origin of ignorance, but it has interesting side-effects. If phenomenal reality is thusness transformed, then ignorance is enlightenment, saṃsāra is nirvāṇa, and phenomena can be affirmed *in toto*. But in this case where is the imperative to seek after enlightenment and nirvāṇa? We shall see later how this attempt to take non-dualism to its logical conclusion led to the development of the concept of 'original enlightenment' (*hongaku* 本覺) in the medieval period, something that had interesting and sometimes disturbing consequences for Japanese Buddhism.

And how does the idea of *sokushin jōbutsu* fit in here?[4] The topic was one of considerable debate and disagreement throughout the tenth century. We have seen that, when Saichō mentioned the possibility of 'realisation of buddhahood in this very body', he used the story of the Dragon King's daughter as an example of someone who had achieved rapid advancement along the path by relying on the perfect teachings of the *Lotus*. This path towards buddhahood was analysed as having six levels, which were called 'identities' (*soku* 即) because one was identifying oneself with the Buddha. Each of these had further subdivisions. 'Realisation of buddhahood in this very body' occurred at the 'first abode' (*shojū* 初住) of the fifth identity, the point when any tendency to backslide was conquered and one deserved the title 'sage'. Not that anyone really expected to reach this in one lifetime; Zhiyi himself stated that he felt he had only reached the third level of identity, although later scholars dismissed this as a case of modesty. When this fifth level was achieved, perhaps after two more lifetimes, the

---

[4]   For more detailed discussion of Tendai views of *sokushin jōbutsu* from Saichō to Annen see Groner 1992.

bodhisattva was thought to have cast off a normal body (*bundanshin* 分段身, subject to karmic transformation) and taken on a dharma-body (*hen'yakushin* 變易身, that could transform itself for the good of others). So how then could the process be really called 'in this body' (*sokushin* 即身)? Saichō left this problem unanswered.

Annen, in his *Sokushin jōbutsu gi shiki* 即身成佛義私記, argued that this change of body at the 'first abode' was not a true abandonment of the body (*jissha* 實捨) but rather a transformation (*tensha* 轉捨), so this was why one could talk of one and the same body. He also argued that 'becoming a buddha' was a process which in fact could start as early as the second identity – when the practitioner had only just heard of the Buddha's teachings. He thereby stretched Saichō's concept of *sokushin jōbutsu* to the limit, opening up the possibility of buddhahood in this life for all sentient beings. Annen was by no means the first scholar to try and argue in this fashion. When Saichō's student Kōjō had earlier questioned the Tiantai master Zongying 宗穎 by letter about the fifth stage, the reply had stated that in order to reach this stage one's state of mind at the end of the fourth stage must already be free of all ignorance. This meant it was therefore logically possible that partial buddhahood might start at the fourth stage. Once this had been admitted, the way was open for those who wished to drive the level even lower, and eventually Tendai monks did start arguing that buddhahood was achievable during one lifetime; the increasing influence of tantric practice in Tendai was certainly partially responsible for such a development (Groner 1992: 444).

A further example of his willingness to extend all boundaries and his unequivocal affirmation of the whole phenomenal world can be found in Annen's espousal of the idea that natural objects might also be able to achieve buddhahood, a concept known as *sōmoku jōbutsu* 草木成佛. Indian Buddhism distinguished quite clearly between sentient and non-sentient, and enlightenment, never mind buddhahood, was only ever a matter for the sentient. In China, the concept of the non-sentient possessing Buddha Nature was tacitly acknowledged by a number of scholars in the Six Dynasties. Jizang 吉藏 (549–623), for example, mentions the idea in the third section of his work *Dasheng xuanlun* 大乘玄論, but perhaps the most influential text in this regard was Zhanran's *Jinbei lun* 金錍論.[5] But here again the emphasis is mainly on the ubiquity of Buddha Nature rather than a discussion of how inanimate objects might have consciousness. It was only Japanese Tendai

---

[5] For a translation and study see Penkower 1993.

monks who took the matter further and presumed that individual objects in nature had mind and could engender an individual inspiration towards enlightenment. As the exchanges in the various 'Tōketsu' letters show, this was largely incomprehensible to the Chinese monks at Tiantai, and it is hard not to assume that the particular interest that Japanese showed in this concept owed much to native Japanese beliefs. Here too Annen was a major influence. His work *Kanjō sōmoku jōbutsu shiki* 斟定草木成佛私記 discusses the matter in great detail and makes a strong case for its logical necessity; it was, of course, possible to go as far as to define the non-sentient as that which had already achieved buddhahood and which therefore had no further need for consciousness. This too was destined to be a powerful and long-lasting element in subsequent Japanese Buddhist doctrine.

Doctrine and practice being indivisible, it is not surprising to find Annen also discussing the rules by which monks were supposed to live. Here, his impact was just as influential, if not more so. It has been argued that it was partly a result of his permissive stance that Tendai continued to show such remarkable laxity as regards monastic discipline, one of the distinguishing characteristics of Japanese Buddhism. We have seen how in his desire to create his own school and in his conviction in the truth of Mahāyāna universalism, Saichō had ended up dismissing the 250 rules of the *vinaya* and instituting the bodhisattva precepts of the *Sūtra of Brahmā's net* as the 'Mahāyāna' precepts for the Tendai tradition. This was accepted soon after his death, but unfortunately this set of ten major and forty minor rules was too vaguely expressed to act as a proper basis for monastic life. It was largely thanks to Annen's ordination manual *Extended commentary on universal ordination with the bodhisattva precepts* (*Futsū-jubosatsukai kōshaku* 普通授 菩薩戒廣釋) that this remained the case for much of subsequent Tendai history. Since in China they were applicable to both monk and layman, they had clearly not been designed simply to replace the *vinaya* (Groner 1990).

The crucial problem with these Mahāyāna precepts was that they were based not so much on action as intention and they were vague enough to need detailed interpretation. Saichō's immediate successors were too busy with tantrism and, although undoubtedly concerned about a lack of discipline, no one before Annen actively turned his mind to fleshing out the precepts. This may well have been because certain elements in tantric ritual demanded that the adept in fact break what would normally be a proscription. We find Annen going even further and placing these precepts below another set, the four *samaya* precepts, which were to be found in the *Mahāvairocanatantra* and were said to have been granted directly to Śākyamuni:

1 not to abandon the true dharma;
2 never to abandon the aspiration to enlightenment;
3 never to refuse to confer Buddhist teachings on someone who sincerely
   wishes to study them;
4 to benefit sentient beings.

By treating these *samaya* precepts as superior, Annen opened the way for the
Mahāyāna precepts to be seen as relative, as themselves little more than
heuristic devices for those with lesser abilities. This meant that they might be
broken in certain circumstances; and if even these rather vague statements
need not hold, then what hope was there for monastic discipline and whither
Tendai? Controls were, of course, imposed, but via piecemeal regulation by
those who ran the temples and monasteries rather than by common precept.
This breakdown was in a sense inevitable once tantric ritual, designed for the
very few and kept secret precisely because it contained such dangers, became
available to all. Once the line between ordinary monk and adept became
obscured, and once intention was allowed to predominate over action, there
were no safeguards and the way was wide open for abuses to find their own
justification. Take the concept of confession followed by forgiveness, link it
to the ideal of compassion, and then mix in the belief that karmic
consequences could be alleviated and even negated by the magical use of
certain dhāraṇī, and one can imagine any crime being accepted as having
been 'unintentional'. This development can be well understood in the context
of Mahāyāna universalism and as a consequence of the rapid spread of
tantrism within Tendai, but the results for monastic discipline were to be dire
and largely irreversible until a reform movement emerged in the thirteenth
century.

7.3   Religious aspects of life at court

Let us step away for a moment from both the politicking of monk and patron
and the picture of scholasticism that the above description might suggest, and
instead ask ourselves how far Buddhist doctrine and practice had permeated
everyday life at court. Most of our information comes from the diaries and
romances that were produced in increasing numbers in the mid-Heian period,
but there is one other important source: the three-volumed *Text to illustrations of the Three Jewels* (*Sanbō ekotoba* 三寶繪詞), compiled by Minamoto
no Tamenori 源爲憲 in 984 (Kamens 1988). The *Sanbō ekotoba* was produced for the nineteen-year-old princess Sonshi 尊子, who had taken initial

vows as a nun in 982 and was ordained by Ryōgen two years later. She clearly needed the most basic information. Book 1 contains thirteen *jātaka* stories about the Buddha in his former existences, stories that are taken from a variety of sources including Zhiyi's *Sijiaoyi* 四教義 (*T*. 1929) and the *Sūtra of golden radiant wisdom*. They all illustrate the importance of self-sacrifice and of compassion: the first six are devoted to the six perfections (*parāmitā*), the next seven are more heterogeneous. Book 2 contains eighteen tales dealing with the introduction and subsequent history of Buddhism in Japan, seventeen of which are taken straight from *Nihon ryōiki*. Again, the effect is to illustrate both the truth of karmic retribution and the need to build up reserves of merit. Book 3 explains to the young woman the importance of making sure that lay men and women pay homage to the community of monks and nuns; this is followed by a calendar of the main Buddhist rites held throughout the year, listed month by month. What Tamenori describes, however, are not the rites themselves but their provenance, giving the princess the kind of historical background that she would not normally have learned. This section is of importance to anyone interested in tracing the origins of certain ceremonies at certain temples, but it should not be assumed that they were all automatically an integral part of lay life at court. On the contrary, Sonshi needed to be informed about them and so they were probably seen as something apart from normal court life. The court had its own busy schedule, which included much that was not specifically Buddhist.

Mention of Sonshi reminds us that women as well as men felt the need for solace and salvation. Nuns had played an important role in the early introduction of Buddhism in Japan and many of the female sovereigns of the Nara period had willingly become influential patronesses. As we have seen, nunneries were set up alongside temples during the reign of Shōmu, for example, and although we do not know much about the official ordination of women, there were clearly many who, privately or not, took certain vows of abstinence and changed their lifestyle accordingly. Some entered nunneries, others simply stayed at home but 'cut their hair' as an outward sign of an inner resolve. As we enter the Heian period, however, official nuns and nunneries begin to disappear from the record. The last time monks and nuns are recorded sitting together at a ceremony is 727 and the last mention of a large number of nuns being ordained is in 828. Both Tendai and Shingon banned women from many of their temple precincts, and hence from their mountains, so by the mid-ninth century it seems that officially recognised nunneries were few and far between. When court women 'cut their hair and became nuns (*ama* 尼)', it was often because of grief, illness or bad fortune, and it was not necessarily an irrevocable step. If a woman was in danger of dying, at childbirth, for example, she might well have her locks cut short as a form of protection against evil spirits. This was certainly the case with Michinaga's daughter Shōshi 彰子 when she was in the midst of a very difficult labour. Sonshi seems to have been an exception, and it is indicative that *Sanbō ekotoba* was written for her not on the occasion of her initial gesture, but when she confirmed her resolve to leave lay life two years later in 984. Increasingly the terms 'taking vows' or 'cutting one's hair' in the Heian period became little more than a metaphor for the act of a woman reaching middle age and moving from the stage of being sexually active to something more contemplative, and occasionally scholastic (Groner 2002: 245–88).

A reading of the diaries written by both men and women during the tenth and eleventh centuries tells us that although Buddhism was firmly entrenched by this time, court life consisted largely in the performance of a series of public and private rites and rituals, only some of which were Buddhist in origin. It is not entirely clear whether the average courtier knew the origin of any particular ritual, and, given the ignorance and lack of interest of most people in most countries of the world in the specific origins of the rituals that govern their lives, this should not be surprising. In a world where medicine was still rudimentary and the majority of events, whether good or bad, were unpredictable, rituals were always best adhered to 'just in case', wherever they came from.

It is convenient to divide these observances into two broad types. Firstly, official court events that either were held at set times every month, or were instituted on special occasions to meet immediate and sudden needs such as illness, epidemic or bad weather; these, of course, could be public or private, although the distinction became more and more difficult to draw as Fujiwara family interests became indistinguishable from those of the state. Secondly, those taboos and observances that were part of everyday life, ranging from the normal ceremonies that marked important stages in the life-cycle, such as birth, coming of age, marriage, death and mourning (forty-nine days), to rituals undergone for specific reasons. These two types were 'broad' in the sense that they too often overlapped. Neither could many of them be marked specifically Buddhist, 'Chinese' or native, although in some cases this would have been obvious. What binds them together is a concern with the here-and-now, with this-worldly benefits. Pain and misfortune came in many guises and forms, but common to them all was the fact that they were beyond human control and could strike at any time. Rituals and observances were almost the only tool one had to build a defence against such evil influences.

Underpinning the official court events was the calendar and almanac that was in the hands of a specific agency called the Bureau of Divination (Onmyōryō 陰陽寮). As the name suggests, the work done here was largely based on a study of Chinese Yin-Yang theory. This is sometimes loosely called Daoism, but this term should be avoided for it suggests elements of a priesthood that are quite out of place in the Japanese context. It was the job of the officials in this bureau to provide assistance on a wide range of matters: 'the observation of the heavens, the recording and interpreting of heavenly movement, signs, and portents, the use of yin-yang techniques of divination, "observing the earth" or geomancy based on five phases (*gogyō* 五行) theory, calendar calculation, and timekeeping' (Bock 1985: 10). The information thus provided was often used in conjunction with purification rites, officials from this bureau working together with diviners from the Jingikan. Their advice was sought whenever an important event was being planned or something untoward such as an eclipse or the discovery of a freak of nature occurred. It is this obsession with ensuring that certain activities took place at the correct time that explains the number of times court diaries describe events happening at all times of the day and night, with no apparent regard for more normal diurnal behaviour.

The official calendar in use for most of the Heian period was the Xuanming Calendar (Senmyōreki 宣明暦) of 822, the seventh of eight calendars produced by the Tang court, brought over by an emissary from Parhae in 859 and adopted in 862. It was a mixed solar-lunar calendar. The natural year (solar) was divided into twelve equal parts known as *setsu* 節, each *setsu* divided into two, giving twenty-four divisions; these were named after agricultural and climatic features distinctive to north China rather than Japan, but they were never changed. The winter solstice (*tōji* 冬至) fell at the midpoint of the first *setsu* of the year, so the solar year began on what is now 21/22 December.

The lunar calendar, with the new moon falling on the first day of the month, deviated from the natural year considerably, necessitating the addition of an intercalary month (*jungetsu* 閏月) one month in every thirty. The beginning of the Japanese civil year was deemed to fall on the first new moon preceding the midpoint of the third *setsu* of the solar year, between what would now be 21 January and 19 February. This dissonance between the official lunar calendar and the natural cycle was often remarked upon: the first poem of the *Collection ancient and modern* (*Kokinshū* 古今集) *c*.905, for example, plays on the fact that the first day of spring (*risshun* 立春, on what would now be 4/5 February) had come 'within the old year'.

Superimposed on this template was a diary of court ceremonial. As one might expect, there was a concentration of ceremonies at the beginning and end of the year, but every month was marked by at least two major festivals. Some were Buddhist; many, such as the Harvest Thanksgiving Festival of the First Fruits (*niinamesai*), were agricultural in nature; yet others were adopted directly from Chinese practice.[6] But as we progress into the period, we encounter the increasing importance of tantric rites offered publicly and privately by both Shingon and Tendai Buddhist monks and a concomitant decrease in the prestige of the officials in the Onmyōryō. It is this phenomenon that is often used to explain why the Japanese continued to use the Xuanming Calendar for the next eight hundred years, despite its increasing inaccuracy. What interest there might have been in the Onmyōryō in astronomy as a science gave way to predictions and the interpretation of a wide range of omens. A new astrology emerged, based on the *Sūtra of constellations and planets* (*Sukuyō kyō* 宿曜經), which had been brought back by Kūkai. This was said to be a translation by Amoghavajra of an Indic original, but it had obviously been embellished with a substantial accretion of Chinese lore. It described the Seven Planets (*shichiyōsei* 七曜星), the Sun 日, Moon 月, Jupiter 木星, Mars 火星, Saturn 土星, Venus 金星, and Mercury 水星, moving through the twenty-eight constellations (or 'lodges' *suku* 宿) of the Indian zodiac.

Ritual gatherings at court and in private gradually became elaborate and costly affairs with multiple daises being constructed, massed groups of monks whose job it was to keep up a constant stream of incantations, and exorcists whose duty it was to draw off evil influences. There was a whole series of rituals to draw on the power of various buddhas, bodhisattvas and other defenders of the Dharma thought particularly efficacious for protecting both state and sovereign from all forms of calamity. There was the Daigensui hō 太元帥法, for example, brought back by Kūkai's student Jōgyō 常曉 and made an annual observance in 851 on the occasion of worries that attacks by pirates from Silla might increase; held to honour Daigensui, master of all demons, one of the eight attendants of Vaiśravaṇa (Bishamon 毘沙門), who was himself one of the Indic protector gods, it involved the presentation of a series of weapons on an elaborate altar (Grapard 1999: 536). And there was the Rite of the Peacock King Sūtra (Kujakukyō hō 孔雀經法), held to

---

[6]   For further details see Hérail 1987–91, vol. I: 50–107. McCullough and McCullough 1980 contains a list of the official dates for the first half of the first month (vol. I: 380–85) and for the second month (vol. I: 400–03).

encourage rainfall in times of drought. Some idea of the pressure generated by such occasions can be gleaned from Murasaki Shikibu's description in her diary of the noise that surrounded the birth of a prince (Bowring 1996: 8–11). And then at the other end of life, mourning the death of a friend or relative was naturally a Buddhist matter, although, as the following description of Go-Ichijō Tennō's funeral in 1036 shows, there were certainly other elements involved as well:

As was customary, Go-Ichijō's funeral procession set out for the cremation site at night. The vanguard consisted of twelve torchbearers and twenty monks in double columns, preceded by a yellow silk banner bearing a Buddhist mantra. Next came twenty men supporting four long silk screens, two on the left and two on the right, which were intended to shield the coffin from vulgar eyes. The coffin, resting on a litter borne by twenty men, and further protected by a second, smaller set of screens, was preceded by two men carrying a 'light litter', on which a lamp burned. The coffin was followed by an 'incense litter', containing a censer and vases of flowers. The bearers of both the light litter and the incense litter marched between the inner and outer screens, as did the Regent, Ministers of State, and other dignitaries, who followed next, wearing mourning garments and straw sandals, and holding peeled-wood staffs. Similarly accoutered, a great throng of lesser officials and minor functionaries streamed along outside the long screens, some carrying torches.

At the cremation site, which was strewn with white sand and guarded by two torii, temporary structures had been erected for the use of the nobles and monks; and tentlike screens, firewood, water, and other necessities were in readiness. Designated nobles removed the coffin lid, inserted firewood, and lit fires. Buddha-invocations were chanted as the body burned. Personal belongings of the Emperor (toilet articles, an armrest, shoes, an inkstone box, etc.) were later consigned to the flames. Around eight o'clock the next morning, the fire was extinguished with rice wine, and the spot was sprinkled by the monks with dirt and sand. After the bones had been ceremoniously sealed in an urn, a Controller set out to take them to a temple, while the other mourners remained for the final rituals at the site, which included the erection of a stone stupa and the planting of trees. The dignitaries then went home, apparently by ox-carriage, stopping at the Kamo River for a brief purification (McCullough and McCullough 1980, vol. I: 373–74).

In a society with an average life expectancy of about thirty, it is hardly surprising that avoidance of illness and disease was a major preoccupation. Major epidemics, probably smallpox, are recorded for the years 947, 974, 993, 994–5, 998, 1020 and 1025. In addition to such figures as Yakushi, to whom the nobles often turned for a cure, there were other gods of more obscure origin who were feared because they were known to be responsible for epidemics (*ekijin* 疫神). Treated properly, they might be prevailed upon to desist. One such was Gozu Ten'ō 牛頭天王, the bull-headed king, with his wife, the Dragon King's daughter Barime no miya 婆梨女宮, and his eight children or Hachiōji 八王子. The origin of this cult is not known but it certainly predates the Heian period and there are a number of signs that it may well be Korean (McMullin 1988). How this cult became established is unclear, but in 863 an epidemic of tuberculosis was put down to the anger of a large number of court nobles who had lost their lives as a result of intense pressure placed on them by the most powerful man at the time, Fujiwara no Mototsune 基經. In an attempt to pacify the anger of their departed vengeful spirits (*onryō* 怨靈), Mototsune organised a large *goryōe* 御靈會 in the palace garden known as the Shinsen'en 神仙苑. This was a large public event at which certain rites were performed in front of six *ryōza* (靈座) or 'spirit seats' that represented six of the individuals concerned. The departed spirits were at once blamed, honoured and appropriated to the Fujiwara cause. Whether this was the first time the cult had been used in this manner we do not know, but *goryōe* of this type were held throughout the Heian period at times of epidemic and other disasters.

Soon after this particular event, the cult of Gozu found a permanent base in the Gion 祇園 temple in Higashiyama, now home to the yearly Gion matsuri, still one of the major festivals of Kyōto. Gion stands for Jetavana, the name of the estate given to Śākyamuni Buddha by the merchant Sudatta, which may or may not explain the presence of a bull-headed deity. The first element to be established in this area of Higashiyama was in fact a temple called Kankeiji 觀慶寺, founded by the monk Ennyo 圓如 in 876. Various divinities then arrived but it took until 926 before a hall, the Tenjindō 天神堂, was built for them. This is a typical example of how the establishment of a Buddhist temple could lead to the worship of other deities and eventually produce what we now think of as a shrine. Kankeiji was affiliated to Kōfukuji in Nara until sometime in the 970s when it was appropriated by Enryakuji, probably thanks to the influence of Ryōgen's patron Morosuke, a relationship that we have discussed earlier in this chapter (McMullin 1987). This started a process by which the original rites were replaced by tantric Buddhist rites and links were created between the Gion divinities and the buddhas and gods on Hieizan.

The second area to be considered, that of taboos affecting the individual, was a mixture of native and Chinese elements. It has been estimated that for various reasons 'the ordinary Heian aristocrat could expect to spend from twenty to seventy days per year in ritual seclusion' (McCullough and McCullough 1980, vol. I: 364). When a period of *monoimi* 物忌, as it was called, was observed by the ruler himself, the whole court fell into a state of paralysis, but they were also of importance to the individual courtier and could be brought about by any number of different things: dreams, unlucky omens, or simply lustration before an important ceremony. Men such as Fujiwara no Michinaga were always consulting diviners as to these matters and recorded the day's events in a diary known as a *guchūreki* 具注暦, which had headnotes in the form of an almanac. From this, one could tell whether the day would be auspicious or not, whether it would be wise to wash one's hair or cut one's nails, and where one's Star of Destiny (*honmyōshō* 本命星) lay. Clearly this kind of information must have come from the Bureau of Divination, or perhaps a private sub-section of it. The following oft-quoted passage from Fujiwara no Morosuke's *Admonitions* (*Kujō-dono no goyuikai* 九條殿御遺戒) of 960 shows the degree to which ritual behaviour ruled the life of the average noble.

Upon arising, first of all repeat seven times in a low voice the name of the star of the year. Take up a mirror and look at your face, to scrutinize changes in your appearance. Then look at the calendar and see whether the day is one of good or evil omen. Next use your toothbrush and then, facing West, wash your hands. Chant the name of the Buddha and invoke those gods and divinities whom we ought always to revere and worship. Next make a record of the events of the previous day. Now break your fast with rice gruel. Comb your hair once every three days, not every day. Cut your fingernails on a day of the Ox, your toenails on a day of the Tiger. If the day is auspicious, now bathe, but only once every fifth day (Sansom 1958: 180).

This shows a remarkable degree of interest in the body as the instrument of ritual, something that links directly to the principles of tantric Buddhism and to native ideas of purity in equal measure. Astrological signs were taken very seriously indeed, since they governed one's whole life. Rites to the Pole Star (*hokuto* 北斗), the *tennō* 天皇 of the heavens, for example, were considered to be of particular efficacy for increasing one's life span, and it was also thought necessary to keep awake all night on the Day of the Monkey once every sixty days in order to stop elements in one's body leaving it to report one's misdoings to the heavenly bureaucracy, a belief known as *kōshin* 庚申.[7] Another particularly interesting set of taboos, known as 'directional inter-dictions' (*kataimi* 方忌), had to do with certain baleful deities such as Taiichi 大一, Taihaku 太白 and Daishōgun 大将軍 (who were both manifestations of Venus), Konjin 金神 and Ōsō 王相, who were constantly on the move both in

---

[7]   Grapard 1999: 549–50. The idea of being reported to a heavenly bureaucracy was Chinese in origin. In Japan a wordplay on 'monkey' (*saru* 申) and the verbal negative suffix *-zaru* gave rise to the three monkeys who were not meant to see, hear or speak about one's misdemeanours to the deity.

the skies and on land, and who had to be carefully tracked to ensure that the individual at risk did not bump into them. This could and did make travel even more troublesome than it already was, because it often necessitated long detours, known as *katatagae* 方違. Not that certain courtiers were above using this as an excuse to prolong a visit to a lover, or to avoid a difficult meeting (Frank 1998).

It might seem from the above account that courtiers of both genders were so hemmed in by ritual activity that they would have been frightened to move far beyond the confines of their immediate surroundings, but such was not the case. Men often had to travel considerable distances as part of their duties, often with large retinues, and we know from women's diaries that they too had the freedom to travel, although they usually needed the excuse that they were going on personal visits to a temple. The advent of Shingon and Tendai led to a growth in the number of important temples that were established in mountains and forests some three or four days' journey from the capital. In order to increase their financial security, these temples, places such as Ishiyamadera, Hasedera, Shiten'ōji, Kiyomizudera and Kōryūji, established festivals and attracted visits by all sections of the population who might want a wish granted or who had special reason to pay their respects to a particular buddha. They were far enough away from the capital to demand some degree of fortitude and perseverance, especially for a woman used to the comforts of the court, but not impossibly distant. Each trip meant considerable pre-paration including abstinence and purification. Such a journey might be motivated by the desire to fulfil a vow, to ask for the birth of a child, to escape from a difficult situation, or even to explore the possibility of becoming a nun. Be they journeys for pleasure or for more serious purposes, such week-long visits to temples in the Yamato area were an accepted part of life at court (Ambros 1990). Something of the solace such journeys might bring is captured in the following passage from *Kagerō nikki* 蜻蛉日記, written by the mother of Michitsuna in the summer of 971:

When I look into the darkness in the shadow of the hills, the fireflies seem to glow with a startling brilliance. Back at home in the old days when I was not so weighed down with sorrow, I used to get annoyed when I couldn't hear the 'voice one will not hear twice'. Here the cuckoo birds sing all over the place to their heart's content. And the water-rails tap out their song; one would think they were right at the door. This is a dwelling where melancholy thoughts are all the more intense . . . The voices signaling the end of the day, the cries of the evening cicadas, the little bells in small monasteries around here calling 'me too, me too' as though competing with each other, and, as there is a shrine to the gods on the hill in front of here, the voices of the priests intoning the sūtras – listening to all of this, I cannot help sinking deep into my thoughts (Arntzen 1997: 237–39).

We also have a detailed record of a rather more elaborate pilgrimage that Michinaga made to Kinpusen 金峰山 at the southern end of the Nara basin in the eighth month of 1007 (Hérail 1987–91, vol. II: 179–87). Kinpusen is the general name for the area of mountains that rise south of Yoshino but it also refers more specifically to Sanjōgatake (1,719 m) in the Ōmine range. Like almost every large mountain in Japan, it was treated as sacred space and had been a centre for mountain ascetics as long as anyone could remember. Legend had it that it contained all the gold that would be used when the future Buddha Maitreya (Miroku) came to restore the world (Tyler 1989: 152). It is mentioned in *Nihon ryōiki* of *c*.820 and there is a record that the deity of Kinpu was given the rank of Junior Third Grade in 852. There seems to have been some form of organisation of ascetics by the time of the monk Shōbō 聖寶 (832–909), who is said to have installed a large image of the tantric deity Kongō zaō 金剛藏王 on the mountain. Somewhat later, a syncretic native-Buddhist deity, Zaō gongen 藏王權現, destined to become the main deity of all such mountain groups, was installed in the Zaōdō on the summit of Sanjōgatake.

After a long period of abstinence (seventy-five days), Michinaga's party left his home at two in the morning on the second of the month, but it was not until about eight o'clock that they finally boarded boats to travel down to Iwashimizu Hachiman. The journey itself (or perhaps one should say 'progress') then took eight days. He reached the Yoshino river on the seventh of the month and stayed overnight on the ninth at a temple called Gion, which may have been near the temple at the foot of the mountains, but may have been halfway between the lower temple and the Zaōdō. The main business of prayer and dedication was carried out on the eleventh. Among the gifts he took were one hundred copies each of the *Lotus sūtra* and the *Sūtra for humane kings* dedicated to members of his family. He also had buried there a copper and gold casket in which he put copies of the *Lotus sūtra*, the three Maitreya sūtras, the *Amida sūtra* and the *Heart sūtra*. These were to ensure not only that he be reborn in Amida's Pure Land but that the teachings would be preserved for the advent of Maitreya when Michinaga would be able to return and achieve final enlightenment. This habit of burying sūtras (known as *maikyō* 埋經) was a characteristic of the mid- to late Heian period and was linked to the concept that the Buddhist Dharma was already in a state of decline and that ways had to be found of ensuring that it was not lost for ever.

Michinaga's own record is unclear as to whether he actually made the gruelling ascent of Sanjōgatake itself or not. One may doubt it, but the fact remains that this very casket was discovered in 1691, buried near the peak of the mountain near the Zaōdō. The journey back to Heiankyō only took two days, partly on horseback and partly by boat.

8   Shrine and state in Heian Japan

8.1   Kasuga

One might be forgiven for assuming from the last few chapters that the native gods were given short shrift during the Heian period, so it is the object of this chapter to correct such an impression. With the move of the capital north, to Nagaoka and thence to Heiankyō, and with the subsequent development of Shingon and Tendai in the ninth century, interaction between native gods and Buddhism increased rather than decreased, and the picture becomes more complex. While it is true to say that the general principle of coexistence was accepted and built upon, this does not mean that the two simply coalesced; they remained two sides of the same coin. Buddhism grew in influence as it gradually made its presence felt in the personal as well as the public sphere, with the result that it eventually entered the bloodstream of Japanese culture at every level. The native *jingi* cults fulfilled quite a different, largely local role, and it is this that allowed them not only to survive but indeed flourish. This was largely thanks to a philosophical flexibility within Buddhism, which recognised the possibility of provisional truths. Buddhism needed local gods to ground itself in new areas via these intermediaries, and in turn it provided local cults (and the families behind these cults) with something of much greater significance, a universal context which became increasingly necessary if the divine right to rule was to be maintained. It was through the medium of Buddhism that local cults began to develop shared characteristics. They needed each other in equal measure.

Kasuga 春日 and the mountain behind it, Mikasayama 三笠山, had been a sacred site well before the Nara period, but at some stage during the eighth century it became the main cult centre for the Fujiwara, who were created out of the Nakatomi. The division between the two was made explicit in 698 and from that time on the role of the two families diverged markedly, the Fujiwara being the secular branch, the Nakatomi remaining as the sacerdotal branch, both serving the ruler at the centre in their own ways. The traditional date for the founding of the shrine at Kasuga is 768. Note in this regard that this is well after the acknowledged date for the founding of the related temple, Kōfukuji (714), so the establishment of a permanent shrine at a sacred site in this fashion may well have come about in response to the presence of Buddhism rather than the other way round. The main shrine houses four deities, ranked in order from east to west, the shrine itself facing south: Takemikatsuchi from Kashima 鹿島, and Futsunushi from Katori 香取, both tutelary deities from eastern Japan; then Amenokoyane, Fujiwara no Kamatari's ancestral deity, and his consort Himegami, who was later treated as representing Ise at Kasuga. In *Koshaki* 古社記, which may be datable to 940 but may also be a product of the mid-Kamakura period, these deities are identified as those gods who helped the Sun Goddess emerge from her self-imposed isolation in the Rock Cave; they thus restored sunlight to the world – symbolic of their role in the Japanese state.[1] At some later stage, these gods realised they were too distant from the capital and decided to move closer, to Kasuga: clearly the mythical expression of territorial gains. The journey of the god Takemikatsuchi from Kashima to Kasuga, riding on a deer, became a common subject of Kasuga devotional art, as is the sacred *sakaki* tree that was connected to the incident at the Rock Cave and was later used by monks and priests at the Kasuga–Kōfukuji complex when they wished to press a complaint against the court.

We know next to nothing about the very earliest rites at Kasuga but they were formalised by the mid-Heian. The following passage that survives from the 'Rituals of the Jōgan era' (872) describes the Grand Rite.

At dawn on the day of the Rite, a member of the Jingikan, accompanied by a young girl whose duty is abstention and purity, cleans the interior of the shrine. Priestly officials decorate the shrines, placing the shrine-treasures in front of the four shrines as well as near the fence running in front of them. The various officials make offerings as usual.

The Chieftain of the House enters the sacred area of the shrine through the Southern Gate in the western corridor, and goes to his seat in the Outer Area. Following him, members of the Fujiwara house who hold the sixth rank and below approach and take their seats, and write their names on the tablets. Tablets, brushes, and inkstones must be prepared in advance by the officials.

During that time the sacral woman leaves her carriage and approaches the shrine. She passes through the Northern Gate in the western corridor. By then those who hold the rank of *tayu*, and who preceded her, have formed a single line ... After the sacral

---

[1]   For a detailed study of these deities and the problem of their origins, see Grapard 1992a: 29–44. Grapard also points out that this arrangement is the exact reverse of that in the Hiraoka shrine dedicated to the ancestors of the Nakatomi, where the ancestral deities outrank the tutelary ones.

woman reaches her seat, those holding the rank of *tayu* leave, while those who hold the rank of *naishi* go to their seats.

At this point the head of the *uchi-kura* orders that the pendant strip offerings must be displayed on a shelf outside the gate, and he waits there for the Elders of the house and of the court. Those who hold the rank of *naishi* take their seats by the shrines and inspect the offerings (Grapard 1992a: 58–59, adapted).

The formula (*saimon* 祭文) proclaimed by the head priest at the Grand Rite makes it clear that at this stage the offerings at Kasuga were to placate the four deities in the interests of the sovereign and that the sovereign expected support from the Fujiwara in return:

By the august decree of the Sovereign, in great awe, we humbly speak in the awesome presence of the four mighty gods, Takemikatsuchi-no-mikoto who resides in Kashima, Iwainushi-no-mikoto who resides in Katori, Ame-no-koyane-no-mikoto and Himegami, who reside in Hiraoka, thus: in the manner in which the mighty gods have ordained, we have planted firmly the pillars of the shrine in the rocks deep under Mt Mikasa of Kasuga. The crossed beams thereof reach toward the heavens, offering a shelter from the gaze of heaven and from the blazing sun. And in it we have prepared and offered these treasures for the gods: august mirror, august sword, august bow, august spear, and august horse; and for sacred raiment, we offer up bright cloth, shining cloth, soft cloth, and coarse cloth. And we place in rows the first-fruits sent in tribute from the provinces in all directions as offerings: the products of the blue sea, things wide of fin and narrow of fin, seaweeds from the deep and seaweeds from the shore, and even unto the sweet herbs and the bitter herbs from mountain and moor. Let the offering jars be filled with *sake* to their brims, yea, let the bellies of the rows of jars be full, and let all manner of goods be heaped up like a range of hills.

Let the surname, clan-rank-title, Court rank, and position of those who are shrine-chiefs be made known. May the choice of great offerings which we present be pleasant offerings, be abundant offerings, and may they be received in tranquillity and pleasure. So we pray as we raise our words of praise to the four mighty gods. Since we serve thus by our worship, we pray that now and in the future our Sovereign may reign in tranquillity and be blessed with a prosperous reign. May it be firm like a solid rock, eternal as an enduring rock, and be caused to flourish. May all the princes and court nobles of all the families from each locality who have participated and served here be at peace. May the August Sovereign flourish in his palace more than the plants and trees which grow, for a reign that prospers, thus we pray as we humbly raise our words of praise (Bock 1970–72, vol. II: 71–72, adapted).

The fortunes of the shrine (and Kōfukuji as well, as we shall see) are closely linked to those of the Fujiwara house itself. Their rise in power and influence is mirrored in the official ranks given to the deities: between 777 and 859, for example, Takemikatsuchi rose from Upper Third to Upper First Rank. Visits to Kasuga by the sovereign began in the late tenth century but it was not until the early twelfth century that the Kasuga cult shifted from being a Fujiwara preserve to something of greater significance. The Buddhist element was important in this development. It is likely that from its inception the shrine was always seen as linked to Kōfukuji, vital for its protection but in the end subsidiary. And when retired sovereigns gave gifts, they were often in Buddhist form. In 1092, for example, the shrine had occasion to rebuke the ex-sovereign Shirakawa, who, in recompense, presented the shrine with a copy of the Buddhist canon and a building in which to house it. Other gifts included two five-storeyed pagodas (in 1116 and 1140). There was no sense of contradiction; it was merely seen as a stronger form of power and protection. Buddhist rites were also held at the shrines, in particular the Biennial Discourses on the *Lotus sūtra* (*niki no gohakkō* 二季御八講) established by 1018 at the latest. It is therefore impossible to discuss the Kasuga shrine without reference to Kōfukuji. When the monk-poet Saigyō visited Kasuga sometime in the middle of the twelfth century he is said to have found the shrine ringing with the Buddha's word (Tyler 1990: 61–62).

Private temples (*ujidera*) such as Kōfukuji were created largely for the protection and worship of the dead. Temple and shrine were complementary in this sense: the one handling the immediately departed, the other handling the divine ancestors and the local deities of place. At Kasuga the two were not antagonistic; they were known to be distinct, but functioned as one unit. As we have seen, Kōfukuji was known as a major centre for Hossō studies but it also adopted tantric practice. Thanks to its patrons, of course, it continued to grow after the capital moved north and built up considerable holdings throughout the early to mid-Heian, appropriating Hasedera from Tōdaiji, for example, in about 990. But it took some considerable time before the gods at Kasuga were directly linked to specific buddhas. In 1016, for example, Fujiwara no Michinaga is said to have proclaimed that the only deity qualified to be called bodhisattva was Hachiman, and the oldest extant documents to contain such associations at Kasuga only date from 1175. Such links were made on various grounds. In the case of Kasuga, the deity Takemikatsuchi, who, as we have seen, travelled from Kashima on a deer, was identified with the bodhisattva Amoghapāśa (Fukūkenjaku 不空羂索) primarily because one of the bodhisattva's iconographical signs was a deerskin thrown over his shoulder. The link may have been entirely fortuitous, but was no less convincing.

As the power of the Fujiwara grew in the eleventh century, so did the landholdings that supported what was now a shrine–temple complex. The Fujiwara ended up by occupying all the senior positions in Kōfukuji's hierarchy. This led to further expansion and the establishment of sub-temples (*inke* 院家) such as the Ichijōin 一條院 (*c.*980) and the Daijōin 大乘院 (1096), which became independent institutions with their own extensive landholdings. This was the phenomenon known as *monzeki* 門跡. From about this time it became commonplace for members of the court aristocracy to create private temples which their sons would occupy until such time as a suitable appointment became available. Most *monzeki* were attached to larger institutions but remained in private hands, and in some cases became richer and more important than their 'parents'. By 1180 these two sub-temples in fact dominated the whole complex. Every time the Fujiwara were 'granted' land for services rendered, part of the grant was offered in gratitude, and much of the land was located in the central regions. By the end of the eleventh century Kasuga-Kōfukuji owned, and therefore governed, almost the whole of the province of Yamato, and Nara itself had grown to be a large city, devoted to its support. So powerful did the priests and monks become, that whenever they were dissatisfied with a decision at court they would threaten to arrive in Heian-kyō with the sacred *sakaki* tree to press their case.

As we near the end of the Heian period, we notice a change. As power at the centre weakened and the relationship between Fujiwara and monarchy began to mean less and less in real terms, the cult centre realised that in order to survive it would have to broaden its base of support. It controlled most of Yamato, but the rituals were still of a private nature, closely tied to the Fujiwara family; this was no longer enough, because what was now needed was a much more direct, emotional, spiritual connection to the ordinary people of the province. So in 1135 an entirely separate shrine, the Wakamiya shrine, emerged, housing a new deity who was claimed to be the son of Takemikatsuchi and Himegami. This in turn created an entirely new cere-mony, the Ō-matsuri. Despite their closeness, the monks had not been able to participate in existing Kasuga rites, which had been held twice a year in honour of the four main deities, but now these new rituals were open to all those in the province under the jurisdiction of the complex, and Kōfukuji imposed a levy throughout the province for its support. A new deity emerged from this process, known as the Kasuga Daimyōjin 春日大明神, a composite figure representing not only the five original deities but also the power of the Kōfukuji as well. We do not know exactly when this happened but the name itself was certainly in common use by 1152 and it was under the protection of this deity that the city of Nara continued to grow in economic significance, becoming itself a 'sacred city'. It was the existence of this more public deity that helped the diffusion of the Kasuga cult throughout the provinces via sub-shrines established on land that belonged to either temple or shrine.

8.2   Cataloguing the native gods

The Heian court took ritual matters extremely seriously, since they affected
the realities of sovereign power vis-à-vis possible rival bases of influence. In
the provinces, rituals were more localised and the sense of being part of a
centralised hierarchy naturally far weaker. We saw earlier how during the
late Nara period there emerged the idea, convenient for those who were
consciously trying to spread Buddhism through Japan, that the local gods not
only were in need of salvation but knew only too well that they were
suffering as unenlightened beings. In Buddhist terms, they had been reborn
into the 'realm of the gods' or *jindō* 神道.[2] The implication of this is that
deities were seen as anthropomorphic beings, not only at court (where it
helps to explain the bestowal of court rank on certain deities), but also in the
countryside and among the population at large. And if a deity was capable of
suffering and of wreaking havoc as a result of such suffering, what better
strategy than to establish a temple in his honour? Hence the establishment of
jingūji 神宮寺, dedicated to bringing succour to the deity in question, in
return for which the deity would become a protector of the Buddhist Dharma.
The gradual process whereby Buddhism married itself to local beliefs by the
simple expedient of offering itself as another, rather more efficacious, form
of worship, is illustrated in a number of stories situated in the ninth century,
and the process was to continue throughout the Heian period. A typical tale
would tell of certain natural disasters that upon investigation turned out to be
curses placed on the locality by a deity in torment. Occasionally this
suffering had been caused by acts in a previous life, and it was only
Buddhism that could solve the difficulties.

In addition to *jingūji* there were *chinjusha* 鎮守社, small shrines set up
either inside temples or in the temple precincts, where the local gods were
worshipped as protectors of the temple. It is possible that these were in fact
the prototype for what later became permanent Shintō buildings. The
installation of Hachiman as the protector of the Tōdaiji in 749 is the typical
example of this process. As we have seen, Hachiman was from the very
beginning a syncretic figure of obscure origins and the earliest non-Buddhist
figure to receive the appellation 'bodhisattva'. He emerges again in 859,
when, as the result of a second oracular pronouncement from Usa, he made it
clear that he wished to be worshipped much closer to the new capital.
Fujiwara no Yoshifusa 良房 linked this to the celebrations for the accession

---

[2]   For further discussion of this term see §16.

of his grandson Seiwa to the throne. This marks the origin of the Gokokuji 護國寺 at Iwashimizu 岩清水 on Otokoyama 男山, at the confluence of the Katsura, Uji and Kizu rivers. It so happened that the individual who had received the oracle was a monk called Gyōkyō 行教 from the Daianji, who was then appointed to run the establishmen at Iwashimizu. Members of his lineage became hereditary *bettō* of this 'palace-temple' (*miyadera* 宮寺) dedicated to Hachiman.

If Iwashimizu was essentially a Buddhist temple set up to honour a deity, there were other cases where the term shrine–temple complex is more appropriate. The earliest reference we have to the idea that a local deity might actually be the incarnation of a buddha is in a petition sent by a Tendai monk to the court in 859, asking for permission for two state-funded monks to offer sūtra recitations for the benefit of the gods of Kamo and Kasuga, but apart from one further reference in 937, we have to wait until the twelfth century for this to become commonplace. The principle is known as *honji-suijaku* 本地垂迹, a term that comes from the *Lotus sūtra*. *Honji* refers to the 'fundamental ground', namely the buddha or bodhisattva concerned, and *suijaku* to the 'dropped footprint (or trace)', the particular form in which he chooses to manifest himself in Japan, a concept that was to dominate religious thinking throughout the medieval period. The resulting deity was known as a *gongen* 權現 or 'provisional manifestation', a term first used at the Atsuta shrine in 1004, at Yoshida in 1007 and at Kumano in 1083.

So what of the relationship between shrine and state during the Heian period? The attempt to impose order on a collection of independent shrines with their attendant cults via the administrative organ of the Jingikan was, as we have already argued, more a matter of hope than reality, and at this remove there is little we can do to verify the degree of its success. This is particularly so because our main source of information on how the system was meant to work, the *Procedures of the Engi era* (*Engishiki* 延喜式), a compendium of ordinances and supplementary legislation compiled in 927 (but not promulgated for some reason until 967), was produced just as the system was on the point of breaking down and giving way to something far more circumscribed. Since this collection presents the culmination of a long process most stages of which we lack, the early years of the Heian period are somewhat of a closed book in this regard, but Books 1–10 of the *Procedures*, devoted to the Jingikan and its associated rituals, do allow us to flesh out the rather sparse details that are provided by the Yōrō Code of 718. The picture it presents shows that no matter how personally involved members of the court might be with Buddhist ritual, no matter how deeply Buddhism penetrated into the ritual of state, local cults were not to be ignored. The welfare of the state as such might be best guaranteed by the activities of tantric masters, but the ability of the centre to impose itself on the rest of Japan depended just as much on its ability to control the cults, those repositories of local power and local allegiances. It is for this reason that although we find no list of temples, of buddhas or bodhisattvas, we do have catalogues of native gods, and Books 9–10 of the *Procedures* present such a catalogue: 2,861 shrines housing a total of 3,132 deities. It is known as the *jinmyōchō* 神名帳 (Bock 1970–72, vol. II: 107–71).

The *jinmyōchō* must be used with caution, since it does no more than reflect conditions in the mid-tenth century and we cannot extrapolate either backwards or forwards with confidence. Indeed we have no way of telling whether all the shrines mentioned still existed at the time or not. It undoubtedly reflected the political ambitions of its compilers. The shrines listed, known as *shikinaisha* 式内社 ('shrines listed in the *Procedures*'), were officially recognised ones, although a number listed in the Nara chronicles are missing. Recognition had been ritually expressed by the yearly presentation of offerings in the form of food and clothing (*heihaku* 幣帛) provided on the occasion of the Toshigoi festival, when an official from each shrine (*hafuribe* 祝部) was supposed to come to the capital to receive the gifts. As an outward expression of control and belonging this was a perfect arrangement, but such an onerous system could not last for long and in 798 the number of shrines involved in this procedure was drastically reduced: 573 shrines (known as *kanpeisha* 官幣社) were to continue to receive offerings direct from the Jingikan, but the rest (known as *kokuheisha* 國幣社) were to receive their gifts from the provincial governor on behalf of the court. The *Procedures* further divides the 3,132 kami into 'major' and 'minor' ones, with an extra category of 285 kami of unusual power and effectiveness, known as *myōjin* 名神. Thirty-eight kami had their cults in the Palace itself and there were three more taken care of in the capital, but the majority were spread around the provinces [see map 8].

The distribution of these official shrines has long been the subject of comment and research, for in places it is counter-intuitive. Among the provinces with the highest concentrations there are some oddities: Yamato (286); Ise (253); Izumo (187); Ōmi (155); Tajima (131); Echizen (126); Yamashiro (122); Owari (121); Kawachi (113); Mutsu (100); and Izu (92). Mutsu is a puzzle that can only be explained as part of the military push to the north that got underway in the early Heian. And the fact that the small islands of Iki and Tsushima on their own contain as many shrines as the

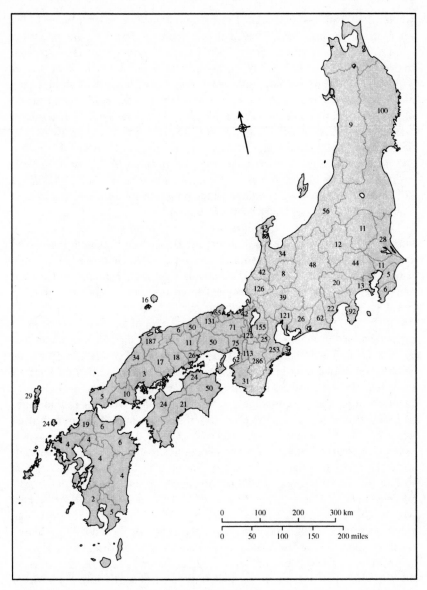

Map 8   Shrines according to the *Engishiki* (927)

whole of Kyūshū must be related to the importance the court placed on the sea routes to the continent. This catalogue, then, reinforces the point that the court's desire to control shrines was as much a political as a spiritual imperative (if we can sensibly distinguish between the two). And just as *Kojiki* and *Nihon shoki* hide more than they reveal, this list of shrines may hide a more mundane truth: that of a rivalry between Nakatomi ritualists and other sacerdotal lineages such as the Inbe 齋部 or 'Abstainers'. The Nakatomi was the house from which the Fujiwara were created as a secular offshoot in 669, so it is hardly surprising that they should still wield considerable power and be creating their own enemies. Inbe no Hironari 廣成, for one, complained bitterly in his *Gleanings from ancient stories* (*Kogoshūi* 古語拾遺) of 807 that the Nakatomi had engineered the omission from official registers of a number of shrines not under their jurisdiction.

The *Procedures of the Engi era* also contains important details on a large number of rituals, ceremonies and shrines. Books 1–3 deal with the annual ceremonial calendar, both fixed and 'extraordinary'. There were five large national ceremonies (Toshigoi, Tsukinami, Kanname, Niiname and Kamo) and thirteen smaller ones, all designed to ensure the orderly flow of a life based largely on agriculture, involving purification rites, offerings of food and drink, and prayers for good harvest. Prevention of untoward events of all kinds from bad weather to illness was the overriding aim. The resources and the ritual activities to be performed were laid down in painstaking detail: the exact amounts of cloth, the weight of the rice, the number of bottles, kinds of utensils and their number. Long lists are given of shrines and deities to be involved in particular ceremonies, such as national prayers for rain in times of drought (*amagoi*) or for the cessation of rain in times of flood, or indeed when emissaries were to be dispatched to China. The demands of such a system, in terms of time, effort and economics, were very heavy indeed. It has been estimated that for the yearly Toshigoi festival alone the Jingikan had to provide offerings to 737 kami, involving such amounts as 75,510 yards of hemp, 737 shields, 737 spearheads, 198 deer antlers, 198 sake jars, 81lb of abalone and 81lb of bonito, among a host of other offerings. As one scholar has put it, 'the maintenance of the realm of the invisible required much visible, material stuff, and just as much work' (Grapard 2000a: 83).

As we have already hinted, there are signs that the system as described in the *Procedures* only worked for a short time (if at all) before the scale of things had to be curtailed; a corrective tonic for anyone who might wish to idealise the situation is provided, yet again, by Miyoshi no Kiyoyuki in his 'Twelve opinions' of 914. He was, at the very least, even-handed in his opprobrium of those involved in 'religion'. Talking of the festivals held to avert natural disasters, he wrote:

the said festival offerings are distributed to the various representatives to present them at their own shrines. The priests should have performed purification and fasting and then reverently bear them to present them each at his own shrine. But, in the very presence of the high nobility, they proceed to take the offerings and silk and tuck them into their bosoms, they throw away the handle of the spear and take only the head, they tip up the bottles of *sake* and drain them in a single draught. Indeed, not one person has gone out of the gates of the Jingikan bearing the offerings intact! How much more so with the sacred horses! Straightway traders outside the Ikuhōmon buy them all and take them and depart. In this situation can the festival deities rejoice in the sacrifices? If they do not rejoice in the sacrifices how can we expect abundance and prosperity? I humbly entreat [your Majesty] to depute one person of the rank of scribe or above, to each of the provinces to take charge of the priests and cause them to receive and take home these festival offerings, and in sincerity to deposit them properly at the home shrine as if they were in the presence of the deities (Bock 1970– 72, vol. I: 13–14).

The first real sign that the court recognised the impossibility of the burden and the need for retrenchment comes in 966, when, on the occasion of a request for prayers for the cessation of rain, we find a list of just sixteen shrines, all located in the Kinai. Three more were added in 991, one more in 994 and two more in 1039, making a final list of twenty-two, and it is by that number that this group is now known.

Upper: Ise, Iwashimizu, Kamo, Matsuno'o, Hirano, Inari, Kasuga
Middle: Ōharano, Ōmiwa, Isonokami, Yamato, Hirose, Tatsuta, Sumiyoshi
Lower: Hie, Umenomiya, Yoshida, Hirota, Gion, Kitano, Nibunokawakami, Kibune

It will be noticed that the seven 'upper' shrines include not only the two shrines connected to the ruling family, Ise and its counterpart in the capital, Kamo, but also the major Fujiwara cult centre of Kasuga and the Hachiman 'palace-temple' at Iwashimizu. The Fujiwara were also represented in the middle set by Ōharano and in the lower set by Yoshida. There are also a number of local cults which must have been included for political reasons that are now impossible to recover with any certainty (Grapard 1988).

It is important to note that many of these shrines were closely associated with *jingūji*, which may, as we have hinted, have predated the shrines themselves. These combinations grew into powerful complexes. At Kasuga a *jingūji* did exist in the area of the shrines but it was soon dwarfed by the overwhelming presence of Kōfukuji nearby, the Kasuga–Kōfukuji complex eventually becoming the major landowner and de facto ruler of the whole province of Yamato. Other such complexes were Hie–Enryakuji, Iwashimizu Hachiman–Gokokuji, Gion–Kankeiji and Kitano–Kannonji. Despite the wish of the court to maintain control, the furthest it went in terms of imposing a hierarchy on shrines was to insist that Ise was supreme, and to catalogue them into 'major' and 'minor'. The localised nature of many of these cults was such that no thought was given to arranging them in tree-and-branch formation according to inter-shrine relationships. Connections between shrines on the ground were not that obvious. Since many of the centres belonged to family cults, their fortunes were dependent on the fortunes of the house, and the shape and status of shrines continually fluctuated throughout Japanese history. Kasuga, for example, gained in autonomy as the Fujiwara became more powerful; Ise, on the other hand, eventually lost its exclusive ties to the royal family. By the twelfth century it had become possible for people other than the ruler to present offerings and to request the performance of rituals, and Ise eventually became a popular site for pilgrimage. In the process, its vision of itself was to change dramatically.

Jingi worship itself remained stubbornly a matter of ritual dedicated to the particular and the local. There was no doctrine, no written scripture apart from the occasional prayer, and no link to the individual per se, since access to a shrine qua sacred ground was severely restricted to the ritualists themselves. One would not, for example, go oneself to pray at a shrine; at most, one might pay a priest to perform a rite. This combination of shrine plus temple was therefore a natural marriage and proved durable, lasting right through to the early Meiji period. The gradual process by which a few of these cultic centres widened their appeal beyond their immediate locale and their specific patrons to become important sacred sites in the popular imagination was intimately connected to loss of patronage from the centre in the later Heian period. Steps had then to be taken to create a broader base for support. As Buddhism moved from being state ritual to something far more 'personal' in terms of both patronage and doctrine, the native *jingi* belief gradually moved from the particular to the more general. But it was a slow process. Nor should we see it as a systematic shift: each shrine and cult changed in its own fashion and for its own reasons. The link between *jingi* worship and a sense of nationalism came very much later.

8.3   The Ise and Kamo shrines

Details of the shrines at Ise are provided in Book 4 of the *Procedures*, which considerably expands on the information given in the only other sources from this period, the *Handbook of ceremonial at the imperial shrine* (*Kōtaijingū gishikichō* 皇大神宮儀式帳) and the *Handbook of ceremonial at the Toyouke shrine* (*Toyouke no miya gishikichō* 豐受宮儀式帳), both produced in 804. At what was later to be called the Inner Shrine (Naikū 内宮) was Tenshō Daijin, with six small 'separate' shrines (*bekkū* 別宮) and twenty-four minor ones. The family that provided the priests (*negi* 禰宜) was the Arakida 荒木田. At the Outer Shrine (Gekū 外宮) resided the food deity Toyouke with one 'separate' shrine and sixteen minor ones, all managed by the Watarai 度會 family. For the purposes of describing festivals and offerings, however, both shrines were usually treated as one. The income for the shrines came from taxes levied on a number of sustenance households (*kanbe* 神戸), which by this time had reached about 1,375, spread throughout nearby provinces. A record dated 806 gives a total of 1,230: Yamato 100, Iga 20, Ise 945, Shima 65, Owari 40, Mikawa 20 and Tōtōmi 40. Although initially the taxes were supposed to be channelled through the Jingikan, in practice the lands were administered by a *gūji* 宮司, who was always drawn from the Nakatomi clan and who ran them like private estates. The *Procedures* also devotes a large amount of space to a catalogue of what was needed during the reconstruction of both shrines, which was scheduled to occur every twenty years. It is not known when this became a requirement, but tradition had it that it started with an edict issued by Jitō Tennō in 689. Since the pillars were of long-lasting Japanese cypress, this regular rebuilding was not in fact an architectural imperative; it may have had more to do with the concept of maintaining purity, although there was another useful side-effect: the buildings themselves may have been simple in style and modest in size (although we do not know this), but the ability to rebuild on such a regular basis was certainly a demonstration of conspicuous consumption and of considerable economic clout (Bock 1970–71, vol. I: 123–50).

Although a messenger was sent from the court on important ceremonial occasions, the sovereign had his own representative at Ise, the Consecrated Princess (*itsukinomiya*, or *saigū* 齋宮). Book 5 of the *Procedures* contains regulations governing her choice, the rituals for her installation, yearly supplies, and her ceremonial duties. The period of purification before she went to Ise was lengthy indeed, involving up to a year secluded in the Palace grounds (the Shosaiin 初齋院), followed by another year spent in a specially built dwelling away from other human habitation, a hut known as the 'Palace in the fields' (Nonomiya 野々宮). It often took her three years to eventually take up her post. Some sense of the seriousness with which this was all taken can be gauged from the following list of words that were taboo in her presence, a restriction that had been imposed *c.*770:

The inner seven words are: the Buddha is the 'Central One', the sutras are 'dyed paper', a pagoda is a 'yew tree', a temple is a 'tiled roof', a monk is a 'long-hair', a nun is a 'female long-hair', a Buddhist meal is 'short rations'. Besides these there are the outer seven words: death is called 'getting well', illness is 'slumber', weeping is 'shedding brine', blood is 'sweat', to strike is 'to caress', meat is called 'mushrooms', a tomb is a 'clod of earth'. There are also other taboo words: a Buddhist hall is called 'incense burner' and an *upāsaka* is called a 'bow-notch' (Bock 1970–72, vol. I: 152–53).

If what we have today is anything to go by, and that is by no means certain, the architecture at Ise was distinctive: not so much the raised floor, since this was a common feature of Japanese buildings designed to counteract heat and humidity, but the fact that it took its shape from a traditional granary. This was, of course, entirely in keeping with the agricultural tone of almost all the rituals. The shrine itself was also unusually modest in its proportions, a simple oblong structure with its entrance on one of the longer sides, facing south. Another distinctive feature was the roof, with ten cylindrical billets placed at right-angles to the ridge pole and exaggerated finials at either end. The contrast with the monumental nature of Buddhist architecture could not be more stark [plates 18–19]. Not only was the shrine hidden from view, an inner sanctum guarded by a series of fences and gates through which only the sovereign and the priests might pass, but there seems to have been little ornament. Even today the sense of monumentality comes rather from the tall trees that surround it than the architecture. Inside the main shrine the deity was represented by a bronze mirror and directly beneath this stood a special pole driven into the ground.[3] Known as the *shin no mihashira* 心御柱, this had nothing to do with the shrine qua granary and all to do with the shrine as cult centre (Naumann 1988: 119–20).

Book 6 of the *Procedures* describes the process of installing a Consecrated Princess (known as the *saiin* 齋院) at the Kamo shrines 賀茂神社. The Upper and Lower Kamo shrines, lying just to the north of the capital of Heian-kyō, were originally part of a triangle of shrines (Matsuno'o to the west and Inari to the east) dedicated to regional deities. The earliest references we have to

---

[3]   For a discussion of the regalia, which included this mirror, see §12.4.

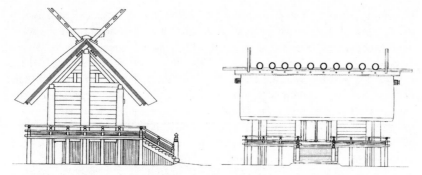

Plate 18   The main Inner Shrine at Ise, side and front elevations.

Plate 19   Aerial view of the Inner Shrine at Ise showing old and new together.

something called a 'Kamo ceremony', which may have been a cross between a folk festival in hope of good weather and ritual pacification of the local deities, occur in 698 and then again in 711. This was preceded by a private ceremony called the *miare* (Bock 1970–72, vol. II: 4–6). The sacerdotal lineage at that time was the Hata 秦, a prominent family who traced their origins back to immigrants from Korea. The crucial change came when the capital itself was moved north from Nara to Nagaoka in 784, at which point the Kamo deity was raised to Junior Second Rank. When the decision was made to move from Nagaoka to what was to become Heian-kyō, even closer to the shrines, his rank was raised even further. Kamo in fact is a classic example of what might happen when a local deity and his shrine were appropriated by and absorbed into a major family cult, in this case that of the ruling family itself. This was of course all part and parcel of the need to 'occupy' the space of the new capital in every sense of the word. The ceremony itself was continued and became one of the most important occasions in the capital, still celebrated today in the form of a large public procession of colourful historical figures through the streets of Kyōto.

The institution of the Saiin was established by Saga in either 810 or 823. Just as in the case of Ise, this was an arrangement whereby a young princess was installed as representative of the sovereign at the shrine, charged with the duty of maintaining the necessary purity and carrying out a series of rituals. The first such princess to be installed was Uchiko 有智子 (807–47); the last one was Reishi 禮子 in 1204. The institution therefore lasted four hundred years and was filled by over thirty-five different young women of royal blood. In this sense, then, Kamo performed the same role at Heian-kyō as Ise did in the wider sphere, but this should not lead us to assume that it was in any way an offshoot or branch of Ise. This is perhaps the clearest example of the kind of autonomy and lack of interconnectedness that we find in early *jingi* worship. The roots of Kamo were entirely unconnected to those of Ise and its distinctiveness was always maintained. At this stage, different cult centres did not see themselves as being linked to each other in either hierarchical or indeed linear fashion. Economic ties in terms of land and other forms of patronage from the centre certainly increased the ostensible hold of the centre over the periphery, but this did little to increase cohesion between the elements themselves. In this sense the 'system' was a mere fiction and the most important shrines are best studied as a collection of cultic sites with as many differences as similarities.

Kamo also happens to provide us with a glimpse of the kind of tensions that could exist between Buddhism and *jingi* worship. In the public arena, this was clearly visible in that nobody other than the sovereign was allowed near the shrines themselves and one could only communicate with those who served in them through intermediaries. In the shrine precincts this was mirrored (as at Ise) by the prohibition on certain words, many of them connected to Buddhism. Of even more interest, however, is what might occur in the private sphere. Senshi 選子 (964–1035), who served at the shrines from 975 till her death, has left us a collection of poetry entitled *Poems on the awakening of faith* (*Hosshinwakashū* 發心和歌集), in which she reveals that privately she looked to Buddhism for personal solace and the possibility of salvation (Kamens 1990). The collection bears eloquent witness to the personal unhappiness that was thus generated between the role she had to play as a ritual representative of the ruler (politico-religious) and her own personal convictions. Nothing could be a better illustration of the distinction between Buddhism and *jingi* worship at this time: they coexisted, avoiding direct conflict because they covered different parts of the religious spectrum. A problem would only emerge, as here, in extremis.

9   The rise of devotionalism

9.1   Turning to face west

It is clear from *Poems on the awakening of faith* (1012) that Senshi, who
served at Kamo for sixty years, found little personal solace in her rituals at
the shrine and was a committed Buddhist, constantly fretting at not being
able to increase her stock of merit through devotion. The bulk of her
collection is devoted to poems linked to lines from the *Lotus sūtra*, for it was
this text that gave her hope of salvation as a woman; but there are a number
of poems that refer to a different object of devotion: 'Though my thoughts
are there, I cannot express it in words, for it is taboo; turn in that direction
and weep, that is all'. The taboos on Buddhist vocabulary we have already
met; the direction in this case is west, the object is the Pure Land, and the
Buddha in question is Amitābha (Jp. Amida 阿彌陀). Senshi was not alone in
her desires. At almost exactly the same time, Murasaki Shikibu finishes off a
letter to a friend with a note of resignation:

Why should I hesitate to say what I want to? Whatever others might say, I intend to
immerse myself in reading sūtras for Amitābha Buddha. Since I have lost what little
attachment I ever had for the pains that life has to offer, you might expect me to
become a nun without delay. But even supposing I were to commit myself and turn
my back on the world, I am certain there would be moments of irresolution before he
came for me riding on his clouds (Bowring 1996: 58–59).

And then we have Michinaga himself. For most of his life he was catholic in
his observances and saw no reason to be exclusive in his devotions. The
reason he buried cylinders containing sūtras on Kōyasan in 1007 was that he
hoped that when he was eventually reborn in Amitābha's Pure Land, he
would be able to return to this world and listen to Maitreya expounding the
Lotus sūtra that he, Michinaga, had buried for the express purpose; he would
then become a buddha himself. By 1019, however, as his illness grew worse,
the specific references in his diary to Amitābha increase in frequency as he

takes vows and starts to build what was to become the Hōjōji 法成寺 with its magnificent Amitābha Hall. He died in 1027, but the very last entries in his diary are for 1021. For the first five days of the ninth month of that year, he records nothing but the number of invocations to Amitābha that he managed: they range from 110,000 up to a fantastic 170,000 per day (Hérail 1987–91: 625). Despite the romanticised account of his death in *A tale of flowering fortunes* (*Eiga monogatari* 榮花物語), we know from other contemporary records that he eventually died in terrible pain and distress, but all accounts show that it was to Amitābha that he turned in his final days:

Altogether detached, it seemed, from worldly concerns, Michinaga fixed his gaze on the nine Amitābha images, which were visible through an opening in the west side of the encircling wall of screens. Even the wisest men are said to feel the three attachments at the time of death, but there was no more room in his mind for worldly splendour – a clear indication of his future state. He had even lost interest in receiving Shōshi and Ishi; although he yielded to their entreaties, he sent them off again after a few minutes. His only desire was to concentrate his thoughts on Amitābha Buddha as death approached. He wished to see no forms other than the signs and attributes of the Buddha, to hear no sound other than the words of the Buddhist teachings, and to think of no object other than his future life. He lay facing west with his pillow to the north, his eyes on the signs and attributes of the Tathāgata Amitābha, his ears filled with holy invocations of the Buddha's name, his heart fixed on the Land of Ultimate Bliss, and his hands grasping the braids held by the Amitābha statue. He looked the very image of a buddha or bodhisattva in human form (McCullough and McCullough 1980, vol. II: 763).

What these examples all illustrate is that Buddhism at the Heian court was not just a matter of grand ritual carried out by priests for peace, prosperity, health and maintenance of the status quo; there was a parallel process by which courtiers absorbed the Buddhist message on an individual level and looked to it for a message of salvation. The trappings of a state religion had already given way to a form of 'privatisation', in the sense that it had become difficult to distinguish between Fujiwara house ritual and state ritual; but here we are talking about something far more personal: devotion to a specific Buddha with the next life in mind. Monk and priest were there to perform certain rituals, but the natural tendency towards universalism within Tendai was giving rise to a much greater involvement of lay people. And with this inward turn, concern with obtaining protection in and for this life became, if not supplanted, then balanced with a fascination with death, an interest in preparing for a future life, and a vision that this life was a form of hell.

9.2   Amitābha's vows

Amitābha means 'Immeasurable Light', although he is also known as Amitāyus, meaning 'Immeasurable Life'. He is clearly a product of the Mahāyāna and is thought to have emerged when Buddhism came into contact with Iranian culture. The tradition that has Amitābha as its main object of devotion is known as Pure Land Buddhism and the three sūtras that Japanese Pure Land Buddhism was to single out for special study and reverence were the *Sūtra on visualising the Buddha of Immeasurable Life* (*Kan muryōju kyō* 觀無量壽經), which has no Indic version and was probably composed in China or perhaps Central Asia (Fujita 1990; Tanaka 1990), the *Smaller Sukhāvatīvyūha* (*Amida kyō* 阿彌陀經), translated into Chinese by Kumārajīva *c*.402, and the *Larger Sukhāvatīvyūha* (*Muryōju kyō* 無量壽經), which exists in five Chinese versions, the favoured one being a fifth-century revision of a third-century translation. Amitābha's Pure Land offers a much easier path to enlightenment than that normally proposed in early Buddhism. Salvation becomes open for all, achievable not through strenuous discipline over an inconceivable timespan by men of extraordinary stamina and self-control, but by lay men and women. Belief and devotion were all that was necessary to lead one into this Pure Land that lay in the west and from where final liberation was guaranteed. Theoretically, the Buddha taught that one could achieve real liberation only from the human state; but what we have here is the development of a half-way house beyond the six courses and the cycle of birth and rebirth that is saṃsāra, a haven from which it is not possible to regress and from which further progress towards nirvāṇa is a foregone conclusion. Note that we should not really say that one was 'reborn' into this Pure Land, because rebirth was part of saṃsāra; one was guided and delivered into it. The majority of believers, of course, could see no further than this first stage, which was more than enough for most mortals to envisage and to strive for.

A good description of Amitābha's Pure Land of Supreme Bliss (Sk. Sukhāvatī) can be found in the *Smaller Sukhāvatīvyūha*. It is a realm of artifice: the ground is made of gold, it is furnished with ponds and steps of precious stones, celestial music is heard, the wind blows softly through jewelled trees, and beautiful birds sing the message of the Buddhist Dharma. But despite this element of physicality in its representation, it is pure, unsullied and ethereal. It would be difficult to locate oneself within it, for example, or to recreate it geographically in the mind's eye, because the description is not architectural. How many believers thought of it as a 'real' place and how many as a state of mind is difficult to gauge of course, but the artificiality is certainly a function of its being seen as something other than simply a beautiful environment. The historical Buddha Śākyamuni, who is the 'presenter' of the description in this sūtra, makes the following promise:

Śāriputra, living beings who hear this should generate an earnest desire, wishing to be reborn in that land. Why? Because in that land one will be able to meet in one place persons of such high virtue as the many living beings I have described here. Śāriputra, one cannot be reborn in that buddha-field, if one depends on the merit of only a few roots of goodness. Śāriputra, if good men or good women hear this explanation of the qualities of the Buddha Amitābha, and embrace his name 執持名号, and keep it in mind single-mindedly and without distraction, be it for one day, or for two, for three, for four, for five, for six, or for seven days, then, when their lives come to an end, the Buddha Amitābha, together with his holy entourage, will appear before them. At the time of their death, their minds free from any distorted views, they will be able to be reborn forthwith in Amitābha Buddha's Land of Supreme Bliss (Gómez 1996: 148).

It is, however, in the *Larger Sukhāvatīvyūha* that we find the famous forty-eight vows made by Amitābha in a previous incarnation as the bodhisattva Dharmākara. Some of the most important are as follows:

1 May I not gain possession of perfect awakening if, once I have attained buddhahood, my land should still have hells, hungry ghosts, or animals.
2 May I not gain possession of perfect awakening if, once I have attained buddhahood, any one among the humans and gods in my land return to one of the three unfortunate paths of rebirth after their normal life span has come to an end.
11 May I not gain possession of perfect awakening if, once I have attained buddhahood, the humans and gods in my land are not assured of awakening, and without fail attain liberation.
13 May I not gain possession of perfect awakening if, once I have attained buddhahood, my life span has a limit, even a limit of hundreds of thousands of million of trillions of cosmic ages.
18 May I not gain possession of perfect awakening if, once I have attained buddhahood, any among the throng of living beings in the ten regions of the universe should single-mindedly desire to be reborn in my land of joy, with confidence, and gladness, and if they should bring to mind this aspiration for even ten moments of thought and yet not gain rebirth there. This excludes only those who have committed the five heinous sins and those who have reviled the True Dharma.
19 May I not gain possession of perfect awakening if, once I have attained buddhahood, any among the throng of living beings in the ten regions of the universe resolves to seek awakening, cultivates all the virtues, and single-mindedly aspires to be reborn in my land, and if, when they approach the moment of their death, I did not appear before them, surrounded by a great assembly (Gómez 1996: 166–68).

If it was believed that Amitābha had vowed to save all humanity for ever by welcoming them into his Land of Supreme Bliss, then Vow 18 was problematic, since it contained what can only be called an exclusion clause. The Chinese monk Shandao 善導 (613–81) provided an answer to this problem in his commentary to the *Sūtra on visualising the Buddha of Immeasurable Life*. It is in this sūtra that Śākyamuni Buddha teaches Queen Vaidehī, who has been imprisoned by her son Ajātaśatru, the consolation of sixteen meditative techniques (思) by which she may visualise the Pure Land and in the end see Amitābha himself. This is followed by a description of nine possible ranks of deliverance in the Pure Land (three sets of three ranks) known as the *kuhon* 九品, which depend on the level of achievement of the individual and range from those with the highest merit right down to those who have committed the worst of crimes, the lowest of the low (*gebon geshō* 下品下生). At this point the Buddha tells the queen that even at this lowest stage, salvation is possible if the person calls out 'Homage to Amitābha' with full sincerity. Shandao asserted that Vow 18 was merely cautionary in nature and that *this* passage constituted an absolute guarantee. There were five practices that could lead to entering the Pure Land of Supreme Bliss: reciting the sūtras, meditation, veneration, the giving of offerings, and lastly, recitation of the name.

9.3   Early Pure Land Buddhism

By the time Buddhism reached China, Amitābha was already an established figure in the Mahāyāna pantheon. The first signs of something approaching a cult come in 402 when Huiyuan 慧遠 (334–416), who had settled at the Donglinsi 東林寺 in Lushan 廬山, collected a group of monks and laymen, 123 in all, in front of an image of Amitābha. They called themselves the White Lotus Society 白蓮社 and together made a vow to help each other reach the Pure Land. The text of the vow and a description of the occasion can be found in Huiyuan's biography in *Biographies of eminent monks*.[1] Much emphasis is placed on the techniques of visualisation that are described in one of the earliest Buddhist texts to be translated into Chinese, the *Samādhi of direct encounter with the buddhas of the present*.[2] Amitābha

---

[1]   Ch. *Gaosengzhuan*, Jp. *Kōsōden* 高僧傳, *T.* 2059, compiled by Huijiao 慧皎 *c*.530. For a full translation see Zürcher 1972, vol. I: 240–53.

[2]   Sk. *Pratyutpannasamādhisūtra*, Ch. *Banzhou sanmei jing*, Jp. *Hanju sanmai kyō* 般舟三昧經, *T.* 416–19.

appears here not as an exclusive figure but merely as a major example, the aim of the exercise being to produce a mental image as if one were standing face-to-face in the Buddha's presence. Huiyuan's death is not recorded as part of his biography, but we do have descriptions of the deaths of his students, descriptions which clearly underlie similar accounts of deliverance into the Pure Land from tenth-century Japan (Zürcher 1972, vol. I: 221–22).

The habit of relying on Amitābha to the exclusion of other buddhas, however, is usually traced back to the figure of Tanluan 曇鸞 (*c*.488–*c*.544) from Wutaishan. We already find here the practice of reciting the name of Amitābha, although it is still just one of many practices or 'entrances' (門) to his compassion. Daochuo 道綽 (562–645) and Shandao (613–81) took this tradition much further by linking it to the emerging idea that the world had already entered the Latter Days of the Dharma, meaning that people were so mentally feeble that devotion to Amitābha in the hope of reaching his Pure Land had become the only hope for salvation for anyone. Shandao is also thought to be the origin of the parable of the 'white way between two rivers' (*niga byakudō* 二河白道), which became the subject of so many illustrations later in Japan. A man is travelling west through land inhabited by wild beasts and robbers. He comes across two rivers: one stretching north is of water, the other stretching south is of fire. Between them lies a narrow white path. The man is convinced he will either drown or be consumed in flames. It is only Amitābha, standing at the other end, who can convince him to tread the narrow path and thereby escape evil for ever.[3]

Pure Land Buddhism as it developed in twelfth-century Japan looked to figures such as Daochuo and Shandao as the patriarchs of their tradition, but Pure Land Buddhism in fact started in Heian Japan from rather different roots. Before the mid-Heian, interest in and devotion to Amitābha was only sporadic. There is the occasional reference in *Nihon shoki* to Pure Land sūtras as early as the mid-seventh century, but statues and images of Śākyamuni and Maitreya far outnumber those of Amitābha until the late eighth century, and even then, Amitābha simply figured as one of a number of buddhas and bodhisattvas to whom one might appeal for help. The halls that were built to hold these statues either were dedicated to the repose of the dead or were to ensure good fortune in this life; there is little evidence that they were geared to the personal salvation of the donor or sponsor. Scholarly consensus is that Amitābha only becomes noticeable in the late Nara period and even then does not stand out in particular from any other buddha or bodhisattva. It is

---

[3] For two good illustrations, see Rosenfield and ten Grotenhuis 1979: 133–37.

not, in fact, until the late tenth century that his cult becomes a serious issue, and when it does emerge it comes not direct from Pure Land practice in China but as an offshoot of Japanese Tendai. One of the religious practices that Zhiyi had encouraged was meditation (*samādhi*), considered necessary preparation for stilling the mind and ridding it of all disturbances. As we saw in §5.3, his manual identified four methods of cultivating *samādhi*. The second of these, the 'constantly walking samādhi' (*jōgyō zanmai* 常行三昧), involved circumambulating an image of Amitābha for ninety days without rest, during which time the practitioner had to try and visualise the image while intoning the name. Two fundamental forms of meditation are dealt with, one that takes three months and another that takes a mere seven days. The relevant section of *Mahāyāna calming and contemplation* presents it as follows:

Speech. When to speak and when to keep silent with the mouth: while the body walks for ninety days without pausing, for ninety days the mouth ceaselessly chants the name of Amitābha Buddha without pausing, and for ninety days the mind recollects [the form and meritorious qualities of] Amitābha Buddha without pausing. One may chant and recollect simultaneously, or first recollect and then chant, or first chant and then recollect. But reciting and recollecting are, nevertheless, to be carried out continually without a moment's pause. The merit that accrues from chanting [the name of] Amitābha is equal to that of chanting [the names of all] the buddhas in the ten directions. However, Amitābha alone is to be regarded as the focus of this practice. Every step, every utterance, and every thought should be centered solely upon the Buddha Amitābha.

Mind. With respect to mind we discuss calming and contemplation. One should mentally recollect the Buddha Amitābha ten trillion buddha lands to the west, in a jewelled pavilion, under a jewelled tree, on an island in a jewelled pond in a jewelled land, expounding sūtras while sitting amid a congregation of bodhisattvas. Recollect the Buddha continually like this for three months. How should you think of him? Mentally recollect his thirty-two marks, one by one in reverse order, from the thousand-spoked wheel on the sole of each foot to the invisible mark at the top of his head. Then you should review all the marks in the proper order, from the mark at the top of his head to the thousand-spoked wheels on his soles and think to yourself: 'Let me come to have these marks as well' (Donner and Stevenson 1993: 239–40).

So how did Pure Land Buddhism spread in the early to mid-Heian period? In 812 Saichō had a hall specially built on Hieizan for the practice of the 'lotus samādhi' (*hokke zanmai* 法華三昧), which formed a part of Zhiyi's third technique, the 'part-walking/part-sitting samādhi', but there is little sign of much interest being shown in the other three forms of meditation. In fact we have to wait until the return of Ennin in 847 to find 'constantly walking' being practised on Hieizan. While on Wutaishan, Ennin had personally experienced a version said to have been devised by Fazhao 法照 in the eighth century, and a few years after his return to Japan, he had a special hall built in the Eastern Pagoda sector so that this technique could be practised. A second such hall was built in the Western Pagoda sector in 893, but Yokawa had to wait until Ryōgen managed to have one constructed in 968. It is known that Fazhao's particular style included chanting Amitābha's name to the accompaniment of music with a special five-tone rhythm. It was a stylish affair; meditation yes, but underpinned by devotionalism.

In the period of over a hundred and fifty years between Ennin's return and the court in which Murasaki Shikibu served, one finds a gradual diversification of meditational techniques as the practice of meditation and devotion was made more accessible to larger numbers of participants. This is mirrored in the development of the halls themselves. It is not known what Ennin's first building looked like, but when it was rebuilt in 883 it is known to have contained five statues (Amitābha plus four bodhisattvas) in the esoteric form that one finds in the Assembly of the Perfected Body (*jōjinne* 成身會) of the Diamond World maṇḍala (see §21). Amitābha is sitting cross-legged deep in meditation. When the Yokawa hall was built some seventy years later, however, we find Amitābha surrounded by Avalokiteśvara (Kannon 觀音), Mahāsthāmaprāpta (Seishi 勢至), Kṣitigarbha (Jizō 地藏) and Nāgārjuna (Ryūju 龍樹), and the esoteric flavour is attenuated. Whether or not Amitābha was standing is not known, but if he were standing this would represent a further shift in emphasis, since it is in this form that he was meant to appear to the dying. From the description given in Minamoto no Tamenori's *Text to illustrations of the Three Jewels* of 984, it is clear that the period normally spent circumambulating was only seven days and that the practice, now called *fudan nenbutsu* 不斷念佛, had turned from being a solitary, demanding ordeal into a rather noisy gathering in which a large number of monks were supposed to take part (Kamens 1988: 342–44). The beginnings of a recognised cult of Amitābha can be dated to the 960s.

At the 'street' level, of course, we have very little information, but, judging from what we know of the figure Kūya 空也 (903–72), there must have been a good deal of activity. Kūya, popularly known as a bodhisattva, was not officially ordained, but was a man in the non-conformist tradition who used a combination of entertainment, prayers, music and dance to spread a message of salvation through devotion to Amitābha to all and sundry. It is known that he took his message through the streets of the capital and, given that he started his activity in Heian-kyō in 938, it may well be that aristocratic interest in Amitābha emerged partly as a result of his activities.

He eventually became properly ordained on Hieizan, but his main concern was still with people in the city. Certainly, Tamenori was sufficiently impressed to write an encomium at his death entitled 'Kūya-rui 空也誄' that praised his work and transformed him into a near-legendary figure.[4]

9.4   Covenanting for salvation

One of the more interesting manifestations of this increasing concern with death and salvation was set in train by the courtier Yoshishige no Yasutane 慶滋保胤 (*c*.931–1002) and the monk Genshin 源信 (942–1017). Yasutane was the guiding spirit behind a fraternity called the Kangaku-e 勸學會, set up in 964 and dedicated to the study of (Chinese) poetry and Buddhism. A group of twenty courtiers and twenty monks met twice a year (on the fifteenth of the third month and the fifteenth of the ninth month) for one day at a temple at Sakamoto at the eastern foot of Hieizan, to listen to lectures on the *Lotus sūtra* in the morning, to chant the name of Amitābha and meditate on him in the evening, and then to compose Chinese poetry on topics from the sūtra throughout the night until dawn the next morning. The group itself seems to have come together fairly regularly and, although attempts to create a permanent meeting place met with failure, some of the meetings were probably accommodated at Rokuharamitsudera 六波羅密寺. The fraternity was disbanded in 986, at which point Yasutane became a monk, taking the name Jakushin 寂心. Although the Kangaku-e has sometimes been treated lightly as an occasional event held by literati dabbling in religion in dilettante fashion, it does represent 'the beginnings of very personal involvement by sincere lay Buddhists in Amidist piety and worship outside the confines of formal monastic ritual, and so marks an important development in the early history of the Pure Land movement' (Kamens 1988: 16). Yasutane is also known as the author of *Deliverance into Supreme Bliss: stories from Japan* (*Nihon ōjō gokuraku ki* 日本往生極楽記), a collection of exemplary biographies of forty-two Japanese figures ranging from Shōtoku Taishi to 'a woman from Kaga' and including Gyōgi, Ennin and Kūya. The reasons for its compilation are set out clearly in the preface:

From my youth I have been mindful of Amitābha Buddha and now that I am over forty years of age this interest has become stronger and stronger. I recite his name and I visualise in my mind his thirty-two major marks and his eighty minor signs. I keep

---

[4]   For a more extended treatment of belief in Amitābha in Japan at this time see Dobbins 1998.

him in mind every waking moment and 'I cleave to this in times of haste and in times of sudden change.' Wherever I find an image of Amitābha or a painting of the Pure Land, be it in temple, on stūpa or mausoleum, I never fail to offer devotion and prayers. Everyone, monk or layman, man or woman, who desires Supreme Bliss and who wishes for deliverance must link themselves [to him]. The sūtras, treatises and other commentaries expound the merit of such and explain the causes thereof; you must always consult them. When the monk Jiacai 迦才 (Kāśyapa) from the Hongfasi of the Great Tang compiled the *Jingtu lun* 淨土論, which contains [the stories of] twenty men who achieved deliverance, he wrote as follows: 'first quote [directly] from the sūtras and treatises. They prove the existence of such deliverance; they indeed make excellent examples. But the wisdom of sentient beings is shallow and they cannot grasp what wise men say. Unless we record [examples of] those who actually attained deliverance, we shall not be able to encourage them.' True indeed! Among the forty-odd people whose stories are told in the *Ruiyingzhuan* 瑞應傳 there are examples such as that of the man who killed cattle and the man who sold chickens, both of whom met virtuous friends and after ten thought-moments attained deliverance. Whenever I see these [examples of] such people my convictions strengthen. Now, on looking through [various] histories and biographies, I have found [examples of] people whose stories were most unusual. I have also asked old acquaintances and I have come across over forty such examples in all. Full of wonder and unable to forget, I have recorded a little of their activities and so now entitle this *Deliverance into Supreme Bliss: stories from Japan*. Those who read this should have no doubts. In the hope that we, along with all other sentient beings, will achieve deliverance in the Land of Peaceful Bliss (Inoue and Ōsone 1974: 11).

Genshin, on the other hand, was a monk through and through. He is now known chiefly as the author of the influential *Essentials of deliverance* (*Ōjōyōshū* 往生要集) of 985, which we shall examine in due course; but he was not influential in a political sense. Far from it. He never sought or gained high office. Some care is needed when discussing his writings, because a great many works that appear to be by him are in fact of much later provenance and have been attributed to him for purposes of legitimation. In the Kamakura period two separate lineages of Tendai initiations emerged, one of which, the Eshinryū 惠心流, traced itself back to Genshin (aka Eshin). An uncritical acceptance of these texts, which all appear in his 'Collected Works', would give a misleading impression of his scholarship, and in fact only about fifteen can be safely attributed to him (Sueki 1991: 320–26). Apart from the short *On visualising Amitābha's ūrṇā* (*Amidabutsu byakugōkan* 阿彌陀佛白毫觀)[5] of 981 and *Essentials of deliverance* itself, they deal with Tendai doctrinal matters.

---

[5]   The *ūrṇā* was a tuft of white hair between the eyebrows of a buddha, from which a strong white light would emerge.

On the twenty-third day of the fifth month of 986, Yasutane, Genshin and a number of other courtiers and monks all put their names to the following vow:

Now the three worlds are all [characterised by] suffering, and the five constituent elements of existence are [all characterised by] impermanence. Suffering and impermanence – who does not abhor them? And yet we have [continued] to be born and to die to no end since the non-beginning [of time] and still we are unable to give rise to a desire for enlightenment (*bodhicitta*), still we are unable to escape the paths of adversity. How sad this is. When shall we [ever be able to] plant firm roots on the path to liberation? Now let us consider what it says in the *Sūtra on visualising the Buddha of Immeasurable Life*:

Or there be sentient beings who enact the five heinous sins and the ten evil acts, laying up all manner of wrong deeds. Foolish men such as these will, because of their bad karma, inevitably fall into adverse ways, where they will linger for many kalpas and suffer without limit. But if, at the very end of his life, someone this evil [is lucky enough to] meet a virtuous friend 善智識, that friend may bring peace and consolation, expound the marvellous Dharma for his sake, and teach him to be mindful of [Amitābha] Buddha 教令念佛. And if that man is too burdened by suffering to [be able to] be mindful of the Buddha, the virtuous friend should say to him: 'If you are unable to concentrate, then [just] call on the name of the Buddha of Immeasurable Life 稱無量壽佛'. If in this fashion he constantly calls out in utter sincerity and completes ten thought-moments 具足十念, calling 'All homage to the Buddha'. because he calls out the name of the Buddha in constant mindfulness, he will escape the sins of birth and rebirth of eight thousand million kalpas; and when he dies he will see appear before him a golden lotus flower bright like the orb of the sun, and in the space of a single thought 如一念頃 he will instantly be born into paradise.

This passage is proof enough of what lies ahead. We have debated among ourselves and can now state as follows:

We now promise to become virtuous friends to each other so that at the last moment of our lives we can help each other be mindful of [Amitābha] Buddha. We hereby proclaim that the number of fellows shall be twenty-five. If one among us falls ill, through the power of our vow to bind ourselves together, we shall ignore whether the day be auspicious or inauspicious, we shall go to wherever he lies, and we shall ask after him and encourage him [to concentrate]. And if it so happens that he achieves rebirth into paradise, through the power of his own vow and through the power of the buddhas and gods, he is to indicate as such to the fellowship, either via a dream or when they are awake. And if it so happens that he has fallen [back] into adverse paths, this too he is to indicate. And the fellowship from time to time with like intent will carry out together those practices that will [help to] lead us to the Pure Land. In particular, every month on the evening of the fifteenth day we shall practice the meditation (*samādhi*) of being mindful of the Buddha 念佛三昧. We shall pray [that we may be able to achieve] the ten thought-moments at the instant of death. Every lifespan has its limit. How can we rely on this life, which is as transient as dew on grass? Success and failure [in this life] are uncertain. Better by far to pin our hopes on being welcomed at the Lotus Seat. Let us strive for diligence. Let us not fall into lax habits (Bowring 1998: 222–23).

The title given to this text is 'Meditations on the twenty-five [states of existence] at the Ryōgon'in – a vow signed by twenty-five founding members'. The Ryōgon'in 楞嚴院 refers to the Shuryōgon'in 首楞嚴院 (The Hall of Heroic Valour (Śūraṃgama)), a building in the Yokawa sector of Hieizan. It started life as a small sūtra repository but was rebuilt in 848 by Ennin, when he decided to develop Yokawa as a religious centre. Genshin was the head monk at the time. The 'meditations on the twenty-five states of existence' refers to twenty-five different meditative states in which one was required to overcome the obstacles presented by the twenty-five states of existence. Why this particular number of *samādhi* was chosen in this particular instance is unclear. It is possible that it was adopted because it reflected the number of participants, although the reverse might also be the case. It does not seem to have any direct relevance to the cult of Amitābha.

The object of the vow of 986 was to bind the signatories in fellowship, and the object of their meetings was to force each other to carry out the extremely difficult practice of intense mindfulness of Amitābha so that at the moment of death each member would be able to concentrate hard enough to fulfil the required 'ten thought-moments' that were needed to achieve rebirth in the Pure Land.[6] Two covenants are extant that show the rules that governed the group. Common to both is a strong concern for collegiality. There is constant reiteration that rules are important and that backsliders will be expelled on very little provocation. This suggests that the members were being asked to do something highly unusual, something that ran counter to common sense. Death and disease were normally to be shunned and it takes a good deal of pressure to persuade otherwise. At first sight it seems curious to find a strong sense of exclusivity being introduced just at the moment that Mahāyāna universalism is being extolled, but this was needed so that a threat of excommunication would have the desired effect. The whole enterprise smacks of insecurity. Despite the apparent reliance on the *Sūtra on visualising the Buddha of Immeasurable Life* and protestations of faith and concentration being the key, there is clearly a strong residual fear of what the individual might face, a fear of death, that was dealt with by dissipating it within the group. The covenants tied them into a series of obligations which

---

[6]   For detailed discussion see Bowring 1998, Horton 2004 and Stone 2004. A full translation of the texts mentioned here can be found in Gülberg 1999.

were meant to increase the chances of success for the individual when his turn came. Dropping everything to go and nurse another would increase one's own store of merit, and mutual support was necessary in the face of an intensely personal struggle. The subheadings for one of the covenants run as follows:

1 On the fifteenth day of every month we shall practise the meditation [involving] contemplation of [Amitābha] Buddha.
2 After the prayers that conclude the contemplation we shall intone the Mantra of Illuminating Wisdom (*kōmyō shingon* 光明眞言) and perform the sand ritual.
3 We shall regulate our minds, keep to the [right] path, discriminate among men and help our fellows to correct their faults.
4 We shall build a separate building called the Hall of Deliverance and when one of the fellows falls ill we shall move him there.
5 While one of the fellowship is ill, the group shall take turns to watch over him.
6 We shall decide on where to place the graves for the fellowship. It shall be called the Mausoleum of the Lotus Seat, and in spring and autumn we shall practise contemplating [Amitābha] Buddha there.
7 We shall always contemplate looking towards the west and endeavour to accumulate great merit.
8 The fellowship shall, after such a death, maintain these principles and continue to practise good deeds.

Item 5 places great stress on the need to nurse the sick and to disregard taboos on uncleanliness:

The sick must be looked after and protected. The suffering mind must be pacified and consoled. Therefore in the *vinaya* the Buddha says: 'From now on you should establish who will nurse the sick; and if there is one who desires to pay me homage, he should first pay homage to the sick.' Much is written of this kind of merit in the sūtras and treatises. It is not merely that [such a deed] is the most laudable in all eight fields of merit, it is even [meritorious enough to be] praised through ten rebirths. For this reason, the fellowship must take turns to watch over a member who falls ill, for the whole period from the onset of his illness to his death.

First, two members shall be appointed to watch over him for just one day and one night. One member should devote himself to encouraging contemplation of the Buddha and allowing the sick man to hear the message of the Dharma. The second should busy himself wherever he must, preparing food and other necessities, which, of course, must be provided depending on the severity of the suffering and the number of people who fall ill. Depending on the sick man's wishes, they should practise meritorious acts according to both the revealed and tantric teachings, they should pray for the power of the Buddha, or they should apply medicines. They must wait for the next group to come to take their turn and then be allowed to leave. In the past Śākyamuni washed the bodies of sick monks with his hands of purple and gold, so we sons of Buddha now must apply ourselves to the task of physician. How can we not [try to] alleviate the suffering of our virtuous friends? We must serve them as if we are serving our parents and our masters. We must never shy away from unclean smells or impurities, and every day when the sun sinks we must carry out the usual tasks. And if it seems as if the candle of his life is flickering in the wind, we should all gather and concentrate our minds on [Amitābha] Buddha. Or, following normal practice, we could chant hymns and dirges as directed in the *vinaya* of the Sarvāstivādins. Or one might ask him what he sees and note it down, as suggested by Daochuo.

Now whether a man travels the path of goodness or evil depends entirely on his concentration at the last moment 臨終一念, and the relationship formed with virtuous friends is exclusively devoted to this one instant. So if we do not wait until the end but simply leave him to die, the whole significance of the fellowship is nullified. Even if you are called to take your turn without warning, you must still be willing to touch impurities, to see him off at the end and to put into effect all that needs to be done: this is what is meant by fellowship.

It is on this that we must set our minds. Others rely deeply on us and we, in turn, rely profoundly on them. If we become estranged from others or if others become estranged from us, the original intention to form a group is already thwarted and the main object – to achieve deliverance – may well be lost. No matter how serious the obstacle, the fellowship must faithfully come and keep turn to serve. Even if one of the group falls ill in quite a different place, we must go and ask after him. But if the journey there and back would take a member more than a day, then that member is exempt from this requirement. This is all extremely important and cannot be ignored (Bowring 1998: 238–39).[7]

Since activities and practices carried out either alone or with the group during one's lifetime were only a help and not a guarantee of success, what happened in the very last moments was of crucial importance. One might expect a desire to produce an atmosphere that was comforting for the dying, but, on the contrary, the whole procedure was imbued with tremendous tension. Yasutane's covenant, for example, suggests the extraordinary scenario of fellows keeping a verbatim record of the dying man's last moments, constantly urging him to concentrate on Amitābha but at the same time pestering him to tell them what he could see and where he was heading, as if one might not only measure success in this way but thereby learn to adjust one's behaviour to maximise the chances when one's own time came. Genshin and his fellows were clearly not ready for simple acts of faith, and we are still some way from later Pure Land Buddhism. This obsession with

---

[7] It is worth noting that at almost the same time Pure Land societies were being set up in Mingzhou. Zunshi 遵式 established one in 996 and Zhili 智禮 in 1013. Although there is a record of scholarly correspondence between Genshin and Zhili, there is little sign of direct influence either way. The coincidence, however, is striking. See Getz 1999.

proof is prefigured in the initial vow of 986, where members are made to promise that they will indicate after death where they have gone, and a good example of how this might work in practice can be found in Genshin's biography, where his death and deliverance to Amitābha's Pure Land is recorded in some detail. The last section is worth quoting in full:

From the second day of the sixth month he stopped taking food or drink. On the fifth he said 'In a dream I saw a monk appear and someone next to him asked "Who are you?" and the monk replied "I have come because I wish to show him correct contemplation." Is this a sign of the end?'

On the ninth, early in the morning, he attached cords to Amitābha's hand and grasped the ends. He chose two *gāthā* from the Buddhist teachings, chanted them himself and asked others to do likewise.

The clear pure entrances to compassion are as numberless as grains of dust;
We are all born in the wondrous aspect of the Tathāgata
Whose each and every aspect is perfect
So he who looks upon it will never tire.

And he also chanted:

His face is good, perfect and pure like the full moon,
A marvellous light like a thousand suns and moons;
His voice is as loud as a drum, as beautiful as the song of the *kokila* bird,
So thus I bow before Amitābha Buddha.

And he chanted 'Homage to the paradise in the west, to the marvellous Pure Land, to Amitābha, great in compassion and pity.' Then he made obeisance again and placed his ends of the cords in front of the Buddha. He ate as normal and urged the others to do likewise. Then he asked them, saying 'Will you know whether I have escaped the death of the fifteen evils by just looking at my face?' And they replied 'Your body shows no sign of suffering; your expression is quite normal. There are no signs that your death will be unpleasant. This shows that all will be well.' Then they cleaned all the dust and dirt away from where he lay, and they washed stains from his body and clothes as if they were preparing [for the final hour].

On the morning of the tenth he ate and drank as usual, then plucked the hair from his nose and cleaned his body and his mouth. He grasped the cords again and concentrated his thoughts on the Buddha; it was as if he had fallen asleep. Those serving him, although close by, merely thought he was resting and so paid no more attention. But then, because he had made no sound for a while, they examined him and found that he had died, his head to the north, his face looking west, lying on his right side. His face looked beatific; his expression like a blossoming flower. In his hand he held the cords and his beads. His hands were together in prayer but had slipped slightly apart.

He had always admonished his students saying 'When I die, you should ask me about important matters: about the production of good and the arising of evil – I will reveal the truth to you.' And on the ninth he had said to one of the monks closest to him, 'I see many things but I do not speak of them to others. [I see] young monks come and sit in groups, now three to a group, now five. They all look composed and they are beautifully clothed. Things like this I can see as soon as I close my eyes. But if I explained it to you in detail, I fear it would sound like madness. At the very moment of death you should ask [me what I see],' he said. 'And other things that occur to me, if you ask, I will tell you of them. Make sure you ask about these final moments, but ask me softly.' But then no one knew when he had died, so who could ask these vital things? For men and for the Dharma, this is deeply to be regretted.

Now there was a student of his called Nōgu, who for some time had been in charge of the Iwakuradera in the county of Kōga in the province of Ōmi. He came in the tenth month in the previous year and announced 'I am now too old and cannot walk. This is the last time that I will be able to pay my respects to my master,' and he returned to his temple. Then Genshin sent a note to him saying 'I must see you [again] either next spring or summer.' But something stopped him from coming and in the end he never fulfilled his master's wish. Then on the tenth day of the sixth month last year about four in the morning he saw a dream. He saw himself entering his master's room. The master was just disappearing into the distance. To the left and right of the path were lines of monks. [Beyond them] stood four young boys, fair of form and garment. The way they stood there to the left and right seemed just like the 'Yokawa welcoming ceremony'.[8] Genshin gestured, saying 'Let the smaller ones line up in front of the taller ones,' and they arranged themselves as he ordered. Then they marched off to the west. Nōgu, in his dream, thought to himself: 'This is strange. They are walking on the ground.' But in that instant they rose up slowly and trod on air as they went. And they chanted 'crossing beyond the three worlds', 'crossing beyond the three worlds', twice and thrice as they left towards the west. Awakening from his dream, he told it to the monk Hōgu and the nun Kenmyō and others, and they said 'Surely this was the master dying, wasn't it?' On the eighteenth a Yokawa monk called Juson arrived. They asked him why he had come and he replied that the master had passed away on the tenth of that month. All were amazed that the dream had been true.

And there was another monk who was a student of the master. After the master's death, he wished to know where he was and so for months he prayed and concentrated. Eventually he saw the master in a dream and asked him whether he had been delivered into the Pure Land. The master replied 'I could say yes and I could say no.' 'Why do you say this?' asked the monk. The master replied 'Because I only just managed to avoid suffering.' The monk said 'What you say is not clear to me. Have you in fact been delivered?' 'Yes,' replied the master. 'Are you not then overjoyed that you have already achieved your original intention?' 'Yes, I am overjoyed.' 'So if you have achieved deliverance, then why did you just tell me "I could say no"?' The master replied, 'When the sainted ones gather like clouds and surround the Buddha, I

---

[8]   The 'Yokawa no mukaekō', said to have been inaugurated by Genshin, was a ceremony open to all at which the coming of Amitābha from the west was enacted as a kind of pageant.

am furthest away [from him]. That is why I said I might say no.' And the monk asked about himself, saying 'Can I achieve deliverance or not?' 'You cannot,' was the reply. 'What have I done wrong that I cannot achieve it?' asked the monk. 'You are too lazy.' 'Is it absolutely impossible?' asked the monk. 'Although you are lazy', said the master, 'you have taken the vow to become a buddha. That is a good thing. You are like a man trapped in a deep dungeon. If he has knowledge, he can escape by himself. To have vowed to become a buddha is like this. Although you are sunk in [the cycle of] birth and death, you can escape.' 'In that case', said the monk, 'can I or can I not achieve deliverance by means of this vow?' 'If you have made the vow but do not practise, it will still be difficult.' 'If I repent of my past mistakes and now redouble my efforts, can I achieve my vow?' At this question, the master held back from replying immediately. He thought awhile and then said 'It will still be difficult . . . to achieve deliverance into the Pure Land is an extremely difficult thing. That is why I myself am on the outer margins.' Hearing this, the monk was very ashamed.

This dream reminds one of something that happened some time ago. The master read the sūtras with care and then created a picture of Amitābha's welcoming. The picture contained many ordinary monks but few bodhisattvas. Someone asked him why there were so few. He replied that he had ambitions for only the lowest lotus [seat]. So why did he not have higher ambitions? asked the man. 'Because that is where I calculate I belong' was the reply.

And if we enquire further into his last moments, he turned to those who were looking after him and said, 'My end is nigh. Ask someone to read the passage about the upper and middle levels of the lowest [third] rank of rebirth from the *Sūtra on visualising the Buddha of Immeasurable Life*.' This must mean the same . . . Now perhaps he has achieved his aim and is sitting on the lowest lotus seat.

Accounts like this, of his appearing and communicating with students, are many; but dreams are difficult to trust and so we should not spread these stories too widely. The master's wisdom and diligence had no peer in this world. The Dharma benefits all sentient beings and its concepts are marvellous. The Buddha's words are not empty. Cause and effect is clearly apparent. So how can we doubt that the master obtained the fruit of peace and bliss? Let us hope that through the power of our relationship we will soon receive his guidance (Bowring 1998: 243–47).

9.5   Visions of heaven and hell

One sure-fire way of persuading people of the importance of preparing for death was to show them the dire consequences of inaction or failure. This was the strategy chosen by Genshin for his work *Essentials of deliverance*, which was completed in the fourth month of 985. It is sometimes claimed that this work was composed as a manual for those who signed the vow of 986; he may indeed have had this group in mind but the work itself is wide-ranging and had an impact beyond the confines of Yokawa, an impact partly a result of its vivid descriptions of the terrible hells, which come at the beginning and are clearly meant to catch both eye and imagination. Life in Japan in the tenth century was as dangerous and precarious as anywhere else, but even so it is not easy to persuade people to turn away from this world en masse and concentrate solely on the next. A visceral fear of the present is needed, and this does not just happen, it has to be manufactured, invented. In the Japanese cultural context this turning away from the here-and-now is not entirely a natural reaction and it needed considerable effort before these concepts, so basic to Buddhism, could be successfully implanted at the personal level.[9]

It is not for nothing, therefore, that *Essentials of deliverance* begins with a long section entitled 'Aversion to this unclean world', which strikes all who read it with such force. The 'unclean world' is saṃsāra, the six courses of birth and rebirth, the opposite of the Pure Land. Genshin's description begins with the horrors of the various hells into which one might easily be reborn. The body in hell with its susceptibility to pain and hurt becomes the central reference point. The horrors of multiple hells are then evinced through a description of pain inflicted in a long series of unending repetitions. Unspeakable tortures are continued for aeons without respite and there is a constant reiteration of extreme violence. Hell is a magnification of pain as felt by the human body. This then forces us back to read the present world in terms of hell and reminds us where the crucial weakness lies: in desire and the body. There is only one redeeming feature of the human condition: salvation is only possible from this particular state, because it is only here that we ever have a chance of hearing the message of the Buddhist Dharma. And now that chance in a million has been offered, it must be taken.

And what of the Pure Land? It is a curious fact that abodes of the blissful are far more difficult to describe than hells, for the former are mostly insubstantial states of mind. As we have already seen, Amitābha's Pure Land was described as a kind of static ecstasy of light and jewels; but to make it real and truly desirable to his audience Genshin is forced to use language, and language by definition is tied to this world. So in the process of being described, the Pure Land turns into a perfect land where the non-existence of desire can only be explained in terms of desire fulfilled. And if all desire is instantaneously gratified, it becomes not so much annihilated as rendered impotent and so inconceivable. But desire presupposes the senses and for

---

[9] Note that a recent study (Horton 2004) accepts that Genshin was well known but questions whether *Essentials of deliverance* was in fact read very widely during his lifetime, or indeed for a century after.

senses to exist at all, there must be a body. This is why, for all the talk of emptiness, Mahāyāna Buddhism is full of bodies. In fact the body, in its pure, pristine form, full of light, becomes itself the object of worship, and visualisation of the body (of Amitābha among others) becomes the path to salvation.

Another reason for the success of this work was that it represented a new kind of Buddhist text, one far more accessible to the layman. The monks had available to them sūtras that had to be studied in the light of commentaries that took the form of scholastic discussions, often of the question-and-answer type, devoted to teasing out the meaning of a word or a passage with the help of liberal quotations from eminent scholastic forebears. But what was there for the layman at court who wished to know at first hand how and why Buddhism might be of importance to him personally? It is here in the late tenth century that a small revolution in attitudes occurs. We notice an increase in texts designed to open up Buddhism for the layman, texts that were obviously written in response to a demand. Yasutane's *Deliverance into Supreme Bliss: stories from Japan*, and Tamenori's *Text to illustrations of the Three Jewels* are perfect examples. A few years previously the monk Senkan 千觀 (918–83) had produced the first extant series of *wasan* 和讃, Buddhist hymns of praise composed in Japanese rather than Chinese, and *Essentials of deliverance* fits well into the same mould. It was, above all, well organised, breaking with the usual pattern of simply following a line of a sūtra with commentary. Part description, part manual, full of practical advice about how one set about a difficult but ultimately rewarding task, it imposed its own distinctive pattern on the material. At times, admittedly, it reads like a patchwork quilt of quotations and examples from previous writings, but one glance at the list of contents shows a new sense of organisation.

1 Aversion to this unclean world
2 Seeking the Pure Land
3 Evidence for the Pure Land
4 The correct practice of *nenbutsu*
5 Aids to *nenbutsu*
6 *Nenbutsu* on particular occasions
7 The benefits of *nenbutsu*
8 Evidence for *nenbutsu*
9 Sundry other practices
10 Question and answer session

After Chapter 3, *Essentials of deliverance* moves from description to manual. Although one occasionally finds Genshin being compared to Dante, it is important to note that the description of the various hells is presented not as a personalised vision but as a truth that drew its authority from the textual tradition. Ironically, its heart lies not in the terrifying descriptions but in the practical chapters that deal with being mindful of Amitābha and how to ensure the best form of rebirth possible. Chapter 4 deals with the five 'entrances': (i) Veneration (*reihaimon* 禮拜門), which is an act of sincere devotion performed in front of an image of Amitābha; (ii) Praise (*santanmon* 賛嘆門), which involves singing hymns and songs of praise; (iii) Making vows (*saganmon* 作願門), which is the arousal of *bodhicitta*, the desire to find enlightenment, without which the process cannot really begin; and (iv) Visualisation (*kansatsumon* 觀察門). It is here that we are given detailed instructions as to how to practise mindfulness, interpreted as an act of contemplation very much in the fashion of Zhiyi's manual. One tries visualising the distinguishing marks of the Buddha Śākyamuni and then one proceeds to Amitābha sitting on his lotus throne, flooding the universe with light. For those who cannot reach this stage, Genshin introduces a series of simpler visualisations, of the Buddha's *ūrṇā*, for example. Finally, for those who cannot manage any form of visualisation at all, there is the activity of constantly 'calling on and keeping in mind (*shōnen* 稱念)' Amitābha. This is the *nenbutsu*. The use of the term *nenbutsu* in *Essentials of deliverance* is not entirely consistent: at times the context demands that it signify all activities of body and mind devoted to Amitābha; at times it seems reduced to the simple intoning of '*namu Amidabutsu*' 南無阿彌陀佛. Genshin clearly saw this latter technique as a last resort for those who were incapable of anything else. The last entrance (v) is Transference of Merit (*ekōmon* 回向門), when whatever merits have come from these practices are dedicated to the salvation of all sentient beings rather than restricted to oneself.

The importance of Genshin's work can be judged from the fact that Michinaga, the most powerful man in his day, owned a copy and used it constantly in his later years. Here was a Buddhist text that could appeal to the layman. The way was gradually opening for wider participation in acts of worship by anyone concerned about the next life, and an increase in the popularity of devotionalism was the natural response. But why at this juncture? Both the texts of Pure Land Buddhism and the Chinese example had been known in Japan for two centuries, but some internal impulse was needed to activate the material. The causes of such a development are, of course, varied. There was a theory that the world was about to enter the

Latter Days of the Dharma during which the Buddhist message would fade and the ability of people to respond would weaken; it was even given the specific starting date of 1052, but it is not at all clear how many people were aware of this concept or how it might have affected them. One might also see it as the result of economic necessity, a response by religious organisations themselves to replace lost state support. When sponsorship was needed from private, and indeed individual, sources, such support could not be expected unless the Buddhist message included clear reference to an offer of personal salvation in return. It would not have been the first or the last time that a message was influenced by such mundane considerations.

10 In a time of strife

10.1 Prophecies of doom fulfilled

The morbid obsession with the next life that we have just described might
initially strike one as being rather unusual, coming at what is by common
consent one of the high points of Japanese cultural history; but there were
good reasons for people to feel pessimistic. As Michinaga's son Yorimichi
頼通 (990–1074) discovered, hegemony at court was a fragile flower of
fortune, subject to such imponderables as the ability of one's daughters to
produce male heirs and the luck of the draw when it came to epidemics. The
history of the late Heian period, those years between the death of Michinaga
in 1027 and the destruction of Tōdaiji in 1180, is one of increasing
factionalism and unrest as the sovereign's family made efforts to gain a
degree of independent action that it had not enjoyed for over a century. And
since religious establishments were vital players in such a game, they too
were inevitably drawn into the conflict. 'Religious' is to be preferred to
'Buddhist' in this context, because by the eleventh century it becomes
increasingly unnecessary, and indeed impossible, to distinguish between
temple and shrine, particularly when discussing major centres such as Hie–
Enryakuji, Hie–Onjōji, and Kasuga–Kōfukuji. The shrines at Ise and Kamo
might remain distinctive, but at the larger shrine–temple complexes the
boundaries were blurred, monks not hesitating an instant to use the spiritual
power of the gods when their help was needed.

We have already seen how the major Buddhist temples had become large
landowners in their own right and were increasingly involved in politics
whether they liked it or not. Private temples proliferated and relations
between various religious institutions were affected by the political affiliation
and status of their sponsors. During Michinaga's lifetime it was not unusual
for a temple to be entirely subservient to the will of the patron, monks being
at the beck and call of their political masters, ritualists with little time for
meditation or study on their own. But as major institutions such as Enryakuji,
Onjōji and Kōfukuji accrued to themselves more and more land and

resources, often at the expense of other members of the aristocracy, their ability to transform this into political muscle grew and they became major centres of secular power in their own right. Although Kasuga–Kōfukuji was meant to be the spiritual base for all those descended from Kamatari, once it reached a certain size, disputes between the complex itself and various different groupings within the larger Fujiwara clan were as numerous as disputes with others.

This was a potentially dangerous situation that needed careful handling, and careful handling was not much in evidence in the late Heian. Disagreements between Enryakuji and Onjōji, for example, simmered throughout the period and often spilled out beyond the confines of Hieizan, threatening peace in the capital itself. Pitched battles were not uncommon and considerable violence and destruction of property was the result. The causes of such difficulties were of long standing and concerned awkward matters of succession and lineage, but they were exacerbated by the willingness of other power blocs in the capital to back one side against another for their own purposes. Such a policy of divide and rule could only exacerbate a friction that was in constant danger of bursting into flame. Much of Onjōji, for example, was destroyed by fire in 1081. Relations between Enryakuji and Kōfukuji were, if anything, even worse, and led to armed conflict on a number of occasions. In the province of Yamato, Kōfukuji was also in almost constant dispute with Tōnomine 多武峰, which enshrined the spirit of Kamatari. The root cause of this particular problem was that in 947 Tōnomine, which had originally belonged to Kōfukuji, had been transferred to Mudōji 無動寺, one of the many temples on Hieizan; this had rankled ever since and Tōnomine was a constant Tendai thorn in the flesh for Kōfukuji, which by this time governed most of the province of Yamato and was understandably jealous of its dominant position.[1]

Each major centre had its own large organisation of peasants and labourers, who could be armed and mobilised at short notice. Not only did they burn down each other's buildings with monotonous regularity, but they carried the demands of their religious masters, whether it be a land dispute or disagreement over appointment to high office, to the capital and the doors of the Palace. This practice, known as 'aggressive appeal' (*gōso* 強訴), started at the end of the tenth century with shrine employees from Ise going to the capital to protest about the actions of the shrine administrator, and became common by the early eleventh. In 1039, for example, 3,000 monks descended

---

[1]   For a detailed account of this period see Adolphson 2000: 75–184.

on the capital from Hieizan to protest about an appointment with which they disagreed, and it took a sizable number of armed men to subdue them. The year 1095 saw the first use by these monks of a palanquin containing the presence of the god of the mountain, Sannō 山王, something that became a common sight whenever monks had a grievance. In 1123, for example, seven of these shrines were carried down into the capital, as a result of which a pitched battle ensued, and in 1165 a disagreement between Enryakuji and Kōfukuji led to the destruction of Kiyomizudera 清水寺, one of Kōfukuji's branch temples in the capital.

Kōfukuji's equivalent to the palanquin was a sacred *sakaki* tree 榊, known as the *shinboku* 神木, which symbolised the presence of the Kasuga deities and was often used to show the 'displeasure' of the gods at decisions that adversely affected temple or shrine. Sometimes just moving the tree-deity from its usual resting place to the main gate of Kōfukuji, an act known as *shinboku dōza* 神木動座, was enough to ensure a favourable decision; sometimes it was taken by carefully choreographed stages all the way to the capital by a large group of peasants and labourers associated with the temple (*shuto* 衆徒) preceded by a similar group connected to the shrine (*jinin* 神人) and left either at the Fujiwara college, the Kangakuin, or at Hōjōji. It was first used in this fashion as early as 1007. Warriors sent to intercept the procession often never lifted a finger to impede the passage of such a potent symbol, and matters were made worse because of a general reluctance to challenge these intimidating groups (Grapard 1992a: 139–41).

The historian George Sansom was in no doubt as to who to blame. 'Any impartial study of Buddhism . . . from 950 to 1150', he wrote, 'is bound to lead to the conclusion that as an institution it failed miserably to provide the moral force that the times demanded, since the influence of the sects with the greatest power and the greatest responsibility in medieval Japan was on the whole an evil influence, breeding disorder, corruption, and bloodshed' (Sansom 1958: 223). One would not want to whitewash the religious institutions, but there were reasons other than mere moral weakness for the speed with which they had recourse to threats and armed intimidation. Although it could be argued that much of the disruption between Enryakuji and Onjōji was local in nature and so essentially beyond the control of the court, in many cases it was in fact events at the centre that precipitated discord: the core problem was one of land rights.

One aspect of government during this period that had not previously existed was the emergence of an entirely new and potentially disruptive power bloc: those sovereigns who 'retired' early. They were ordained, but continued to control events through their own private offices. This system, which was later given the name *insei* 院政 or 'government from the cloisters', was set in train by Go-Sanjō 後三條 (r. 1068–72, ret. 1072–73), but the two really dominant figures were Shirakawa 白河 (r. 1072–86, ret. 1086–1129) and Go-Shirakawa 後白河 (r. 1155–58, ret. 1158–92). The reasons for such a complicated arrangement were clear to everyone: it was an attempt by the ruling family to wriggle out from under the control of the Fujiwara regents and to gain an independence they had long lost. But outside the immediate confines of the capital, this had unforeseen repercussions. Land was, of course, the key to power. Traditionally the family of the sovereign had not been a landowner, since ostensibly it was the recipient of tax returns from all public land. But now one had relatives of the sovereign whose main aim in life was achieving financial independence. The key policy of both Shirakawa and Go-Shirakawa was to build up large private landholdings, and they proceeded to take much of this land from the large religious establishments. Land thus acquired was designated as *chokushiden* 勅旨田, which maintained the pretence that this was public land, but in fact it became the property of the ex-sovereign and his family. That this provoked a strong reaction is not surprising. New conflicts at the centre, then, were just as much to blame for the unrest that followed.

Shirakawa did not register the land in his own name. Instead he used the names of female relatives and retainers whom he wished to reward. His boldest move, however, was the creation of an entirely new group of six temples, built and governed by his family. His father had already taken the first steps in this direction in 1070 by setting up his own *goganji*, Enshūji 圓宗寺, part of whose remit was to organise a new set of rituals that were meant to take the wind out of the sails of Kōfukuji, which still ran the most prestigous assemblies, including the Yuima-e. The main role of Shirakawa's six temples, the largest of which was Hosshōji 法勝寺, begun in 1075 and finished in 1083 with the addition of an octagonal nine-storey pagoda eighty-two metres high, was to act as recipient for the large amount of land that was appropriated by the ex-sovereign. All six were placed under the general control of Ninnaji, the Shingon-related temple that had always been in royal hands. Shirakawa also created a new title, that of Hōshinnō 法親王, destined for princes of royal blood who subsequently became ordained. Shirakawa's third son Kakugyō 覺行 (1074–1104) was the first to be given this title on the occasion of his being made head abbot of Ninnaji. Measures such as these were seen as provocative in the extreme, a grave threat to both the prestige and financial muscle of places like Enryakuji and Kōfukuji. And these centres were right to be concerned. The lavish expenditure on these six temples and the Buddhist images held within them could not have been sustained without the accumulation of vast amounts of capital.

As a coda here, it is worth drawing attention of the situation at Hiraizumi 平泉 in Mutsu, the site of a remarkable 'provincial capital' of the north that was built during this period, only to be destroyed by the Minamoto forces at the end of the twelfth century. Many of the Buddhist buildings that rivalled the best built in the home provinces are thought to have been inspired by the spectacular results of the building programme of Shirakawa and those who came after him (Yiengpruksawan 1998).

Some seventy years later, Go-Shirakawa found himself pursuing the same land policies as his great-grandfather Shirakawa, but because his position at court was rather less secure and factionalism even worse than before, he found himself increasingly reliant on military retainers, chief among them, of course, Taira no Kiyomori 平清盛 (1118–81). He also went further than his predecessors in trying to control Enryakuji, appointing his uncle Saiun 最雲 法親王 to the post of head abbot (*zasu*) in 1156. This particular move, the first time a prince had been appointed to this role, happened to be successful, but other efforts to impose members of the sovereign's family on temples could meet with stiff resistance; it was a habit that proved extremely disruptive and caused great unhappiness within the institutions concerned. Not only was it a break with tradition, but they were also provided with substantial private means of support, the proceeds of which were not given to the temple but kept for the abbot's exclusive use. This was not designed with harmony in mind.

Eventually the relationship between Go-Shirakawa and Kiyomori broke down and, as if to illustrate the truth of *mappō*, the home provinces were engulfed in open warfare. On 1180.12.28, a punitive Taira force under the command of Taira no Shigehira attacked the monks of Kōfukuji in Nara and in the ensuing battle both Kōfukuji and nearby Tōdaiji, Shōmu's magnificent monument, were reduced to ashes. At Tōdaiji only the Shōsōin and Sangatsudō survived. Over 3,000 men and women are said to have died in the flames and the huge statue of Vairocana was damaged beyond repair. This was a disaster for Japan on an unimaginable scale, confirmation that Dharma must be in decline. As Kujō Kanezane 九條兼實 (1149–1207) wrote in his diary *Gyokuyō* 玉葉:

All seven great temples [in Nara] are in ashes. This reflects the decline of both the Buddhist and the Sovereign's Dharma for the people in this world. I cannot find words, nor can I find the characters to write what I feel. When I hear these things, my heart feels as if it has been butchered . . . I now see the destruction of our clan before my very eyes . . . Tōdaiji, Kōfukuji, Enryakuji, and Onjōji: these are our traditions. Both Tendai centres have already been in ashes several times, but it has never happened to the temples of Nara before. Because of these things, it is evident that these are evil times, undoubtedly an era of decline (Adolphson 2000: 166, adapted).

10.2   Pilgrimages to Kumano

If Shirakawa's trademark was six new royal temples with the enormous expense that this entailed, Go-Shirakawa is known for a rather different kind of expenditure of time and money: the elaborate pilgrimages he made to Kumano, far away at the southern end of the Kii peninsula. Why Kumano, which even today is very difficult of access? The route lay not down the central spine of mountains but around the western shoreline to Tanabe and then up through difficult terrain to reach Hongū 本宮, a large shrine constructed on an island in the Kumano River. Hongū was the first of the three famous Kumano sites (Kumano sanzan 熊野三山), the others being a shrine at Shingū 新宮 and a spectacular waterfall with its shrine at Nachi 那智 [map 9]. It is difficult to say exactly when this tradition of visiting the Kumano region began; we know that retired sovereign Uda went in 907, and Kazan went to Nachi in 987, but it only became of major importance in the late eleventh century. Although Kumano was later to become a centre of pilgrimage for people from every walk of life, the tradition was created 'top-down'.

The beginnings were in 1090 when retired sovereign Shirakawa made the first of nine journeys to Kumano. Following on from this, Toba went twenty-three times, Go-Shirakawa thirty-four times and Go-Toba twenty-nine times, always in their role as retired but very active sovereigns. This was no ordinary pilgrimage; it took some thirty days to complete and was an elaborately choreographed spectacle with all the elements of a royal progress, 'the circulation of both symbolic and material capital' (Moerman 1997). It was also ruinously expensive. The ex-sovereign's retinue would set out from the Toba Detached Palace on the Kamo River and although the main actor himself would be dressed in white clothes with sandals and a staff, just like any other mountain ascetic, his retinue was large and no expense was spared. The road was marked by ninety-nine small shrines, known as 'princes' (*ōji* 王子); there were performances, poetry competitions and much entertainment at each stop on the way. It was a ritual show of conspicuous consumption, so much so that its arrival was feared by the local populace, who were often ruined by the demands placed upon them as the procession passed through.

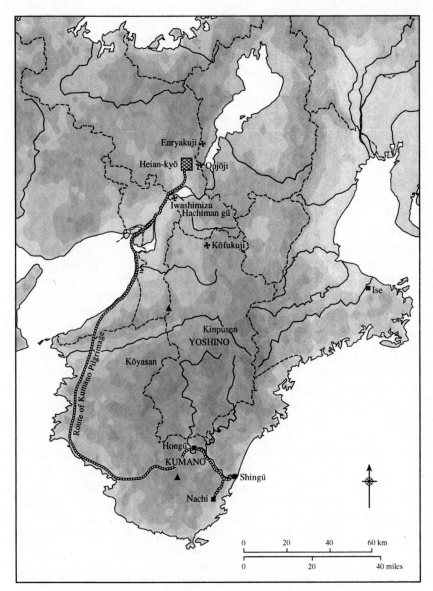

Map 9   Route of the pilgrimage to Kumano

So why Kumano? Kumano is mentioned in *Nihon shoki* as being the burial site of Izanami, the place where Susano-o lived before joining his mother, and the area which saw a change in the military fortunes of Jinmu Tennō. In the *Procedures of the Engi era* of 927 both Hongū and Shingū are already listed as important shrines and in 940 their main deities were both raised to the highest court rank possible. The details are not clear but it would seem that both had strong maritime links and were given the duty of keeping routes through the Inland Sea free from piracy. Warriors from Kumano also had a fearsome reputation. But Kumano was also one of the first places where we can find *honji suijaku* in action. Although in this case it might seem as though the shrines were more prominent, in fact the term used was Kumano sanzan, which clearly refers to Buddhist temples. The deities were certainly treated as manifestations of certain buddhas: at Hongū: Ketsumiko–Amitābha; at Shingū: Hayatama–Bhaiṣajyaguru; and at Nachi: Fusumi–Avalokiteśvara of the Thousand Arms. We find the term 'provisional manifestation' being used as early as 1086 and the commonest form of ritual at Hongū was in fact the recitation of Buddhist scriptures in the presence of the deities. To travel to Kumano was to enter sacred space and catch a foretaste of a Buddhist Pure Land in a native Japanese environment. Indeed, so strong was this sense of the sacred that it was not unknown for people to set out in small boats from the coast by Nachi in the forlorn hope of reaching what was thought to be Avalokiteśvara's Land of Immortality (Sk. Potalaka, Jp. Fudaraku 補陀落), a practice known as *fudaraku tokai* 補陀落渡海 (Moerman 1997: 356).

If retired sovereigns in the late Heian had a problem apart from finances, it was that of legitimation. The institution of *insei* grew out of a desire to revive the fortunes of the sovereign family by wresting power away from entrenched interest groups. Such were the restrictions on the person of the sovereign himself, however, that this could only be done by retiring and ruling from behind the scenes. But simply acting in this fashion was not enough; the retired sovereign needed spiritual backing for such a move. How, in other words, could one justify the existence of a power higher than that of the sovereign, no matter how young and inexperienced the latter might be? In this sense, Kumano became the equivalent for the ex-sovereign of what Ise was for the ruling sovereign; or perhaps it would be better to say what Kasuga–Kōfukuji was for the Fujiwara. Shirakawa on his first pilgrimage in 1090 instituted the position of Overseer of the Kumano Temples (Kumano sanzan kengyō 檢校) and from that point on tied the fortunes of the Kumano region to those of his family. As a result of this patronage, Kumano grew in landholdings and other riches and the cult of what one might call the second spiritual centre of the state naturally expanded outwards wherever new land was obtained. This, in turn, led to the tradition of pilgrimages for more than just the aristocracy. Origin narratives were written, showing the miraculous nature of the site, linking the story back into China and as far as India. The Buddhist element was crucial to the whole enterprise, enabling a distinction to be made between a this-worldly ruling sovereign tied to the rituals of his office and the retired sovereign, fulfilling a more spiritual role as a wise Buddhist king.

The role of Kumano at this stage reminds us of the importance of mountains in the religious life of Japan. In a tradition that goes back far beyond the advent of Buddhism but which was only strengthened by Buddhist tradition (particularly after the return of Saichō and Kūkai), mountains were sacred places, the source of water and ultimately life and death. And as such, they were far too dangerous for ordinary mortals to enter. Those men (and it seems to have usually been men) who ventured into the mountains and manage to survive there for extended periods of time undergoing severe hardship, were known by the term *yamabushi* 山伏 or 'those who sleep in the mountains' and their practice came to be called Shugendō 修験道, the 'Way of [ascetic] practice and miraculous results'. Special powers attained by living a life of deprivation gave these men the ability to act as healers, exorcists, diviners and prayer leaders among the people.

The previous discussion of *jingi* worship stressed (possibly overstressed) the degree to which it was politicised: not a religion of the individual but rather a series of ritual sites that had as their main reference point the state or the family, with a priest as medium. It is useful to think of Shugendō as being the individual, personalised, depoliticised aspect of native beliefs, while always acknowledging that precisely because it was not subject to political imperatives, it could freely adopt rituals and practices that it found useful. Such is its flexibility that already by the mid-Heian period it had developed into a complex mixture of native, Chinese and particularly tantric Buddhist practices and beliefs. The gaining of special powers was, for example, overlaid with the idea that for some special individuals enlightenment in this very existence was possible; those who had survived the experience of mountain training and had managed to rid themselves of all human passions and desires, identifying themselves, for example, with a spirit such as Fudō myōō 不動明王, were themselves treated as buddhas.

In a sense, of course, a religious activity such as this is only given a name once it has already become semi-institutionalised, and there are signs that this was already happening in the late Heian period. It is for this reason that we should resist the temptation to regard Shugendō as folk religion as distinct from the written tradition; the picture is far more complex, particularly where Kumano is concerned, where the tradition of pilgrimage was very much a top-down institution. The power these ascetics represented was something worth appropriating. So we have the growth of a written tradition, underlining practice, the production of shrine and temple histories (*engi* 緣起) and symbolic paintings of the sites themselves (known as Kumano 'maṇḍala', using the term in a loose sense) where miraculous origins were put into writing, enabling them to become, in their turn, documents, 'proof' of veracity. The degree to which this activity could be linked to wider questions of the sacred nature not just of certain mountains but even of Japan itself can be seen in a work such as *Shosan engi* 諸山緣起 'The history of various mountain [sects]', thought to have been composed in the late twelfth century. This document not only gives details as to which deities were honoured on which mountain, but explicitly describes the path the adept must take through the mountains in terms of travelling through a maṇḍala: the Diamond World in the case of Yoshino–Kinpusen; the Womb World in the case of Kumano. The whole area was presented as the manifestation on earth, in Japan, of the entire mental universe of tantric Buddhism (Grapard 1982). As Grapard has pointed out, Japan eventually became a 'patchwork quilt' of such sacred areas, which could be 'entered' (the term is *nyūbu* 入峰) and where union with the sacred could be obtained. As pilgrimage became more popular in later centuries these sacred sites merged with each other, resulting in the concept that the whole of Japan was sacred space and Japan a sacred nation.

10.3   Japanese monks in Song China

The picture we have painted so far in this chapter, of battles over land rights, a Buddhist establishment trapped almost in spite of itself in an increasingly violent world, and a complex system of government with a series of sovereigns retiring to spend vast resources on prestige projects of various kinds, might well suggest that every monk and every priest had been seduced into an obsession with secular concerns. Such was, of course, not the case. Many monks, perhaps the majority, were still true to their calling and, as so often happens, a time of turmoil can also be a time of intellectual ferment. This period also saw a revival of interest in travel to China and further significant doctrinal changes, particularly as regards the continued penetration of tantric modes of thought and action.

Following the collapse of the Tang Dynasty at the beginning of the tenth century, safe travel in China could no longer be guaranteed and although pilgrimage to Tiantai and Wutaishan was still a draw, such had been the destruction in the Huichang suppression of the 840s that the lure of obtaining newer and better texts was no longer operative. Indeed, when Japanese monks did start travelling to China again in the eleventh century they knew that the most treasured gifts they could take with them were copies of the numerous sūtras and treatises that were no longer available on the continent. A number of scholarly traditions that remained strong in Japan, such as Hossō, had to all intents and purposes died out in China. But the fortunes of Buddhism changed with the rise of the Song Dynasty in 960 and the reimposition of central authority. Although the Japanese court itself was never again to institute formal missions, travel became feasible. Once a monk had received permission to leave, it was not difficult for him to find a means of passage, usually on Song trading ships that plied regularly between Kyūshū and the coast of south-central China. And by the late tenth century, there was a strong revival in Buddhist fortunes in China. Both Emperor Taizu 太祖 (r. 960–76) and Taizong 太宗 (r. 976–97) were patrons of Buddhism and devoted large resources to the reconstruction of temples. Most interesting of all was an institute for the translation of Buddhist scriptures 譯經院 that was established in 980–82 in the grounds of the Taiping xingguosi 太平興國寺 in the new capital Kaifeng 開封. Late in 983 it was renamed the Institute for the Transmission of the Dharma 傳法院 and a printing house was added. It was here that the 130,000 woodblocks were used to produce the first printing of the Buddhist canon, an event of major importance in the history of the printed word. Obtaining a copy of this work became a tantalising prospect for many Japanese monks.

The first man to succeed in this endeavour was Chōnen 奝然 (938–1016), a monk from Tōdaiji (Wang 1994). Although the diary covering his trip is not extant, we do know that he obtained approval and support from a number of Fujiwara nobles and left Japan together with six companions in the eighth month of 983. He visited Tiantai and reached the capital by the twelfth month. He was extremely fortunate in arriving when he did. The Song state was particularly interested in fostering good relations with its neighbours so that even private visitors tended to be treated as public guests. Chōnen was granted an imperial audience within two days of his arrival, a far greater honour than he could have dreamed of receiving. He then made a pilgrimage to Wutaishan during 984, returning to the capital in the third month of 985. It was here at a second audience with Taizong that he was granted his request for a complete copy of the newly printed Buddhist canon (known as the Kaibao edition 開寶版), which included 5,048 volumes and 41 newly translated works. He arrived back in Japan the next year. Of his later life, we know little except that he was made Tōdaiji bettō in 989 and died in 1016. The canon was stored in Michinaga's own temple, Hōjōji 法成寺, and there served as a master copy until it was lost in the fire that destroyed the temple in 1058. Chōnen is also known for having brought back a copy of a famous life-size red sandalwood image of Śākyamuni said to have been carved in India on the orders of King Udāyana in the sixth century BCE; it (or a copy) was kept in the Imperial Palace in Kaifeng. Although probably not of Indian origin, this unusual image shows influences from Gandhāra and Chinese Turkestan, especially in the fashioning of the hair. The copy Chōnen brought back with him was eventually installed in the Seiryōji 清涼寺 in 1019, after his death. It was to have a life of its own, in that it was copied many times from the thirteenth century onward as part of a movement to establish yet another cult of Śākyamuni (Henderson and Hurvitz 1956; McCallum 1994: 127–29).

The second monk of note is Jakushō 寂昭 (962–1034), who was ordained in 988, studied Tendai doctrine under Jakushin and Genshin, and Shingon ritual at Daigoji. He travelled to Tiantai in 1002, taking with him the set of twenty-seven questions that Genshin had addressed to Zhili. He was also interviewed by Emperor Zhenzong 眞宗. Initially intending to return to Japan with the replies received from Zhili, he was eventually persuaded to stay and found other means to return the letters. While resident in China he carried on a correspondence with members of the Japanese court, including Fujiwara no Michinaga, and eventually died in Hangzhou in 1034.

For our purposes, however, the third and most interesting figure to visit China during this period was Jōjin 成尋 (1011–81), who left Japan in 1072. Although he never returned, he did leave us a detailed diary of his voyage which is of considerable importance for students of the Northern Song, the *San Tendai Godaisan ki* 參天臺五臺山記 (Borgen 1987; Verschuer 1991). By the time Jōjin reached Kaifeng the translation work at the Institute was in decline and there was only one Indian left who could really understand Sanskrit (Bowring 1992a). Jōjin was given access and left a record of what he saw there. He was also given permission to leave with a large number of newly translated sūtras for transmission to Japan, although he failed to repeat Chōnen's success in obtaining a printed copy of the whole canon. It is perhaps here that his greatest significance lies. Although the list of works he obtained and sent back with his companions is not extant, we do know the kind of texts that were being translated in Kaifeng at this time and they are of particular interest. Fully 40 per cent of the works translated between Chōnen's visit in 985 and Jōjin's arrival in 1072 were tantric, and, what is more, they included a number of the so-called 'higher tantras', such as the *Guhyasamājatantra* (translated by Shihu 施護 in 1002) and the *Hevajratantra* (translated by Fahu 法護 in 1054–55), both of which are fundamental to the Tibetan tradition and which contain the kind of sexual references which were largely absent from the tantric material brought back by Saichō and Kūkai. As is well known, the higher tantras are in fact marked by their absence from the Chinese canon and those that are included are bowdlerised (Willemen 1983: 29). Entry into the printed canon was by no means automatic and it is possible that a large number of works actually translated at the Institute never saw their way into print. How many of these Jōjin may have obtained is unknown, but we shall have occasion to draw attention to this fact later, when we discuss the emerging role played by sexual tantrism in Japan.

10.4   The spread of tantric modes of thought

We saw in §6.5 that Shingon as an institution ran into difficulties soon after the death of Kūkai. As tantric ritual began to permeate all areas of aristocratic life and formed a major component of Tendai practice, so the very existence of Shingon as a separate tradition came into question. Annen, for example, had purloined its very name. Doctrinally it saw itself as distinct, with a different set of priorities mirrored in its own particular *kyōhan* system, but it is doubtful whether many at court not directly involved in these matters really understood the subtlety of such distinctions. Matters were made worse with the outbreak of tension between Kōyasan and Tōji. Kōyasan was really too remote from the centre of power and fell into rack and ruin during the tenth century. The main stūpa was destroyed by lightning in 994 and not rebuilt until 1103. No monks at all are recorded as living on the mountain between 1001 and 1006, and Kōyasan's role was usurped by temples closer to the centre, such as Ninnaji and Daigoji 醍醐寺, each of which in turn spawned its own lineage of both teaching and ritual, leading to increased factionalism. In the end it was Michinaga himself who was persuaded to help in the preservation of Kōyasan; he made the strenuous climb in 1023 and pledged funds so that restoration could commence. Kōyasan represented for

him the site of the Tuṣita heaven on earth and he had sūtras buried here as
well as at Kinpusen, so that the Buddhist message would be heard anew
when Maitreya eventually arrived.

From about 1070 the situation began to improve and it became a habit for
monks from Ninnaji to retire to Kōyasan. Shirakawa in retirement made a
pilgrimage there in 1088. Another factor that helped its survival was the
process by which Kūkai himself became deified. Gradually it came to be
believed that he had not in fact died but had achieved enlightenment and
gone into a form of suspended animation in his mausoleum. It is from about
this time too that we begin to notice the emergence of religious figures of a
peripatetic persuasion known as *hijiri* 聖 . Since the very beginnings of
Buddhism in Japan there had been those deeply spiritual individuals who had
found it hard to fit into institutional life. From the point of view of the state,
they were an embarrassment; from the point of view of the general populace,
they were regarded with awe, especially when they brought with them a
reputation of being doers of good works, such as constructing bridges and
ensuring better irrigation. In a very real sense, they brought Buddhism to the
people in a form they could readily appreciate: the message was that of the
possibility of salvation for the common man, but they also offered simple
exorcism, chanting passages from the *Lotus sūtra*, and recitation of the
nenbutsu. The larger monastic institutions showed no particular animosity to
hijiri and indeed employed them for a variety of purposes. Although they
were free spirits who did not exactly fit with the kind of submissiveness that
was often the mark of a monk's life, they were men of considerable moral
courage and physical stamina. There was undoubtedly a degree of admiration
for them and they were allowed to find their place within the system. Men
like Gyōgi and Kūya come to mind as figures who were at first treated as
outcasts, but who proved to have such large followings that it was thought
wiser in the end to incorporate them. These two are prominent because they
find mention in the official records, but there were countless others of like
persuasion. The term *hijiri* is an inclusive one, taking in monks who had
decided to leave the confines of a monastery as well as semi-illiterates, who
performed a variety of tasks for the temple authorities.

By the eleventh century, the number and influence of *hijiri* had increased
to the point that they constituted a major group, although 'group' is perhaps
misleading, given that they were so individualistic in outlook. Perhaps the
term 'mendicant order' is more appropriate. The poet Saigyō (1118–90), for
example, was of aristocratic birth and kept his ties to poets and others at
court, but he studied at various monasteries, travelled widely, and was not to

be pinned down. It would be wrong to mark him, or others like him, as being 'anti-establishment', however. Many were welcomed at monasteries when they needed refuge. As traditional sources of patronage became difficult to maintain, religious establishments found they needed to look elsewhere for a different kind of support, and recognised that *hijiri* offered an opening to a larger world; eventually they were employed as travelling fund-raisers. When not on the road, they lived in small temples called 'other places' (*bessho* 別所), such as Ōhara 大原, tucked in at the western foot of Hieizan, or on the slopes of Kōyasan. Indeed it was these *bessho hijiri* who were in good measure responsible for the successful reconstruction of Kongōbuji, and their presence on the mountain may go some way towards explaining why the revived community there began to adapt the cult of Amitābha to its own tantric framework. Two monks in particular are central to this development of what became known as the 'secret *nenbutsu*' (*himitsu nenbutsu* 秘密念佛): Jichihan (or Jippan 實範, *c.*1089–1144) and Kakuban 覺鑁 (1095–1143).

Not that a tantric master would need an excuse to be interested in Amitābha's Pure Land. A maṇḍala was a diagrammatic representation of a Pure Land or series of Pure Lands and Amitābha is a major presence in both the Diamond World and Womb World maṇḍala. He was also connected to two tantric texts that were already well known in Japan: Amoghavajra's commentary on the *Scripture of the guiding principle* (*Rishushaku* 理趣釋, *T.* 1003), the fourth chapter of which contains a discussion of Amitābha and the merits of his seed syllable *hrīḥ*, visualisation of which could help in this life and ensure deliverance (Astley-Kristensen 1991: 142–44), and the *Manual for services and offerings when visualising Amitābha* (*Muryōju nyorai kangyō kuyō giki* 無量壽如來觀行供養儀軌, *T.* 930). Although at first sight there might seem to be a contradiction between the kind of Pure Land belief that underpins Genshin's *Essentials of deliverance*, with its stress on the impurity and suffering of this body, and tantric Buddhism, for which the body was the very instrument of salvation, the aim of reaching the Pure Land was the same; it was merely that one needed different vehicles for people at different stages of spiritual development.

As one might expect, Jichihan's early work is very much influenced by Genshin and the Tendai tradition. Later works, however, show a movement towards the tantricisation of practice: *How to practise while ill* (*Byōchū shugyōki* 病中修行記), for example, which deals with deathbed *nenbutsu* techniques and is written with Shingon practitioners in mind, advising them to meditate on the four aspects of Amitābha's Absolute Body, the four forms of his maṇḍala, and to try and realise enlightenment by achieving mystic union by identifying one's own 'three mysteries' with those of the Buddha (Buijnsters 1999: 65). The Pure Land itself is the maṇḍala and when Jichihan talks of visualisation, he is referring not to the image normally envisaged in Pure Land practice but to the form that appears in the Assembly of the Perfected Body in the Diamond World. The technique Jichihan recommended was visualisation of the syllable '*a*', which was then linked to the two syllables '*mi*' and '*da*' in such a way that to go through the steps necessary to visualise '*a*' correctly was the same as visualising Amitābha (Amida) himself, and if that was achieved then one had, there and then, achieved one's goal.

The figure most closely associated with Amitābha in a tantric context, however, is Kakuban. Through family connections he started his career as a monk at Ninnaji, studying with the master Kanjo 勘助 (1057–1125), who was involved in trying to restore Kōyasan and in particular in revitalising Shingon scholarship, which had become so factionalised. With the encouragement of retired sovereign Shirakawa, in 1109 Kanjo revived the seminar tradition at Tōji known as the *denpōe* 傳法會. A number of his writings deal in great detail not with minor differences between Shingon masters but with the larger differences that distinguish what Kūkai had labelled the 'revealed' teachings (*kengyō* 顯教) from his own tantric teachings (*mikkyō* 密教).

Kakuban first visited Kōyasan in 1114. Once he had received his final initiation from Kanjo in 1121, he decided to move from Ninnaji to Kōyasan on a permanent basis, but not before studying at as many Shingon centres as he could, intent on reversing the fragmentation of ritual and practice. Through his links with retired sovereign Toba, he soon became the most influential monk on Kōyasan, aligning himself closely with the *hijiri* groups. In 1126 he obtained funds to institute a *denpōe* on Kōyasan and by 1132 he had constructed a number of buildings on the mountain, including the Daidenpō'in 大傳法院, designed to be a study centre for doctrinal matters, and the Mitsugon'in 密嚴院, for the practice of visualisations.

Kakuban was now in direct competition for patronage and influence with the monks already established at Kongōbuji. Not only was he having inordinate success in raising funds, but there was something uncomfortable about the growing closeness between the retired sovereign and the *hijiri*. Matters came to a head when Toba Tennō proclaimed that the administration of all temples on the mountain was to be unified under Kakuban. Tōji, which had traditionally controlled Kongōbuji, complained and started a campaign against Kakuban. In 1135, giving no explanation, he suddenly retired to the Mitsugon'in to enter a punishing period of meditation. By 1140 it had become clear that he could no longer remain on the mountain; there was violence and he was forced to flee west to Negoro 根來 with 700 of his followers. There he died in 1143. Two requests were made for him to be granted the title of 'Great Master' in 1168 and again in 1540, but it was not until 1690 that he was given the title Kōgyō Daishi 興教大師 (van der Veere 2000: 43–44).

Kakuban's writings are not extensive, but they do cover a variety of tantric topics. As one would expect of a Shingon master, there are a number of meditation manuals, such as *Contemplating the disc of the moon: a secret interpretation* (*Shingachirin hishaku* 心月輪秘釋) and *Visualising the syllable A* (*Ajikan* 阿字觀), that discuss visualisation techniques. There are also commentaries, such as *Hokekyō hishaku* 法華經秘釋 on the *Lotus sūtra*, that explore the main Mahāyāna sūtras from a tantric perspective. Also of interest are those texts on such deities as Aizen myōō 愛染明王 and Kangiten 歡喜天, which suggest that Kakuban was prepared to deal with the more overtly sexual aspects of tantric doctrine that stemmed from an interest in and analysis of passion and lust. But his central importance lies in his analysis of what was later labelled *himitsu nenbutsu*. In this context the important works are *Secrets of the crucial moment of death* (*Ichigo taiyō himitsu shū* 一期大要秘密集), *Amitābha: a secret interpretation* (*Amida hishaku* 阿彌陀秘釋), and *Mantras of the five spheres and nine syllables: a tantric interpretation* (*Gorin kuji myō himitsu shaku* 五輪九字明秘密釋), none of which can be dated with any accuracy but which were probably written at Negoro. The first two were clearly written under the direct influence of Jichihan; they contain the same kind of explanation of the significance of the three syllables in Amitābha's name, for example, although Kakuban went further and specifically identified him with Mahāvairocana.[2]

The fact that the tantric adept can have direct access to Amitābha here and now via ritual identification means that the *nenbutsu* is 'seen not as an invocation to some external divinity, but rather as a constituent element of the human body, innate, perfect, inherently pure. The *nenbutsu* was identified with breath, life force, or both at once, so that to live at all, simply to produce the two-part instinctual rhythm of breathing in and out, becomes a constant intoning of the *nenbutsu*' (Sanford 2004: 121). As he explained in his discussion of breathing (*juzokukan* 受息觀) in *Aizen-ō kōshiki* 愛染王講式:

When one opens one's mouth and closes one's lips, the two syllables *a* and *hūṃ* are spontaneously generated; when one raises a hand and moves a leg the two great

---

[2] For Kakuban's explanation of the meanings of the syllable '*a*' see Yamasaki 1988: 212–14.

elements of wind and consciousness of necessity arise. Fix one's mind intently, count one's breaths, and concentrate on the seed character of the main image. This is the profound secret of the mystery of yoga, the most direct path to achieve instant enlightenment in this very body . . .

At the moment of exhalation, this syllable *hūṃ* leaves the lotus seat of the heart and, guided by our great compassion, reaches out to all worlds in the ten directions without exception, comes into contact with the three karmic activities of all sentient beings, and both purifies and eliminates obstacles present since the non-beginning of time . . .

At the moment of inhalation, this syllable *a* penetrates throughout the body, destroys the three negative passions of one's [pure] nature, fixes itself in its appointed palace, and there rests at the level of enlightenment that is without thought (Rambelli 1992, vol. I: 141–43; Sanford 1994).

Since breathing is the classic example of intentionless activity common to all sentient beings, all activity is salvific in its effect, both for oneself and for the world at large. Once faith was present and initiation had taken place, then salvation was guaranteed to all. It should be obvious why such teachings as these were only vouchsafed to a minority of advanced practitioners. Tantric Buddhism was originally designed as a 'dangerous' path, a shortcut to enlightenment via intense ritual activity carried out with body and mind, but a shortcut limited to the very few. Simply opened out to all, it would fail to provide any incentive for meritorious activity. The very compassion that motivates the revelation of a shortcut to all humankind would be in danger of rendering compassion meaningless and unnecessary. As Kakuban writes in *Secrets of the crucial moment of death*:

According to the kind of tantra 儀軌 performed at the moment of death, even monks and nuns who have broken the precepts will obtain deliverance. Those men and women who have done evil too will assuredly be welcomed into Sukhāvatī. How much more so then those who have wisdom and who have kept their vows! How much more so men and women of virtue! This is the result of the tantric contemplation known as *shingon*. Have deep faith in this and do not harbour any doubts! (Rambelli 1992, vol. I: 144).

It should be clear that Kakuban prefigures much of what was to follow in the Kamakura period, although the kind of Pure Land belief that was to come rejected the validity of tantric ritual in an age of decline and its doctrine remained at the level of the common man.

To espouse a doctrine of non-duality and claim that one's system is all-encompassing, one must be prepared to absorb a whole raft of apparently heterogeneous elements. Nowhere is this better illustrated than in Kakuban's *Mantras of the five spheres and nine syllables*, where he presents nothing less than an explanation of the basic principles that govern the *dharmakāya*, the cosmos and all that it contains. The key number is, of course, five. The 'Preface' explains:

In my humble opinion, the 14 maṇḍala [of the five spheres and nine syllables] are the inner realisation of Lord Mahāvairocana, and the essence of Amitābha, the honoured one; the universal entrance to great awakening in this present existence, the single path to deliverance. You ask why? Those who see only a little and hear only a little will still succeed in seeing the Buddha and hearing the Dharma in this very existence, and those who perform just one visualization or are mindful for just one thought-instant will achieve freedom from suffering and bliss in this very body. How much more so those whose roots of faith are pure and clean and who devote themselves to ascetic practice? They will reach the level of enlightenment of Mahāvairocana Tathāgata himself with ease; they can expect deliverance into the Pure Land of Amitābha the Perfect by [simply] calling on his name. Such is the benefit of calling on his name; how could the merit of contemplating reality ever be in vain?

The revealed teachings [tell us that] Amitābha exists apart from Śākyamuni Buddha, but in the tantric teachings Mahāvairocana is none other than Amitābha, lord of the teachings of Sukhāvatī. You should know that the Pure Lands in all ten directions are all transformed lands of the one Buddha; all the Tathāgatas are none other than Mahāvairocana. Vairocana, Amitābha: these are different names for the same entity. Sukhāvatī, 'Secret Grandeur' (Mitsugon 密嚴): these are different names for the same place. Through the divine strength of empowerment (*kaji* 加持) of Mahāvairocana's ultimate wisdom (*myōkanzatchi* 妙觀察智), the aspect of Amitābha is manifest above the body of Mahāvairocana. Therefore if you succeed in this visualization, [you will realize that] from the buddhas, bodhisattvas and saints, down to men, gods, nagas, demons and other protectors of the Dharma, there is not a single one that is not the body of Mahāvairocana Tathāgata.

If you open the entrance of the five spheres, the *dharmakāya* as essence (*jishō hosshin* 自性法身) will be manifest. If you set up the entrance of the nine syllables, the *sambhoghakāya* as enjoyer of bliss (*juyūhōjin* 受用報身) will show himself. We already know that the two buddhas are equal. How in the end can the wise and the saintly disagree? The Pure Land and the Tuṣita Heaven are the playgrounds of the same buddhas. 'Secret Grandeur' and 'Flower-store' (Kezō 華藏) are the lotus-throne of the one mind. How regrettable that the wise ones of old fought over difficult and easy ways to reach the [Pure] Land in the West. How marvelous that even those of dull wits in our age can attain deliverance. I have written this secret commentary for one reason: [to show] that the difficulty of deliverance is caused by clinging to existence (Nasu 1970: 13–14; Rambelli 1992, vol. II: 24–26; van der Veere 2000: 135–38).

Of the 'three mysteries', body, speech and mind, that were the key to obtaining tantric enlightenment, Kakuban paid most attention to that of speech, *gomitsu* 語密. But to see this term as referring to sound alone would be an error. What Kakuban meant by *gomitsu* was all the activities that surrounded the use of 'seed syllables' and the *siddham* script. As we have seen, these graphs were at a double remove from Japanese and were treated as being beyond language, uncontaminated by ordinary meaning. They were central to Kakuban's thought, an ideal medium for representing in visual and verbal form matters such as the nature of non-duality and the constitution of the universe; they could be manipulated, 'spoken', written, memorised, visualised and explained like a language, but remain alien. It is not difficult to imagine that in lesser hands, they might quickly take on aspects of the fetish.

Taking his cue from the sixth section of the *Mahāvairocanatantra*, entitled 'The manifestation of siddhi' 悉地出現品, and using other sources such as Amoghavajra's commentary on the same tantra and Śubhākarasiṃha's *Manual for the destruction of hells* (Jp. *Hajigoku giki* 破地獄儀軌), Kakuban devoted a good part of his *Mantras of the five spheres and nine syllables* to an exhaustive exploration of the five-syllable mantra of Mahāvairocana, *āḥ-vi-ra-hūṃ-khaṃ* (Jp. *a-bi-ra-un-ken*). These five syllables in their *siddham* form are seen to hold the key to understanding the make-up of the universe and hence to achieving buddhahood in this very existence. The *dharmakāya* consists of five elements 五大, which in turn are linked by analogy to a whole series of other 'sets of five', all symbolised by these five graphs. To enumerate all these sets is by definition to describe the cosmos, and as the goal of the adept is to identify with the cosmos, this can best be done via visualisation of, and identification with, these graphs that contained within them all things. This homology on a truly vast scale is possible because of what one might call 'tantric logic', whereby similarity becomes proof of identity. A single point of contact can be enough to link two aspects together as part of an underlying pattern.

In order to achieve his aim, Kakuban makes full use of traditional Chinese sets based on the theory of the Five Elements, five shapes, five colours, five viscera and so on. His system is not entirely waterproof and there are signs of various conflicting 'lists', but, by and large, the following chart shows how the analysis proceeds:

Seed syllable	Element	Shape	Colour	Human body
kha or *khaṃ*	Air	Jewel	All colours	Top of head
ha or *haṃ*	Wind	Crescent	Black	Head to throat
ra or *raṃ*	Fire	Triangle	Red	Throat to heart
va or *vaṃ*	Water	Circle	White	Trunk
a	Earth	Square	Yellow/gold	Lower body

The above list does not exhaust the series by any means. Kakuban, whose own name means 'becoming enlightened to *vaṃ*', goes on to describe a maṇḍala for each syllable and how visualisation should take place. Perhaps the most interesting step is the inclusion of the five sections of the body. Though by no means his own innovation, it allows him to clarify in a concrete way how the practitioner can identify himself with the cosmos. In tantric doctrine the human body is seen not as a pile of filth and excrescence, but as *the* prime, privileged instrument for the attainment of enlightenment and salvation. This is made visually explicit early on in the work when we come across the illustration of a series of 'maṇḍala' which actually consist of stūpas with five spheres, one of them in the shape of a human being. This is now known as a *gorintō* 五輪塔 and is to be found in almost every cemetery in Japan today. We do not know for certain, but it is thought that Kakuban may well be responsible for this particular shape being so common [plate 20]. The latter part of this work turns to deal with a nine-syllable dhāraṇī invocation to Amitābha: *Oṃ-amṛta-tese-hara-hūṃ* (*on-amirita-teizei-kara-un*). These nine syllables are explained in similar fashion to the five and their ritual use is linked explicitly to the nine levels of rebirth (*kuhon*) of Pure Land belief.

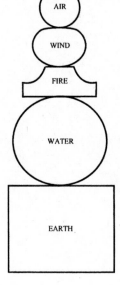

Plate 20   *Gorintō* grave markers

Part III

From the destruction of Tōdaiji to the fall of
Go-Daigo (1180–1330)

Plate 21   Kūya
This wooden carving of the itinerant Kūya (aka Kōya 空也, 902–72) was carved by
Kōshō 康勝, fourth son of Unkei 運慶 (d. 1223), in the early Kamakura period. Height
1.18 m. Kyōto, Rokuharamitsudera.

Although Kūya himself lived 250 years prior to this carving, he clearly symbolises
the ideals behind popular Amidism that were so prevalent during the Kamakura
period. Here he stands holding a staff topped with a stag's antler in his left hand and
sounding the gong that hangs round his neck with his right. The six small statues
emerging from his mouth are six figures of the Buddha Amida, representing the six
characters of the *nenbutsu* chant: *namu Amidabutsu* 南無阿彌陀佛.

Chronology

1180	Tōdaiji and Kōfukuji destroyed.
1181	Chōgen begins plans to rebuild Tōdaiji. Kiyomori dies.
1185	New buddha at Tōdaiji completed. Battle of Dannoura.
1187	Eisai travels to Song China for the second time.
1191	Eisai returns.
1192	Yoritomo takes over as Seii Taishōgun. Go-Shirakawa dies.
1194	Eisai refused permission to establish Zen as a separate school.
1197	Bakufu offers up 84,000 stūpas to commemorate the dead.
1198	Hōnen composes *Senchakushū* but keeps it secret.
1199	Shunjō travels to Song China. Mongaku banished to Sadō. Yoritomo dies.
1200	Dōgen born. Bakufu bans the *nenbutsu*.
1201	Shinran converts to Pure Land.
1202	Eisai founds Kenninji.
1206	Myōe establishes Kōzanji. Chōnen dies. Rise of the Hōjō regents.
1207	Hōnen banished to Tosa, Shinran to Echigo.
1208	Establishment of the Tsurugaoka Hachiman *jingūji*.
1211	Shunjō returns from China. Hōnen settles at Ōtani in Higashiyama.
1212	Hōnen dies. Myōe's *Zaijarin*.
1214	Dōgen leaves Hieizan.
1220	Jien's *Gukanshō* written about this time.
1221	Jōkyū disturbance. Go-Toba sent into exile.
1223	Dōgen goes to China. Continued pressure from Bakufu on *nenbutsu* sects.
1227	Hōnen's grave destroyed. Dōgen returns from China.
1228	Continual conflict between Hieizan and Kōfukuji around this period.
1232	Death of Myōe.
1238	Daibutsu erected at Kamakura.
1239	Go-Toba dies in exile.
1243	Founding of Tōfukuji.
1244	Dōgen moves to Echizen.
1246	Lanqi Daolong arrives in Japan.
1248	Ippen becomes a mendicant.
1253	Nichiren begins proselytising. Dōgen dies. Kenchōji established.
1256	Shinran disinherits Zenran.
1260	Nichiren composes *Risshō ankokuron*.
1262	Shinran dies.
1263	Hōjō Tokiyori dies. Wuan Puning asks to return to China.
1271	Nichiren banished to Sado.
1272	Honganji founded at Ōtani.
1274	Nichiren founds Kuonji. Ippen goes to Kumano. First Mongol invasion.
1278	Lanqi Daolong dies.

1279   Wuxue Zuyuan arrives from China.
1281   Second Mongol invasion.
1282   Nichiren dies. Enkakuji founded.
1289   Ippen dies.
1290   Eizon dies.
1294   Nichizō establishes the Hokkeshū in Kyōto.
1302   Bakufu places a banning order on the Ikkōshū.
1322   Kokan Shiren's *Genkō shakusho*.
1324   Daitokuji founded.
1325   Musō Soseki becomes abbot of Nanzenji.
1331   Go-Daigo fails in his attempt to win power.
1332   Go-Daigo banished to Oki.
1333   Go-Daigo returns to Kyōto.

11   For and against exclusive practice of the *nenbutsu*

11.1   Hōnen

Go-Shirakawa is said to have remarked that only three things refused to obey his decree: the River Kamo, dice, and the monks of Enryakuji. The history of the late twelfth century is one of almost constant strife between Enryakuji and Onjōji, with Kōfukuji frequently involved. Time and time again these temples sent some of their workforce into Heian-kyō, using the threat of divine retribution from the native deities to cow the court into submission and overturn decisions that were not in their favour. The court often felt itself trapped between the demands of these rival temples and began to call on the services of its own troops to counter what was an increasing threat. It was this kind of violence that had culminated in the destruction of both Tōdaiji and Kōfukuji at Nara in 1180. Go-Shirakawa might – if he had been prescient enough – have also added the military to his list, for it was his dependence on armed groups under the command of Taira no Kiyomori 平清盛 that was to bring about his downfall. This was followed by the rise of Minamoto no Yoritomo 源頼朝 and the establishment of a very different kind of power base far to the east in Kamakura.

It is not surprising that there were some monks who felt disillusioned with such easy recourse to confrontation and with the more worldly interests of the institutions to which they nominally belonged. The mountain that was Hieizan was large enough to support a good number of such men, who found refuge in the various small *bessho* scattered in the high valleys and in the foothills, where they could concentrate on their meditation exercises and their devotions; and it was from among such a group that there emerged the figure of Hōnen 法然 (1133–1212).

Hōnen was trained as a Tendai monk on Hieizan from 1147 to 1175. As a matter of course, he was introduced to Genshin's *Essentials of deliverance*, and at some point during his training, spurred on by independent study of

Shandao's commentaries on the main Pure Land sūtras, he became convinced that Japan was now so far advanced into the Latter Days of the Dharma (*mappō*) that what Genshin had talked of as a last resort for those incapable of other forms of meditation – namely intoning the phrase '*namu Amidabutsu*' – was in fact the only path to salvation left. Single-minded attention to this one practice *(senju nenbutsu* 專修念佛) was the last remaining technique. Textual proof for such a doctrine was later provided in his tract *Choosing the nenbutsu as the fundamental vow: a collection of quotations (Senchaku hongan nenbutsushū* 專擇本願念佛集), thought to have been written for his most influential supporter Kujō Kanezane, but which was kept secret and not made public until just after Hōnen's death in 1212. *Senchakushū*, as it is known for short, is a scholarly compendium of selected passages from a variety of Pure Land texts interpreted largely through the prism of Shandao's commentaries, which aims to prove that verbal recitation of Amitābha's name was the highest form of practice. The passage usually taken to encapsulate his argument comes near the end of the work, in which the term 'Saintly Path' refers to traditions other than those that propose deliverance into Amitābha's Pure Land:

Upon reflection, I realise that, if people wish to escape quickly from saṃsāra, then of the two excellent teachings they should, for the time being, ignore the Entrance of the Saintly Path (*shōdōmon* 聖道門) and choose instead the Entrance of the Pure Land (*jōdomon* 淨土門). And if they do so, then of the two main categories of practice, the [five] correct ones 正 versus other diverse practices 雜, they should, for the time being, abandon the latter and choose instead to rely on the former. And if they do so, then they should ignore the secondary set of such practices and concentrate single-mindedly on the definitive one. And by 'definitive' we mean recitation of the Buddha's name. If they recite his name, they will be delivered into the Pure Land without fail, for this is the fundamental vow of the Buddha (Ōhashi 1971: 158).[1]

Leaving Hieizan for good in 1175, Hōnen settled closer to the capital, where he must have already gained some form of patronage, since he was soon able to construct two small buildings. Not a *hijiri* in the sense of someone constantly on the move, actively spreading the word among the people, Hōnen preferred a sedentary life, hardly ever moving from his temple. Over the next fifteen years he gradually won recognition for his learning and grudging respect for his rejection of Tendai politicking and occasional violence. By 1190 he was a prominent figure, well liked by a wide range of nobles, most conspicuously Kujō Kanezane, one of the most powerful states-

---

[1]   Trans. adapted from Dobbins 1989: 14 and Senchakushū English Translation Project 1998: 147–48. See also the extended discussion in Tanabe 1992: 84–95.

men of the time. But only five years later he was being bitterly attacked as a radical for his teachings, and much worse was to follow. How was it that this quiet monk, who had the best of intentions and the backing of some of the highest of the land, ended up causing so much trouble and dissent?

The problem lay in the implications of such an extreme simplification of practice. On a theoretical level, it could be justified as the logical extension of Mahāyāna universalism and it might also be welcomed as a vital step forward in the spread of Buddhism throughout Japan at all levels. In this sense it can be seen as the culmination of the process of making Buddhist practice relevant to a wider and wider audience that we have noted in our analysis of the situation in the late Heian. On a practical and political level, however, Hōnen was opening up Pandora's box.

There were two major problems. The first was his belief that it was too late to choose other approaches to salvation and that recitation of the phrase '*namu Amidabutsu*' was the only answer. Although the quotation above shows that Hōnen himself was in fact quite careful not to dismiss other paths out of hand, using the phrase 'for the time being' (*shibaraku*) twice, the term *senju* 'single-minded practice' could be (and was) interpreted as 'exclusive practice', and it was this charge of exclusivity that was most frequently brought against him. What was more, Hōnen was one of the few Buddhists in Japan to dismiss native deities out of hand and openly denigrate their worship. Never before had there been such doctrinal intolerance that damned non-practitioners to a lesser fate. This was seen by many as un-Buddhist by its very nature.

The second problem was, if anything, more serious. The key to salvation was being offered to everyone, with no reference to class, karma or present activity. It applied equally to the simplest peasant and to the wisest monk. Hardly surprising that such an optimistic message found a ready and wide audience, but hardly surprising too that it provoked a powerful backlash. It was fine in theory, but it struck at too many vested interests, questioning the very heart of the whole monastic enterprise and annulling the distinction between ordained member of the saṅgha and layman. After all, if immediate salvation was guaranteed to the lowest of the low through a simple act of verbal repetition, why submit oneself to difficult practice? What was the point of the saṅgha at all?

A strong reaction to this kind of teaching, then, was only to be expected. More difficult to fathom is Hōnen's role in all of this. The sources leave us with a contradictory picture of a blameless, well-intentioned man who initiated an awkward movement almost by accident. Despite the kind of high-level support on which he could rely, and despite his own care to maintain good relations, friction between his supporters and the Buddhist establishment inevitably grew. The crisis came in 1204 when Tendai monks appealed to their head abbot to prohibit the 'exclusive practice of the *nenbutsu*'. The immediate cause of this demand is not known, but there is no doubt that by this date Hōnen was already thought of as having 'followers', many of whom were in fact answerable to no one but themselves. At this stage, it may have simply been that the religious establishment was taking umbrage at the setting up of what looked like a separate sect, since official permission still had to be obtained before a new religious group was allowed to operate, but in fact Hōnen's response to this appeal suggests that things were indeed getting out of hand. He immediately issued what are known as the 'Seven injunctions' (*shichikajō seikai* 七箇條制誡), a document which was duly signed by 190 of his *nenbutsu* practitioners:

To all those *nenbutsu hijiri* who call themselves my followers (門人):

1 Do not denigrate other buddhas or bodhisattvas, or attack Shingon and Tendai, if you have not yet studied a single one of their teachings. To partake in disputation one must first be a scholar. It is not for fools. And moreover, those who slander the true Dharma are eliminated from Amitābha's [eighteenth] vow. You will fall into hell as a result. Is this not the height of folly?

2 Ignorant as you are, do not indulge in doctrinal disputes with men of wisdom or when you encounter monks from other persuasions. The discussion of principles is for wise men, not fools. Disputation itself gives rise to much suffering. The wise man maintains a distance of one hundred *yojanas* [from such activity]. How much more so the practitioner of the single-minded *nenbutsu* 一向念佛.

3 Do not, in your ignorance and inclination, tell those of other persuasions and other practices that they should abandon their activities, and do not subject them to wanton ridicule. It is fitting to work hard at one's own practice without interfering in the practice of another. In [Guiqi's] *Xifang yaojue* 西方要決 it is written: 'Always show respect to those of other persuasions and practices. If you denigrate them, you will incur a limitless burden.' How can you possibly break this rule? And what is more, Shandao himself was particularly severe on this matter. Not to know the proscription of the founder 祖師 is folly indeed.

4 Do not proclaim that those who practise the *nenbutsu* have no interest in the precepts; do not label those who indulge in lascivious behaviour, drink alcohol, eat meat and only very rarely observe the precepts simply 'performers of diverse practices' (*zōgyōnin* 雜行人), and do not teach that those who rely on Amitābha's fundamental vow need have no fear of doing evil. The precepts are the foundation of the Buddhist Dharma. Practices are various, but all give priority to the precepts. This is why Shandao never raised his eye to look upon a woman. The aim of this document is at one with the prohibitions of the *vinaya*. Those who do meritorious acts must follow these rules or lose the Tathāgata's teachings. To deviate is to turn one's back on the founder. Is there anyone who does not depend on the teachings?

5   Do not, as an ignoramus not yet able to distinguish between right and wrong, deviate from the sacred teachings; do not rashly give your opinion of what is not taught by your master; do not earn the scorn of the wise by disputing without cause, and do not try to mislead the foolish. The ignorant [heterodox] Mahādeva is now reborn in Japan and talks heresies at random; not a whit different from the 'ninety-five kinds of non-Buddhist doctrines'. This is greatly to be lamented.

6   Do not, in your ignorance and dullness, take special delight in proselytizing; do not, in your ignorance of the True Dharma, spread heresies or try to convert ignorant priests or laymen. To become a teacher without having achieved liberation oneself is to break the bodhisattva precepts. Those who live in darkness desire to show off their talents, treat the Pure Land teachings as a performance, are avid for fame, desire patronage, expound their own ideas blindly, and both ridicule and mislead the people. The punishment for slandering the Dharma is grave indeed. Such people are bandits, rather.

7   Do not expound heresies that have nothing to do with the teachings of the Buddha as if they were the true teaching; do not deceive by calling them your master's teachings. Everyone explains matters according to his own understanding, but *in toto* they are blamed on me alone. To sully the teachings of Amitābha and to besmirch the name of the master is the grossest of evils, to which nothing can compare (Ōhashi 1971: 232–35).

This is an extraordinary document and a number of scholars have had difficulty accepting that Hōnen could have issued it, since it places his followers in such a bad light. But if it is genuine, then it shows that the political chaos of these years was being used by some to justify a breakdown of morals across the board. Hōnen's message was in this sense too all-embracing, too optimistic, and too simple, leading inevitably to the kind of antinomian behaviour at which he hints in these injunctions. There is a lot of wringing of hands here, as if Hōnen knew that the belief that repetition of 'namu Amidabutsu' alone would guarantee the Pure Land had lit a spark of permanent carnival-like activity that he was powerless to extinguish. But how are we to explain the fact that Hōnen continued to teach as before and yet, at the same time, became so worried about the possible effect of his teachings that he made sure the tract *Senchakushū* never saw the light of day until after his death? Some have simply accused him of duplicity, but a more charitable explanation would be that while being genuinely convinced that he had discovered the one and only path to fit the present age, and that he was doing the right thing by broadcasting this message as widely as he could, he was at the same time genuinely dismayed at the anarchic effect his teachings were having. The seven injunctions suggest that the Buddhist authorities had good reason to be concerned and were right in asking for some sort of ban, although we have no independent evidence as to the scale of the problem.

And what of Hōnen himself? Even allowing for the hagiographic haze that surrounds him, he seems to have been beyond reproach. Such were his connections and his standing that this public acknowledgement of difficulties won him some time; but it was to be no more than a temporary reprieve. A year later, in 1205, Jōkei 貞慶 (Gedatsubō 解脱坊, 1155–1213) attacked what he saw as a heretical sect by writing a petition to court, known as the *Kōfukuji sōjō* 奏状. Jōkei had been trained at Kōfukuji, although he had left the main temple compound by this time and was living in relative seclusion at Kasagidera 笠置寺 to the northeast. It is fair to say that at Kōfukuji the adherence to the Hossō view that there was a class of incorrigibles, who could never reach full enlightenment no matter how hard they tried, had become considerably attentuated by this stage. Jōkei himself was certainly eclectic in his interests, encouraging the worship of relics, devotion to Śākyamuni, Avalokiteśvara and Maitreya, as well as trying to revive study of the *vinaya* (Ford 2002). What made him most unhappy was what he saw as the sheer exclusivism of Hōnen's teachings and the threat this posed to the institutional status quo. He drew up nine charges against what was now being seen as a newborn tradition:

1 The error of establishing a new tradition without proper court recognition.
2 The error of designing new images for worship. In particular for allowing an image of the Pure Land in which only followers of the exclusive *nenbutsu* are bathed in Amitābha's light and everyone else is excluded.
3 The error of slighting Śākyamuni Buddha by arguing that there is none other than Amitābha.
4 The error of rejecting all other ways of cultivated merit apart from the *nenbutsu*.
5 The error of turning one's back on the native deities.
6 The error of denying that diverse other religious practices may lead to rebirth in the Pure Land.
7 The error of misunderstanding the *nenbutsu* by claiming that its verbal form is superior to its meditative form.
8 The error of harming the Buddhist order by maintaining that violation of the precepts is no obstacle to rebirth in the Pure Land.
9 The error of bringing disorder to the country by undermining other Buddhist teachings (Morrell 1987: 66–88).

The threat posed by the invention of a new tradition was real. We know from *Senchakushū* that Hōnen was intent on providing himself with a lineage running back into China on which the legitimacy of his brand of Pure Land teaching could be established, a teaching that was distinct from the kind of practice that had developed slowly and organically within Tendai. And in this attempt to prove that the new was old, he was spectacularly successful, for the lineage that he invented eventually became accepted as historical truth.[2] Somewhat surprisingly, no immediate action was taken as a result of this doctrinal attack by Jōkei, but the next year a number of Hōnen's most prominent followers were accused of using *nenbutsu* sessions with court women as a cover for sexual activity, and two of them were summarily executed in the second month of 1207. Hōnen himself was exiled to Tosa but allowed back into the capital four years later, partly because it was accepted that he himself had not been entirely responsible, and partly because he still had influential backers. He died in Kyōto in 1212.

We are fortunate in having an account of this affair written not long after the event by Kanezane's elder brother, the abbot of Enryakuji, Jien 慈圓 (1155–1225). It appears in his *Selections from the brush of a fool* (*Gukanshō* 愚管抄), a history of Japan written in 1219. This account is of particular interest because Jien was both a member of the Buddhist establishment most directly affected and yet a sympathetic ally, who had in fact helped Hōnen find somewhere to live when he returned to the capital in 1211.

And in the Kan'ei era (1206–07) there was a holy man called Hōnenbō. About this time, while resident in the capital, he established the *nenbutsu* tradition, calling his teachings the 'exclusive practice of the *nenbutsu*'. 'All you need to do is say *"Namu Amidabutsu"*. Do not bother with other practices, revealed or secret,' he would proclaim. Strangely ignorant, foolish nuns and priests were delighted by this teaching, and it began to flourish beyond all expectations and to grow in popularity. Among them was the monk Anrakubō 安楽房, a retainer who had served with [Takashina] Yasutsune 泰經. Upon ordination he became a practitioner of the single-minded *nenbutsu*, and, together with Jūren 住蓮, he advocated the practice of Shandao, singing praises [to Amitābha] six times a day. There were numerous people, among them nuns, who turned to this teaching and placed their trust in it. And what is more, they went around proclaiming that if you joined them, Amitābha would never ever chastise you, even if you were to indulge in sexual relations or eat fish or fowl; that once you had entered this path of single-minded practice and placed your faith in the *nenbutsu* and that alone, he would come to welcome you at the end. As people in both capital and countryside were all becoming converted, a lady-in-waiting at the detached palace of the retired sovereign, along with the mother of the Ninnaji priest [Dōjo 道助], joined in as believers. They summoned Anrakubō and others in secret to have them explain the teachings. He proceeded to visit them together with his companions, and even stayed overnight. I know not what to say. The upshot was that both Anrakubō and Jūren were beheaded, and Hōnen ended up exiled, unable to remain in the capital.

And so the affair was dealt with and it seemed for a while that things had settled down. But Hōnen had not really been a participant and so he was pardoned. He

[2] Sharf 2002: 298–301. Such was the influence of this invention that it is only now that scholars are challenging the picture it paints of Pure Land movements in China.

eventually died at Ōtani in Higashiyama. And as he passed away, they all gathered round, discussing his deliverance into the Pure Land, but there is no proof that it actually came to pass. The ceremonies at his deathbed were nothing like those reported when Zōga died. The effects of all this are felt to this very day; and perhaps because this single-minded practice with its tolerance of meat eating and sexual relations remains largely unchecked, many monks at Enryakuji have now risen up and are threatening to drive out the *nenbutsu* group led by Kūamidabutsu [1156–1228] (Okami et al. 1967: 294–95).

Perhaps the most interesting aspect of this passage is Jien's unwillingness to blame Hōnen for the excesses of those who were 'delighted by this teaching'. It suggests a reluctance to face the fact that the teachings must ultimately have been to blame, since they inevitably challenged the legitimacy of the Buddhist order and threatened to privilege layman over monk no matter how carefully Hōnen stepped. The essential difficulty at the heart of Hōnen's teaching is here transformed by Jien into a question of public order, as if he found it difficult to look any closer. Perhaps this is hardly surprising, since the concept of salvation for all based on a single verbal ritual act was both a natural consequence of Mahāyana optimism and a path that was to lead to considerable political difficulties. In this sense, Hōnen's teachings served to bring into relief a contradiction that had been present in Mahāyāna Buddhism from the very beginning. It is in this light that we should interpret the fact that there are at least twelve documented instances of suppression of one or more Pure Land factions in the years between 1207 and 1330, all instigated by monks (Dobbins 1989: 20). In 1227, for example, Tendai monks came down from Hieizan, destroyed Hōnen's grave at Ōtani, and publically burned copies of *Senchakushū*. The sangha felt under threat.

It is instructive to compare Hōnen with Kakuban. Kakuban taught the certainty of salvation to all in the knowledge that the involuntary act of breathing itself was by definition salvific, but this was to a limited audience of specialised practitioners. He was subjected to vilification and banishment of a kind, but not because of his doctrine. Hōnen, on the other hand, ran the danger of persecution precisely because he taught a simple path to everyone, sangha member and layman alike. It was always going to be difficult for the Buddhist establishment to face up to the fact that it was losing exclusive access to the rights of salvation.

Was Hōnen then a revolutionary? There is one interpretation that sees in him a kind of Japanese Luther, a defender of everyman, insisting that salvation was universally available and not in the gift of an essentially aristocratic authority. A recent book even talks of Pure Land teaching as the 'liberation theology' of medieval Japan, taking religion away from the state and vested interests and giving it gratis to the people (Machida 1999). There is a grain of truth in this. Replace Hieizan and Kōfukuji with the church of Rome, and Amitābha's vows by the word of the Bible, and one does begin to see one or two similarities. That Hōnen's teachings were fundamentally as troublesome as Luther's there can be no doubt, exposing, as they did, a major paradox, and although there was no Japanese Reformation at the time, the subversive potential of Pure Land Buddhism survived to become a real threat to secular power in later centuries; but as far as the individuals themselves are concerned, we do not have enough reliable material on Hōnen the man, and what we do have is contradictory and heavily overlaid with centuries of tendentious commentary. Certainly there was much to protest about in the venal conduct of religious affairs, and the results of Hōnen's teaching were seen to be rather frightening: but turn to the type of practice recommended and what do we find? A traditional recipe: a mantra of sorts. Not a mantra in the tantric sense, but still a phrase which if repeated over and over again was believed to have remarkable effects. One occasionally finds Pure Land teachings being described as 'rational', but the image that really sticks in the mind is a famous carving made about this time of Kūya [see page 241], the early Heian forerunner of Hōnen. Emerging from Kūya's half-open mouth are six small statues of Amitābha strung out along a line of wire; an evocative statement of the magical potential of sound, the very embodiment of *nenbutsu*.

11.2   Myōe

The unhappiness generated by the wider implications of Hōnen's teachings, which seemed to be so at odds with the lifestyle of the man himself, was given even greater impetus with the publication of *Senchakushū* in the months after his death. Criticism was registered right across the monastic institutions, but perhaps the most famous response came from the monk Myōe 明惠 (1173–1232), who immediately wrote a highly charged rebuttal entitled *A wheel to crush heresy* (*Zaijarin* 摧邪輪), accusing Hōnen of having played fast and loose with his sources. He too, however, reveals the contemporary puzzlement at the contradiction between what people knew of the man and what was revealed in the teachings:

Of late, a saintly monk has written a book; it is called *Senchaku hongan nenbutsushū*. [In it] he flounders around in the scriptures and makes fools of us all. His intention is to create a tradition devoted to practices to ensure deliverance [in the Pure Land], but in fact he ends up creating obstacles to such practice. For many years now I myself have had deep admiration for this monk and I used to attribute the numerous heresies one hears about to irresponsible statements by lay men and women taking his name in vain. Never once have I tried to ridicule him, and, although I have heard tales told, I have never once believed them. But now, having recently read this *Senchakushū*, I find myself saddened beyond belief.

When I first heard the title, I looked forward to paying honour to his skilful commentary; but, having read the work, I now feel resentment that the true meaning of the *nenbutsu* has been so misrepresented. Now I know for certain that the heretical views held by his myriad followers, both lay and ordained, have all arisen from his work. Now that he is dead and gone, these practices have become even more popular. Once committed to writing, it becomes a treasure for future generations. Transmitted to followers, it becomes revered as if it were the words of the Buddha himself. All believe it to contain the essence of the Pure Land tradition (往生宗), to be the treasure chest of those who practise the *nenbutsu*. And so, if you dare to criticise it, you are immediately saddled with criticising the *nenbutsu* itself. And when you occasionally meet a believer, merit is seen to consist of [exclusive] belief in this one practice. Eventually the single taste of the Dharma rain will become divided into sweet and sour, and the community of monks will be driven to schism, a great error. How greatly this is to be deplored! So, I recently took the opportunity of a lecture on the Dharma to destroy [the thesis of] this work by presenting two major criticisms:

1 The error of rejecting [the importance of the arousal] of *bodhicitta*
2 The error of likening those who enter the Entrance of the Saintly Path (*shōdōmon*) to robbers (Kamata et al. 1971: 44–46).

Myōe proceeds to explain how *Zaijarin* was first drafted as a private critique, only to be then made public at the behest of a patroness. One of his main complaints was that Hōnen had been extremely selective in his use of quotations from Daochuo and Shandao, hiding the fact that neither of them had ever actually argued that the verbal form of the *nenbutsu* was the one and only practice possible; they had always taken care to see it as one of a whole range of practices. Hōnen, he argued, was misrepresenting the Pure Land tradition for his own ends. Myōe was a careful scholar and knew his Pure Land texts well, so his criticisms were always apposite. He was also concerned that the absolute necessity of *bodhicitta*, the initial aspiration for enlightenment, had simply been discarded. Without this, he argued, the process could hardly begin; the Pure Land was not so much a place to which one was translated, but rather a state of mind into which one would be transformed. This kind of criticism, whereby Myōe took the stance of a defender of Pure Land orthodoxy, was particularly damaging, since it could not be simply put down to a monk fighting for his own vested interests, or trying to maintain the line between monk and layman for this-worldly reasons.

Who was the author of such a bitter denunciation? The question is much easier to ask than to answer. Myōe is one of the most interesting figures in the history of Japanese religious life, but in the usual historical surveys he receives only cursory treatment, mainly because he was neither the founder of a tradition nor a major political force. This marginalisation is especially regrettable because he is that rare creature – a Japanese monk who allows us to see something of the person behind the role. For most of his life he kept a written record of his dreams. This is a unique document, giving us a glimpse into the inner life of a Buddhist monk of intense personal religiosity.[3] There is, however, another reason to draw attention to his life and work. Eclectic in both doctrine and practice, he represents what one might call a conservative radicalism: someone committed to traditional learning and scholarship, unhappy with the militant exclusionism that was emerging, and yet maintaining a firm resolve not to become personally absorbed into the Buddhist establishment. He preferred the role of monk as hermit.

Myōe was born in 1173 in the west-central area of the Kii peninsula. His parents both died when he was young and he entered Jingoji 神護寺 on Takaosan 高尾山 to the northwest of Kyōto in the care of his uncle Jōgaku 上覺 as early as 1181. This temple had figured prominently in the early Heian period and had been Kūkai's first base, but had since fallen into disuse. Most of its treasures had been transferred to the Ninnaji and it was little more than a ruin when Jōgaku and Mongaku 文覺 arrived to restore it in 1168. In 1188 Myōe became a monk, receiving his full ordination (*gusokukai*) at Tōdaiji. From the beginning he showed an interest in both Kegon doctrine and tantric ritual, and by 1193 he had become recognised for his learning. In that year, the head of the Sonshōin 尊勝院 Kegon seminar asked him to represent Kegon at the annual court lectures (*kujō* 公請). Typically he turned down the offer, a clear sign that he had no wish to proceed with an official career.

He soon became disillusioned with monastic life and in 1195 went into seclusion at Shirakami 白上 in Kii. It was during this time that intense efforts brought on a severe mental crisis, which ended with him slicing off his right ear in front of a portrait of Buddhalocanā (Butsugen Butsumo 佛眼佛母), in order to show his utter devotion to the task of achieving enlightenment. We are told that blood spattered over the portrait. A portrait – it may or may not be the very one – survives with a poem and the following inscription that shows Myōe's state of mind:

---

[3]   For this reason his writings have been of particular interest to psychologists; see, for example, Kawai 1992.

The mother of the earless monk. Homage to the mother of all buddhas! Take pity on me! Do not ever leave me, in this life or those that follow! Homage to mother, oh mother! Homage to mother, oh mother! (*namu haha gozen*). The beloved son to whom Śākyamuni bequeathed the Dharma upon his death. Jōben (Brock 1984: 333).

Three years later Myōe returned to the area around Jingoji, but there too he felt unhappy and soon returned to Kii, where he was to spend the next nine years in seclusion, with one or two companions and supported by his mother's family, the Yuasa. It was now that he started writing on Kegon doctrine. It was also during this time that he became obsessed with the idea of travelling to India. There were two periods in particular when this obsession reached a peak and on both occasions he was only saved from his madness by a manifestation of the deity at Kasuga, who persuaded him that Buddha was not in India and could equally well be reached in Japan. In 1210 the sovereign Go-Toba granted him a *bessho* at Toganoo 栂尾 near Jingoji, where he was to remain for the rest of his life, winning a reputation as an incorruptible monk of great learning and compassion and also gaining a number of patrons, among them some very highly placed women. The *bessho* eventually became the temple we now know as Kōzanji 高山寺. In 1212 came the controversy over Hōnen and the writing of *Zaijarin*. From this time onwards Myōe became increasingly involved in tantric ritual, but we know that he also made himself available to the public on many occasions. In a diary entry for 1229.5.15, the famous scholar Fujiwara no Teika 定家 wrote in his usual self-pitying mode:

About eight [in the evening] my wife and daughter went on a private visit to Toganoo. Myōe administers the precepts there on the fifteenth and the last day of the month. Monks, nuns and laymen all gather together there as if the Buddha himself were alive, they say. Although I realise how important it is to link oneself to one's karma, I hate crowds, so – poor lonely outcast that I am – I ended up by missing his teachings. This was indeed most regrettable. On this occasion they went with Kōshin as guide and returned at about four [the next afternoon]. Apparently everyone had been jammed into such a small room that they had no idea who else might have been there, except that someone did tell them that Lord Tamenaga had been present. And, in particular, I heard that Lord Morikane and Lord Sadataka had been there. As usual, this outcast was missing from their number (Imagawa 1977–79, vol. V: 27–28).

Myōe lives in the Japanese imagination not so much through his own writings as through his biography, which presents the classic picture of an incorruptible medieval monk leading a life of strenuous self-examination, extreme self-imposed hardship and meditation, and totally dedicated to the search for enlightenment in a Mahāyāna context. The primary sources for the historian are a series of works known as *gyōjō* (行状) or 'records of conduct', the most important of which was written by his companion Kikai 喜海 (1178–1250). This source, as one might expect, is inescapably hagiographic in intent and yet less obviously full of legendary material than many other sources. But, as one might expect of a man who went out of his way to fashion a life as a particular kind of quest, ultimately in the image of Śākyamuni, the process of creating a legend started with Myōe himself. Hardly surprising, then, that it accelerated after his death. The picture presented is largely that contained in *Myōe shōnin denki* 明惠上人傳記, which, although also attributed to Kikai, is of indeterminate authorship and probably dates from the late thirteenth century. It is here that one encounters the legendary feats of meditation in trees, what can only be called a 'love letter' written to an island on which he secluded himself, and meetings with eminent figures that he may not actually have met. He emerges as Buddhist hero-monk, not typical of any school or sect but certainly meant to be typical of the period in which he lived.[4]

To turn from biography to autobiographical material is to face the *Dream diary* itself. This remarkable document, which was kept secret in Kōzanji and not made available until fairly recently, records dreams and visions experienced over a period of forty years.[5] Many have to do with his frustrations stemming from religious passion and uncertainty, but many more are obviously sexual in nature. The intensity of his practice is only rivalled by his overwhelming chagrin at not having been born during the lifetime of Śākyamuni himself. Occasionally he adds his own interpretations to the record. Dreams were very much seen as legitimate signs of one's spiritual progress, whether they arrived by chance, or whether they were actively encouraged by visualisations and states of trance. Indeed the line between active visualisations, meditation and dream becomes extremely difficult to draw, especially at the degree of magnification we find with Myōe, and there is little sign that he himself felt moved to draw such distinctions. There can be no doubt that he was particularly susceptible to creating and recalling dreams, and the evidence of this diary would suggest that he was the visualiser par excellence. As a young monk, he had copied out extracts from texts that specifically dealt with this subject. Entitled *Mukyōshō* 夢經抄, these

[4]   On this subject see 'Kegon's Myōe as a popular religious hero', and 'Zeami's *Kasuga ryūjin* or *Myōe shōnin*' in Morrell 1987. The letter is translated in Tanabe 1995.
[5]   See Girard 1990, which contains a full translation of all known fragments of the diary together with a detailed introduction on the subject of dreams in Buddhism; also the English translation in Tanabe 1992.

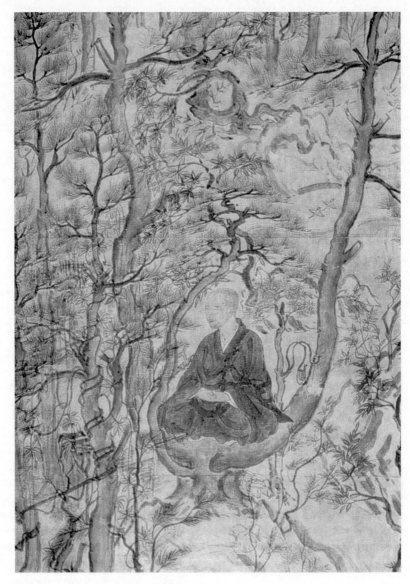

Plate 22   Myōe meditating in the forest.

passages discussed how to obtain dreams, how to interpret them and recount them, how to distinguish between 'real' as opposed to 'illusory' dreams, and how to deal with dreams of bad omen.

The ability to remember dreams is not given to all, and not everyone is able to write them down. To record a whole lifetime of dreams demanded an extraordinary feat of mental energy. It is difficult to choose examples that will not distort, since they range from the cryptic to the prolix and rambling, but the following entries should give some idea of the richness of this record:

In a dream, there were two great golden Peacock Kings, which were larger in size than a man's body. Their heads and tails were decorated with an assortment of jewels, and from their entire bodies came a fragrant force that permeated the entire world. The two birds frolicked and flew through the sky, and from the jewels came a great voice of sublime beauty resounding throughout the world. The sound of that voice recited a verse: 'The 84,000 teachings and the means for countering [ignorance] are the wonderful Dharma preached by Śākyamuni, the honoured one.' A man was there and he said, 'These birds always dwell on Vulture Peak; they have great affection for the unsurpassed Mahāyāna in which they delight, and they are far removed from attachment to worldly matters.' After the birds recited the verse, I held two sūtra scrolls in my hands. On one scroll was written the title, 'Buddhalocanā Tathāgata', and on the other was written 'Śākyamuni Tathāgata'. I thought of how I had obtained these two sūtras from the peacocks, and a feeling of great joy arose when I heard the verse. As I chanted 'Praise be to Śākyamuni Tathāgata! Praise be to Buddhalocanā Tathāgata!', tears of joy began to flow and I rejoiced at holding the two scrolls. When I awoke from my dream, the bottom of my pillow was soaked with tears.

I was staying with Military Guard Sakiyama. As I was tired, he took my pillow and placed *shikimi* leaves under my head. In a dream after that, there was a large rock whose pinnacle had no end. Sea water flowed from above like a waterfall. It was a most excellent token that I experienced with great delight.

There was a living thing shaped something like an octopus, which I thought to be the soul of the priest Shōgi. It was moving into the house; and Girin grabbed it, hacked at it with a sword, and threw it limp into a pond. It resembled a turtle in shape, and wanted to go to the other shore, but sank to the bottom.

In a dream on the night of the sixth day of the eleventh month (during my early evening meditation when I sat in meditation and wanted to practise tantric methods), there was a very dignified, beautiful lady in a room. Her clothing was marvelously exquisite, but she showed no sign of worldly desire. I was in the same place with this noble lady. Not having any feelings for her, I ignored her. She was fond of me and did not want to be separated. I ignored her and left. Still she showed no sign of worldly desire. She held a large single mirror around which she wrapped some wire. She also held a large sword. Interpretation: the woman was Vairocana; that is, she was certainly a queen (Tanabe 1992: 161, 166, 168, 185).

Myōe has a reputation for being one of the restorers of the Kegon tradition, but this is somewhat misleading. While it is true that he picked out the *Flower garland sūtra* for particular study and so in one sense turned the spotlight on to it and away from the Pure Land texts or the *Lotus*, he did not contribute in any meaningful sense to the further development of Kegon doctrine.[6] He chose it for his own purposes mainly because it was considered to be the first of the Buddha's teachings and was therefore closest to Śākyamuni himself in time. It also happened to be the most difficult of sūtras. True to his tantric training, however, and true to the spirit of the age, he used the sūtra not so much as something to study and decipher but as an object of devotion and meditation.

When dealing with Kegon (Huayan) there is always the problem of whether one is talking of the teachings or the sūtra itself, for the relationship between the two is not entirely straightforward. It is generally understood that the sūtra was an illustration of the main Buddhist truths, but Huayan doctrine soon became a philosophy in its own right that could be studied independently. Myōe was unusual in his insistence on concentrating on the sūtra itself rather than the doctrinal tradition, and given the vast and amorphous nature of the work, it was inevitable that if he was to use it as an object of devotion (somewhat in the manner that elements of the Tendai tradition treated the *Lotus*), it should suffer reduction. In the work *Sanji sanbōrai shaku* 三時三寶禮釋 (1215), Myōe discussed a set of three phrases that expressed praise for the moment of *bodhicitta* and for the Three Jewels; this was intended to be written on a scroll, hung up, and used for veneration and recitation. It may well be, of course, that this kind of thing was directly affected by the emergence of the *nenbutsu* and other methods that advertised themselves as short, easy paths, although whether or not Myōe produced it in direct response to '*namu Amidabutsu*' is difficult to judge.

Myōe continued to develop these simple techniques for encouraging mindfulness in the common man, making particular use of two rituals that have already been described: the 'Mantra of radiant wisdom' (*kōmyō shingon* 光明眞言) and the 'Visualisation of Buddha's *ūrṇā*' (*bukkōkan* 佛光觀). The mantra, which Genshin had used during funeral rituals, was recited over purified sand that was in turn spread on the person's grave to release the light of Vairocana over the body and ensure salvation. The practice of visualising the bright light that emerged from the tuft of hair on the Buddha's forehead

---

[6] See Girard 1990: 58ff for a discussion of the revival of the Kegon seminar at Tōdaiji under the monk Bengyō 辨曉 (1138–1202).

was something that Myōe borrowed from the heterodox Huayan thinker Li Tungxuan 梨通玄 (635–730), whose writings helped Myōe understand how Huayan might be transformed into a devotional practice as well as being a source of intellectual excitement (Tanabe 1992: 143–52; Gimello 1983).

Yet one further tie between Myōe and Kegon is revealed by the existence at Kōzanji of what is known as the *Narrative scroll of the origins of Hwaŏm* (*Kegon engi emaki* 華嚴緣起繪卷). This tells the story of how Huayan (Kr. Hwaŏm) teachings were brought to Korea by two monks, Ŭisang 義湘 and Wŏnhyo 元曉. The primary source for this material was the biographies of these two men in the *Song biographies of eminent monks* of 988. A major role in the story of Ŭisang is played by the Chinese maiden Shanmiao 善妙, who falls deeply in love with him but is in turn converted by him. When Ŭisang returns to Korea, Shanmiao not only secures him safe passage by turning into a dragon to carry his ship across the stormy waves, but also helps him to found the first Hwaŏm temple at Pusoksa. As we have seen, Myōe had a special concern for women and after settling at Kōzanji built a nunnery in 1223 at Hiraoka for the widows created by the civil wars that had raged during his lifetime. He named it Zenmyōji 善妙寺 after the heroine of the story, Shanmiao.[7]

Myōe also had a special relationship with the Kasuga deity. While in Kii he had occasion to pray for the survival of his aunt in pregnancy. She survived the ordeal, which was considered to be a result of his successful intervention with the evil spirits that had been trying to drag her away. This woman must have had psychic powers herself, because when Myōe announced in 1203 that he wished to go to India she started a fast during which she became possessed by the Kasuga deity and demanded that he stay in Japan. India would come to him in the form of visions, and, in any case, since all was mind, there was no need to travel. At this point Myōe is said to have visited Kasuga a number of times to converse with the deity.

A similar encounter took place two years later when he was again planning a journey to India. This time he went as far as to calculate the distance between Chang'an and Magadhā and worked out how long it would take him to reach his goal. Sickness overwhelmed him at this point, however, and the deity again intervened. It now became clear to Myōe that the Kasuga deity was in fact a manifestation of Śākyamuni; he could now comfort himself that the Buddha himself had come to Japan:

---

[7] For a full study of this scroll and how it might be linked to Myōe, see Brock 1984. The scrolls are normally dated 1224–25, although Brock suggests a slightly earlier date, prior to the founding of the nunnery.

This August Deity is the king of the teaching in this age of five defilements. It is the representative manifestation of the Tathāgata Śākyamuni. Truly, every single practice and ritual indicates its relationship as the incarnation of Śākyamuni, the honoured one. The descent of the Great August Deity is a marvel in this latter age and a superior thing for our country (Tanabe 1992: 38–39).

How very different from Hōnen, who was so convinced of the rightness of his belief in *mappō* and Amitābha that he rejected native cults out of hand. Myōe had no compunction in having recourse to this homegrown deity, whom he now knew was actually the manifestation of the Buddha in Japan.

11.3   Shinran

The logic at work in Hōnen's belief in the efficacy of the *nenbutsu*, linked to the conviction that such a path was in fact the only conceivable one for those living in an advanced state of *mappō*, was carried even further by Shinran 親鸞 (1173–1262). Shinran underwent the usual Tendai training on Hieizan, but left the mountain for good in 1201, becoming a committed follower of Hōnen. Both men were separated by the 1207 banishment, Hōnen being sent to Tosa and Shinran to Echigo, and their paths were not to cross again. Why Shinran was exiled is not known, although it is thought that he took a wife somewhere about this time, which may well have been taken as illustrative of precisely the kind of outrageous behaviour Hōnen's teachings were encouraging. Certainly it would be difficult to exaggerate the importance of this act, for it broke a fundamental rule of monastic life. But things were never this clear cut in Japan. There were always religious figures who found it impossible to survive in the regimented world of the monastery: like Hōnen before him, Shinran could leave Hieizan and yet continue to live a life that was recognised by others as being different from a normal lay life. What was different in Shinran's case was the openness with which he married and the fact that despite taking such a drastic step, he remained a revered figure accepted by a growing audience.

From 1207 to 1214 Shinran stayed in exile in Echigo. Then in 1214 he moved east to settle at Inada 稲田 in Hitachi, where he stayed until about 1235. It was here in eastern Japan that he set about proselytising his faith in Amitābha among the farmers and peasants of the region. Although figures are hard to come by, his following (known by the generic term *monto* 門徒) was largely among the rural poor and the illiterate. Ignoring almost entirely the distinction between monk/priest and layman, he cultivated a form of worship that was protestant in nature. Believers would form 'congregations' (*kō* 講) which met at regular intervals in meeting houses (*dōjō* 道場) under the guidance of a leader (*otona* 乙名). Here, often in the presence of an inscription reading '*namu Amidabutsu*', or some variant thereof known as the *myōgō honzon* 名号本尊, they would practise common devotions, chant the *nenbutsu*, listen to simple sermons, and (at a somewhat later stage) chant *wasan* 和讃 or short Japanese hymns. This kind of practice undoubtedly had its roots in local custom and nurtured a strong sense of participation in a communal act of worship. It can be imagined how far this was from the traditional behaviour of monks in temples. The leader of the group must have had some education and status, but Shinran's ideal was democratic and he fought all his life against the doctrine of the primacy of the monk. He founded no temples. Although he did not discourage the use of images of Amitābha, it was the *nenbutsu* that lay at the heart of practice; the act of gratitude for the gift of faith. Whether or not there were congregational rules at this early stage we do not know, because the earliest extant ones date from 1285 (Dobbins 1989: 67).

Shinran seems to have continued preaching in this fashion until about 1235, at which point we find him moving back to the capital. It is thought that this came about because in that year the military authorities placed a ban on any *nenbutsu* teaching in and around Kamakura, so he may have felt that it would only be a matter of time before similar pressure was applied even further east in Hitachi. Whatever the reasons, he was back in Kyōto by 1237, although he had no fixed residence and was supported largely by gifts in kind sent from congregations in the Kantō. There were a number of well-defined groups by this time: the Takada 高田 *monto* in Shimotsuke, the Yokosone 横曽根 in Shimōsa, the Kashima 鹿島 in Hitachi, and the Ōami 大網 in Mutsu to the north. He had secured a strong base in eastern Japan and most of his extant letters are addressed to these groups. The fact that he never returned there, however, suggests that he may well have been ordered out in the first place, although there is no specific record of this happening. The last fifteen years of his life were divided between writing and dealing with a series of disputes. In response to the emergence of antinomianism among certain groups in the Kantō, for example, he sent his son Zenran 善鸞 east to solve the problem. Unfortunately, Zenran proved to be overbearing and out of sympathy with Shinran's own egalitarianism, causing such tensions that in 1256 Shinran was forced to go so far as to disinherit him.[8]

[8]   Details here and elsewhere on Shinran taken largely from Dobbins 1989.

Difficulties such as these stemmed directly from the nature of Shinran's own teachings. Most of his writings are in the form of letters, tracts and commentaries written in Japanese but there is one major doctrinal work, a difficult text written in classical Chinese entitled *Selected passages revealing the true teaching, practice and attainment of the Pure Land* (*Ken jōdo shinjitsu kyōgyōshō monrui* 顯淨土眞實教行証文類), known as *Kyōgyō-shinshō* 教行眞証 for short. Six fascicles cover six topics: teaching, practice, faith, attainment, 'the land of the true Buddha' 眞佛土, and 'the land of the Buddha in his transformed body' 化身土. The form resembles Hōnen's *Senchakushū*, in the sense that it largely consists of a series of quotations of key illustrative passages, and it can be seen as a defence of Hōnen's work against the kind of attack that we have seen coming from Myōe, although it certainly takes the argument much further.

According to Shinran's calculations, the world was already in the 683rd year of *mappō*, which meant that previous practice was now of no use; belief in the power of Amitābha's vow was the only choice. No human being could be pure at such a time, and that included the community of monks. Anything that smacked of the self, including self-help, was suspect. Even 'cultivating all the virtues' (from the nineteenth vow) would, in his view, only lead to a kind of provisional Pure Land, from which it was still possible to backslide, because it was based on the belief that self-help (*jiriki* 自力) was possible. Similarly, to 'cultivate the basis of all virtue' (from the twentieth vow) by chanting the *nenbutsu* was certainly efficacious but was not perfect, because it retained an element of self-help. The only true answer was 'the vow that Amitābha singled out' (the eighteenth vow), which talks of nothing but faith, pure and simple. This for Shinran is the ultimate teaching, because it was based on the correct understanding that salvation was at root a gift from Amitābha. Everything was a result of his beneficent power, help from the other (*tariki* 他力). The faith that underlies the conviction that the *nenbutsu* can lead one straight to the Pure Land comes not from individual effort, but is itself bestowed on us by Amitābha, as part of his vow. In this sense, faith does not come from within. Unlike Hōnen, Shinran saw the *nenbutsu* in terms of a simple act of gratitude, not as an act that had meritorious effect in and of itself. He also shifted the emphasis entirely away from the earlier belief in the importance of one's state of mind at death; the onset of faith, he claimed, might occur at any stage. It is worth noting that to make his argument stick Shinran had occasionally to adjust the syntax of the classical Chinese in his reading of the sūtras to prove that faith was bestowed rather than spontaneously generated in the mind of the believer (Dobbins 1989: 34).

Although the basic concept was simple, Shinran's arguments were subtle and not always correctly understood. This goes not only for his largely illiterate audience but also for the more intellectual among his congregations. Nowhere is this clearer than in the tract called *Notes lamenting deviations* (*Tannishō* 歎異抄), which consists of a collection of ten statements attributed to Shinran himself, followed by a discussion of eight common misunderstandings. It is now treated as a concise guide to Shinran's teachings. It is not known who compiled these notes, but it may have been a follower called Yuienbō 唯圓坊, who is mentioned in the text. What emerges from this discussion is the radical nature, one might say the purity, of his thought. The problem was how to maintain the pristine nature of this vision.

In Amitābha's principal vow there is no distinction between young and old or good and evil persons. We should realize that faith alone is necessary. His vow is therefore aimed at saving the sentient being who is steeped in wrongdoing and blazing with evil inclinations. Consequently, if one has faith in the principal vow, no other good is necessary, since there is nothing so good that it can surpass the *nenbutsu*. Nor should one fear evil, since there is nothing so evil that it can obstruct his principal vow (Dobbins 1989: 75).

The logic is that since faith is a gift, to strive for faith simply shows that one lacks faith; to believe in the possibility of self-help is to believe in a self, which is anathema. Faith must be detached from practice, since one must not actually intend anything; it is by its very nature unplanned.

There are a number of interesting consequences that can follow from such a doctrine, and it naturally gave birth to a whole series of heresies. How does one recognise true faith? And if salvation is guaranteed, what then? Faith being the result of the mind of Amitābha being implanted into the mind of the believer means, does it not, that we are filled with Amitābha and are ourselves therefore buddhas. And since he vowed to save all sentient beings before he accepted full buddhahood himself, and since we know that he has already reached this stage, it follows that all sentient beings are already saved. It was this that led Shinran to claim that Amitābha's eighteenth vow was designed above all for the doer of evil, the incorrigible. From here it is but a short step to arguing that it matters little what we do in this life as long as we have faith; that, on the contrary, to do good deeds and follow lay precepts in the attempt to save oneself through one's own effort was an indication of one's *lack* of faith in Amida's ability to lead one to salvation come what may.

Given that Shinran addressed himself to a largely illiterate audience, it is hardly surprising that such teachings could be misconstrued. Certain aspects could easily lead to what became known as the principle of licensed evil (*zōaku muge* 造惡無碍). Since salvation was assured, why bother to practise devotion or act within accepted norms? After all, Shinran himself had broken the precepts and raised a family. Antinomian activity was constantly emerging, and this in turn gave rise to suppression of what was clearly a dangerous doctrine being spread in the lowest of social classes. Things were made worse by Shinran's somewhat dismissive attitude to other buddhas and gods. He tolerated them at best. It is not surprising that his followers were regarded with suspicion by both the Buddhist and secular authorities, and subjected to considerable pressure.

As we have seen, Hōnen himself had been plagued by a tendency to antinomianism among some of his followers, something that was often tied to what he saw as the heresy of the 'single *nenbutsu*' (*ichinengi* 一念義), which claimed that a single intonation of the *nenbutsu* was itself enough to guarantee salvation on its own (Dobbins 1989: 49–53). By and large Hōnen tried to argue for the maintenance of the precepts. Shinran went much further, rejecting outright the distinction between lay and clerical, both in his own life and in his teachings. But it was the very purity of his radicalism that made it so difficult for him to deal with excess on the part of his followers. The argument against antinomian behaviour was that to intend to do wrong was to seek to please the self; since faith came not from the self but from Amitābha, it would never arrive unless the self were annihilated. This from a man who had broken the precepts by getting married and who believed that no human activity could be pure in an age of *mappō*. It is hardly surprising that his followers occasionally found his logic difficult to follow.

12 Religious culture of the early 'middle ages'

12.1 Baking the cake

The terms 'middle ages' and 'medieval' come, of course, from the example of European culture, and one baulks a little at using such loaded terms in an utterly different context. Nevertheless, it has proved useful to cultural historians of Japan in their attempt to characterise that long period that starts with the creation of another centre of gravity at Kamakura in the Kantō at the end of the twelfth century and comes to a close with martial law in the late sixteenth. The unity of such a huge time span must, of course, be in large measure illusory, stemming more than anything else from the clarity of what happened before and after, and yet the term has stuck and we shall stay with it. And what characterises this period? If one is allowed a metaphor, by the end of the Heian period most of the ingredients of the Japanese cultural cake had been assembled and mixed together. Now they were to be placed in the oven.

A balanced appraisal of this period, however, is sometimes difficult to find. There is a natural tendency to overestimate the influence of the new, such as the radical Pure Land beliefs just discussed, partly because they were new, and partly because in time these groups evolved and became themselves part of the mainstream, writing the history of the medieval period in their own image in the process. But this should not blind us to the continuing presence and power of the older ingredients that remained as the bedrock of medieval life and culture. Minamoto no Yoritomo, for example, was careful to pay due honour to both buddhas and the gods. He carried with him a rosary (*gonenju* 御念珠) and a small silver statue of Kannon in his hair. He performed Buddhist and local rites every day, and depended on diviners to advise when his army should mount an attack. Special reverence was paid to the composite deity Izu Gongen 伊豆權現, whose centre of devotion was at Sōtōzan 走湯山 on the Izu peninsula. The hub of ritual life in Kamakura, however, was the shrine to Hachiman, the adopted *ujigami* of the Minamoto. What may have been just a small family shrine when Yoritomo first arrived in Kamakura eventually became a large temple, the Tsurugaoka Hachiman gūji, the centre of a major cult, the symbol of warrior unity in the Kantō, and an official Bakufu institution. As we have come to expect of Hachiman temples, the rituals were Buddhist, the two largest events being the Hōjōe 放生會 and (after 1221) the Ninnōe 仁王會. Pure Land Buddhism was seen as destructive of public order, little more than a nuisance to be dealt with. Of Zen, Yoritomo was largely ignorant (Collcutt 1996).

It is at this stage that we find tantric attitudes and tantric logic expanding to fill every nook and cranny of Japanese spiritual life. The increasing pressure on royal institutions that came in the wake of the establishment of rival power bases, first in the form of retired sovereigns and then in the form of military rule from Kamakura, led to a crisis of confidence, which was slowly overcome by a deliberate regime of myth-making, the end result of which was a redefinition of Japan's origins and a ratification of Japan's place in the world. An explosion of histories known as *engimono* 緣起物 that recounted the foundation legends of a particular temple or shrine, a revision of the tale told of the origins of Japan in the *Nihon shoki*, the emergence of new composite deities, and above all the heroic efforts of Buddhist scholar-monks to unify the spiritual landscape by firmly grounding local cults in an overarching tantric theory; these are the signposts that will help to guide us through this period.

12.2   Tōdaiji and Ise

It might be thought, for example, that when the Taira troops destroyed both Kōfukuji and Tōdaiji at the end of 1180, that would be that. Far from disappearing from the scene, however, they both emerged stronger than before. Almost before the ashes were cold, moves were afoot to rebuild both of them. Kōfukuji being the main clan temple of the Fujiwara, the task was left largely to them, but Tōdaiji presented a different kind of problem. From the very beginning this huge temple had been a sovereign's project and it had been built with state funds. Times had changed and this was now no longer a feasible option. Nor could matters be left to the temple itself. All its land holdings were now in the hands of the Taira and its revenues were barely enough to support normal running costs, let alone a major rebuilding programme. Go-Shirakawa was well aware that it was in his interests if blame for the disaster could be laid entirely at the door of the Taira, and if the temple could be restored under his auspices. Funds were therefore sought not only from enemies of the Taira but also through a form of solicitation of public funds known as *kanjin* 勸進, which was carried out on a national scale. The project eventually succeeded largely through the efforts of the monk Chōgen 重源 (1121–1206), who was put in change of fund-raising and construction in the eighth month of 1181. At first sight, Chōgen seems to have been an odd choice. He was of obscure origin and had no formal connection to Tōdaiji whatsoever, but it is known that he had already supervised the construction of two smaller temples and as a *Kōya hijiri* he had a special connection to the office and person of the retired sovereign. His slightly marginal status gave him access to a much wider public than might have been available to a more ordinary aristocratic monk, which in turn facilitated the running of a successful money-raising campaign.

This particular *kanjin* campaign was carried out by a large group of *hijiri*, who travelled throughout Japan, accompanied by six substantial carts (with, one assumes, armed guards) in which various donations in the form of money, precious materials or other goods were stored. Legitimacy was given to the enterprise by a formal written document issued by the court. In return for a small amulet, or certificate, donors were made to feel part of a great 'national' religious effort. It is thought possible that as part of this process Chōgen adopted the practice of giving himself another name containing the word 'Ami' or 'Amidabutsu'. It was a habit that was to spread into a fashion among lay landowners and itinerant monks alike.

Although there is no doubt that Chōgen did succeed in raising substantial funds from men and women of substance who wished to gain merit in this way, and also from enemies of the Taira such as Minamoto no Yoritomo, who contributed a thousand bolts of silk, a thousand *ryō* of gold dust, and ten thousand *koku* of rice, it is unlikely that he managed to raise large amounts of money from peasants and farmers; but since the main aim of this effort was to produce the impression that the whole project belonged to everyone, this did not in the end matter. The full reconstruction of the temple complex was to take almost a century to complete, but the image of Vairocana was ready by 1185, cast under the guidance of a Chinese craftsman called Chen Heqing 陳和卿.[1] The next stage was to create the main building to house the image,

---

[1] The architecture of this reconstruction is discussed in Coaldrake 1986: 33–47. Tōdaiji was destroyed again in 1567, so the only parts of Chōgen's work to survive today are the Kaisandō, the outer hall of the Sangatsudō and the Nandaimon. For details of the administration of Tōdaiji during the Kamakura period, see Piggott 1982.

which took until 1203 and involved bringing timber from the far end of the Inland Sea. After the death of Go-Shirakawa in 1192, it was in fact Yoritomo who gave full support in both material and logistics. It undoubtedly suited his purposes to be seen to be recreating something that his rivals had destroyed, particularly when that something was a national, state project, and in the end he probably benefited most of all.[2]

Tōdaiji was not able to recover the majority of its landholdings until the defeat of the Taira at Dannoura 壇ノ浦 in 1185 and even then this provided nowhere near what was necessary for construction. It was at this point that the temple was given the province of Suō 周防; not just the few estates it already owned there, but all the public property (*kokugaryō* 國衙領) as well. This can be seen as an extension of the habit of shifting public, state-owned land into private hands which had been used so successfully by Go-Shirakawa as part of his campaign to regain power and authority. Tōdaiji now had ownership of a whole province and it was from there that most of the wood necessary for reconstruction came, although the project was so large that resources from the provinces of Bizen and Harima also had to be marshalled to complete the main hall. Apart from a short hiatus from 1206 to 1231, Tōdaiji continued to own most of the province of Suō for the next six hundred years. This privilege brought a huge increase in yearly income, but also brought with it the necessity to deal with administrative matters on a day-to-day basis, which in turn ensured that the temple authorities would continue to be plagued with the kind of land disputes that had made the late twelfth century so unhappy for many temples (Arnesen 1982).

It will be recalled that when Shomu first built Tōdaiji, such was the magnitude of the task that Hachiman had to be brought from Usa to Nara to offer divine assistance. Chōgen now turned to Ise for the same kind of help. Nothing illustrates better the eagerness with which Buddhism embraced the local gods in this period than his pilgrimage to Ise in the fourth month of 1186, recorded by the monk Keishun 慶俊 in a description entitled *Tōdaiji shuto sankei Ise Daijingū ki* 東大寺衆徒参詣伊勢大神宮記. Chōgen himself had gone to Ise in the second month of that year and had passed the night at Mizugaki 瑞垣, where Tenshō Daijin appeared to him in a dream and complained that it had been feeling very weak of late and had not been able to accomplish much of value. In return for succour, it promised to help him complete the rebuilding of Tōdaiji. He returned to Nara, had two copies of the *Daihannya kyō* made and decided to take them back personally to Ise.

---

[2]   For more details on the campaign to rebuild Tōdaiji, see Goodwin 1994: 67–106.

The group left on the twenty-third day of the fourth month, having bathed and cleansed themselves for three days. There were sixty monks in all with a total retinue of over seven hundred. On the twenty-fifth they arrived at the entrance on the Miyagawa, where they were met by large crowds. They stayed the night at Jōkakuji 成覺寺, then, at the urging of the chief priest of the Outer Shrine, Watarai Mitsutada 度會光忠, moved to the Jōmyōji 常明寺, the *ujidera* of the Watarai. The visit to the Outer Shrine was performed at the dead of night, so the monks saw very little of the shrine itself. The next day the party set off for the Inner Shrine, where they were allowed to pay their respects. The account tells us that all the monks received this privilege, and Keishun records being overwhelmed by the experience. There is a story that on this occasion Chōgen also dreamed that a woman aristocrat gave him two jewels, one red and the other white, which he found in his hand when he awoke. The jewels he took back to Nara and enshrined in the new head of the Buddha.[3] The monks then went on to Futamigaura 二見浦, where they spent the night at the Tenkakuji 天覺寺, built by Arakida Shigenaga 荒木田成長. It is of particular interest that although Tenshō Daijin is often referred to in this account, nowhere do we find the name Toyouke. It may well be that the existence of this deity at the Outer Shrine was either unknown or thought to be of very little significance (Yamamoto 1998: 13–17).

It is interesting to note how many Buddhist temples there were in the environs of Ise; temples, moreover, that belonged to the families of those priests who were in charge of the shrines. The imposition of restrictions against Buddhism at and near Ise that were introduced after the downfall of Dōkyō was very short-lived indeed. The ties between Buddhism and the local gods (in this case directly linked to the sovereign) were far too strong. Just as in the case of the priestess at the Kamo shrines in the early eleventh century, working as a ritualist for the native gods in this life by no means precluded making efforts through Buddhism to secure one's own salvation in the next.

Until the early ninth century all tax revenues for the shrines at Ise were channelled through the Jingikan. Worship was the prerogative of the sovereign alone, and even other members of the royal family had to obtain special permission to approach the deities. Those 'sustenance households' (*kanbe* 神戶) and shrine lands (*shingun* 神郡) that supported the upkeep of the shrines were administered by a head priest (*gūji* 宮司), who was always drawn from the Nakatomi family. Shrine lands did increase in number, from three in 897, to seven in 1019, and finally to eight in 1185, but compared

---

[3] Ruppert 2000: 183–84.

with the wealth of the main temples this was very small scale indeed. As the administrators of these lands themselves became more powerful and started to treat them as private holdings, the priests who actually ran the shrines found themselves in difficulty because of an insufficient flow of income from the estates (Teeuwen 1996: 22).

As the main source of patronage coming directly from this source dried up, the shrines were forced to look elsewhere for support. Of course, they tried to increase their landholdings, which led to friction, but they also turned to a wider audience with a number of new strategies to encourage patronage from wherever it might be available. This was eventually to lead to the popularisation of pilgrimages to Ise. One of the most interesting results of these various changes at Ise was a shift in the nature of ritual. Whereas before, ritual had been concentrated on the relationship between ruler and deity with priest as ritualist, with the breakdown of this exclusive link, anyone who could pay could have prayers said on his or her behalf. Chōgen's grand procession of 1180 was only the most conspicuous of an increasing number of pilgrimages to Ise at this time. The impetus seems to have come from Buddhist monks, who used what I have described as tantric logic to translate Ise from its role as the centre of the royal cult in Japan into a much wider Buddhist context, in which it could be defined as the pivot of the universe. In time, this was to lead in interesting directions as the relative weight accorded to buddhas versus gods changed, but at this point the drive for further accommodation undoubtedly came from the Buddhist side.

One sign that matters were moving in this direction is a text entitled *A reading and explanation of the Nakatomi purification formula* (*Nakatomi harae kunge* 中臣祓訓解). Recent research suggests that it was composed sometime prior to 1191, the earliest date we have for a colophon.[4] The author was probably a Buddhist monk who had close ties with the priesthood at Ise and it is worthy of special attention because it clearly shows how tantric Buddhism was already becoming fully engaged in the task of explaining native ritual in such a way as to accommodate it in the larger Buddhist picture. The starting point is a ritual prayer or *norito* known as the 'great purification formula' (*ōharae no kotoba*), which was recited by the Nakatomi on the last days of the sixth and twelfth months of the year. The earliest extant text of this formula is recorded in Book 8 of the *Procedures of the Engi era*. It would appear that by the mid-twelfth century its recitation had

---

[4]   For further detailed discussion see Teeuwen and van der Veere 1998, who show that the text is in several layers. This discussion here concentrates on the earliest layer; other layers will be dealt with later.

been transformed from its original use as state ritual into something that priests could perform for individuals. The earliest record of this happening is 1180, when Yoritomo's prayer master (*kitōshi* 祈禱師) used it as part of the prayers for success in battle. By the 1190s it was in common use for various rituals at both the Inner and Outer Shrines. A Buddhist interpretation was necessary precisely because of this transformation. The text begins with an explanation that the formula is more than it seems; it is not just that it consists of words used by the deity Amenokoyane:

[The words] are the beneficent truth that one's own mind is pure; they are Sanskrit words of Maheśvara (Daijizaiten 大自在天); they are helpful techniques of all the buddhas of past, present and future, a field of bliss for all sentient beings; they contain the extensive and great wisdom that springs from the mind, and the great teaching that in essence is pure; [this formula] is a dhāraṇī that dispels fear (*mufui darani* 无怖畏 陀羅尼) and a divine spell of repentance for one's transgressions.

The ritual objects used are also carefully given Buddhist equivalents:

The form of the *ōnusa* 大麻 is a representation (*samaya*) of the purity of one's own original nature and a symbol of the *samādhi* of [Dainichi's] Universal Presence (*fugen* 普現). Wearing a robe of endurance, and holding a *shaku* 笏 of uprightness, [the celebrant] sweeps away the three poisons and the seven calamities, and liberates [the sponsor] of the five impurities and the eight sufferings. The ritual robe is an armour of endurance. When one holds the *shaku* while resisting evil thoughts, it will become a sword of wisdom that deters all enemies. Its form is straight; its working is perfect.

Purification is interpreted in terms of enlightenment and ritual recitation as an exercise in meditation, which, of course, it always was in Buddhist terms. The formula was thus transformed into a technique, an aid to the attainment of salvation:

To perform *harae* is to purify oneself from all transgressions and divine wrath by means of the mystic ritual formula; this is the same as to return to the wondrous state in which everything is originally unborn, represented by the syllable '*a*', and to realize the real wisdom of the subtle brightness of one's own nature. The duality of pure and impure does not arise in reality. And so, the conditioned is in fact attachment, which is impure, and the unconditioned is in fact the entity which is pure. This [the unconditioned] is the essence of our minds. If one practices meditation, one's mind will gradually become pure. Because of this, when one makes reverence and recites this [formula] seven times, one will not be defiled by the mud of the passions that accompany the state of ignorance. When one does worship at a stream and touches it seven times, the waves of the [wisdom-]water from the pond will cleanse you and the source of your mind will become pure. Thus one will escape from the net of the ten passions and not be caught in the three existences. This is called 'purification'. It is a secret technique to extinguish transgressions, to produce good, and to achieve immediate enlightenment (Teeuwen and van der Veere 1998: 20–25, adapted).

The reference to worshipping at a stream reveals that this formula must have been used during the ritual known as the *rokuji karinpō* 六字河臨法, which is first mentioned in 1043. This was a ritual that lasted seven days, on the seventh day of which a *goma* fire stage was moved onto a large boat, which passed through seven rapids, a tantric ritual involving six seed-syllables being performed at each rapid (Teeuwen and van der Veere 1998: 58). Rituals originally designed for exclusive royal use were now being used by priests at Ise in more individual settings and given a Buddhist framework. If we remind ourselves of the way in which tantric masters at the Tang court spent their time amalgamating Indian and Chinese rituals, this should come as no surprise.

12.3   Of deer and monkeys

And what of Kasuga–Kōfukuji? In §8.3 we left this joint institution developing from a house temple and shrine into a major power base, with considerable local authority and increasing landholdings. The conflagration of 1180 proved to be little more than a temporary setback, and the process by which the complex grew to control the whole of the province of Yamato was hardly interrupted. The area had always been sacred ground, of course, but the creation of the Wakamiya shrine with the composite figure of Kasuga Daimyōjin in the mid-twelfth century (often seen as an invention of Kōfukuji to extend its power over shrine matters), and the large, expensive public festival which came in its wake, led to something qualitatively different. It was the development of this deity that allowed Kōfukuji to use the *shinboku* as a political weapon throughout this period.[5] It has already been shown how men like Kujō Kanezane, and Jōkei (Gedatsu Shōnin) became involved with this deity, and there were many others: Myōe, for example, had a relationship with it that bordered on the erotic. As mentioned previously, the early fourteenth-century *Miracles of the Kasuga Deity* (*Kasuga gongen genki* 春日權現驗記) describes in detail how in the first month of 1203 the deity took the form of a woman in order to persuade him to give up his obsessive desire to travel to India:

[5]   See Grapard 1992a: 100–18 for a description of the administration of both shrine and temple.

'There is not one of the gods, good monk', she then continued, 'who does not protect you. The Great Deity of Sumiyoshi and I attend you particularly. And I, especially, am always with you in the centre of your body, so that even if you were across the sea we would not be parted, and I would not personally mind. But when I remember all the people who can be inspired by you to faith, as long as you are in Japan, my happiness at the thought turns to grief that you should mean to undertake so long a pilgrimage' . . . Then she descended from the ceiling as silently as a swan's feather falling. The fragrance as she spoke had grown still more pronounced. Though not musk or any such scent, it was very rich, and quite unlike any fragrance of the human world. Transported with delight, those present licked her hands and feet, which were as sweet as sweetvine. One woman's mouth had been hurting for days, but when she licked her the pain was gone. Despite everyone pressing in to lick her, the lady kept her loving expression and seemed not to mind. She never moved. In colour she was as bright as crystal, and every detail of her was beyond the ordinary. Her wide-open, unblinking eyes showed much less pupil than white. Everyone was weeping. 'Never before have I shown my true form this way and come down into human presence', she said, 'and I never will again. I have done so now, good monk, because I have such supreme regard for you' (Tyler 1990: 272–74).

The symbolic link used to 'prove' the connection between Buddhism and the local cult at Kasuga had previously been to identify the resident of the first shrine, Takemikatsuchi, with Fukūkenjaku via the sign of the deerskin; we now find a quantum leap whereby the sacredness of the whole locale gains a new Buddhist dimension. Tantric logic, by which we mean the belief that surface similarities, however slight, are the key to an underlying identity, seized on the presence of deer, which had long been a symbol of Kasuga. And where had the Buddha set the wheel of the Dharma in motion with his first sermon? In the Deer Park outside Benares. This was proof that the fundamental ground of Buddhism had now shifted to Japan; the Kasuga–Kōfukuji complex was the Buddha's Land in Japan and hence represented a Pure Land on earth. When one remembers that it was Hossō Buddhism for which Kōfukuji was famous, with its basic premise that all reality is nothing but mind, one can see how it became possible to create the concept of a Pure Land in the here-and-now: since the Buddha had once lived in this world of ours, it must be pure; only those of impure mind saw it as impure. So this sacred area became somewhere to visit, a place of pilgrimage. Here you could touch purity. People started to come to Kasuga in the hope that they might be able to experience dreams and visions of a Pure Land.

Clearly such a development puts the shrine–temple complex on an entirely different level. It moves it from being a private Fujiwara cult centre to being the object of public fascination, and it is at this point that private rituals

Plate 23   A Kasuga 'deer maṇḍala', showing the moon of enlightenment held in the branches of the sacred *sakaki* tree, entwined with wisteria, the symbol of the Fujiwara.

become public festivals, giving birth to a number of new art forms, the most important of which is the kind of dance and theatre (*dengaku* 田楽) that was eventually to develop into Nō. There also emerged a new kind of devotional art, known as Kasuga maṇḍala, which made it possible to pay obeisance from afar. These paintings are not of the deity itself but of the Kasuga–Kōfukuji landscape. We are fortunate to have an account by Kujō Kanezane himself of how one of these paintings might be used. In his diary *Gyokuyō* 玉葉 for the fifth month of 1184 we read as follows:

16th: Today there is a divine taboo, so we will pay our respects to the painting that depicts the august shrine [Kasuga] tomorrow.

17th: Rain. I was sent a scroll painting depicting the august shrine from the abbot in Nara. Having bathed early in the morning and thus purified myself, I put on my ceremonial dress (with the belt and sword, as usual), took up the purifying wands (six small ones for indoor use with short streamers), and, standing in front of this treasure from the august shrine, I performed my devotions as usual with two paces and two bows. Then, still wearing the ceremonial dress and standing in front of the treasure, I offered up a thousand short repetitions of the *Heart sūtra*. And after that, I picked up each wand and waved it in front of each shrine in turn (the four main shrines, plus the Wakamiya and Isakawa shrines). I then retired and laid aside my dress. This was an extremely difficult practice. From today for a period of seven days the whole family will offer up together 10,000 short readings. Every day I will enter my hall (with purified ceremonial dress). Today the General [my son] did the same devotions (but since he was in ordinary court dress he did not offer the wands).

24th: At dawn today (as I had not done on the intervening six days) I bathed and purified myself. Wearing ordinary court dress, I stood in front of the treasure, picked up the wands and offered them up. Then I immediately returned the painting, adding a mirror as a treasure for the gods. It was made of gold and silver in the shape of a Chinese lion, and so took a long time to make and was sent later. In due course both I and others dreamed that the august shrine itself had come to us. I do indeed believe it did (Nara kokuritsu hakubutsukan 1964: 16; Grapard 1992a: 91).

This extract is the first record we have of the use of a devotional painting of the shrine for practice in absentia. One might have thought that here lay an instrument of propagation ready for use, but the emergence of cheap talismans lay far in the future.[6] What Kanezane receives is obviously both representation and the object itself at one and the same time; not only does he go through exactly the same motions as he would if physically present at the shrine itself, but he and others of his family dream that the shrine had in fact come to them, and it is the dream that proves that it did.

---

[6] I am referring here to *sansha takusen* of the Edo period. Note, however, that the term *sansha*, which covers Ise, Iwashimizu and Kasuga, is already in use by this time.

Developments further to the north on Hieizan, home of the great rival institution of Enryakuji, were entirely different but of no less import. Here one is dealing not with a small sacred hill but with a series of interconnected valleys high in the mountains northeast of the capital. The name Hiei 比叡 is thought to be a sinification of the original name of the mountain, namely Hie 日吉. The term Hie Taisha 日吉大社 refers to a series of seven shrines: there are four in the eastern group, Ōyamagui and Kamo-tamayori-hime with two shrines each (two at the top of the mountain and two at the foot) both linked to the Eastern Pagoda and the Medicine King (Yakushi nyorai); one in the western group, Ōnamuchi, identified with Ōmononushi, son of Susano-o, the main deity of the Ōmiya Shrine in Yamato, linked to the Western Pagoda and Śākyamuni; one called the Usa Shrine, which honoured Hachiman, and was linked to Yokawa and Amitābha; and one called Shirayama, linked to the Hakusan cult. These seven shrines were eventually associated with a whole series of 'sevens', the seven Buddhas of the past, the seven stars of Ursa Major, and the seven orifices in the human head, in an attempt to prove that Mt Hiei was a microcosm of the universe (Grapard 1987: 220).

Thanks to the destruction wrought by Hideyoshi's troops in the sixteenth century, older records about Hieizan and the Hie shrines are few and far between. There is, however, one text entitled *Record of a shining heaven* (*Yōtenki* 耀天記), which has been dated to 1223 and is of particular value in this regard. The text is in two distinct parts: a collection of short entries dealing with the history of certain shrines, names and rituals, and then a longer piece of connected prose entitled 'On the god Sannō' ('Sannō no koto' 山王事). This second section shows us that by the beginning of the thirteenth century the interpenetration of buddhas, bodhisattvas and gods was fully developed on Hieizan, to the point that, as at Kasuga, a composite deity called Sannō had emerged. It was, of course, no accident that Sannō (Ch. Shanwang) was the name given to the deities who protected Mt Tiantai in China, from whence the whole Tendai movement had sprung.

It is stated somewhere in the Chinese Classics that the essential energy of the sage is called *shen* 神, but the truth we call *shen* is [in fact] the advent of Sannō. There are many proofs for this. In the beginning, this country of Japan was first ruled by seven generations of heavenly gods and five generations of earthly gods; and then Tenshō Daijin manifested itself in the province of Ise. It called the Inner Shrine Kōtai jingū and the Outer, Toyouke, united their brightness, protected the hundred kings, and took care of the people of the land. Then, gradually, the gods of the four directions, beginning with those at Kamo, Kasuga, Matsuo and Sumiyoshi, took possession of every province and every place, protected the ruler's palace and the houses of the people. But to say, as people have a habit of saying, that this is due to the fact that

Japan is the land of the gods shows an ignorance of the Tathāgata's true intentions. He himself through his great, deep compassion knew that the three worlds are all one, and so, because he was a great teacher, he knew that unless he himself planned it, no buddha, bodhisattva or sacred being would ever occupy land in Japan or bring to fruition the vow to save all living beings. He also knew that if they were to mingle their radiance with the dust of this world, take possession of the shrines and raise auspicious fences, their presence would be thanks to acts of good merit by the Tathāgata himself.

With this in mind, he said: 'I intend to manifest myself in Japan as the god Sannō of Hie. I shall work for the salvation of all living beings and I shall protect the greatest of all teachings, the perfect Dharma of the Buddha. But first I shall send you all before me so that you may manifest yourselves as gods. Then Japan will become a land full of gods and I will cause them to believe in these gods and make them hold them in awe. Only then will I soften my radiance, manifest myself as a god, and work for the salvation of all living beings.' This he told to the great masters of the Dharmakāya, with the intention of manifesting himself under the name of Sannō at the foot of Hieizan (Kageyama 1983: 73).

Mention of Tenshō Daijin here should not mislead us into believing that the monk who wrote this passage subscribed to the view that the Hie shrines were in any way subordinate to those at Ise, along the lines laid down by the Jingikan centuries earlier. It was accepted that the ruling family could trace itself back to Tenshō Daijin, but claims made for Hieizan were far greater. The composite deity Sannō was the Buddha himself, who had filled Japan with gods with the ultimate aim of salvation in mind; it clearly outranked Ise. It was on such a basis that the Sannō cult continued to strengthen and it was this aspect of the cult that allowed it to be linked much later to the deification of the early Tokugawa rulers in the Edo period.

Yōtenki makes considerable use of what we have found to be a staple of Japanese logic, a logic that looks for signs on the surface for clues as to what correspondences might lie beneath. Relationships and connections can reveal themselves in surprising ways, often involving magic. Language and writing plays a large part in this kind of relevation of the truth of a relationship. What might be ignored as serendipity and chance is, in this system, claimed as the key to truth. As regards the name Sannō, for instance, this deity is directly linked to Tendai thought by analysing the way the name is written. Both 山 and 王 consist of three lines linked by a fourth. This must relate to the Tendai concept of *santai ichijitsu* 三諦一實 'the three provisional truths are all one truth' and so can be used as proof of his existence on the mountain. Similarly, in a discussion that tries to identify various clues as to how and why it was that the origin of Sannō lay in Śākyamuni, we find the following explanation that actually defines the term *kami* as 'the advent of Sannō' by using the habitual association of Hieizan with the monkeys that are indigenous and have always been the symbol of the mountain:

This is something that happened when the Yellow Emperor was ruling China, before the Tathāgata was born. One of his ministers called Cang Xie 蒼頡 was a [prior] manifestation of Śākyamuni. They say that before any of the *kami* had appeared, this minister was ordered by the Yellow Emperor to create writing. Many scholars created characters thereafter, I am told, but writing was invented in the time of the Yellow Emperor. It is difficult to be certain. Be that as it may, the character for *kami* 神 is made up of *saru* 申 and *shimesu* 示. The character for *saru* can be used to write 'Hiyoshi monkeys (*saru*)' and the character *shimesu* can be used to write [part of] the word 'manifest [himself]' (*jigen* 示現). Since the word *kami* 神 is written with the radical 示, the character *kami* means 'manifest himself to the monkeys'. So the character for *kami* was created by Cang Xie, who looked into the future and described the advent of Sannō by means of writing, knowing that when Śākyamuni Tathāgata was about to manifest himself as the god Sannō he would reveal the true face of reality, good and bad, to the monkeys (Kageyama 1983: 81).[7]

12.4   A dream of swords and sheaths

Jien's *Selections from the brush of a fool* (*Gukanshō*) of 1219 was quoted earlier in the context of Hōnen's banishment, but Jien's work is important for many other reasons. It is the first narrative history in Japan to do more than simply chronicle events; it asked why those events had happened as they had, and it gave what Jien understood to be a rational explanation. It is not hard to find the reasons for this. It looked very much as though succession to the throne was in danger and the country was falling into chaos, one armed conflict following another in rapid succession. The times were out of joint. Jien began his work just when it seemed that his own branch of the Fujiwara, the Kujō family, might succeed in unifying the two power centres of Kyōto and Kamakura. In 1218 a great-grandson of his brother Kanezane was made crown prince and the next year another great-grandson, Kujō Yoritsune 賴經 (1218–56), was adopted as the next head of the Minamoto house. It was important to justify this position and to show why it was a historical inevitability. In retrospect, of course, history did not prove to be so kind.

Jien's argument is grounded in two axioms, both of which have to do with support for the monarchy. Firstly, that the privileged position of the Fujiwara as regents was entirely a result of a pact that had been agreed between

---

[7] The translation hides yet one more play, since the character for *saru* 申 is also used in the recurring phrase 'the character for *kami*' (*kami to mōsu moji* 神と申す文字).

Tenshō Daijin and Amanokoyane, the *ujigami* at the Kasuga shrine, that the Fujiwara house would guard the palace and help the monarch rule. This much was clear from the account in *Nihon shoki* and subsequent history. The times when the state, in the form of the monarchy, had flourished coincided exactly with those times when the Fujiwara regency had also been active. Secondly, that the Buddha's Dharma (*buppō* 佛法) had been introduced into Japan during the reign of Kinmei Tennō for the express purpose of protecting the Royal Dharma (*ōbō* 王法) (Okami et al. 1967: 137). Much of the chaos of the early thirteenth century had arisen precisely because both of these truths had been forgotten. The chronicle section with which Jien begins his history does not touch the 'Age of the gods' at all, but plunges straight into the earliest Chinese dynasties, followed by Japanese rulers starting with Jinmu Tennō. This suggests that although fully receptive to native deities, Jien was far more interested in the politics of succession to the throne than in early myth and legend. He was concerned to reveal the principles that underpinned what had happened in the past. Not that he was very optimistic about the future. How could he be, since he firmly believed that Japan had indeed entered the age of *mappō* in 1052 and was on a path of gradual decline from a golden age? The best he could hope for was a temporary improvement as long as the Fujiwara were again allowed to play their predestined, allotted role. The second, discursive part of *Selections* begins with an explanation of the theory of 'a hundred kings' (*hyakuō* 百王), which stated that Japan would be no more after a hundred reigns, of which there were now only sixteen remaining.

Jien, like Myōe, is also of interest for his dreams, and one in particular. There exists a record, together with a series of self-interpretations, of a dream he had in 1203. Whenever he was in attendance at the palace, part of his duties as a 'protector monk' (*gojisō* 護持僧) involved a ritual called the Kannon ku 觀音供, the performance of which was meant to safeguard the monarch's health during the night (*yorui kaji*). This was carried out in the Futama, a room that contained an image of Kannon which held in its hand a 'wish-fulfilling jewel' (*nyoi hōju* 如意寳珠). The Futama was right next to the room where the monarch slept and where replicas of the sacred sword and 'seal' were kept on a table (Teeuwen 2000: 107).

In the year Kennin 3 (1203) at dawn on the 22nd day of the 6th month I had a dream that of the two royal treasures, the divine seal (*jinji* 神璽) and the treasure sword (*hōken* 寳劍), the divine seal was the jewel woman 玉女, and this jewel woman was the body of the sovereign's wife, the queen. When the king enters the body of the jewel woman, who is pure in and of herself, and they have intercourse, both actor and recipient are free from fault! And it is for this reason that the divine seal is a pure jewel. The dream revealed this to me and then came to an end. Thereafter, while drifting in and out of sleep, I began thinking about these matters from various angles. This is none other than the sword and sheath mudrā of Acalanātha![8] The sword is the treasure sword, the body of the king. The sheath is the divine seal, the body of his queen. Their union signifies the attainment of his mudrā! Acalanātha, the revered one, should be treated as the cult image of the king! And I went on to speculate – the divine seal is the jewel woman, the mother in the Buddhalocanā section [of the maṇḍala]. The Saintly King of the Golden Sphere 金輪聖王 is to be identified with the One-Syllable Golden Sphere (Ichiji Kinrin 一字金輪). This means that this deity, also known as the Golden Sphere of Buddha's Pate (Kinrin butchō 金輪佛頂) unites with Buddhalocanā. The treasure sword is the Saintly King of the Golden Sphere! It is for this reason that during the ritual of Buddhalocanā the sword of knowledge is placed on the altar. It is driven in and out eight times into the eight spokes of the wheel. This sword and seal signify attaining the unity of heaven and earth. That which brings to fruition the Buddhist Dharma and the Royal Dharma to regulate the state and profit the people is the king's treasure. The room called the Naishidokoro also goes by the name of 'divine mirror'. This is the son of heaven [the prince?], born from these two seeds [the sword and the sheath], the august body of Tenshō Daijin, who is in turn Mahāvairocana; and Mahāvairocana manifests himself as the One-Syllable Golden Sphere for the benefit of sentient beings. This golden sphere is within the Diamond World and the King of the Golden Sphere is the origin of the king. This is why he manifests himself as such, taking his significance from the Buddha World. Now Shingon originates in phenomena and reveals the path that benefits sentient beings; its function is to reveal the significance of everything in this world. And it is said that during the ceremony of enthronement of the king of this land, the world, when he is placed on a high throne he mimics the King of the Golden Sphere, the manifestation of Mahāvairocana, and clasps his hands in the mudrā of the Knowledge Fist. This is Mahāvairocana from the Diamond World emerging from the origin and revealing his traces to benefit sentient beings. When this occurs, Mahāvairocana is treated as the cause and the King of the Golden Sphere as the result. The deep significance of Shingon's highest teaching can hereby be known. Acalanātha [Fudō myōō] is the aspect of Mahāvairocana known as the Sphere of Instruction. Among his fourteen basic mudrā, the one that gives rise to all phenomena is the sword and sheath mudrā. This is equivalent in meaning to the sword and jewel. Buddhalocanā, Golden Sphere, Acalanātha, these three revered ones, are what gives rise to the king, and to the land (Akamatsu 1957: 318–19).[9]

There is far too much in this dream to unwrap, but the outlines should be clear. Jien is trying to unravel the underlying significance of what are now known as the regalia: the sword, the jewel and the mirror. The 'original' sword was kept at the Atsuta shrine and the 'original' mirror at Ise. He sees

---

[8]   Reading 不動 for 不釣 .

[9]   The names with the common element 'Golden Sphere' are aspects of the deity Butchō 佛頂, an anthropomorphic representation of the protuberance on Śākyamuni's head, the *uṣnīṣa*.

the sovereign and his queen as two different manifestations of Mahāvairocana, one from the Diamond World and the other from the Womb World maṇḍala. The sword and the seal (as jewel) are their *samaya*, or symbols. The sexual imagery of the sword and sheath mudrā, which belongs to Acalanātha (Fudō) in his role as the instructional aspect of Mahāvairocana, presents sovereign and queen as generators of the world. The mirror is their offspring.

Following on from this dream there are two interpretive passages, in the first of which Jien describes what happened when, on the first day of the following year, he showed a record of his dream to retired sovereign Go-Toba and his nephew Yoshitsune 良經. When Yoshitsune draws his attention to a passage from the first book of *Nihon shoki* that actually describes the divine seal as being a jewel, he expresses great joy at finding proof of the veracity of his dream. It might seem rather odd that someone of Jien's education and interests had not read this crucial passage, but we know from other sources that even sovereigns could be hazy as to the real identity of the 'divine seal': as late as 1320, retired sovereign Hanazono noted a similar ignorance in his diary (Akamatsu 1957: 325). Why?

In fact the history of the regalia in Japan is not as straightforward as it might seem. There is only one early reference in *Nihon shoki* to 'three treasures' 三種寶物 that Amaterasu presents to Ninigi as he prepares to descend to earth: the curved jewel (Yasakani no magatama 八坂瓊曲玉), the mirror (Yata no kagami 八咫鏡) and the sword (Kusanagi no tsurugi 草薙劍), and this passage appears not in the main text but in a quotation 'from another source' (Sakamoto et al. 1967, vol. I: 147; Aston 1972: 76). From that time on, we only find references to two treasures in relation to the accession ceremony until a much later date. The ritual text *Kogo shūi* 古語拾遺 of *c.*807 compiled by Inbe no Hironari 齋部廣成, for example, lists only a mirror and a sword as the 'sacred treasures' (*jinpō* 神寶); the *Engishiki* of 927 does the same, calling both of them the sovereign's 'heavenly seals' (*amatsushirushi* 天璽 or *jinji* 神璽). *Sendai kujihongi* 先代舊事本紀 mentions as many as ten treasures, which were probably sets of mirrors and swords. In 960 a disastrous fire destroyed the Unmeiden 溫明殿 where most of the treasures were held and it was later reported that one of the sacred mirrors had survived, flying away by itself from the flames. It has been suggested that the reintroduction (if that was what it was) of a third treasure in the form of a jewel was a result of Buddhist influence, possibly as early as the ninth century (Ruppert 2002). Although the initial short reference in *Nihon shoki* must have played its part, the coming of tantric practice introduced the

Plate 24   'Acalanātha's sword'. During a battle between Acalanātha (Fudō) and a non-believer, both beings changed into flaming swords. Acalanātha then changed again into the black dragon Kulika (Kurikara ryūō 倶利迦羅龍王) and finally extinguished the flames of his opponent.

worship of Buddha relics (*busshari* 佛舍利), which usually consisted of bone fragments, pieces of natural glass, quartz and other chips of polished jewels, housed in expensively fashioned reliquaries. The veneration of a 'wish-fulfilling jewel' held by the statue of Nyoirin Kannon 如意輪觀音 that stood in the Jijuden 仁壽殿 may have been an added influence, and there seems to have been a tendency to conflate this kind of jewel with the *magatama* curved jewel. Worship of Kannon in this guise was seen to be particularly efficacious in the granting of wishes. Sometime in the early eleventh century another figure of Kannon was installed in the Futama, which is where Jien would have performed his rites on behalf of the sovereign. But we are still faced with the interesting problem that when Jien had his dream, he claimed he was uncertain as to what the term 'divine seal' (*jinji* 神璽) referred to.

Immediately after this account, Jien adds what he sees as further proof of his interpretation by recalling the story of what was supposed to have happened at Dannoura in 1185, when Kiyomori's wife took the young Antoku Tennō 安德天皇 in her arms and jumped into the sea. Both perished. What were now undoubtedly three regalia were with the young boy. The mirror was saved and brought back to the capital by Taira no Tokitada; the sword sank to the bottom of the sea and was lost for ever; but the 'seal' floated in its box and was later retrieved by a warrior who, not knowing what it might be, opened it in the presence of a lady-in-waiting. Together they discovered that the box was in two layers, each layer holding four jewels. Jien expresses his delight in remembering this, which gave further proof for his dream, although he does not comment on the fact that there was more than one jewel. He is also concerned to know why history has allowed the sword to be lost, especially since as a result of the dream, he knows what it stands for; he concludes that it must also have symbolised military protection for the throne, which is no longer needed given the presence of warriors from the east.

One thing that stands out in this dream and Jien's understanding of it is the overt use of sexual imagery. This had been present, of course, from the very beginnings of tantric practice in the Tang court and Kūkai's Shingon was full of images of the unification of opposites and the interpenetration of phenomena. Kūkai was very well aware of the dangers of such vocabulary and it was probably for this reason that he had once refused to lend the commentary to the *Rishukyō* to Saichō on the grounds that it would need a trained teacher to explain its true meaning. But the more explicit type of tantric texts did not even exist in Chinese translation until well after Kūkai. We do not know for sure when they arrived, but it is possible that they formed part of the group of texts that Jōjin collected in the 1070s. In any case there can be no doubt that by this time in the late twelfth century such modes of thought were commonplace in tantric circles, and lay at the heart of much of the speculation directed at discovering the true origin of Japan and the nature of the monarchy. We shall investigate this again in due course.

It is also instructive to note what Jien says about the accession ceremony: he understands that the monarch forms the mudrā of the wisdom fist, which not only belongs to Mahāvairocana but is clearly sexual in its symbolism, involving as it does the right hand making a fist around the upward extended index finger of the left hand (see plate 16, p. 144). We do not know exactly when this mudrā was first used in such a context, but it is part of a development whereby the older form of ceremony, the Daijōsai, was replaced with a tantric form of consecration, called the *sokui kanjō* 即位灌頂. It is almost as if what Kūkai had hoped for, a tantric state with tantric masters advising the monarch, had finally come to pass four hundred years later, with Buddhist monks of high standing taking a close interest in matters to do with the sovereign, the regalia and the succession. It might seem as though Ise was in some danger of being written out of the picture altogether.[10]

---

[10] Kamikawa 1990 analyses a series of references to *sokui kanjō* and comes to the conclusion that it was probably not in actual use until Fushimi Tennō's accession in 1288. Interestingly, Jien's dream record was often quoted as proof of precedent despite the fact that he was careful to note that he did not really know the truth of the matter.

13   Chan Buddhism

13.1   The early development of Chan

Before the impression is produced that medieval Japan was interested in little more than its own problems of governance, succession to the throne, and the creation of a national myth, it is important to backtrack a little and attend to matters on the continent. In the midst of all the ferment, and the slow baking of the cake, something new arrived from China that was to have a lasting impact on Japanese life and culture: that form of Buddhism known in China as Chan 禪, and in Japan as Zen. Unfortunately, such is the degree of misunderstanding about the realities of Chan/Zen that it has proved necessary to insert here a fairly lengthy excursus into the history of Chan in China, to provide some idea of the kind of institutions that Japanese encountered when they started travelling to the continent again in the late twelfth and early thirteen centuries. Zen itself will be taken up in the next chapter.

The history of Chan is difficult to untangle for two main reasons. Firstly, Song 宋 period Chan historians and apologists present us with a picture of Chan in the earlier Tang period that is largely of their own making; and secondly, Japanese Zen historians have found it difficult to avoid projecting their own sectarian concerns back into the past. The outline that follows is therefore somewhat tentative and relies on recent Western scholarship to an unusual degree (Yampolsky 1967; McRae 1986; Faure 1997). The origins of Chan and the story of its early growth are unclear. All we can say with any certainty is that sometime around 624–74, in the early years of the Tang dynasty, a community of monks in a monastery in Huangmei County 黃梅縣 (Hubei Province) in south-central China began to attract attention as a centre dedicated specifically to the practice of meditation. It was this, rather than the study of sūtras or the performance of ritual, that would bring one closest to the experience of Śākyamuni himself. The centre grew in popularity, largely because of the personal charisma of the monk Hongren 弘忍 (601–74). Students would come to study with him for limited periods, so it was not a 'school' so much as a centre known for the teaching and dissemination of a particular practice. Hongren himself may have concentrated on teaching techniques of meditation, but his students were interested in many different aspects of Buddhism.

A number of impressive monks emerged from this centre, which became known as the Community of Dongshan 東山, the most important of them being Shenxiu 神秀 (606?–706), the author of a work entitled *On contemplating mind* (Ch. *Guanxin lun* 觀心論). Shenxiu's move to Luoyang in 701 marks the emergence of Chan into the limelight. He was favoured by Empress Wu Zetian, lionised by the court for his magic powers, and given an elaborate funeral at his death. He was succeeded in this role by Laoan 老安, Xuanze 玄頤, Yifu 義福 (658–736) and Puji 普寂 (651–739), and it was thanks to his students that the theory and practice of Chan spread to the southwest and northeast of China. The monk Moheyan, for example, who represented China at the famous debate with the Indian Buddhists in Lhasa in the 790s, had studied under Yifu, and Daoxuán 道璿 (702–60), who brought some early Chan texts to Japan and taught Gyōhyō 行表 (720–97), who in turn taught Saichō, was a student of Puji. Puji was also master for a time to Yixing (685–727), already mentioned in the context of Chinese tantrism; he produced a major commentary to the *Mahāvairocanatantra* and was known for his scientific interests. The degree to which tantric practice may have influenced Chan meditation techniques is an interesting but as yet open question.

It was during this period that the sense of a Chan identity slowly began to develop, resulting in the emergence of the earliest Chan histories, in particular the *Record of transmission of the Dharma jewel* (*Chuan fabao ji* 傳法寶紀), by Dufei 杜胐,[1] and the *Record of the masters and students of the Laṅkāvatāra [tradition]* (*Lengqie shizi ji* 楞伽師資記), compiled by Jingjue 淨覺. Both of these works date from the period 710–20 and clearly belong to what we might call the 'Shenxiu faction'. The first of these is a short work listing some patriarchs of Chinese Chan together with brief biographies taken largely from *Biographies of eminent monks, continued* (*Xu gaosengzhuan* 續高僧傳). The second takes this further and establishes a numbered series of patriarchs beginning with Gunabhadra (394–468), translator of the *Laṅkāvatārasūtra*, and proceeding via Bodhidharma, Huike 慧可 (*c.*485–*c.*575), Sengcan 僧璨 (d. 606), Daoxin 道信 (580–651) and Hongren 弘忍 (601–74) to Shenxiu and Puji. At a slightly later stage a whole series of legendary Indian patriarchs was added going back to Śākyamuni himself. Other Chan

---

[1]   Translated in McRae 1986: 255–69.

traditions denied Gunabhadra a place in the lineage, but all acknowledged the semi-legendary figure of Bodhidharma, who was said to have brought the teachings from India during the reign of Emperor Wu of the Liang (r. 502–49) and who was reputed to have died at the age of 150. The concept of a patriarchal succession may well have emerged at this point partly because Shenxiu and his students needed to bolster their sense of legitimacy in the face of the rival popularity of Huayan doctrines at court, but also because it was a central tenet of Chan that the teachings could not be learned from scripture, but had to be handed down from master to student via a process of personal transmission. It was on the concept of this direct *personal* line back to Śākyamuni that Chan based its claim to be the one and only true teaching. This emphasis on lineage did not necessarily mean that there existed the concept of a 'school'; at this stage we are still talking of a series of independent masters united by virtue of their interest in meditation.

It is not difficult to imagine the kind of problems that such an emphasis produced, problems that were to plague Chan throughout its history. One important but rather awkward by-product of the reliance on personal transmission rather than textual study or ritual was the emergence of the enlightened master as a perfect figure, whose every act and deed bespoke his special status, all the more important since transmission was understood to occur from mind to mind rather than verbally. This led inexorably to a cult of the master. It also led to problems of legitimation. Since transmission was an essentially secret affair, it was open to abuse. The chosen successor was supposed to receive some form of certification (*yinke* 印可) from the master, but how could such a form of transmission ever be policed? Since it was supposed to occur from mind to mind, how could it ever be verified? This was fertile ground for disagreement and factionalism.

As one might expect, Shenxiu's faction was not without its rivals. In 730 a monk called Shenhui 神會 (684–758) began to launch a series of public attacks on Puji, which culminated in a lecture given at the Great Dharma Assembly at the Dayunsi 大雲寺 in Huatai 滑臺 (Henan Province). His accusation was that Shenxiu had usurped the line of succession and that his followers were propagating incorrect teachings. Shenhui accepted the legitimacy of Hongren as Fifth (Chinese) Patriarch, but argued that the mantle of true succession had then passed not to Shenxiu, but to Shenhui's own master, Huineng 慧能 (638–713), who was therefore the 'real' Sixth Patriarch. This meant, of course, that Shenhui himself was the rightful heir to the Chan tradition. As part of this attack Shenhui seems to have invented some traditions of his own: the idea of a mantle or robe passed down from

Bodhidharma as symbolic of the line of succession; his accusation that Puji had plotted to cut off the head of Huineng's mummified body; and his labelling of Shenxiu's followers as the 'Northern Tradition' 北宗. Both the robe as symbol and the name 'Northern Tradition' were to stick, and they appear regularly thereafter.

Another charge that was also quite unfair but nevertheless stuck was that the 'Northern Tradition' stressed sitting in meditation for long periods to the exclusion of other practices, believing only in the possibility of a gradual method of attaining enlightenment by pacifying the mind and practising arduous concentration. This, Shenhui argued, restricted enlightenment to those who had the opportunity and ability, and energy, to engage in long years of practice, and so it hardly differed from Hīnayāna teachings. He contrasted this with his own 'sudden' method: true enlightenment coming as an unexpected breakthrough to a state of no-mind. There is no real evidence that his accusations were at all justified; the motivation was largely political and factional, and Shenxiu's thought was actually appropriated rather than negated. Shenhui's attack proved effective, however, and he seems to have achieved his aim of establishing his particular version of the story as the dominant one for the rest of the eighth century, although he himself slips from view. Certainly, by the middle of the eighth century Shenxiu and his 'Northern Tradition' had been written out of the picture as heterodox. Although his students did not simply disappear into thin air, the centre of gravity gradually shifted away from the cities in the north to the south and east, where the prestige that Shenxiu had gained at court counted for less (McRae 1986: 242–43).

It should not be thought that there were only two factions at this stage. There were probably as many factions as there were self-styled 'masters', since the concept of personal transmission was so open to challenge and adaptation. A document from Dunhuang 敦煌 entitled *Genealogical record of the Dharma jewel* (*Lidai fabao ji* 歷代法寶記), for example, with a date of *c.*780, comes from yet another group, which was influenced by both Shenxiu and Shenhui factions in the way it listed the patriarchs, but which was intent on creating its own line of legitimacy (Yampolsky 1967: 39–45). The Huayan scholar-monk Zongmi 宗密 (780–841) accepted both the paradigm of 'sudden' versus 'gradual' and the legitimacy of the Huineng–Shenhui succession, since he saw himself as direct in line from Shenhui; nevertheless, he still felt it necessary to list no fewer than seven distinct Chan factions. Later Song historiography, however, was to present just two lineages, ignoring Shenxiu (and Shenhui) altogether:

Caoxi Huineng 曹溪慧能 (638–713)

Nanyue Huairang 南嶽懷讓 (?–?)	Qingyuan Xingsi 青原行思 (?–740)
Mazu Daoyi 馬祖道一 (709–88)	Shitou Xiquan 石頭希遷 (700–90)
Baizhang Huaihai 百丈懷海 (749–814)	Yaoshan Weiyan 薬山惟儼 (745–829)
Huangbo Xiyun 黄檗希運 (?–856?)	Yunyan Tancheng 雲巌曇晟 (782–841)
Linji Yixuan 臨濟義玄 (?–867)	Dongshan Liangjie 洞山良价 (807–69)

So by the mid-eighth century, Shenxiu had been forgotten, Huineng had become fully accepted as the legitimate Sixth Patriarch, and a number of legends had already grown up around him, now transformed into the Chan hero par excellence. A highly embellished biography, *Caoxi dashi biezhuan* (Jp. *Sōkei daishi betsuden* 曹溪大師別傳), was brought back to Japan by Saichō,[2] but perhaps the best-known hagiographic work of this kind is the *Platform sūtra of the Sixth Patriarch* (*Liuzu tanjing* 六祖壇經), which gives a dramatised account of the putative rivalry between Shenxiu and Huineng.[3] This sūtra has been dated to about 780, although it is clearly a composite text created over a fairly long stretch of time.

The first part of the *Platform sūtra* presents a sketch of Huineng set in the form of an autobiographical sermon. He lost his father when young and was reduced to selling firewood to support himself and his mother. He was illiterate. One day he heard some verses from the *Diamond sūtra*, realised his vocation, and set out to study under Hongren at the Eastern Mountain. Hongren recognised his potential immediately but said nothing and set him to work with the other monks. He was given the job of treading rice, and one version has it that he was so light that he had to wear a heavy stone around his neck. About eight months later the master called the monks together and asked each one to prepare a verse. On the basis of this verse he was to decide who was to be his Dharma successor. All were convinced that Shenxiu would be the chosen one and so left the verse writing to him, but Shenxiu was still rather unsure of himself, and so wrote his poem secretly at midnight on a wall of the south hall:

The body is the bodhi tree,
The mind is like a clear mirror.
At all times we must strive to polish it,
And must not let the dust collect.

---

[2] This text did not survive in China. The copy brought back by Saichō is dated 803.
[3] This work arrived in Japan at a fairly early stage. It can be found, for example, in Ennin's catalogue of 847. See Yampolsky 1967: 91–92.

When Hongren saw the verse in the morning, he told Shenxiu that he had not yet reached perfect understanding.[4] Huineng, still consigned to the kitchen, happened to hear another monk reciting Shenxiu's poem, asked to be taken to see it, had it read out to him, realised that it did not express full awareness, and immediately produced his own poem:

Originally there is no tree of enlightenment,
Nor is there a stand with a clear mirror.
From the beginning not one thing exists;
Where, then, is a grain of dust to cling?

That night Hongren conferred on him the patriarchal robe and made him his successor. Everything was done in secret and Huineng was forced to flee for his life. Eventually, however, largely as a result of Shenhui's campaign on his behalf, he was recognised as the true Sixth Patriarch.

Such is the core myth of Chan as it emerged in the mid-eighth century: an illiterate, the lowest of the low, managing to achieved enlightenment simply through intuition and without the help of scripture. The master, also using intuition, acknowledging his achievement in secret, man to man, but passing on the robe as something that Huineng could eventually use as proof. And it is worth keeping in mind that although it is presented rhetorically as a form of transmission, nothing is in fact transmitted except the succession: it is merely that the master formally recognises that the student has awakened to his true nature. In this story of the prototypical Chan hero, we have many of the contradictions that were to plague Chan henceforth. By apparently (but only of course 'apparently') denying a role for scripture, one is thrown back on mind-to-mind transmission, which leads in turn to great stress on the master–student relationship and lineage. This is Chan's claim to truth, and so lineage cannot be allowed to admit mistakes. As an institution, proof is needed, but given the nature of the master–student relationship such proof can never be foolproof. It is highly significant that the *Platform sūtra* argues that the transmission of the robe came to an end with Huineng, to be replaced with transmission of the sūtra itself; a sign of the terrible strain that denial of scripture would place on the whole enterprise.

It is now generally accepted that the *Platform sūtra* was in fact written not by anyone connected with the Shenhui faction, but by a member of a dif-

---

[4]   The traditional interpretation of this poem – that the 'polishing' represented a slow process of clarification – is based on an acceptance of Shenhui's characterisation of Shenxiu's method as 'gradual', but, as we have argued above, this is highly suspect. It could equally represent an effort to maintain an already achieved state of clarity. See McRae 1983: 222.

ferent group altogether, possibly the Ox Head tradition (Ch. *Niutou*, Jp. *Gozu* 牛頭), which took its name from a mountain south of Nanjing (in Jiangsu Province), where tradition has it that a Chan meditation centre had been established in 642. It is likely that this group in fact emerged sometime in the early eighth century and, like all such Chan factions, proceeded to invent its own origins, since the first time we hear of them is in an epitaph written in 754. Whatever the truth of the matter, the *Platform sūtra* represents an attempt to find a way through the crisis that Shenhui had precipitated, and it does this by carefully avoiding significant reference to Shenhui himself, and attributing his views directly to Huineng instead.[5]

13.2   Chan meditation techniques

Before discovering how Chan developed after the fall of the Tang in 907, it is important to know what the early teachings actually were. The earliest text we have is the short 'On the two entrances and four practices' (Ch. *Erru sixing lun* 二入四行論), attributed to Bodhidharma himself, which was circulating during the late 600s. The term 'two entrances' refers to two ways of entering enlightenment (Ch. *rudao* 入道), one via principle 理 and the other via practice 行. Entry via principle involves first having the faith that all sentient beings have Buddha Nature, and that one's own Buddha Nature can be revealed by something called 'wall contemplation' (Ch. *biguan* 壁觀). Enlightenment is in fact the moment of revelation, when one understands the true nature of phenomenal reality and comes to a realisation of one's own purity. The term 'wall contemplation' has been subject to a number of different interpretations, ranging from the mind 'being like a wall' (but does this means 'steadfast' or 'unconscious'?) to a more explicit 'sitting in meditation facing a wall'. It is from this undefined term that we get the well-known legend of Bodhidharma sitting facing a cave wall in meditation on Mt Song 嵩山 for nine long years. It is not known what kind of meditation was involved, but it is generally assumed that it was quite different from traditional Indian practice, being an attempt to transcend ratiocination entirely and contemplate a state of no-mind. Certainly, written teachings were to be eschewed. The object of meditation is 'to be without discrimination, serene and inactive' (McRae 1986: 103). The entry via practice is analysed under four headings, involving the acceptance of karma,

---

[5]   For further discussion of Shenhui see McRae 1987.

remaining unmoved by outward circumstances, striving to be rid of craving, and coming to a realisation of ultimate non-dualism.

The next doctrinal text that is of any help is 'On the essentials of cultivating mind' (Ch. *Xiuxin yaolun* 修 心 要 論), which purports to be representative of Hongren's teaching, but which in fact tells us about Chan meditation in the early eighth century. This too stresses the essential purity of the mind – it is like the sun covered in cloud. By maintaining awareness of mind (Ch. *shouxin* 守心), one will force the clouds to dissipate. There is no point in thinking or relying on buddhas outside the self; one becomes enlightened by discerning one's mind, which is done by sitting in meditation. At such times all sorts of strange psychological states will arise, but the object of meditation is to negate these by concentrating on the operation of mind itself, thereby coming to a realisation that all is illusion.

Gently quiet your mind. I will teach you [how to do this] once again: make your body and mind pure and peaceful, without any discriminative thinking at all. Sit properly with the body erect. Regulate the breath and concentrate the mind so it is not within you, not outside of you, and not in any intermediate location. Do this carefully and naturally. View your own consciousness tranquilly and attentively, so that you can see how it is always moving, like flowing water or a glittering mirage. After you have perceived this consciousness, simply continue to view it gently and naturally, without [the consciousness assuming any fixed position] inside or outside of yourself. Do this tranquilly and attentively, until its fluctuations dissolve into peaceful stability. This flowing consciousness will disappear like a gust of wind (McRae 1986: 130).

Note that this is not simply wiping the clouds away but rather concentrating on the sun and then concentrating on the clouds of illusion, which eventually melt away, for they are not really there. This is more a matter of clarity of vision than of cleansing something. Clearly the term *shouxin* is crucial here. What seems to be asked for is being constantly aware of one's own consciousness without consciously doing so, since all ratiocination is impure. One concentrates on impurity and ignorance until all discrimination ceases and the mind can then respond perfectly and naturally to outside stimuli, although by this time one also realises that there is no inside or outside. There is much that is Daoist here, although the influence is more general than specific.

Early Chan texts are difficult to understand precisely because they were trying to put across something difficult: how to contemplate mind with mind and in the end achieve a realisation that the object of one's concentration was non-substantial. Buddhism before Chan had been more to do with interpreting texts, devotion to an image, producing material offerings, and performing certain prescribed rituals; Chan saw itself as trying to replicate the experience of Śākyamuni himself. No wonder the message was difficult to put across. Various techniques were tried, such as an explicitly metaphorical analysis and interpretation of previous texts (Ch. *guanxin shi* 觀心釋), which attempted to show, for example, that accepted Buddhist activities and descriptions were actually only ways of explaining the technique of meditation, but in the end this too proved problematic and inevitably led Chan in the direction of non-linguistic, non-verbal methods of explanation (McRae 1986: 198–201).

13.3 Chan after the end of the Tang

It is only because of the chance finds at Dunhuang that we have as much information as we do about the history and development of early Chan. The situation post-800 is, if anything, even more problematic. Our main sources for developments over the next two hundred years were compiled well into the Song (Northern Song 960–1127; Southern Song 1127–1279) and must therefore be read as having their own strong agendas. To see Song Chan literature as providing a reliable history of Chan for the period 800–1000 is unwise. The narrative of lineages and the biographical vignettes, for example, are constructs reflecting Song Chan interests and concerns. They create a strong backdrop – a late Tang 'golden age' – against which they define themselves as a school and a tradition. 'The Song construction of the "Chan lineage" and its history was so ingenious and convincing that it succeeded magnificently in drawing attention away from its own creativity and directing it instead to the ostensible glories of the past' (Foulk 1993: 149). There is therefore actually very little we can say with any certainty about the late Tang except that Chan survived the Huichang suppression rather better than any other Buddhist group, for the greatest destruction was wrought in the north and in the cities. After the demise of Shenxiu, the main centre of gravity for Chan shifted to the south and out to the provinces. What is more, transmission from master to student of the kind that Chan espoused could do without large libraries, expensive sūtra repositories, and the kind of critical mass of specialists in certain difficult philosophical texts that made the other, more scholastic groups so vulnerable to the destruction of their material surroundings.

As it is impossible to present a coherent narrative of what may have been, it seems wisest simply to reflect the Song sources and present the Chan of this period as a collection of memorable masters, via whom the tradition transmitted itself. Although each instance of transmission is given a concrete historical context, the end result is curiously ahistorical, since each individual's moment of realisation is but the iteration of the first such moment, when the Buddha achieved his own enlightenment. From that point on, transmission was understood as being mind-to-mind as illustrated by the myth of the primal scene where Śākyamuni is said to have silently offered a flower to his disciple Mahākāśyapa, who received it with an enigmatic smile and nothing more (Jp. *nenge mishō* 拈華微笑). These masters and their dialogues come to us in such collections as the *Anthology of the Patriarch Hall* (Ch. *Zutang ji*, Kr. *Chodang chip* 祖堂集) of 952, the *Song gaoseng zhuan* compiled by Zanning (919–1001), and two early Song Chan 'transmissions of the flame': the *Jingde chuandeng lu* 景德傳燈錄 of 1004 and the *Tiansheng guangdeng lu* 天聖廣燈錄 of 1036.[6] The three most prominent figures in this tale are Mazu Daoyi 馬祖道一 (709–88), Shitou Xiqian 石頭希遷 (700–90) and Linji Yixuan 臨濟義玄 (810?–66), who, since we have no contemporary accounts, are best taken out of time and interpreted as paradigmatic figures representing various approaches to Chan practice, many of them marked by a lack of restraint and a deliberate wildness.

These biographical collections, all set in a familiar pattern dealing with the difficult path to enlightenment, battles with the master, later life as a teacher, and ending with a miraculous death, also contain anecdotes presented in the vernacular and relating to master–student interaction, the so-called 'encounter dialogues' (Ch. *jiyuan wenda* 機緣問答). They were later to be excerpted to become collections of 'sayings' (Ch. *yulu*, Jp. *goroku* 語錄), ostensibly verbatim transcriptions of short sermons by a master, mixed in with master–student dialogues, verbal and non-verbal. It is likely that much of this literature was written, or at best rewritten, by the Song compilers.

The realism that characterises the records of the patriarchs' words is often so finely detailed that it betrays the works as fiction. The point is particularly apt in cases where not only the exact words but also the unspoken thoughts of a master are quoted verbatim . . . Another factor that suggests that in many cases the use of realistic, concrete settings is a purely literary device is that the descriptions of the monastic environment of the Tang masters often contain anachronistic details. Tang masters are depicted in monastic settings with facilities, officers, and activities characteristic of Song-style monasteries (Foulk 1993: 153).

In this fashion the conscious attempt to depict the idealised practice of these late Tang masters gave birth to a new form of literature that was at once

---

[6]   For the justification of the translation 'flame' rather than 'lamp', see Foulk 1993: 200, n. 20.

entertaining and instructive. Chan masters became the new cultural heroes, allowed to indulge themselves within the special confines of the Chan temple in the kind of behaviour that would normally have been seen as detrimental to public order and decency.

So the Song sources present us with a drama of what may have been. Mazu takes on the role of the unpredictable one, known as the major exponent of what one could legitimately term 'organised violence' in Chan, mixing shouts, rudeness and beatings with strange paradoxical language to break down rational modes of thought in his students. Simply sitting in meditation was for him a futile exercise.

[One day when Mazu] was walking in attendance on Bojang, a flock of wild geese flew off overhead. Mazu asked Bojang, 'What is that?' Bojang replied, 'Wild geese, master.' Mazu: 'Where did they go?' Bojang: 'They've flown away.' Mazu turned his head and, seizing Bojang's nose, violently tweaked it, so that Bojang cried out in pain. The master asked, 'How could you say that the wild geese have flown away? They have been here from the very beginning.' Through these words, Bojang awakened (Buswell 1987: 337).

Shitou took the role of the quieter figure, often appearing as a foil to Mazu. Linji, who lived somewhat later (d. 866), represents the culmination, the ideal master and the paradigmatic teacher. His activities are described in the *Linji lu* 臨濟錄, usually dated *c.*1120 (note that this is a full 250 years after his death, although an earlier version of his biography can be found in the *Tiansheng guangdeng lu* of 1036). It is an anthology of pungent sayings and short sermons, the aim being to make the student look into his or her true nature and discover the Buddha Nature within. This is all done in a style peculiar to Chan, 'brisk, barking sentences in the colloquial language of the period, earthy, at times coarse or vulgar in expression' (Watson 1993: xxiii).

The Master ascended the hall and said, 'Here in this lump of red flesh there is a True Man with no rank. Constantly he goes in and out the gates of your face. If there are any of you who don't know this for a fact, then look! Look!' At that time there was a monk who came forward and asked, 'What is he like – the true Man with no rank?' The Master got down from his chair, seized hold of the monk and said 'Speak! Speak!' The monk was about to say something, whereupon the Master let go of him, shoved him away, and said, 'True Man with no rank – what a lump of dried shit!' The Master then returned to his quarters.

Followers of the Way, if you want to get the kind of understanding that accords with the Dharma, never be misled by others. Whether you're facing inward or facing outward, whatever you meet up with, just kill it! If you meet a buddha, kill the buddha. If you meet a patriarch, kill the patriarch. If you meet an arhat, kill the arhat. If you meet your parents, kill your parents. If you meet your kinfolk, kill your kinfolk.

Then for the first time you will gain emancipation, will not be entangled with things, will pass freely anywhere you wish to go (Watson 1993: 13, 52).

For later Chan teachers and students alike, these works, which chronicle in various forms the practice of former masters, became the canon, largely replacing traditional Buddhist sūtras. But this process of committing these activities and sayings to paper had unforeseen results. By its very nature, it betrayed the original enterprise: not only did it run counter to the underlying early Chan principle that language itself was at the root of the problem, but once a tale of wild and violent methods had become a permanent record to be revered and memorised, it lost its immediacy. One studied, one did not emulate. Institutionalisation had again taken its toll. And yet, there is another possibility that must be considered. The wild and violent methods may only have ever existed on paper and we may be dealing with myth-making on a grand scale.[7] In this sense, it is wise to resist the pressure exerted by the texts themselves to persuade us that Song realities had been subject to an inexorable process of degeneration from High Tang practice. The idea of a pure Chan that is now forever lost and can only be grasped as past example rather than experienced as present action is itself a Song invention, a natural response by those who were engaged in the difficult task of institutionalising a practice that grounded itself in the denial of institutions.

By the latter half of the Northern Song (960–1127), it is safe to say, the group that traced itself back to Linji had become orthodox Chan, although its apparent prominence, especially in the eleventh century, may again be partly a result of the fact that the influential *Tiansheng guangdeng lu* (1036) was compiled by a monk of this persuasion. As one might expect, factions continued to come and go throughout the period. It was also during this time that Chan began to develop its own monastic codes called 'pure rules' (Ch. *qinggui*, Jp. *shingi* 清規), which eventually supplanted the *vinaya* in all public monasteries and became the norm in China (Yifa 2002). Here too, Chan monks promoted the idea that such codes dated from the Tang period, although in fact the earliest description we have is a brief section of the *Jingde chuandeng lu* of 1004 entitled *Chanmen guishi* 禪門規式 and the oldest code that survives in toto dates from 1103, the *Chanyuan qinggui* 禪苑清規 compiled by Zongze 宗賾.[8] It has been persuasively argued that the Chan tradition that attributes the creation of specifically Chan monasteries to

[7]   This is essentially the approach taken by Faure 1991.
[8]   See Collcutt 1983. Collcutt analyses these two sets of rules to discover what changes occurred between 1004 and 1103.

the monk Baizhang Huaihai (749–814) in the mid-Tang is another myth and that there is no sign whatsoever of such institutions in the Tang sources. The myth was needed in order to provide a proper historical foundation for what was in fact an unprecedented rise to prominence of Chan in the Song period (Foulk 1993: 156–57).

Quite how Chan came to dominate the scene is not yet entirely clear, because we do not know enough about developments in the early years of the Northern Song to be able to trace its rise with any precision. Certainly, by the early eleventh century, with the two 'transmissions of the flame' in 1004 and 1036, the latter compiled by the son-in-law of an emperor, the process must have been well under way. A major reason for Chan's success lies in the way it managed to identify itself as being Chinese rather than foreign. As the Chan master began to supplant the Buddha as the source of all wisdom, so there developed a canon that consisted not of translations from Indic languages but of vernacular Chinese. The slogan 'special transmission beyond doctrine' (Ch. *jiaowai biezhuan*, Jp. *kyōge betsuden* 經外別傳) allowed Chan to distance itself from the traditional canon but in the process gave rise to another kind of dependence on texts. During the early Northern Song period Chan masters became fully accepted members of the literati. This allowed them to carry Buddhist values into the heart of Chinese culture in a way that had not happened in the Tang, and the influence thus gained was enormous. But there was a price to pay. In return for the influence, Chan masters found themselves developing what has become known as 'lettered Chan' 文字禪, a term that was often used pejoratively to refer to an excessive interest in literary pursuits and erudition that could easily undermine the religious message. The fact remains, however, that Chan would not have survived and prospered had it not linked itself to mainstream Chinese literati culture in this way. It was through the activities of men like Faxiu 法秀 (1027–90), also known as Yuantong Chanshi 圓通禪師, that Chan became the predominant Buddhist institution in the Song and the beneficiary of state patronage.[9]

During the early years of the Northern Song the state began to draw a clear distinction between public and private monasteries, the abbacy of the latter being based on hereditary principles. A large number of these originally hereditary monasteries were converted to public ones, known as *shifang juchi yuan* 十方住持院, and simply redesignated as 'Chan'. The abbot of such a monastery had to be a recognised enlightened master but did not have to be

---

[9] See in this connection the discussion of Faxiu in Gimello 1992.

from a particular branch of the main lineage. So in many ways Chan became the public face of Buddhism, patronised and supported by the state. This naturally led to a need to satisfy government regulations:

There was in the Song an elite group of Buddhist monks (and a few nuns and laypersons) who were regarded as living members of the Chan lineage by virtue of the fact that they had formally inherited the Dharma from another recognized member of the lineage in a ritual of dharma transmission. In the accounts of the early generations of the lineage in China, the flame histories depict the patriarchs handing over robes and bowls to their disciples as proof of dharma transmission – visible signs that the formless Dharma had indeed been vouchsafed. In the Song, however, it was only by the possession of an 'inheritance certificate' (*sishu* 嗣書), a kind of diploma received in the ritual of dharma transmission, that a person was recognized as a member of the Chan lineage (Foulk 1993: 159).

It can be imagined how sought after these certificates might be; they became objects of power in themselves, the outward symbol of something intangible yet desirable. By the time we reach the Southern Song (1127–1279), then, Chan had become predominant in China and fully integrated into Chinese intellectual life. It had also adapted to its role and contained a strong admixture of the kind of ceremonial, ritual and magic that Chan masters of the mid-Tang had been so insistent on rejecting. Rather than 'blaming' this on the adulteration of a purer Chan, it is probably more correct to see the very concept of 'pure' Chan itself as a Song invention; the admixture had been there all along and was an inevitable consequence of success. It would not have been so influential if it had actually insisted on the kind of purity that it invented for its own past.

What else was there apart from Chan? In Kaifeng the translation bureau was funded by the state and produced a large amount of material that was tantric in nature and kept to a limited circle. This activity did not survive the move south in 1127. Then there was Tiantai. Tiantai had lost much of its influence as a result of the Huichang suppression and was reduced to requesting copies of some of its major texts from Korea and Japan in order to recreate itself. The major figures of the Tiantai revival in the Song were Zhili 知禮 (960–1028) and Zunshi 遵式 (964–1032), who between them secured its survival and indeed its rebirth. But this was an uphill struggle in the Northern Song, because Tiantai was very much a regional phenomenon, largely confined to the area around Mingzhou, Hangzhou and Mt Tiantai itself. Special permission had to be sought from the court, for example, for the inclusion of Tiantai texts in the newly planned printed version of the canon, and people like Zunshi relied heavily on contacts with influential bureaucrats.

13.4 Chan in the thirteenth century

It is at this point that we can link back to things Japanese. The two founders of Zen in Japan are usually said to be Myōan Eisai 明庵榮西 (1141–1215), who went to China in 1168 and again in 1187–91, and Eihei Dōgen 永平道元 (1200–53), who was there from 1223 to 1227. What kind of situation did they encounter? The pre-eminent figure in Southern Song Chan was undoubtedly Dahui Zonggao 大慧宗杲 (1089–1163) of the Linji lineage. Dahui's rise to prominence dates from 1134. Before that time he had lived and studied in relative seclusion, but in 1125 he went to study under Yuanwu Keqin 圜悟克勤 (1063–1135), the compiler of *Emerald Cliff record* (Ch. *Biyanlu*, Jp. *Hekiganroku* 碧巌録, 1128), the first major collection of 'cases' (Ch. *gong'an*, Jp. *kōan* 公案). For some time Chan monks had been in the habit of extracting snippets from the 'records' (*yulu*) of past masters, isolated them as 'ancient precedents' (Ch. *guze*, Jp. *kosoku* 古則), and commenting on them, sometimes in verse, sometimes in prose. By the mid-eleventh century the core situation was known as a 'case to be investigated' or a *gong'an*.[10] The process was incremental and difficult to stop. Yuanwu's *Emerald Cliff record*, for example, took a previous eleventh-century collection entitled *Master Xuetou's verses on a hundred old cases* (Ch. *Xuetou heshang baize song'gu* 雪竇和尚百則頌古) and added an introduction (Ch. *chuishi*, Jp. *suiji* 垂示) and extensive commentary to each 'case', sometimes also dropping in comments on the appositeness, or more usually inappositeness, of the relevant verse, so becoming in his turn 'magistrate'.[11] A *gong'an* collection, therefore, reveals many layers, all of them dedicated to undercutting the stability of language while at the same time playing a complex game of competing authorities. Herein lies their fascination.

It was while working with Yuanwu that Dahui is said to have achieved his first experience of enlightenment. Eventually, in 1134, he ended up in Fuzhou and it was here that he began to emerge as an important teacher (Schlütter 1999; Levering 1999). His approach to the use of *gong'an* was somewhat different from his master. In particular, he was worried that a student might be led astray by the erudition and word-play of verse and commentary. There was even a legend that he tried to have the blocks of the

[10] See Foulk 2000 for a discussion of the history of this term, which originally referred to a magistrate's table or bench and by extension a legal 'case'.

[11] For an example of a typical *Emerald Cliff record* entry see Foulk 2000: 29–30. Also on Yuanwu see Hsieh 1994.

Emerald Cliff record destroyed (Buswell 1987: 345). In order to disrupt this intellectual interest in the literary form of a *gong'an*, Dahui is known to have advocated concentrating on one crucial phrase (*huatou* 話頭). This led to what is known as 'contemplating phrases' (Ch. *kanhua*, Jp. *kanna* 看話), which shifted the use of *gong'an* from being a heuristic device to an object of meditation. Rather than puzzling over an exchange or over an odd juxtaposition of prose and verse, one concentrated on a short phrase or even a word, hoping thereby to pierce through to the mind of the master who made it. This was sometimes expressed as using poison (language) to counteract poison and has clear parallels in tantric attitudes to the same phenomenon (Buswell 1987: 347–48). As Dahui put it:

A monk asked Zhaozhou: 'Does even a dog have Buddha Nature?' Zhaozhou answered: 'No!' (*wu* 无).
   Whether you are walking or standing, sitting or lying down, you must not for a moment cease [to hold this no/*wu* in your mind]. When deluded thoughts arise, you must also not supress them with your mind. Only just hold up this *huatou*. When you want to meditate and you feel dull and muddled, you must muster all your energies and hold up this word. Then suddenly you will be like the old blind woman who blows [so diligently] at the fire that her eyebrows and lashes are burned right off (Schlütter 1999: 115).

Before we return to the situation in Japan, there is one other major Chan lineage of the Southern Song to be discussed, the Caodong (Jp. Sōtō 曹洞). The name of this lineage is drawn from two monks, Caoshan Benji 曹山本寂 (840–91) and Dongshan Liangjie 洞山良价 (807–69), who were claimed as its founding patriarchs. Dahui was not particularly happy with their approach:

In recent years there has been a bunch of heretical teachers who preach Silent Illumination Chan. They teach people to do this all day without regard to anything else, ceasing and resting, not daring to make a sound and afraid to waste any time. Often literati, who because of their intelligence and keen aptitude strongly dislike boisterous places, are being made by these heretical masters to do quiet-sitting (*jingzuo* 靜坐). They see that they can save effort [doing this kind of practice] and so regard it as correct. They do not even seek wondrous enlightenment but only regard silence as the highest principle (Schlütter 1999: 111).

The two most important Caodong masters of the Southern Song were Hongzhi Zhengjue 宏智正覺 (1091–1157) and Zhenxie Qingliao 眞歇青了 (1088–1151). From their point of view, Chan was first and foremost a matter of ridding oneself of all the corrosive habits of discursive thinking. Dahui's complaint was that they overemphasised the importance of 'silent illu-mination' (Ch. *mozhao* 黙照), and so saw enlightenment as a state of mind.

Simply by pacifying the mind, one would reach the point of full realisation of one's own original enlightened state, one's own Buddha Nature. But for Dahui enlightenment was not so much a state as an event that had to be worked towards. It seemed to him that they saw the act of meditation itself as the actualisation of enlightenment *tout court*. Although there was undoubtedly some element of caricature in Dahui's description of Caodong practice, not unrelated to the degree of competition for support among local literati, it is true that they advocated sitting in meditation and emptying the mind until it was a clear mirror. For them one's Buddha Nature manifested itself in the very process of emptying the mind and there was no striving needed; indeed striving could damage and interrupt the process. Buddha Nature as the inherent state of man had to be 'experienced' in this sense, rather than 'realised'. In the end, it is a question of degree, since we know that Hongzhi himself did use other means, including *gong'an*, of which he compiled two collections. Whether Dahui's criticism was fair or not, Caodong did become associated with sitting in passive silence – quietening the mind and suppressing thought – inducing a state of unreflective calm, which could not, in Dahui's eyes, lead to the individual achievement of enlightenment. Disagreements such as these would surface again in Japan.

14   Zen Buddhism

14.1   The beginnings of Zen in Japan

Although knowledge of Buddhist techniques of meditation had, of course, been introduced into Japan at an early date, one cannot really talk of the formation of Japanese Zen until the late twelfth century. Chan teachings were indeed known as early as the eighth century, following the arrival of Daoxuán, who taught the monk Gyōhyō who, it may be remembered, was Saichō's first mentor. What is more, Saichō claimed to have received instruction from a monk called Xiuran 脩然 at the Chanlinsi on Mt Tiantai, who identified himself as a follower of the Ox Head tradition. Among the texts that Saichō brought back with him to Japan was a copy of Shenxiu's *Guanxin lun* and the biography of Huineng, *Caoxi dashi biezhuan,* mentioned earlier. Although both Saichō and, indeed, Ennin, who came across some rather unruly Chan monks while he was in China, were familiar with early Chan, this was simply incorporated within the Tendai tradition as one element of the practice known as 'constantly-sitting' (*jōza zanmai* 常座三昧), and the term *zensō* 禪僧 that one comes across in Heian texts meant 'monk adept at meditation' or 'monk whose duties include meditation'. It was not until Japanese started going to China again in the late twelfth and thirteenth centuries that they discovered that in their absence Chan had become the major force in Song Buddhism. Apart from late tantrism and a greatly weakened Tiantai, the older philosophical traditions had almost died out.

The figure usually credited with introducing Song Chan into Japan is Myōan Eisai (§13.4), although this happened more by serendipity than by design. Certainly, he, and others like him, did not travel to China with a view to importing an entirely new set of Buddhist ideas and practices, but were more concerned with finding some way of revitalising their own institution. Eisai arrived in 1168 to find that most state-supported Buddhist institutions were now run by Chan abbots, and it was in these monasteries that he found the kind of strict adherence to regulations for which he was looking. His first visit to China, in 1168, lasted only six months. The dominance of Chan meditation practices and the decline in Tiantai and other forms of scholarship with which he must have been familiar came to his attention, of course, but on his return to Japan he continued to study and practise Tendai ritual as normal. On revisiting China almost twenty years later in 1187, however, he first of all asked permission from the Chinese authorities to travel on to India and when that request was refused, he decided to stay on the southeast coast at Wan'niansi 萬年寺 on Mt Tiantai, where he studied for three years under the Chan master Xu'an Huaichang 虛菴懷敞, returning to Japan in 1191 with the necessary certificate showing that he was now a registered Chan master. He began by establishing one or two meditation halls in Kyūshū, but on reaching Kyōto ran into considerable opposition from Enryakuji. They did not see why yet another tradition should be given official approval; they were also somewhat resistant to the idea that their discipline might be in need of reform. Eisai was in fact seen as a threat. In 1194 the Tendai establishment secured a temporary ban on his attempts to promote his views, which in turn provoked him to produce the polemical work *On protecting the nation through the encouragement of Zen* (*Kōzen gokokuron* 興禪護國論). Driven out of Kyōto, he arrived in Kamakura, where his rejection by the monks at Enryakuji was seen as more of a recommendation than a bar and where his knowledge of things Chinese was recognised to be an important asset. Hōjō Masako 北條政子 (1157–1225), Yoritomo's wife, became his patroness and appointed him founder abbot of Jufukuji 壽福寺. Eventually the backing of the shogunate allowed him to return to Kyōto, where he oversaw the building of Kenninji 建仁寺, completed in 1205. In 1214 he wrote *Kissa yōjōki* 喫茶養生記 for the third shōgun Sanetomo (1192–1219) 實朝 introducing the culture of tea drinking for the first time.

Eisai and men like him were employed by the Kamakura shogunate firstly because they had up-to-date knowledge of China and secondly in their role as ritualists. Perhaps their chief asset was the hostility shown them by the Tendai establishment, for the Hōjō were not supporting Zen per se; they were simply taking advantage of a new source of knowledge and spiritual power that had no existing ties to any other centre of power in Japan to give their rule authority and prestige. Eisai himself was very far from being an advocate of meditation practice to the exclusion of all else – indeed normal Tendai ritual was maintained at both Jufukuji and Kenninji, the latter not even being provided with a hall for communal meditation (*sōdō* 僧堂), which was usually the focal point in a Zen monastery.

The temporary ban imposed on Eisai in 1194 shows that it was not just Pure Land Buddhism that was in danger of prohibition. Part of his self-defence in *Kōzen gokokuron* involved a careful explanation of the fundamental differences between what he understood as Zen and the Zen of the monk Dainichi Nōnin 大日能忍, who was already infamous as the prime exponent of a movement called the 'Daruma tradition' 達磨宗. Daruma stands for Bodhidharma, but who was Nōnin? Until reconstructed by recent scholarship, this group had been effectively written out of history, but we now know that it was quite influential and remained a substantial force until well into the thirteenth century. Certainly, when Nichiren 日蓮 (§15.3) attacked Zen (among others) eighty years later, he was referring not to Eisai, but to Nōnin.

Hōnen and Dainichi (Nōnin) both appeared during the Kennin period [1201–03], and they gave rise to the Nenbutsu and Zen traditions. Hōnen said: 'Since we have entered the period of the final Dharma, not even one man in a thousand has obtained any benefit from the *Lotus sūtra*.' Dainichi said: 'The transmission [of truth] is something special, independent of teachings.' The country is filled with these two teachings. The scholars of Tendai and Shingon flatter and fear the patrons of Nenbutsu and Zen; they are like dogs wagging their tails in front of their masters, like mice afraid of cats.[1]

The scholar-monk Kokan Shiren 虎關師練 (1278–1348), also writing somewhat tendentiously in his *History of the Śākyamuni [tradition, written] in the Genkō era* (*Genkō shakusho* 元亨釋書) of 1322, explained Nōnin's role as follows:

Having heard of the popularity of the [Chan] school in Song China, a certain Nōnin sent his disciples there to question the *dhyāna* master Fozhao [De]guang of Ayuwang shan. Impressed by the faith of these strangers, [Fo]zhao took pity on them and offered them a Dharma-robe and a picture of Bodhidharma. Nōnin, bragging of these courtesy gifts, began to spread Chan teachings. But since he lacked a direct transmission from a master as well as a disciplinary code, the people of the capital scorned him.

When Eisai began to preach the mind, the nobility and common people alike confused him with Nōnin and wanted to reject him . . . [Finally] Hieizan monks supported his Zen preaching. Eisai debated several times with Nōnin on doctrinal matters and eventually defeated him (Faure 1987: 29).

Kokan Shiren's bias is probably responsible for the disappearance of Nōnin from history. It is generally accepted that Nōnin did in fact send two students to meet Choan [Fozhao] Deguang 拙庵[佛照]德光 (1121–1203), who had studied under Dahui Zonggao, their mission being to request certification of Nōnin as a Chan master. Bizarrely, this request was granted and on the

---

[1]   From *Kaimokushō* 開目抄, quoted in Faure 1987: 28, the source of much that follows.

strength of this he became a well-known figure in Japan. Exactly how he became interested in Chan in the first place and how he first conceived of setting up as a master in his own right is not known. But then, given that Chan was so prominent in Song China, it might seem surprising that this move came so late in the day. What comes as no surprise is the response of the Buddhist establishment in Japan. They saw any move to isolate what they saw as one element of Tendai practice, 'constantly-sitting', and to transform it into a separate tradition as a threat, above all a political problem. Nōnin was an obvious and easy target because the claim that he had received legitimate transmission was preposterous, and other claims, such as the idea that his 'school' was in possession of various important Buddhist relics, for example, were also open to attack.

Among the recently discovered Daruma texts is one entitled 'On the attainment of bodhisattva awakening' (*Jōtō shōgakuron* 成等正覺論). This text is made up of three sections: a history of Chan, starting with the usual legendary material about Bodhidharma and ending with the arrival of Zen in Japan with Nōnin's students; a discussion of the phrase 'the mind itself is the Buddha'; and lastly, a description of the benefits that reciting the text itself would bring. The discussion in the second section makes great play of the idea that one simply looks for one's own Buddha Nature to achieve enlightenment. From the attacks made on Nōnin by Eisai and others, it would seem that his understanding of Zen had certain antinomian elements, which could easily fall into the assumption that practice and meditation were unnecessary. This would explain, of course, why he had popular appeal and why his success was viewed with such anxiety. Not surprisingly, Eisai tried to distance himself from precisely this aspect:

Someone asked: 'Some people recklessly call the Daruma tradition Zen. But they themselves say that there are no precepts to follow, no practices to engage in. From the outset there are no passions; from the beginning we are enlightened. Therefore do not practice, do not follow the precepts, eat when hungry, rest when tired. Why practice *nenbutsu*, why give maigre feasts, why curtail eating? How can this be?' Eisei replied that the adherents of the Daruma tradition are those who are described in the sūtras as having a false view of emptiness. One must not speak with them or associate with them, and must keep as far away as possible (Faure 1987: 39).[2]

Another aspect of this early form of medieval Zen was the cult of Buddha relics which, it was said, had been brought back from China by Nōnin's

---

[2] From the chapter entitled 'On solving the doubts of worldly people' 世人決疑論 in *Kōzen gokokuron*.

students. These were enshrined in the Sanbōji 三寶寺, a Tendai temple in Settsu Province, as further proof of legitimacy, and, together with a robe supposedly handed down through Fozhao Deguang, they soon became the object of intense worship. The influence of this Daruma tradition was felt most strongly among the followers of the monk Dōgen (1200–53).

14.2   Eihei Dōgen

Dōgen 道元 studied first as a Tendai monk on Hieizan, moving to Kenninji in 1217 to study under one of Eisai's students, Myōzen 明全 (1184–1225). In 1223 he accompanied Myōzen to China, to the Jingdesi 景德寺 on Mt Tiantong 天童山, where they studied under a Linji master called Wuji Liaopai 無際了派. Myōzen died there two years later and when Dōgen returned to Japan in 1227 he brought Myōzen's ashes back with him. There are two traditional sources for our information about Dōgen in China: the *Record from the Baoqing era [1225–27]* (*Hōkyōki* 寶慶記), which purports to be a record of notes taken at the time, but which is now accepted to be an edited version of Dōgen's reminiscences produced by the Daruma monk Koun Ejō (孤雲懷弉, 1198–1280) soon after Dōgen's death; and *Kenzei's record* (*Kenzeiki* 建撕記), a hagiography written by the fourteenth abbot of Eiheiji 永平寺, Kenzei (1415–74), but read in modern times in the form of a heavily annotated edition (*Teiho Kenzeiki* 訂補建撕記), produced by the Tokugawa-period scholar-monk Menzan Zuihō 面山瑞方 (1683–1769). The narrative we glean from these texts tells us that Dōgen had considerable difficulty in finding a Chan master with whom he felt an affinity, and that he travelled to a number of monasteries in Zhejiang Province, including visits to Tiantai and Jingshan 徑山, in his quest for the right teacher. What he was looking for was an answer as to why practice and meditation were necessary, if all we were being asked to do was realise that we were already enlightened; in other words, why was the Daruma tradition wrong? A full two years later he finally returned to the Qingdesi, where he 'discovered' the master Tiantong Rujing 天童如淨 (1163–1228), who had been appointed abbot there in late 1224. Rujing, it turned out, was a trenchant critic of most Southern Song monks and monasteries, considering them far too lax; as a monk of the Caodong lineage he had a particular dislike of the use of *kōan*, preferring to stress instead the virtues of silent meditation (Jp. *shikan taza* 只管打坐). Dōgen knew immediately that this was the master with whom he wished to achieve enlightenment, an aim in which he eventually succeeded, casting off body and mind (Jp. *shinjin datsuraku* 身心脱落). He received a certificate of succession and a robe, and returned to Japan as a fully fledged Zen master with a recognised lineage. Just as Kūkai had returned to Japan four hundred years earlier embodying within himself the succession of Shingon, so Dōgen embodied the flame of the line of Caodong, which was not just transmitted but bodily transferred to Japan.

The problem with this account, as with so many other stories that deal with Japanese monks in China, is that very little of it is verifiable from contemporary sources. No one has yet tried to argue that Dōgen never went to China at all, but there is little sign in his writings that he travelled very widely, or that he ever left Jingdesi for any length of time (Heine 2003). What is more, the presentation of Rujing as a revered master who had passed on to Dōgen the one true form of Chan practice is only attested in Japanese writings that date from well after Dōgen's return to Japan. Rujing himself is hardly mentioned in standard histories of Chinese Chan and seems to have been little more than simply one of the abbots of an important monastery; he belongs to history as Dōgen's teacher, in much the same way that Huiguo is chiefly known as Kūkai's master. What remains of his teachings, as preserved in two short collections that only survive in Japanese editions of the seventeenth and eighteenth centuries, gives little sign that he had ever been dismissive of normal Linji practice.[3] So one needs to be aware that Rujing lives almost entirely through Dōgen. There seems to be no doubt that he was of the Caodong lineage, but, as we have seen in Chapter 13, the automatic link that is often made between Caodong and the advocacy of exclusive silent meditation is highly problematic. But more of this later.

Back in Kyōto in 1227, Dōgen first stayed at Kenninji but moved south three years later to Fukakusa, where he eventually established a small monastery of his own, the Gokurakuji 極楽寺. It is thought that he may have written an early version of his manual on meditation techniques, the *Universal promotion of the principles of seated meditation* (*Fukan zazengi* 普勧座禪儀), about this time, although the earliest extant copy is an autograph dated 1233. In 1231 he wrote 'Bendōwa' 辨道話, a series of questions and answers that explain his understanding of Zen Buddhism in Japanese. From the very beginning he was determined to be independent of Tendai and to transmit what he considered to be the true way to enlightenment. This allowed him doctrinal freedom, but by the same token cut him off from

---

[3] Bielefeldt 1985: 27. We are told that a copy of Rujing's 'recorded sayings' only reached Dōgen in 1242.

traditional forms of patronage. Nevertheless, he managed to raise enough funds to start building a meditation hall at Fukakusa and in 1236 he renamed the growing complex Kōshōji 興聖寺.[4] Two years earlier, in 1234, he had been joined by Ejō, whose record of Dōgen's teaching at Fukakusa, *Zuimonki* 隨聞記, is still used today as a beginner's introduction to Zen, despite the fact that it reveals areas of fundamental disagreement between Dōgen and Ejō. Ejō himself was joined in 1241 by a further group of Daruma followers, together with their master Ekan 懷鑒.

Suddenly, late in 1243, Dōgen upped sticks, left Kōshōji, and moved his whole group to a new and extremely isolated area in Echizen. The reasons for this abrupt departure are not known: it may have been that pressure from Hieizan became too intense, particularly since he was now harbouring members of a group that was considered heterodox and disruptive, but another factor may have been his discovery of an entirely new source of patronage, the locally based warrior class on which he was to rely for the rest of his life. His chief support from this time on was a man called Hatano Yoshishige 波多野義重, a Kamakura Bakufu retainer, who offered him both land and the resources to start building. In 1246 the monastery was given the name Eiheiji 永平寺.

During the last seven years of his life Dōgen concentrated on writing a series of works on monastic regulations. These dictate in close detail the correct way to comport oneself within the monastery on a daily basis, how to work, eat and indeed defecate. Based on the principle that all actions were connected to enlightenment and that one of the best ways to express the concept of non-self was to subject oneself to strict regulations, they formed the basis of what is now known as the *Eihei Code* (*Eihei shingi* 永平清規). Perhaps the most important of these tracts was 'Bendōhō' 辨道法, which set down rules as to how monks were to sit, sleep, move about in the meditation hall and meditate (Beilefeldt 1988: 50). He also encouraged the participation of local lay men and women in rituals such as the recitation of the precepts, so that Eiheiji soon became recognised as an important place of spiritual power. That said, however, he was not interested in collapsing the distinction between monk and lay supporter and in fact strengthened it as time went on. How Dōgen managed to coexist with members of the Daruma tradition who came with Ejō and Ekan is still a mystery, for there was undoubtedly considerable tension, as the following exchange between Ejō and Gikai (dated *c.*1254) illustrates; both men were originally Darumashū adherents:

[4]   This name was a reference to Xingsheng wanshousi 興聖萬壽寺 on Jingshan.

Gikai: My Dharma comrades of past years would say: 'The Buddhist [expression],
"All evil refrain from doing; all good reverently perform" (*shoaku makusa shuzen
bugyō* 諸惡莫作衆善奉行) actually means that within [true] Buddhism all evil
ultimately has been refrained from and all activities are Buddhism . . .' Therefore
merely lifting an arm or moving a leg – whatever one does, whatever phenomena one
produces – all embody [true] Buddhism . . .

Ejō: In our master's [i.e. Dōgen's] community there were some who spread such
heterodox views. That is why he cut off all contact with them while he was still alive.
Clearly the reason he expelled them was because they held these false doctrines.
Those who wish to honour the Buddhism [taught by] our master will not talk or sit
with such [heretics]. This was our master's final instruction (Bodiford 1993: 34).

This suggests that in the end those who insisted on retaining their antinomian
beliefs and refused to submit to Dōgen's strict regime were forced to leave
the community, but we simply do not have enough information to be sure.

There is much that is contradictory in Dōgen's writings, for the main
reason that his attitude to Zen theory and practice seems to have undergone a
series of changes after his return to Japan. Take, for example, his attitude to
his putative master Rujing. Before 1240, Rujing is mentioned only
occasionally in Dōgen's writings and lectures, and even then he is not singled
out for particular praise. Neither is there any overt criticism of Dahui
Zonggao. In 'Bendōwa', for example, Dōgen writes of five lineages without
any sign of opprobrium:

The Sixth Patriarch had two 'supernatural feet': Huaizhang of Nanyue and Xingsi of
Qingyuan. Both carried on the transmission of the Buddha seal, becoming the teachers
of men and gods. As their two factions developed, they opened five gates: the schools
of Fayan, Guiyang, Caodong, Yunmen, and Linji. Today in the great Song, it is the
Linji school alone that dominates everywhere. The five houses differ, but they all
[bear] the one Buddha mind seal (Bielefeldt 1985: 31, adapted).

From 1240 onwards, however, we find a marked shift; the Caodong lineage,
and Rujing in particular, is given increased emphasis as Dōgen felt the need
to carve out a space for himself. By 1243 and the tract 'Butsudō' 佛道 this
had developed into a militant claim that Caodong was the only true line and
that names for various lineages 宗 should be abandoned entirely, since they
were misleading: there was only one transmission, the rest were fictions.

The treasury of the eye of the true Dharma of the Old Buddha [Huineng] was
correctly transmitted only to the Eminent Patriarch Qingyuan. Even if we concede
that [Huineng] had two 'supernatural feet' equally possessed of the way, the Eminent
Patriarch [Qingyuan] represents the sole pace of the true supernatural foot . . . The
Great Master Dongshan [Liangjie] was the legitimate successor in the fourth generation after Qingyuan. He correctly received the transmission of the treasury of the

eye of the true Dharma and opened the eye of the marvelous mind of nirvāṇa. There is no other transmission; there is no other school (Bielefeldt 1985: 31–32, adapted).

It is at this point that Dōgen, in the essay 'Sesshin sesshō' 説心説性 (1243), for example, attacks the degeneracy of Southern Song Chan as exemplified by Dahui and his student Choan Deguang, and in the process he begins to exaggerate the degree of antagonism between the various traditions. Why? It will be remembered that Deguang was the master from whom Nōnin had claimed succession. It has been suggested, most plausibly, that it was the presence of Daruma monks in his community that led Dōgen to pick a doctrinal fight with Deguang and, by extension, with the whole Dahui lineage. The criticism itself was certainly doctrinal, but the motive was political. Neither should we forget that if Dōgen was trying to carve out an authoritative position for himself, he had also to define himself vis-à-vis other groups of Zen monks, who, as we shall see from the next section, were rapidly outpacing his own group in terms of influence, patronised by the good and the great. His own Kōshōji, for example, was dwarfed by the new Tōfukuji which had been built just next door. He was thus inexorably led to define his own vision of what Zen should be in contrast to those who traced their own lineage back to Linji (Jp. Rinzai), making use of Rujing and the Caodong label for what was largely domestic purposes.

   This exaggerated stance was taken up much later in the writings of Tokugawa Sōtō sect apologists, in particular Menzan Zuihō, who strengthened the polarity of the argument and claimed that Dōgen had only ever been interested in 'quiet meditation' (*shikan taza*) to the exclusion of all else. Dahui, in particular, who had championed the cause of contemplating short phrases (*kanna zen* 看話禪) and criticised Caodong practice as mere passive quietism that forgot the importance of sudden enlightenment, was treated as being quite beyond the pale. Unfortunately, although this may well have served the immediate interests of Menzan, who was involved in a difficult struggle of his own with other Zen sects, such a view of Dōgen does not fit the facts as we now have them. If Dōgen was indeed critical of the use of *kōan*, how was it that while still in Kyōto in 1235 he produced a collection of *kōan* cases, entitled *Eye of the true Dharma: three hundred precedents* (*Shōbō genzō sanbyakusoku* 正法眼藏三百則), the title of which was probably taken from a similar collection edited by none other than Dahui himself? And how was it that a few years later he began a project to write extended commentaries on these cases? In the end, the nature of the enterprise changed somewhat and the result was the large collection of essays in Japanese entitled *Eye of the true Dharma* (*Shōbō genzō* 正法眼藏), written over the period 1231 to 1253, for which he is so famous. The fact remains, however, that many of these essays are rooted in a discussion of one or two *kōan*.[5]

On more careful analysis, it turns out that the criticism of Dahui, which had admittedly been started by Dōgen himself and then picked up by Menzan and exaggerated, was really limited to Dahui's arguments in favour of *kanna zen* and his concentration on the short word or phrase (*watō* 話頭). It was not that Dōgen decried the use of *kōan* per se; he merely had different ideas as to how they should be best used. The idea of *kanna zen* had emerged from a desire to negate the intellectualism that came from the study of such a complex literary product as a *kōan*, with its multiple voices, its interlocking layers of authority, and its fascination with language. This worry was such that, as already mentioned, a myth had even grown up that Dahui had tried to destroy the woodblocks of Yuanwu's *Emerald Cliff record*. Dōgen, in his turn, saw yet another way to use *kōan*. If Dahui was concerned to condense the case into a single word and then to concentrate on that one word, the Dōgen that we find operating in the *Eye of the true Dharma* did exactly the opposite, adding his own particular brand of complexity, embracing the fertility and plurality of language itself in order to produce in the individual an awareness of the shifting sands on which his thought always stood.

Perhaps the best example of this is the essay 'The ungraspable mind' (*Shinfukatoku* 心不可得), which deals with the case of the Zen master Deshan 德山, an expert on the *Diamond sūtra,* who stopped one day to buy some refreshments (Ch. *dianxin*, Jp. *tenshin* 點心) by the roadside. The old woman asks him: 'According to the *Diamond sūtra*, the past mind is ungraspable, the present mind is ungraspable, and the future mind is ungraspable. So, where is the mind 心 that you now seek to refresh 點 with rice cakes?' Deshan is simply struck dumb at this sophisticated piece of wordplay. The general response to this *kōan* was to praise the old woman as being enlightened. The *kanna zen* response to this would have been to concentrate on the word '*tenshin*', but Dōgen takes the opportunity to expand. He criticises the *kōan* for stopping at that point and proceeds to invent a further conversation that builds on it. No point, he says, in just praising the enlightenment of the old woman. Better to retort and ask her: 'As past mind is ungraspable, present mind is ungraspable, and future mind ungraspable, where is the mind that now makes the rice cakes used for refreshment?', in which case the old woman could have responded: 'You know that one cannot refresh the mind with a rice cake. But you do not realise that the mind refreshes the rice cake,

---

[5] The following discussion makes much use of Heine 1994.

or that the mind refreshes the mind.' And so on, and so on (Heine 1994: 254–56).

Just as Dōgen's collection of 300 *kōan* are given quite straightforward commentaries rather than the juxtaposition of cryptic phrases that one finds in more normal *kōan* collections, so the essays and sermons in the *Eye of the true Dharma* are prolix rather than cryptic, discursive rather than disjointed. Dōgen is not afraid of explaining at length. This does not really make him any less difficult, but it does pull Zen prose in quite a new direction; there is a poetic quality to his writing. Take, for example, the following from '*Kōan* as manifest activity' (*Genjō kōan* 現成公案):

Enlightenment is like the moon that dwells in water. The moon does not get wet and the water is not broken. It is a broad, bright light but dwells in a foot or an inch of water. The whole moon, the whole sky dwells in the dew on the grass, in a single drop of water. Enlightenment does not break the person, just as the moon does not break the water. Just as the man does not stop enlightenment, so the dew drop does not hinder the sky or the moon. Depth can be measured as height; time can be measured by volume of water and by breadth of sky and moon (Terada and Mizuno 1970, vol. I: 37).

But what of Dōgen's attitude to what is usually considered the most important activity for Zen monks, the act of seated meditation (*zazen* 座禪) itself? We must not be misled by Tokugawa Sōtō masters trying to tell us that Dōgen's special form of 'just sitting' (*shikan taza*) was unique, somehow different from all other techniques of meditation. One text that has occasioned a good deal of study in this regard is his meditation manual *Fukan zazengi*. As already stated, although it is possible that a manual was written immediately after Dōgen's return to Japan, the earliest example we have is an autograph dated 1233 (the so-called Tenpuku MS), which is in fact little more than a revision of the section on meditation entitled 'Zuochan yi' 座禪儀, in the standard *Chanyuan qinggui* of 1103. It in fact had no influence because it remained in manuscript form until quite recently. The commonly available text (*rufubon*) of *Fukan zazengi*, however, is of much later provenance and represents a revision of this first manual. This second version, still in use today, was first extracted by Menzan from *Eihei kōroku*, a collection of Dōgen's discussions and writings edited by Ejō and published by Manzan Dōhaku (1636–1715) in 1673 (Bielefeldt 1988: 36). It has been dated somewhere between 1242 and 1246, just at the time Dōgen was establishing himself, attacking Dahui, and drawing legitimacy from a newly defined role given to Rujing and the Caodong/Sōtō lineage as the true heirs of the patriarchal tradition.

The key question as regards meditation was how the monk was supposed to control the mind during practice. Whereas someone like the Tiantai master Zhiyi had gone into considerable technical detail about how one should go about preparing oneself mentally for the ordeal, Zongze's rather simple text pays little attention to this aspect and even runs the risk of appearing to support an entirely passive approach to simply clearing the mind. In the second version of *Fukan zazengi*, Dōgen puts it as follows:

Sitting fixedly, think of not thinking. How do you think of not thinking? Nonthinking. This is the essential art of *zazen*. *Zazen* is not the practice of *dhyāna* (trance): it is just the entrance to the Dharma of ease and joy. It is the practice and verification of ultimate bodhi. The *kōan* realized, baskets and cages cannot get to it (Bielefeldt 1988: 181, adapted).

Whether this really helps us to understand is a moot point, because it somewhat begs the question of how we can think of non-thinking, how we can use the mind against itself, detach ourselves from the stream of discursive thoughts that the mind continually provides us with when awake (or asleep). What is clear, however, is that Dōgen was as concerned as other Zen masters to counteract any idea that simply emptying the mind and avoiding all thought was the answer, because that would be too easy, an example of 'mental vacuity' (*kyōkin buji* 胸襟無事) or of 'suspending thoughts and freezing the mind' (*sokuryo gyōshin* 息慮凝心) (Bielefeldt 1988: 136). To think of non-thinking had to be an active procedure, whereby every thought that arises is not so much killed as dissolved within itself, turned back on itself in a radical form of reflexivity. This was, of course, one of the reasons why no Zen master could seriously ignore the use of *kōan*, which provided a mode of discourse that forced the mind to think against itself, whether via the path of building up a creative intellectual impasse or via concentration on a single word.

When Dōgen died in 1253, the community at Eiheiji was faced with a problem. He left no obvious monk to fill his shoes and his success had been largely built on his own charisma as a teacher. Ejō took over the leadership, but he lacked Dōgen's authority and was not immune from challenge. Somehow, however, the group held together. Dōgen's senior students, men like Giin 義尹 (1217–1300) and Gikai 義介 (1219–1309), both of whom used the character '*gi*' that identified them as Daruma followers, spread out into various parts of Japan founding a series of monasteries. Giin founded Daijiji 大慈寺 in Kyūshū in 1282, patronage for which came from a warrior family with close ties to the Hatano. He had studied in China in 1264–65 and had gone there, so it is said, to obtain Chinese recognition for Dōgen's *goroku*.

Gikai had studied under Ekan and had strong local ties in the Echizen region. After making efforts to finish the construction of Eiheiji and being appointed third abbot from 1267 to 1272, he then moved northeast into Kaga to found Daijōji 大乗寺. It was here that he was joined by Keizan Jōkin 瑩山紹瑾 (1264–1325), who succeeded him as abbot in 1298 and whom many see as the 'second founder' of what would eventually become known as the Sōtō tradition. By 1300 there were five largely independent groups based on five monasteries: Daijiji in Kyūshū, Daijōji in Kaga, Eiheiji in Echizen, Hōkyōji 寶慶寺 also in Echizen, and Yōkōan 永興庵 in Kyōto.

Much of the history of this period from Dōgen's death to 1300 is obscure, and things are made much more difficult by the fact that what sources we do have are tendentious in the extreme. What is clear, however, is that these monks had discovered a rich and relatively untapped source of patronage: local warriors and local farmers who had become wealthy landowners in their own right. It was a combination of this discovery and the willingness (indeed positive desire) of the monks themselves to travel throughout rural Japan and proselytise in areas remote from the traditional bases of power that laid the foundation for what was to become one of the largest Buddhist organisations in the land.

There were two other reasons for its eventual success. Firstly, the nature of the monks themselves. Up to this point the higher echelons in monasteries had been those scholar-monks (*gakuryo* 學侶) who were capable of reading difficult doctrinal texts and sūtras; those who were given jobs such as performing menial tasks and routine rituals such as chanting sūtras or sitting in meditation were distinctly second class (Bodiford 1993: 16). Dōgen, however, reversed these priorities: he wrote essays on the importance of cooks and bothered himself with the minutiae of everyday life. The ability to meditate was given a much higher profile than before and knowledge of the written tradition thereby reduced in importance. Huineng, after all, had been an illiterate. All these differences drew in a different kind of monk, the kind of person who was quite happy to live away from the main centres of population. Secondly, although Dōgen and his followers might have been exclusive about their own practice, they were only too willing to fit in to what was a very eclectic landscape, taking care not to denigrate local spirits, and becoming closely involved with mountain cults wherever they found themselves. Without this flexibility and the awareness of what was felt to be sacred in the population at large, this sect would never have achieved the popularity it did.

14.3   Official patronage

Dōgen and those who came after him made a conscious choice to stay away from the centres of power and seek life and patronage in the provinces; and this turned out to be the source of much of their strength. But there was another very different kind of Zen institution developing, one patronised by the new rulers in Kamakura for largely political ends. Not that members of the Kyōto aristocracy were uninterested. They in fact became great patrons themselves, but as an institution the court was too closely identified with Tendai and Shingon to be able to lay exclusive claim to Zen for their own. Kamakura, on the other hand, needed a new spiritual backing for its new authority, and Southern Song Zen offered interesting possibilities. Not only was it a form of Buddhism free from ties to Kyōto, but the monks involved were men who had recent experience of living in China; they were a valuable commodity.

Once it became clear that Kamakura was interested in becoming patron to a new group of religious advisers, the number of monks travelling to China increased rapidly. We have seen how Eisai was given protection by Hōjō Masako and allowed to set up operations at Jufukuji in the very early years of the century. Dōgen went to China in 1223. Enni Ben'en 圓爾辨圓 (1202–80), who came from a similar background, left Japan in 1235 and stayed for six years studying at Jingshan under the Linji master Wuzhun Shifan 無準師範 (1177–1249). This choice, if choice it really was, was to have interesting consequences. Wuzhun Shifan happened to belong not to the dominant lineage that traced itself back to Dahui Zhonggao, but to a rival group that claimed its lineage from Huqiu Shaolong 虎邱紹隆 (1077–1136). The Huqiu tradition was in turn split into two factions, one descended from Poan Zuxian 破菴祖先 (1136–1211) and the other from Songyuan Chongyue 松源崇岳 (1132–1202). Later, in the fourteenth century, this question of affiliation was to have important political ramifications.

After his return to Japan in 1241, Enni continued to correspond with his Chinese master, with the result that a large number of Japanese monks were to receive their training at Jingshan. Obtaining the patronage of Kujō Michiie (1192–1252), for whom he wrote *Shōichi hōgo* 聖一法語 to explain the essentials of Zen, he managed to resist pressure from Enryakuji and eventually became the founder of the impressive complex in Kyōto known as Tōfukuji 東福寺. He was eclectic in his practice and continued the Japanese tradition of lecturing on tantric texts alongside the practice of meditation, but at least Tōfukuji was organised as a Zen monastery under the correct regulations, with Zen ritual, bureaucratic structure, and four daily sessions of mandatory *zazen*.[6] Staying for most of the time in Kyōto rather than Kamakura, Enni was fortunate in his patron and kept close ties with the aristocracy. One of his students, Mukan Gengo 無關玄悟 (1212–91), in turn became the founder of Nanzenji 南禪寺.

It was at this stage, in the mid-thirteenth century, that something entirely unexpected happened: a number of Chinese Chan masters decided to move to Japan. By no means all of them were actually invited, and each one of them must have had his own reasons. In some cases the perceived threat from the Mongols was enough to persuade them to move; in others it may have been as a result of factional rivalry and marginalisation. Whatever the causes, one should not underestimate either the dangers of the voyage or the boldness of the move. It was to have a lasting impact on Japan, for it was really a result of the arrival of these men, more than a dozen in all, that Zen eventually took such strong root in Japan and was not simply re-absorbed into Tendai. The man who did more than anyone to bring this about was the fifth regent Hōjō Tokiyori 北條時賴 (1227–63). 'Tokiyori was the first member of the Hōjō family, and one of the first Japanese laymen, to explore fully the religious and philosophical assumptions of Zen, to devote himself seriously to the practice of Zen meditation and confrontation with a Zen master (*mondō*), and to finance the building of monasteries in which Song Zen monastic discipline and practice were enforced' (Collcutt 1981: 58). It is important to remember, however, that men like Tokiyori looked to Zen masters to provide cultural and spiritual prestige; the positing of some natural affiliation between Zen principles and the warrior ethos is little more than a modern myth.

The first such Chinese master to arrive was Lanqi Daolong 蘭渓道隆 (1213–78), who came in 1246. Making his way up to Kamakura, he soon came to the attention of Tokiyori, who built for him Kenchōji 建長寺. This was to be the first Zen monastery in Japan properly modelled on Song lines, with no concessions being made to either Tendai or Shingon practice. He soon had an enrolment of several hundred monks. Lanqi stressed daily meditation sessions and discussion of *kōan*, together with strict observance of the regulations. Tokiyori also extended his patronage to Wuan Puning 兀庵普寧 (1197–1276), a renowned master who was already in his sixties when he arrived in Japan. He became the second abbot of Kenchōji, allowing Lanqi to move to Kyōto to transform both Kenninji and Tōfukuji into more recog-

---

[6]   Collcutt 1981: 45. Collcutt is the source for much that follows.

nisable Song-style Zen monasteries. Wuan Puning found Tokiyori a good disciple and granted him a seal of transmission (*inka* 印可), thereby recognising his achievement of enlightenment; in the end, however, he found it very difficult to adapt to life in Japan and after Tokiyori died in 1263 he requested to be allowed to return to China. When Lanqi himself died in 1274, Tokiyori's son Hōjō Tokimune 時宗 (1251–84) sent for a replacement, Wuxue Zuyuan 無學祖元 (1226–86). This too turned out to be a fruitful relationship, although we should not be too quick to paint a picture of a military ruler debasing himself in front of a Chinese monk. The following tale probably illustrates more accurately what the real relation was between these two men:

In their encounters, the Chinese monk, Zen master though he was, did not forget that he was dealing with the most powerful warrior in Japan. Discussions on Zen were conducted through an interpreter. When the master wished to strike his disciple for incomprehension or to encourage greater effort, the blows fell on the interpreter (Collcutt 1981: 72).

This points up an extraordinary fact that is easily forgotten: more often than not, when a Chinese master was involved, Zen was not taught verbally but via written dialogue (*hitsudan* 筆談). Interpreters were available for a man like Tokimune, of course, but within a monastery the only language that master and student normally had in common was written Chinese. Little wonder then that Zen in the larger official monasteries patronised by the Kamakura authorities became increasingly involved with the ability to read and write classical Chinese, which in turn demanded a good knowledge of Chinese culture. Somewhat ironically for a practice supposedly based on the spoken word and direct person-to-person interaction, texts became even more important in Japan than they had been in China. The monk Mingji Chuzhun 明極楚俊 (1264–1336) put it well when he sent a poem to his patron Ōtomo Sadamune that read in part:

> Not long after I arrived to live nearby as a guest
> We made good friends and got to know each other well.
> To communicate my feelings I used a brush to transmit my speech
> And you grasped my meaning by using your eyes to hear my words.
>
> (Pollack 1985: 157, adapted).

And what of the life within these monasteries?

The Zen monastery and its lifestyle are today so accepted as Japanese that it is difficult to realize how exotic the new Zen monasteries must have seemed in the thirteenth century. Not only were monastery buildings different in style, disposition, and furnishing from anything existing in Japan; the robes of Zen monks, their manner of walking and bowing, their etiquette before and after eating, bathing, and even defecating were also distinctive. So too were the sounds of the Zen monastery: the signals on bells, clappers, and gongs that regulated the meditative pattern of daily life; the musical accompaniment of the ceremonies and chants; even the style of sūtra chanting. The vocabulary of Zen monastic life included hundreds of terms unfamilar to Japanese ears. And, as a final reminder of the foreign origin of the institution, spoken Chinese was heard frequently . . . until the end of the thirteenth century, and the Chinese literary flavour continued to thicken in the fourteenth. The new Zen monasteries were outposts of Chinese religion and culture in medieval Japanese society (Collcutt 1981: 171–72).

The three most important buildings in the monastery were the Buddha Hall (*butsuden* 佛殿), the Dharma Hall (*hattō* 法堂) and the Monks' Hall (*sōdō* 僧堂). Of these the Buddha Hall housed images and was used for devotional prayers. The Dharma Hall was similar to the lecture halls in traditional temples except that it was designed not for disquisitions and lectures on the sūtras but for discussion between the abbot and monks in open assembly. It was the Monks' Hall, however, that was peculiar to Zen. Previously in Japan monks had lived in separate small cells. In a Zen monastery the rule was communal living and it was in the Monks' Hall that they all sat in meditation, ate their meals and slept. Their personal living space was restricted to one mat on a long knee-high platform, just deep enough to allow them to stretch out and sleep when necessary (Collcutt 1981: 206–15).

The life of all monks was rigidly governed by rules and regulations, which helped to bring home to the monk a number of Buddhist 'truths': that every daily activity of whatever hue was an enlightened act; that enlightenment would only be found through strenuous exertion and the willingness to undergo privation; and that the self did not exist. These rules were central to Zen of no matter what persuasion and ranged from instructions on how to meditate to how to eat, wash and carry oneself.

15   Reform from within and without

15.1   The Saidaiji community

Both Hōnen and Shinran were ordained, but had become disillusioned with the way in which the Tendai tradition had allowed itself to become mired in secular and political matters; they questioned the relationship between Buddhism and secular authority, re-evaluated the *raison d'être* of the saṅgha, and professed a radical egalitarianism. Both men were convinced that their brand of popular devotion was the only path to salvation in a degenerate age; it was precisely this strength of conviction that ensured they became sectarian founders but it also ensured that they incurred the enmity of both the ecclesiastical authorities and those who ruled Japan. There was an open recognition that their radicalism amounted to a denial of the saṅgha: it was too dangerous to gain wide support. But not all such reformers caused antagonism. We also have examples of priests and monks who had just as strong convictions, but who preferred to work within the system, putting their ideas into practice with the active help of at least some sections of the establishment. They knew only too well that standards in monasteries were lax and that the very success of Buddhism, especially as regards its relationship with the state, had led to a secularisation with which they were uncomfortable. One such was Eison 叡尊 (1201–90).

Eison was the son of a Kōfukuji scholar-monk, something that should give pause for thought precisely because it sounds so normal. Shinran was excoriated for taking a wife but in fact it was only too common in the older monasteries. Eison received the usual precepts at Tōdaiji and spent his early years studying tantric practice at Daigoji, but then at some stage he began to have serious doubts as to whether his ordination had been really valid according to a strict interpretation of the rules, and in 1234 he was given permission to join a small band of six monks at the Hōtōin 寶塔院 at Saidaiji 西大寺 who were engaged in a strict regime of observing the precepts to the letter (Groner 2001 and 2004). Attending lectures on the four-part *vinaya* at Tōdaiji, he became more and more convinced that his ordination had indeed been invalid, since the monks who had carried it out had not themselves been correctly ordained and were not themselves living according to the precepts. Many were, like his father, married. This laxity had been the norm ever since the tradition created by Jianzhen lapsed, but it was only now, when the country and its traditions seemed to be falling apart around their ears, that some members of the saṅgha began to take matters into their own hands. Eison himself began to prepare very carefully for a self-ordination ceremony (*jisei jukai* 自誓受戒), memorising and chanting the precepts, performing rituals of confession, and looking for a dream or a sign that he was ready. Finally, in 1236, he broke out of the normal pattern and in the company of some monks of like mind, including Kakujō 覺盛 (1194–1249), Enjō 圓晴 (1180–1241) and Ugon 有嚴 (1186–1275), he performed the ceremony in front of a statue of Avalokiteśvara in the Hokkedō 法華堂 at Tōdaiji. A statue, given the right environment and the right practitioners, was felt to have the presence and power to confer precepts on a monk. Self-ordination of this type had been generally accepted for the shorter Mahāyāna precepts (the *bosatsukai*) but this occasion was rather different, since Eison and his companions were taking upon themselves the full 250 *gusokukai*. Since the procedure was not officially sanctioned and relied on private conviction, he knew it would be a highly contentious act and took great care to make a record of the event and the activities leading up to it.

Eison and his companions knew that they had taken an extremely radical step, particularly as it had been performed at Tōdaiji, where he had previously been ordained on the more usual, 'correct' platform. It could be seen as inviting chaos, and it could also be taken as an insult to other monks; hardly surprising that he and his fellow monks found life at Kōfukuji difficult as a result. He moved to the Kairyūōji 海龍王寺, where he hoped to be able to settle. The monks in this temple were devoted to a set of precepts that had been brought back from China by Shunjō 俊芿 (1166–1227). Shunjō had studied in the Hangzhou–Mingzhou area from 1199 to 1212, returning with a large number of texts (327 *vinaya*, 716 Tendai, 175 Kegon, 256 Confucian or Neo-Confucian). Unfortunately not even a list of these works is extant, but we know that they were eventually brought to a temple in Higashiyama, formerly named Hōrinji 法輪寺 but restored for Shunjō and then renamed Sennyūji 泉涌寺.[1] In the end, however, Eison fell out with these monks as well and moved on to the dilapidated grounds of Saidaiji, which he set about

---

[1]   Walton 1989. It became a tradition to inter the ashes of sovereigns at Sennyūji. This began with Shijō Tennō, who died in 1242, and ended with Kōmei Tennō in the early Meiji period.

restoring. Here he created a new order of monks, which over the years has been given a number of different and highly tendentious labels; we shall call it the 'Saidaiji order'.

Eison set about instituting the correct procedures for fortnightly assemblies, as stipulated in the *vinaya*. He ran into criticism from both Kōfukuji and Tōdaiji, of course, for being so literal, but in general the attacks on him were not as virulent as one might expect. Perhaps there was a recognition that, unlike Hōnen, he was not denying the validity of the saṅgha; he was actually devoted to strengthening it. Neither was the position at Saidaiji without its own contradictions. Once a new order had been established, it was in the interests of monks like Eison and Kakujō not to encourage any further such activity, since this would have led to a plethora of new orders and eventual breakdown. Indeed, although in the beginning he made no distinction between different kinds of precepts, offering a comprehensive one (*tsūkai* 通戒) for all monks entering his community, he eventually returned to the kind of ordination conferred at Tōdaiji. The details of these shifts (although of major importance to those who were involved) cannot be dealt with here; suffice it to say that Eison and his community were committed to following the precepts to the letter, which was unusual enough for them to stand out.

The restoration of the serious study and practice of the *vinaya* that began in the Saidaiji community was mirrored by a revival in religious establishments for women. It has been shown in the course of this history that official nunneries all but died out in the early Heian period, but this should not lead one to assume that women were thereby unduly discriminated against. Admittedly, one or two sacred mountains – Hieizan for example – were barred to them, but there were many others – the royal temple of Daigoji for example – to which they had free access. They may not have been treated by the state as nuns in an institutional sense, but there were in fact large numbers of court women in the Heian period who led a religious life as a matter of choice. Some created their own private institutions; others decided that patronage offered a more powerful model of religious practice than entering a religious order (Meeks 2003: 205).[2] But now, about the same time that Eison started his work, there was a revival of interest in the creation of nunneries. It began with Hokkeji 法華寺, the nunnery that had initially been created to stand alongside Tōdaiji. By the 1230s it was in a dilapidated state but still

---

[2] This remarkable thesis has corrected a large number of misconceptions about women and Buddhism in this period, putting the subject on an entirely new footing.

home to a small, active community of women, former ladies at court, widows, and daughters of priestly families committed to living a life of ritual and meditation.

Encouraged, perhaps, by the success Eison was having in raising awareness of the importance of the *vinaya* for monastic revival and in raising money to support this endeavour, the women at Hokkeji approached him to help them rebuild an order of nuns. In 1245 a small group of them received from him the 348 precepts. Strictly speaking, he was doing the impossible, because the rules stipulated that ten fully ordained nuns had to be present for an ordination to be correct and such a situation had never pertained in Japan, but the value of the act was felt to far outweigh this technical problem. By 1249 there were 26 women living at a revitalised Hokkeji, 12 of them fully fledged nuns (*bikuni* 比丘尼) and a private precepts platform for nuns had been established. By 1280 the number had risen to 183, with 48 *bikuni* and over 100 laywomen also listed as supporters. We have the names of 16 such women, including Kūnyo 空如, who is thought to have been Hachijō'in Takakura, a poet of some repute. Other women were sometimes single, sometimes the widows of scholar-monks, and must have included former concubines. Abutsuni, the author of *Diary of a waning moon* (*Izayoi nikki* 十六夜日記) stayed there around 1252 (Hosokawa 1999). The community at Hokkeji continued to strengthen and in many respects began to take on the characteristics of a literary and artistic salon, of the type that had been common in the mid-Heian but which had been more difficult to maintain in the disturbed climate of the late twelfth century. Hokkeji was only the first of a whole series of such establishments that were revived at this time, including the old Hōryūji nunnery of Chūgūji 中宮寺, where the central figure was a nun called Shinnyo 信如 (1211–?).

The Saidaiji order became a magnet for a number of men of like mind, monks who felt that the grand establishments had lost their way amid secularism and warfare, and that it was essential to rediscover the true vocation of a member of the saṅgha. This involved embracing a lifestyle that had more in common with the European friar than the monk. It is generally considered that the driving force behind this particular aspect of their work, social welfare and charity, was Eison's student Ninshō 忍性 (1217–1303), although it is known that Eison himself was constantly on the move, drawing large crowds, holding public services, offering the bodhisattva precepts to laypeople of all types, and declaring that no animals should be killed in certain designated locales. It involved mixing with the lowest in society, beggars, lepers and the like, and bringing to them salvation, alms, medical help, and a message of hope for the future. It involved creating bath houses, visiting prisons, providing basic food in times of famine and difficulty, and using medicines; but it also presupposed a willingness to become involved with burying the dead at all levels.

Buddhism had always played a central role in funerals and mortuary rites ever since its arrival in Japan but until the end of the Heian period this was limited by and large to those who could actually afford such rites. Official state-sponsored temples such as Tōdaiji were not involved in funerals at all but the *raison d'être* for most *ujidera* that were built in great numbers around the capital was precisely to commemorate deceased members of important families. A typical aristocratic funeral might involve a procession from the home to a designated spot on a hillside. If the body was cremated, the ashes might be buried there and then under a mound or small stūpa, or perhaps brought to the grounds of the *ujidera* to be interred. Any pollution would have been cleansed in the burning and in any case it was thought that the sacred ground cleansed the bones as opposed to the bones polluting the ground. This was certainly the case on Kōyasan. If the family wished to bury the whole body without cremation, matters were a little more complicated; they might have to wait until the body had entirely decomposed some years later before performing a second burial and bringing the remains into the temple grounds. As far as the sovereigns themselves were concerned, their burial mounds were dotted around the hillsides of the capital and there was no specific burial ground until Sennyūji became the designated area in 1242.

Funeral services and proper burial were completely beyond the means of the majority of the population, who were often driven to leave corpses rotting by the side of the road or cast them into rivers to be carried to the sea. Cremation would have been an expensive business. Mid-Heian court diaries are full of entries where courtiers are caught unawares in the presence of death and have then to ask for advice as to the precise degree of contamination they have incurred. Only with the advent of the Saidaiji order in Yamato (and Sōtō Zen in the provinces) do we find the development of common grave sites open to those of little or no rank. The willingness of the Saidaiji order to become involved in this work was presumably part and parcel of the 'rediscovery' of what it was to be a member of the saṅgha.

Charity work needed money and the Saidaiji community became known for its ability to raise money for such projects. Having newly established temples, the monks did not have large landholdings and so were forced to introduce *kanjin* techniques to survive and to do their work. Mortuary rites also brought in funds, particular when the population at large became convinced that one could help the dead by commissioning prayers and ceremonies at certain defined stages after death. One might wish to argue that none of this was very new and that men like Hōnen and Shinran had been dedicated to precisely this kind of work, but secure information of their activities in this regard is remarkably sketchy and their message of salvation was, after all, geared almost entirely to the afterlife. The Saidaiji order made great play of the compassionate role of the bodhisattva and Eison himself was posthumously known as Bodhisattva Kōshō 興正菩薩. A dedication to working amongst the lowest of the low, outcasts and those known as 'non-humans' (*hinin* 非人), lay at the heart of the revised vision of what a monk should be, and it is reasonable to credit him and his order with bringing the concept of salvation to the large underclass of those who worked in trades that were considered most polluting. There are signs that this mission recommended itself to the powers in Kamakura, for it was in the interests of public order if nothing else, but much research remains to be done on this order to gauge its true effect.

One of the doctrinal underpinnings for this kind of work was worship of Mañjuśrī, whose *sūtra* (*Monjushiri hatsunehangyō* 文殊師利般涅槃經, *T.* 463) explained how he might at times appear as a *hinin* to test compassion. The usual rationale for discriminating against outcasts was that a person's present situation must, by definition, be a result of something they had done in the past; they had earned their present state and could do little to change their lot. But Mañjuśrī offered a way to alleviate this condition; if one placed one's trust in him and worshipped him, he had the wisdom and the power to negate such karma.

The Saidaiji community is known to history for this series of innovations and the revival of the serious study and practice of the *vinaya* (the order is known as Shingonritsu 眞言律, but this label was invented in the sixteenth century), but Eison's own activities were much broader than this might suggest. He is known, for example, to have commissioned a large number of images. In 1255 he had an image of Mañjuśrī made for a temple near Nara called Hannyaji 般若寺, which was dedicated to the salvation of the *hinin* who lived in the area. In his *Kanjin gakushōki* 感身學正記, he records the difficulty he had raising the necessary funds:

I had this image carved in order to make it the focus of reverence for all living beings. Originally I intended to conduct a *kanjin* campaign among the rich and poor, and use their donations to obtain materials for the image. However, the city and the countryside have become saturated with those seeking alms from the faithful. Since *kanjin* has become commonplace, it will not necessarily arouse the deep faith [that inspires donations]. Therefore we did not circulate *kanjin* appeals but have instead relied on spontaneous contributions (Goodwin 1994: 119).

The main public image at Saidaiji was one of Śākyamuni, completed in 1249, almost an exact replica of the Seiryōji Buddha (§10.3). This image was important because it was said to be life-size; it was packed inside with a large number of texts, relics, a roster of 6,670 names, and five silk viscera in a symbolic attempt to bring the image alive, to represent Śākyamuni still active in this world (Groner 2001: 121–33). Eison's personal object of devotion (*gojibutsu* 護持佛), however, was not Śākyamuni at all but Aizen myōō 愛染明王, the King of Lust. There is a well-known image of Aizen that Eison had commissioned in 1247, still housed at Saidaiji. Aizen was worshipped for a wide variety of different reasons. He could, for example, bring disaster on your enemies (and it was said that Eison used him against the Mongols) or make someone fall passionately in love with you. In other words there was a 'voodoo' tinge to his worship. He was also used in tantric rites of a more obviously sexual nature. It is probable that Eison used this image for more orthodox reasons: it had the power to crush desire and free one from lust, rather than indulging in lust itself.

Plate 25   Aizen myōō

15.2   Dancing to salvation

The other order that emerged at this time could hardly have been more different. It was inspired by one man, Ippen 一遍 (1239–89), who was a charismatic but never ordained. Committed to circumventing the established order by going straight to the people and ignoring institutions, Ippen differed from both Hōnen and Shinran in one crucial aspect: he was eclectic to the point of carelessness, tolerant of any and all gods on the implicit understanding that ultimately they were all manifestations of Amitābha. This also meant that his ties to the plethora of cults were such that he cannot be identified with any particular one.

With a figure such as Ippen, one is talking not of someone performing a series of discrete pilgrimages but of someone whose whole life was a pilgrimage. There was undoubtedly a pathological element in Ippen's constant wanderings, as if he were incapable of staying put in one place for long, but in his movement from one cultic site to another, in the willed denial of stasis, the mundane becomes translated into the sacred and the traveller performs his own salvation. And in the wider sphere of things, it is almost as if his own mission was put into the service of linking together a whole series of sacred locations in one unifying movement. This was similar to the activity of a *kanjin hijiri*, but was not tied to a specific site and not connected to the raising of funds for that site; it was something far more spiritual, at least in the beginning. It had the effect of shifting the emphasis away from sacred sites per se and into the traveller himself. It stemmed from a deeply rooted conviction that itineracy had been the path chosen by Śākyamuni: to travel the land and spread the message of the Buddhist Dharma was the only true path for the believer. There are strong connections here with the Tendai practice of *jōgyō zanmai* or the 'constantly walking samādhi'. It also fulfilled another function, of course: that of the missionary.

Ippen's career as an itinerant priest began quite late in life, when he was already in his thirties. He was born into an important warrior family and retained throughout his life an understanding that native deities and familial gods were an integral and implicit part of the sacred in Japan. His early study of Buddhism was as a member of a Pure Land confraternity, the Seizanha 西山派, which had been founded by Shōkū 証空. This particular branch of Pure Land Buddhism taught that the moment of chanting the *nenbutsu* was the moment of one's symbolic death and deliverance. It was in this sense that one could be said to be able to reach salvation in this very life and in this very body. But it was also thought that this state of blessedness lasted only as long as one chanted. The result was that the chanting had to be continuous to be truly effective. It was out of such a belief system that Ippen's own brand of practice was to emerge. He was married at one stage but eventually 'left the household' in 1270, travelling first to Zenkōji 善光寺, the important cultic centre devoted to Amitābha. From this point on, he began his life of constant motion, a group beginning to form around him from about 1274. Legend has it that it was at Kumano that he had the revelation that was to provide one of the more distinctive elements of his devotional practice.

The sources we have about Ippen are, of course, hagiographic in nature and some of them (such as the collection of his sermons and sayings) date from as late as the eighteenth century; he left no doctrinal writings. He must have had natural charisma, since he attracted a small band of devoted followers who gave themselves to the same form of hardship in travel. By 1278 he had gathered round him seven or eight committed followers, among them Ta'amidabutsu Shinkyō 他阿彌陀佛眞教 (1237–1319), who joined in 1277 as they were passing through Bungo Province and who was to be a significant figure after Ippen's death. In 1279 the group adopted a form of ecstatic dance, which became known as *nenbutsu odori* 念佛踊. Part showman, Ippen encouraged this dance as an integral element of devotion, linked of course to the chanting of the *nenbutsu* itself. In the early stages this seems to have been a truly spontaneous outbreak of ecstatic expression, but even during his lifetime it was already turning into a staged event, a draw for crowds, an enticement to what was seen as the main act, which was known as *fusan* 賦算, the distribution of amulets or *fuda* 札 on which was written the words 'Homage to Amitābha Buddha: deliverance guaranteed for all' (*namu Amidabutsu: ketsujō ōjō rokujūmannin* 南無阿彌陀佛決定往生六十萬人). The revelation received at Kumano had been that the simple act of receiving such a *fuda* with this phrase printed on it would create a bond (*kechien* 結緣) between the individual and Amitābha and so ensure a welcome into the Pure Land. Not only did Ippen therefore go one step further than his teacher Shōkū and imbue the written, rather than the spoken, word with ultimate power, he even denied the necessity of faith in the recipient. All that was needed was to abandon the idea of self and give oneself fully to the word in spoken or written form; although one might legitimately question whether it was possible to 'give up any idea of self' without a strong drive of faith. As with the other Pure Land movements, the antinomian possibilities of such a creed are only too clear, but Ippen, known as 'the saint who had cast all away' (*sutehijiri* 捨て聖), was very well aware that for this kind of *nenbutsu* to be effective one had to be prepared to sacrifice everything. It was a tough life that he demanded from his followers, who had to entrust themselves to him entirely.

It is not until 1280 that we find the term Jishū 時衆 being used (by Ippen himself) about the group, so it was probably around this period that he began to see himself as the leader of an order. There were perhaps twenty to twenty-five members, who were sworn to follow him and obey him in return for the secure knowledge of their absolute salvation. The origin of the term *jishū* itself is obscure, but it is probably a short form of *rokuji nenbutsushū* 六時 念佛衆 meaning 'the group that chants the *nenbutsu* for six *ji* [twelve hours]', referring to the way the group would divide into groups and take turns to chant, so that the end result was almost an endless recitation. The group was not without its setbacks, of course. Arriving in Kamakura in 1282 at an awkward time, just as Hōjō Tokimune was about to leave the city, they were unceremoniously thrown off the public highway, looking and probably sounding like beggars. Then later that year, having licked their wounds, they moved to Kyōto, where their arrival caused a near riot. Hardly surprising that many people were less than complimentary, accusing them of being little more than a band of monkeys.

It was only in the last years of Ippen's life (1280–89) that moves were made to create a more coherent order. The lack of a clear distinction between the priestly and the lay, which was fundamental to his early appeal, gave way to a clearer demarcation. A distinction became apparent between those who had given everything up to travel with him (*dōjishū* 同時衆), those lay adherents who had received the amulet, practised the *nenbutsu*, but were not mendicants (*zokujishū* 俗時衆), and lastly lay supporters (*kechienshū* 結緣衆), who offered hospitality to the *dōjishū* and gave them financial support. Clearly the last group far outnumbered the first and by the time of Ippen's death it was said to have numbered half a million, although this probably meant little more than that they had heard of the order and were willing to help.

One of the distinctive elements in the Jishū armoury was the death registers (*kakochō* 過去帳). The first entry in the *Jishū kakochō* is dated 1279. Not that these registers were themselves a new phenomenon, but in the hands of Shinkyō and those who came after him they were transformed into a remarkable tool for both proselytising the faith and controlling followers. The *kakochō*, of which there were fair numbers, were registers of those who had died and achieved deliverance. Soon, however, it became common to have one's name written in *before* one's death in order to secure salvation in advance, although the head of the community had the power to rescind this promise by the simple but powerful expedient of adding the cruel words 'no deliverance' (*fuōjō* 不往生) to the entry. In the very beginning only *dōjishū* were eligible for registration but in the course of the fourteenth century this was extended to the *zokujishū*, so numbers steadily increase into the thousands. These registers were a symbol of the absolute power wielded by the head of the order.

Efforts were made to standardise things such as dress, and the dances became formal events rather than spontaneous outbursts, but serious moves to create an organisation started only after Ippen's death in 1289. When he died, seven of his followers drowned themselves and Shinkyō himself initially decided to lead the rest of the followers in a pact to starve themselves to death but, it is said, he was eventually persuaded by a local warrior to carry on the work of distributing *fuda*.

Shinkyō began by travelling, as his master had done, although he did not range so widely and kept, by and large, to central and eastern Japan. After some sixteen years he settled down in the Kantō region and established a meeting house (*dōjō* 道場) at Muryōkōji 無量光寺 in Taima 當麻, Sagami Province, not far from Kamakura, handing over the travelling duties to his chosen successor, Chitoku 智得 (1260–1320). A branch of the order, later known as the Shijōha 四條派, was also set up in Kyōto under Shinkan 眞觀 (1268–1341). So began an inevitable process of institutionalisation by which the Jishū became a curious mixture of the itinerant and the sedentary, with the head of the order remaining in the main temple and the itinerant second-in-command based at a different centre but devoting most of his energy to emulating Ippen the traveller and dispenser of *fuda*. An organisation needed a base and it was under the guidance of Shinkyō that a series of meeting houses were built by powerful warrior families in central and eastern Japan such as the Hōjō, in return for the provision of religious and pastoral services. Certainly one reason for the success of the Jishū among the warrior class was its habit of being entirely open to native deities; warriors had never been very happy with the exclusivism of Hōnen and Shinran. By 1306 Shinkyō had managed to create an organisation centred on about one hundred of these meeting houses, spread out over a wide area from Echizen to Sagami, all administered from Muryōkōji. While a strong element of itinerancy was maintained, the order was essentially transformed into a sedentary one and they took on pastoral roles much like parish priests. An almost total reliance on the goodwill of patrons had a dampening effect on their behaviour and led to a loss of the eccentricity that had been so marked in the founder. The order became fully domesticated and encorporated into the structure of social life.

Shinkyō's campaign to propagate the order and his role as sole master took textual form in the illustrated scroll known as *Ippen shōnin ekotobaden* 一遍上人繪詞傳 of 1303–04. This 'proved' Shinkyō's right to take over the mantle from Ippen and included a substantial number of sermons given in the form of answers to letters from lay supporters. The *Ekotobaden* became the central scripture of the order. Each house had a copy which was revered and which was used for teaching purposes. In typical Japanese fashion this 'scripture' is not a revealed text but one that talks of origins, lineage and legitimation. In this way, Shinkyō managed to put his own stamp on the order and raise himself to a position of even greater importance than Ippen himself. He succeeded in creating a solid economic base using the patronage of local warriors by stressing that the *nenbutsu* could overcome even the taboo on taking life; salvation was secure even though one had died fighting.

When Shinkyō died in 1319, his chosen successor, Chitoku, took over the headship, but he died the next year and the headship then shifted to Shinkō 眞光 (1280–1333). This was to cause considerable trouble. Another follower, Donkai 吞海 (1265–1327), who had been put in charge of a meeting house in Kyōto, protested that Shinkō could not become the head of the order for the simple reason that he had no experience of mendicancy. This led to a split in 1325 between the Taima group, based on Muryōkōji, and the so-called Yugyō 遊行 group, which was based in Kyōto but soon had a Kantō base as well in the form of Shōjōkōji 清淨光寺 at Fujisawa. In the end, it was really Donkai who founded what became known as the Yugyōha and there then emerged a dual leadership: the Yugyō shōnin, based in Kyoto, whose job it was to travel and dispense *fuda*, with a retinue that was to reach substantial proportions in the Tokugawa period; and the Fujisawa shōnin based in Fujisawa, who ran the organisation and was the titular head. This was supposed to allow for elements of the itinerant origins of the movement to survive the shift towards institutionalisation. In the end, of course, such a compromise could never work well, for the simple reason that this particular order needed a charismatic leader, the inevitable consequence of which was constant fragmentation.

15.3   Worshipping the *Lotus*

The phenomenon of militant exclusionism that we have seen generated in this period, a phenomenon that ran counter to the general open-mindedness of most Buddhist doctrine and practice and not unnaturally upset the established

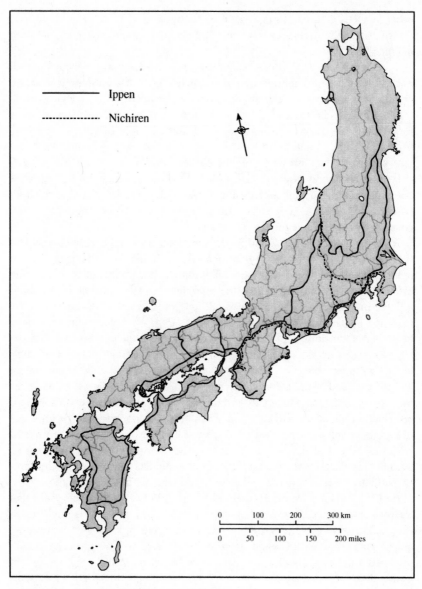

Map 10   The travels of Ippen and Nichiren

order, reaches a climax in the figure of Nichiren 日蓮 (1222–82), notorious for the strength of his convictions and for the uncompromising way he pursued his goals.

Whether through conscious erasure or not, contemporary documents do not in fact mention Nichiren by name: all we have of a biographical nature are his own doctrinal essays and his numerous pastoral letters, which must be used with the usual caution. The extant corpus contains 498 items, of which a remarkable 115 survive in his own hand and 25 more of which were destroyed in a fire as late as 1875.[3] No student or follower who actually knew him personally has left a record; the earliest biography, *Goden dodai* 御傳土代, was written by Nichidō 日道 (1283–1341), who was born the year after Nichiren's death. A later source entitled *Genso kedōki* 元祖化導記, written by Nitchō 日朝 (1422–1500) in the fifteenth century and first printed in 1666, contains much that is legendary in nature.

It is hardly surprising to find legends encrusted around such a charismatic figure, a man who attracted a loyalty as fierce as his own character. Unlike other important clerics of the time, Nichiren was assuredly not of aristocratic birth. He was to make much of the humbleness of his origins in a fishing village, in what is now south Chiba, although the fact that he was sent to be educated at the local temple, Kiyosumidera 清澄寺, suggests he may have been more than simply the son of a fisherman. Nevertheless, he was certainly a provincial with no contacts and no expectation of patronage. His intellectual abilities were such, however, that he soon exhausted what the temple had to offer and at the age of sixteen left for Kamakura. He stayed there for four years and then moved to Kyōto and Nara. We have very little hard information about the next sixteen years and it is not possible to trace his exact movements, but he must have spent a number of years on Hieizan, and we know he was also at Kōyasan for a period. It was during this time that he became convinced that salvation lay not in Amitābha nor indeed in any form of Buddhist practice other than the study and worship of the *Lotus sūtra*.

In 1253 Nichiren returned east. Relying entirely on his willingness and ability to preach, he slowly gathered together a series of what we might again call 'congregations', many of his followers being laymen and laywomen, only a small fraction of whom were either able or willing to become fully ordained. Such was his self-confidence that he proclaimed the right to ordain monks himself. This alone would have been enough to brand him a sub-

---

[3]   It should be noted that the authenticity of quite a number of these essays is in question. See Sueki 1999 for a discussion of the considerable difficulties this can cause.

versive, but Nichiren was convinced of his legitimacy, even going as far as to express pride that many of his followers were, in official eyes at least, unordained or *mukai* 無戒.

Certain in his own mind that the reason for continued natural disasters and political unrest was the fact that the *Lotus sūtra* was not being given its rightful place in the nation's affairs, either by the Buddhist establishment or indeed by the leadership in Kamakura, Nichiren wrote the tract for which he is best known, *On establishing the true Dharma to bring peace to the nation* (*Risshō ankokuron* 立正安國論) in 1260 and sent it directly to Hōjō Tokiyori (1227–63), the former regent who was now living in retirement at a Zen temple. Written in the form of a dialogue between 'a visitor' and 'the master', it is openly critical of the country's leaders, calling on them to castigate all those who propagate Pure Land teachings or who profess to practise Zen; he warns of terrible disasters if the *Lotus sūtra* is not given its full due. There is no sign that anyone in authority took this outburst seriously, but someone took care that its contents became known, with the result that Nichiren's house was destroyed and he barely escaped with his life. Such attacks only served to strengthen his resolve to continue his mission and in less than a year he was back proselytising in the streets of Kamakura. At that point, it was decided that his presence constituted too great a threat to public order (and to himself), and he was immediately arrested and banished to the Izu peninsula.

Risshō ankokuron is important for two main reasons: its unblinking critique of the status quo, and the fact that it contained a prophecy that came to pass. As we have seen throughout this study, there never was a time in Japanese history when Buddhism did not have a complex and difficult relationship with the state, but the received wisdom up to this point had been that Buddhist institutions were politically important because they gave protection to the ruler, and, by extension, to the state (*chingo kokka* 鎮護國家). Nichiren turned this logic on its head and placed the onus firmly on the ruler. We all desire peace and stability, but this can only be ensured if the nation and the ruler pay due respect to the correct Buddhist Dharma (namely, the *Lotus sūtra*) and actively fight the spread of useless falsehoods. As long as the authorities fail to do this, they are at fault; and when calamity does strike, as it surely will, it is they who will be to blame.

Then there was the matter of prophecy. Using a series of quotations not only from the *Lotus* but from such sources as the *Sūtra for humane kings*, Nichiren described what was bound to happen to a state that continued to ignore the correct teachings. Many of the disasters he listed had naturally already occurred in Japan, but not yet a foreign invasion. The prediction of military conquest and overthrow of the ruler by outside forces is common to a large number of Mahāyāna sūtras: in essence it often acted as self-advertisement, part and parcel of the attempt to secure state support and patronage. In this case, Nichiren could hardly have been more fortunate, for his particular prophecy was to come true. He returned from Izu in 1264, but was clearly still in considerable personal danger, because we find him daring to enter Kamakura itself only four years later, in 1268. This was about the time that the Bakufu received its first threatening missive from Khubilai Khan. We do not know enough about the flow of information to know whether someone of Nichiren's marginal status could have had much inkling of what was happening on the continent, so he may well have been as surprised as everyone else at this turn of events, but, in any case, to him it was absolute proof that he had been correct all along. He gained some notoriety as a prophet and increasing confidence in his mission. Although the authorities in Kamakura never gave any sign of having taken his thesis seriously, the way in which his predictions seemed to have validity helped swell the ranks of those willing to follow him.

In 1271 the pressures he continued to create for himself by his relentless verbal attacks on all who failed to see his point of view eventually proved too great and the Bakufu was forced to banish him yet again on grounds of sedition. This time he was sent to the island of Sado, a move that may well have saved his life. While on Sado he produced a large number of pastoral letters to his congregations in the Kantō and continued refining his own vision of how the Japanese people might best achieve salvation. Eventually pardoned in 1274, the date of the first Mongol attack, he returned to Kamakura to be questioned about his views. Unhappy that the authorities continued to be unresponsive to his message, however, he gave up 'direct action' and retired instead to Mt Minobu 身延, where he established a temple to look after his growing band of clerical disciples and student priests.

Who were his followers? Neither the number of monks who worked with him nor the number of the lay communities that supported him is known, but they were not large and it is important not to be misled by the later success of the Hokkeshū, the Nichiren sect that traced itself back to his initial inspiration. The majority were middle- and lower-ranking samurai and local landowners, many of whom must have first encountered his teaching while they were serving in Kamakura. Convinced, one assumes, by his force of character, they returned to the countryside and formed the nuclei of communities throughout the Kantō region (Stone 1999c). The 'professional' followers or priests were of three types: those who were based at local Tendai temples but who travelled to the homes of supporters to preach and elaborate on the content of Nichiren's pastoral letters; those who had richer patrons and who served as religious advisers on their estates; and lastly those who led a monastic existence and went to study with Nichiren at Mt Minobu from 1274 onwards (where there were, he claimed, more than one hundred by 1279). Nichiren made every effort to instil a sense of belonging into this thinly spread congregation, which was constantly subjected to official censure and, occasionally, outright violence. They were constantly buoyed up both by Nichiren's own charisma and by the self-fulfilling prophecy of the sūtra itself, that in the Latter Days of the Dharma those who tried to maintain the correct teaching would inevitably be subjected to persecution and ridicule; although quite why a middle-ranking samurai should choose to belong to a community under such pressure is a difficult question to answer. Was it that Nichiren came from the Kantō and spoke their own dialect?

His pastoral letters, which occasionally contained doctrinal arguments but more often than not simply gave thanks for gifts or acts of kindness always followed by words of encouragement, were an important tool of propagation. The tone of these letters is one of a preacher bringing advice and succour to his flock. It would seem that a large number of his lay supporters were women, not surprisingly perhaps since the *Lotus* paid particular attention to their fate and offered the clear example in the Dragon King's daughter of a girl who had managed to achieve enlightenment faster than any man. In one remarkable passage he advises the wife of a follower on whether she could continue reading and studying the sūtra while menstruating. Since it was not pollution from an external source but merely a characteristic of the female sex related to procreation, he could find no doctrinal basis for such a taboo, he said, and urged her to continue with her devotions (Yampolsky 1996: 255).

The degree to which Nichiren politicised religion was unprecedented, particularly the way in which he linked the possibility of personal salvation to the creation of an ideal state. This might sound suspiciously like nationalism but that would be very far from the truth, because for Nichiren the very definition of an ideal state was one that upheld the practice of the *Lotus*. Buddhism had always taught that doctrine was dependent on differences in time and place, but Nichiren was particularly interested in the element of time. He accepted the premise of *mappō* but saw it not as an occasion for pessimistic resignation but as a marvellous chance. How? Because the *Lotus* which gave humanity the one best chance of salvation tells

us that it will only be expounded in this world and only in a time of *mappō*.
The proper, ideal time was therefore here and now. A Buddha Land on this
earth was within everyone's grasp:

When all people throughout the land enter the one Buddha vehicle and the Wonderful
Dharma alone flourishes, because the people all chant '*namu-myōhō-renge-kyō*' as
one, the wind will not thrash the branches nor the rain fall hard enough to break clods.
The age will become like the reigns of Yao and Shun. In the present life, inauspicious
calamities will be banished, and the people will obtain the art of longevity. When the
principle becomes manifest that both persons and dharmas 'neither age nor die', then
each of you behold! There can be no doubt of the sūtra's promise of 'peace and
security in the present world' (Stone 1999a: 291–92).

Obviously, it must be the duty of the authorities in power to facilitate this and
when the state refused to recognise this fact, it was doomed. The arrival of
threats from the Mongols was clear proof:

Because all the people of the land of Japan, from high and low without a single
exception, have become slanderers of the Dharma, Brahmā, Indra, Tenshō Daijin, and
the other deities must have instructed the sages of a neighbouring country to reprove
that slander . . . The entire country has now become inimical to the Buddhas and
deities . . . China and Korea, following the example of India, became Buddhist
countries. But because they embraced Zen and *nenbutsu* teachings, they were
destroyed by the Mongols. The country of Japan is a disciple to those two countries.
And if they have been destroyed, how can our country remain at peace? . . . All the
people in the country of Japan will fall into the Hell without Respite (Stone 1999b:
413–14).

So Japan fully deserved the punishment that was to come. No wonder that the
authorities came to see Nichiren as a threat, for this kind of politicised
radicalism might so easily spill over into civil discontent, hardly what the
country needed when the Mongols were knocking at the door. He was also a
potential liability since, far from being nationalistic about the enterprise, he
was actually welcoming the invasion as proof of divine retribution. It
increasingly becomes a wonder that Nichiren was treated quite so leniently as
he was by the authorities, although it is more than likely that our sources
exaggerate the threat and that in fact he hardly registered in the larger scale
of things.

    Although in his direct criticisms of the authorities Nichiren was
pessimistic about Japan's ability to withstand attack, doctrinally he knew
there was hope, and that hope lay in one man: himself. He himself was living
proof that the true Buddhist teachings still survived in the world in one
place – Japan; and if his message was heard and Japan mended its ways, it

could become the source for regenerating Buddhism throughout the world. What had arisen in India and come east would return from east to west with renewed splendour.[4] This optimistic vision can be seen as a strategy for countering the essentially pessimistic doctrine of *mappō*, and marks another point where Nichiren differed from Hōnen. Pure Land Buddhism, based on a thoroughgoing dualism, saw no possibility of hope in this world, preferring to stress the irredeemably vile nature of life in the here-and-now, and arguing that a guarantee of enlightenment was only available in the next life.

So what was the message of the *Lotus* that made it of such central importance? As we have already seen, although the sūtra had been central to Tiantai Buddhism in China, by Nichiren's time Japanese Tendai had become inextricably involved with tantric ritual and Pure Land beliefs. Nichiren saw himself as the reviver of a 'purer' Tendai, restoring the *Lotus* to its rightful place at the pinnacle of the Buddha's teachings. It will be recalled that the sūtra had two major but interlinked messages. Firstly, that salvation in the form of buddhahood is potentially available to all. Of course, this became a creed common to Mahāyāna in general, but in this particular case salvation was to be obtained through devotion to the sūtra itself. Secondly, that more than one Buddha can exist at any one time and they are in essence transcendental beings; Śākyamuni, the historical Buddha, did not disappear but is with us always, offering his guidance. He may no longer be present in physical form, but he is eternally present within the Dharma. In this sense, the Tathāgata is the sūtra. Hardly surprising then that Nichiren eventually chose the teachings rather than the teacher as his object of devotion.

One of the rhetorical tricks by which the *Lotus sūtra* tried to ensure its survival at the heart of Buddhist teaching was the extent to which it predicted its own dire fate in the Latter Days of the Dharma, when it would be shunned, its teachings ignored, and those who defended it would be subject to persecution. Devotees of the *Lotus* had to be constantly on their guard against anyone who 'slandered the Dharma', by which was meant anyone who treated the sūtra with anything less than complete faith and anyone who was attached to other, provisional, teachings. But it also put forward the proposition that it was precisely in such an age that it would come into its own, being specifically designed to fit the capabilities of those born in such an age. To this extent, those born at this point were paradoxically considered fortunate, since the ultimate teaching had been reserved for them.

---

[4] See in particular his 'Kenbutsu miraiki', translated as 'On the Buddha's prophesy' in Yampolsky 1996: 73–81.

It is difficult not to conclude that in many respects Nichiren was drawn to a text that mirrored his own character – militant and with a highly developed persecution complex. The warnings in the sūtra were to be taken quite literally. A devotee of the truth in an age of *mappō* must, by definition, encounter and indeed encourage persecution for his or her faith. Not only must one be prepared to give one's life in defence of the sūtra, one is duty-bound to attack all wrong thoughts and ill-founded beliefs in a constant battle to defend the truth, a process known as *shakubuku* 折伏.

[If] even one with deep faith does not rebuke the enemies of the *Lotus*, no matter what great good he may produce, even if he recites and copies the *Lotus* a thousand or ten thousand times, or perfects the way of contemplating the three thousand realms in one thought-moment, if he fails to rebuke the enemies of the *Lotus*, then it will be impossible for him to realize enlightenment. To illustrate, even if one has served the court for ten or twenty years, if, knowing of the ruler's enemies, he fails to report them or to oppose them himself, then the merit of his service will all be lost and he will instead be guilty of a crime. You must understand that the people of today are slanderers of the Dharma (Asai 1999: 250).

But what does it mean to worship and pay homage to a text rather than a Buddha? Perhaps the question is misplaced, because, as we have just seen, to Nichiren the text was the body. So it is not so much privileging the Dharma over Buddha as recognising the Buddha in the Dharma and seeing them as indivisible. There can be no doubt that Nichiren believed that to read and pay homage to the *Lotus* was the only way one could encounter the body of the Tathāgata in the age of *mappō*. It was therefore imperative to give all humankind the opportunity to carry out such devotions, and it was with this in mind that Nichiren developed the idea, perhaps as early as his exile in Izu, that chanting the title (*daimoku* 題目), in other words reciting the phrase 'Homage to the *Lotus sūtra*' ('*namu myōhō renge kyō*' 南無妙法蓮華經), was the best way of showing one's devotion. Although this might be seen as an extremely 'easy' practice, the equivalent of Hōnen's 'easy' *nenbutsu*, Nichiren did not see it in this light. For him it was difficult, because such practice would inevitably bring with it persecution.

How was it that the title of a sūtra came to be imbued with such power? There is good evidence that chanting the *daimoku* was practised as a form of religious exercise throughout the late Heian period. In Genshin's time, for example, reading and discussing the *Lotus* formed an integral part of devotions that ended with recitation of the *nenbutsu* (Bowring 1998), and there are records from the late twelfth century that suggest extended recitations of the title alone were practised. But it remained largely a private practice among aristocrats. There were in fact good doctrinal grounds, starting with passages in the sūtra itself, for considering the title to represent its essence in a unique way not found with other texts: the whole of Zhiyi's *Fahua xuanyi* 法華玄義 had been an investigation of this very phenomenon. But Nichiren went further: he transformed recitation of the *daimoku* into a practice for all; he claimed exclusive efficacy for this practice and damned the rest; and he maintained that this form of recitation was not second best to reading the whole, but was itself the ultimate practice.

In Nichiren's later writings, chanting the *daimoku* is presented not as a beginning step or accommodation to those incapable of the greater practice of reciting the sūtra, but as the highest form of practice, the ultimate of the Buddha's teaching, which he had embodied in the title of the *Lotus sūtra* specifically for the Final Dharma age when people would need it most. The *daimoku* contains all good precepts and the merit gained by observing them. All the practices undertaken by the Buddha over countless kalpas and the enlightenment he consequently attained are contained within the sūtra's title and 'spontaneously transferred' to those who embrace it (Stone 1998: 138–39).

It is at this point that Nichiren's relationship to Pure Land and tantrism comes into question. To the outsider, influence from both would seem undeniable, and yet it is well known that Nichiren saw them both as the 'enemy' and constantly railed against them. As far as Pure Land practice is concerned, one could well argue that Nichiren invented the *daimoku* to be the substitute or equivalent of the *nenbutsu* as a ritual recitation designed to lead the believer to enlightenment. The crucial difference lay not in the form of practice but in the doctrinal foundation of that practice. Perhaps a key to his violent denunciation of Pure Land practice lies in this very closeness. A similar reaction can be seen vis-à-vis tantrism, although here the relationship is a little more complicated. The main reason why we find Nichiren critical of both Tendai and Shingon was that they failed to understand the overriding importance of the *Lotus* and downgraded it in their systems of classification, and for Nichiren there could be no graver crime. One of his explanations as to why a ruler such as Go-Toba had failed was that he had paid undue attention to tantric ritual and thus ignored the 'true' teachings. This was equally the problem with the government in Kamakura. But this sectarian stance should not blind us to the fact that there is much in Nichiren's own practice that draws fundamental inspiration from tantrism. As the marginal notes on his own copy of Kumārajīva's text show,[5] he read widely in tantric treatments of

---

[5] Nichiren's personal copy is known simply as *Chū hokekyō* 注法華經. On the subject of Nichiren and tantrism is general see Dolce 1999 and 2002.

this and other sūtras, and his very first extended essay (*Kaitai sokushin jōbutsu gi* 戒體即身成佛義) was a discussion of the *Lotus* from a tantric perspective.

The tradition of using the *Lotus* as a tantric text can be traced back to Śubhākarasiṃha, but the extensive use of a Lotus maṇḍala, which is based on the fact that a Lotus Hall lay at the very centre of the Womb World maṇḍala, is really a product of the mid-Heian period. The rites connected with this important example of a *besson mandara* 別尊曼荼羅 are known as *hokkehō* 法華法, and they are dealt with in considerable detail in the two major collections of ritual texts from this period, Kakuzenshō 覺禪鈔 of 1217 and Asabashō 阿沙縛抄 of *c*.1240. At the centre of the *hokke mandara*, of course, we find the jewelled stūpa with Śākyamuni and Prabhūtaratna sitting inside; but the central figure in the Womb World maṇḍala is Mahāvairocana. Although for sectarian reasons, Nichiren tried to distinguish between Mahāvairocana and Śākyamuni, in fact he was led to adopt the tantric identification of these figures on the basis of what was said in the second half of the sūtra (chapters 15–28, 'entrance of origin' *honmon* 本門, see §5.3) about Śākaymuni being eternally present. This in turn led Nichiren to place much more emphasis on the *honmon* section of the sūtra than any of his predecessors. It was here, he argued, that one found expressed both the concept of 'the three thousand worlds in one thought-moment' (*ichinen sanzen* 一念三千) and the idea that enlightenment was to be found not so much in the contemplation of principle (*ri* 理) but rather in activity or actual practice (*ji* 事).

In addition to the *daimoku*, then, Nichiren also created his own form of maṇḍala; not iconographic but logographic, in line with his belief that the text of the Dharma had to be the object of devotion (*honzon* 本尊). It would seem that Nichiren worked on this idea while in exile on Sado, although most of the surviving maṇḍala in his own hand (and 128 examples from the years 1271–82 do survive) are from his later Mt Minobu period. Each one is individual and distinct, and no images are involved, the whole object being made up of a collection of titles and *siddhaṃ* seed syllables. In the centre is always the *daimoku* phrase surrounded by a symmetrical arrangement of names written vertically and leading away from the centre, perhaps with a stūpa shape in mind. Śākyamuni is always on the immediate left of the *daimoku* and Prabhūtaratna to the right; these are followed in turn by the names of certain bodhisattvas central to the sūtra, although sometimes one also finds figures inscribed who do not appear in the *Lotus sūtra* itself, such as Dainichi, Fudō and Aizen. Some of the larger maṇḍala were clearly meant to be hung up and treated as devotional objects, whereas others were small enough to be carried on the person as talismans. Being gifts from Nichiren himself, they could be seen as performing a social role as well, perhaps marking the entry of a person into the community of believers and supporters, as many of them are inscribed with the name of the 'owner'.

16   The emergence of Shintō

16.1   Japan in 1280

By the late thirteenth century, the developments that were discussed in §12.1–12.4 had strengthened considerably. The investigation into the origins of Japan and speculation as to the nature of the sovereign's power at a time of double rule was now given an unforeseen catalyst – the threat of invasion from the continent. Jien had interpreted the Kamakura part of the new power structure in a positive light – he saw it as a transformation of the sword that had been lost at Dannoura. He had not foreseen how soon this new sword would be asked to respond.

Khubilai Khan first made direct contact with the rulers of Japan in 1266. A letter addressed to the 'King of Japan' arrived in Kyūshū and was forwarded from Dazaifu to Kamakura. It then found its way back to the capital. There was general paralysis at court and in the end it seemed best to ignore it, so no reply was forthcoming. The Japanese authorities continued to ignore Mongol envoys and their threatening messages in the hope they might simply go away. The first attempt at an invasion did not in fact materialise until 1274, and when it happened it was a somewhat desultory affair. Later Mongol and Japanese accounts inflate the number of warriors involved by a factor of at least ten, and recent research suggests that no more than 3,000 warriors were involved on either side. The Mongols were probably outnumbered and failed to make much impact, being forced to return to the Korean peninsula at the head of a strong easterly wind. Japan was much better prepared for the second attempt in 1281, surprising the Mongols with forward defences that gave them little room to land. On this occasion adverse weather conditions made things worse and the Mongols again retreated after less than six weeks of skirmishing (Conlan 2001). Such was the rather banal reality, somewhat at odds with the frightening image created by later chronicles and by courtiers willing to exaggerate at the time. It was widely reported that Japan had only been saved from certain destruction by the many prayers and rituals carried out at temples and shrines, and that salvation had come in the form of a typhoon that was later interpreted as a 'divine wind' (*kamikaze* 神風), a term that is first met in the early poetry collection *Man'yōshū* 萬葉集 used as a descriptive epithet for the shrines at Ise. This is an early sign that the role of Ise was to change radically during this period.

It may be useful to be reminded what else was happening in 1280. Dōgen had been dead for some thirty years and, although his successors were making some headway in the provinces, the future of his particular Zen tradition was not at all secure and would remain uncertain until the emergence of Keizan Jōkin at the turn of the century. Other Zen institutions, far more interested in locking themselves into the structures of power, were becoming established not only with the Hōjō in Kamakura but also with a number of influential Kyōto nobles; even so, the future here was also uncertain and would remain so until the ranks of Zen masters were joined by an influx of Chinese emigrés. Ippen was active, in constant motion, spreading the gospel of Amitābha along with an eclectic approach to native deities. Nichiren in the east had only two more years to live. Elsewhere, devotion to the buddhas and rituals for the gods were becoming increasingly difficult to distinguish, and the metaphor of two sides of the same coin is increasingly fitting. Hieizan and Kōfukuji were still at loggerheads, and whenever they wished to petition in the capital against some decision they continued to bring the local dieties with them in the form of either a *mikoshi* or a *sakaki* tree. Was there a nascent sense of nationalism? Perhaps. But one should resist drawing a direct connection between such events as the Mongol invasions and the rise of a sense of nationhood among the warriors, for example. Their interests were by and large parochial and they fought with material rewards in mind. On the other hand, two ideological movements were about to emerge that certainly were firmly rooted in the idea that Japan was special in both a physical and a spiritual sense. The first of these was essentially Buddhist in nature; the second could not have existed without Buddhist influence, especially the tantric variety, but showed signs of wishing to strike out on its own. Eventually it was to give rise to anti-Buddhist sentiment.

16.2   The maṇḍalisation of Japan

On Hieizan, monks and exegetes were busy developing those ideas first expressed in *Yōtenki* in 1223 (§12.3), especially as regards the deity Sannō. The best guide here is the collection entitled *A gathering of leaves from the valley mists* (*Keiran shūyōshū* 渓嵐拾葉集, *T.* 2410), which was compiled between the years 1311 and 1348 by the monk Kōshū 光宗 (1276–1350). Only about one-third of this work is extant but even in its present state it can be described as encyclopedic. The approach taken here is almost entirely tantric and the existence of popular Pure Land sects is entirely ignored. Indeed, it would be misleading if one tried to characterise this vision as a rejection of, or even just a reaction to the phenomenon of Hōnen or Shinran, for their existence is not even recognised. The world revealed here is one dedicated to the protection and maintenance of an ideal system, revealing subtle patterns that were seen as lying just beneath the surface and proving that the status quo was not only inevitable but permanent. Justification for much of this was found in an important play on words, the kind of paronomasia that we have come to expect of tantric logic.

It so happened that the characters 大日本國 could either be read *Dai Nihonkoku*, in which case they would mean 'The great land of Japan', or *Dainichi [no] hongoku*, in which case they could mean 'The original land of Mahāvairocana (Dainichi)', who in his manifestation as Tenshō Daijin ('the great deity of heavenly brilliance' being obviously the same as 'the great shining one') had his seat at Ise. Once the concept behind the double reading of the term 大日本國 was understood and accepted, the whole geography of Japan could be analysed along tantric lines, in much the same way as we have seen in the case of Kumano (§10.2). This leads to what has been called the 'maṇḍalisation' of Japan, whereby shapes of Buddhist ritual objects, in particular the *vajra*, could be shown to underlie its geography (Grapard 1998; *T.* 2410: 626b) [plate 26]. In this way further proof could be excavated to show that the body of the land was indeed the body of Dainichi. One is reminded somewhat of the belief that the whole of southern England is criss-crossed by a web of ancient, mythical, force fields known as 'ley lines', linking ancient monuments such as Stonehenge and Avebury, although the example of Japan contained much more potential in this regard. The recognition of identity in spatial terms was mirrored by a concomitant collapse of temporal distinctions, since the gods and buddhas that stood at the origin of a particular shrine or temple could be contacted and brought into the present through the simple act of pilgrimage and the observance of certain prescribed rites. History, and therefore by definition karma, could be transcended in this fashion, so that Japan as the abode of Dainichi could be treated not only as the centre of the universe but as eternal and beyond time. *Keiran shūyōshū* was, among other things, a guide to Hieizan showing how every square inch could be interpreted as the manifestation of some aspect of Tendai doctrine.

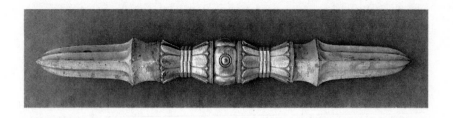

Plate 26   Japan in the shape of a *vajra*, south at the top.

This set of correspondences, showing that physical reality was sacred in and of itself, was mirrored in more philosophical form in another series of secret texts, only a small proportion of which have ever been published. They go now under the generic but not entirely helpful title of 'original enlight-enment discourse' (*hongakuron* 本覺論), essentially an investigation of the central tenet that all sentient beings, and indeed the non-sentient, are always already enlightened, hence the term '*hongaku*'. Such a doctrine of extreme optimism is in marked contrast to the inbuilt dualism on which Pure Land Buddhism was based.

There are a number of interesting consequences if this doctrine is accepted, all of them unsettling (Stone 1999a). It was, of course, recognised that this tantric overcoming of the law of cause and effect, and the conditioned nature of all elements of existence, was a particularly difficult mode of thought that could only be vouchsafed to initiates. Firstly, if non-dualism is taken to its logical conclusion and there is no way of distinguishing between nirvāṇa and saṃsāra, then the world as we see it is both enlightened and enlightenment. This means that the status quo is a Pure Land that never changes, since it is by definition eternal. From here it is but a short step to moving beyond a position of simple equivalence – mind equals empirical reality – to a position whereby empirical reality is not simply affirmed but actually valorised above mind, ritual activity given preference over meditation.

From the standpoint of nonduality, there is no hierarchy whatsoever among the three truths, because one truth encompasses three truths, and the three truths are implicit in one. But from the standpoint of duality, the truth of conventional existence is superior, while those of emptiness and the middle are inferior. The truth of conventional existence is the realm before our eyes, the myriad phenomena, the body of what is originally unborn . . . Emptiness and the middle are the adornments of conventional existence (Stone 1999a: 201).

The ramifications of such a view have much in common with the effects that stem from the maṇḍalisation of Japan. There is also, as we shall see a little later, a sense in which this chimes with the development of an intellectual, philosophical strain of Shintō.

Secondly, if liberation is to be defined simply as coming to a full realisation that one was already enlightened, what is the point of the saṅgha and what is the point of practice? Time, after all, had no meaning. As one can imagine, there were considerable disagreements as to how to deal with this particular problem, which in the end came down to how easy, or difficult, it might be to achieve such a realisation. One could always try and save the situation by arguing that serious practice was needed for realisation to be achieved, but one could equally see it from another angle: if the end result of treading an arduous path was to discover that none of it had really been necessary, since to stand at the beginning of the path was actually to stand already at the end, then why start down that path in the first place? Hardly surprising that these texts were not broadcast widely, since to have done so would have immediately led to yet more antinomian behaviour.

Perhaps it is also not surprising to find Buddhist concepts wrapping themselves around local cults on Hieizan, where the Buddhist element was already predominant, but this was also happening elsewhere, with increasingly interesting results. As far as Ise is concerned, the earliest date we have for the next major step in the Buddhist appropriation of local tradition, and in particular, of course, the two shrines most closely associated with the sovereign, is the group of tales and anecdotes entitled *Collection of sand and pebbles* (*Shasekishū* 沙石集) compiled by Mujū Ichien 無住一圓 (1226–1312). In a section dated about 1262, he wrote:

We have come to identify the deities of the Inner and Outer Shrines with Dainichi of the Two Maṇḍala; and that which is called the Rock Door of Heaven is the Tuṣita Heaven, also called the High Plain of Heaven. Events which took place during the Age of the Gods all have their [Buddhist] interpretation. In the Shingon view the

Tuṣita Heaven, indeed, is spoken of as the Dharma World's Palace of Inner Realisation, the Land of Secret Grandeur (*mitsugonkoku* 密嚴國). Dainichi emerges from his capital of Inner Realisation and leaves his trace (*ato o tare* 跡ヲ垂レ) in the land of the sun [Japan]. So the deity of the Inner Shrine is Dainichi of the Womb World [maṇḍala]; and patterned after this maṇḍala of the four enclosures are the several shrine fences: *tamagaki, mizugaki, aragaki* etc. Similarly there are nine billets (*katsuo'gi* 鰹木) [on the roof], which symbolise the nine Honoured Ones of the Womb World. The deity of the Outer Shrine is Dainichi of the Diamond World maṇḍala, or sometimes identified as Amida. There are five moon discs there, presumably to symbolise the five wisdoms of the Diamond World. When the two maṇḍala, Womb and Diamond, are seen in terms of Yin and Yang, because the Yin is the female and the Yang the male, the Womb World has an eight-petalled [lotus pattern] which corresponds to the eight [inner] shrine maidens. And this is why there are five male kagura dancers [in the outer shrine] corresponding to the five wisdom males in the Diamond World (Watanabe 1966: 60; trans. adapted from Morrell 1985: 73–74).

This theory, which was later to be labelled 'Shintō of the two maṇḍala' (Ryōbu Shintō 兩部神道) by Yoshida Kanetomo in the late fifteenth century, may have been in circulation for some time. Dainichi had long been associated with Tenshō Daijin, because of the similarity in their names, but this was now extended much further to include the idea that Japan was in fact the centre of the universe. Since the two tantric maṇḍala identified with 'principle' and 'wisdom' made up the universe, the shrines could be described in like fashion; together and in union they symbolised the birth of Japan.[1]

Ties between the sovereign and Ise had been slackening for some time, a classic symptom of which was the collapse of the system of the consecrated priestesses, which fell into disuse in the mid-thirteenth century. With the exception of two very short interludes, from 1246 onwards no representative of the court was sent to Ise and the arrangement was never revived. The monk Tsūkai 通海, visiting Ise in 1286, recorded his shock at finding the shrines in a terrible state of decay. It is hardly surprising that faced with such a drastic decline in their main source of patronage, the shrines were forced to look elsewhere for support. The priests turned to a much wider audience and tried a number of new strategies to encourage patronage from wherever it might be available. One outcome of this financial need was the encouragement of pilgrimages to Ise, which had started with Chōgen's large retinue of 1186. Pilgrimages of this size were, of course, somewhat rare, but there was another upsurge a hundred years later in 1272–86. Gradually the circle widened so that by 1318 we have evidence of the first rules for visitors (from

---

[1]   For a more detailed discussion of the two Shingon maṇḍala, see Appendices.

the provinces of Mino and Owari), rules which were needed to protect them from the various entrepreneurial ventures that had sprung up to take advantage of this new phenomenon. It is important to recognise that Buddhist monks were just as involved in this movement as the Ise priests themselves, if, indeed, that distinction makes any sense at this stage (Teeuwen 1996: 80).

The shrines had to be careful, however. Much of their appeal and ultimate justification came from the fact that the main deity of the Inner Shrine was indissolubly linked to the monarch and his lineage, to the court, and thereby to the state. Without this special relationship much of Ise's *raison d'être* would have disappeared. But this had to be run in parallel with making the shrines more accessible. It was, for example, inevitable that once the shrines started to spread their appeal to the rising warrior class in the east, the ban on offering prayers for anyone but the monarch would fall into abeyance. There emerged men and women who went by the name of *nottoshi* 祝詞師 or *kitōshi* 祈禱師, who were paid to convey (or perhaps one should say purvey) a benefactor's private prayers to the gods. The Ise shrines were beginning to create their own path to wealth and Japan-wide prominence. In the process, new forms of ritual had to be developed, since no tradition of offering services for individuals existed. These new rituals and the mantra that went with them employ a mixture of Buddhist and Yin-Yang terminology, and mark a shift from purification seen as cleansing the state of impurities, to purification as a means of attaining individual enlightenment (Teeuwen 1996: 96). As the word 'enlightenment' suggests, the influence of Buddhism was still very strong. The passage from *Nakatomi harae kunge* quoted in §12.2 shows that this was already the norm in Ise by the late twelfth century.

The increasing influence of tantric Buddhist concepts and vocabulary on Ise and the ease with which priests became monks after their retirement, suggests that compared, say, with the degree of antagonism between Enryakuji and Kōfukuji, the strains between Buddhism and the native tradition at Ise were few and far between. A way was even found to explain the taboos against certain items of Buddhist vocabulary and against allowing monks close to the shrines that had been instituted after Shōtoku Tennō's death and the banishment of Dōkyō in 770. These restrictions could not be simply ignored, since they were expressed so clearly in texts such as *Procedures of the Engi era*. The best-known account of how this awkward fact of life was rationalised can be found again at the beginning of Mujū's *Shasekishū*.

While I was on a pilgrimage to the Great Shrine during the Kōchō era [1261–64], an official explained to me why words associated with the Three Jewels of Buddhism were forbidden at the shrine, and why monks could not closely approach the sacred buildings.

In antiquity, when this country did not yet exist, the deity of the Great Shrine, guided by a seal [*mudrā*] of Mahāvairocana inscribed on the ocean floor, thrust down the august spear. Brine from the spear coagulated like drops of dew, and this was seen from afar by Māra, the Evil One, in the Sixth Heaven of Desire. 'It appears that these drops are forming into a land where Buddhism will be propagated and people will escape from the round of birth and death,' he said, and came down to prevent it.

Then the deity of the Great Shrine met with the demon king. 'I promise not to utter the names of the Three Jewels, nor will I permit them near my person. So return quickly back to the heavens.' Being thus mollified, he withdrew.

Monks to this very day, not wishing to violate that august promise, do not approach the sacred shrine, and the sūtras are not carried openly in its precincts. Things associated with the Three Jewels are referred to obliquely: Buddha is called 'The Cramp-Legged One' [*tachisukumi*]; the sūtras, 'coloured paper' [*somegami*]; monks, 'longhairs' [*kaminaga*]; and temples, 'incense burners' [*koritaki*], etc. Outwardly the deity is estranged from the Dharma, but inwardly it profoundly supports the Three Jewels. Thus, Japanese Buddhism is under the special protection of the deity of the Great Shrine (Watanabe 1966: 59; Morrell 1985: 72–73).

So much for an explanation of an apparent anti-Buddhist theme in the rituals at Ise; but the quotation above contains some oddities. 'In antiquity, when this country did not yet exist, the deity of the Great Shrine, guided by a seal [*mudrā*] of Mahāvairocana inscribed on the ocean floor, thrust down the august spear.' This is a classic example of how Buddhists managed quietly to rewrite the myths as presented in the early chronicles. It is admittedly rather difficult to explain the gross error here – was it not common knowledge that the spear was thrust down by Izanami and Izanagi, not their offspring? – but the important element is the tantric seal lying on the bottom of the sea, placed there by Mahāvairocana as a guide. This is entirely a medieval invention.

16.3 Watarai Shintō

What of the second ideological movement? It may come as a surprise to discover the term 'Shintō' appearing so late in this book and some explanation for this decision is probably due. Up to this point non-Buddhist elements have been identified either as '*jingi* worship' or just 'local cults'. The official term was always *jingi* and the term 'Shintō' does not occur very often in the sources: in fact between 720 and 1604 only 186 occurrences of the word have been found, just over twenty examples per century (Teeuwen 2002). It appears four times in *Nihon shoki*, never in *Kojiki*, once in the lengthy *Shoku Nihongi*, and only sporadically thereafter. In this early period it is often used in contrast to the Buddhist Dharma (*buppō* 佛法) signifying 'the realm of the local deities/cults'. A classic case of the term being used in a derogatory sense can be found in the early Heian description of a *jingūji*, *Ise no kuni Tado jingūji garan engi narabi ni shizaichō* 伊勢國多度神宮寺伽藍緣起並資材帳, where the kami of Tado admits that because of kalpas of sinful karma he has received retribution in the form of being born in the realm of the gods (受神道報). One might say, therefore, that it is a Buddhist term for the local cults, borrowed from its usage in such Chinese texts as the *Biographies of eminent monks*, with the term 道 being used as it appears in *rokudō* 六道, in a Buddhist sense. If the word had slightly negative connotations, this would explain why it is not found in official contexts.

Use of the term 'Shintō', therefore, has been held back until now (1280–1320), because it is only at this point that one encounters the beginnings of a self-conscious discourse. A tradition that had been almost entirely based on ritual now found it politic to develop a textual basis, an intellectual justification which would help it claim equality with (and eventually supremacy over) Buddhism. Such a development does not, of course, come out of the blue, but there is very little in the way of texts between the late twelfth-century *Nakatomi harae kunge* and the first products of what is now known as Ise or Watarai Shintō 度會神道. The significance of the 'discovery' that Mahāvairocana and Tenshō Daijin were one and same deity had tremendous importance for the shrines at Ise, of course. It meant that the gods were not simply the traces of a Buddhist original but were original in themselves, and from there it was not going to be a large step to reversing the equation. But one of the difficulties we have in tracing how this came about is the awkward fact that many of the prime movers were Buddhist priests; there is also considerable evidence to suggest that not only were Buddhist works studied at Ise but shrine priests prided themselves on keeping the precepts. Many of them, of course, retired to temples and monasteries. Much work remains to be done before the picture becomes clearer (Bodiford 1998).

As it turned out, however, the reassertion of the native tradition, when it did come, started as an internal squabble between the Outer and Inner Shrines (Teeuwen 1996). In the drive for self-preservation, each shrine needed a secure independent base of funding and this inevitably led them into economic competition with each other. The Outer Shrine, which had up to that point been considered the subordinate partner, laboured under a major handicap: neither the shrine itself nor its main deity, Toyouke 豐受, was mentioned in *Nihon shoki* and, although both deity and shrine are mentioned in later sources such as the *Toyouke no miya gishikichō* 豐受宮儀式帳 of 804 and *Procedures of the Engi era* of 927, they were seen as having little or no pedigree. In order to prove that they were at least the equal of the Inner Shrine, the priests of the Watarai house began to produce a series of sacred texts during the course of the thirteenth century that set out to rewrite history, reverse the order of precedence, and prove that the Outer Shrine was rightfully the dominant member of the pair. They also contain new traditions about the origin of Japan and its monarchy. The best-known of these texts were: *Hōki hongi* 寶基本記, *Yamatohime no mikoto seiki* 倭姫命世記, *Gochinza denki* 御鎮座傳記, *Gochinza hongi* 御鎮座本紀, *Gochinza shidaiki* 御鎮座次第記 and *Jingi fuden zuki* 神祇譜傳圖記. The first five of these were later singled out for special attention by Yamazaki Ansai 山崎闇斎 (1618–82), but there are many more that have yet to be studied in any detail.

The *Gishikichō* of 804 describes how Tenshō Daijin asked that Toyouke, the deity who was in charge of food (*mike* 御饌), be moved from Mt Hiji in Tanba to serve at Ise, and this event was generally accepted to be the origin of the Outer Shrine. Then Toyouke was gradually provided with a new identity, becoming identified with Uka no mitama 倉稲魂, a food deity who does appear in *Nihon shoki* as a child of Izanami and Izanagi and could therefore be seen to be the equal of Tenshō Daijin (Teeuwen 1996: 39–40). It then became associated with the discovery and use of fresh water for sustaining life. When Tsūkai visited in 1286 he reported that the Inner Shrine was related to fire and the Outer to water, and *Gochinza denki* has:

Izanagi and Izanami . . . first gave birth to the eight great islands [of Japan], next to the deity of the sea, next to the deity of the wind, and so forth; later, although ten thousand years had passed, the working of water still had not appeared, and the world was famished. Then the two deities . . . offered the beautiful Yakasa Jewels to the Nine Halls, thus producing a deity called Toyouke Kōdaijin. By way of a thousand changes and ten thousand transformations, [this deity] received the working of water (*suitoku* 水德) and brought forth the knowledge to maintain life. There it is called Mike-tsu-kami (Teeuwen 1996: 42–43).

The next passage goes on to make the bold claim that an alternative name for Toyouke was Ame no Minakanushi 天御中主. This sleight of hand is in fact a gross contradiction because it serves to raise Toyouke above the parents. Amenominakanushi occurs only twice in the early chronicles, but in the most exalted position of all: in *Kojiki* it is the very first deity to be mentioned, and in *Nihon shoki* it is listed once, very briefly, in a variant passage at the beginning. In this way Toyouke is shown to be the first of all deities and the closest Japanese culture has to a progenitor. This then allowed the Outer

Shrine to claim that Toyouke had always acted in conjunction with Tenshō Daijin and that they were equals at the very least. As a passage in *Yamatohime no mikoto seiki* put it:

The Two Imperial Great Shrines of Ise are [the dwelling of] the gods honoured by Izanami and Izanagi, the gods of the mausolea of the ancestors and the shrines of the state (*sōbyō shashoku* 宗廟社稷). They are the ancestors of all gods, the progenitors of the Hundred Kings. They are the One and Highest. All the other gods are their children and their servants. Who would dare resist them? (Ōsumi 1977: 31; Teeuwen 1996: 62, adapted).

Of the two 'Chinese' terms being used here, *sōbyō* refers to the Inner Shrine as the ancestral shrine and *shashoku* to the Outer Shrine dedicated to the gods of land and food. The rivalry between the two shrines broke out in earnest in 1296–97 when the Outer Shrine first dared to use the term 'sovereign deity' (*kōdaijin* 皇大神) about Toyouke in a letter to the court. This then led to legal action brought by the Inner Shrine, which naturally wished to guard its special status. Neither side seems to have won the legal argument, but the most important outcome of the disagreement was the emergence of the texts we have just mentioned, which claimed to be of great antiquity but were in fact written by members of the Watarai house.

16.4   New myths of origin

If the native tradition was beginning to flex its muscles and claim supremacy, what, one might well ask, was it going to do about doctrine? It was never going to be possible for Shintō to produce a doctrine to rival that of Buddhism. For one thing, it lacked the vocabulary. It is more fruitful to think of the native equivalent of doctrine – we might call it 'Shintō theory' – as being a new discourse of origins, mirrored in the explosion of interest in stories about the founding of temples, shrines, sacred sites and indeed Japan itself. But this should not be taken to mean that Shintō theorists shied away from doctrine altogether. They concentrated on the concept of purity, gradually transforming it into something much closer to a morality. Take, for example, the following text that is often seen as central to medieval Shintō. It comes in the form of an oracle:

The mind-god is the fundamental basis of heaven and earth. The body is a transformation of the Five Elements. You must therefore make the origin the origin, and rest in the original beginning; you must make the basis the basis, and depend upon your basic mind (*honshin*). To receive divine beneficence, you must give priority to prayer; to obtain protection, you must make uprightness the basis. If you respect heaven and serve the earth, revere the gods and honour the ancestors, the Ancestral Temple [*sōbyō*] will never cease to sustain the sovereign's reign. Furthermore, you must cover your breath concerning the Buddhist Dharma and worship the gods. The sun and the moon circulate the four continents and illuminate the earth, but they will [especially] shed their light on the upright (Ōsumi 1977: 30; Teeuwen 1996: 101).[2]

Ransacking both Buddhism and Chinese Yin-Yang discourse to transform their own vocabulary, Shintō ideologues tried to create a metaphysics of the base, origin, uprightness and purity, which may well have been influenced by ideas stemming from Tendai *hongaku*. Certainly they share the same interests in treating the here-and-now as sacred, returning to the origin, and nullifying the effects of history by proclaiming the reality of an eternal present. But it is instructive to see that even here they found it impossible to break away from a concern with sovereignty; the argument inevitably drifts back to matters of lineage. In this sense, Shintō was tied to political realities from its inception and always found it difficult to escape into something of more universal significance, without the aid of Buddhism.

It is in the context of the development of a metaphysics that the question of how the compound 神道 was actually pronounced becomes of interest. It is possible that until the late fourteenth century the word was pronounced '*jindō*' rather than '*shintō*', and that the shift to '*shintō*' mirrors the new obsession with origins and purity of intent. A passage from a somewhat later text, lectures on *Nihon shoki* by the monk Ryōhen 良遍 dated 1419, reads:

On the term 神道: we do not read this *jindō* but *shintō*, with purity (*sumute* 清ムテ). This signifies straightforwardness (*sugu naru gi*). And straightforwardness means 'just as it is' (*ari no mama*). So the shrines at Ise manifest the deep significance of Shintō by not cutting the reeds or brushwood [on the roofs], not shaving the rafters, not adorning boats or carts, and not wearing patterned clothes. And another text says: do not play flutes or drums, and do not deal in bright colours; which means that at Ise they do not cut the ends of the reeds, they lay rafters of unshaven wood, and they do not play sacred music with either flute or drum (Tamura and Sueki 1990: 517; Teeuwen 2002: 242).

There is an interesting use of linguistic terminology here. The word *jindō* displays voicing on both syllables and the Japanese word for 'voicing' is *nigoru*, which also means 'to muddy'. To devoice from *jindō* to *shintō* is

[2] Note that the phrase 'cover your breath concerning the Buddhist Dharma' (*buppō no iki o kakushite* 佛法ノ息ヲ屛シテ) is ambiguous. Here it is likely to mean 'show utmost respect to', but in the Edo period it was interpreted to mean the exact opposite: 'do not mention'.

therefore to purify, precisely the metaphor that governed Shintō discourse from now on. Whether this was a new reading of the term or not, however, is difficult to fathom from one isolated example. Ryōhen may simply have been explaining a fact rather than proposing something radical.[3]

'Returning to the origin' also involved a more literal revisitation of the earliest Japanese sources. There were, of course, many reasons for this desire to rewrite the past in order to redefine the present, and the drive by the priests of the Outer Shrine to reverse the order of precedence at Ise is but one of what turned out to be an outpouring of origin tales of shrines and temples throughout Japan. Certainly, Watarai priests were only one of many groups interesting in performing radical surgery on the oldest of sources. Not only was the logic behind *Nihon shoki* now quite alien, being so much a product of its own time, but newer gods were needed. Invention in the guise of rectification was again the order of the day as the records were subjected to an imaginative re-reading. It will be recalled that *Kojiki* itself had, to all intents and purposes, disappeared. No tradition of its decipherment had ever been instituted and it had lain largely untouched and unstudied; this was a condition that was to last a long time, until the rise of a radical native philological movement in the seventeenth century. *Nihon shoki*, on the other hand, could boast an almost continuous tradition of reading and commentary, a tradition that had been kept alive by the Urabe 卜部 family and which culminated in *Shaku Nihongi* 釋日本紀 produced by Urabe Kanefumi 兼文 and his son Kanekata 兼方 some time between 1275 and 1300. Kanekata also produced his own *Nihon shoki: jindai no maki* 神代巻 of roughly the same date. These works are not straightforward commentaries. Concentrating almost entirely on the 'Age of the gods', they often invent their own versions of events and feel little compunction in usurping the role of the original: not a difficult procedure when the text itself was, if not exactly secret, then not widely disseminated.

Take, for example, myths that deal with the origin of the universe. What stands out here is the central role given to two deities, Amenominakanushi and Kunitokotachi. In *Nihon shoki* these names, redolent of centrality on the one hand and foundations on the other, are just that, names, and they disappear from the rest of the chronicle. But in the medieval tradition they emerge from obscurity to play major roles. The rather vague statements at the

---

[3]   Another example of the reading *jindō* can be found in tale 7.3 in the early twelfth-century *Konjaku monogatarishū* (Yamada Yoshio et al. 1959–63, vol. II: 124). The editors state that their *furigana* readings were chosen to reflect late Heian pronunciation as far as possible, but the whole question calls for further investigation.

beginning of *Nihon shoki* were clearly unsatisfactory in a Japan that had fully absorbed tantric Buddhism and the concept of Mahāvairocana. There was a strongly felt need for a more coherent narrative with an identifiable figure standing at the origin. Even so, one searches for a core story in vain; it was as if everyone felt free to invent his or her own version. The opening section of the collection of tales entitled *Kokon chomonjū* 古今著聞集, compiled by Tachibana Narisue 橘成季 in 1254, is a fairly straightforward paraphrase of the beginning of *Nihon shoki*:

Before heaven and earth were divided, [the cosmos] was like a congealed egg. The clear parts floated up to form heaven and the murky parts sank and stagnated to form earth. Then something appeared between heaven and earth, the shape of a reed shoot (*ashikabi* 葦牙). It then transformed into a deity. This was Kunitokotachi no mikoto 國常立尊. In the intervening period there have been seven generations of heavenly deities and five generations of earthly deities. The age of man began with Jinmu Tennō, the son of the deity Hikonagisa takeugayafuki awasezu. It was in his reign, in the ninth month of the twenty-eighth year, that all the deities were first honoured (Nagazumi et al. 1966: 49).

But turn to *Yamato katsuragi hōzanki* 大和葛城寶山記 and we get an entirely different tale:

It is said that the creation of heaven and earth involved water vapour changing and becoming heaven and earth. The winds of the ten directions blew against each other and protected the waters. And on the waters a deity was born with a thousand heads and two thousand hands and feet. It was called the Spirit King of Eternal Compassion (Jōjūjihishinnō 常住慈悲神王) and also Viṣṇu (違細). From the navel of this deity in human form sprang a golden Lotus of the Marvellous Dharma with a thousand petals. Its light was exceeding bright as if shining like ten thousand moons. Within the flower a deity in human form sat in the Lotus position. His gaze was immeasurably bright and he was called Brahmā. From his heart came eight children and from them were born the people of heaven and earth. They were called heavenly deities or the ancestor gods of the monarch of heaven (Yamamoto 1998: 36–37).

Later on in this text, we find this Spirit King being identified with Ameno-minakanushi/Toyouke. The reference to Indic deities here may be thought curious but should not come as too much of a surprise since, as we have seen before, Buddhism had absorbed many such a deity as *gohō zenjin*. This passage is in fact borrowed from a collection of tales entitled *A miscellany of metaphors and examples* (*Zōhiyu kyō* 雜譬喩經, *T*. 204).

As far as the creation of earth itself is concerned, we also find a series of rewritings that usually incorporate tantric Buddhist elements and begin to interpret *Nihon shoki* passages in ways that make the underlying symbolism explicit. Mujū, it will be remembered, described a *mudrā* lying on the ocean floor. This crops up again in a text called *Jingi hishō* 神祇秘抄:

> The two deities Izanagi and Izanami opened up Mt Sumeru and looked into the sea below but there was neither land nor island. So they thrust down the 'reversed spear of Heaven' (*ame no sakahoko*) and stirred and searched. The drips from the spear hardened and became an island, and the five characters *A-bi-ra-un-ken* appeared. Then a strange wind arose and the 'five-cornered island' was created. This was Awajishima. And many deities lived there (Yamamoto 1998: 87).

Since the *mudrā* is Mahāvairocana's own seal, not only is the land sacred from the very beginning but they are searching for something already present, finding it rather than creating it. In *Nihon shoki*, the island, called Onogorojima, becomes itself the 'pillar of heaven', but in the early Heian text *Sendai kujihongi* the spear becomes the pillar, the centre of the world, and it is this version that becomes commonly used in the thirteenth century. By the time we reach the fourteenth century, the spear has become a *vajra* (*kongōshō* 金剛杵) dipping into a sea that is shaped like an eight-leaved lotus flower (Yamamoto 1998: 97).

16.5   The literal reading of metaphor

As the graphic image of a spear dipping into the centre of the lotus lying at the heart of the Womb World maṇḍala suggests, origins (or rebirths for the Buddhist) have to do with procreation and sex. In the orthodox tantric tradition it was taken for granted that the kind of language used in these contexts was by its very nature metaphorical, but it was also recognised that language was a slippery beast and that there was an ever-present danger that such phrases as 'passions are enlightenment' could easily be taken literally. It is about this time that we find the emergence of a heterodox tradition, now known as Tachikawa ryū 立川流, that is supposed to have taken the message literally and equated sexual bliss with the achievement of buddhahood in this very body (*sokushin jōbutsu*). The history of this tradition is obscure, partly because of the secrecy that surrounded it, and partly because in the 1470s it was proscribed and many of its texts destroyed. Most of our knowledge comes from two treatises which were written to counteract its influence and so should be treated with considerable caution: Shinjō's 心定 *On receiving the Dharma with circumspection* (*Juhō yōjinshū* 受法用心集) of 1272 and the later *Jewelled mirror* (*Hōkyōshō* 寶鏡鈔) of 1375, written by Yūkai 宥快

(1345–1416).[4] In fact, very little is known about Tachikawa except that heterodox tantric practices certainly existed in Japan and that the texts that do survive show yet again a willingness to link tantric Buddhist explanations to Shintō myths of origin.

There is a question as to the provenance of this tradition. Shinjō's work, in particular, contains a graphic and detailed explanation of a Skull Ritual involving necromancy and the use of sexual fluids of both male and female which is much more explicit than even the more advanced Indo-Tibetan tantras, but the *Hevajratantra*, to give just one example, was translated into Chinese at a fairly late date (1054–55), and even then in a somewhat bowdlerised form. It is entirely possible that some of these works were sent back to Japan by Jōjin in 1073, or perhaps came with other monks at a later stage, but there is no proof (Bowring 1992a). Perhaps these practices had been common at court throughout the late Heian period and had been kept so secret that there is no record of them. All that can really be said is that they seem to break surface in the thirteenth century. Mujū Ichien, who has been quoted more than once in this chapter, was moved to complain about these 'strange aberrations' in 1280. The fact that this tradition received at least semi-public recognition at this juncture may well be related to the emergence of a discourse of origins that was both tantric and revolved around Ise.

The first text to show clear influence of heterodox ideas is in fact a literary commentary. A substantial number of courtiers were both poets and Buddhist priests and a large of number of them had an intimate knowledge of tantrism. Since it is in the very nature of tantric thought to discover connections hidden beneath the surface, it is perhaps not surprising that the culture of secrets and initiations would have held a particular attraction. The habit of collecting mysteries was not, of course, unconnected to economics; but that is not to say that everyone was doing this simply for financial gain. Two literary works, in particular, lay themselves open to this form of interpretation: the tenth-century *Tales of Ise* (*Ise monogatari* 伊勢物語) and *Collection ancient and modern* (*Kokinshū* 古今集), although it was probably the first of these that set the ball rolling. *Tales of Ise* had been a problematic text from at least the mid-Heian period. It consists of a series of discrete sections, each one involving a poem or set of poems with a prose context. There appears to be only a minimal attempt to link these sections together, but the need to discover a coherent principle in the text was present from quite early on.

[4] For *Juhō yōjinshū* see Sanford 1991a. *Hōkyōshō* is translated in Vanden Broucke 1992. Faure 1998: 126ff and 2000 deals mainly with later manifestations of this tradition.

Various strategies of reading were employed, the main one being to see the work as a poetic biography of the politically marginal but culturally central court figure of Ariwara no Narihira 有原業平 (825–80), a reading that was already common by the early eleventh century. A second, more troublesome, problem, however, was the title. Apart from the fact that one short section dealt with Narihira's illicit liaison with the priestess of the Ise shrines, it was not at all obvious to what the title referred. In the context of the kind of discourse described above, a tantric, explicitly sexual, interpretation was generated. Given that the two shrines at Ise were by now firmly identified with the two main Shingon maṇḍala, 'I' 伊 was marked as the female principle and 'Se' 勢 as the male principle, and the title was explained as an oblique reference to the union of sexual opposites. The subject matter of *Tales of Ise* was therefore the power of poetic language in the context of the erotic.[5] A poetic treatise of the early thirteenth century, *Waka chikenshū* 和歌智顯集, explains it as follows:

Narihira is the bodhisattva known as Batō Kannon 馬頭觀音, the bodhisattva of song and dance in paradise . . . Seeing the plight of humanity in the world . . . he eventually brought comfort to 3,733 women. He kept records of his activities, writing down what had happened to him in order to proclaim the meaning of the erotic for later generations.

The bird inquires: I am greatly puzzled by this explanation. The scriptures say that to approach a female is the ultimate karmic act, thus all Buddhas warn about this in particular, called it either 'fixing the mind on boundless kalpas' or 'one cause leading to five hundred births'. What kind of bodhisattva is it who tries to encourage escape from suffering by urging people to take the path of which others have made such dire warnings? This is strange indeed.

The wind replies: If people are of one accord, the way to become a Buddha is indeed to practice the austerities of the six perfections, to offer up prayers, to honour and succor one's parents and superiors, and thus to achieve immediate rebirth in paradise; but people are by nature many and various and find it difficult to believe in Buddhist precepts to the exclusion of all else. Since they do not believe, they are fated to wander in the dark for generations. It is for this reason that the Buddhas have divided into myriad forms and encourage escape from suffering by adapting to human propensities. The bodhisattva in question is not, of course, insisting that we all cast aside the practice of austerities and enter instead upon this particular path; it is rather that, since we now live in degenerate times, in the Latter Days of the Dharma, humanity has become bored with good intentions and prefers evil ways – so all now enter upon this way to the exclusion of all else.

The way is known as the 'Principle of Union between the Two Fluids, of Womb and Egg', and there are many who believe that it is an activity that, if one studies well

---

[5]   For more on this subject see Bowring 1992b and Klein 1997, 1998 and 2002.

and achieves awareness, will eventually lead to a state of buddhahood in this existence. Because people are constantly warned that this path is neither austerity nor good practice but simply the karmic act of eternal rebirth, many are confused; so it is that this bodhisattva came into this world to show people, to impart to others (if only a little) the true, deep significance of the act.

No phenomenon is divorced from the Union of the two Fluids, of Womb and Egg. If the male becomes heaven by carrying out the austerities of the womb, the female becomes earth by virtue of the diamond-hard body. Heaven and earth – the names differ but in fact it is the union of male and female. Though the earth holds the seeds of grasses and trees, not a single shoot will develop unless heaven bestows the blessing of rain and dew. Though the female holds the place of birth within her womb, there will be no humanity unless the male bestows the seeds of his essence. So the male should prepare to nurture rain and dew in the image of heaven and care for the female; and the female should, in the image of earth-woman, nurture the grass and trees and honour the heaven-male . . . this is why Narihira tried to encourage people towards enlightenment by treating this practice as the ultimate austerity (Bowring 1992b: 436–37).

It was secrets like this that were imparted at poetry initiation ceremonies (*waka kanjō* 和歌灌頂) that became common at court in the thirteenth century and that are associated with the figure of Fujiwara no Tameaki 爲顯 (*c.*1230– *c.*1300), grandson of the famous scholar Teika. They represent an amalgam of literary secrets with the tantric connotations of the term/place 'Ise' and show that the myths of origin that we have described in the previous section were well known and well used at court. This is made absolutely clear in a slightly later text, *Ise monogatari zuinō* 髓腦, that has been dated to about 1320. Here we find the sexual vocabulary of origins made even more explicit. An explanation of the pillow-word *chihayaburu* (usually written 風速振), that was commonly found in early poetry attached to the word '*kami*' but whose meaning was in fact unclear, shows how the interpretation of poetry was intimately linked to the new role that Shintō was beginning to claim. By dint of some imaginative use of characters and by equating the lotus with female genitalia, the secret meaning behind an obscure word could be related to Shintō metaphysics.

The phrase *chihayaburu* 千葉破 means 'emerging from the womb', it refers to the process by which the soul, having been conceived in human form, is born. The form of the five viscera and six entrails of the mother closely resemble petals of the lotus flower. Conceived in the lotus, when born in the tenth month, the child emerges by tearing 破る those thousand-petaled 千葉 membranes . . . A person's *tama* is referred to as a '*kami*'. The word '*kami*' does not refer to something awe-inspiring outside of ourselves. It is said that [the *kami* are] the karmic link of the Buddhist divinities dimming their splendour and mingling with the dust of this world (和光同塵); when [the *kami*] is in a state of no-aspect and no-mind (*musō munen* 無相無念) and has no body or thought, it is a buddha. The *kami* is a buddha who mingles its light with the dust in order to guide people. Your psyche is called a buddha when it is in the midst of the sky-void because it had neither body or consciousness to acknowledge anything. It is called a *kami* when it becomes a human being in order to guide other people (Klein 1998: 29–30, adapted).[6]

This was not the only link between poetry and the religious tradition. At times they were almost treated as one and the same thing. The 5-7-5-7-7 form of the *waka* was seen as something divinely inspired and it was known that the earliest example, which significantly had to do with producing sacred space and enclosing a loved one, was recorded in *Kojiki* as having been produced by the god of Izumo, Susano-o. Ki no Tsurayuki in his preface to *Kokinshū* of 905 had proclaimed that *waka* had the divine ability to calm the human spirit. Now, with the spread of tantric thought, there was much reference to *waka* being the dhāraṇī of Japan. The five phrases were related to the five-syllable *mudrā* of Dainichi, *A-bi-ra-un-ken*, and arguments were found to prove that the act of producing a poem was tantamount to producing a buddha: a *waka* had thirty-one syllables plus the meaning, which corresponded to the thirty-two aspects of a Tathāgata (Bowring 1992b: 439–46).

---

[6]   See Sanford 1997 for an important introduction to the more medical aspects of what he terms 'fetal Buddhahood in Shingon'.

17   Taking stock

17.1   Buddhist historiography

The period from the second Mongol invasion of 1281 to the fall of the Kamakura Bakufu in 1333 was not a stable one at either Kamakura or Kyōto. Signs of lawlessness were everywhere and constant interference by Kamakura in matters of succession meant that the court was unable to settle down. Indeed, from the time of Go-Saga 後嵯峨 (r. 1242–45) the succession had switched back and forward between the families of his two sons, giving rise to two rival groups, one known as the Daikakuji faction 大覺寺統 and the other, the Jimyōin faction 持明院統. This situation lasted until the accession of Go-Daigo 後醍醐 in 1318. Taking advantage of a period of disunity in Kamakura, Go-Daigo made a move to restore full power to the sovereign's line. He failed, of course, and in the process opened the way for the rise of the next military family, the Ashikaga. His eventual flight to Yoshino in 1336 led to the setting up of two rival courts; sporadic fighting continued for the rest of the century.

Monks at the main Tendai and Shingon centres – Enryakuji, Kōfukuji, Tōdaiji, Tōji – and the temples more closely tied to the sovereign such as Daigoji and Ninnaji, continued to be involved in matters political and indeed military. But if one can speak for Buddhism as an institution in general, it was a period of consolidation. No new tradition emerged from the continent and nothing radically new developed in Japan either. There was certainly a need to take stock, and it is at this juncture that we encounter the first histories in Japan to deal with matters from a largely religious perspective. These scholar-monks, however, were not interested in the role that Buddhism as a whole had played in Japanese history to date; their interests were more parochial. They were chiefly concerned with matters of lineage and genealogy. There was a recognition that the kind of Pure Land Buddhism that had developed within Japan and the various forms of Zen that had been newly imported from the continent were not going to go away; it was time to incorporate them into the general picture.

The problem was that the Buddhist historian is not particularly well equipped to deal with innovation and change. Since all expressions of legitimacy involve proof of a genealogy leading from Śākyamuni to the present, change can only be dealt with in terms of heuristic devices (*hōben*): the explanation of a new doctrine has to be that different audiences of differing capabilities call for different kinds of message. This can be documented, of course, but to do this well one needs an interest in the social and political environment that generates the need for change, and this interest was conspicuous by its absence. There is also a natural tension between providing legitimation in the form of a clear line back to the beginnings and acknowledging the role of certain individuals in the continuation of this link. Does one extol the 'eminent monk' as a prime mover or should he be treated as little more than an empty vessel through which the tradition and the doctrine perpetuated itself? One notices at this time a tendency to go for the latter option, an inevitable consequence of placing such weight on transmission. It was possible to argue, for example, that neither Saichō nor Kūkai was the first to introduce his respective doctrine, which would lead to a downgrading of their role. In the case of Kūkai this even generated a story that Śubhakarasiṃha himself had come to Japan to propagate Shingon.

The outstanding scholar of his generation was the Tōdaiji monk Gyōnen 凝然 (1240–1321), who achieved the unprecedented accolade of receiving the title 'national master' (*kokushi* 國師) during his lifetime. Today he is best known for one of his earliest works, the short introduction to Japanese Buddhist teachings known as *Essentials of the eight traditions* (*Hasshū kōyō* 八宗綱要) of 1268, which is still used today; but he was a prolific writer and had a wide range. Given the bodhisattva precepts on Hieizan at the age of sixteen, he left soon afterwards and moved to Tōdaiji where we find him being ordained again as a novice in the newly restored Kaidan'in 戒壇院, taking the full 250 precepts in 1259. He then started a life of scholarship, which culminated with the abbotship of the Kaidan'in, a post that he held from 1277 until his death in 1321. Given this position, it is not surprising that he was closely involved in the renewal of interest in and scholarship of the *vinaya*, a concern that was shared by many of his contemporaries such as Eison. Although just one of many, the work that stands out in this context is the comprehensive *Bonmō kaihon sho nichijushō* 梵網戒本疏日珠鈔 (1318), an extensive subcommentary on Fazang's interpretation of the bodhisattva precepts. Fazang was in fact one of his permanent interests and formed the basis of another monument to scholarship, the *Mirror revealing the meaning of the Dharma world according to Kegon* (*Kegon hokkai gikyō* 華嚴法界

義鏡) of 1295, which proved to be by far the most sophisticated treatment of Kegon doctrine to date.[1]

The *Essentials of the eight traditions* presents a short account of the development of Buddhism in India, China and Japan and then launches into a highly compressed exposition of Buddhist teaching, divided into what was generally accepted to be the eight major doctrinal traditions: Kusha, Jōjitsu, Ritsu, Hossō, Sanron, Tendai, Kegon and Shingon. It is even-handed in that Gyōnen refused to express a preference for one doctrine over another, but this was very much in the nature of scholarship at Tōdaiji. The temple and its precincts had by this time fully recovered from the disasters of 1180 and regained its reputation as an important centre for Buddhist scholarship where all subjects could be studied. As already pointed out, these eight traditions (八宗) were not so much schools or sects but academic subjects of study such as Hossō phenomenology or Kegon philosophy, and it was common for monks to remain 'non-denominational' for many years and to study a number of them at different institutions. These subjects all had their genealogies and were seen as complementary. Indeed, this was precisely the point Jōkei had made much earlier when he attacked Hōnen for his tendency to exclusivism. By the same token, however, the number 'eight' had by this time become fixed in the institutional mind as the agreed number of acceptable traditions in Japan and any inflation of this figure was bound to cause dissent. When first Pure Land Buddhism and then Zen emerged, a challenge to their legitimacy was to be expected on these grounds alone. By Gyōnen's time, however, it was impossible to deny their right to exist. In *Essentials*, he fudged the matter and simple added them somewhat perfunctorily at the end almost as an afterthought, but it was obvious that this was an unsatisfactory stopgap and he eventually produced something far more substantial, particularly as regards Pure Land beliefs.

On the origin and development of Pure Land doctrine (*Jōdo hōmon genrushō* 淨土法門源流章) of 1311 was a sympathetic history of Pure Land's origin and development. It pins its colours to the mast right at the beginning:

The Pure Land teachings originate in the distant past. It was at Rājagṛha where a special meeting was held concerning the wondrous Pure Land [doctrine]. In the grove of Jetavana, the Buddhas expressed their approval by [extending] their tongues in affirmation. With the translation of the *Jingtu-lun* 淨土論 [knowledge of] the twenty-nine adornments [of the Pure Land] began to spread to China 神州, and the commentarial tradition was then transmitted to Japan 日域.

---

[1] For discussion of Gyōnen's significance vis-à-vis Kegon see Girard 1990: 60–67.

The [doctrine of the] Forty-eight Vows has been widely acclaimed. From its origin it has spread far and wide over long distances, its roots deep and its branches thick. Now I will give a summary, presenting its origin and development, here roughly and there minutely, describing the large and small branches. I will delineate names and meanings, illustrating themes and their conclusions (Blum 2002:145–46, adapted).

Gyōnen starts by describing the various Pure Land sūtras and their Chinese versions. He then discusses the development of Pure Land ideas from India, through China and into Japan, the first part ending with the advent of Hōnen. His aim is clearly to provide scholarly justification for treating Pure Land as a legitimate tradition, and in this sense it can be seen as a long-distance response to Jōkei's concerns from the viewpoint of an impartial scholar. Hōnen, of course, had defended himself vigorously. Having placed Hōnen firmly in a doctrinal lineage, Gyōnen then goes on to analyse the doctrinal disagreements that emerged among his followers. He was obviously fascinated by such differences, although he is again scrupulous in not voicing a preference. He structured his presentation on the major doctrinal positions: whether, for example, practice of the *nenbutsu* should be constant or whether a single correct instant was enough to secure rebirth in the Pure Land. It is in fact because of his account that we know as much as we do about the kind of arguments that developed in the century after Hōnen's death. There are some interesting lacunae, however. Neither Shinran nor Ippen is mentioned, for example, perhaps because their denial of the legitimacy of the saṅgha was a step too far.

Another one of Gyōnen's many works is *A history of the transmission of Buddhism through the three lands* (*Sangoku buppō denzū engi* 三國佛法傳通緣起) of 1311. Yet again, the picture concentrates on doctrine and lineage, and avoids almost all mention of social and political conflict. As the term 'three lands' suggests, he ignored all the spaces in between, such as Central Asia and Korea, and was mainly concerned to ratify the position of Japan as the equal of India and China. Not surprisingly, despite his intellectual interest in Pure Land teachings, the concept of *mappō* held no legitimacy for him. Providing a secure genealogy back through China to India was vital for each tradition, but the movement of Buddhism to the east had a purpose: Japan was now the home of these traditions and it was the duty of scholars such as himself to keep them all alive and in good health. There is a sense of confidence here that found the idea of *mappō* inconvenient and even a little distasteful.

One possibly unintended consequence of concentrating on specific traditions was to encourage the process by which each 'approach' (宗) slowly transformed itself into a distinct school, something that finally happened only in the Edo period. For this reason, it may indeed be a little misleading to entitle this section 'Buddhist historiography' because it suggests that 'Buddhism' was a recognisable concept at this time, which is open to doubt. Or perhaps it would be fairer to say that the way a scholar-historian such as Gyōnen approached his subject tended to isolate traditions from one another and thereby caused the particular to loom much larger than the whole. This is a phenomenon that was recognised by the Zen monk Kokan Shiren (1278–1346), who tried to counteract it in his *History of the Śākyamuni [tradition, written in] the Genkō era* (*Genkō shakusho*), that appeared in 1332, the year after Gyōnen's death. *Genkō shakusho* is in three unequal parts: biographies (*den* 傳), annals (*hyō* 表) and miscellaneous accounts (*shi* 志). The first two of these, at least, explore entirely different ways of presenting the past (Bielefeldt 1997). The annals give a chronological account of important events in the development of Buddhism in Japan from 538 to 1221, although not without some bias towards Zen near the end. The biographies follow the usual division into ten sections that one finds in the series of three Chinese 'biographies of eminent monks' to which Kokan Shiren would have had access: monks were listed in groups, which were named after their chief claim to fame. But Shiren's titles were idiosyncratic: 'transmitting knowledge' (傳智), 'wisdom in exegesis' (慧解), 'purity in meditation' (淨禪), 'zeal in obtaining supernatural response' (感進), 'patience in observance' (忍行), 'illuminating the commandments of morality' (明戒), 'fostering charity' (檀興), 'accommodations of skilfulness' (方應), 'vigour in journeying' (力遊) and 'miscellanous vows' (願雜) (Ury 1970: 130).

Shiren was abbot of Tōfukuji and a Zen scholar of major repute. The underlying message of this work – that the Zen tradition was in fact the oldest and should rank above all others – is clear from the very beginning, since he begins his account boldly with a biography of Bodhidharma. But he chose not to follow Gyōnen down the road of emphasising the separateness of traditions by designing his work along quite different lines. By taking as his framework the Chinese example and so reverting to the biographical mode, he managed to suggest the possibility of rising above sectarian differences and treating Buddhism as an entity, even while continuing to extol the role of Zen in particular. The difference between this approach and Gyōnen's obsession with doctrine could hardly be more striking.

17.2   Metropolitan Zen

The previous discussion of Zen masters and their relationship with the Hōjō regents in Kamakura (§14.3) led up to Wuxue Zuyuan (1226–86), who served Hōjō Tokimune. Within two years of his arrival, the Mongols had launched their second attempt at invasion and a new temple had been created at Kamakura dedicated to the memory of those who had died in the fighting. This was Engakuji 圓覺寺, where Wuxue was installed as founder abbot in 1282. Documents dated 1283 record that there were already one hundred monks, one hundred assistants, twenty attendants with ceremonial duties, four laundry workers and six assistants at the abbot's headquarters, but numbers were to rise rapidly in the early fourteenth century (Akamatsu and Yampolsky 1977: 325). Clearly, if this level of staffing and organisation could be arranged from the beginning, Zen was now firmly established in Japan. But it was still very much the preserve of the elite and successive regents encouraged the study of more than just religious texts. To patronise Zen was to patronise Chinese learning in general, with all that meant in terms of prestige. Zen monasteries flourished as a result, but at the same time, they themselves had to submit to increasing supervision and strict regulation, for the Bakufu wished to avoid the growth of another Hieizan at all costs, a centre of spiritual and indeed military power that might one day come to threaten their own position of dominance. In 1303, for example, Hōjō Sadatoki was sufficiently concerned about the possibility of this occurrence that he banned assistants at Engakuji from carrying swords, and in 1327 Hōjō Takatoki (1303–33) created an office whose specific remit it was to handle disciplinary matters to do with monks and monasteries. The Ashikaga in their turn were to become equally concerned to control the power of the Zen monasteries they patronised. It was from about this time that the official system known as the 'five mountains' (*gozan* 五山) seems to have come into being, the first extant use of the word being in 1299, when the Jōchiji 淨智寺 in Kamakura was given this rank. The Gozan system itself was not properly established, however, until fifty years later under the Ashikaga, and it is at that point that it will be described in more detail.

By the beginning of the fourteenth century, therefore, Zen was firmly established as a religious foundation under the patronage of the masters in Kamakura, and it had become a matter of status for an important political figure to have a Zen master at his beck and call. Hōjō Sadatoki (1271–1311), for example, had Yishan Yining 一山一寧 (1247–1317), who seems to have arrived as a Mongol envoy in 1299. He was a trained scholar and, once installed, began to encourage the serious study of Chinese literature and painting, habits that eventually led to the kind of culture we normally associate with Zen temples. One of the tasks he gave aspiring monks, for example, was a test of their ability to compose Chinese poetry. The increasing flow of Chinese masters provided Kamakura with the trappings of high culture, the study and practice of Chinese literature and painting. It was this aspect too that encouraged the higher strata of warriors in the provinces to patronise their own monasteries (usually by the simple procedure of converting an existing institution to Zen by fiat), although Pure Land Buddhism and the Lotus movement still held sway with most warriors and peasants.

Zen as an institution proved to have strong enough roots to survive the fall of the Hōjō. If it had been too closely and exclusively linked to them, it would have died with the collapse of the Kamakura shogunate, but in fact it was just about to hit its stride. First Go-Daigo and then the Ashikaga shōguns were to patronise influential Zen monks and use them to full advantage. A key figure in this process was the monk Musō Soseki 夢窓疎石 (1275–1351) (Collcutt 1997). History has not been kind to Musō. He has usually been portrayed as an opportunist who did not really understand Zen and who insisted on sullying it with tantric and other ritual. After much early wandering he was ordained at Tōdaiji in 1292 under the guidance of the *vinaya* master Jikan. He then turned to Zen, studied at Kenninji, and began again the peripatetic lifestyle of a typical young Zen monk. He succeeded in passing the tests set all prospective students by Yishan Yining in Kamakura, but despite trying on two different occasions, failed to strike up the kind of relationship with this master that he felt was necessary, and he reverted to a life of wandering for ten years or more, becoming known for little more than his peripatetic and reclusive lifestyle. Eventually he came to the notice of Go-Daigo, who persuaded him to become abbot of Nanzenji in 1325. Like many Kyōto aristocrats, Go-Daigo's interest in Zen was closely linked to what it offered in terms of a window onto Chinese culture, and Musō's acknowledged expertise in this area may well have brought him to Go-Daigo's attention. But Musō's arrival in the capital caused a good deal of upset and he was subjected to withering criticism by the retired Hanazono and his protegé Shūhō Myōchō 宗峰妙超 (Daitō 大燈, 1282–1337). Two years later he was back in Kamakura, where he remained until the fall of the Hōjō in 1333. This then propelled him back to Kyōto and Nanzenji. After Go-Daigo fled the city, Musō came under the protection of Ashikaga Takauji and his younger brother Tadayoshi, who had particular regard for him and for whom he wrote a guide to Zen for the warrior layman *Dialogues in dreams* (*Muchū mondō* 夢中問答) in 1344. The rest of Musō's career was devoted to the building of Tenryūji 天龍寺 to the west of Kyōto, a Zen temple devoted to Go-Daigo's memory. Economic support was provided not only through grants of land but also via a new source of funds, earmarking the profits from trading missions to Yuan China. All this was achieved in the teeth of opposition from Enryakuji.

The first truly self-confident Japanese master, confident in the sense that he felt no need to go to China or indeed receive transmission from a Chinese master, Musō secured the future of Zen as a major national institution. Zen masters became important not only as cultural advisers but also in trade and finance, used by successive rulers in diplomacy and commerce. What they gained in prestige, however, they lost in freedom, subject as they were to increasing interference in every aspect of their administration. One Enryakuji and one Kōfukuji was clearly enough for any country. And it should not be forgotten that the Tendai authorities were constantly on their guard during this period, sniping at Zen temples whenever possible, at times with brute force, and jealously trying (and failing) to keep their pre-eminent role.

Musō's great rival was Daitō, the founder abbot of Daitokuji 大徳寺, who traced himself back through his teacher Nanpo Jōmyō 南浦紹明 to a different Chinese Zen tradition known as the Songyuan lineage 松源派. If Musō has been treated rather badly by history, seen unfairly as a politician rather than a monk, it may simply be because Daitō's lineage eventually became the dominant one in the Tokugawa period. Certainly Daitō has the reputation of having been the perfect monk, proof that it was no longer necessary to study in China to become a Zen master (Kraft 1992). His early study was with Kōhō Kennichi 高峰顯日 in Kamakura, where (his chroniclers tell us) he showed a precocious ability to handle the special language of Zen encounters between master and student. In 1304 he went to study in Kyōto with Jōmyō, who had studied in China for eight years. Working on several difficult *kōan* under his guidance, he achieved enlightenment and then spent some ten years in relative obscurity, studying and meditating. This period of seclusion only served to enhance his reputation, so that by 1319 he had been persuaded to become the abbot of a newly planned temple in the north of the city. In 1323 he had the first of many meetings with Hanazono and was then helped to found Daitokuji by not only Hanazono but also Go-Daigo. The Dharma Hall was finished in 1326 and the temple was officially opened in the winter of that year. He remained as abbot of this temple until his death in 1337. Daitō is known chiefly through his own writings and commentaries, and through later hagiographies. It is clear from the former, however, that he was unusually proficient in classical Chinese and developed a form of commentary known as 'capping phrases' (*agyō* 下語, *jakugo* 著語), a device whereby one showed one's understanding of a *kōan* or an exchange by producing a line or phrase (often taken from Chinese poetry) that encapsulated an insight and sparked insight in others. This method of teaching, Daitō made his own.

It is worth noting here that the Mongol intrusion into the north of China, its attacks on Japan, and its eventual conquest of the Southern Song in 1279, did very little to stop the movement of monks back and forth between Japan and China. In fact the number of monks travelling to study under Chinese Zen monks peaked in the first two decades of the fourteenth century. This is an interesting phenomenon that has yet to be studied in any depth. North China had been under the control of the Jurchen since the fall of Kaifeng in 1127 and not many Japanese are known to have ventured into what was then known as Chin 金 territory. Both Eisai and Dōgen travelled in the south and after them most Japanese concentrated on the area around the Southern Song capital of Hangzhou. The arrival of the Mongols in the north (they occupied the Chin capital of Yanjing 燕京 in 1265) did not change matters much, but one might have thought that when they occupied Hangzhou in 1276, such travel would have ceased. It is hardly surprising that travel tailed off during the turbulent period in the 1270s, but once the threat of an invasion had subsided the number of monks moving between Japan and China increased. This speaks volumes for the degree to which Buddhism was actively supported in Yuan Dynasty China. At court and in the north, of course, it was Tibetan Buddhism that held sway, particularly under the Imperial Preceptor 'Phags-pa (1235–80), but Chan Buddhism was also allowed to flourish. Japanese monks concentrated on the area around Hangzhou, intent on studying under the two major figures of Yuan Chan, Kulin Qingmo 古林清茂 (1261–1329) and Zhongfeng Mingben 中峰明本 (1263–1323) (Yü 1982).

17.3   Zen in the countryside

So much for the kind of Zen Buddhism that was patronised by warrior rulers and courtiers alike, with its pronounced Chinese flavour and its close ties to the centres of power. Turn to the countryside and the provinces, however, where Dōgen's Sōtō Zen monks had deliberately placed themselves to avoid such political interference, and we find the growing influence of an entirely different kind of Zen, drawing its inspiration from Chinese example, of course, but developing rituals and beliefs that incorporated much from the medieval spiritual environment just described. The most influential figure in Sōtō Zen after Dōgen was undoubtedly Keizan Jōkin (1264–1325), who became abbot of Daijōji in 1298 (§14.2). It is not known why Keizan left Daijōji but he did so in 1317, founding a monastery called Yōkōji 永光寺 at Hakui 羽咋 on the western coast of the Noto peninsula 能登半島, where his ability to raise money and gain patronage soon created one of the most powerful monasteries of the whole group. He is also known for his writings, two in particular: *A record of transmission of the flame* (*Denkōroku* 傳光錄) and *A record from Tōkoku* (*Tōkokki* 洞谷記). The first of these seems at first glance to be nothing more than a straightforward history of the transmission of enlightenment from Śākyamuni to Dōgen and Ejō in fifty-three chapters, but it is more than this. Each chapter begins with an encounter dialogue that, in many but not all cases, led the monk in question to realise enlightenment. This is followed by a discussion of the significance of the particular event or the relationship between master and student, a discussion that is often not easy to grasp. Each chapter finishes with a verse in Chinese that is supposed to encapsulate the point made. We do not know for certain, but it would seem to be a set of extended *kōan* that Keizan used for instruction (Cleary 1990).

A record from Tōkoku is autobiographical and deals in essence with the founding of Yōkōji. It is particularly valuable since it includes Keizan's dreams and has been used most effectively as the raw material for an investigation into the mental and spiritual life of a Zen monk of this time. What emerges from such a study is an extraordinarily rich picture, which shows us that religion in practice was far more interesting and far less coherent than in theory. It is not surprising that Tokugawa Sōtō apologists, who were busy creating their own vision of a 'pure' Dōgen-style Zen, accused Keizan of a betrayal of what Sōtō Zen was meant to be; but it was this rich mixture, of course, that allowed Sōtō Zen monasteries to prosper in the first place and reach out into all corners of the Japanese countryside.

Chan/Zen takes as its position the rejection of all imagination. But the universe in which Keizan lived was no less impregnated with the marvellous, structured by the imaginary than that of his contemporary Dante Alighieri. This contradiction is only one surface sign, one manifestation of a deep tension that we shall meet again and again. Keizan's Zen is, as we might expect, aporetic and therefore paradoxical: it is at the same time elitist and popular, idealistic and realistic, sudden and gradual (or, if you like, immediate and mediate), unlocalized and localized, obsessed with the idea of unity and besotted with multiplicity (Faure 1996: 8).

A Zen master was by definition enlightened, therefore a buddha, and so blessed with supranormal powers that stemmed from his mastery of meditation. This explains the ease with which Keizan can discuss his own past lives in such matter of fact terms:

As for me, it was in the past, at the time of the Buddha Vipaśyin, that I realized the fruit of Arhatship. I was living on the Himalayas, to the north of Mount Sumeru. At that time I was the deity of a Kuvala tree. With the head of a dog, the body of a kite, and the belly and tail of a serpent, I was a four-footed animal. Although I was only a humble tree deity, I nonetheless received the fruit [of Arhatship]. From that time on, I lived in the Himalayas, in the northern continent of Uttarakuru, with Suvinda, the fourth Arhat. This is why I am now reincarnated here [in the north of Japan]. Owing to my karmic affinities with the [northern] regions, I managed to be reborn as an *ujiko* of Hakusan . . . Since achieving the fruit of Arhatship, I have been reincarnated through five hundred existences in order to spread the Dharma and bring profit to all beings (Faure 1996: 30).

Since he is now a buddha, it is not surprising that his birth and life-course was patterned on that of Śākyamuni. The following passage that describes a miraculous birth must be read as the record not of a megalomaniac but of a quietly confident believer.

Moreover, when she was thirty-seven, my merciful mother dreamed that she was swallowing the warmth of the morning light, and when she woke up she found she was pregnant. She then addressed the following prayer to the Venerated [Kannon]: 'Let the child I am carrying become a holy man, or a spiritual guide. If he is to become a benefit to men and *deva*, give me an easy delivery. If not, O Kannon, use your great divine power to make the insides of my womb rot and wither away.' With this prayer on her lips, for seven months she prostrated herself 1333 times each day, and recited the *Kannon sūtra*. At the end of this time, she had a natural, painless childbirth. Thus I was born in a property belonging to the Kannon temple of Tane, in Echizen Province. Later, all the events that marked my life were determined by maternal prayers to the Venerable [Kannon]. I was able to reach adulthood without any problems, leave my family and study letters, cultivate the Way and produce wisdom, and finally inherit the Dharma and become an abbot, and come to the aid of men and *deva* – all this due to the prayers to Kannon (Faure 1996: 35).

We find Keizan building a funerary mound behind his new monastery, a mausoleum into which he placed five relics: a copy of Rujing's discourses, part of Dōgen's skeleton, a sūtra that Ejō had copied in his own blood, Gikai's documents of succession (*shisho*) and some Mahāyāna scriptures in Keizan's own hand. This is an interesting mixture, which shows him intent on producing a distinct 'Sōtō' lineage as well as trying to increase the spirituality of the place. But alongside this strong statement and recognition of the continental roots of Zen, his rules for life in the monastery show a high degree of sensitivity to the native tradition. When Yōkōji was consecrated, the invocation read as follows:

The vast merits that have been accumulated, we offer them respectfully to Tenshō Daijin, who created this country, to the seven generations of heavenly *kami*, to the five generations of earthly *kami*, to the ninety-six generations of human emperors, to the primordial star that governs the ultimate fate of the present monarch, to the seven luminaries, to the nine luminaries and twenty-eight mansions of the year in its round, to the various *daimyōjin* who protect the capital, to the great and small divinities of the five home provinces and of the seven districts, to the great ridgepole of the Dharma, Hakusan Myōri Daigongen, to the past and future protectors of this district, to the great bodhisattvas of the two sanctuaries, the various shrines of this county and community, to the tutelary god of this mountain, to the dragon-king of this mountain . . . to the god Katoku of the south, to the group of stars in the fire section, to the eighteen gods who protect this monastery, to the members of the category of the great Bodhisattva Kita of Ichinomiya in this province, to the members of the category of the great Bodhisattva Shohō Shichirō Daigenshuri, Tamonten, Karaten, the Acolyte with the Blue Face [Seimen dōji] . . . to the various celestial emissaries robed in white, to the ancient tutelary god Inari Daimyōjin, and to the great Bodhisattva Hachiman who gave his protection [during the conquest of] Silla (Faure 1996: 110, adapted).

Reading through this list it almost seems as though Keizan was simply making sure that no one was left out. The range is impressive and not just restricted to local deities, such as the god of Hakusan 白山, the main sacred mountain of the area. Hakusan was, however, extremely important, since this cult had already spread to many other parts of Japan (the deity was present at Hie, for example), a fact that was of considerable help to the spread of Sōtō monasteries. Japanese Zen monasteries in general inherited some rather surprising cults from Chinese Chan. There is, for example, the cult of the arhats (*rakan* 羅漢). These figures, 'auditors' (Sk. *śrāvakas*) who had achieved enlightenment by being direct disciples of the Buddha, were emblematic of Hīnayāna Buddhism and, one might have supposed, were looked down on by the Mahāyāna tradition. But in Sōtō Zen they were treated as honorary bodhisattvas. Perhaps they were considered important because they provided a definite link to the historical Buddha Śākyamuni, who stood, after all, right at the beginning of the Zen lineage. It has been suggested that the cult to arhats started in China with the figure of Piṇḍola, who became the spirit of the monastery kitchen and bathrooms. The number of arhats in fact varies considerably. In Tendai Buddhism, 500 arhats were supposed to have their abode on the other side of a famous stone-bridge on

Mt Tiantai; in Chan the number is usually sixteen. In 1200, for example, Eisai had performed a ceremony to open the eyes of sixteen images commissioned by Hōjō Masako (Faure 1996: 88–96).

The example of Keizan therefore provides us with an extraordinarily complex series of interrelated cults and rituals designed to cover almost any eventuality, and belies the usual picture one has of Zen masters sitting in quiet contemplation, teaching students with severity, and ignoring what was happening in the outside world. One area that was common to all Zen monasteries, however, was the ritualisation of daily life. To a certain extent this can be seen as a reflection of the profound Mahāyāna belief in essential non-dualism, so that any act became an enlightened act; but it can also be seen heuristically as an important tool whereby the non-existence of the self could be inculcated on a moment-to-moment basis; but the other side of the coin is, of course, the danger that all may become simply thoughtless habit and nothing more.

The secret of the success of Sōtō Zen in the provinces was undoubtedly its willingness to engage fully with local beliefs, encourage eclecticism and offer a source of spiritual power to a series of local elites. Drawing its patrons from middle-ranking landowners and local lords, it gradually became the main source of religious experience for large swathes of the provinces, and it is only really in this sense that we can call Zen a religion of the samurai class, if at all. These monasteries provided a whole series of services, ranging from the usual prayers for good weather, good harvests, good health and good fortune to the provision of funerals. Indeed, as we shall see, it could be argued that it was this last element, providing funerals for the layman, that became one of their principal roles as they continued to spread throughout the countryside.

Part IV

From the fall of Go-Daigo to the death of
Nobunaga (1330–1582)

Plate 27   Reaching the Pure Land through the ten worlds. This seventeenth-century woodblock print explains the Kegon concept of ten worlds and then reconciles this with belief in the Pure Land. The devotee is supposed to fill in one small circle each time he or she has chanted the *nenbutsu* 10,000 (or preferably 100,000) times. When the whole process has been completed and all the circles filled in, deliverance into the Pure Land is all but guaranteed.

観心十方界図

華厳経ニ云々　曰ク三世一切ノ仏應ニ観法界性
一切唯心造ト云フ大仏頂首楞厳経ニ自ノ覚路ヲ来
シ慈雲大師此大文ニ依テ観ス十界界ノ親ヲ第一ニ
仏ノ相王敏若人作テ流通ヲ給ヘ識ヲ給ヲ給ルル
仏ヲ見第七第地獄鬼界界界界ニ墮ト善々令知
七八念ヲ第第念界界七豆仏仁起ト観界界ヲ起ス
キ念ハ即チ此界ニ墮ト本界ニ墮ト一念仏界ヲ起
ラ念ハ仏界ヲ観トル本界ニ墮ト一念地獄ノ念ヲ
由リ此地獄ノ念ニ依テ仏界ヲ識ト一念各念各界ヲ
境ニ住ス仏界ノ微妙ヲ楽ヲ楽ト八地獄猛火ノ
善悪ノ性ハ時々刻々念ヲ首ヨリ唯我我心ノ
ス煩悩六道界ヲ心ニ由テ外ニ有ラ仏界ヲ六道
得タリ極楽浄土ヲ外ニ安養極楽ト観ジ自性
生シ浄土ヲ浄土ト信ス此界々ヲ一仏界ヲ浄楽ト
十二願ニ此浄土ニ安養ト界々ト決定シ十六
増セテ行ズル所仏佛弥陀如来ノ大道
キ道理ヲ信ス是真ノ信念仏ニテ
十二願ニ信ヲ信ズ念々佛々ノ信ハ
其功徳弘深不可思議利益弥陀如来一
同心テ此国ニ依リ唯心ノ理ヲ信ズ佳キ
キ誓願ノ部ニ信願已ニ国々ノ所信
モ彼ニ在ルヲ知ルレバ若彼ヲ八唱テ佛ト信
千過万通ヲ至十万上云ヘト国テ国々佛
黙ヲ消シ共歓ノ記ニ三百尚過テ
決定往生疑ナカルベシ矣

寛文己酉仲冬

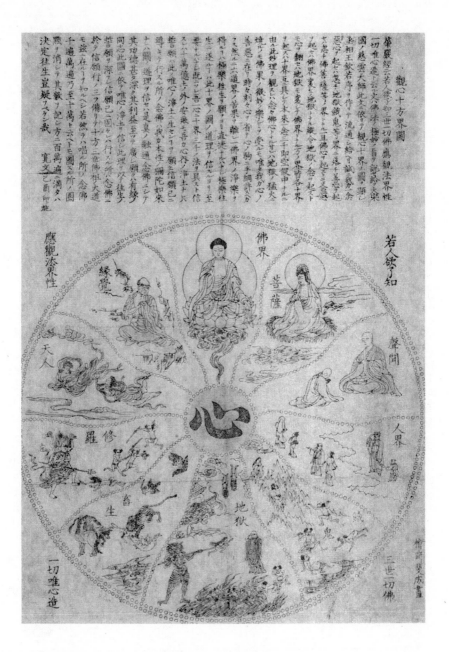

Chronology

1331	Go-Daigo fails in his attempt to win power.
1332	Watarai Ieyuki's *Ruiju jingi hongen* presented to court.
1332	Go-Daigo banished to Oki.
1333	Go-Daigo returns to Kyōto.
1336	Go-Daigo defeated by Ashikaga Takauji. Start of the Ashikaga shogunate.
1339	Go-Daigo dies. Kitabatake Chikafusa starts work on *Jinnō shōtōki*.
1351	Musō Soseki dies.
1368	Start of the Ming Dynasty in China.
1375	The Urabe family formally adopts the name Yoshida.
1390	Shakunyo founds Zuisenji in Etchū.
1392	Northern and Southern Courts reconciled.
1396	*Meitokuki*.
1400	Rise of Nō as art form.
1404	Official tally trade with Ming China begins.
1408	Ashikaga Yoshimitsu dies.
1441	Assassination of Ashikaga Yoshinori.
1457	Rennyo becomes abbot of Honganji.
1467	Start of the Ōnin war. Sesshū travels to China.
1474	Ikkyū becomes abbot of Daitokuji.
1475	The first *ikkō ikki*.
1477	Ōnin war ends.
1479	Rennyo starts building Honganji at Yamashina.
1482	Bukkōji joins forces with Honganji.
1485	Taigenkyū built at Yoshida in Kyōto.
1488	Province of Kaga taken over by Shinshū adherents; *ikkō ikki*.
1499	Rennyo dies.
1506	Sesshū dies.
1532	Rise of the Hokkeshū in Kyōto. Destruction of Yamashina Honganji.
1536	*Hokke ikki* destroyed by Hieizan forces.
1543	First Portuguese traders arrive
1549	Francis Xavier arrives in Japan.
1560	Oda Nobunaga begins his rise.
1568	Nobunaga enters Kyōto.
1570	Cabral becomes Jesuit Mission Superior.
1571	Destruction of Hieizan by Nobunaga.
1579	Arrival in Japan of Valignano.
1580	Ishiyama Honganji surrenders to Nobunaga.
1582	Death of Nobunaga. Valignano leaves Japan with a 'diplomatic mission' of four youths.

18   Two rival courts

18.1   Class as a factor

Periodisation is a necessary evil for the historian: necessary because it
provides essential structure; evil because the structure quickly becomes too
imperious in its demands and can hide as much as it reveals. The long period
of some 250 years between the fall of Go-Daigo and the death of Oda
Nobunaga in 1582 is particularly awkward in this respect. Not that one has
any problem in deciding about the beginning or the end, which both form
reasonably sharp junctures. It starts with the failure of the sovereign to win
back power and prestige, and it ends with the wholesale destruction of the
temples on Hieizan in 1571 and of the Jōdo Shinshū stronghold of Ishiyama
Honganji soon after, events that changed forever the relationship between
religious institutions and the state. In between, however, there is a sense of
dislocation and upheaval, which makes it difficult to find one's bearings.

   Initially there is a period of fifty-six years (1336–92), during which two
rival courts coexisted with anything but equanimity. In the years that
followed, there remained the constant threat of instability that had as many
socio-economic as political causes and eventually led to the destruction of a
large part of Kyōto in the Ōnin wars of 1467–77. The same can be said of
most of the sixteenth century, when all pretence of centralised control was
lost and, in the midst of the turmoil, the first Catholic missionaries arrived,
adding their startling presence to the complications. But, on the other hand,
this whole period saw Japanese culture reach new heights, at first under the
generally benign guidance of the early Ashikaga shōguns, and later under the
patronage of the many daimyō. As if to compensate for the regular bouts of
destruction in Kyōto itself, a number of provincial capitals emerged, each
intent on making itself a 'little Kyōto', and some of the most important artists
and poets of this period actually lived most of their lives in the provinces.
Amid all the unrest there emerged art forms such as the Nō theatre, some of
the most exquisite painting and architecture Japan has ever produced, and a
revival of interest in Chinese culture and scholarship centred on the great Zen

monasteries. Even at the height of the troubles, there seems to have been hardly any let-up in the production of art and artefacts for pleasure, relaxation and everyday use. In the latter half of the period, the merchants (particularly of Kyōto and Sakai) had a much greater say in what was imported, and they imprinted their own tastes on what was produced. Looked at from this angle, it seems at times that the constant emphasis of the historian on destruction and dislocation may be somewhat misjudged.

The pattern of change in religious institutions is also difficult to see clearly; partly, no doubt, because much from this period remains to be investigated in depth. The older established institutions and temples such as Enryakuji, Onjōji and Kōfukuji spent much of their time trying to adjust to a new environment in which their traditional status as guardians and protectors of the state had been all but usurped by Zen temples and abbots, who were intentionally used as a counterweight by the Ashikaga shogunate. Given the habit historians have of spending time on the new at the expense of the old, perhaps it is not surprising that these older institutions have not in fact figured as prominently as they might in the history of the fifteenth and sixteenth centuries. They remained powerful landowners, but they lost the ability to hold on to far-away estates that were simply expropriated by local interests over which the centre could exert less and less control as time went by. Buddhist scholarship certainly continued, but there were no major doctrinal innovations. The internecine strife that had been so common between Enryakuji and Kōfukuji died away, but this was chiefly because they had discovered a common foe. But all these negatives hide a considerable presence and, to some extent, it is precisely because they continued as a normal part of the landscape that they find so little mention. The loss of control over land was compensated for as their administrators moved into newer areas of commerce. Enryakuji, for example, had some 80 per cent of the sake-brewers and money-lenders in the capital on its books and controlled many of the trades and guilds that began to make Kyōto a major financial centre. It continued to draw substantial revenues from land to the east and operated a series of tolls on the main routes. The toll at Katada 堅田, for instance, was particularly lucrative, since all goods passing via Lake Biwa into the capital had to pass this point (Gay 2001: 66). Looking at Kyōto today, it is easy to forget that for much of the fifteenth and sixteenth centuries it was the powerhouse of Japan's mercantile economy. Kōfukuji suffered some loss of control over the southern part of the province of Yamato, but it retained its title as governor of this vital central region. The Ashikaga never found it possible simply to ride roughshod over its demands and Enryakuji, in particular, was still a powerful enough presence at the end of the sixteenth century to present Oda Nobunaga with a major headache (Adolphson 2000: 288–345).

The popular movements that had emerged in the Kamakura period slowly increased their influence until by the end of the sixteenth century they had become major political entities in their own right. In absolute numbers, temples continued to increase and the percentage of the population that participated directly in religious activities of one sort or another also grew. In this context, it is very tempting to describe the situation in terms of class distinctions, although one must also be aware that regional differences played an important role and the identification of class and sect might well differ depending on what part of Japan one is discussing. It is also true that class becomes less useful as a guide from the mid-fifteenth century on. As a very rough guide, the upper class was represented on the one hand by the new phenomenon of metropolitan Zen, very much in the control of the Ashikaga shōguns and looking at times like an arm of government, and on the other hand by the older established institutions such as Enryakuji, Onjōji and Kōfukuji, whose traditionally close relationship with the aristocracy continued, but who suffered a drop in status and power, exacerbated by the loss of traditional sources of economic support. There were also temples such as Ninnaji, Daigoji and Tōdaiji, closely connected to the figure of the sovereign; their fortunes fluctuated but they survived. Kōyasan, Tōji and Negoroji each maintained strong power bases in their respective localities. The lower class was represented by various Pure Land groups such as Jōdo Shinshū, which was active among the peasants and lower echelons of the warriors, especially in the more agriculturally advanced areas such as the home provinces and the Kantō, and also by the Jishū, who took it upon themselves to minister directly to men in the field of battle, but at times had a considerable following in Kyōto itself. This leaves us in the middle with two very different types of institution: in the rural areas further away from the centres of power, Sōtō Zen temples continued to expand throughout Japan, providing services to a wide variety of different social groups; and among the merchants and the artisans in cities such as Kyōto, we have the Lotus sects (Hokkeshū 法華宗) that traced themselves back to the teachings of Nichiren and who were known for their strident anti-authoritarianism.

18.2   Go-Daigo's legacy

Go-Daigo (1288–1339) came to power at the age of thirty in 1318. Taking advantage of considerable disarray in Kamakura and understandably annoyed at the way that the Bakufu continued to interfere in matters of succession to the throne, he set out to restore the fortunes of his own lineage. In 1331 a short attempt to bring Kamakura to its knees by military means failed rather badly and he was banished to the island of Oki 隠岐 off the Japan Sea coast. His son, Prince Morinaga, managed to revive anti-Bakufu sentiment two years later. Go-Daigo himself escaped from exile, and for a time it seemed as though he might succeed in his aim of restoring the monarchy to full power. Ashikaga Takauji 足利尊氏, sent by Kamakura to quell the uprising, turned against his masters, Nitta Yoshisada moved against Kamakura in the Kantō, and the Bakufu fell. But it was not long before the relationship between Go-Daigo and Takauji soured, due in good measure to an unwillingness on Go-Daigo's part to recognise the role that the warriors had played in his success. By 1336, Takauji was in control of the home provinces and Go-Daigo had been forced to retire south to the hills and mountains of Yoshino, where he established what became known as the Southern Court. Takauji set up a puppet replacement in Kyōto, the Northern Court. Go-Daigo himself died in 1339, but the north–south split survived until reconcilation came in 1392.

Go-Daigo's failed attempt to restore the power and authority of the sovereign that had been lost centuries before had interesting consequences. Almost by accident, the centre of gravity switched back to Kyōto, as the Ashikaga rulers abandoned Kamakura and transferred their operations back to the centre. The Zen temples in Kyōto regained the status they had temporarily lost to those in Kamakura, and the Ashikaga soon found themselves absorbed into the ways of the aristocracy, becoming themselves the arbiters of taste and fashion, and ruling like kings. In a geographical sense, then, two power centres, one cultural and one military, had become one. But almost in the same breath the court itself broke into two rival camps that became physically separated north and south. This led to two sorts of confusion. To the outsider, particularly China under the Yuan (and, after 1338, under the Ming) and Korea in the form of the Koryŏ Dynasty, the Ashikaga shogunate were obviously the authority with whom they had to negotiate, although in religious and cultural circles within Japan, the duality of the structure was still clearly marked. To the insider, matters were further confused because one side of the pair had become doubled. It is hardly surprising that during this period matters of genealogy and lineage became close to an obsession, mirroring the concern with origins that we have previously identified as being a marked characteristic of Shintō discourse at this time. The genealogy entitled *Bloodlines of the noble and the base* (*Sonpi bunmyaku* 尊卑文脈), which dealt with the complex interrelationships between aristocratic and military families, is a product of these years, as is *A record of the correct lineage of gods and sovereigns* (*Jinnō shōtōki* 神皇 正統記), written by Kitabatake Chikafusa 北畠親房 (1293–1354) in 1339 and revised in 1343. Chikafusa's early life is not entirely clear, but it is known that he had already taken initial Buddhist vows before he was drawn into public life in 1318, when he was appointed tutor to Go-Daigo's son. He retired again in 1330 when the boy died, went north with his own son, who had been appointed governor of Mutsu, visited Ise in 1336, lived from 1338 to 1341 in Hitachi, where he wrote the first draft of the *Correct lineage*, and ended up as the chief administrator of the Southern Court in Yoshino from 1344 until his death in 1354.

Since Chikafusa's *Correct lineage* deals with matters of succession and since it was written at a difficult time when two courts were in existence, it became a key text for state Shintō in the early twentieth century, when the concept of 'divine sovereigns' was fundamental to the new ideology. It therefore needs to be treated with some care. It has, for example, been read as a specific defence of the Southern Court. It is true that Chikafusa was concerned to identify the correct line of descent and clearly felt that the Southern Court had legitimacy, but he was not an uncritical admirer of Go-Daigo's policies. Indeed, he clearly felt that individual sovereigns should be held responsible for their decisions and actions, and he was quite willing to castigate a ruler for his mistakes. Yōzei 陽成, for example, is described as being 'of bad disposition and unfitting to be a ruler' (性悪ニシテ人主ノ器ニ タラズ) and Kazan 花山 is diagnosed as 'unbalanced' (御邪気アリ) (Iwasa et al. 1965: 122, 136). It is in this context that the title itself is of some interest. *Shōtō* means 'correct lineage', but what about the term '*jinnō*'? Bohner's German version of 1935 has 'wahren Gott-Kaiser-Herrschafts-Linie' and Tsunoda's English version of 1958 translates it as 'Legitimate succession of the divine sovereigns' (Bohner 1935; Tsunoda et al. 1958: 267). Both of these interpretations are very much products of their time. Chikafusa himself made a clear distinction between the deities of heaven, the deities of earth, and the human sovereigns beginning with Jinmu, and there is no sign that he believed that Japanese sovereigns were in and of themselves divine. Indeed, in many cases they proved themselves to be only too human. Numerous cases of unusual succession are recorded and then explained in terms of the system correcting itself in the long run thanks to the benevolence of the gods, but the rulers themselves are never referred to as being divine. 'Gods and sovereigns' would seem to be the best answer (Varley 1980).

A slightly different problem arises with the famous first sentence, which reads 大日本者神國也. This is a good example of the kind of difficulties to which the Japanese writing system can sometimes give rise. We do not know how Chikafusa intended this to be read. The most commonly used edition today reads '*Ōyamato wa kami no kuni nari*' (Iwasa et al. 1965: 41), which would give either 'Japan is the land of the gods', or possibly 'Japan is a land of the gods', and suggests a land under the protection of the *kami*. But if it were read in Sino-Japanese fashion as '*Dainihon wa shinkoku nari*', the effect would be quite different. This encourages us to interpret the compound 神國 as a concept and so suggests 'divine land', which is in fact how most translators take it.[1] But did Chikafusa mean to go this far? This is a contentious issue. The term 神國 first appears in that section of *Nihon shoki* that treats of Empress Jingū's putative exploits in Korea and can be found in regular use in Heian records and diaries, where there is no sign that it was used in any other sense than simply 'a land under the protection of the gods'. But it is precisely because of his use of this term in this sentence that Chikafusa is often quoted as being a key figure in the process by which a fairly straightforward descriptive phrase turned into the concept of 'a divine land ruled by god-sovereigns', with all that means in terms of exclusivism and latent nationalism. As we do not know how 神國 was read, there is always a danger of producing a circular argument.

Starting his work by describing Japan baldly as 'the land of the gods', Chikafusa goes on to try and define the nature and character of the country by investigating the series of different names by which it has been known in the early chronicles, but none of them really provides the answer as to what makes Japan special. He then shifts to describe Japan's geographical position vis-à-vis India and China. Recognising that each country has its own myth of origin, despite the fact that the world must have been created at the same time everywhere, he launches into a substantial description of the Indian account of the genesis of heaven and earth; the Chinese equivalent is then non-chalantly dismissed as being derivative. Before going on to start the section on Japan by retelling the creation myths as presented in the medieval version of *Nihon shoki* touched on earlier, he describes what it is that gives Japan its

---

[1] Bohner translates 'Japan ist Gottheits-Reich', Tsunoda, 'the divine country', and Varley, 'the divine land'. 'A divine land' would also be possible.

unique quality in the world. Unlike the situation in India or China, where the norm was unspeakable discord and where the position of king or emperor had constantly changed hands, Japan had managed to maintain an uninterrupted line of succession from the very beginning. It was this that gave Japan its uniqueness, its special quality. What is more, this rule from a single 'seed' had been guaranteed by Tenshō Daijin to continue for ever, for as long as the regalia remained in Japan. Chikafusa was only too aware that the succession had not always been smooth and on occasions had gone collaterally instead of directly, but he believed that thanks to the benevolence of the gods it had always eventually returned to the 'correct' path, the *shōtō* 正統, that he was about to describe for posterity.

Whether such a position justifies a translation of 神國 as 'the divine land' or not is a matter of debate, but it is entirely in keeping with the essentially political nature of *jingi* worship as it had existed since the Nara period: namely, that it is the sovereign's lineage that defines Japan as Japan, setting it apart and distinct from all other lands. Given Japan's position as a small island, 'no larger than a millet seed', apparently lying at the eastern extremity of a clear line of cultural influence, a fact of which Chikafusa was only too aware, perhaps this was the only way that he could give his country a pre-eminent role. Culture, in the form of Confucianism, Buddhism and writing itself, may not have arisen in Japan, but it had made its home in Japan because only here would it be able to survive in difficult times. The influence of these two intellectual and spiritual systems had only become necessary because there had been a falling off everywhere from the purity and straightforwardness that had characterised original rule; the object was to return to an uprightness, a purity within the polity. In direct contrast to the concept of *mappō*, and so in contrast to the thought that underlay Jien's *Gukanshō*, for example, Chikafusa's view of history was fundamentally optimistic: since the gods had founded Japan and the rulers could still trace a link back to those gods, rule in Japan would always be fundamentally good. There would be vicissitudes and wrong turnings as there had been in the past, and occasionally it might seem as though one were indeed in an age of decline (he uses the term *masse* 末世 rather than *mappō* 末法), but Tenshō Daijin's promise guaranteed that Japan would always return to the right path in the end. Japan was a land of the gods and would remain so forever. Rule by a heavenly ordained sovereign line was, by definition, eternal. There were obvious parallels with a Confucian-style Rule of Heaven, but in comparison to the violence of dynastic change in China the Japanese case was far more benign and pure.

There are plenty of signs in the *Correct lineage* that Chikafusa saw absolutely no contradiction in remaining a Buddhist monk while at the same time absorbing much of the newly emerging Shintō 'doctrine'. He knew the priest Watarai Ieyuki and went to Ise in late 1336, staying there for two years. It was there that he wrote his *Treating the origin as the origin, a compilation* (*Gengenshū* 元元集). This turns out to be a patchwork of quotations from Ieyuki's own compendium *The origins of the gods, a classification* (*Ruiju jingi hongen* 類聚神祇本源), written in 1320 and presented to the court in 1332. The strange title *Treating the origin as the origin* comes directly from the oracular statement in *Yamatohime no mikoto seiki* quoted in §16.4. Chikafusa clearly found the new vocabulary of Shintō congenial and fitting for his task. It appears again prominently in the section of the *Correct lineage* that deals with the reign of Ōjin Tennō 應神天皇.

And so if you wish to know what lies at the heart of the two ancestral shrines [Ise and Iwashimizu Hachiman], it is first and foremost rectitude, nothing more. All men between heaven and earth have received the spirits of Yin and Yang, but unless they have probity they cannot survive. Particularly in this land, a land of the gods, whoever deviates from the way of the gods will never enjoy for even a day [the light of] the sun or moon. Yamatohime no mikoto gave her oracle as follows: 'Reject the blackness of heart, be pure and obey the taboos with a [clear] heart of cinnabar. Serve the great deity by not moving to the right that which is to the left, or to the left that which is to the right. Let left be left and right be right. Be correct in all things, whether turning to the left or turning to the right, because the origin is the origin, and the base is the base 元元本本故ナリ.'

Indeed. Remember! This is [the correct way] to serve your lord, serve the gods, rule the land and teach the people . . . To deal with all eventualities by casting off one's desires and thinking of how you may benefit others; to be clear and undeluded like a reflecting mirror; is this not the true way 正道? There is no need to despise ourselves 'in an age of decline'. The principle should be: 'the beginning of heaven and earth is this very day' 天地ノ始ハ今日ヲ始トスル理ナリ (Iwasa et al. 1965: 82–83; Bohner 1935, vol. I: 233–34; Varley 1980: 108–10).

The argument here begins with an exhortation to rectitude and uprightness that has by this time become the definition of what best characterised the fundamental doctrines of Shintō; it then develops in the direction of the rectification of names, whereby probity is defined as keeping things in their appointed place and not going counter to 'nature'; and it ends with a quotation from the Chinese classic *Xunzi* 荀子. The *Xunzi* reference is to the chapter entitled 'Nothing indecorous': 'Accordingly, the essential nature of 1,000 or 10,000 men is in that of a single man. The beginnings of Heaven and Earth are still present today. And the way of all True Kings is in that of the Later Kings.'[2] Note, however, that the meaning has been transformed from one of scepticism to something much more enigmatic. This difference in interpretation may have come about because Chikafusa had probably not read the whole *Xunzi* text but relied on the series of long extracts contained in the thirty-eighth chapter of the Tang anthology of philosophical writings entitled *Junshu zhiyao* 郡書治要. The object of the whole Japanese passage here is to exalt the principle of purity and sincerity that will help us return to the unadulterated origin, and in the process it expresses a utopian optimism that comes from a belief that we can also negate the workings of time.

How did this close relationship between Chikafusa, the Southern Court and Watarai Ieyuki affect matters at Ise itself? Ieyuki provided considerable practical support during the long period of strife, allowing the Southern Court access to the port of Ōminato 大湊, which was not far from the Outer Shrine. But there was also considerable disagreement within the Watarai clan as to which court to support, with the result that the whole province was subject to constant depredation, which had a severe effect on the economic situation of both shrines. What changed things radically and loosened the ties between Ise and the sovereign even further was the beginning of pilgrimages on a large scale. The shōgun Yoshimitsu started visiting almost every year, although in his case it clearly served a double purpose, since he made sure he was always accompanied by large numbers of troops to give an impression of majesty. At roughly the same time we see the appearance of the first Ise-kō 伊勢講, local groups who raised funds among themselves to organise pilgrimages, which became popular even among farmers and villagers by the early years of the fifteenth century. The attraction of the Ise shrines was obviously connected to what they stood for, but at the same time this drastic shift in patronage changed the nature of the shrines and of ritual practice. The sixteenth century saw the rise of *onshi* 御師. These were Ise priests who not only helped to arrange and guide these organisations but were themselves itinerant and, as part of an attempt to proselytise in the Buddhist manner, took to rural areas talismans and other small ritual objects which they would then distribute with prayers and incantations.

The widening of patronage that came in the wake of these developments brought with it other unforeseen consequences. On the one hand merchant families in the two towns of Yamada and Uji began to take control of the economics of the whole region away from the Watarai and Arakida, and on

[2] 故千人萬人之性、一人之性是也。天地始者、今日是也。百王之道、後王是也。trans. Knoblock 1988: 179.

the other hand friction between the two shrines showed little sign of decreasing. Although money poured into the area, there was an increasing reluctance to spend it on the shrines themselves, with the result that when the Outer Shrine burned to the ground in 1486 and the Inner Shrine collapsed soon after, very little was done to rebuild either structure for over 120 years. Clearly the situation at Ise was not at all stable and was susceptible to sudden changes in fortune (Teeuwen 1996: 133–77).

One other legacy of Go-Daigo's attempted restoration was the emergence into the limelight of a cult based at Miwa. Mt Miwa 三輪山 was an ancient sacred site situated at the south of the Yamato basin just at the point where the southern road to Ise plunges east into the valley created by the River Hase 長谷. Not only was this a vital transport node but the mountain dominated the eastern skyline of the old capital at Asuka. The god of Miwa, known variously as Ōkuninushi, Ōmononushi or Ōnamuchi was conspicuous in *Nihon shoki* as a major Izumo deity, eventually pacified by Yamato. As part of the process of healing, it was agreed that he would be for ever honoured with a shrine at Miwa. Unusually, the sacred object (*shintai* 神體) in this case was not an object within the shrine but the mountain itself. Little is known of Miwa during the Heian and Kamakura periods and it is only about this time that it re-emerges. The main contemporary text is entitled *Miwa daimyōjin engi* 三輪大明神緣起 which has a colophon dated 1318, the year of Go-Daigo's accession to the throne, although like many such dates it is open to doubt. This tale of Miwa's origins makes a series of large claims regarding its deity, arguing that it was at least the equal of Tenshō Daijin and one with Sannō. The study of this cult is still in its infancy but we do know that it was generated by Buddhist monks and priests who were part of the Saidaiji order. We do not know, however, quite why it emerged into the limelight at this time or why it felt strong enough to challenge Ise as being the heart of Japan. It would seem likely that there is a connection to questions of the legitimacy of the Southern Court, but further research is needed before anything definite can be said.

Some scholars argue for Eison as the author of the *engi*. There were certainly close links between Saidaiji and the Miwa shrine, which are well documented, and the presence at Miwa of large numbers of outcasts (*hinin*) would also suggest a connection. In the Edo period the Miwa cult became associated with initiation rites for a series of artisan groups, and Ōnamuchi became the god of doctors, but the links back to this Miwa cult of the fourteenth century are not at all clear.

18.3   Saving the souls of warriors

What of the life and beliefs of the ordinary fighting man, whose services were constantly in such demand? It is doubtful whether he would have had much knowledge of Zen meditation, or much interest in the subtleties of the sovereign's correct lineage; his main concern was that his allotted role in this life was almost guaranteed to damn him to an extremely uncomfortable time in the next. The need for encouragement and comfort was obvious and was partly met by the wandering priests of the Jishū order, who traced themselves back to Ippen but who had been first organised into a legitimate group by Ta'amidabutsu Shinkyō (§15.2). Not long after the death of the third head of the order, Donkai, in 1327, the north–south wars broke out and the order found itself being drawn into the conflict, acting as chaplains on the battlefield, ministering to dying warriors with their own particular message of salvation. This tradition is celebrated in such works as *Taiheiki* 太平記 (*c.* 1375), *Meitokuki* 明德記 (1396) and the *Yūki senjō monogatari* 結城戰場物語 (post-1451) (Thornton 1988: 102ff), although the earliest reference we have to these activities is 1333, when two hundred of them were reported working with the Hōjō armies beseiging the castles of Akasaka and Chihaya. When Kamakura itself fell that same year, the Fujisawa Shōnin 藤澤上人 of the time (1279–1337) described the scene in his temple grounds as follows:

Although Kamakura was in great uproar, it was particularly quiet at the temple, because all the men who had come in swarms had departed for the battlefield; the place having been deserted except for the monks, nothing untoward happened. Even in the thick of the fighting, the men were all chanting the *nenbutsu*, the attacking force and the defenders. In the aftermath, men were executed for fighting against their own side; our priests went to the beach, all led *nenbutsu* believers in the chanting of the *nenbutsu* and caused them to achieve deliverance. Since the battle, having witnessed what we did, people have been increasing their faith in the *nenbutsu*. I hope I live [long enough] to write to you again (Thornton 1999: 101).

Despite the taboo on holding arms, there were many occasions when the absolute dependence of these men on their patrons put considerable strains on their role in the order. A letter known as the 'Nagano gosho' of 1353, written to a constable in Ise Province by the seventh head, Takuga 託何, in defence of his men who had been bringing solace to the constable's enemies after a siege, clearly refers to the need for the order to maintain independence of action, difficult though that might be (Thornton 1999: 182–83). Indeed, there are signs that their activities on the battlefield declined during the early years of the fifteenth century precisely because the headship of the order discovered it was no longer possible to guarantee neutrality. But warriors continued to make use of the order's meeting places as places to rest and prepare for death or suicide if they had been wounded in battle. The tradition of Jishū saving the souls not only of warriors but of angry spirits (*goryō*) became a staple of their tradition, given artistic expression in such Nō plays as 'Sanemori' 實盛, 'Seiganji' 誓願寺 and 'Yugyō yanagi' 遊行柳. The process by which famous warriors of the past (including Yoshitsune, Benkei and the Soga brothers) found their way into Jishū death registers by appearing to the head of the order as ghosts to be pacified and given guarantees of salvation reached its height with Sonne 尊恵 (1364–1429), who used this technique to increase substantially the power of his order to minister to warriors. To say as much, however, would be to ignore other elements. Although the outward propaganda produced the image of semi-martial control wielded by a head of the order who was called the *chishiki* 知識 or 'good friend', who saw himself as the representative of Amitābha in this world, guaranteeing rebirth for those of his followers who kept to the precepts and recited the *nenbutsu*, in practice it was not possible to impose such iron discipline. It should not be forgotten that Ippen's original group had appeared as a rabble of eccentrics and this element was difficult to erase entirely. If Takuga's admonition to the members of his order of 1342 entitled *Tōzai sayōshō* 東西作用抄 is anything to go by, the habits of the average member left a good deal to be desired. He complained about:

wearing outdoors clogs in the corridors, entering the temple by banging the shoulder against the sliding doors, going to the bathroom with the door open, during services chanting too loudly, leaning against the pillars and walls and gossiping, pushing and shoving to get the first rows and looking every which way but front; rumpled clothing, fancy clothing, fancy fans, sloppy posture; ogling the nuns and other women, visiting nuns alone; running around with parishioners, favoring the talented and high-born among them, getting involved in their fights; talking about the time before becoming a *jishū*; rudeness to the elderly; telling naughty stories about monks and nuns in front of the Chishiki, improper posture before the Chishiki, insufficient attendance on the Chishiki, insufficient gratitude to the Chishiki, and insufficient zeal and alacrity on obeying the orders of the Chishiki (Thornton 1999: 81).

It was during the tenure of the fourth, fifth and sixth Ashikaga shōguns, Yoshimochi, Yoshikazu and Yoshinori (all of whom had themselves entered in the death registers), that the Yugyōha subgroup of the order finally managed to establish itself as a major force. In 1400 they were recognised as a Buddhist school in their own right and despite considerable internal dissension, maintained Bakufu patronage both in Kyōto and Kamakura, where the Betsuganji 別願寺 became the official family temple of the Ashikaga deputies (*kubō* 公方). As a result, of course, the fortunes of the order tended to fluctuate with those of the Ashikaga, especially in the latter part of the fifteenth century. This kind of patronage was particularly important for them if they were to continue their traditional itineracy, for which permission was necessary. In times of war and dislocation a shogunal directive allowing free passage was of inestimable value. Of all the Pure Land groups, the Jishū order was by far the closest to the authorities, if only because it catered for the warriors so well. Not having extensive land-holdings, they relied on support from the *kechienshū* but also on patronage from the shogunate. This was given partly because of the special links with the warrior class, but it must have also been helpful that the activities of the missions were never seriously subversive; handing out amulets and saving souls was conducive to maintenance of the status quo and was no threat whatsoever to the authorities, whoever they might be. It is also the case that a number of priests became important in various cultural spheres such as poetry and the tea ceremony. The renga poet Ton'a 頓阿, for example, was from the meeting house at Shijō. It also became common for Nō actors, physicians and other artistic companions of the Muromachi elite to append the typical Jishū suffix *-ami* to their names, but this may be misleading and we cannot simply assume that men like Kan'ami and Zeami were members of the order; it may well have been little more than a fashion among a particular group, or it may have been used as a way to give a certain standing to artists and performers, the majority of whom were of very low rank.

It will be recalled that there was a clear distinction between the active Jishū mendicants on the one hand and the *kechienshū* supporters on the other. The numbers of the latter could be infinitely expanded through the distribution of amulets. It is therefore extremely difficult to gauge the number of people involved in this order, since a lay supporter could quite easily be a member of another sect at the same time. Numbers are in this sense of little significance. There can be no doubt, however, that this sect and the Jōdo shinshū were aiming for roughly the same constituency, so that numbers tended to drop in one sect as they rose in the other. This may help to explain why the Jishū found itself attracting back members it had lost when Honganji was finally brought to its knees by Nobunaga.

18.4   The growth of Pure Land congregations

What of the other Pure Land groups, which appealed to quite a different constituency and did not particularly endear themselves to anyone in authority? When Shinran died in 1262 the majority of his followers (known as *monto* 門徒) were in the Kantō, the most influential of them being the group based at Takada 高田 in the province of Shimotsuke 下野. Shinran left no instructions as to the future organisation of the groups he left behind. Since he had always denied the need for a priestly rank and believed passionately in equality before Amitābha, he must have decided that it was simply their collegiate responsibility to make their own decisions and to elect their own leader (*otona*). As had been the case with Ippen and his order, it was Shinran's followers who fashioned an institution, raising the founder to a semi-divine status and designating his teachings as sacred texts. One inevitable consequence of this was a sharp rise in factionalism and a betrayal of his doctrine of pure faith. One might indeed be tempted to characterise Jōdo Shinshū 淨土眞宗, as it became known, as a social organisation of the lower classes first, and as a religious group only secondarily. Operating among the poorest and least educated of people, it grew into a power of considerable potential. Hardly surprising, then, that in the late sixteenth century it attracted the attentions of Nobunaga, who saw this sect as one of his most awkward adversaries.

The process towards institutionalisation was slow but sure. It began in 1272 with the building of a tomb for Shinran's cremated remains at Ōtani 大谷 (just east of what is now Higashiōji-Gojō) on land owned by the second husband of Shinran's daughter Kakushinni 覺信尼. At her husband's death she inherited title, and when she died in 1277 she willed ownership of the site to the whole *monto* community on condition that her descendants be granted custodial rights (*rusu-shiki* 留守式) (Weinstein 1977: 337). There then followed a period of unseemly strife within the family as to who was to have the honour of holding the site, and it was not until 1309 that Kakunyo 覺如 (1270–1351), Kakushinni's grandson, managed to gain custody. Even so, he had to sign a draconian agreement with the leaders of the Kantō *monto* that restricted him to a purely nominal role (Solomon 1972: 72–74). There is some evidence to suggest that Kakunyo made far too much of his aristocratic heritage, which rankled with the Kantō groups, who were far from aristocratic themselves and had a particular interest in maintaining Shinran's principle of egalitarianism; but they were also worried that the heredity principle was about to be put into effect. They were right to be concerned, for this is exactly what transpired. Kakunyo eventually succeeded in gaining full control over Ōtani and turning it into a full-fledged temple that at some stage prior to 1321 became known as Honganji 本願寺. In 1334 he finally won legal independence. Kakunyo it was who wrote a biography of Shinran and transformed Ōtani into a mausoleum devoted to the cult of the founder. It was under his leadership that Honganji evolved for the first time in Japan a system whereby temple leadership was inherited by tradition from father to son, a move only made possible, of course, because Shinran himself had completely rejected his vows of celibacy.

It would be a mistake, however, to stress the importance of Honganji at this early stage in the proceedings. It was to be over a hundred years before it became the hub of a state within a state, for the good reason that Shinran had specifically rejected the whole idea of institutional controls over what he preferred to see as a community of believers. Admittedly, it always had the advantage of being Shinran's resting place, but there were a number of rival institutions that were equally, if not more, powerful. Bukkōji 佛光寺, for example, founded by Ryōgen 了源 (1295–1335) at Shibutani 澁谷 further up in the hills east of Ōtani and south of Kiyomizu, was a major rival in Kyōto itself, and in fact entirely overshadowed Honganji until the fifteenth century. This establishment won the majority of converts because it borrowed a number of key elements from Jishū practice, including the use of salvation registers (*myōchō* 名帳) and portrait lineages (*e-keizu* 繪系圖) of important priests; this signified a revival of the reality of priest as arbiter of salvation, something that ran counter to Shinran's teachings. Quite rightly, these practices were branded as heresies by those at Honganji, and it was to stop such developments that Kakunyo wrote his *Notes rectifying heresy* (*Gaijashō* 改邪鈔). As well as using to the full his blood relationship to Shinran, Kakunyo also invented a tradition of a secret transmission in a work entitled *Kudenshō* 口傳鈔, in 1331. This represented another betrayal of Shinran's ideals, of course, but was in line with normal Japanese practice. Successive custodians at Honganji used this semi-mythical tie as a major weapon in the battle to claim exclusive rights over what was and what was not orthodox. Although one must naturally be sceptical about such claims, since heresy can often simply be defined as the beliefs and practices of those who lose the battle for supremacy, there seems to be no doubt that Honganji did try to keep as close as it could to the purity of Shinran's ideals, while inevitably betraying them in the very act of creating and maintaining an institution.

Zonkaku 存覺 (1290–1373), Kakunyo's eldest son, was not chosen as his successor, partly because of his friendship with Ryōgen. It is ironic that having established the principle of hereditary rule, Kakunyo should disagree so violently with his son Zonkaku as to disinherit him twice as a heretic, once in 1322 and again in 1342. This kind of factionalism was an inevitable consequence of having a series of loosely knit organisations with different figureheads vying for the attention of a common pool of believers. Zonkaku's main heresy was his unwillingness to accept the purity of Shinran's thought; he was far more in the mainstream of Pure Land belief, demanding practice and intention as well as faith, and in contradistinction to his father's *Notes rectifying heresy*, his own polemic, entitled *Notes assailing heresy and revealing truth* (*Haja kenseishō* 破邪顯正鈔), was a more general defence of Pure Land Buddhism per se rather than a discussion of orthodoxy and heresy within the Shinran tradition itself.

The period from 1351 to 1457, namely between the death of Kakunyo and Rennyo's installation as abbot (*hossu* 法主), was characterised by a gradual increase in Honganji's influence, not least via the policy of establishing branch temples in Hokuriku to the north. One oddity of Honganji that had to be addressed if it was to play a major role as a temple was that it lacked a *honzon* 本尊 or central image. Shinran had preferred the written sign as symbol rather than the human image, and it was left to Kakunyo's grandson Zennyo 善如 to install an image of Amitābha. His son Shakunyo 綽如 did much travelling as part of his tenure at Honganji and founded Zuisenji 瑞泉寺 at Inami in Etchū in 1390, so encroaching on Takada affiliated territory. Chōshōji 超勝寺 was founded in Echizen during the tenure of Gyōnyo 教如, and his son Zonnyo 存如, who was *rusu-shiki* from 1436 to 1457, began the process by which Honganji cemented relations with its outlying temples and meeting houses by the systematic distribution of the sacred inscription. It was also about this time that two of Shinran's works were given the status of sacred scriptures: *Sanjō wasan* 三帖和讚, a collection of short poems or 'hymns' explaining doctrine in a simple format designed for chanting, and *Shōshinge* 正信偈, a distillation of the sect's central tenets.

It should not be thought that Jōdo Shinshū had a monopoly; Hōnen's Pure Land sect, for example, continued to exist. And there were others. Although the history of the various sects is often presented in terms of schools and their subdivisions, it makes better sense to picture multiple congregational centres, be they temples or the far more numerous meeting houses, all claiming devotion to Amitābha but owing allegiance to one or other lineage. These groups were in competition with each other for the affections and support of large swathes of the Japanese peasant population. As usual, it is impossible to disentangle the religious from the social and the economic. Since they were fighting over essentially the same constituency, disagreement could be acrimonious. When Hōnen died in 1212 his tomb at Higashiyama Ōtani became a sacred place. After the attack by monks from Hieizan in 1227, the decision was made to cremate the body and distribute the ashes among his principal followers. A large number of factions emerged from this process and a major element in their strategies for survival was whether or not they had custody of these relics. Each faction also tended to have its own understanding of what constituted the *nenbutsu*, whether it had to be recited only once or repeatedly, and what the role of faith in practice should be. This factionalisation along essentially personal lines was an inevitable consequence of the reliance on the individual master. Within the structure of a temple or a monastery, be it Tendai, Shingon or Zen, such tendencies were usually kept in check, but in the context of large lay congregations and in a sect that at root denied the need for the saṅgha at all, it was unavoidable. Continual branching became the rule, and it was only when one group had a particularly active leader that it started to gain adherents at the expense of the others; it could then lose them just as easily in the next generation. The long-term future of the Chinzeiha 鎮西派 subdivision of the Pure Land sect, for example, was secured by Shōgei 聖冏 (1341–1420), who from his base in Kamakura turned his back on traditional Pure Land exclusionism and instead accepted kami as manifestations of Amitābha. They stressed practice of the *nenbutsu* over faith and presented themselves as being the closest to Hōnen's original teachings. This put them in direct conflict with Shinran, although it would be a mistake to put down the growth of factions to pure disagreement over doctrine. Personalities had at least as large a part to play.

18.5   The Lotus sects

As Pure Land Buddhism took firm root among the farmers and peasants of provincial Japan during the fourteenth and fifteenth centuries, the Lotus sects (Hokkeshū 法華宗) were developing among a rather different social group, the low- to mid-ranking warriors and (as time went on) the burgeoning merchant class in Kyōto. It would be an exaggeration to say simply that Jōdo Shinshū was rural and the Lotus urban, but an element of this had certainly developed by the sixteenth century.

Nichiren's first follower was a Tendai priest called Jōben (Nisshō 日昭), who came to join him in the winter of 1254. He was closely followed by his twelve-year-old nephew (Nichirō 日朗). Nichiren had taken it upon himself to ordain his followers himself, which shows the degree of his self-confidence and his disdain for other systems. His followers were divided into those few disciples who were actively to spread the message and those lay believers who gave financial support and who established small temples in their own homes, where recitation of the *daimoku* could be accomplished in a communal setting. During the 1270s the number of lay converts increased rapidly and came under increasing pressure because of their intransigent behaviour. Mt Minobu became the centre of this sect and by 1278 there were between forty and sixty disciples resident. It was here that they built a tomb for Nichiren (it was to become Kuonji 久遠寺), and when he died, his six leading followers agreed to look after it in turn.

The history of the Lotus sects (or what is also termed in general Nichirenism) from that point on was one of internal disagreements, intolerance towards others, and persecution. The six split up and went their separate ways, each founding his own lineage, each certain of his correctness. Disputes ranged from how to deal with Shintō deities to doctrinal questions as to which sections of the *Lotus sūtra* were primary and which secondary. What emerged was not a cohesive institution but rather a series of groups tied together by little more than their belief in the power of the *Lotus*, their veneration for the founder, and their religious practice, which consisted of repeating the *daimoku*, meditating in front of Nichiren's 'maṇḍala', and spreading the faith in militant fashion by adopting the method known as 'breaking and subduing' (*shakubuku*), which involved rigorous doctrinal argument and explicit rejection of the views and beliefs of others. It meant that the true follower of Nichirenism had to be prepared to preach, debate and fearlessly submit memorials to government authorities (*kokka kangyō* 國家 諫曉) whenever necessary. Although a number of sects in the Kamakura period had made claims for being exclusive, Nichiren was unique in his integration of confrontation into the very structure of his thought (Stone 1994: 233). It became a test of orthodoxy. As we have seen in §15.3, he believed that the persecution he received as a result of his intransigence was proof of the righteousness of his cause, a kind of self-fulfilling argument for conflict that had far-reaching consequences. His followers often found it extremely difficult to maintain such purity of motive in practice.

For example, the only way in which Nichizō 日像 (1269–1342), who arrived in Kyōto in 1294 to begin converting people in the capital, could make much leeway was to ingratiate himself with Go-Daigo. Even so, it took until 1321 to found his first temple, Myōkenji 妙顯寺. His relationship with Go-Daigo was crucial to the success of the mission and yet it was seen by many of his peers, those who owed allegiance to Nikkō 日興 (1246–1333) for example, as a compromising betrayal. The number of Hokkeshū priests who courted imprisonment and torture by repeated memorialising of the authorities throughout the Muromachi is extraordinary. It became a badge of honour. Many of these priests entered the annals of Hokkeshū lore, such as Nisshin 日親 (1407–88), who became known to posterity as Nabekanmuri shōnin 鍋冠り上人 because he had a red-hot iron kettle jammed over his head to stop him reciting the *daimoku* (Stone 1994: 239). The wonder is that the movement survived at all.

19   Muromachi Zen

19.1   The five mountains

By the time Daitō died in 1337, and Musō Soseki in 1351, a substantial number of large and powerful Zen temples had become established and the link between these institutions and the new rulers of Japan was secure. Kōgon 光嚴 of the Northern Court was the first sovereign to be given a formal Zen funeral in 1336. As the centre of gravity shifted back to Kyōto, patronage moved with it, with the result that although the temples in Kamakura remained influential, those in Kyōto came to dominate. Given the special relationship that had existed between both Ashikaga Takauji and Tadayoshi 直義 and a number of Zen masters, in particular Musō, it was only natural that their successors would follow suit. Zen temples and their abbots became to the Ashikaga what Enryakuji and Kōfukuji had been to the court and the sovereign, a guarantee of their prestige and legitimacy. Although it is doubtful whether any shōgun ever spent all his time in meditation or trying to solve kōan, they certainly sponsored literary and artistic events, and used the temples as a door to the wider world of Song–Ming culture, including Neo-Confucianism. Zen was for them a mixture of education and entertainment. But this was by no means all. Zen monks were extremely useful to the shogunate when it came to matters of diplomacy and commerce; they had a good command of written Chinese, and often had direct experience of dealing with Chinese officialdom. They were also willing to become involved in finance, often becoming an important source of funds for the Bakufu.

Experience showed that if religious institutions were allowed too much unfettered power they became a threat. Tadayoshi took some care to exercise control over the temples, setting up an office of commissioners (Zenritsugata 禪律方), and as early as 1338 an attempt was made to establish a nationwide network, to be known as *ankokuji* 安國寺, which was intended to symbolise the establishment of a new peace and help to pacify the spirits of those who had died in battle in the previous decade. In most cases, of course, this simply involved the official re-registering of an already existing Zen temple. In addition, an order went out for the construction of a series of pagodas or *rishōtō* 利生塔 to be built in the precincts of major Tendai and Shingon temples, as a sign that they too were to be brought within the general remit of the new Ashikaga power structure. The political intent behind these moves is clear: it was another way of extending authority over the military governors (*shugo* 守護), who formed the backbone of provincial government and who, by their very nature, tended to be independent of both mind and action. As it happens, these *rishōtō* did not survive the death of Takauji in 1358, and the *ankokuji* were simply absorbed into the larger system that became known as the *gozan* 五山 or 'five mountains'.

Of the new temples that were built at this time, perhaps none is more important than Tenryūji 天龍寺. When Go-Daigo died in 1339, Musō persuaded Takauji that it would be wise to ensure that the spirit of the disappointed sovereign was properly pacified; the potential for trouble was too great. Kōgon agreed to donate a detached palace in the Arashiyama district northwest of Kyōto, but not enough funds were allocated at the outset, with the result that work had to be stopped well before completion. Eventually it was decided to send two ships to China on a trading mission, the proceeds of which would go to building this memorial for Go-Daigo. The mission, the first of what became known as Tenryūjibune 天龍寺船, left in 1342 and returned having made a handsome profit, allowing the temple to be completed in 1344. What is more, another important precedent was set when Enryakuji complained about the lavish ceremonies that were planned in honour of Go-Daigo at its opening. For the first time, the Bakufu simply rejected their protestations out of hand and threatened to confiscate whatever they might bring into the streets of the capital.

Recent research has questioned whether there was a system of 'five major temples' in Southern Song China, but, whatever its historical validity, this is certainly where the term was thought to have originated. In Japan the number 'five' came to denote not the number of temples but five ranks in a hierarchical system that was brought into full operation under Ashikaga Yoshimitsu (1368–94). The system changed quite rapidly. In 1334 the order was:

1   Nanzenji 南禪寺 (*Kyōto*)
2   Tōfukuji 東福寺 (*Kyōto*)
3   Kenninji 建仁寺 (*Kyōto*)
4   Kenchōji 建長寺 (*Kamakura*)
5   Engakuji 圓覺寺 (*Kamakura*).

By 1341 this had changed to:

1 Kenchōji (*Kamakura*); Nanzenji (*Kyōto*)
2 Engakuji (*Kamakura*); Tenryūji (*Kyōto*)
3 Jufukuji 壽福寺 (*Kamakura*)
4 Kenninji (*Kyōto*)
5 Jōchiji 淨智寺 (*Kamakura*); Tōfukuji (*Kyōto*).

Under Go-Daigo in 1334, Kyōto clearly outranked Kamakura, but the first Ashikaga order in 1341 was more evenly balanced. Yoshimitsu changed it yet again when he founded Shōkokuji 相國寺 as the Ashikaga family temple in Kyōto, and by 1386 the following balance had been achieved, with Nanzenji at the apex.

	Nanzenji	
	Kyōto	*Kamakura*
1	Tenryūji	Kenchōji
2	Shōkokuji	Engakuji
3	Kenninji	Jufukuji
4	Tōfukuji	Jōchiji
5	Manjuji 萬壽寺	Jōmyōji 淨妙寺

Below the top level of *gozan* were the 'ten temples' (*jissatsu* 十刹), of which there was at least one per province by the mid-fifteenth century; and under these was a large group of miscellaneous temples (*shozan* 諸山), smaller provincial temples, often simply redesignated as Zen from some other affiliation such as Tendai or Jōdo, and associated with major local families, the majority of which were of the military governor class, provincial agents of the Ashikaga Bakufu (Collcutt 1990: 600–10). It was along the route provided by these connections that the practice of Zen and contact with Kyōto culture spread throughout Japan, although one should keep in mind that its influence was limited to a relatively small group, and it was always going to be seen as the domain of an elite class. From the point of view of the Bakufu the *gozan* system made sense both in terms of overall control and in terms of economics, since temples had to pay substantially for the privilege of being included. From the point of view of the provinces, it brought prestige and encouraged patronage of high culture within what became provincial capitals of considerable wealth and sophistication. Zen monks were in great demand throughout the country, since by installing a monk as abbot into one's own converted *ujidera*, one might gain much in terms of influence and contacts. By the mid-fifteenth century there were 300 main temples listed within the system and a much larger number of affiliates (Collcutt 1981: 115–16).

This rapid growth was fuelled partly by the habit of allowing abbots to retire to their own sub-temples, known as *tatchū* 塔頭, which proliferated in the grounds of larger temples and which often became important cultural centres in their own right, and partly by the habit of warrior families sending their sons to be educated in temples. The authorities were constantly worried about such matters as size and discipline. The notional limit of 500 monks per establishment was exceeded on a regular basis, but the Bakufu did not always help the situation by selling abbacies as often as possible to the highest bidder to fill their own coffers. Where they do seem to have succeeded was in keeping Zen institutions from becoming a source of armed threat. Discipline was also of importance, especially because the *gozan* temples were the one Buddhist institution over which they had real control. The legal codes known as *Kenmu shikimoku* 建武式目 (1352) contain a number of regulations aimed specifically at Zen temples. Article 141 of the supplementary legislation, for example, reads:

Both elders and ordinary monks must be carefully checked for [attendance at] the three daily services. [If they are absent] they must be removed from the temple rolls, and elders must not be promoted. In the Zen sect, advancement comes with the practice of Zen discipline (*zazen*), and those who have been repeatedly negligent shall be expelled from the temple (Collcutt 1990: 607).

It is usually argued that Zen meditation and *kōan* practice suffered increasingly as we progress through the fifteenth century. Whether or not this growth did in fact lead to a decline in practice and meditation is difficult to gauge, but what is true is that *gozan* temples became known more for their contributions to culture in general, painting, architecture and Chinese poetry, than for a rigorous training in meditation. This should come as no surprise, given that such emphasis was placed on the ability to understand classical Chinese references when dealing with *kōan* and the commentarial tradition. Musō Soseki, for example, was even drawn to criticise monks whose knowledge of Chinese was less than adequate for devoting too much of their time to meditation (Bodiford 1993: 147).

In 1379 direct control over the *gozan* temples was delegated back to the monks in the form of the Registrary General for the Saṅgha (Sōroku 僧錄), the first monk to be appointed to run this office being the Tenryūji abbot, Shun'oku Myōha 春屋妙葩 (1311–88). From 1383 his offices were based in a subtemple of Shōkokuji called the Rokuon'in 鹿苑院, which also served as a drafting office for much of the official diplomatic correspondence exchanged with the Korean and Chinese authorities. A number of highly influential monks were to hold this post of Registrar, including Zekkai Chūshin 絶海中津 (1336–1405), Zuikei Shūhō 瑞渓周鳳 (1391–1473) and Keijo Shūrin 景徐周麟 (1440–1518). Although individual *gozan* temples continued to retain a good deal of autonomy, it was through this office that abbots were appointed and regulations enforced. In principle the system required abbacies to be open to all (*jippōsatsu* 十方刹), but in practice Japanese habit prevailed and by and large abbots were chosen from within the lineage established by the founder, in which case they were known as *tsuchien* 度弟院. Tenryūji and Shōkokuji, for example, only installed abbots who could trace their learning back to Musō Soseki. Although this close relationship between *gozan* monks and the Bakufu administration worked to the advantage of both parties, it had the disadvantage of tying their fates together and ensured that as the central authority itself weakened over the years, the prestige and effectiveness of those temples in the *gozan* system would decline as well.

19.2   'Those below the grove'

By no means every Zen temple became part of the *gozan* system. The generic term for those who were either excluded or stayed outside on purpose was 'those below the grove' (*rinka* 林下), to distinguish them from the *gozan* temples which were known collectively as 'the grove' (*sōrin* 叢林). This might give the impression that they were situated well away from urban areas, which is true of many Sōtō temples, but there were many others, including two large urban foundations in Kyōto itself, Daitokuji 大徳寺 and Myōshinji 妙心寺, that stayed fiercely independent and accepted no patronage or support from the shogunate. Nevertheless, they formed a crucial element in the life and culture of metropolitan Zen. Their patrons came from the court, lesser provincial families and wealthy townspeople in Kyōto and Sakai 境. Daitokuji had been founded by Shūhō Myōchō, who was Musō's rival in many ways, and this may have been one of the many reasons why successive Daitokuji abbots kept aloof from the *gozan* system, preferring to keep a certain distance between them and the Ashikaga. They saw themselves as having special ties to the sovereign and indeed were the only group of abbots to be allowed to wear purple robes. Although Daitokuji itself was burned down in 1453 and then again in the Ōnin wars, it was revived thanks to the fund-raising efforts of Yōsō Sōi 養叟宗頤 (1376–1458). An unashamed populariser, he even went as far as granting certificates of enlightenment to lay people who attended mass meditation sessions at which *kōan* were 'solved' by transmission of the secret correct answer rather than through rigorous meditative exercise (Collcutt 1990: 614). Somewhat bizarrely, the infamous Ikkyū Sōjun 一休宗純 (1394–1481), who became abbot in 1474, also managed to attract financial support, especially from merchants in the port city of Sakai. But the real period of prosperity for Daitokuji came later, in the sixteenth century, when it attracted a number of former *gozan* temples that at best found themselves marooned and at worst completely gutted in the widespread destruction of the mid-fifteenth century. It became a major centre of cultural activity for painters, renga poets and especially masters of the tea ceremony. Both the renga poets Saiokuken Sōchō 柴屋軒宗長 (1448–1532) and Yamazaki Sōkan 山崎宗鑑 (1465–1553) were connected to Daitokuji, as was the famous tea master Sen no Rikyū 千利休 (1522–91). It was to survive and prosper in the sixteenth century, counting as many as two hundred branch temples throughout the country by the 1580s.

Myōshinji was founded by Kanzan Egen 關山惠玄 (1277–1360) at the request of Hanazono. Like his mentor Shūhō Myōchō, Kanzan made a name for himself as an uncompromising monk with rigorous standards for Zen practice and little interest in preferment. Closed down in 1399 because Ashikaga Yoshimitsu believed that the abbot had offered help to the rebel Ōuchi Yoshihiro, Myōshinji was re-established about forty years later by Nippō Sōshun 日峰宗舜 (1408–86) and it too eventually grew to be one of the largest Zen establishments in the country. The period of its real growth was later, in the sixteenth century, when it outgrew even Daitokuji and took over some fifty defunct *jissatsu* and *shozan* temples. It is important to note that present-day Rinzai Zen traces itself back not to the *gozan* temples, which faded out as the Ashikaga lost power and prestige, but to this Myōshinji line via the monk Hakuin Ekaku 白隠慧鶴 (1685–1768). One other group deserves a mention at this point, the lineage that became known as Genjūha 幻住派, named after Zhongfeng Mingben's hermitage, the Huanju'an 幻住庵. This included a number of monks, such as Onkei Soyū 遠渓祖雄 (1286–1344), Kosen Ingen 古先印元 (1295–1374) and Muin Genkai 無隠元晦 (d. 1358), who had all studied with the reclusive Zhongfeng. This group saw itself as forming an entirely separate lineage and shared with Sōtō Zen a dislike of secular authority in general.

And what of Sōtō temples in the tradition that had been started by Dōgen and owed its institutionalisation to Keizan Jōkin (1268–1325)? They kept themselves aloof from the *gozan* and grew rapidly in more rural environments. Having founded Yōkōji, Keizan moved on again and near the end of his life, in 1324, founded yet another centre, a temple some sixty kilometres north of Hakui called Sōjiji 総持寺. This was eventually to rival Eiheiji itself, forming the core of a very large organisation of sub-temples numbered in the thousands. Gasan Jōseki 峨山韶碩 (1275–1366) was installed as its first abbot. Sōjiji had originally been a Shingon temple and from the beginning of its new incarnation Sōtō abbots showed a willingness to incorporate both tantric and Pure Land rituals into their belief and practice; partly, of course, to fit in with their patron's wishes. As we have already mentioned, later sectarian scholarship has often castigated these men for diluting Zen 'proper', but the secret of the success of Sōtō Zen as an institution lay precisely in its willingness to engage fully with local beliefs, encourage eclecticism, and offer a source of spiritual power and sustenance to a series of local elites. Drawing its patrons from middle-ranking land-owners and local samurai lords, it became the main source of religious experience for this class in the countryside.

The presence of Gasan at Sōjiji and his ability to attract benefactions meant that this temple prospered throughout the late fourteenth century such that by the end of the century it challenged Yōkōji in both size and significance. Rivalry between the two erupted in a major conflict in the 1370s, although the actual reasons for dispute remain obscure because of the highly tendentious nature of the sources that remain. The nub of the problem was the question of status: which temple had priority and what procedures should be followed for the appointment of abbots at both institutions. Much time was spent adjudicating between different factions, factions that grew out of the usual obsession that Zen had with master–student lineages (Bodiford 1993: 101–07). Sōjiji learned its lesson from these disagreements, however, and eventually managed to control a large number of potential factions by making sure that the abbotships of temples rotated through various sub-lineages.

It was in the main Gasan's students who started the expansion of Sōtō Zen from the main base in Kaga and Noto, spreading throughout Japan, setting up small temples wherever they could and so ensuring that by 1400 their tentacles had spread to no fewer than seventeen provinces. The growth continued. It has been estimated that in the two hundred years between 1450 and 1650 on average more than forty-three Sōtō Zen temples appeared each year: a phenomenal rate of growth (Bodiford 1993: 110). In part this can be explained by the habit of re-assignment, whereby a temple that had originally been linked to a Shingon or Tendai main temple had somehow lost that tie (in many cases because of the loss of power and influence at the centre); Sōtō monks simply filled the gap. None of this would have happened, of course, if the monks themselves had not been willing to travel far and wide, taking over local, often derelict, temples in the remote areas they visited. But to do this they needed to obtain the permission and sponsorship of local leaders, who were the only ones wealthy enough to fund temple building and interested enough to use them as centres of power and authority. Their persuasive powers must have been considerable. In contrast to the monks of the *gozan* temples, who impressed through their learning, Sōtō Zen monks had much more in common with traditional mountain ascetics and the order as a whole was associated with two sacred mountains in particular, Hakusan in Kaga and Sekidōzan in Noto.

Mountain pilgrimage is a standard motif in many Sōtō biographies and temple histories. The founding of Zuisenji by Tenshin Yūteki (1341–1413), illustrates how Sōtō monks appropriated the cultic power of sacred mountains. Tenshin had been living in seclusion in Kinsei Village (Chikusen Province) when the local residents first asked him to found a new temple. But he could not accept their request without a divine sign. Tenshin journeyed to the nearby Mt Hiko to practice austerities. Later, when Tenshin returned to Kinsei Village, a rock fell out of the sleeve of his robe. Just as the rock hit the ground a three-foot-tall man suddenly appeared – the spirit of the mountain. This apparition was the proper sign, and construction of the new temple began (Bodiford 1993: 113).

So in many ways Sōtō Zen monks became the equivalent of parish priests, offering sermons and whatever services the community wished. After all, it was not as if Chan had been devoid of prayers and rituals for prosperity and good luck in this world. Far from keeping to themselves in temples and cultivating increasingly effective meditational techniques, the monks saw it as their role to take the message out into the villages. They transformed, for example, the rite of ordination into something approaching baptism for all. Although Dōgen himself had shown no hesitation in ignoring the old institutional controls over the ordination process, claiming for himself and his followers the right to ordain their own, he had in fact been somewhat equivocal about which precepts Sōtō monks should use and placed far more emphasis on a close observance of the monastic codes (Bodiford 1993: 170–72). This weakening of the tie between ordination and the status of monk allowed ordination to shift its ground, and it came to be seen as something that could be conferred on lay people in much the same way that tantric practice used the initial *kechien kanjō* initiation for the layman. Perhaps the most remarkable feature of Sōtō Zen was the degree to which the lay community was actively encouraged to partake in various ceremonies. They were invited, for example, to join in the monthly recitation of the precepts, for which a fee was charged. The monks also arranged group ordinations for their lay supporters (*jukai'e* 受戒會), which seem to have become common in the sixteenth century. The participants shared in the work of the monks for a few days, after which they were given a certificate in the form of a lineage-chart (*kechimyaku-zu*). This not only gave the layperson an insight into the life of the temple but also created a link from him or her to the Buddha himself through the chart and the person of the abbot. Records show that all sections of society were encouraged to attend these events, so deepening the link between Zen monks and the rural population (Bodiford 1993: 179–84).

Another important aspect of Sōtō Zen proselytisation was in the matter of funerals, for which they became particularly well known. Buddhist funerals for laypersons were the exclusive preserve of the nobility until about the thirteenth century. We do not know enough about funeral practices among the rest of the population at this stage, although it is clear that in many cases corpses, particularly those of young children and those whose family members had also died, were simply interred or otherwise left to decay. One important gift that Sōtō Zen monks brought to the rural areas in which they settled was the opportunity for families at all levels of society to bury their dead in such a fashion as to secure their future salvation. The Pure Land and Nichiren groups had their own ceremonies, but most other Buddhist orders were to adopt Zen funeral services as the norm.

The rites as they were prescribed in the Sung Chan codes were restricted to ordained monks and were informed by Chinese practice; laypeople could be offered memorial services but not funerals. But once Sōtō became firmly established in Japan it was not long before funeral rites were being offered to lay patrons. At a later stage this service was extended to all laypersons of no matter what status, although the scale of the ceremony was naturally reduced, depending on the resources available. This shift whereby rites originally due to a monk were given to laypersons was justified by the device of posthumous ordination. Once that had been achieved, and it was usually done in a simple initiation ceremony, the person could be treated as if he or she were a monk or a nun.

From the point of view of the layman the only difference between a Zen monk and a Tendai or Shingon monk was that the former was thought to draw his spiritual strength from meditation rather than knowledge of esoteric ritual. It is probably true to say that standards of practice and meditation were far higher in Sōtō temples than in metropolitan ones, which had become centres of cultural rather than spiritual excellence. Story after story is told of the strictness of Sōtō abbots, both for themselves and for others. Observance of the rules that governed every tiny aspect of a monk's life was an essential part of training the mind and counteracting the belief in a self. The use of *kōan* was also central, although in this case, given the background of most Sōtō monks and the difficulty of the *kōan* texts themselves, the kind of systematisation and rote learning that we have described in relation to *gozan* practice must have been the norm and must have set in much earlier. One of the main reasons a monk might prefer to be at a *rinka* rather than a *gozan* temple was precisely the realisation that the possibility of reaching enlightenment should not be tied so closely to one's ability to handle classical Chinese. There was much memorisation of set responses according to a fixed curriculum and it is difficult to avoid the conclusion that for the majority of monks the study of *kōan* had been reduced to an exercise in familiarising oneself with Zen lore. When the correct answers had been learned, and these answers might be non-verbal in nature, one passed on to the next *kōan*, and in the end one 'graduated'.

This sounds somewhat dismissive, but in its own way this kind of study could impart the necessary message. Take, for example, this record of an exchange in which the abbot takes the student on a mental tour of the temple. The abbot performs both sides of the exchange and the student just listens (hence the term 'substitute'), but, even so, much is imparted in the process:

Teacher: 'First, the abbot's building?'
Substitute: 'Prior to the Great Ultimate [there is] the abbot's building.'
Teacher: 'Nothing exists prior to the Great Ultimate. How can [you] say that the abbot's building exists?'
Substitute: 'This answer means that the master dwells in the place of non-being.'
Teacher: 'A verse?'
Substitute: 'No bright brightness; in the dark, darkness.'
Teacher: 'Next, the storehouse? . . . ' (Bodiford 1993: 156).

19.3   Three men of Zen

Perhaps the best way to illustrate some of the main facets of Zen culture during the Muromachi is to take three figures who are representative of three different aspects: Daitō (1282–1337) for his teaching and his use of *kōan*, Ikkyū Sōjun (1394–1481) for his behaviour, and Sesshū Tōyō 雪舟等楊 (1420–1506) for his mastery of the brush.

The central place that study of *kōan* still has in Zen is in large measure a result of the example of Daitō, the founder of Daitokuji. He came to be seen as the paradigmatic Zen master and his 'final admonitions' are still chanted in Rinzai temples to this day, but it is as well to be aware that this reputation is largely the result of historical accident. As has just been pointed out, present-day Rinzai Zen traces itself back to him via the Tokugawa monk Hakuin, and it is for this reason that he looms so large. Much of what we are told of his early life is the usual hagiography with the quirky touches that were an intrinsic part of the role that a Zen master was supposed to play. All we really know is that after having gained his first experience of enlightenment studying with Kōhō Kennichi (1241–1316), he lived in a small temple called Ungoan 雲居庵 from 1309 to 1319 and then in 1319 became the founding abbot of Daitokuji, where (unusually) he remained for the rest of his life. A commonly accepted embellishment is that he lived as a beggar for many years before finally coming to the notice of the sovereign Hanazono. This gives him the proper flavour of a Zen master while also providing proof of the perspicacity of the sovereign.

It is said that he really spent [these years] living among the beggars under the Gojō Bridge in Kyōto, quite indistinguishable from his ragged associates. Eventually, so the story has it, Hanazono heard of him, and wished to invite him to preach at his palace. Having also heard that this unusual beggar was fond of a certain melon known as *makuwa-uri*, he went to the Gojō Bridge in disguise carrying a large basket of the fruit. There he handed the melons to the beggars one by one, carefully scanning each face as he did so. Noticing one with unusually bright eyes, he said, as he offered the melon, 'Take this without using your hands.' The immediate response was, 'Give it to me without using your hands' (Kraft 1992: 42, adapted).

Hanazono was not the only admirer. Go-Daigo was also enamoured of his intelligence and his sheer presence, as we can tell from an inscription written by Go-Daigo on one of Daitō's portraits: conventional though it undoubtedly is, the fact remains that Daitō was seen as a charismatic teacher by two sovereigns from rival camps.

Swifter than a flash of lightning, he brandishes his stick as he pleases. Faster than ever before, he forges buddhas and patriarchs on his anvil. When he deals with his monks, there is no place for them to seize hold. He was a teacher to two sovereigns, yet never once revealed his face to them. His severe and awe-inspiring manner made it impossible for anyone to approach him. A single point of spiritual radiance – who presumes to see it? (Kraft 1992: 126).

Daitō's teaching involved both meditation (*zazen*) and use of *kōan*, although it is his use of the latter for which he is best known. Of *zazen*, he said:

'Sweep away all thoughts!' means one must do *zazen*. Once thoughts are quieted, the Original Face appears. Thoughts can be compared to clouds – when clouds vanish, the moon appears. The moon of suchness is the Original Face. Thoughts are also like the fogging of a mirror – when you wipe away all condensation, a mirror reflects clearly. Quiet your thoughts and behold your Original Face before you were born (Kraft 1992: 117).

But in line with the strictures voiced most strongly by Dahui Zonggao, Daitō was also concerned lest this be interpreted as simply an attempt to become mindless. Enlightenment, he argued, would not be gained by simply sitting still and cutting off thought altogether. *Zazen* would not in and of itself guarantee enlightenment, since that might well come out of the blue at any time. It was in an attempt to counteract this impression that he paid great attention to the use of *kōan* and especially the use of 'capping phrases'. It may be remembered that Dahui had advocated concentrating on a single phrase (*kanna* 看話) in order to fight the tendency to slide back into intellectualisation. Daitō's trick was similar. Keeping to the spirit of a work like the *Emerald Cliff record*, he offered comments not in the form of a sentence or two of normal language, which would have been a betrayal of the whole enterprise, but in the form of a 'capping phrase'. These were designed not as discursive explanations but as interlinear comments, as pointers to an understanding; it was then the job of the student to work on his own in the gap between *kōan* and phrase, and meditation might well involve battling with a *kōan* and its capping phrase for many months (Kraft 1992).

What is not clear is how Daitō or his students actually used these phrases. Modern Rinzai practice, stemming from Hakuin, involves the student in a good deal of research. He is given the *kōan* to consider and is supposed to go away and find a *jakugo* that he feels captures its essence. He does this by combing through a series of handbooks and collections of phrases for something that fits. There is, of course, no one right answer and he might have to return many times before the master judges that he has grasped and internalised the import of the *kōan*. It is the master's role to take the student through a series of these *kōan* much as a teacher might guide a student through a set curriculum. Gradually the student will memorise the contents of the collections and become proficient at what is, in essence, an exercise and a training. In the process, the spontaneity and cut and thrust of an actual encounter dialogue that is still the ideal of Zen training tends to be lost, and in many cases the young monk simply learns a series of fitting, correct responses by rote. This method might have its own rationale in terms of a kind of training of the mind, but it probably began as a rather mundane attempt to deal with rather more practical problems, problems of a linguistic rather than religious nature. All the literary material involved is in Chinese and the fact that some of the language is colloquial Chinese of the Song period makes matters doubly difficult. Even if the Chinese is verbalised in the Japanese manner, it is still difficult to understand unless seen at least once and memorised.

Were matters any different in Daitō's time? It is difficult to tell. Reliable sources are limited to his *goroku*, which were first published somewhere between 1426 and 1467 and which record his talks and discussions, and to the collections of capping phrases that he left, perhaps the most important being the commentary on the *Emerald Cliff record*, from which he stripped out both layers of prior annotation, replacing them with his own phrases. So despite Daitō's reputation as a master who managed to inspire students in much the same spirit as the Tang masters envisioned for us in Song texts, intent on fighting language with language, we have no information on how this performance might have worked. Here again, the catch is linguistic. How would the following set of *kōan* plus capping phrases (in italics) have been used?

Wuzu [Fa]yan said, 'An ox passes through a window. His head, horns, and four legs all go through. But why can't the tail pass too?'
One game, two victories.
Under a peony, a kitten naps.
Someone else would not have been able to trace the footprints (Kraft 1992: 193).

This is all in Chinese. How much of it could have been oral? Did the master write the phrases down and show them to the student, asking him to go away and mull them over? In which case the written has priority and to use the term 'dialogue' (*mondō* 問答) of such a procedure is to stretch it to breaking point. And what happened when the student felt as though he had the answer? Was he supposed to return and superimpose his own, new capping phrase? The language of everyday discussion must have been Japanese but perhaps the *kōan* and phrases were read in what passed for Chinese pronunciation. If so, they must have been learned and could hardly have been spontaneous. The nature of the whole exercise meant that the pressure to base the performance on a written text must have been irresistible, and we should err on the side of supposing that formalisation set in at an early stage.

It is extremely difficult to give an account of the activities of Zen monks in the Muromachi period that is not coloured to a large extent by the hagiographic writings of their students. This is certainly true of a man like Ikkyū Sōjun (1394–1481), whose present reputation as a free spirit (everyone

Plate 28   A portrait of Ikkyū by Bokusai.

knows Ikkyū-san, who can always be relied upon to turn the tables with a witty or sometimes cheeky remark) is based on a series of stories that were developed around his persona during the Tokugawa period. But there seems to have been plenty of fertile ground from which such an image managed to sprout. He was known during his lifetime as a monk of highly uncon- ventional views and behaviour, the reincarnation of the kind of wild Zen master of the Tang prototypes, the embodiment of integrity. We have three main sources: his own writings, mostly in the form of a collection of Chinese poetry entitled *Kyōunshū* 狂雲集; a biography by the painter Bokusai 墨齋, who knew him well; and a famous sketch from life by the same man, which is one of the most revealing of all pre-modern Japanese portraits [plate 28].

The biography suggests that Ikkyū was in fact the unacknowledged offspring of the sovereign Gokomatsu. He was sent to work in a temple at the age of five and proved to be extremely quick. For his training he chose to study under a man called Ken'ō Sōi 謙翁宗爲, who was known for his uncompromising attitude to meditation and monastic life and whose allegiance was to the Daitokuji–Myōshinji lineage rather than the *gozan* system, so it is clear from the beginning that Ikkyū was not interested in establishing himself within the Buddhist hierarchy. When Ken'ō died in 1414, Ikkyū moved on to train with Kasō Sōdon 華叟宗曇 (1352–1428), another demanding master who lived and worked at Katada, on the western shores of Lake Biwa. He is said to have had his first experience of enlightenment sitting on a boat in the lake in 1420. In 1432 we find him in the port city of Sakai, where it would seem he gave free rein to his bohemian habits, becoming famous as a monk who drank with gusto and made frequent visits to the brothels along the waterfront. He endeared himself to the merchants of the town, who were growing wealthy from trade with China and were willing to support those Zen temples that were outside official Ashikaga control. This stood him in good stead later, when, somewhat surprisingly, he rebuilt broken fences with his own lineage and was eventually chosen to become abbot of Daitokuji, just in time to rebuild it after the destruction of the Ōnin wars.

Two stories will show us the character of the man. The first is from Bokusai's biography and refers to a Chinese Zen story about rebirth and the possibility of coming back as a cow:

One day Ikkyū entered the home of a parishioner and found an old cow in the courtyard. As a joke he hung a poem from the tip of its horn:

Well and fine, to be a beast.
Potential depends on State, and State depends on Potential.
Born anew, I forget my former path,
And forget my monkly name of former years.

That evening the cow died. The next day its owner came and teased the master by claiming that he had eulogized the animal to death. Ikkyū just smiled (Sanford 1981: 36).

The second story, which comes from a later collection, tells how Ikkyū paraded around the capital on New Year's Day carrying a human skull on the end of a long pole wishing everyone best wishes for the coming year. This hinges on a word play: 'best wishes' in Japanese is *omedetō* 御目出度う, which can also be read to mean 'eyes popped out'. Clearly the gruesome sight had a very serious intent. Indeed a seriousness of purpose seems to have underlain his constant drive to break the boundaries of normal behaviour, to break taboos. It came from a rare singlemindedness that is always unsettling and yet draws admiration. Unlike most of his fellow men, he was serious in living out the difficult and dangerous belief that this world was indeed identical to nirvāṇa and that all distinctions were in the ultimate analysis untenable.

It should not surprise us to find that Ikkyū was full of contradictions. He was at home with intellectuals and was known to many of the major cultural figures of his day: the Nō master Konparu Zenchiku 金春禪竹, the renga master Iio Sōgi 飯尾宗祇 (1421–1502), and the tea master Murata Shukō 村田珠光 (1422–1502). His poetry is difficult and full of allusions to Chinese culture, but hidden there are also passionate love poems written when he was in his seventies to a woman in her forties, together with many blunt expressions of lust. He impresses by the sheer honesty with which he faced his own desires. He loved and hated with equal intensity. And yet he is also a symbol of the transformation of Zen Buddhism into a popular religious form (Sanford 1981: 36–37). His antinomian behaviour and his refusal to dissimulate mark him as one of the first home-grown Japanese Zen-monk heroes, a sign that Zen had by this time become something of interest to a much wider audience than just those who ruled. Ikkyū is a classic example of the truth that all our heroes are taboo breakers of some kind or other.

Since Zen masters had achieved enlightenment and deepened that experience over many years, they were seen as being buddhas in their own right. It is partly for this reason that the Zen canon placed more emphasis on the records of their dialogues and sermons than on sūtras. It is therefore not surprising that one of the major forms of art in *gozan* temples was portraits and images of these revered masters. The portraits, known as *chinzō* 頂相,[1] were done both as paintings and sculptures, although the former predominated, because although every temple of any size had within it an atelier, sculptors were peripatetic. The object of such portraits being to preserve the likeness of the master in remembrance and reverence, the Kamakura interest in realistic images continued and every effort was made to represent these characters warts and all. Indeed, it was common to insert the person's ashes or fingernails inside a carving as a sign that the image was in a certain sense alive, retaining the capacity for compassion and guidance that had existed in life.

This kind of art, if the word 'art' is even appropriate in such a devotional context, is not what would normally be thought of as 'Zen art'. What is usually signified by this term is painting that is seen to express in some form or other the essence of Zen teachings. It may or may not be produced by Zen monks, although in the period we are discussing it almost always was. The reason why painting became such an important medium among *gozan* Zen

---

[1]   This word originally signifies the protuberance on Buddha's head (*uṣṇīṣa*), in which case it is normally read *chōsō*.

monks and their patrons was twofold. Firstly, this kind of painting had a long and distinguished Chinese heritage and the practice of this art was seen as a prestigious cultural pursuit in its own right. Secondly, painting offered a medium through which a message could be expressed in non-verbal terms, and as such it was a perfect vehicle. Kūkai had said as much and Shingon used diagrams and sounds that were divorced from an immediate transparent meaning. Zen, on the other hand, preferred to use pictorial representations of the natural world in such a way as to make the teaching immediately apprehensible; it was a perfect medium, in fact, for presenting the world as both phenomena and mind.

There were limitless ways in which this kind of effect could be achieved. One might present a picture of Buddha or Bodhidharma in a few simple strokes, thereby making reference to the all-important Zen lineage while at the same time proving the illusory nature of all reality; an image conjured up by a few strokes on paper. One might illustrate a famous incident in the tradition or the behaviour of a Zen master, such as the painting in plate 29,

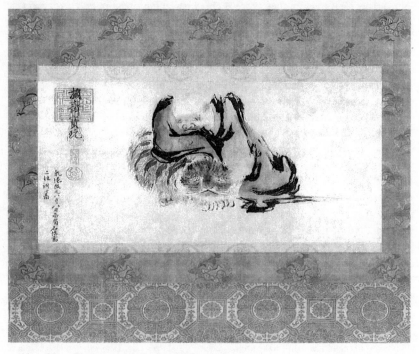

Plate 29   The eccentric Fenggan, after Shike.

which was probably painted in the thirteenth century but in the style of the Chinese artist Shike 石恪, who flourished in the tenth century. Despite an inscription that describes the figure in the painting as one of two patriarchs, it is in fact the legendary eccentric Fenggan, who had a tiger as an inseparable companion. Here there is both humour and depth, portrayed with the kind of brushwork that could be equally employed depicting a rock formation.

Or one might produce a landscape in which the ideals of Buddhism were expressed not via a devotional image, nor with a complex abstract maṇḍala, but in the way that man and nature are presented and seen in the artist's imagination: as in plate 30 [p. 418], for example, perhaps the most famous painting by the master Sesshū Tōyō. This is one of what was probably a set of four paintings depicting the four seasons, only two of which remain: autumn and winter. It clearly owes much to Chinese prototypes, but is stamped just as clearly with the personality and vision of Sesshū. Sesshū was a young Zen monk at Shōkokuji, where he studied under the painter Tenshō Shūbun 天章宗文 (fl. 1420–60). Sometime in the mid-1460s he left Kyōto and established himself in Yamaguchi under the patronage of the Ōuchi family, who controlled the province of Suō. The Ōuchi also controlled most of the China trade and had ploughed their profits into creating a mini-Kyōto at Yamaguchi. In 1467 he travelled with a trade mission to China, where he came into contact with a whole range of Chinese styles that were new to him, many of which he copied.

The brushwork that we see in this late work is remarkable for its roughness. Sharp, uncompromising angles, thick strokes and branches like thorns seem to threaten the lone figure on all sides. Falling snow is represented by randomly placed blobs of black ink. But what is most striking is the way in which the perspective developed at the bottom of the painting disappears into a flattened geometrical pattern at the top. An extraordinary dark gash down the middle marks a cliff face that has no visible means of support but simply hangs from a dull, grey sky. No soft mists or slowly receding series of lakes and mountains here. We are faced with the prospect of the whole rock pulling down the sky on both man and his dwellings. A winter scene indeed, where the soul of a painter who saw nothing but foreboding seems to have triumphed over the soul of a monk.

Plate 30   A winter scene, Sesshū Tōyō.

20   The end of the medieval

20.1   Yoshida Shintō

The process by which a self-conscious Shintō discourse continued to develop
after the emergence of Watarai Shintō in the thirteenth century was given
added impetus by the activities of Yoshida Kanetomo 吉田兼倶 (1434–1511).
It was under the guidance of this man that the ideal hierarchical system for
which the Jingikan had originally been created began to look feasible for the
first time at a practical level. It is indicative of the degree to which the
authority of the court was no longer taken seriously that such a move was
made not by the sovereign or the court, but by one of the priestly families
themselves. So this new attempt to create a system to incorporate all shrines
in the country occurred under essentially private auspices. This was, after all,
a time when central authority had collapsed and the court's finances were so
stretched that even simple enthronement ceremonies could not be afforded.
When Hosokawa Masamoto 細川政元, who was in control of the central
provinces from 1493 until his assassination in 1507, was asked by the court
for financial support, he is said to have refused, saying: 'Even if the enthronement ceremony is held, the common people will not know the sovereign is
sovereign; and even if it is not held, I will know the sovereign is sovereign'
(Berry 1994: 62, adapted).

The Urabe family, from which the Yoshida had emerged, was one of two
sacerdotal lineages (the other being the Nakatomi) who were in charge of
divination. They occupied certain positions in the Jingikan and were
responsible for a number of important shrines in the vicinity of Heian-kyō, in
particular the Yoshida shrine in the northeast of the capital, which had been
built by Fujiwara no Yamakage 山影 in 859 to represent the interests of the
Kasuga shrine, and was listed in 1081 as one of the twenty-two major shrines
to received court sponsorship (Grapard 1992b: 33). In the thirteenth century
the Urabe began to play a major role in the study of the earliest chronicles,
Urabe Kanefumi 兼文 writing the earliest known commentary on *Kojiki*,
Kojiki uragaki 古事記裏書, in 1273 and his son Kanekata 兼方 producing the

419

influential *Shaku Nihongi* 釋日本紀. But perhaps the most famous member of the Yoshida branch is Urabe Kenkō 兼好 (d. 1350?), author of *Tsurezuregusa* 徒然草, although his brother, the Tendai monk Jihen 慈遍, also produced a number of important works dealing with the theory and practice of *honji suijaku*. Jihen is, for example, thought to have been one of the first openly to suggest inverting the theory and claiming that buddhas and bodhisattvas were emanations of the *kami*.[1]

In 1375 Urabe Kanehiro 兼熙 formally adopted the name Yoshida. In 1398 he placed copies of *Nihon shoki*, *Kogo shūi* and *Engishiki* in the Yoshida shrine as a gesture to mark them out as 'sacred texts', which, as has been repeatedly argued, they were not. As was the case at Ise, it was obviously strongly felt that a textual tradition was a necessary adjunct to ritual if the dominance of Buddhism was ever to be properly challenged. Near the end of his life, however, Kanehiro followed precedent and retired to the shrine's temple Jinkōji 神光寺 and devoted himself to Amitābha (Grapard 1992b: 38).

It was Kanehiro's grandson Kanetomo who, in the late fifteenth century, succeeded in creating a new form of Shintō, which aimed at nothing less than hegemony over all shrines in the land. It was to prove remarkably resilient. Kanetomo succeeded in obtaining moral and financial support from Hino Tomiko 日野富子, the wife of Ashikaga Yoshimasa 義政, and after the destruction of the shrine in the Ōnin wars he managed to gain enough patronage to rebuild the whole site at Yoshida along new lines in accordance with his newly designed cult. The most important of these buildings he called the 'Shrine of the palace of the great origin' (Taigenkyū saijōsho 太元宮斎場所), which was created in 1485 for the specific purpose of symbolising the unification of all shrines in Japan under one roof, and for which he designed three new rituals, each with its own altar. It still stands today at Yoshida, behind Kyōto University, although few understand its significance and not many people now visit the site. The structure is unique, a hexagonal building standing in the middle of a courtyard that contains 3,132 small shrines.

The crossbeams (*chigi*) . . . are cut differently from the norm: in the front (southern side), the extremities are cut horizontally to symbolize the Yang aspect of the universe, and in the back (northern side) they are cut vertically to symbolize the Yin aspect. The *katsuogi*, which stand horizontally across the summit of the roof, are also arranged in a symbolic manner. There are three groups of three round beams to the south (the number three and the circle are Yang emblems), and two groups of two

---

[1]   Among his works are *Kogorui yōshū* 古語類要集, *Tenchi jingi chin'yōki* 天地神祇鎭要記, *Sendai kujihongi gengi* 先代舊事本義玄義, and *Toyoashihara shinpū waki* 豐葦原神風和記, written for Go-Daigo's consort.

square beams to the north (the number two and the square are Yin emblems). In the middle of the summit of the roof stands a decoration that marks the centre of the shrine and symbolizes the *yata no kagami* mirror, one of the regalia. The decoration is embedded in a seven-petalled lotus and this receives rain water, which flows through a hole in the roof and down the central vertical beam of the shrine. This beam is set in an octagonal base on which an octagonal wheel is placed vertically, and the base stands on a bed of black pebbles whose number, 3,132, corresponds to the number of *kami* mentioned in the *Engishiki* (Grapard 1992b: 54).

The next year, 1486, the Outer Shrine at Ise caught fire and burned to the ground. Three years later in 1489, Kanetomo took the opportunity to tell the court that a number of strange portents had been seen over Mt Yoshida and that 'a numinous object' had dropped from the skies. This, he claimed, was the sacred object (*shintai* 神體) of the Outer Shrine at Ise, which had flown to Kyōto for safety. The *shintai* of the Inner Shrine miraculously followed a few days later. He then managed to persuade the sovereign to endorse this identification and both objects were installed in the Yoshida shrine. Despite protestations, the shrines at Ise were not influential enough to be able to countermand this decision and in one bold sweep Kanetomo appropriated for himself and his family the potential to administer those court rites that had previously been carried out at Ise. He then gave himself an impressive sounding title and proceeded to abrogate to himself the authority to issue ranks and titles to shrines, first of all in the home provinces and then further afield. It was an extraordinary coup.

Kanetomo's main theoretical work is entitled *Essentials of the name and doctrine of the One and Only Shintō* (*Yuiitsu Shintō myōbō yōshū* 唯一神道名法要集) written about 1485 and passed down in secret until modern times.[2] In it he distinguished his own version – which he described as 'Shintō as origin and foundation' (*genpon sōgen shintō* 元本宗源神道) – from two other kinds of Shintō that were bound too closely to Buddhism: the kind that saw the gods as emanations of the buddhas and concerned itself with the origin of specific shrines; and the kind that identified Tenshō Daijin with Dainichi. Kunitokotachi he accepted as progenitor. Yoshida Shintō was therefore the culmination of a trend to reverse the *honji-suijaku* equation and state bluntly that both Buddhism and Confucianism were secondary manifestations of a Shintō original. In order to rationalise the textual tradition, Kanetomo identified the three chronicles *Kojiki*, *Nihon shoki* and *Sendai kuji hongi* as the 'revealed' part of the teachings, but he was still faced with the age-old problem that these works were clearly not doctrinal. He therefore invented

[2] For a translation into English see Grapard 1992c, and into German Scheid 2001.

(just as Watarai before him) a set of three secret texts to carry the doctrine. As had been the case with his predecessors, the vocabulary he employed was concocted from a mixture of tantric Buddhist and Daoist writings. One Daoist text in particular that was ransacked for its terminology was the *Sacred scripture of the eternal life of the original spirit of the Pole Star* (Ch. *Taishang yuanling beidou benming yansheng miaojing* 太上玄靈北斗本命延生妙經).

Of much greater significance than the new doctrine itself, however, which was to all intents and purposes secret, was the success Kanetomo had in establishing a single political framework that could accommodate all shrines and priests in the country. Having obtained the approval of the court to issue titles and to appoint to office, the Yoshida family quickly secured a monopoly and took on the task of running a nationwide Shintō institution. Given the local nature of shrines and their cults, this was no mean achievement, particularly as it was carried out not by court officials or the Jingikan, which had been all but disbanded, but by the Yoshida themselves. This tells us how much the nature of the relationship between shrine and locality had changed, otherwise they would never have succeeded. Perhaps the reasons were as much economic as anything else. In a time of constant strife and quickly shifting allegiances that meant that land could change hands many times without warning, many shrines must have lost patronage and certainly felt isolated. In such an environment they would have been only too willing to submit to any form of central authority that could claim sovereign permission, so long as it gave some guarantee of financial support. It should be stressed, however, that not enough is known at present about the means by which Yoshida Shintō expanded its control for this to be anything other than speculation. The fact remains that by the beginning of the Tokugawa period, the Yoshida family was in prime position to be chosen by the new military rulers to run shrines on a nationwide basis.

To describe how the shrines at Ise survived this attempt to appropriate their spiritual power would take us too far into the new century. Suffice it to say that although Yoshida Shintō was given the bureaucratic role of imposing a system on the shrines, it never really succeeded in dimming the light from Ise, which re-emerged at the end of the sixteenth century as a centre for popular pilgrimage on a large scale. The Outer Shrine was rebuilt in 1562 and the Inner in 1585, after well over 120 years of total neglect. In both cases the prime mover was a Buddhist nun (Teeuwen 1996: 190–91).

20.2   The rise of Honganji

The Jōdo Shinshū congregations had been slowly developing amid internal rivalry between Honganji and Bukkōji in Kyōto and between various independent *monto* groups in the provinces, both in the Kantō and Hokuriku. A major change to the balance of power came about in 1457, when Rennyo 蓮如 (1415–99) was appointed abbot of Honganji; it was to be under his guidance that Honganji emerged as the heart of a powerful religious organisation, so powerful indeed that it was to cause considerable problems for the first 'unifier of Japan', Oda Nobunaga in the late sixteenth century.

Once installed as abbot, Rennyo began an aggressive campaign to win new converts to the Honganji cause, mainly through a technique learned from his father, Zonnyo, the presentation of *myōgō honzon* from Honganji to a large number of meeting houses. He expanded further into the province of Ōmi to the northeast of Kyōto, helped in particular by two groups of *monto*, those at Kanegamori and those at Katada. Katada in particular was a staunch ally, an important commercial town on Lake Biwa that spawned the large Shinshū temple of Honpukuji 本福寺. But this expansion into Ōmi was dangerous: it meant that he was trespassing into Hieizan's backyard and in 1465 Enryakuji struck back, sending soldiers down to the capital from the Western Pagoda to destroy Honganji and force Rennyo into a peripatetic existence for a number of years. He ended up in the grounds of Onjōji in Ōtsu where he built a temple, Kenshōji 顯証寺, to house Shinran's portrait. The communities in Katada and Kanegamori were also subject to pressure, although they resisted with some success. Then, in 1471, Rennyo decided to move away from the area and relocate to a small village in Echizen called Yoshizaki 吉崎, just south of what is now Kaga City.

This period spent in Hokuriku (1471–75) was very fruitful for Rennyo indeed. Within two years the area around Yoshizaki had blossomed into a thriving trading centre. A strong base already existed in the region in the form of Zuisenji at Inami in Etchū and Chōshōji in Echizen; but he was not without rivals in Hokuriku: the Takada *monto*, who had moved their main temple Senjuji 専修寺 west to Isshinden in Ise Province in 1465, had a good deal of influence in this area as well and were equally as convinced as Honganji was of the orthodoxy of their own ideas and practice. Pilgrims and believers flocked to be near Rennyo, and for those communities who found it difficult to travel he communicated by means of his famous pastoral letters (*ofumi* 御文), which were written in straightforward Japanese. Over two hundred of these letters are extant; they were copied and handed on, eighty being published as a set in 1537. Many of them are simply exhortatory but a fair number are clearly attempts to counteract heterodox ideas: such misunderstandings as the belief that the *nenbutsu* was equally effective without faith (*mushin shōmyō* 無信稱名); that the grace of Amitābha could be taken for granted (*jikkō hiji* 十劫秘事); or that devotion was unnecessary (*fuhai hiji* 不拝秘事) because salvation was guaranteed. There was also the everpresent problem of priests being seen as having special powers, something that went entirely against Shinran's ideals but was almost impossible to eradicate. The message of pure faith was, after all, a difficult one to comprehend and to practise.

Success at Yoshizaki was not unalloyed: order was breaking down throughout Japan and, affected by the general atmosphere of social unrest, the *monto* themselves became increasingly unruly. The old estates had been dissolving for some time, replaced by a combination of local warrior-owned land and semi-autonomous villages. The *monto* represented a potential series of peasant farmer–warrior alliances that from their very size became willy-nilly a major part of the power structure. To some it felt like anarchy and certainly social revolution. One disgruntled Enryakuji monk wrote in 1482:

Looking carefully at the actions of the followers of Honganji, we see that they slander the true doctrines of Buddhism, destroy the images of the Buddha and the holy scriptures, and overturn shrines and temples. They are an unprecedented bane, and what they preach has nothing to do with Buddhism. Moreover, in Kaga recently the high officials have been swept aside and the province is without a leader. So topsy-turvy is the situation that the peasants are taking charge of administering affairs, and the prospects of the officials of the shogun and the constable are precarious. It is as if the sun and the moon are falling into the mud before our eyes (Solomon 1972: 229).

The *monto* were inexorably drawn into local disputes which involved them in military activity; in 1475 they took part in what is known as the first *ikkō ikki* 一向一揆, a term that originally meant 'leagues of the single-minded' but which soon came to signify violent uprisings by peasants who refused to pay their taxes or submit to any form of authority. Rennyo found himself trapped between a desire to continue ministering to his followers and his unhappiness at the highly problematic social consequences of disorder. His precise role at this juncture is a matter of some debate, but it is most unlikely that he actually wished to foment violence. He decided to return to Kyōto at this point, unable to do much more than censure those of his followers who became involved. It was to no avail. In 1488 the Honganji *monto* defeated the military governor of Kaga, Togashi Masachika 富樫政親, and took control of the whole province. They were to remain in power there for the next century.

The difficulties of controlling these groups in Hokuriku do not seem to have done material damage to Rennyo's cause, however. Contributions in the form of cash donations must have increased, because by 1483 he had completed the construction of an imposing new Honganji at Nishino 西野 in Yamashina, in the small valley that lies between Kyōto proper and Ōtsu on Lake Biwa. The main source of funds was cash donations from supporters, who channelled them directly to Honganji, avoiding the creation of a middleman who might have profited. By this time Rennyo was also close to Hosokawa Masamoto who became an important patron of the temple (Solomon 1978). The Yamashina Honganji included both an imposing Amitābha Hall and the Mieidō 御影堂, which contained the portrait of Shinran that had been kept at Ōtsu for safekeeping in the interim. It was here at Yamashina that Rennyo finally created an organisation with a sound financial base of such prestige that eventually it acted as a kind of overlord for all elements of the sect. One of his main tools was the creation of the Ikkeshū 一家衆, a council of immediate family members. Rennyo had five wives and twenty-seven children. Not all the children survived into maturity, of course, but those who did were placed in charge not only of existing temples but of new temples set up for the express purpose of exerting control over congregations in the provinces. Marriage had its uses and for Honganji blood relations became a guarantee of legitimacy and orthodoxy in a way not seen in religious circles before. It was in fact after Rennyo's death that the Ikkeshū came into its own as a governing body, using the threat of excommunication and the promise of guaranteed salvation (*goshō gomen* 後生御免) as powerful tools of control over its followers. It is clear how far they had moved away from Shinran's ideal.

Why was Honganji so successful? Partly it was a matter of good organisation but largely it was because the social circumstances were particularly fitting for such growth. It was just as much a social as a religious phenomenon. The breakdown of the old estates and the emergence of semi-autonomous corporate villages (*sōmura* 惣村) in central Japan had been going on since the mid-fourteenth century. This kind of structure, with a village headman, was an ideal focus for the kind of religious propagation that lay at the heart of Honganji's enterprise. Once converted to this form of Pure Land Buddhism, the headman had the time and resources to run a meeting house, which in turn gave him prestige. The backing of a large religious organisation specifically aimed at bringing a message of salvation to the lowest strata of society was also of great political use. It gave the village an extra resource on which to rely in case of local dispute. In addition there was an organisational level below the meeting house, namely the *kō* 講 discussion group. Although one meeting house might accommodate a number of discussion groups, the members of the groups were not necessarily from the same village.

The growth of Honganji from this time on was relentless. Not only did it absorb a large number of non-Jōdo Shinshū temples but it also absorbed rival temples within the movement itself. The most spectacular addition was Bukkōji itself, which joined Honganji in 1482. Rennyo himself retired in 1490, but he remained active, writing further *ofumi* and *myōgō honzon* scrolls that were so useful in cementing ties throughout the larger enterprise. It was in fact with the gifts received in return that he built yet another temple. On this occasion he chose Ishiyama 石山, not far from Sakai, and it was to be around this area that the new city of Ōsaka was to grow over the next century. Largely as a result of Rennyo's close connection to Hosokawa Masamoto, Honganji found it difficult to turn down requests for military aid and assistance, which happened first in Kawachi in 1505 and on a much larger scale in Etchū and Echizen in 1506. This was a fateful development and from this time on Honganji found itself becoming increasingly embroiled in the conflicts that tore central Japan apart for the next seventy years.

20.3   Playing with fire

The whole social fabric was now in flux, the clearest manifestation of which was the ability of peasants to show their collective anger at an oppressive tax burden in times of famine by forming leagues (*ikki*). Every one or two years a league would invade Kyōto and cause considerable destruction before usually obtaining amnesty for their debts. This was in essence class warfare, and it continued intermittently throughout the fifteenth century.[3] As far as the shogunate was concerned, matters began to slide downhill with the assassination of Ashikaga Yoshinari in 1441, which eventually led to the Ōnin wars (1467–77). The causes of this anarchy are less important than its results. Kyōto became little more than a battleground. The wealthy and the aristocracy fled, and any semblance of public order was lost as the two opposing forces settled down to a conflict of attrition. Sporadic, unpredictable acts of violence continued for ten years, and by the end of it about half the city was left in ruins, although, except for the odd occasion, the actual casualties seem to have been remarkably low. Fire was the main danger. It was to be twenty

---

[3]   See Gay 2001: 133 for a list of these so-called *tokusei ikki* running from 1428 to 1532.

years before Kyōto managed to recover, and when it did the townspeople discovered that they had to organise and look after themselves; it was clear that no one else would do it for them.

The reasons for the breakdown in law and order which began in the mid-fifteenth century and dragged on for most of the sixteenth century are, of course, many and various, and the gradual slide into anarchy cannot be laid solely at the door of a weak shogunate. It must be admitted that large, powerful organisations such as Honganji were equally to blame. The fundamental mission of Jōdo Shinshū, to bring the message of salvation through Amitābha to all sections of society (and especially the most disadvantaged), was laudable, but the message that faith alone was a sufficient key did not carry with it enough moral imperatives. Or perhaps it would be fairer to say that the moral imperatives were easily drowned out, the noisier things became. It was inevitable that when a large group of the most disadvantaged sections of society found common cause and common justification for upsetting the status quo, trouble would ensue. Just like Hōnen before him, Rennyo discovered that his followers had minds of their own; and the very lack of a priestly class that was such a proud tenet of the sect contributed to the problem. The problem that Jōdo Shinshū confederacies posed was that they soon became a state within the state, answerable to no one but their leaders and largely self-sufficient. They are best explained as being the equivalent of a daimyō's province, but consisting of people rather than land, united across provincial boundaries and other loyalties by a common religious conviction. Those whose salvation was assured made rather fearsome enemies.

But Pure Land Buddhists were not the only groups to find themselves drawn into a culture of violence and lawlessness. The followers of Nichiren were, if anything, more prone to such behaviour, given that intolerance of others and a delight in being obstreperous was one of their (less attractive) trademarks. Attention has already been drawn to the curious way in which Nichirenism, or the Hokkeshū as it was now known, managed to survive in the face of constant persecution by treating persecution as its birthright. From the early fourteenth century it had begun to create a base in Kyōto, especially among the artisans and merchants of the city. It is commonly said that the Hokkeshū proved popular with merchants because it was this-worldly and offered profit in return for devotion and practice, but this is not a convincing argument. The reasons were far more complex. Perhaps the strong streak of anti-authoritarianism struck a chord with a new urban class that found itself with financial power that far outweighed its status in society. Perhaps too, the traditional antagonism between the Hokkeshū and the Tendai stronghold of Enryakuji with its aristocratic links, was a contributing factor. Certainly, the wealth of many a merchant family was put to funding Hokkeshū temples, of which there were eventually twenty-two, most of these in the southern sector of Shimogyō 下京.

Once Kyōto found its feet again after the trauma of the Ōnin wars, the townspeople began to organise themselves into self-governing groups, which coalesced around the Hokkeshū temples, many of which took on the aspect of a fortress. One need not try to explain this by analysing what it was within Nichirenism that particularly appealed to them: it was a local marriage of convenience. The Hokkeshū temples were, quite naturally, eager to attract adherents; the townspeople for their part needed an organisation that was used to standing up for itself, was not a friend of Enryakuji or the peasant leagues, and was not tied to aristocratic culture. It is not therefore surprising that once they had organised themselves defensively in this fashion, they should take the offensive if and when necessary.

By the 1530s the atmosphere of mutual mistrust between the Hokkeshū groups in Kyōto and the Jōdo Shinshū confederates in the surrounding provinces had reached such a stage that the slightest rumour could spark conflict. In 1532 stories of an impending attack on Kyōto galvanised the Hokkeshū into pre-emptive action and with the help of other forces they attacked and destroyed the Yamashina Honganji, forcing Jōdo Shinshū to move its headquarters to Ishiyama. As a result of this success, the Hokkeshū *monto* set up what amounted to an autonomous government in Kyōto that lasted for four years. But there are still many imponderables. Was it a religious war? Where did the townspeople get their fervour? What was it about the Hokkeshū that really brought so many of them together at this time?[4]

This state of affairs was not to last. Late in 1536 Enryakuji decided to act and managed to create a temporary alliance which gave them a much larger force than could be raised by the combined Hokkeshū leagues. They invaded the city, burned every Hokkeshū temple, and turned much of the southern part of Kyōto into a wasteland, doing more damage than had been done in ten years during the Ōnin wars. This might look like a religious war, but in fact it was merely a case of the traditional ruling forces striking back and regaining a position of ascendancy that they had temporarily lost.

---

[4]   On the difficulty of analysing what really held these groups together and what motivated them see Berry 1994: 145–70.

It was clearly time for order to be restored, time for one daimyō among the many to rise above the rest and impose his authority on his peers, the court and the shogunate. This task was begun with some relish by the first of what are known as the 'three unifiers', Oda Nobunaga 織田信長 (1534–82). Nobunaga did not become a powerful daimyō until about 1560, at which point he managed to gain control over most of his own province of Owari, but in the period of twenty-two years from 1560 to his death in 1582 he changed the religious landscape of Japan forever, redefining the relationship between Buddhist institutions and the state, and consigning the principle of their mutual dependency to history. His ruthless treatment of those institutions that stood in his way was a by-product of his desire to gain absolute control. The temples were major political and economic powers that had to be subdued. Unlike secular powers before him, Nobunaga seemed to have nothing but contempt for threats of divine retribution. He was not out to destroy all Buddhist institutions for the sake of it, and it is worth remembering that he left them with far more than Thomas Cromwell had left the monasteries in England just thirty years previously. He was on good relations with a number of Zen temples, in particular Daitokuji, and only treated harshly those who crossed him or who represented a threat. In a way, then, one might argue that it was only those temples and sects that had become too politicised for their own good that brought down retribution upon themselves.

Most institutions wisely acquiesed to his demands or adapted themselves to his land policies, but two of the proudest refused to abandon their role as defenders of the faith and paid a terrible price as a result. Enryakuji was the first to go in what was undoubtedly Nobunaga's most notorious act. In 1570 he had warned the Tendai monks that if they allied themselves with his enemies they would be destroyed. Unfortunately the monks gambled and lost. Late in 1571 he arrived at the base of the mountain and set up camp in the grounds of Onjōji, ordering his troops to move up the mountain and destroy everything in their path. He was intent on using Enryakuji as an example to any other Buddhist organisation that might dream of confronting or plotting against him. In the space of two days every building on the mountain was destroyed, together with all the contents, priceless manuscripts, pictures, images that they contained. The fires burned for four days and stood as a dire warning to those watching from the capital to the west. Between three and four thousand priests and laity were slaughtered over a period of a week, among them a large number of women and children, and Hieizan's vast landholdings were redistributed among Nobunaga's supporters. The medieval period in Japan was well and truly over.

The second great institution was Ishiyama Honganji. This was a more difficult proposition, since it was built like a fortress. It was also well defended and had an extensive network of confederacies on which it could rely for military support. Conflict was inevitable, because Honganji was far too autonomous for Nobunaga to be able to countenance its existence or its intransigence for long. It is said that it took him ten years to subdue, from 1570 to 1580, but this was mainly because he went about the task methodically, clearing other provinces of supporters first and gradually starving Honganji of its main resource. Not that this was an easy task, and for a time it seemed as though he might fail; but eventually it became clear that the head of the order, Kennyo, had backed the wrong horse and he capitulated in 1580. Unfortunately, although Kennyo signed the agreement and left Honganji, his son refused to do so for a while and when his followers did in the end leave, they set the citadel alight and destroyed it. Nobunaga was left with a burned-out shell but he was also now in full control of the home provinces.[5]

When one looks back at the early and mid-sixteenth century from the standpoint of the 1570s, it is clear that some Buddhist institutions were carving out for themselves semi-autonomous realms within the state, just as a number of cities, such as Sakai, had become largely self-governing entities. It is quite natural that they should be brought to heel. The Hokkeshū were not to escape Nobunaga's anger either. Not that this is surprising either, given their belief that 'admonishing the ruler' was a bounden duty. No one admonished Nobunaga more than once. And what he left undone, Hideyoshi finished for him, reducing Negoroji to rubble in 1585 and causing Kōyasan to submit soon afterwards.

20.4   Jesuits

The first contacts between Japan and Europe had been made as early as the middle of the sixteenth century, when two Portuguese traders arrived on a Chinese ship at Tanegashima 種子島 in 1543. Tanegashima lay just to the south of Kyūshū, where a number of daimyō families such as the Shimazu, Ōtomo and Ōuchi were vying for overall control. The muskets brought by these traders were soon being copied and used to deadly effect. It was in the middle of all this confusion and warfare that the Jesuits arrived, carried on the same kind of trading vessels. The first Christian missionary to arrive in

[5]   See McMullin 1984b: 100–45 for a detailed treatment of this conflict.

Japan was the Basque Jesuit Francis Xavier who arrived from Malacca with two Spanish companions in 1549, landing in Kagoshima. He was carried on board a Chinese ship that was indulging in illicit trading, his only guide and interpreter a man called Yajirō, a somewhat suspect character who seems to have initially left Japan as a fugitive from justice. He was illiterate and his knowledge of his own religion left a good deal to be desired. The beginnings were hardly propitious. Xavier was received with courtesy at the main Zen temple in Kagoshima but immediately made himself a laughing stock when he read out a summary of Christian doctrine that had been translated for him by Yajirō into language that was far too rough and colloquial for such a setting. The only reason he was taken at all seriously was because he was rumoured to have arrived from 'India' and Yajirō had translated the word 'Deus' as 'Dainichi'. He was clearly bringing a new, previously unknown form of Buddhism to Japan and so was worth listening to. It took Xavier a full two years before he discovered the implications of this disastrous translation, and in the meantime his Buddhist adversaries had armed themselves with a nicely judged cross-linguistic pun: 'Deus' was the '*dai uso*', a great lie (Elison 1973: 36).

Xavier and his companions were welcomed by various Kyūshū daimyō for one reason and one reason only: it was understood that there was a strong link between the Jesuits and the Portuguese traders and it was this trade that they were after. To welcome one was to attract the other. The Jesuits were, of course, aware of this and used it to their full advantage. But Xavier also discovered that he needed ambassadorial trappings if he was going to make any impact. On his first attempt to visit Kyōto, he was refused audience with anyone of importance; he had no letter of introduction, no retinue and was shabbily dressed. On his second visit to Ōuchi Yoshitaka 大内義隆 in Yamaguchi in 1551, he made sure he had all the necessary accoutrements in order to impress. In return he received permission to preach in all domains under Ōuchi control. This was a major achievement, but the success was only apparent. A rebellion in the province soon rendered the permission invalid and Xavier left Japan that year. The Jesuits were beginning to realise the difficulty of their task. They desperately needed the support and permission of a strong local daimyō, but in the climate of mid-sixteenth-century Japan, no daimyō could be counted on to last for very long, and the very fact that a daimyō had consorted with them could easily prove his downfall.

Xavier had better luck with Ōtomo Sōrin Yoshishige 大友宗麟義鎮, the daimyō of Bungo on the northeastern coast of Kyūshū, who remained on good terms with the Jesuits until his death in 1587, gaining considerable profit (and munitions) from trade and allowing them to set up their head-quarters at Funai 府内. It was in fact a letter of introduction from him in 1560 that gained Gaspar Vilela access to the shōgun Yoshiteru, who in turn granted him limited approval for missionary work. This led to some success in converting a number of important figures in the home provinces in 1564. To put things into perspective, however, by 1564 there were still only ten Jesuits resident and working in Japan and after some fifteen years of hard work there were only a few thousand Japanese who could be considered converts. A stubborn refusal to compromise with Buddhism that often went as far as demanding that temples be demolished and images destroyed was not entirely helpful. Neither was the unbending attitude of Francisco Cabral, Mission Superior from 1570 to 1581. He had very little good to say about the Japanese and was convinced they could never become missionaries.

If one does not cease and desist admitting Japanese into the Society . . . that will be the reason for the collapse of the Society, nay! of Christianity, in Japan, and it will later hardly prove possible to find a remedy . . . I have seen no other nation as conceited, covetous, inconstant, and insincere as the Japanese . . . Among the Japanese it is considered a matter of honour and wisdom not to disclose the inner self, to prevent anyone's reading therein. They are trained to this from childhood; they are educated to be inscrutable and false (Elison 1973: 16).

So much for empathy. It is doubtful whether Christianity of any kind would have survived as long as it actually did with such a man at the helm. Fortunately in 1579 there arrived the Italian Alessandro Valignano (1538–1606) in the role of 'visitor', with full powers over the local superior. He soon realised that Cabral's attitude had been utterly counterproductive, and during his first sojourn in Japan (1579–82) he transformed the way the Jesuits interacted with the Japanese. He discovered, for example, that no attempt had been made to educate the missionaries in things Japanese and there was no seminary, but he soon managed to establish a novitiate at Usuki 臼杵 in Bungo where he had both Portuguese and Japanese taught for the first time. The perspicacity of Valignano is most evident in two tracts: *Advertimentos e avisos acerca dos costumes e catangues de Jappão* (1581)[6] and *Sumario de las cosas de Japon* (1583). Japan was still very strange to him but he understood that unless the Jesuits conformed to Japanese customs, they would simply fail. The three major points he emphasised tell us perhaps more about the Jesuits at the time than about the Japanese: the Japanese, he said,

---

[6]   The curious term *catangues* in this title is not a Portuguese word but an adaptation of the Japanese *katagi*, meaning 'characteristics' or 'habits'. It is restricted to Jesuit writings about Japan in this period.

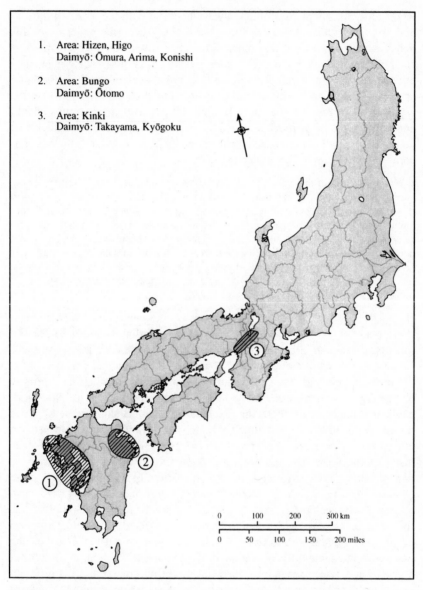

1. Area: Hizen, Higo
   Daimyō: Ōmura, Arima, Konishi

2. Area: Bungo
   Daimyō: Ōtomo

3. Area: Kinki
   Daimyō: Takayama, Kyōgoku

Map 11   Areas of Christian influence in Japan, late sixteenth century

were fastidious about cleanliness, always behaved with the utmost courtesy, and expected those in authority to look the part. The obverse of this behaviour was, however, that inner virtue on its own was not recognised as such without the outer signs. The *Advertimentos* was in essence a manual of etiquette containing much detail about how to behave in accordance with the strictest of Japanese norms in almost everything except morality, where the Japanese were found to be sadly lacking. He urged that the Jesuits should adopt titles used by different levels of the *gozan* Zen monks, so that their rank could be properly appreciated. The *Sumario* contains the following encomium of the people he was dealing with:

If we are to speak of the requisite capacity in virtues and letters, then I frankly do not know how there could among men be found a better. For the Japanese by nature make it a point to be masters of their passions, agreeable, docile, prudent and very circumspect, and modest and serious beyond measure. They are much given to ceremony. They are great endurers of hunger and cold and inured to rigors and personal maltreatment (even the kings and great lords glory in this), and are sublimely forbearing in the loss of their estates and in persecutions, without taking recourse to murmur and resentment; and in all this, and even unto death, they demonstrate a most noble and valiant heart and soul (Elison 1973: 72).

By the same token, however, Valignano was not a starry-eyed romantic and drew attention to what seemed to be an extraordinary disregard for the sanctity of human life, whether it be killing another or killing oneself. Infanticide was commonly practised apparently without moral qualms.

The best guide to how the Jesuits saw their task in doctrinal terms is Valignano's *Catechismus* written in 1580. The second half of this work explains Catholic doctrine but the first half deals with Buddhism. In the main, his attack on Buddhism was aimed at its 'obvious' failure to provide a strong ethical basis for action. The proof was in the pudding. Of course, it was historical accident that the Jesuits had turned up in Japan at a time of unprecedented civil strife and discord, with fidelity being a concept more honoured in the breach; in another time Japanese morality may well have appeared in a much better light. Be that as it may, the root of the problem was for him the very ease with which salvation was offered. Without delving too deeply into Buddhist philosophy, he also managed to put his finger on the one unsurmountable difference between the two modes of thought: Buddhism accepted and indeed proclaimed the principle of multiple truths and different levels of awareness in the individual that gave rise to different levels of understanding. Added to this was the quasi-physical nature of the Pure Land, the concept of rebirth, and the idea that everything had within it Buddha

Nature. It was an impersonal universe. None of this could ever be accepted by a Christianity that drew a definite distinction between man and his soul on the one hand and the rest of creation on the other, and that envisaged the creator as being separate from that which he had created.

When Valignano left Japan at the end of his first stay in February 1582, he took with him four Japanese boys who were to act as the first Japanese diplomatic mission to Europe. Although he was aware of the fragile nature of the Jesuits' toehold in Japan, he must have felt that with luck the mission had a reasonable future ahead of it. A local lord had been persuaded to give the Jesuits free rein to transform the small fishing village of Nagasaki into a major deep-water port to accommodate Portuguese ships. This culminated in 1580, when they were allowed to take formal possession of the town and its immediate environs. This extraordinary development must have looked like a tremendous success at the time. But it was, perhaps, their worst mistake. What the Jesuits did not know was that a few weeks before this agreement had been signed, Oda Nobunaga had succeeded in subjugating Ishiyama Honganji after ten years of prolonged warfare that he had pursued precisely on the grounds that autonomy (let alone extraterritoriality) by any sect could not be tolerated. Although Jesuits in Japan now numbered some sixty and the future looked much more secure than it had done only a few years previously, their troubles were in fact only beginning. In June 1582 Nobunaga was assassinated and his place was taken by a man with even greater ambitions; they were about to encounter Toyotomi Hideyoshi. But the fate of the Jesuits and of Christianity in Japan belongs to another chapter in another book.

Appendices: Reading Shingon's two maṇḍala

In §6.2 we touched on the use of maṇḍala in tantric practice. What follows is a somewhat more detailed treatment of the two main Shingon maṇḍala, the Diamond World (Kongōkai 金剛界) and the Womb World (Taizōkai 胎藏界), which use a combination of circles, squares and certain symbolic forms and figures to impose a pattern upon chaos. Further information can be found in Snodgrass 1988, ten Grotenhuis 1999 and Yamasaki 1988.

The Diamond World maṇḍala

The Diamond World represents wisdom, the *vajra* (*kongō* 金剛) being the symbol of wisdom, adamantine in its hardness, a thunderbolt that can pierce the darkest of clouds and smash ignorance and error, revealing that the whole universe is the body of Mahāvairocana. The maṇḍala is in the form of a square and whether it is placed on the ground or hung on a wall, the top is always treated as being west [plates 31–32]. In the centre of this square is a circle, which represents the disc of the full moon; here sits Mahāvairocana (Dainichi 大日) on a lotus, surrounded by four female figures, representing four perfections. His mudrā is not one of meditation but rather the wisdom fist (*chiken-in* 智拳印) with its obvious sexual connotations.[1] This disc is surrounded by four more discs, which contain four buddhas: to the west (top), Amitābha (Amida), who signifies that through meditation one can both realise enlightenment and at the same time engender in oneself the compassionate resolve to help others; to the east, Akṣobhya (Ashuku 阿閦), signifying the arousal of bodhicitta, the initial desire to achieve enlightenment; to the north (right), Amoghasiddhi (Fukūjōju 不空成就), who represents activity arising out of compassion; and to the south (left), Ratnasaṃbhava (Hōshō 寶生), who strengthens resolve and breaks down the concept of self. Each one of these is surrounded in turn by four bodhisattvas.

[1] For a full study of these gestures see Saunders 1960.

Akṣobhya, for example, is supported by Vajrasattva (Jp. Kongōsatta 金剛薩埵), who breaks down suffering, Vajrarāja (Jp. Kongōō 金剛王), who pulls people in with his hook, Vajrarāga (Jp. Kongōai 金剛愛), who shoots arrows that cause us to awaken to the truth, and Vajrasādhu (Jp. Kongōki 金剛喜), who causes the mind that results from this action to feel pleasure.

This group of five buddhas is then held within a larger circle, made of *vajra* laid end to end, which is held in place by the deities of Wind, Water, Fire and Earth, the whole combination held within a thick square double border, the inner border filled with tightly packed images of the thousand buddhas, the outer one containing twenty protecting deities. What might seem a static arrangement is in fact treated as being full of movement. In response to activity generated from Mahāvairocana at the centre, the four buddhas produce the four female figures that surround him. In response to this, Mahāvairocana produces the bodhisattvas who sit in small discs at the four corners of the large circle. They represent joy (*ki* 嬉), a diadem (*man* 鬘), song (*ka* 歌) and dance (*bu* 舞). In return, the four buddhas produce the four outer bodhisattvas who sit at the four corners of the inner border: incense (*kō* 香), flowers (*ke* 華), lamps (*tō* 燈) and powders (*zu* 塗). Mahāvairocana then produces the four bodhisattvas sitting at the midpoint gates of the same border, representing hook (*kō* 鉤), cord (*saku* 索), chain (*sa* 鎖) and bell (*rei* 鈴), metaphors for 'catching' sentient beings. All this activity is called paying 'mutual homage' (*kuyō* 供養), which is understood to be a euphemism for sexual intercourse, symbolised by the 'wisdom fist' at the very heart.

The full Diamond World maṇḍala is a large diagram consisting of nine of these 'assemblies' (*e* 會) each a transformation of the basic design, which is known as the Assembly of the Perfected Body (*jōjinne* 成身會). The maṇḍala can be read in two spiral movements, either from the centre out or from the outside inwards. Let us start at the centre and follow the spiral, which works like the *kana* の. This is to follow the process by which energy generated at the centre produces the universe, the process by which Mahāvairocana becomes a human being. The format of the centre assembly is repeated in all but the three at the top. Immediately below lies the Samaya Assembly (*samaya-e* 三昧會), which replaces the buddha and bodhisattva figures with physical objects that reveal their intentions and special powers. This is the universe in its physicality. In the next assembly, Subtle Discernment (*misai-e* 微細會), each figure sits inside a three-pointed *vajra*. This is the universe as light and sound, radiation and vibration. Rising next to the Assembly of Homage (*kuyō-e* 供養會), where all the figures except the buddhas are female in form and in different poses, we enter the universe as bodily movement.

Plate 31   Diamond World maṇḍala, Tōji. Heian period. 1.83 × 1.63m.

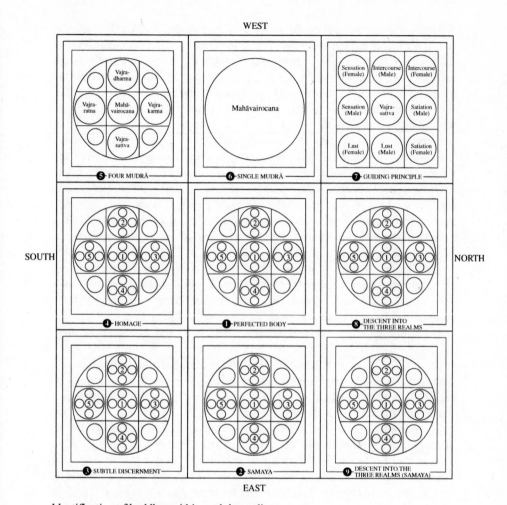

Identification of buddhas within each large disc.
1   Mahāvairocana
2   Amitābha
3   Amoghasiddhi
4   Akṣobhya
5   Ratnasaṃbhava

Plate 32   Diamond World maṇḍala (diagrammatic outline).

The assemblies on top are different. The Four Mudrā (*shiinne* 四印會), top left, is a simpler design, the moon disc at the centre having been expanded to fill the whole assembly and only Mahāvairocana and four bodhisattvas are present. It is an abbreviated digest of the preceding four assemblies and might have been used as a way of consolidating the practice attained so far, showing that the four were indivisible. Top centre we find the Assembly of the Single Mudrā (*ichiinne* 一印會), which is further truncated, containing only one deity, Mahāvairocana himself, although in some versions the deity is Vajrasattva. Perhaps at this point it was important to be reminded of the source of all things. Top right is the Assembly of the Guiding Principle (*rishu-e* 理趣會), where we are faced with nine squares, with Vajrasattva in the very centre surrounded by lust (*yoku* 欲), physical sensation (*shoku* 触), sexual intercourse (*ai* 愛) and satiation (*man* 慢), with the corresponding feminine forms occupying the four corners. Mahāvairocana is not present. We are getting closer to the world as we know it. This section is a graphic representation of the principle that 'delusion and enlightenment are identical'; normal human energy and desire is also what drives us to seek enlightenment and buddhahood; sexual intercourse is one with our desire for union with Mahāvairocana. We then proceed to the final two assemblies, the Descent into the Three Realms (*gōzanze-e* 降三世會) and its *samaya* version. We are now in the world of human beings, full of passion, desire and anger, Gōzanze (Trailokyavijaya) being the wrathful manifestation of Vajrasattva, who is, in his turn, a manifestation of Mahāvairocana. The deities here can be seen both as representing our own passions and, perhaps, as Mahāvairocana's fierce opposition to the evils he finds here.

To follow the spiral the other way is to travel from the human state to ultimate union with Mahāvairocana at the centre. The sentient being, sunk in passion and ignorance in the first two assemblies, awakens to the idea of original enlightenment and begins to resist, to cut through delusion. When he reaches the Assembly of True Meaning, he understands that human desires are also the energies that generate enlightenment. This is the classic Mahā-yāna formulation: desires are themselves enlightenment. At the Assembly of the Single Mudrā the individual realises that he must take refuge in the eternal buddha and he begins to practise various visualisations and then travels on towards an understanding of bodily motion, sound and physical objects, finally reaching the ultimate wisdom at the centre.

The Womb World maṇḍala

The Womb World maṇḍala represents compassion [plates 33–34]. It uses the same combination of circles and squares, but is a very different shape and can perhaps best be seen as a two-dimensional representation of a huge three-dimensional stepped altar or Indian stūpa. At its centre/summit Mahā-vairocana sits in a bright disc, which forms the central bud of an open, red, eight-petalled lotus set in a square. This is the Hall of the Central Dais with Eight Petals (*chūtai hachiyōin* 中臺八葉院). Red is the colour of the human heart and the lotus here is a representation of the heart, forming the primary symbol of the whole maṇḍala. Mahāvairocana is dressed not like a buddha but like a bodhisattva with jewels across his body, golden armbands and an elaborate crown. His mudrā shows him deep in meditation. He is surrounded at the cardinal points by four more buddhas, identifiable as such by their simple robes and bare heads; they have emanated from the centre. Reading from the top in clockwise fashion with the top being east, they are: to the east, 'Jewelled Banner' (Hōdō 寶幢), who is red, has the mudrā of 'fulfilling of the vow' (*segan-in* 施願印), and stands for the initial arousal of bodhicitta; to the south, 'King of the Spreading Lotus' (Kaifuke-ō 開敷華王), who is yellow, with the mudrā of 'granting the absence of fear' (*semui-in* 施無畏印), and stands for practice; to the west, 'Eternal Life' (Muryōju 無量壽), who is blue-green, with the mudrā 'concentration' (*jō-in* 定印), and is Amitābha in his Pure Land signifying the achievement of enlightenment; and to the north, 'Drumming in the Heavens' (Tenkuraion 天鼓雷音), who is black, with the mudrā of 'touching the ground' (*sokuchi-in* 觸地印), and stands for the achievement of nirvāṇa. Between these four buddhas sit four bodhisattvas: Samantabhadra (Fugen), Mañjuśrī (Monju), Avalokiteśvara (Kanjizai), Maitreya (Miroku), each holding a symbolic object. In the four corners of the square stand four treasure vases, which symbolise the four virtues of Dainichi Nyorai: enlightened mind, wisdom, compassion and useful techniques. Eight three-pointed *vajra*s are revealed at the point at which each petal overlaps its neighbour. These symbolise wisdom.

Although the centre might again seem to be static, it is interpreted as being in motion. The inner eight-petalled design shows in clockwise fashion how the mind becomes a buddha in five transformations (*goten* 五轉). Starting at the top, one arouses the desire for enlightenment; one then undergoes practice; one then comes to a realisation of enlightenment, finding it within one's grasp; one then achieves enlightenment or nirvāṇa; and then one finally arrives at the centre, where one puts one's achievement into practice; full

Plate 33   Womb World maṇḍala, Tōji. Heian period. 1.83 × 1.64m.

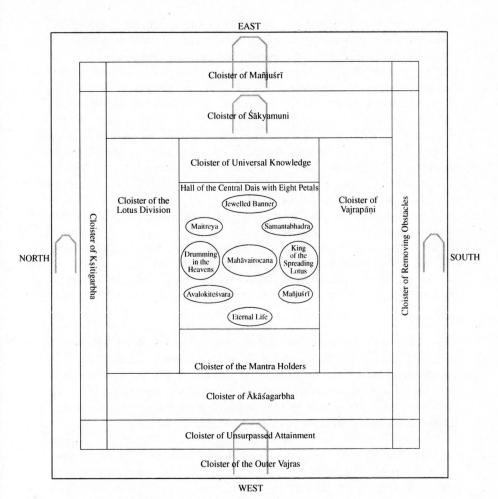

Plate 34   Womb World maṇḍala (diagrammatic outline).

enlightenment is not an absence but rather an activity whereby one partakes in the process by which all beings are saved. It is compassion in action. In other words, having reached the centre, compassion radiates out again.

This central 'stūpa' is surrounded by a series of cloisters (*in* 院), which contain a galaxy of bodhisattvas and deities, like the groundplan of a temple. The cloisters are arranged in layers, three on each side and four at the top and bottom. Beneath the centre square is the Cloister of the Mantra Holders (Jimyō-in 持明院). In the three-dimensional version this is where the initiate would stand. In the painting this position is occupied by the six-armed bodhisattva Prajñā (Hannya) with the mudrā of appeasement (*an'i-in* 安慰印), accompanied by four wrathful deities, Acala (Fudō 不動), Trailokyavijaya (Gōzanze 後三世), Yamāntaka (Daiitoku 大威德) and Trailokyavijaya in another form (Shōzanze 勝三世). It is here that error and delusion is burned in fire and frightened into submission.

Above the centre square is the Cloister of Universal Knowledge (Henchiin 遍知院). Two protective bodhisattvas on the right and two fecund female deities on the left surround a swastika within a flaming triangle surrounded by another circle of fire, above which hover two small figures. This is a *homa* (*goma* 護摩) altar and the two figures are two of the three Kāśyapa brothers whom Śākyamuni converted by quenching their fires of desire with his own fire. The *goma* rite is one of the most important of all Buddhist rituals. To the right of the centre lies the Cloister of Vajrapāṇi (Kongōshu-in 金剛手院), who is supported by twenty-one large deities and twelve smaller ones. It is here that one is given the knowledge to fight for enlightenment. To the left is the Lotus Division (Rengebuin 蓮華部院) with Avalokiteśvara as the central deity. Here one is promised compassion to help in the struggle.

The next layer out also consists of four halls, dedicated to similar activities to those at the first level but a stage closer to phenomenal reality. At the top is the Cloister of Śākyamuni (Shaka-in 釋迦印), with the manifestation of the eternal Buddha in human form at a specific time in history. He sits under a ceremonial gate and is accompanied by thirty-eight deities including his most important disciples, Ānanda and Kāśyapa, together with deities that symbolise parts of his body. To the right is the Cloister of Removing Obstacles (Jogaishō-in 除蓋障院), to the left the Cloister of Kṣitigarbha (Jizō-in 地藏院), dedicated to the bodhisattva who saves those suffering in hell. At the bottom lies the Cloister of Ākāśagarbha (Kokūzō-in 虚空藏院), whose name means 'holding emptiness within'.

The third layer consists of only two spaces, which may have been simply designed to give the maṇḍala visual balance. At the top is the Cloister of

Mañjuśrī (Monju-in 文殊院), where sits the bodhisattva of wisdom on a blue lotus, surrounded by many attendants. At the bottom is the Cloister of Unsurpassed Attainment (Soshitchi-in 蘇悉地院) with eight bodhisattvas but no central figure. The whole is then enclosed by another uniform layer, the Cloister of the Outer Vajras (Gekongōbuin 外金剛部院). Depicted here are 202 deities, kings and mythical creatures, many of them from Indic mythology. It is here, for example, that we find the god Gaṇeśa.[2] The job of these deities, the closest of all to the world of sentient beings, is to defend the whole edifice, while finding refuge in the Buddhist Dharma. Each side of the maṇḍala has a large gateway.[3]

These cloisters are also involved in activity and motion. On the one hand a constant series of waves radiate out from the centre to show how Mahāvairocana gives rise to the whole universe or mind and matter. The essence at the core spontaneously gives rise to compassion, which gives rise to activity, which moves towards the periphery becoming more and more concrete and phenomenal. On the other hand there is a corresponding flow coming inwards from layer to layer showing how the individual being at the periphery can proceed through stages eventually to arrive at the origin. Enlightenment is the discovery of the essential purity of Buddha Nature that exists at the heart.

Maṇḍala in use

How were these diagrams actually used in the ninth century? Although the linking of both maṇḍala as a pair was attributed to Huiguo (§6.1), the concept that they represent the dual aspect of the Dharmakāya, the Diamond World expressing the workings of the Dharma Body of Knowledge 智身 and the Womb World expressing the workings of the Dharma Body of Principle 理身, seems to have been a Shingon invention, as was the habit of hanging them on either side of an altar. There is no sign that they were originally created to be a set and it is preferable to deal with them as separate entities.

The path that we took through the Diamond World, starting at the centre, dropping east and then moving clockwise, exiting bottom right, comes from a description in a tenth-century Japanese commentary by Gengō 元杲 (914–95) called *Kongōkai ku'e mikki* 金剛界九會密記 (*T.* 2471), on the basis of which

---

[2] For a discussion of Gaṇeśa in Japan see Sanford 1991b: 287–335.
[3] Note that the Sanskrit for these gateways is *toraṇa*, which is thought by some to be the origin of the Japanese word *torii*, a Shintō gate.

later Shingon exegetes developed an elaborate description of the mental journey that this spiral of energy involved (Sharf 2001). On reaching each assembly, the practitioner was expected to perform a rite, involving a *mudrā*, a prayer or spell and a contemplation. One presumes that the painting was thought of as representing a three-dimensional layout and that the practitioner performed the rites while facing it. When Gengō's description is analysed, it turns out that in most cases the rite and the assembly do not always correspond, the ritual manual only partially fitting the image it is meant to explicate. This, in turn, mirrors another oddity: the normal expectation is that a maṇḍala has a 'mother' text, which it is in some way illustrating. In the case of the Diamond World, this is the large *Assembled reality of all the tathāgatas*; but it has always been known that this is not an exact fit either, since it deals with only six of the main nine deities. There are in fact a large number of variant maṇḍala designs, which suggests that they were not always related to a specific text but may often have been designed by different tantric masters for *ad hoc* purposes. Certainly, the maṇḍala that Kūkai brought back with him included layers of Chinese elements not reflected in the Sanskrit text. The distinctive pattern of nine assemblies in the Diamond World, for example, has convincingly been traced to the nine palaces of Daoist rather than Indic origin (Orzech 1998: 171–74). A similar situation arises in the case of the Womb World maṇḍala, whose mother text is assumed to be the *Mahāvairocanatantra*; in fact it contains numerous extraneous elements, which come from a variety of other sources.

As we know from Kūkai's own account, the primary initiation was little more that the casting of a flower or sprig of anise onto a flat maṇḍala to create a link between the self and a particular deity. Subsequent ceremonies led the practitioner further into a complex series of rites, full control over which was a prerequisite for certification as a tantric master. The maṇḍala, with its insistent, abstract geometry offset by a bewildering riot of body forms, each with its own implement or identifying sign (*samaya*), its own *mudrā*, and its own sound or seed syllable (*bīja*), was not only a graphic demonstration of how the unity at the centre manifests itself in a vast array of discriminations, it was itself sacred space into which the practitioner was supposed to enter. Each rite was built around the scenario of entertaining a guest (the deity). Careful preparations are made and the practitioner (as host) cleanses himself physically and mentally. The area is secured and made sacred, the deity's presence requested and offerings made. The heart of the rite is when the practitioner identifies himself with the deity, performing each of the three mysteries. While a mantra is intoned, for example, one imagines the syllables circulating through the body of the deity, out of its mouth and into one's head and then within one's own body. The rite is closed with a return of the space to its normal mode.

The relationship between ritual and image is therefore not as straightforward as one would suppose. There were no doubt occasions when a practitioner gazed upon the single image of a deity in order to meditate on what lay behind, or to activate some latent power, but tantric ritual tended to the formulaic and often involved imagining a series of transformations. Take, for example, the following directions from the 'contemplation of the sanctuary' (*dōjōkan* 道場觀), part of a Shingon ritual involving Nyoirin Kannon 如意輪觀音:

Assume the 'tathāgata fist' *mudrā* . . . Contemplate as follows: in front of me is the syllable *ah*. The syllable changes into a palatial hall of jewels. Inside is an altar with stepped walkways on all four sides. Arrayed in rows are jewelled trees with embroidered silk pennants suspended from each. On the altar is the syllable *hrīh*, which changes and become a crimson lotus blossom terrace. On top is the syllable *a*, which changes and becomes a full moon disk. On top is the syllable *hrīh*, and to the left and right there are two *trāh* syllables. The three syllables change and become a vajra jewel lotus. The jewel lotus changes into the principal deity, with six arms and a body the colour of gold. The top of his head is adorned with a jeweled crown. He sits in the posture of the Freedom King, assuming the attribute of preaching the Dharma (Sharf 2001: 164, adapted).

This is not meditation in order to still the mind; this is a very active process, an attempt to drive the imagination through a series of transformations from syllable to form and back again in order to counteract the insidious tendency to reify. The role of the specific image in front of one is therefore problematic, because the effect of the transformations one is performing is to deconstruct it the moment it is reached.

References

Abe Ryūichi 1999. *The weaving of mantra* (New York: Columbia University Press).
Adolphson, Mikael S. 2000. *The gates of power: monks, courtiers, and warriors in premodern Japan* (Honolulu: University of Hawai'i Press).
Akamatsu Toshihide 1957. *Kamakura bukkyō no kenkyū* (Kyōto: Heirakuji Shoten).
Akamatsu Toshihide and Philip Yampolsky 1977. 'Muromachi Zen and the Gozan system', in John Whitney Hall and Toyoda Takeshi (eds.), *Japan in the Muromachi age* (Berkeley: University of California Press): 313–29.
Ambros, Barbara 1990. 'Liminal journeys: pilgrimages of noblewomen in mid-Heian Japan', *Japanese Journal of Religious Studies* 24.3–4: 301–45.
Aoki Kazuo, Inaoka Kōji, Sasayama Haruo and Shirafuji Noriyuki (eds.) 1989–98. *Shoku Nihongi*, Shin Nihon koten bungaku taikei (Tōkyō: Iwanami Shoten).
Arnesen, Peter J. 1982. 'Suō province in the age of Kamakura', in Jeffrey P. Mass (ed.), *Court and Bakufu in Japan* (New Haven: Yale University Press): 92–120.
Arntzen, Sonja (tr.) 1997. *The kagerō diary* (Ann Arbor: University of Michigan Center for Japanese Studies).
Asai Endō 1999. 'Nichiren's view of humanity', *Japanese Journal of Religious Studies* 26.3–4: 239–59.
Astley-Kristensen, Ian 1991. *The Rishukyō*, Buddhica Brittanica Series Continua III (Tring, UK: Institute of Buddhist Studies).
Aston, W. G. (tr.) [1896] 1972. *Nihongi: chronicles of Japanese from the earliest times to AD 697*, 2 vols. (Tōkyō: Tuttle).
Batten, Bruce L. 1986. 'Foreign threat and domestic reform: the emergence of the ritsuryō state', *Monumenta Nipponica* 41: 199–219.
Bender, Ross 1979. 'The Hachiman cult and the Dōkyō incident', *Monumenta Nipponica* 34: 125–53.
Berry, Mary Elizabeth 1994. *The culture of civil war in Kyōto* (Berkeley: University of California Press).
Bielefeldt, Carl 1985. 'Recarving the dragon: history and dogma in the study of Dōgen', in Willam R. LaFleur (ed.), *Dōgen Studies* (Honolulu: University of Hawai'i Press): 21–53.
    1988. *Dōgen's manuals of Zen meditation* (Berkeley: University of California Press).
    1997. 'Kokan Shiren and the sectarian uses of history', in Jeffrey P. Mass (ed.), *The origins of Japan's medieval world* (Stanford University Press): 295–317.
Bingenheimer, Marcus 2001. *A biographical dictionary of the Japanese student-monks of the seventh and early eighth centuries*, Buddhismus-Studien 4 (Munich: Iudicium Verlag).

Birnbaum, Raoul 1979. *The healing Buddha* (Boulder, CO: Shambhala).

Blum, Mark L. 2002. *The origins and development of Pure Land Buddhism: a study and translation of Gyōnen's* Jōdo hōmon genrushō (Oxford University Press).

Bock, Felicia G. (tr.) 1970–72. *Engi-shiki, procedures of the Engi era*, 2 vols. (Tōkyō: Sophia University Press).

——— (tr.) 1985. *Classical learning and Taoist practices in early Japan*, Occasional paper 17 (Tempe: Arizona State University Center for Asian Studies).

Bodiford, William M. 1993. *Sōtō Zen in medieval Japan* (Honolulu: University of Hawai'i Press).

——— 1998. 'Review of Teeuwen 1996', *Journal of Japanese Studies* 24.2: 361–77.

Bohner, Hermann (tr.) 1935. *Jinnō shōtōki: Buch von den wahren Gott-Kaiser-Herrschafts-Linie*, 2 vols. (Tōkyō: Japanisch-Deutsches Kultur-Institut).

Borgen, Robert 1982. 'The Japanese mission to China, 801–806', *Monumenta Nipponica* 37.1: 1–25.

——— 1987. 'San Tendai Godai san ki as a source for the study of Sung history', *Bulletin of Sung-Yuan Studies* 19: 1–16.

Bowring, Richard 1992a. 'Buddhist translations in the Northern Sung', *Asia Major*, 3rd series, 5.2: 79–93.

——— 1992b. 'The *Ise monogatari*: a short cultural history', *Harvard Journal of Asiatic Studies* 52.2: 401–80.

——— (tr.) 1996. *The diary of Lady Murasaki* (Harmondsworth: Penguin).

——— 1998. 'Preparing for the Pure Land in late tenth-century Japan', *Japanese Journal of Religious Studies* 25.3–4: 221–57.

Breen, John and Mark Teeuwen (eds.) 2000. *Shinto in history* (Richmond, Surrey: Curzon).

Brock, Karen L. 1984. 'Tales of Gishō and Gangyō: editor, artist and audience in Japanese picture scrolls', Ph.D. dissertation, Princeton University.

Brown, Delmer M. (ed.) 1993. *The Cambridge history of Japan*, vol. I (Cambridge University Press).

Buijnsters, Marc 1999. 'Jichihan and the restoration and innovation of Buddhist practice', *Japanese Journal of Religious Studies* 26.1–2: 39–82.

Buswell, Robert E. Jr. 1987. 'The "short-cut" approach of k'an-hua meditation: the evolution of a practical subitism in Chinese Ch'an Buddhism', in Peter N. Gregory (ed.), *Sudden and gradual: approaches to enlightenment in Chinese thought* (Honolulu: University of Hawai'i Press): 321–77.

Chen, Jinhua 1998. 'The construction of early Tendai esoteric Buddhism: the Japanese provenance of Saichō's transmission documents and three esoteric apocrypha attributed to Śubhākarasiṃha', *Journal of the International Association of Buddhist Studies* 21.1: 21–76.

Chou Yi-liang 1945. 'Tantrism in China', *Harvard Journal of Asiatic Studies* 8: 241–332.

Cleary, Thomas (tr.) 1990. *Transmission of light* (San Francisco: North Point Press).

Coaldrake, William M. 1986. 'The architecture of Tōdai-ji', in Yutaka Mino (ed.), *The Great Eastern Temple* (The Art Institute of Chicago): 33–47.

450   *References*

Collcutt, Martin 1981. *Five mountains: the Rinzai Zen monastic institution in medieval Japan* (Cambridge, MA: Harvard University Press).

1983. 'The early Ch'an monastic rule: *ch'ing kuei* and the shaping of Ch'an community life', in Whalen Lai and Lewis L. Lancaster (eds.), *Early Ch'an in China and Tibet* (Berkeley: Asian Humanities Press): 165–84.

1990. 'Zen and the Gozan', in Yamamura Kōzō (ed.), *The Cambridge history of Japan*, vol. III (Cambridge University Press): 583–652.

1996. 'Religion in the life of Minamoto Yoritomo and the early Kamakura Bakufu', in P. F. Kornicki and I. J. McMullen (eds.), *Religion in Japan: arrows to heaven and earth* (Cambridge University Press): 90–119.

1997. 'Musō Soseki', in Jeffrey P. Mass (ed.), *The origins of Japan's medieval world* (Stanford University Press): 261–94.

Conlan, Thomas D. 2001. *In little need of divine intervention: Takezaki Suenaga's scrolls of the Mongol invasions of Japan* (Ithaca, NY: Cornell University East Asia Program).

Cranston, Edwin A. (tr.) 1993. *A waka anthology*, vol. I (Stanford University Press).

Davidson, Ronald M. 2002. *Indian esoteric Buddhism: a social history of the tantric movement* (New York: Columbia University Press).

Deal, William E. 1999. 'Hagiography and history: the image of Prince Shōtoku', in George J. Tanabe Jr. (ed.), *Religions of Japan in practice* (Princeton University Press).

de Bary, Wm. Theodore, Donald Keene, George Tanabe and Paul Varley (eds.) 2001. *Sources of Japanese tradition*, 2nd edn, vol. I (New York: Columbia University Press).

de Groot, J. J. M. (tr.) [1892] 1967. *Le code du Mahāyāna en Chine* (Vaduz: Saendig Reprint Verlag).

Dobbins, James C. 1989. *Jōdo shinshū: Shin Buddhism in medieval Japan* (Bloomington: Indiana University Press).

1998. 'A brief history of Pure Land Buddhism in early Japan', in Kenneth K. Tanaka and Eisho Nasu (eds.), *Engaged Pure Land Buddhism* (Berkeley: WisdomOcean Publications): 113–65.

Dolce, Lucia 1999. 'Criticism and appropriation: Nichiren's attitude toward esoteric Buddhism', *Japanese Journal of Religious Studies* 26.3–4: 349–82.

2002. 'Esoteric patterns in Nichiren's interpretation of the Lotus Sūtra', Ph.D. dissertation, University of Leiden.

Donner, Neal and Daniel B. Stevenson 1993. *The great calming and contemplation* (Honolulu: University of Hawai'i Press).

Ebersole, Gary L. 1989. *Ritual poetry and the politics of death in early Japan* (Princeton University Press).

Elison (Elisonas), George 1973. *Deus destroyed: the image of Christianity in early modern Japan* (Cambridge, MA, Harvard University Press).

Emmerick, R. E. (tr.) 1970. *The sūtra of golden light* (London: Luzac).

Endō Yoshimoto and Kasuga Kazuo (eds.) 1967. *Nihon ryōiki*, Nihon koten bungaku taikei (Tōkyō: Iwanami Shoten).

Faure, Bernard 1987. 'The Daruma-shū, Dōgen and Sōtō Zen', *Monumenta Nipponica* 42.1: 25–55.

1991. *The rhetoric of immediacy: a cultural critique of Chan/Zen Buddhism* (Princeton University Press).

1996. *Visions of power: imagining medieval Japanese Buddhism* (Princeton University Press).

1997. *The will to orthodoxy: a critical genealogy of Northern Chan Buddhism* (Princeton University Press).

1998. *The red thread: Buddhist approaches to sexuality* (Princeton University Press).

2000. 'Japanese tantra, the Tachikawa-ryū and Ryōbu Shintō', in David Gordon White (ed.), *Tantra in practice* (Princeton University Press): 543–56.

Foard, James H. 1977. 'Ippen Shōnin and popular Buddhism in Kamakura Japan', Ph.D. dissertation, Stanford University.

1980. 'In search of a lost reformation: a reconsideration of Kamakura Buddhism', *Japanese Journal of Religious Studies* 7.4: 261–91.

Ford, James L. 2002. 'Jōkei and the rhetoric of "other-power" and "easy practice" in medieval Japanese Buddhism', *Japanese Journal of Religious Studies* 29.1–2: 67–106.

Foulk, T. Griffith 1993. 'Myth, ritual, and monastic practice in Sung Ch'an Buddhism', in Patricia Buckley Ebrey and Peter N. Gregory (eds.), *Religion and society in T'ang and Sung China* (Honolulu: University of Hawai'i Press): 147–208.

1999. 'Sung controversies concerning the "separate transmission" of Ch'an', in Peter N. Gregory and Daniel A. Getz Jr. (eds.), *Buddhism in the Sung* (Honolulu: University of Hawai'i Press): 220–94.

2000. 'The form and function of kōan literature', in Steven Heine and Dale S. Wright (eds.), *The kōan: texts and contexts in Zen Buddhism* (New York: Oxford University Press): 15–45.

Frank, Bernard 1998. *Kata-imi et Kata-tagae: étude sur les interdits de direction à l'époque Heian* (Paris: Collège de France, Institut des hautes études japonaises).

Fujita Kōtatsu 1990. 'The textual origins of the *Kuan wu-liang-shou ching*', in Robert E. Buswell (ed.), *Chinese Buddhist apocrypha* (Honolulu: University of Hawai'i Press).

Gardiner, David L. 1994. 'Kūkai and the beginnings of Shingon Buddhism', Ph.D. dissertation, Stanford University.

1996. 'Maṇḍala, maṇḍala on the wall: variations of usage in the Shingon school', *Journal of the International Association of Buddhist Studies* 19.2: 245–79.

2000. 'The consecration of the monastic compound at Mount Koya by Kūkai', in David Gordon White (ed.), *Tantra in practice* (Princeton University Press): 119–30.

Gay, Suzanne 2001. *The moneylenders of late medieval Kyōto* (Honolulu: University of Hawai'i Press).

Getz, Daniel A. Jr. 1999. 'T'ien-t'ai Pure Land societies and the creation of the Pure Land patriarchate', in Peter N. Gregory and Daniel A. Getz Jr. (eds.), *Buddhism in the Sung* (Honolulu: University of Hawai'i Press): 477–523.

Gimello, Robert M. 1976. 'Chih-yen and the foundations of Hua-yen Buddhism', Ph.D. dissertation, Columbia University, NY.

1983. 'Li T'ung-hsüan and the practical dimensions of Hua-yen', in Robert M. Gimello and Peter Gregory (eds.), *Studies in Ch'an and Hua-yen* (Honolulu: University of Hawai'i Press): 321–89.

1992. 'Mārga and culture: learning, letters and liberation in Northern Sung Ch'an', in Robert E. Buswell Jr. and Robert M. Gimello (eds.), *Paths to liberation* (Honolulu: University of Hawai'i Press): 371–437.

Girard, Frédéric 1990. *Un moine de la secte Kegon à l'époque de Kamakura, Myōe (1173–1232)* (Paris: École française d'extrême-orient).

Gómez, Luis O. 1996. *The land of bliss* (Honolulu: University of Hawai'i Press).

Goodwin, Janet R. 1994. *Alms and vagabonds: Buddhist temples and popular patronage in medieval Japan* (Honolulu: University of Hawai'i Press).

Grapard, Allan G. 1982. 'Flying mountains and walkers of emptiness: toward a definition of sacred space in Japanese religions', *History of Religions* 20.3: 195–221.

1987. 'Linguistic cubism: a singularity of pluralism in the Sannō cult', *Japanese Journal of Religious Studies* 14.2–3: 211–34.

1988. 'Institution, ritual, and ideology: the twenty-two shrine-temple multiplexes of Heian Japan', *History of Religions* 27.3: 246–69.

1992a. *The protocol of the gods: a study of the Kasuga cult in Japanese history* (Berkeley: University of California Press).

1992b. 'The Shinto of Yoshida Kanetomo', *Monumenta Nipponica* 47.1: 27–58.

1992c. '*Yuiitsu Shintō Myōbō Yōshū*', *Monumenta Nipponica* 47.2: 137–61.

1998. '*Keiranshūyōshū*: a different perspective on Mt Hiei in the medieval period', in Richard K. Payne (ed.), *Re-visioning 'Kamakura' Buddhism* (Honolulu: University of Hawai'i Press).

1999. 'Religious practices', in Donald Shively and William H. McCullough (eds.), *The Cambridge history of Japan*, vol. II (Cambridge University Press): 535–36.

2000a. 'The economics of ritual power', in John Breen and Mark Teeuwen (eds.), *Shinto in history* (Richmond, Surrey: Curzon): 68–94.

2000b. 'Precepts for an emperor', in David Gordon White (ed.), *Tantra in practice* (Princeton University Press): 146–64.

2002. 'Shrines registered in ancient Japanese law,' *Japanese Journal of Religious Studies* 29.3–4: 209–32.

2003. 'The source of oracular speech: absence? presence? or plain treachery?: the case of *Hachiman Usa-gū gotakusenshū*', in Mark Teeuwen and Fabio Rambelli (eds.), *Buddhas and kami in Japan* (London: RoutledgeCurzon): 77–94.

Grayson, James H. 2002. 'Susa-no-o: a culture hero from Korea', *Japan Forum* 14: 465–87.

Gregory, Peter N. (ed.) 1987. *Sudden and gradual: approaches to enlightenment in Chinese thought* (Honolulu: University of Hawai'i Press).

1991. *Tsung-mi and the sinification of Buddhism* (Princeton University Press).

Gregory, Peter N. and Daniel A. Getz Jr. (eds.), 1999. *Buddhism in the Sung* (Honolulu: University of Hawai'i Press).

Groner, P. 1984. *Saichō*, Berkeley Buddhist Studies Series 7 (Berkeley: Institute of Buddhist Studies).

1987. 'Annen, Tankei, Henjō and monastic discipline in the Tendai school: the background of the *Futsū jubosatsukai kōshaku*', *Japanese Journal of Religious Studies* 14.2–3: 129–59.

1989. 'The *Lotus sutra* and Saichō's interpretation of the realization of buddhahood with this very body', in George J. Tanabe Jr. and Willa Jane Tanabe (eds.), *The Lotus sutra in Japanese culture* (Honolulu: University of Hawai'i Press): 53–74.

1990. 'The *Fan-wang ching* and monastic discipline in Japanese Tendai: a study of Annen's *Futsū jubosatsukai kōshaku*', in Robert E. Buswell Jr. (ed.), *Chinese Buddhist apocrypha* (Honolulu: University of Hawai'i Press): 251–90.

1992. 'Shortening the path: early Tendai interpretations of the realization of buddhahood with this very body (*sokushin jōbutsu*)', in Robert E. Buswell Jr. and R. M. Gimello (eds.), *Paths to liberation: the mārga and its transformations in Buddhist thought* (Honolulu: University of Hawai'i Press): 439–73.

2001. 'Icons and relics in Eison's religious activities', in Robert H. Sharf and Elizabeth Horton Sharf (eds.), *Living images: Japanese Buddhist icons in context* (Stanford University Press): 114–50.

2002. *Ryōgen and Mount Hiei* (Honolulu: University of Hawai'i Press).

2005. 'Tradition and innovation: Eison's self-ordinations and the establishment of new orders of Buddhist practitioners', in William M. Bodiford (ed.), *Going forth: visions of Buddhist vinaya* (Honolulu: University of Hawai'i Press): 210–35.

Gülberg, Niels 1999. *Buddhistische Zeremoniale* (kōshiki) *und ihre Bedeutung für die Literatur des Japanischen Mittelalters*, Münchener Ostasiatische Studien 76 (Stuttgart: Franz Steiner Verlag).

Guth, Christine M. E. 1988. 'The pensive prince of Chūgūji', in Alan Sponberg and Helen Hardacre (eds.), *Maitreya, the future Buddha* (Cambridge University Press): 191–213.

1999. 'Mapping sectarian identity: Onjōji's statue of Shinra Myōjin', *RES* 35: 111–24.

Hakeda, Yoshito S. 1972. *Kūkai: major works* (New York: Columbia University Press).

Hare, Thomas Blenman 1990. 'Reading, writing and cooking: Kūkai's interpretative strategies', *Journal of Asian Studies* 49.2: 253–73.

Hayami Tasuku 1975. *Heian kizoku shakai to bukkyō* (Tōkyō: Yoshikawa Kōbunkan).

Heine, Steven 1994. *Dōgen and the kōan tradition* (Albany, NY: State University of New York Press).

2003. 'Did Dōgen go to China? Problematizing Dōgen's relation to Ju-ching and Chinese Chan', *Japanese Journal of Religious Studies* 30.1–2: 27–59.

Henderson, Gregory and Leon Hurvitz 1956. 'The Buddha of Seiryōji', *Artibus Asiae* 19.1: 5–55.

Hérail, F. (tr.) 1987–91. *Notes Journalières de Fujiwara Michinaga*, 2 vols. (Paris: Librarie Droz).

Horton, Sarah 2004. 'The influence of the *Ōjōyōshū* in late tenth- and early eleventh-century Japan', *Japanese Journal of Religious Studies* 31.1: 29–56.

Hosokawa Ryōichi 1999. 'Medieval nuns and nunneries: the case of Hokkeji', in

Tonomura Hitomi, Anne Walthall and Wakita Haruko (eds.), *Women and class in Japanese history* (Ann Arbor: University of Michigan Center for Japanese Studies): 67–79.

Hsieh, Ding-hwa Evelyn 1994. 'Yuan-wu k'o-ch'in's (1063–1135) teaching of Ch'an *kung-an* practice: a transition from the literary study of Ch'an *kung-an* to the practical *k'an-hua* Ch'an', *Journal of the International Association of Buddhist Studies* 17.1: 66–95.

Imagawa Fumio (ed.) 1977–79. *Kundoku Meigetsuki*, 6 vols. (Tōkyō: Kawade Shobō Shinsha).

Inoue Mitsusada and Ōsone Shōsuke (eds.) 1974. *Ōjōden, Hokke genki*, Nihon shisō taikei (Tōkyō: Iwanami Shoten).

Inoue Mitsusada, Seki Akira, Tsuchida Naoshige and Aoki Kazuo (eds.) 1976. *Ritsuryō*, Nihon shisō taikei (Tōkyō: Iwanami Shoten).

Inoue Nobutaka, Itō Satoshi, Endō Jun and Mori Mizue 2003. *Shinto – a short history* (London: RoutledgeCurzon).

Iwasa Masashi and Tokieda Motoki (eds.) 1965. *Jinnō shōtōki, Masukagami*, Nihon koten bungaku taikei (Tōkyō: Iwanami Shoten).

Janousch, A. 1999. 'The emperor as bodhisattva: the bodhisattva ordination and ritual assemblies of Emperor Wu of the Liang Dynasty', in Joseph P. McDermott (ed.), *State and court ritual in China* (Cambridge University Press).

Kageyama Haruki (ed.) 1983. *Hie*, Shintō taikei: jinjahen, vol. XXIX (Tōkyō: Shintō taikei hensankai).

Kamata Shigeo and Tanaka Hisao (eds.) 1971. *Kamakura kyūbukkyō*, Nihon shisō taikei (Tōkyō: Iwanami Shoten).

Kamens, Edward 1988. *The Three Jewels*, Michigan monograph series in Japanese Studies, no. 2 (Ann Arbor: University of Michigan Center for Japanese Studies).

   1990. *The Buddhist poetry of the Great Kamo Priestess*, Michigan monograph series in Japanese Studies, no. 5 (Ann Arbor: University of Michigan Center for Japanese Studies).

Kamikawa Michio 1990. 'Accession rituals and Buddhism in medieval Japan', *Japanese Journal of Religious Studies* 17.2–3: 143–80.

Kawai Hayao 1992. *The Buddhist priest Myōe: a life of dreams* (Venice, CA: The Lapis Press).

Kidder, J. Edward 1999. *The lucky seventh: early Hōryūji and its time* (Tōkyō: International Christian University, Hachiro Yuasa Memorial Museum).

Klein, Susan Blakeley 1997. 'Allegories of desire: poetry and eroticism in the *Ise monogatari zuinō*', *Monumenta Nipponica* 52.4: 441–65.

   1998. '*Ise monogatari zuinō*: an annotated translation', *Monumenta Nipponica* 53.1: 13–43.

   2002. *Allegories of desire: esoteric commentaries in medieval Japan* (Cambridge, MA: Harvard University Press).

Knoblock, John (tr.) 1988. *Xunzi*, vol. I (Stanford University Press).

Kornicki, Peter F. 1998. *The book in Japan* (Leiden: Brill).

Kraft, Kenneth 1992. *Eloquent Zen: Daitō and early Japanese Zen* (Honolulu: University of Hawai'i Press).

Kurano Kenji and Takeda Yūkichi (eds.) 1958. *Kojiki, Norito*, Nihon koten bungaku taikei (Tōkyō: Iwanami Shoten).

LaFleur, William R. 1983. 'In and out of the *rokudō*: Kyōkai and the formation of medieval Japan', in *The karma of words* (Berkeley: University of California Press): 26–59.

Lancaster, Lewis 1988. 'Maitreya in Korea', in Alan Sponberg and Helen Hardacre (eds.), *Maitreya, the future Buddha* (Cambridge University Press).

Levering, Miriam 1999. 'Miao-tao and her teacher Ta-hui', in Peter N. Gregory and Daniel A. Getz Jr. (eds.), *Buddhism in the Sung* (Honolulu: University of Hawai'i Press).

Liscutin, Nicola 1990. 'Daijōsai: the great festival of tasting the new fruits', *Transactions of the Asiatic Society of Japan*, 4th series, 5: 25–52.

McCallum, Donald F. 1994. *Zenkōji and its icon* (Princeton University Press).

McCullough, William H. and McCullough, Helen Craig (tr.) 1980. *A tale of flowering fortunes*, 2 vols. (Stanford University Press).

Macé, François 1986. *La mort et les funérailles dans le Japan ancien* (Paris: Publications orientalistes de France).

Machida Sōhō 1999. *Renegade monk: Hōnen and Japanese Pure Land Buddhism* (Berkeley: University of California Press).

McMullen, I. J. 1996. 'The worship of Confucius in ancient Japan', in Peter F. Kornicki and I. J. McMullen (eds.), *Religion in Japan* (Cambridge University Press): 39–77.

McMullin, N. 1984a. 'The Sanmon-Jimon schism in the Tendai school of Buddhism: a preliminary study', *Journal of the International Association of Buddhist Studies* 7.1: 83–105.

  1984b. *Buddhism and the state in sixteenth-century Japan* (Princeton University Press).

  1987. 'The Enryakuji and the Gion shrine-temple complex in the mid-Heian period', *Japanese Journal of Religious Studies* 14.2–3: 161–84.

  1988. 'On placating the gods and pacifying the populace: the case of the Gion goryō cult', *History of Religions* 27.3: 270–93.

  1989a. 'The Lotus sūtra and politics in the mid-Heian period', in George J. Tanabe and Willa J. Tanabe (eds.), *The Lotus sūtra in Japanese culture* (Honolulu: University of Hawai'i Press): 119–41.

  1989b. 'Historical and historiographical issues in the study of pre-modern Japanese religions', *Japanese Journal of Religious Studies* 16.1: 3–40.

McRae, John R. 1983. 'The Ox-head School of Chinese Ch'an Buddhism', in Robert M. Gimello and Peter N. Gregory (eds.), *Studies in Ch'an and Hua-yen* (Honolulu: University of Hawai'i Press): 169–252.

  1986. *The Northern School and the formation of early Ch'an Buddhism* (Honolulu: University of Hawai'i Press).

  1987. 'Shen-hui and the teaching of sudden enlightenment in early Ch'an Buddhism', in Peter N. Gregory (ed.), *Sudden and gradual: approaches to enlightenment in Chinese thought* (Honolulu: University of Hawai'i Press): 227–78.

Matsunaga, Daigan and Alicia 1974. *Foundation of Japanese Buddhism*, 2 vols. (Tōkyō: Eikyōji Foundation).

Matsunaga Yūkei 1973. *Mikkyō no sōjōsha* (Tōkyō: Hyōronsha).

Meeks, Lori Rachelle 2003. 'Nuns, court ladies, and female bodhisattvas: the women of Japan's medieval Ritsu-school nuns revival movement', Ph.D. dissertation, Princeton University.

Miller, Roy Andrew 1975. *'The Footprints of the Buddha': an eighth-century Old Japanese poetic sequence* (New Haven: American Oriental Society).

Moerman, David 1997. 'The ideology of landscape and the theater of state: Insei pilgrimage to Kumano (1090–1220)', *Japanese Journal of Religious Studies* 24.3–4: 347–74.

Morrell, Robert E. (tr.) 1985. *Sand and pebbles* (Albany, NY: State University of New York Press).

   1987. *Early Kamakura Buddhism: a minority report* (Berkeley: Asian Humanities Press).

Morse, Samuel C. 1986. 'Sculpture at Tōdai-ji', in Yutaka Mino (ed.), *The Great Eastern Temple* (The Art Institute of Chicago): 49–63.

Nagazumi Yasuaki and Shimada Isao (eds.) 1966. *Kokon chomonjū*, Nihon koten bungaku taikei (Tōkyō: Iwanami Shoten).

Nakamura, K. M. (tr.) 1973. *Miraculous stories from the Japanese Buddhist tradition* (Cambridge, MA: Harvard University Press).

Nara kokuritsu hakubutsukan 1964. *Suijaku bijutsu* (Tōkyō: Kadokawa Shoten).

Nara rokudaiji taikan kankōkai 1968–72. *Hōryūji*, 5 vols. (Tōkyō: Iwanami Shoten).

Nasu Seiryū 1970. *Gorin kuji hishaku no kenkyū* (Tōkyō: Rokuyaon).

Naumann, Nelly 1988. *Die einheimische Religion Japans*, vol. I (Leiden: Brill).

   1994. *Die einheimische Religion Japans*, vol. II (Leiden: Brill).

   2000. 'The state cults of the Nara and early Heian periods', in John Breen and Mark Teeuwen (eds.), *Shinto in history* (Richmond, Surrey: Curzon): 47–67.

Ōhashi Shunhō (ed.) 1971. *Hōnen, Ippen*, Nihon shisō taikei (Tōkyō: Iwanami Shoten).

Okami Masao and Akamatsu Toshihide (eds.) 1967. *Gukanshō*, Nihon koten bungaku taikei (Tōkyo: Iwanami Shoten).

Orzech, Charles D. 1989. 'Seeing Chen-yen Buddhism: traditional scholarship and the Vajrayāna in China', *History of Religions* 29.2: 87–114.

   (tr.) 1995. 'The legend of the iron stūpa', in Donald S. Lopez Jr. (ed.), *Buddhism in practice* (Princeton University Press): 314–17.

   1998. *Politics and transcendent wisdom: the Scripture for humane kings in the creation of Chinese Buddhism* (University Park, PA: Pennsylvania University Press).

Ōsumi Kazuo (ed.) 1977. *Chūsei shintō ron*, Nihon shisō taikei (Tōkyō: Iwanami Shoten).

Penkower, Linda L. 1993. 'T'ien-t'ai during the T'ang Dynasty: Chan-jan and the sinification of Buddhism', Ph.D. dissertation, Columbia University, NY.

Philippi, Donald L. (tr.) 1968. *The Kojiki* (Princeton University Press).

Piggott, Joan R. 1982. 'Hierarchy and economics in early medieval Tōdaiji', in

Jeffrey P. Mass (ed.), *Court and Bakufu in Japan* (New Haven: Yale University Press): 45–91.

1987. 'Tōdaiji and the Nara imperium', Ph.D. dissertation, Stanford University.

1997. *The emergence of Japanese kingship* (Stanford University Press).

Pollack, David (tr.) 1985. *Zen poems of the five mountains* (Decatur, GA: Scholars Press).

Rambelli, Fabio 1992. 'Segni di diamante: aspetti semiotici del buddhismo esoterico giapponese di Kakuban', 2 vols., Ph.D. dissertation, Università degli Studi di Venezia.

Reischauer, Edwin O. (tr.) 1955a. *Ennin's diary: the record of a pilgrimage to China in search of the law* (New York: The Ronald Press Company).

1955b. *Ennin's travels in T'ang China* (New York: The Ronald Press Company).

Robert, Jean-Noël 1990. *Les doctrines de l'école japonaise tendai au début du IXe siècle: Gishin et le Hokke-shū gi shū* (Paris: Maisonneuve et Larose).

Rocher, Alain 1997. *Mythe et souveraineté au Japon* (Paris: Press universitaires de France).

Rosenfield, John M. and ten Grotenhuis, E. (eds.) 1979. *Journey of the three jewels: Japanese Buddhist paintings from Western collections* (New York: The Asia Society).

Ruch, Barbara (ed.) 2002. *Engendering faith: women and Buddhism in premodern Japan*, Michigan monograph series in Japanese Studies, no. 43 (Ann Arbor: University of Michigan Center for Japanese Studies).

Ruppert, Brian D. 2000. *Jewel in the ashes: Buddha relics and power in early medieval Japan* (Cambridge, MA: Harvard University Press).

2002. 'Pearl in the shrine: a genealogy of the Buddhist jewel of the Japanese sovereign', *Japanese Journal of Religious Studies* 29.1–2: 1–33.

Sakamoto Tarō, Ienaga Saburō, Inoue Mitsusada and Ōno Susumu (eds.) 1967. *Nihon shoki*, 2 vols., Nihon koten bungaku taikei (Tōkyō: Iwanami Shoten).

Sakurai Tokutarō, Hagiwara Tatsuo and Miyata Noboru (eds.) 1975. *Jisha engi*, Nihon shisō taikei (Tōkyō: Iwanami Shoten).

Sanford, James H. 1981. *Zen-man Ikkyū* (Chico, CA: Scholars Press)

1991a. 'The abominable Tachikawa skull ritual', *Monumenta Nipponica* 46.1: 1–20.

1991b. 'Literary aspects of Japan's Dual-Gaṇeśa cult', in Robert L. Brown (ed.), *Ganesh: Studies of an Asian god* (Albany, NY: State University of New York Press): 287–335.

1994. 'Breath of life: the esoteric *nenbutsu*', in Ian Astley (ed.), *Esoteric Buddhism in Japan*, Seminar for Buddhist Studies Monograph 1 (Copenhagen: Seminar for Buddhist Studies): 65–98.

1997. 'Wind, waters, stupas, mandalas: fetal buddhahood in Shingon', *Japanese Journal of Religious Studies* 24.1–2: 1–38.

2004. 'Amida's secret life: Kakuban's *Amida hishaku*', in Richard K. Payne and Kenneth K. Tanaka (eds.), *Approaching the Land of Bliss: Religious praxis in the cult of Amitābha* (Honolulu: University of Hawai'i Press).

Sansom, G. B. 1924. 'The imperial edicts in the Shoku-Nihongi', *Transactions of the*

Asiatic Society of Japan, 2nd series, 1: 5–39.

1934. 'Early Japanese law and administration (Part II)', *Transactions of the Asiatic Society of Japan*, 2nd series, 11: 122–27.

1958. *A history of Japan*, vol. I (Stanford University Press).

Saunders, E. Dale 1960. *Mudrā* (New York: Pantheon Books).

Scheid, Bernard 2000. 'Reading the *Yuiitsu shintō myōbō yōshū*', in John Breen and Mark Teeuwen (eds.), *Shinto in history* (Richmond, Surrey: Curzon): 117–43.

2001. *Der Eine und Einzige Weg der Götter: Yoshida Kanetomo und die Erfindung des Shinto* (Vienna: Verlag der Österreichischen Akademie der Wissenschaften).

Schlütter, Morten 1999. 'Silent illumination, *kung-an* introspection, and the competition for lay patronage in Sung Dynasty Ch'an', in Peter N. Gregory and Daniel A. Getz Jr. (eds.), *Buddhism in the Sung* (Honolulu: University of Hawai'i Press): 109–47.

Senchakushū English Translation Project (tr.) 1998. *Hōnen's Senchakushū* (Honolulu: University of Hawai'i Press).

Sharf, Robert H. 2001. 'Visualization and mandala in Shingon Buddhism', in Robert H. Sharf and Elizabeth Horton Sharf (eds.), *Living images: Japanese Buddhist icons in context* (Stanford University Press): 151–97.

2002. 'On Pure Land Buddhism and Ch'an/Pure Land syncretism in medieval China', *T'oung Pao* 88: 282–331.

Snellen, J. B. 1934. 'Shoku Nihongi', *Transactions of the Asiatic Society of Japan*, 2nd series, 11: 169–70.

Snodgrass, Adrian 1988. *The Matrix and Diamond World mandalas in Shingon Buddhism*, 2 vols. (New Delhi: Aditya Prakashan).

Solomon, Ira M. 1972. 'Rennyo and the rise of Honganji in Muromachi Japan', Ph.D. dissertation, Columbia University, NY.

1978. 'The dilemma of religious power: Honganji and Hosokawa Masamoto', *Monumenta Nipponica* 33.1: 51–65.

Stevenson, Miwa 1999. 'The founding of the monastery Gangōji and a list of its treasures', in George J. Tanabe Jr. (ed.), *Religions of Japan in practice* (Princeton University Press): 299–315.

Stone, Jacqueline I. 1994. 'Rebuking the enemies of the *Lotus*: Nichirenist exclusivism in historical perspective', *Japanese Journal of Religious Studies* 21.2–3: 231–59.

1998. 'Chanting the august title of the *Lotus sūtra*: daimoku practices in classical and medieval Japan', in Richard K. Payne (ed.), *Re-visioning 'Kamakura' Buddhism* (Honolulu: University of Hawai'i Press): 116–66.

1999a. *Original enlightenment and the transformation of medieval Japanese Buddhism* (Honolulu: University of Hawai'i Press).

1999b. 'Placing Nichiren in the "big picture": some ongoing issues in scholarship', *Japanese Journal of Religious Studies* 26.3–4: 413–14.

1999c. 'Biographical Studies of Nichiren', *Japanese Journal of Religious Studies* 26.3–4: 443–58.

2004. 'By the power of one's last *nenbutsu*: deathbed practices in early medieval Japan', in Richard K. Payne and Kenneth K. Tanaka (eds.), *Approaching the*

Land of Bliss: Religious praxis in the cult of Amitābha (Honolulu: University of Hawai'i Press).

Sueki Fumihiko 1991. *Annen, Genshin,* Daijō butten: Chūgoku Nihon hen (Tōkyō: Chūō Kōronsha).

1994. 'Annen: the philosopher who Japanized Buddhism', *Acta Asiatica* 66: 69–86.

1999. 'Nichiren's problematic works', *Japanese Journal of Religious Studies* 26.3–4: 261–80.

Swanson, Paul L. 1989. *Foundations of T'ien-t'ai philosophy* (Berkeley: Asian Humanities Press).

(tr.) 1995. *The collected teachings of the Tendai Lotus School,* BDK English Tripiṭaka (Berkeley: Numata Center for Buddhist Translation and Research).

Takakusu Junjirō 1928–29. 'Le voyage de Kanshin en orient (742–754),' *Bulletin de l'école française d'extrême-orient,* 28: 1–41, 441–72; 29: 47–62.

Tamura Kōyū 1985. 'The doctrinal dispute between the Tendai and Hossō sects', *Acta Asiatica* 47: 48–81.

Tamura Yoshirō and Sueki Fumihiko (eds.) 1990. *Shintō taikei, Tendai Shintō jō* (Tōkyō: Shintō Taikei Hensankai).

Tanabe, George J., Jr. 1992. *Myōe the dreamkeeper: fantasy and knowledge in early Kamakura Buddhism* (Cambridge, MA: Harvard University Press).

1995. 'Myōe's letter to the island', in Donald S. Lopez (ed.), *Buddhism in practice* (Princeton University Press): 88–91.

Tanaka K. K. 1990. *The dawn of Chinese Pure Land Buddhism* (Albany, NY: State University of New York Press).

Teeuwen, Mark 1996. *Watarai Shintō: an intellectual history of the Outer Shrine* (Leiden: CNWS).

2000. 'The kami in esoteric Buddhist thought and practice', in John Breen and Mark Teeuwen (eds.), *Shinto in history* (Richmond, Surrey: Curzon): 95–116.

2002. 'From *jindō* to *shintō*: a concept takes shape', *Japanese Journal of Religious Studies* 29.3–4: 234–63.

Teeuwen, Mark and Hendrik van der Veere 1998. *Nakatomi harae kunge: purification and enlightenment in late-Heian Japan,* Buddhismus-Studien 1 (Munich: Iudicium Verlag).

Teiser, Stephen F. 1994. *The scripture on the ten kings and the making of purgatory in medieval Chinese Buddhism* (Honolulu: University of Hawai'i Press).

ten Grotenhuis, Elizabeth 1999. *Japanese mandalas* (Honolulu: University of Hawai'i Press).

Terada Tōru and Mizuno Yaoko (eds.) 1970. *Dōgen,* 2 vols., Nihon shisō taikei (Tōkyō: Iwanami Shoten).

Thornton, Sybil A. 1988. 'The propaganda traditions of the *yugyō ha*', Ph.D. dissertation, University of Cambridge.

1999. *Charisma and community formation in medieval Japan: the case of the Yugyō-ha (1300–1700)* (Ithaca, NY: Cornell East Asia Series, no. 102).

Toby, Ron P. 1985. 'Why leave Nara?: Kenmu and the transfer of the capital', *Monumenta Nipponica* 40.3: 331–47.

Tsunoda Ryūsaku, Wm. Theodore de Bary and Donald Keene (eds.) 1958. *Sources of*

Japanese tradition, 1st edn, vol. I (New York: Columbia University Press).

Tyler, Royall 1989. 'Kōfukuji and Shugendō', *Japanese Journal of Religious Studies* 16.2–3: 143–80.

(tr.) 1990. *The miracles of the Kasuga deity* (New York: Columbia University Press).

Ury, Marian B. 1970. '*Genkō shakusho*: Japan's first comprehensive history of Buddhism: a partial translation, with introduction and notes', Ph.D. dissertation, University of California, Berkeley.

Vanden Broucke, Pol (tr.) 1992. *Hōkyōshō* (Gent: Rijksuniversiteit Gent, Vakgroep Oost-Azië).

van der Veere, Henny 2000. *A study into the thought of Kōgyō Daishi Kakuban* (Leiden: Hotei Publishing).

Varley, Paul (tr.) 1980. *A chronicle of gods and sovereigns* (New York: Columbia University Press).

von Verschuer, Charlotte 1991. 'Le voyage de Jōjin au mont Tiantai', *T'oung pao* 77.1–3: 1–48.

Walton, Linda 1989. 'Sino-Japanese cultural relations in the early thirteenth century: the Buddhist monk Shunjō (1166–1227) in China, 1199–1212', in *Ryū Shiken [Liu Tzu-chien] hakase shōju kinen: sōshi kenkyū ronshū* (Tōkyō: Dōbōsha): 569–82.

Wang Zhenping 1994. 'Chōnen's pilgrimage to China, 983–986', *Asia Major*, 3rd series, 7.2: 63–97.

Watanabe Tsunaya (ed.) 1966. *Shasekishū*, Nihon koten bungaku taikei (Tōkyō: Iwanami Shoten).

Watson, Burton (tr.) 1993. *The Zen teachings of Master Lin-chi* (Boston: Shambhala).

Weinstein, Stanley 1973. 'Imperial patronage in the formation of T'ang Buddhism', in Arthur F. Wright and Denis Twitchett (eds.), *Perspectives on the T'ang* (New Haven: Yale University Press): 265–306.

1977. 'Rennyo and the Shinshū revival', in John Whitney Hall and Toyoda Takeshi (eds.), *Japan in the Muromachi age* (Berkeley: University of California Press): 331–58.

1987. *Buddhism under the T'ang* (Cambridge University Press).

1999. 'Jordan lectures in comparative religion', SOAS, London, unpub. seminar papers 1–4.

Willemen, Charles (tr.) 1983. *The Chinese Hevajratantra*, Orientalia Gandensia 8 (Gent: Rijksuniversiteit).

Yamada Yoshio, Yamada Tadao, Yamada Hideo and Yamada Toshio (eds.) 1959–63. *Konjaku monogatarishū*, 5 vols., Nihon koten bungaku taikei (Tōkyō: Iwanami Shoten).

Yamamoto Hiroko 1998. *Chūsei shinwa*, Iwanami shinsho 593 (Tōkyō: Iwanami Shoten).

Yamasaki Taikō 1988. *Shingon: Japanese esoteric Buddhism* (Boston: Shambhala).

Yampolsky, Philip B. 1967. *The platform sutra of the sixth patriarch* (New York: Columbia University Press).

(ed.) 1996. *Letters of Nichiren* (New York: Columbia University Press).

Yiengpruksawan, Mimi Hall 1998. *Hiraizumi: Buddhist art and regional politics in twelfth-century Japan*, East Asian Monograph 171 (Cambridge, MA: Harvard University Press).

Yifa 2002. *The origins of Buddhist monastic codes in China* (Honolulu: University of Hawai'i Press).

Yü Chün-fang 1982. 'Chung-feng Ming-Pen and Ch'an Buddhism in the Yüan', in Hok-lam Chan and Wm. Theodore de Bary (eds.), *Yüan thought: Chinese thought and religion under the Mongols* (New York: Columbia University Press): 419–77.

Ziporyn, Brook 2000. *Evil and/or/as the Good: omnicentrism, intersubjectivity, and value paradox in Tiantai Buddhist thought* (Cambridge, MA: Harvard University Press).

Zürcher, Eric 1972. *The Buddhist conquest of China*, 2 vols. (Leiden: Brill).

Index